The Information Age
Economy, Society and Culture

Volume III
End of Millennium

Para mi hija, Nuria Castells, alegría de mi vida, con la esperanza de que su milenio sea mejor que el mío

End of Millennium

Second Edition

Manuel Castells

Copyright © Manuel Castells 1998, 2000

The right of Manuel Castells to be identified as author of this work has been asserted in accordance with the Copyright, Designs and Patents Act 1988.

First edition published 1998
Reprinted 1998 (three times)
Revised and updated edition published 1999
Second edition published 2000

2 4 6 8 10 9 7 5 3 1

Blackwell Publishers Ltd
108 Cowley Road
Oxford OX4 1JF
UK

Blackwell Publishers Inc.
350 Main Street
Malden, MA 02148
USA

British Library Cataloguing in Publication Data

A CIP catalogue record for this book is available from the British Library.

Library of Congress Cataloging-in-Publication Data has been applied for

ISBN 0-631-22139-5 (pbk)

Typeset in 10.5 on 12 pt Sabon
by Ace Filmsetting Ltd, Frome, Somerset
Printed in Great Britain by T.J. International Limited, Padstow, Cornwall

This book is printed on acid-free paper

Contents

Figures

Tables

Charts

Acknowledgments

This volume closes 12 years of research effort to elaborate an empirically grounded, cross-cultural, sociological theory of the Information
Age. At the end of this journey, which has marked, and to some extent
exhausted, my life, I want to publicly express my gratitude to a number
of persons and institutions whose contribution has been decisive for
the completion of this three-volume work.

My deepest gratitude goes to my wife, Emma Kiselyova, whose love
and support gave me the life and energy I needed to write this book,
and whose effective research work has been essential in several chapters, particularly chapter 1 on the collapse of the Soviet Union, which
was researched by us both, in Russia and in California. It could not
have been written without her personal knowledge of the Soviet experience, her analysis of Russian-language sources, and her correction
of the many mistakes I made in successive drafts. She was also the
primary researcher for chapter 3 on the global criminal economy.

Chapter 4 on the Asian Pacific relied on the input and comments of
three colleagues who, over the years, have been constant sources for
my ideas and information on Asian societies: Professor You-tien Hsing
of the University of British Columbia; Professor Shujiro Yazawa of
Tokyo's Hitotsubashi University; and Professor Chu-joe Hsia of Taiwan National University. Chapter 2 on social exclusion relied on the
outstanding research assistance of my collaborator Chris Benner, a
doctoral student at Berkeley during 1995–7.

Several people, besides those named above, provided their generous
contribution, in information and ideas, to the research presented in
this volume. For this, I particularly thank Ida Susser, Tatyana
Zaslavskaya, Ovsey Shkaratan, Svetlana Natalushko, Valery Kuleshov,
Alexander Granberg, Joo-Chul Kim, Carlos Alonso Zaldivar, Stephen

Cohen, Martin Carnoy, Roberto Laserna, Jordi Borja, Vicente Navarro, and Alain Touraine.

I would also like to thank those colleagues who commented on drafts of this volume, and helped to rectify some of my mistakes: Ida Susser, Tatyana Zaslavskaya, Gregory Grossman, George Breslauer, Shujiro Yazawa, You-tien Hsing, Chu-joe Hsia, Roberto Laserna, Carlos Alonso Zaldivar, and Stephen Cohen.

Throughout the years, a number of research institutions have provided essential support for the work presented here. I thank their directors and the colleagues in these institutions who taught me much of what I have learned about societies around the world. Foremost among these institutions is my intellectual home since 1979: the University of California at Berkeley, and particularly the academic units in which I worked during these years: the Department of City and Regional Planning, Department of Sociology, Center for Western European Studies, Institute of Urban and Regional Development, and the Berkeley Roundtable on the International Economy. Other institutions that have supported my work on the themes covered in this volume in the past decade are: Instituto de Sociologia de Nuevas Tecnologias, and Programa de Estudios Rusos, Universidad Autonoma de Madrid; Russian Sociological Association; Center for Advanced Sociological Study, Institute of Youth, Moscow; Institute of Economics and Industrial Engineering, Soviet (then Russian) Academy of Sciences, Novosibirsk; University of California, Pacific Rim Research Program; Faculty of Social Sciences, Hitotsubashi University, Tokyo; National University of Singapore; University of Hong Kong, Center for Urban Studies; Taiwan National University; Korean Institute for Human Settlements; Institute of Technology and International Economy, The State Council, Beijing; Centro de Estudios de la Realidad Economica y Social, Cochabamba, Bolivia; International Institute of Labour Studies of the International Labour Office, Geneva.

I reserve a special mention for John Davey, former editorial director at Blackwell Publishers. For over 20 years he has guided my writing and communicating skills, and has thoroughly advised me on publishing. His personal contribution in commenting on the conclusion to this volume has been decisive. My written work can never be separated from my intellectual interaction with John Davey.

I also wish to name a few people who have been essential in my overall intellectual development throughout the past 30 years. Their work and thinking is, in many ways, but under my exclusive responsibility, present in the pages of this book. They are: Alain Touraine, Nicos Poulantzas, Fernando Henrique Cardoso, Emilio de Ipola, Jordi Borja, Martin Carnoy, Stephen Cohen, Peter Hall, Vicente Navarro,

Anne Marie Guillemard, Shujiro Yazawa, and Anthony Giddens. I have been fortunate to evolve together, in a global network, with an exceptional generation of intellectuals committed to both understanding and changing the world, while keeping the necessary distance between theory and practice.

Finally, I would like to thank my surgeons, Dr Peter Carroll and Dr James Wolton, and my physician, Dr James Davis, all of the University of California San Francisco Medical Center, whose care and professionalism gave me the time and energy to finish this book.

May 1997   Berkeley, California

The author and publishers gratefully acknowledge permission from the following to reproduce copyright material:

Tables 1.1, 1.2, 1.3 and Figures 1.1 and 1.2: from Mark Harrison, *Europe–Asia Studies* 45, 1993 (Carfax Publishing Company, reprinted by permission of Taylor and Francis, Abingdon, Oxon, 1993);
Table 1.4: from *The Soviet Economy: Problems and Prospects*, compiled and elaborated by Padmai Desai (Blackwell Publishers, Oxford, 1987);
Table 1.6: from D. J. B. Shaw, *Post-Soviet Geography*, 34, 1993 (© V. H. Winston and Son Inc., 1993);
Table 2.2: from Peter Gottschalk and Timothy M. Smeeding, "Empirical evidence on income inequality in industrialized countries," Luxembourg Income Study working paper, no. 154, 1997; elaborated by Lawrence Mishel, Jared Bernstein, and John Schmitt, *The State of Working America 1998/99*. Reprinted by permission of M. E. Sharpe, Inc. Publisher, Armonk, NY 10504;
Table 2.10: Congressional Budget Office data analyzed by Center on Budget and Policy Priorities;
Figure 2.3: from *The Economist* (September 7, 1996);
Figure 2.5: reprinted by permission of the US Bureau of the Census;
Figures 2.6a, 2.6b, 2.7, and 2.8: from Lawrence Mishel, Jared Bernstein, and John Schmitt, *The State of Working America 1998/99*. Reprinted by permission of M. E. Sharpe, Inc. Publisher, Armonk, NY 10504;
Figure 3.1: from International Centre for Migration Policy Development; elaborated by *The Economist* (October 16, 1999);
Figure 4.1: from *The Economist* (June 27, 1997);
Chart 3.1: from *The Economist* (August 28, 1999);
Extract from "Too Many Names" from *Extravagaria* by Pablo Neruda,

translated by Alastair Reid (Farrar, Straus and Giroux Inc., 1974, translation copyright © by Alastair Reid: Carmen Barcells Literary Agency and Farrar, Straus and Giroux Inc.).

A Time of Change

The turn of a millennium is thought to be a time of change. But it is not necessarily so: the end of the first millennium was, by and large, uneventful. As for the second, those awaiting some kind of fateful lightning had to content themselves with the emotions aroused by the anticipation of the Y2K global computer collapse – which never happened. Moreover, while most people celebrated the change of millennium at midnight on December 31st, 1999, in strictly chronological terms, the second millennium ended on December 31st, 2000. Furthermore, this was a change of millennium only according to the Gregorian calendar of Christianity, a minority religion that is bound to lose its pre-eminence in the multiculturalism that will characterize the twenty-first century.

And, yet, this is indeed a time of change, regardless of how we time it. In the last quarter of the twentieth century, a technological revolution, centered around information, transformed the way we think, we produce, we consume, we trade, we manage, we communicate, we live, we die, we make war, and we make love. A dynamic, global economy has been constituted around the planet, linking up valuable people and activities from all over the world, while switching off from the networks of power and wealth, people and territories dubbed as irrelevant from the perspective of dominant interests. A culture of real virtuality, constructed around an increasingly interactive audiovisual universe, has permeated mental representation and communication everywhere, integrating the diversity of cultures in an electronic hypertext. Space and time, the material foundations of human experience, have been transformed, as the space of flows dominates the space of places, and timeless time supersedes clock time of the industrial era. Expressions of social resistance to the logic of informationalization and globalization build around primary identities, creating defensive communities in the name of God, locality, ethnicity, or family. At the same time, founding social institutions as important as patriarchalism and the nation-state are called into question under the combined pressure of globalization of wealth and information, and localization of identity and legitimacy.

These processes of structural change, which I have analyzed in the two previous volumes of this book, induce a fundamental transformation of the macropolitical and macrosocial contexts that shape and condition social action and human experience around the world. This volume explores some of these macro transformations, while attempting to explain them as a result of the interaction between processes characterizing the Information Age: informationalization, globalization, networking, identity-building, the crisis of patriarchalism, and of the nation-state. While I do not claim that all important dimensions of historical change are represented in this volume, I believe that the trends documented and analyzed in the following chapters do constitute a new historical landscape, whose dynamics are likely to have lasting effects on our lives, and on our children's lives.

It is no accident that the volume opens with an analysis of the collapse of Soviet communism. The 1917 Russian Revolution, and the international communist movement that it sparked, was the dominant political and ideological phenomenon of the twentieth century. Communism, and the Soviet Union, and the opposite reactions they triggered throughout the world, have marked decisively societies and people for the span of the century. And yet, this mighty empire, and its powerful mythology, disintegrated in just a few years, in one of the most extraordinary instances of unexpected historical change. I argue that at the roots of this process, marking the end of an historical epoch, lies the inability of statism to manage the transition to the Information Age. Chapter 1 will try to provide empirical grounding for this statement.

The end of Soviet communism, and the hurried adaptation of Chinese communism to global capitalism, has left a new brand of leaner, meaner capitalism alone at last in its planetary reach. The restructuring of capitalism in the period from the 1970s to the 1990s showed the versatility of its operating rules, and its capacity to use efficiently the networking logic of the Information Age to induce a dramatic leap forward in productive forces and economic growth. Yet, it also displayed its exclusionary logic, as millions of people and large areas of the planet are being excluded from the benefits of informationalism, both in the developed and developing worlds. Chapter 2 documents these trends, relating them to the uncontrolled nature of global capitalist networks. Furthermore, on the fringes of global capitalism, a new collective actor has appeared, possibly changing the rules of economic and political institutions in the years to come: global crime. Indeed, taking advantage of the world disorder that followed the disintegration of the Soviet empire, manipulating populations and territories excluded from the formal economy, and using the instruments of global networking, criminal activities proliferate throughout the planet, and link up with each other, constituting an emergent, global criminal economy, that penetrates financial markets, trade, business, and political systems in all societies. This perverse connection is a significant feature of informational, global capitalism. A feature whose importance is usually acknowledged in the media, but not integrated in social analysis, a theoretical flaw that I will try to correct in chapter 3 of this volume.

At the same time, there has been an extraordinary expansion of capitalist growth, which includes hundreds of millions in the development process, particularly in the Asian Pacific (chapter 4). The process of incorporation of dynamic areas of China, India, and of East and South-East Asia, in the wake of Japanese development, into an interdependent global economy, changes history, establishing a multicultural foundation of economic interdependence: this signals the end of Western domination, which characterized the industrial era from its outset. Yet the volatility of new global capitalism was also revealed in the dramatic change of fortune in the Asian Pacific, shaken by the 1997–8 financial crisis. The analysis given in chapter 4 presents the interaction between development and crisis in Asia as an expression of the growing tension between globalization and the state.

Faced with the whirlwind of globalization, and with the shake up of the cultural and geopolitical foundations of the world as it used to be, European countries came together, not without problems, in the process of European unification, which aims symbolically to unify their currencies, and thus their economies, around the turn of the millennium (chapter 5). However, the cultural and political dimensions, essential to the process of European unification, are still unsettled, so that the fate of Europe will ultimately depend, as for other areas of the world, on solving the historical puzzles posed by the transition to informationalism, and by the shift from the nation-state to a new interaction between nations and the state, under the form of the network state.

After surveying these macrosocial/political transformations, which define some of the major debates of our time, I shall conclude in a more analytical vein. Not just about the themes presented in this volume, but about the connections between these themes and the social processes analyzed in the preceding two volumes. With the reader's benevolence, the conclusion of this volume will propose some materials to construct an open-ended, social theory of the Information Age. That is to say that, after exploring our world, I shall try to make sense of it.

1

The Crisis of Industrial Statism and the Collapse of the Soviet Union

When the Soviet Union will produce 50 million tons of pig iron, 60 million tons of steel, 500 million tons of coal, and 60 million tons of oil we will be guaranteed against any misfortune.

Stalin, Speech in February 1946[1]

The contradiction which became apparent in the 1950s, between the development of the production forces and the growing needs of society on the one hand, and the increasingly obsolete productive relations of the old system of economic management on the other hand, became sharper with every year. The conservative structure of the economy and the tendencies for extensive investment, together with the backward

This chapter was researched, elaborated, and written jointly with Emma Kiselyova. It relies mainly on two sets of information. The first is the fieldwork research I conducted between 1989 and 1996 in Moscow, Zelenograd, Leningrad, Novosibirsk, Tyumen, Khabarovsk, and Sakhalin in the framework of research programs of the Programa de Estudios Rusos, Universidad Autonoma de Madrid, and of the University of California's Pacific Rim Program, in cooperation with: the Russian Sociological Association; the Institute of Economics and Industrial Engineering, Russian Academy of Sciences, Siberian Branch; and the Center for Advanced Sociological Study, Institute of Youth, Moscow. Four major research projects were co-directed by myself with O.I. Shkaratan, V.I. Kuleshov, S. Natalushko, and with E. Kiselyova and A. Granberg, respectively. Specific references to each research project are given in the footnotes corresponding to each subject. I thank all my Russian colleagues for their essential contribution to my understanding of the Soviet Union, but I certainly exonerate them from any responsibility for my mistakes and personal interpretation of our findings. The second set of information on which this chapter is based refers to documentary, bibliographical, and statistical sources, primarily collected and analyzed by Emma Kiselyova. I also wish to acknowledge the thorough and detailed comments provided on the draft of this chapter by Tatyana Zaslavskaya, Gregory Grossman, and George Breslauer.
1   Cited by Menshikov (1990: 72).

system of economic management gradually turned into a brake and an
obstacle to the economic and social development of the country.
        Abel Aganbegyan, *The Economic Challenge of Perestroika*, p. 49

The world economy is a single organism, and no state, whatever its
social system or economic status, can normally develop outside it. This
places on the agenda the need to devise a fundamentally new machinery
for the functioning of the world economy, a new structure of the inter-
national division of labor. At the same time, the growth of the world
economy reveals the contradictions and limits inherent in the traditional
type of industrialization.
        Mikhail Gorbachev, Address to the United Nations, 1988[2]

We will realize one day that we are in fact the only country on Earth
that tries to enter the twenty-first century with the obsolete ideology of
the nineteenth century.
        Boris Yeltsin, *Memoirs*, 1990, p. 245[3]

The sudden collapse of the Soviet Union, and with it the demise of the
international communist movement, raises an historical enigma: why,
in the 1980s, did Soviet leaders feel the urgency to engage in a process
of restructuring so radical that it ultimately led to the disintegration of
the Soviet state? After all, the Soviet Union was not only a military
superpower, but also the third largest industrial economy in the world,
the world's largest producer of oil, gas, and rare metals, and the only
country that was self-reliant in energy resources and raw materials.
True, symptoms of serious economic flaws had been acknowledged
since the 1960s, and the rate of growth had been decreasing since
1971 to reach a standstill by 1980. But Western economies have experienced a slowdown trend in productivity growth, as well as negative
economic growth at some points in the past two decades, without
suffering catastrophic consequences. Soviet technology seems to have
lagged behind in some critical areas, but overall, Soviet science maintained its level of excellence in fundamental fields: mathematics, physics, chemistry, with only biology having some difficulty in recovering
from Lysenko's follies. The diffusion of this scientific capacity in technological upgrading did not seem out of reach, as the advance of the
Soviet space program over NASA's dismal performance of the 1980s
seems to indicate. Agriculture continued to be in permacrisis, and shortages of consumer goods were customary, but exports of energy and

2 Reprinted in a special supplement of *Soviet Life*, February 1989, and Tarasulo (1989:
331).
3 Our translation into English.

materials, at least until 1986, were providing a hard currency cushion for remedial imports, so that the living conditions of Soviet citizens were better, not worse, in the mid-1980s than a decade earlier.

Furthermore, Soviet power was not seriously challenged either internationally or domestically. The world had entered an era of relative stability in the acknowledged spheres of influence between the superpowers. The war in Afghanistan was taking its toll in human suffering, in political image, and in military pride, but not to a greater level than that of the damage inflicted by the Algerian War on France or the Vietnam War on the United States. Political dissidence was limited to small intellectual circles, as respected as isolated; to Jewish people wanting to emigrate; and to kitchen gossip, a deeply rooted Russian tradition. Although there were a few instances of riots and strikes, generally associated with food shortages and price increases, there were no real social movements to speak of. Oppression of nationalities and ethnic minorities was met with resentment, and in the Baltic republics with open anti-Russian hostility, but such feelings were rarely articulated in collective action or in parapolitical opinion movements.

People were dissatisfied with the system, and expressed their withdrawal in different forms: cynicism, minor larceny at the workplace, absenteeism, suicide, and widespread alcoholism. But with Stalinist terror long superseded, political repression was limited and highly selective, and ideological indoctrination had become more of a bureaucratic ritual than an ardent inquisition. By the time the long Brezhnevian rule had succeeded in establishing normalcy and boredom in the Soviet Union, people had learned to cope with the system, going on with their lives, making the best of it, as far away as possible from the hallways of the state. Although the structural crisis of Soviet statism was brewing in the cauldrons of history, few of its actors seem to have realized it. The second Russian revolution, which dismantled the Soviet empire, so ending one of the most daring and costly human experiments, may be the only major historical change brought about without the intervention of social movements and/or without a major war. The state created by Stalin seems to have intimidated its enemies, and succeeded in cutting off the rebellious potential of society for a long period.

The veil of historical mystery is even thicker when we consider the process of reform under Gorbachev. How and why did this process go out of control? After all, against the simplistic image conveyed in the Western press, the Soviet Union, and before it Russia, had gone "from one *perestroika* to another," as Van Regemorter entitles his insightful historical analysis of reform processes in Russia.[4] From the New

4 Van Regemorter (1990).

Economic Policy of the 1920s to Kosygin's reforms of economic management in the late 1960s, passing through Stalin's dramatic restructuring of the 1930s, and the revisionism of Khrushchev in the 1950s,
the Soviet Union had progressed/regressed by leaps and bounds, making a systemic feature of alternating between continuity and reform.
Indeed, this was the specific way in which the Soviet system responded
to the issue of social change, a necessary matter for all durable political systems. Yet, with the major exception of Stalin's ruthless ability
to constantly rewrite the rules of the game in his favor, the party apparatus was always able to control the reforms within the limits of the
system, proceeding when necessary to political purges and changes of
leadership. How, in the late 1980s, could such a veteran, shrewd party,
hardened in endless battles of managed reform, lose political control
to the point of having to resort to a desperate, hurried coup that ultimately precipitated its demise?

My hypothesis is that the crisis that prompted Gorbachev's reforms
was different in its historical nature from the preceding crises, thus
impinging this difference on the reform process itself, making it riskier,
and eventually uncontrollable. I contend that the rampant crisis that
shook the foundations of the Soviet economy and society from the
mid-1970s onwards was the expression of the structural inability of
statism and of the Soviet variant of industrialism to ensure the transition towards the information society.

By statism, I understand a social system organized around the appropriation of the economic surplus produced in society by the holders of power in the state apparatus, in contrast to capitalism, in which
surplus is appropriated by the holders of control in economic organizations (see volume I, prologue). While capitalism is oriented toward
profit-maximizing, statism is oriented toward power-maximizing; that
is, toward increasing the military and ideological capacity of the state
apparatus to impose its goals on a greater number of subjects and at
deeper levels of their consciousness. By industrialism, I mean a mode
of development in which the main sources of productivity are the quantitative increase of factors of production (labor, capital, and natural
resources), together with the use of new sources of energy. By
informationalism, I mean a mode of development in which the main
source of productivity is the qualitative capacity to optimize the combination and use of factors of production on the basis of knowledge
and information. The rise of informationalism is inseparable from a
new social structure, the network society (see volume I, chapter 1).
The last quarter of the twentieth century was marked by the transition
from industrialism to informationalism, and from the industrial society to the network society, both for capitalism and statism, in a pro-

cess that is concomitant with the information technology revolution. In the Soviet Union, this transition required measures that undermined the vested interests of the state's bureaucracy and party's *nomenklatura*. Realizing how critical it was to ensure the transition of the system to a higher level of productive forces and technological capacity, the reformers, led by Gorbachev, took the gamble of appealing to society to overcome the *nomenklatura*'s resistance to change. *Glasnost* (openness) displaced *uskorenie* ([economic]acceleration) at the forefront of *perestroika* (restructuring). And history has shown that once Russian society comes into open political ground, because it has so long been repressed, it refuses to mold to pre-packaged state policies, takes a political life of its own, and becomes unpredictable and uncontrollable. This is what Gorbachev, in the tradition of Stolypin, learned again at his expense.

Furthermore, opening up political expression for Soviet society at large unleashed the contained pressure of national identities – distorted, repressed, and manipulated under Stalinism. The search for sources of identity different from the fading communist ideology led to the fracturing of the still fragile Soviet identity, decisively undermining the Soviet state. Nationalism, including Russian nationalism, became the most acute expression of conflicts between society and the state. It was the immediate political factor leading to the disintegration of the Soviet Union.

At the roots of the crisis that induced *perestroika* and triggered nationalism was the incapacity of Soviet statism to ensure the transition to the new informational paradigm, in parallel to the process that was taking place in the rest of the world. This is hardly an original hypothesis. Indeed, it is the application of an old Marxian idea, according to which specific social systems may stall the development of productive forces, admittedly presented here with an ironic historical twist. I hope that the added value of the analysis submitted to the reader's attention in the following pages will be in its specificity. Why was statism structurally incapable of proceeding with the necessary restructuring to adapt to informationalism? It is certainly not the fault of the state *per se*. The Japanese state, and, beyond the shores of the Sea of Japan, the developmental state, whose origins and feats are analyzed elsewhere (see chapter 4), have been decisive instruments in fostering technological innovation and global competitiveness, as well as in transforming fairly traditional countries into advanced information societies. To be sure, statism is not equivalent to state interventionism. Statism is a specific social system oriented toward the maximization of state power, while capital accumulation and social legitimacy are subordinated to such an overarching goal. Soviet communism (like all communist systems) was built to ensure total control by the party over the state, and by the state over society via the twin levers of a centrally planned economy and of Marxist–Leninist ideology enforced by a tightly controlled cultural apparatus. It was this specific system, not the state in general, that proved incapable of navigating the stormy waters of historical transition between industrialism and informationalism. The whys, hows, and ifs of this statement make the stuff of this chapter.

The Extensive Model of Economic Growth and the Limits of Hyperindustrialism

We have become so used to demeaning accounts of the Soviet economy in recent years that it is often overlooked that, for a long period of time, particularly in the 1950s and until the late 1960s, Soviet GNP grew generally faster than most of the world, albeit at the price of staggering human and environmental costs.[5] To be sure, Soviet official statistics grossly overestimated the growth rate, particularly during the 1930s. The important statistical work of G.I. Khanin,[6] fully recognized only during the 1990s, seems to indicate that Soviet national income between 1928 and 1987 did not grow 89.5 times, as Soviet statistics would make us believe, but 6.9 times. Still, by Khanin's own account (that we should consider the lower limit in the range of estimation: see tables 1.1–1.3 and figures 1.1 and 1.2), average annual growth of Soviet national income was 3.2 percent in the 1928–40 period, 7.2 percent in 1950–60, 4.4 percent in 1960–65, 4.1 percent in 1965–70, and 3.2 percent in 1970–75. After 1975 quasi-stagnation settled in, and growth became negative in 1980–82, and after 1987. Yet, overall, and for most of the existence of the Soviet Union, its economic growth was faster than that of the West, and its pace of industrialization one of the fastest in world history.

Furthermore, a system's performance must be evaluated according to its own goals. From such a perspective, the Soviet Union was for half a century an extraordinary success story. If we put aside (can we

5   See, among other works, Nove (1969/1982); Bergson (1978); Goldman (1983); Thalheim (1986); Palazuelos (1990). For the debate on statistical accuracy in analyzing the Soviet economy, see Central Intelligence Agency (1990b).
6   Khanin (1991a). Khanin has been, for many years, a researcher at the Institute of Economics and Industrial Engineering, Russian Academy of Sciences, Siberian Branch. In addition to the reference cited, which corresponds broadly with his doctoral dissertation, much of his work has been published in the economic journal of the above-mentioned Institute, *EKO*; for example, see issues 1989(4); 1989(10); 1990(1); 1991(2). For a systematic review, in English, of Khanin's decisive contribution to the economic statistics of the Soviet Union, see Harrison (1993: 141–67).

Table 1.1 Soviet national income growth, 1928–87: alternative estimates (change over period, percentage per year)

Period	TsSU[a]	CIA	Khanin
1928–40	13.9	6.1	3.2[b]
1940–50	4.8	2.0	1.6[c]
1928–50	10.1	4.2	2.5
1950–60	10.2	5.2	7.2
1960–65	6.5	4.8	4.4
1965–70	7.7	4.9	4.1
1970–75	5.7	3.0	3.2
1975–80	4.2	1.9	1.0
1980–85	3.5	1.8	0.6
1985–87	3.0	2.7	2.0
1950–87	6.6	3.8	3.8
1928–87	7.9	3.9	3.3

[a] TsSU: Central Statistical Administration (of the USSR).
[b] 1928–41.
[c] 1941–50.
Sources: compiled by Harrison (1993: 146) from the following sources – TsSU; Khanin: net material product, calculated from Khanin (1991b: 85); CIA: GNP, calculated from CIA (1990a: table A-1)

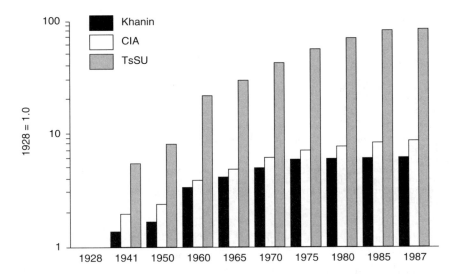

Figure 1.1 Soviet national income, 1928–87: alternative estimates
Source: compiled from figures in table 1.1 by Harrison (1993: 145)

Table 1.2 Soviet output and inflation, 1928–90 (change over period, percentage per year)

	Real product growth			Wholesale price inflation	
	Industry	Construction	National income	True	Hidden
TsSU[a]					
1928–40	17.0	–	13.9	8.8	–
1940–50	–	–	4.8	2.6	–
1950–60	11.7	12.3[b]	10.2	−0.5	–
1960–65	8.6	7.7	6.5	0.6	–
1965–70	8.5	7.0	7.7	1.9	–
1970–75	7.4	7.0	5.7	0.0	–
1975–80	4.4	–	4.2	−0.2	–
1980–85	–	–	3.5	–	–
1985–87	–	–	3.0	–	–
1928–87	–	–	7.9	–	–
Khanin					
1928–41	10.9	–	3.2	18.5	8.9
1941–50	–	–	1.6	5.9	3.2
1950–60	8.5	8.4[b]	7.2	1.2	1.8
1960–65	7.0	5.1	4.4	2.2	1.6
1965–70	4.5	3.2	4.1	4.6	2.6
1970–75	4.5	3.7	3.2	2.3	2.3
1975–80	3.0	–	1.0	2.7	2.9
1980–85	–	–	0.6	–	–
1985–87	–	–	2.0	–	–
1928–87	–	–	3.3	–	–
1980–82	–	–	−2.0	–	–
1982–88	–	–	1.8	–	–
1988–90[c]	–	–	−4.6	–	–

a TsSU: Central Statistical Administration (of the USSR).
b 1955–60.
c Preliminary.
Sources: compiled by Harrison (1993: 147) from the following sources – TsSU; 1928–87: 'National income' calculated from Khanin (1991b: 85); 'other columns' calculated from Khanin (1991a: 146, industry; 167, construction; 206, 212, wholesale prices; 1980–90: calculated from Khanin (1991b: 29)

really?) the tens of millions of people (60 million?) who died as a result of revolution, war, famine, forced labor, deportation, and executions; the destruction of national cultures, history, and traditions (in Russia and the other republics alike); the systematic violation of human rights and political freedom; the massive degradation of a rather

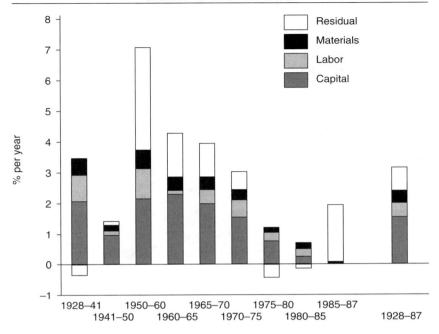

Figure 1.2 Soviet national income: role of inputs in output growth
Source: compiled from figures of Khanin (1991a, b) by Harrison (1993: 149)

pristine natural environment; the militarization of the economy and the indoctrination of society; if, for one analytical moment, we can view the historical process with Bolshevik eyes, it can only be amazement at the heroic proportions of the communist saga. In 1917, the Bolsheviks were a handful of professional revolutionaries, representing a minority fraction of the socialist movement, itself only a part of the broader democratic movement that enacted the February 1917 Revolution almost exclusively in the main cities of a country whose population was 84 percent rural.[7] Yet, they were able not only to seize power in the October coup, eliminating competition from all political forces, but still to win an atrocious revolutionary war against the remnants of the Tsarist army, the White Guards, and foreign expeditionary forces. They also liquidated in the process the anarchist Makhno's peasant army and Kronstadt's revolutionary sailors. Moreover, in spite of a narrow social base in a meager urban industrial proletariat, barely joined by scores of intelligentsia, the Bolsheviks went on to build in

7   See, among other works, Trotsky (1965); Conquest (1968, 1986); Cohen (1974); Antonov-Ovseyenko (1981); Pipes (1991).

Table 1.3 Soviet inputs and productivity, 1928–90 (change over period, percentage per year)

	Stock of fixed assets	Capital productivity	Output per worker	Materials intensity
TsSU[a]				
1928–40	8.7	4.8	11.9	−0.3
1940–50	1.0	3.1	4.1	−0.2
1950–60	9.4	0.8	8.0	−0.5
1960–65	9.7	−3.0	6.0	−0.2
1965–70	8.2	−0.4	6.8	−0.4
1970–75	8.7	−2.7	4.6	0.6
1975–80	7.4	−2.7	3.4	0.0
1980–85	6.5	−3.0	3.0	0.0
1985–87	4.9	−2.0	3.0	0.4
1928–87	7.2	0.5	6.7	−0.2
Khanin				
1928–41	5.3	−2.0	1.3	1.7[b]
1941–50	2.4	−0.8	1.3	1.1
1950–60	5.4	1.6	5.0	−0.5
1960–65	5.9	−1.4	4.1	0.4
1965–70	5.1	−1.0	3.0	0.4
1970–75	3.9	−0.6	1.9	1.0
1975–80	1.9	−1.0	0.2	1.0
1980–85	0.6	0.0	0.0	1.0
1985–87	0.0	2.0	2.0	−0.5
1928–87	3.9	−0.6	2.2	0.8
1980–82	1.5	−3.6	−2.5	2.5
1982–88	1.9	−0.2	1.4	0.7
1988–90[c]	−0.5	−4.1	−4.1	3.4

[a] TsSU: Central Statistical Administration (of the USSR).
[b] 1.7–2%.
[c] Preliminary.
Sources: compiled by Harrison (1993: 151) from the following sources – TsSU; 1928–87: calculated from Khanin (1991b: 85); 1980–90: calculated from Khanin (1991b: 29)

record time, and despite international isolation, an industrialized economy that was developed enough in just two decades to provide the military hardware capable of crushing the Nazi war machine. In a relentless determination to overtake capitalism, together with a somewhat understandable defensive paranoia, the Soviet Union, by and large a poor country, managed to become quickly a nuclear power, to maintain strategic military parity with the United States, and to pull ahead in the space race by 1957, to the shocked astonishment of Western governments which had believed their own mythology about communism's inability to build an advanced industrial economy.

Such undeniable feats were accomplished at the price of deforming the economy forever.[8] At the root of Soviet economic logic was a set of cascading priorities.[9] Agriculture had to be squeezed of its products to subsidize industry and feed cities, and emptied of its labor to provide industrial workers.[10] Consumer goods, housing, and services had to concede priority to capital goods, and to the extraction of raw materials, so that socialism could rapidly be made self-sufficient in all indispensable production lines. Heavy industry itself was put at the service of military industrial production, since military might was the ultimate purpose of the regime and the cornerstone of statism. The Leninist–Stalinist logic, which considered sheer force as the *raison d'être* of the state – of all states in the final analysis – permeated down through the entire institutional organization of the Soviet economy, and reverberated throughout the whole history of the Soviet Union under various ideological forms.

To enforce such priorities under the strictest conditions, to "bring politics to the command posts of the economy," as the communist slogan runs, a centrally planned economy was established, the first of its genre in world history, if we except some centrally controlled preindustrial economies. Obviously, in such an economy, prices are simply an accounting device, and they cannot signal any relationship between supply and demand.[11] The entire economy is thus moved by vertical administrative decisions, between the planning institutions and the ministries of execution, and between the ministries and the production units.[12] Links between production units are not really horizontal since their exchanges have been preestablished by their respective parent administrations. At the core of such central planning, two institutions shaped the Soviet economy. The first was Gosplan, or State Board for Planning, which established the goals for the whole economy in five-year periods, then proceeded to calculate implementation measures for each product, for each production unit, and for the whole country, year by year, in order to assign output targets and supply quotas to each unit in industry, construction, agriculture, and even services. Among other details, "prices" for about 200,000 products were centrally set each year. No wonder that Soviet linear programming was among the most sophisticated in the world.[13]

8   Aganbegyan (1988).
9   Menshikov (1990).
10   Johnson and McConnell Brooks (1983).
11   For a theoretical understanding of the logic of the centrally planned economy, see the classic work of Janos Kornai (1986, 1990).
12   Nove (1977); Thalheim (1986); Desai (1989).
13   Cave (1980).

The other major economic institution, less notorious but more significant in my opinion, was Gossnab (State Board for Materials and Equipment Supply), which was in charge of controlling all supplies for every transaction in the whole country, from a pin to an elephant. While Gosplan was preoccupied with the coherence of its mathematical models, Gossnab, with its ubiquitous antennae, was in the real world of authorizing supplies, actually controlling flows of goods and materials, and therefore presiding over shortages, a fundamental feature of the Soviet system. The Gosbank, or central bank, never played a substantial economic role, since credit and money circulation were the automatic consequence of Gosplan decisions, as interpreted and implemented by the state in accordance with the party's central committee instructions.[14]

To accomplish fast industrialization, and to fulfill the targets of plans, the Soviet state resorted to full mobilization of human and natural assets of an immense, resource-rich country, accounting for one-sixth of the earth's surface.[15] This extensive model of economic growth was characteristic of the Soviet Union not only during the phase of primitive accumulation in the 1930s,[16] but in the post-Stalin period.[17] Thus, according to Aganbegyan,

> in a typical post-war five-year period, usually in these five years the basic application of funds and capital investment increased one and a half times, the extraction of fuel and raw materials by 25–30 percent, and a further 10 to 11 million workers were recruited in the national economy, a large proportion of whom moved into new branches of production. This was characteristic of the whole period from 1956 to 1975. The last five-year period which involved a large growth in the use of resources was 1971–75. In that period a composite index for the increase of all resources used in production showed a growth of 21 percent.[18]

Thus, the Soviet model of economic growth was typical of an early industrial economy. Its rate of growth was a function of the size of capital investment and labor inputs, with technical change playing a minor role, thus potentially inducing diminishing returns as the supply of resources wears down (see table 1.4 and figure 1.3). In econometric terms, it was a model of growth characterized by a constant elasticity production function with constant returns to scale.[19] Its fate

14   Menshikov (1990).
15   Jasny (1961); Nove (1977); Ellman and Kontorovich (1992).
16   Wheatcroft et al. (1986).
17   Palazuelos (1990).
18   Aganbegyan (1988: 7).
19   Weitzman (1970: 63), cited by Desai (1987: 63)

Table 1.4 Growth rates of Soviet GNP, workforce, and capital stock, with investment–GNP and output–capital ratios

Year	GNP (%)	Workforce in man hours (%)	Capital stock (%)	Gross investment– GNP ratio (%)	Output–capital ratio (average)
		Growth rate of			
1951	3.1	−0.1	7.7		0.82
1952	5.9	0.5	7.5		0.81
1953	5.2	2.1	8.6		0.78
1954	4.8	5.1	10.5		0.74
1955	8.6	1.6	10.6		0.73
1956	8.4	1.9	10.3		0.72
1957	3.8	0.6	9.9		0.68
1958	7.6	2.0	10.0		0.66
1959	5.8	−1.0	9.7		0.64
1960	4.0	−0.3	9.2	17.8	0.61
1961	5.6	−0.7	8.9	18.1	0.59
1962	3.8	1.4	8.8	17.9	0.56
1963	−1.1	0.7	8.8	19.3	0.51
1964	11.0	2.9	8.6	19.1	0.52
1965	6.2	3.5	8.2	18.9	0.51
1966	5.1	2.5	7.7	19.2	0.50
1967	4.6	2.0	7.2	19.9	0.49
1968	6.0	1.9	7.1	20.2	0.48
1969	2.9	1.7	7.2	20.3	0.46
1970	7.7	2.0	7.8	21.0	0.46
1971	3.9	2.1	8.1	21.7	0.45
1972	1.9	1.8	8.2	22.9	0.42
1973	7.3	1.5	8.0	22.3	0.42
1974	3.9	2.0	7.8	23.0	0.40
1975	1.7	1.2	7.6	24.6	0.38
1976	4.8	0.8	7.2	24.5	0.37
1977	3.2	1.5	7.0	24.6	0.36
1978	3.4	1.5	6.9	25.2	0.35
1979	0.8	1.1	6.7	25.2	0.33
1980	1.4	1.1	6.5	25.4	0.31

GNP and investment (information for which is available from 1960) are in terms of 1970 rubles, whereas capital stock data are in terms of 1973 rubles. The output–capital ratios are average ratios, derived by dividing the absolute values of output and capital during a given year. The latter is the average of the capital stock at the beginning of two consecutive years.
Source: compiled and elaborated by Desai (1987: 17).

was dependent upon its capacity either to keep absorbing additional resources or else to increase its productivity through technological advance and/or the use of comparative advantages in international trade.

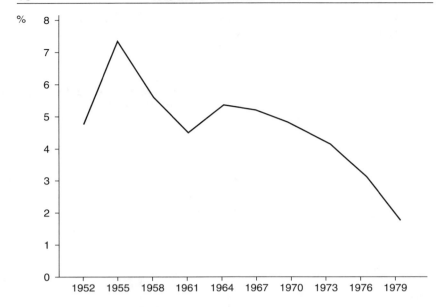

Figure 1.3 Soviet GNP growth rates, 1951–80. The annual growth rates are averaged over three years and plotted at the mid-year of each period.
Source: elaborated from table 1.4, col. 2

Yet, the Soviet economy developed in autarky, and for a long time in a hostile world environment that generated a siege mentality.[20] Trade was reduced to essential items, and always conditioned, both in imports and exports, by security considerations. Predatory acquisition of additional resources was never really an option for the Soviet Union, even after the Yalta Treaty acknowledged its occupation of Eastern Europe. Its vassal states, from East Germany to Cuba and Vietnam, were considered political pawns rather than economic colonies, some of them (for example, Cuba) being, in fact, very costly for the Soviet budget.[21] Interestingly enough, this priority of political over economic criteria was extended to the relationships between Russia and the non-Russian Soviet republics. The Soviet Union is a unique case of national domination in which there was reverse discrimination in the regional share of investment and resources, with Russia distributing

20   Holzman (1976); Desai (1987: 163–72; 251–73); Aganbegyan (1988: 141–56); Menshikov (1990: 222–64).
21   Marrese and Vanous (1983). For a critique (which I find questionable) of this analysis, see Desai (1987: 153–62).

to the other republics far more resources than it obtained from them.[22] Given the traditional Soviet distrust of foreign immigration, and with the belief in the unlimited potential of resources in the Asian and northern areas of the country, the *economic* emphasis was not on extending geographically the imperial reach but in mobilizing Soviet resources more fully, both natural and human (putting women to work outside the home; trying to make people work harder).

The shortcomings of this extensive model of economic growth followed directly from those features that assured its historical success in its politically assigned goals. The sacrifice of agriculture, and the brutal policy of enforced collectivization, hampered forever the productivity of the countryside, not only in cultivation, but in harvesting, in storing, in distributing.[23] Very often, crops were left to rot in the fields, or were spoiled in warehouses, or on the long journey to distant silos, located as far as possible from peasant villages to prevent pillage by a distrusted, resentful rural population. Tiny private plots of land systematically contributed much higher yields, but they were too small, and too often submitted to controls and abuses, to make up for the difference in an otherwise ruinous agriculture. As the Soviet Union moved from a state of emergency to a society trying to feed its citizens, agricultural deficits became an onerous burden on the state budget and on Soviet imports, gradually taking away resources from industrial investment.[24]

The centrally planned economy, extremely wasteful, yet effective in mobilizing resources on priority targets, was also the source of endless rigidities and imbalances that decreased productivity as the economy became more complex, technologically advanced, and organizationally diversified. When the population was allowed to express consumption preferences above the level of survival, when technological change forced the transformation of established work procedures, and when the sheer size of the economy, functionally interdependent on a vast geographical scale, eluded the programming skills of Gosplanners, the command economy began to be plagued by systemic dysfunctions in the practice of implementing the plan. Vertical, heavy-handed bureaucracies, stranded in an age of flexibility, became increasingly aloof, wandering along the paths of their own interpretation of the plan's assignments.

This system also discouraged innovation at a time of fundamental technological change, in spite of the vast resources that the Soviet Union dedicated to science and research and development (R&D), and in

22 See, among other sources, Korowkin (1994).
23 Volin (1970); Johnson and McConnell Brooks (1983); Scherer and Jakobson (1993).
24 Goldman (1983, 1987).

spite of having a higher proportion of scientists and engineers in the working population than any other major country in the world.[25] Because innovation always entails risk and unpredictability, production units at every level were systematically discouraged from engaging in such risky ventures. Furthermore, the accounting system of the planned economy represented a fundamental obstacle to productivity-enhancing innovation, both in technology and in management. Let us explain. The performance of each unit was measured in the gross value of production measured in rubles. This value of output (or *valovaya produktsiya, val*) included the value of all inputs. The comparison of *val* between years determined the level of fulfillment of plan and, eventually, the premium for managers and workers. Thus, there was no interest in reducing the value of inputs in a given product, for instance by using better technology or better management, if the *val* system could not translate such improvements into higher value added.[26] Furthermore, the vertical organization of production, including scientific production, made it extremely difficult to establish synergistic linkages between production and research. The Academy of Sciences remained by and large isolated from industry, and each ministry had its own research support system, often separate from that of other ministries, and rarely working in cooperation. Piecemeal, *ad hoc* technological solutions were the rule in the Soviet economy at the very moment when uncharted technological innovation was breaking ground in advanced capitalist economies at the dawn of the Information Age.[27]

Similarly, the priorities politically assigned to each branch and sector of the economy allowed for the realization of the Communist party's goals, not the least being the achievement of superpower status in about three decades. But systemic priorities led to systemic imbalances between sectors, and chronic lack of adjustment between supply and demand in most products and processes. Since prices could not reflect such imbalances because they were set by administrative decision, the gap resulted in shortages. Shortages of everything became a structural feature of the Soviet economy.[28] And with shortages also came the development of methods to deal with shortages, from the consumer to the store, from the manufacturer to the supplier, and from one manager to another. What started as a pragmatic way of circumventing shortages, in a network of reciprocal favors, ended up as a vast system of informal economic exchange, increasingly organized on the basis of

25 Aganbegyan (1988).
26 Goldman (1987).
27 Golland (1991).
28 On the analysis of systemic generation of shortages in the command economy, see Kornai (1980).

illegal payments, either in money or in goods. Since allegiance to and protection from supervising bureaucrats was a prerequisite for the system to work outside the rules on such a large scale, the party and the state became immersed in a gigantic shadow economy, a fundamental dimension of the Soviet system, which has been thoroughly investigated by Gregory Grossman, one of the leading scholars on the Soviet economy.[29] It has been sometimes claimed that such a shadow economy smoothed the rigidities of the system, creating a quasi-market mechanism that permitted the real economy to operate. In fact, as soon as managers and bureaucrats discovered the benefit of the shortage-ridden economy, shortages were constantly induced by strictly applying the rigid rules of the plan, thus creating the need for the softening of the system – at a price. The shadow economy, which grew considerably during the 1970s with the compliance of the party's *nomenklatura*, deeply transformed Soviet social structure, disorganizing and making more costly a planned economy that, by definition, was no longer allowed to plan, since the dominant interest of "gatekeepers" throughout the administrative apparatus was to collect their shadow rents rather than to receive their bonuses from the fulfillment of planned targets.[30]

The international isolation of the Soviet economy was functional to the system because it made possible the operation of the plan (not feasible practically in an open economy) and because it insulated production from external competitive pressures. But precisely for the same reason, Soviet industry and agriculture became unable to compete in the world economy, just at the historical moment of formation of an interdependent, global system. When the Soviet Union was forced to import goods, whether advanced machinery, consumer goods, or grain to feed cattle, it discovered the damaging limits of its scarce capacity to export manufactured goods in exchange. It resorted to massive exports of oil, gas, materials, and precious metals, which by the 1980s represented 90 percent of Soviet exports to the capitalist world, with oil and gas alone accounting for two-thirds of such exports.[31] This external trade structure, typical of underdeveloped economies, is susceptible to the secular deterioration of commodity prices *vis-à-vis* the prices of manufactured goods, and is excessively vulnerable to fluctuations in the price of oil in world markets.[32] This dependence on exports of natural resources diverted energy resources and raw materials from investment in the Soviet economy, further undermining

29 Grossman (1977).
30 Grossman (1989).
31 Menshikov (1990).
32 Veen (1984).

the extensive model of growth. On the other hand, when the price of oil fell, in 1986, the import capacity of the economy was severely damaged, increasing shortages of consumer goods and agricultural inputs.[33]

Yet, perhaps the most devastating weakness of the Soviet economy was precisely what was the strength of the Soviet state: an over-extended military–industrial complex and an unsustainable defense budget. In the 1980s, Soviet defense expenditure could be evaluated at about 15 percent of Soviet GNP, more than twice the equivalent proportion in the US at the peak of Reagan's defense build up. Some estimates put it at an even higher level, at about 20–25 percent of GNP.[34] About 40 percent of industrial production was defense related, and the production of enterprises that were engaged in the military–industrial complex reached about 70 percent of all industrial production. But the damage of such a gigantic military industry to the civilian economy went deeper.[35] Its enterprises concentrated the best talent in scientists, engineers, and skilled workers, and were also provided with the best machinery, and access to technological resources. They had their own research centers, the most technologically advanced in the country, and they had priority in the allocation of import quotas. Thus, they absorbed the best of Soviet industrial, human, and technological potential. And once these resources were allocated to the military sector, they were hardly returned to civilian production or applications. Technological spin-offs were a rarity, and the proportion of civilian goods to the total production of military enterprises was usually lower than 10 percent. Even so, most television sets and other electronic consumer goods were produced by military enterprises, as a by-product of their activity. Needless to say, attention to consumer satisfaction was minimal, given the organic dependence of such enterprises on the Ministry of Defense. The military–industrial sector operated as a black hole in the Soviet economy, absorbing most of the creative energy of society and making it disappear in an abyss of invisible inertia. After all, the militarization of the economy is a logical attribute of a system that assigns absolute priority to the power of the state for the sake of the power of the state. That an impoverished, massively rural, and barely developed country like the Soviet Union at the beginning of the century could become one of the greatest military powers in history in just three decades had necessarily to take its toll on the Soviet civilian economy and on its citizens' everyday life.

The Soviet leadership was not unaware of the contradictions and bottlenecks that were developing in the planned economy. Indeed, as

33   Aganbegyan (1988).
34   Steinberg (1991).
35   Rowen and Wolf (1990); Cooper (1991).

mentioned above, Soviet history has been dominated by periodic efforts of reform and restructuring.[36] Khrushchev tried to bring the achievements of socialism closer to people's homes by improving agricultural production, and giving more attention to consumer goods, housing, and social benefits, especially pensions.[37] Furthermore, he envisaged a new kind of economy, able to unleash the full development of productive forces. Science and technology would be put to the service of economic development, and the natural resources of Siberia, the far east and the central Asian republics would be brought to fruition. In the wake of the enthusiasm generated by the successful launching of the first sputniks, the 21st Party Congress, extrapolating on the basis of growth indicators, predicted that the USSR would reach economic parity with the United States in 20 years. Accordingly, the overall strategy to vanquish capitalism shifted from the inevitability of military confrontation to the stated policy of peaceful coexistence and peaceful competition. Khrushchev actually believed that the demonstration effect of the achievements of socialism would ultimately bring communist parties and their allies to power in the rest of the world.[38] Yet, before engaging the international communist movement in such a grandiose perspective (contested by Chinese communists), he knew that changes had to be made in the bureaucracy of the Soviet state. With the party hardliners put on the defensive by the revelation of Stalin's atrocities in the 20th Congress, Khrushchev eliminated the economic ministries, limited Gosplan's power, and transferred responsibility to regional economic councils (*sovnarkhozy*). The bureaucracy responded, predictably, by reconstructing informal networks of top-down control and management of scarce resources. The ensuing disorganization of the planning system led to falls in production, and to a substantial slowdown in the growth of agriculture, the core of Khrushchevian reforms. Before Khrushchev could react to the sabotage of his policies, admittedly flawed with excessive voluntarism, the party apparatus staged an internal coup that ended Khrushchev's tenure in 1964. Immediately afterwards, Gosplan's powers were reinstated, and new branch ministries were created, through which planning authorities could enforce their directives.

Economic reform was not completely stalled, but reoriented from the level of state administration to the level of the enterprise. The 1965 Kosygin reforms,[39] inspired by economists Liberman and Nemchinov, gave greater freedom of decision to enterprise managers, and experi-

---

36   Van Regemorter (1990).
37   Gustafson (1981); Gerner and Hedlund (1989).
38   Taibo (1993b).
39   Kontorovich (1988).

mented with a price system to pay for resources in production. More attention was also paid to consumer goods (whose production, for the first time, grew faster than that of capital goods in 1966–70). Incentives were provided to agriculture, resulting in a substantial increase in output in the 1966–71 period. Yet, when confronted with the logic of the planned economy, these reforms could not last. Enterprises that improved their productivity by using their newly obtained freedom found themselves assigned higher production quotas the following year. Entrepreneurial managers and workers (as in the enterprise that became the role model of the reforms in 1967, the chemical complex of Shchekino in Tula) felt trapped into being, in fact, punished with an intensification of their work pace while firms that had kept a steady, customary level of production were left alone in their bureaucratic routine. By the early 1970s, Kosygin had lost power, and the innovative potential of the halfhearted reforms faded away.

Yet, the first ten years of the Brezhnev period (1964–75)[40] witnessed moderate economic growth (above 4 percent per year, on average), coupled with political stability, and a steady improvement in the living conditions of the population. The term "stagnation" (*zastoi*), usually applied to the Brezhnev years, does not do justice to the first part of the period.[41] Relative stagnation did not settle in until 1975 onwards, and a zero growth level was reached in 1980. The sources of such stagnation seem to have been structural, and they were the immediate factors prompting Gorbachev's *perestroika*.

Padma Desai has provided empirical evidence, as well as an econometric interpretation, of the retardation in the growth of the Soviet economy (see figure 1.3), whose main reasons seem to be the declining rate of technical change, and the diminishing returns of the extensive model of accumulation.[42] Abel Aganbegyan also attributes the slowdown in economic growth to the exhaustion of the model of industrialization based on extensive use of capital, labor, and natural resources.[43] Technological backwardness led to decreasing returns in the oil and gas fields, in the coal mines, in the extraction of iron, and rare metals. The cost of exploring new resources dramatically increased with distance and with the geographical barriers created by the inhospitable conditions in the northern and eastern areas of the Soviet territory. Labor supply dwindled in the Soviet economy as birth rates declined over time, as a result of education and economic development, and as women's incorporation into the labor force was almost

40   Goldman (1983); Veen (1984); Mitchell (1990).
41   Van Regemorter (1990).
42   Desai (1987).
43   Aganbegyan (1988).

complete. Thus, one of the pillars of the extensive model of accumulation, steady quantitative increases in labor, disappeared. Capital inputs were also limited by decreasing returns of investment under the same production function, characteristic of an earlier stage of industrialization. To produce the same quantity, under the new economic conditions, more capital had to be used, as the dramatic decline in output–capital ratio indicates (see table 1.4).

Retardation was also linked to the inherent dynamics and bureaucratic logic of the model of accumulation. Stanislav Menshikov, together with a team of young economists at the Institute of Economics of the Academy of Sciences in Novosibirsk in the 1970s, developed an intersectoral model of the Soviet economy. In his words:

> Economic analysis showed that our investment, production, and distribution decision-making was not, in fact, aimed at increasing the well-being of the population, promoting technological progress and keeping growth rates sufficiently high to maintain economic equilibrium. Rather, decisions were made with a view to maximizing the power of ministries in their struggle to divide up the excessively centralized material, financial, labour, natural, and intellectual resources. Our economic–mathematical analysis showed that the system had an inexorable inertia of its own and was bound to grow more and more inefficient.[44]

This inefficiency became particularly blatant when consumption demands from an increasingly educated, by now self-assured, population, started to put pressure on government, not in the form of social movements challenging the system, but as the loyal expression of the citizens' request for the gradual delivery of promised well-being.[45]

Yet, two major structural problems seemed to impede the ability of the system to reform itself by the 1980s. On the one hand, the exhaustion of the extensive model of economic growth implied the need to shift to a new production equation in which technological change could play a greater role, using the benefits of the unfolding technological revolution to increase substantially the productivity of the whole economy. This required that a share of the surplus could be set aside for social consumption without jeopardizing the updating of the military machine. On the other hand, the excessive bureaucratization of economic management, and the chaotic consequences of its corollary, the growth of the shadow economy, had to be corrected by shaking up the planning institutions, and by bringing under control the parallel circuits of appropriation and distribution of goods and services. On

44 Menshikov (1990: 8).
45 Lewin (1988).

both counts – technological modernization and administrative regeneration – the obstacles to reckon with were formidable.

The Technology Question

In spite of the shortcomings of centralized planning, the Soviet Union did build a mighty industrial economy. When, in 1961, Khrushchev launched to the world the challenge that by the 1980s the USSR would produce more industrial goods than the United States, most Western observers ridiculed the statement, even in the wake of the sputnik shock. Yet, the irony is that, at least according to official statistics, in spite of economic retardation and social disarray, in the 1980s the Soviet Union produced substantially more than the US in a number of heavy industrial sectors: it produced 80 percent more steel, 78 percent more cement, 42 percent more oil, 55 percent more fertilizer, twice as much pig iron, and five times as many tractors.[46] The problem was that, in the meantime, the world's production system had shifted heavily toward electronics and specialty chemicals, and was tilting toward the biotechnology revolution, all areas in which the Soviet economy and technology were lagging substantially.[47] By all accounts and indicators, the Soviet Union missed the revolution in information technologies that took shape in the world in the mid-1970s. In a study I conducted in 1991–3, with Svetlana Natalushko, on the leading firms in microelectronics and telecommunications in Zelenograd (the Soviet Silicon Valley, 25 km from Moscow),[48] the immense technological gap between Soviet and Western electronic technologies became apparent, in spite of the generally high technical quality of the scientific and engineering personnel we interviewed. For instance, even at such a late date, Russian enterprises did not have the capability to design sub-micron chips, and their "clean rooms" were so "dirty" that they could not even produce the most advanced chips they could design. Indeed, the main reason we were given for their technological underdevelopment was the lack of appropriate equipment for semiconductor production. A similar story can be told about the computer industry, which, according to the observations of another study I conducted in the research institutes of the Siberian Branch of the Academy of Sciences in Novosibirsk, in 1990, seemed to be about 20 years behind the American or Japanese

46   Walker (1986: 53).
47   Amman and Cooper (1986).
48   Castells and Natalushko (1993).

computer industry.[49] The PC revolution completely bypassed Soviet technology, as it did in fact with IBM. But, unlike IBM, the Soviet Union took more than a decade to start designing and producing its own clone, suspiciously looking like an Apple One.[50] At the other end of the spectrum, in high-performance computers, which should have been the strong point of a statist technological system, the aggregate peak performance of Soviet machines in 1991 – the highest year of such production in the USSR – was over two orders of magnitude less than that of Cray Research alone.[51] As for the most critical technological infrastructure, the evaluation by Diane Doucette of the Soviet telecommunications system in 1992 also showed its backwardness in relation to any major industrialized nation.[52] Even in key technologies with military applications, by the late 1980s the Soviet Union was well behind the US. In a comparison of military technology between the US, NATO, Japan, and the USSR, conducted by the US Defense Department in 1989, the Soviet Union was the least advanced country in 15 out of 25 technologies evaluated, and was not in parity with the US in any technological field.[53] Malleret and Delaporte's evaluation of military technology also seems to confirm this fact.[54]

Here again, there is no obvious, direct reason for such backwardness. Not only had the Soviet Union a strong scientific basis, and a technology advanced enough to have overtaken the US in the race to space in the late 1950s,[55] but the official doctrine under Brezhnev brought the "scientific and technical revolution" (STR) to the core of Soviet strategy to overtake the West and build communism on a technological foundation spurred by socialist relations of production.[56] Nor was this stated priority a purely ideological discourse. The importance given to the STR was backed by massive investment in science, R&D, and the training of technical personnel, with the result that, by the 1980s, the USSR had more scientists and engineers, relative to the total population, than any other major country in the world.[57]

Thus, we are left anew with the idea that "the system," not the people, and not the lack of material resources devoted to scientific and technical development, undermined its foundations, provoking tech-

49   Castells (1991); for an abridged version of this analysis, see Castells and Hall (1994: ch. 4).
50   Agamirzian (1991).
51   Wolcott and Goodman (1993); see also Wolcott (1993).
52   Doucette (1995).
53   US Department of Defense (1989), compiled and cited by Alvarez Gonzalez (1993).
54   Malleret and Delaporte (1991).
55   *US News and World Report* (1988).
56   Afanasiev (1972); Dryakhlov et al. (1972). For an English summary of these themes, see Blyakhman and Shkaratan (1977).
57   See Fortescue (1986); Smith (1992: 283–309).

nological retardation precisely at the critical moment of a major paradigm shift in the rest of the world. Indeed, until the early 1960s there
is no evidence of substantial Soviet lagging behind in the main technological fields, with the major exception of biological sciences, devastated by Lysenkoism.[58] But, as soon as discontinuity took place in
technological evolution, as it did in the West from the early 1970s,
scientific research could not help technological progress, and efforts at
learning through reverse engineering engaged the Soviet Union in a
doomed race against the acceleration of technological innovation in
America and Japan.[59] "Something" happened during the 1970s that
induced technological retardation in the USSR. But this "something"
happened not in the Soviet Union, but in the advanced capitalist countries. The characteristics of the new technological revolution, based
on information technologies and on the rapid diffusion of such technologies in a wide range of applications, made it extremely difficult
for the Soviet system to assimilate and to adapt them for its own purposes. It was not the crisis of the Brezhnevian stagnation period that
hampered technological development. Rather, it was the incapacity of
the Soviet system actually to integrate the much-vaunted "scientific
and technical revolution" that contributed to its economic stagnation.
Let us be specific about the reasons for this incapacity.

The first reason was the absorption of economic resources, science
and technology, advanced machinery, and brainpower into the industrial–military complex. This vast universe, which accounted in the early
1980s for about two-thirds of industrial production, and received,
together with the armed forces, between 15 and 20 percent of Soviet
GNP,[60] was a wasteful repository for science and technology: it received the best talent and best equipment available, returning to the
civilian economy only mediocre electrical appliances and consumer
electronics goods.[61] Few of the advanced technologies that were discovered, used, or applied in the military–industrial complex were diffused into society, mainly for security reasons, but also for the sake of
controlling information which made the military enterprises virtual
oligopolies of advanced industrial know-how. Furthermore, the logic
of military enterprises, in the East as in the West, was and is, overall,
to please their only client: the Defense Ministry.[62] Thus, technologies
were developed, or adapted, to fit the extremely specific requirements

58   Thomas and KruseVaucienne (1977); Fortescue (1986).
59   Goldman (1987).
60   Sapir (1987); Audigier (1989); Alexander (1990: 7620); Steinberg (1991).
61   Alvarez Gonzalez (1993).
62   Fieldwork by Manuel Castells, Svetlana Natalushko, and collaborators in electronics
firms in Zelenograd (1991–3). See Castells and Natalushko (1993). On the problems of
technological spinoffs from the defense industry in Western economies, see Kaldor (1981).

of military hardware, which explains the considerable difficulties of any conversion project both in Russia and in the US. Who needs, in the industrial or consumer market, a chip designed to withstand a nuclear blast? What saved American electronics defense industries from rapid obsolescence was their relative openness to competition from other American companies, as well as from Japanese electronics producers.[63] But Soviet enterprises, living in a closed economy, without incentive to export, and with no other purpose than to follow the specifications of a not necessarily up-to-date Ministry of Defense, were engaged in a technological trajectory increasingly removed from the needs of society and from the processes of innovation of the rest of the world.[64]

The logic imposed by military requirements on technological performance was largely responsible for the demise of Soviet computers, which were not far behind their Western equivalents between the mid-1940s and mid-1960s, and were a key element in the progress made by the early Soviet space program.[65] Computer design began at the Academy of Sciences in Kiev in the 1940s, under the direction of Professor S.A. Lebedev.[66] The first prototype, the MESM, was built in 1950, only four years after the first American computer, the UNIAC. From such prototypes developed, in the late 1950s and 1960s, a whole family of mainframes: the M-20, BASM-3M, BASM-4, M-220, and M-222. This line of development reached its peak in 1968 with the production of a powerful machine, the BESM-6, capable of 800,000 operations per second, which became the workhorse of Soviet computing for the next two decades. Yet, this was the last major breakthrough of an endogenous Soviet computer industry. In 1965, under pressure from the military, the Soviet government decided to adopt the IBM model 360 as the core of the Unified Computer System of the Council of Mutual Economic Assistance (the Soviet-dominated Eastern European international organization). From then on, IBM and digital computers, and later some Japanese computers, became the norm in the Soviet Union. Instead of developing their own design and production line, Soviet electronic R&D centers and factories (all under the Ministry of Defense) engaged in the smuggling of computers from the West, proceeding to reverse engineering and to reproduce each model, adapting them to Soviet military specifications. The KGB was given, as a priority task, the acquisition of the most advanced Western

63 Sandholtz et al. (1992).
64 Cooper (1991).
65 Fieldwork by Manuel Castells in Novosibirsk (1990) and in Zelenograd (1992–3); see also Hutching (1976); Amman and Cooper (1986).
66 Agamirzian (1991).

technological know-how and machines, particularly in electronics, by whatever means.[67] Open and covert technology transfer from the West, both in design and in equipment, became the main source for the information technology revolution in the Soviet Union. This necessarily led to retardation, since the time lag between the moment that a new computer hit the world market (or even became available to KGB agents) and the moment that Soviet factories were able to produce it became increasingly longer *vis-à-vis* the state of the art, especially given the acceleration of the technological race in the late 1970s. Since the same procedure was followed for all electronics components and software, retardation in each segment of the industry interacted with each other, thus multiplying the technological lag. What had been a situation close to parity in computer design in the early 1960s became, in the 1990s, a 20-year difference in design and manufacturing capability.[68]

A similar development took place in software. Soviet machines of the 1960s were working on the endogenously developed ALGOL language, which would have paved the way for systems integration, the current frontier of computing. Yet, in the 1970s, in order to operate American-like computers, Soviet scientists developed their version of FORTRAN, quickly made obsolete by software developments in the West. Finally, they resorted to copying, without legal permission, whatever software appeared in America, thus introducing the same retardation mechanism to a field in which Russian mathematicians could have pioneered the world's scientific frontier.

Why so? Why, paradoxically, did the Soviet military and the KGB choose to become technologically dependent on the US?! The researchers I interviewed in the Academy of Sciences' Institute of Informatics Systems in Novosibirsk gave a convincing argument, drawn from their own experience. The development of Soviet computer sciences in isolation from the rest of the world was too uncertain in a field largely unexplored to satisfy the worried military and political leadership. What would happen to Soviet power, based on computing capacities, if their researchers missed a crucial new development, if the technological trajectory in which they were locked diverged dangerously from the West in an untested course? Would it not be too late to change course if the US one day realized that the Soviet Union did not have the real computing capacity to defend itself effectively? Thus, the So-

67 Andrew and Gordievsky (1990: 521ff.).
68 Evaluation by the director of the Institute of Informatics Systems, Russian Academy of Sciences, Siberian Branch. This evaluation was confirmed by six engineers and managers in telecommunications and electronics institutes in Zelenograd during my fieldwork; see Castells and Natalushko (1993); Castells and Hall (1994: ch. 4).

viet leadership (probably a high-level decision informed by the KGB) opted for a conservative, safe approach: let us have the same machines as "they" have, even if we take some extra time to reproduce "their" computers. After all, to activate Armageddon a few years' technological gap in electronic circuitry would not really be relevant, as long as it worked. Thus, the superior military interests of the Soviet state led to the paradox of making the Soviet Union technologically dependent on the United States in the crucial field of information technology.

However, Japanese electronics companies also proceeded to copy American technology in the early stages, and succeeded in catching up in several key areas in one or two decades, while the Soviet Union experienced the opposite result. Why so? The main reason seems to be that Japanese (and later other Asian countries) had to compete with the firms from whom they were borrowing the technology, so they had to keep apace, while the rhythm of technological development in Soviet enterprises was dictated by military procurement procedures and by a command economy that emphasized quantity over quality. The absence of international or domestic competition removed any pressure on Soviet firms to innovate faster than was needed in the view of the planners of the Ministry of Defense.[69] When the military-oriented technological acceleration of the "Star Wars" program made evident the much-feared technological gap between the Soviet Union and the US, the alarm of the Soviet high command, as expressed most openly by the chief of staff Marshal Ogarkov, was one of the factors that prompted *perestroika*, in spite of the political fall of Ogarkov himself.[70]

However, the Soviet Union had sufficient scientific, industrial, and technological resources outside the military sector to have been able to improve its technological performance even in the absence of military spinoffs. But another layer of statist logic precluded such development. The functioning of the command economy, as mentioned above, was based on the fulfillment of the plan, not on the improvement of either products or processes. Efforts at innovation always entail a risk, both in the outcome and in the ability to obtain the necessary supplies to engage in new areas of production. There was no incentive built into the system of industrial production toward such a goal. Indeed, there was the possibility of failure inscribed in any risk-taking initiative. Technological innovation had no rewards but could result in sanctions.[71] A simplistic, bureaucratic logic presided over techno-

69   Goldman (1987).
70   Walker (1986).
71   Berliner (1986); Aganbegyan (1989).

logical decision-making, as in all other areas of economic management. A revealing anecdote may help to illustrate the argument.[72] Most US chip leads are spaced ¹⁄₁₀ inch apart. The Soviet Ministry of Electronics, in charge of copying American chips, mandated metric spacing, but ¹⁄₁₀ inch is equivalent to an odd metric measure: about 0.254 mm. To simplify things, as is often the case with the Soviet bureaucracy, rounding was decided upon, creating a "metric inch": 0.25 mm spacing. Thus, Soviet chip clones look like their American equivalents, but they do not fit in a Western socket. The mistake was discovered too late, with the net result that, even in 1991, Soviet semiconductor assembly equipment could not be used to produce Western-sized chips, thus excluding potential exports for Soviet microelectronics production.

Furthermore, scientific research and industrial production were institutionally separated. The powerful and well-provided Academy of Sciences was a strictly research-oriented institution with its own programs and criteria, disconnected from the needs and problems of industrial enterprises.[73] Unable to rely on the contributions of the Academy, enterprises used the research centers of their own ministries. Because any exchange between these centers would have required formal contacts between ministries in the context of the plan, applied research centers also lacked communication between each other. This strictly vertical separation, imposed by the institutional logic of the command economy, forbade the process of "learning by doing" that was critical in fostering technological innovation in the West. The lack of interaction between basic science, applied research, and industrial production led to extreme rigidity in the production system, to the absence of experimentation in scientific discoveries, and to a narrow application of specific technologies for limited uses, precisely at the moment when advancement in information technologies was predicated on constant interaction between different technological fields on the basis of their communication via computer networks.

Soviet leaders became increasingly concerned about the lack of productive interaction between science and industry, at least from 1955, when a conference convened by Bulganin met to discuss the problem. During the 1960s, Khrushchev, and then Brezhnev, were betting on science and technology to overtake capitalism. In the late 1960s, in the context of cautious economic reforms, "science–production associations" were introduced, establishing horizontal links between en-

---

72   Reported by Fred Langa, chief editor of the journal *BYTE*; see the April 1991 issue, p. 128.
73   Kassel and Campbell (1980).

terprises and research centers.[74] The results, again, were paradoxical. On the one hand, the associations won some autonomy and increased the interaction between their industrial and scientific components. On the other hand, because they were rewarded by their differential increase in production *vis-à-vis* other associations, they developed a tendency to be self-sufficient, and to cut off ties with other production associations, as well as with the rest of the science and technology system, since they were only accountable to their own parent ministries. Additionally, ministries were not keen to cooperate outside their controlled turfs, and the Academy of Sciences resisted any attempt at curtailing its bureaucratic independence, skillfully using the fears of regressing to the excessive submission of the Stalinist era. Although Gorbachev tried later to revive the experience, horizontal linkages between scientific research and industrial enterprises never really worked in the planned economy, thus precluding effective application of technological discoveries using different channels from vertically transmitted ministerial instructions.

A case in point, which illustrates the fundamental inability of the centrally planned economy to accommodate processes of rapid technological innovation, is the experiment of the science city of Akademgorodok, near Novosibirsk.[75] In 1957, Khrushchev, upon his return from the United States, aimed at emulating the American university campus model, convinced that, given the right conditions, Soviet science could surpass its Western equivalent. On the advice of a leading mathematician, Lavrentiev, he launched the construction of a science city in the Siberian birch forest, on the shores of the artificial Ob lake, adjacent to, but deliberately separated from, the main Siberian industrial and political center, Novosibirsk. Some of the best, young, dynamic scientific talent in the Soviet Union were given incentives to settle there, away from the academic bureaucracy of Moscow and Leningrad, and somewhat freer from direct ideological control. In the 1960s, Akademgorodok flourished as a major scientific center in physics, mathematics, informatics, advanced materials, and economics, among other disciplines. At its peak in the 1980s, Akademgorodok was home to 20 Institutes of the Academy of Sciences, as well as to a small, elite university, Novosibirsk State University. Altogether there were almost 10,000 researchers and professors, 4,500 students, and thousands of auxiliary workers and technicians. These scientific institutions operated on the cutting edge of their disciplines. Indeed, in economics and sociology, Akademgorodok provided some of the first

74   Kazantsev (1991).
75   Castells and Hall (1994: 41–56).

intellectual leaders of *perestroika*, including Abel Aganbegyan and Tatyana Zaslavskaya. Yet, regardless of the scientific excellence achieved by the Siberian science city, its link up with industry never took place. And this was in spite of its proximity to the Siberian industrial center, where were located major defense plants, including electronics and aircraft factories. The separation between the two systems was such that the Academy of Sciences established its own industrial workshops in Akademgorodok to produce the machines needed for scientific experimentation, while Novosibirsk electronics enterprises continued to rely on their Moscow-based research centers. The reason, according to the researchers I interviewed in 1990–2, was that industrial firms were not interested in state-of-the-art technology: their production plans were adjusted to the machinery they already had installed, and any change in the production system would mean failure to meet production quotas assigned to them. Therefore, technological change could happen only through the impetus of the corresponding Gosplan unit, which would have to order the introduction of new machines at the same time as it determined a new production quota. But Gosplan's calculations could not rely on potential machinery resulting from cutting-edge research in the academic institutes. Instead, Gosplan relied on off-the-shelf technology available in the international market, since the more advanced Western technology procured secretly by the KGB was reserved to the military sector. Thus, one of the boldest experiments of the Khrushchev era, designed to link up science and industry to form the core of a new development process in one of the world's richest regions in natural resources, ultimately failed under the inescapable burden of Soviet statism.

Thus, when technological innovation accelerated in the West, during the 1970s and early 1980s, the Soviet Union increasingly relied on imports of machinery and technology transfer for its leading industrial sectors, taking advantage of the cash bonanza resulting from Siberian oil and gas exports. There was considerable waste. Marshall Goldman interviewed a number of Western business executives engaging in technology exports to the Soviet Union in the early 1980s.[76] According to their accounts, imported equipment was poorly utilized (at about two-thirds of Western efficiency for the same machines); the Ministry of Foreign Trade attempted to save its scarce hard currency resources, while major enterprises had a vested interest in stockpiling the most recent equipment and large amounts of spare parts whenever they were authorized to proceed with imports; distrust between ministries made it impossible to harmonize their import policies, resulting

76   Goldman (1987: 118 ff.).

in incompatibility between equipment; and long periods of amortiza-
tion for each type of equipment imported in a given factory led to
technological obsolescence, and to the painful coexistence of machinery and procedures of highly diverse technological ages. Moreover, it
soon became evident that it was impossible to modernize the technology of one segment of the economy without revamping the entire system. Precisely because the planned economy made its units highly
interdependent, it was impossible to remedy technological lag in some
critical sectors (for example, electronics) without enabling each element of the system to interface with the others. To close the circle, the
logic of using scarce foreign technology resources for a shrunk, indispensable segment of the system, reinforced the priority given to the
military–industrial sector, and firmly established a sharp separation
between two increasingly incompatible technological systems, the war
machine and the survival economy.

Last, but not least, ideological repression and the politics of information control were decisive obstacles for innovation and diffusion of
new technologies precisely focused on information processing.[77] True,
in the 1960s the excesses of Stalinism were left behind, to be replaced
by the grand perspectives of "scientific and technical revolution" as
the material basis of socialism. Lysenko was dismissed shortly after
Khrushchev's fall, although only after exercising intellectual terror for
20 years; "cybernetics" ceased to be considered a bourgeois science;
mathematical models were introduced in economics; systems analysis
was favorably commented upon in the Marxist–Leninist circles; and,
most significantly, the Academy of Sciences received strong material
support and considerable bureaucratic autonomy to take care of its
own affairs, including exercising its own ideological controls. Yet,
Soviet science and technology continued to suffer from bureaucracy,
ideological control, and political repression.[78] Access to the international scientific community remained very limited, and available only
to a select group of scientists, closely surveilled, with the ensuing handicap for scientific cross-fertilization. Research information was filtered,
and the diffusion of findings was controlled and limited. Science bureaucrats often imposed their views on challengers and innovators,
finding support in the political hierarchy. KGB presence in major scientific centers continued to be pervasive until the end of the Soviet
regime. Reproduction of information, and free communication among
researchers, and between researchers and the outside world, remained
difficult for a long time, constituting a formidable obstacle to scien-

77 Smaryl (1984).
78 Fortescue (1986).

tific ingenuity and technological diffusion. Following Lenin's genial instinct to control paper supply as the basic device for controlling information in the aftermath of revolution, Soviet printing, copying, information processing, and communication machines remained under tight control. Typewriters were rare, carefully monitored devices. Access to a photocopying machine always required security clearance: two authorized signatures for a Russian text, and three authorized signatures for a non-Russian text. Use of long-distance telephone lines and telex was controlled by special procedures within each organization. And the very notion of a "*personal* computer" was objectively subversive to the Soviet bureaucracy, including science bureaucracy. Diffusion of information technology, both of machines and of the know-how, could hardly take place in a society where the control of information was critical to the legitimacy of the state, and to the control of the population. The more communication technologies made the outside world accessible to the imaginary representation of Soviet citizens, the more it became objectively disruptive to make such technologies available to a population which, by and large, had shifted from submissive terror into passive routine on the basis of a lack of information and of alternative views of the world. Thus, as its very essence, Soviet statism denied itself the diffusion of information technologies in the social system. And, without this diffusion, information technologies could not develop beyond the specific, functional assignments received from the state, thus making impossible the process of spontaneous innovation by use and networked interaction which characterizes the information technology paradigm.

Thus, at the core of the technological crisis of the Soviet Union lies the fundamental logic of the statist system: overwhelming priority given to military power; political–ideological control of information by the state; the bureaucratic principles of the centrally planned economy; isolation from the rest of the world; and an inability to modernize some segments of the economy and society technologically without modifying the whole system in which such elements interact with each other.

The consequences of this technological backwardness at the very moment when advanced capitalist countries were involved in a fundamental technological transformation, were full of meaning for the Soviet Union, and ultimately became a major contributing factor in its demise. The economy could not shift from an extensive to an intensive model of development, thus accelerating its decline. The increasing technological gap disabled the Soviet Union in world economic competition, closing the door to the benefits of international trade beyond its role as supplier of energy and materials. The highly educated population of the country found itself trapped in a technological system that was increasingly distant from comparable industrial societies. The application of computers to a bureaucratic system and to a command economy increased the rigidity of controls,[79] verifying the hypothesis according to which technological rationalization of social irrationality increases disorder. Ultimately, the military machine itself came to suffer from a growing technological gap *vis-à-vis* its competing warriors,[80] thus deepening the crisis of the Soviet state.

The Abduction of Identity and the Crisis of Soviet Federalism

Many of our national problems are caused by the contradictory nature of the two principles which were laid as the cornerstones of the Russian Federation: the national-territorial principle and the administrative-territorial principle.

Boris Yeltsin, *Rossiyskaya gazeta*, February 25, 1994

Gorbachev's reforms were explicitly aimed, at their inception, at economic restructuring and technological modernization. Yet, these were not the only faults of the Soviet system. The foundations of the multinational, multi-ethnic, multilayered, Soviet federal state were built on the shaky sand of reconstructed history, and barely sustained by ruthless repression.[81] After massive deportations of entire ethnic groups to Siberia and central Asia under Stalin,[82] an iron-clad prohibition was imposed on the autonomous expression of nationalism among the more than a hundred nationalities and ethnic groups that populated the Soviet Union.[83] Although there were isolated nationalist demonstrations (for example, Armenia, April 1965; Georgia, April 1978), sometimes crushed by force (for example, Tbilisi, March 1956), most nationalist expressions were subdued for a long period, and only taken up by dissident intellectuals in rare moments of relative tolerance under Khrushchev or in the late 1970s.[84] Yet, it was the pressure of nationalism, utilized in their personal interest by the political elites of the republics, that ultimately doomed Gorbachev's reformist experiment, and led to the disintegration of the Soviet Union. Nationalism, including Russian nationalism, provided the ideological basis for social

79   Cave (1980).
80   Walker (1986); Praaning and Perry (1989); Rowen and Wolf (1990); Taibo (1993a).
81   Carrere d'Encausse (1978).
82   Nekrich (1978).
83   Motyl (1987); Lane (1990).
84   Simon (1991).

mobilization in a society where strictly political ideologies, not relying on historical–cultural identity, suffered the backlash of cynicism and disbelief generated by seven decades of indoctrination in the themes of communist utopia.[85] While the inability of Soviet statism to adapt to the technological and economic conditions of an information society was the most powerful underlying cause of the crisis of the Soviet system, it was the resurgence of national identity, either historically rooted or politically reinvented, that first challenged and ultimately destroyed the Soviet state. If economic and technological problems prompted the Andropov–Gorbachev reforms of the 1980s, the explosive issue of insurgent nationalism and federal relationships within the Soviet Union was the main political factor accounting for the loss of control of the reform process by the Soviet leadership.

The reasons for this irrepressible resurgence of nationalism in the Soviet Union during the *perestroika* years are to be found in the history of Soviet communism. It is, in fact, a complex story that goes beyond the simplistic image of sheer repression of national/ethnic cultures by the Soviet state. Indeed, it is argued by one of the leading historians of non-Russian nationalities in the Soviet Union, professor of Armenian history Ronald Grigor Suny, that:

> Lost in the powerful nationalist rhetoric is any sense of the degree to which the long and difficult years of Communist party rule actually continued the "making of nations" of the pre-revolutionary period. As the present generation watches the self-destruction of the Soviet Union, the irony is lost that the USSR was the victim not only of its negative effects on the non-Russian peoples but of its own "progressive" contribution to the process of nation building . . . The Soviet state's deeply contradictory policy nourished the cultural uniqueness of distinct peoples. It thereby increased ethnic solidarity and national consciousness in the non-Russian republics, even as it frustrated full articulation of a national agenda by requiring conformity to an imposed political order.[86]

Let us try to reconstruct the logic of this powerful political paradox.[87]

The Soviet Union was founded in December 1922 and its multinational, federal state was enshrined in the 1924 Constitution.[88] Originally it included: the Russian Soviet Federated Socialist Republic (RSFSR), itself incorporating, besides Russia, a number of non-

85   Carrere d'Encausse (1991); Khazanov (1995).
86   Suny (1993: 101, 130).
87   For a theoretical analysis of the relationship between nationalism and mobilization by Leninist elites, see Jowitt (1971, esp. part I), which sets his analytical foundation in a comparative perspective.
88   Pipes (1954).

Russian autonomous republics; the Ukrainian Soviet Socialist Republic; the Byelorussian Soviet Socialist Republic; and the Transcaucasian Federated Socialist Republic, a potentially explosive, artificial entity that brought together centuries-old inimical peoples, such as Georgians, Azeris, Armenians, and a number of smaller ethnic groups, among whom were Ingushis, Osetians, Abkhazians, and Metsketyans. Membership of the Union was open to all existing and future Soviet and Socialist Republics in the world. In the Fall of 1924, two additional republics were incorporated: Uzbekistan (formed by the forced territorial integration of the Uzbek population in Turkestan, Bukhara, and Khoresm), and Turkmenia. In 1936, three new Union Republics were created under the names of Tajikistan, Kirghizia, and Kazakhstan. Also in 1936, Transcaucasia was divided into three republics, Georgia, Armenia, and Azerbaijan, leaving inside each one of the three republics substantial ethnic enclaves that acted eventually as nationalist time bombs. In 1940, the forced absorption into the USSR of Estonia, Latvia, Lithuania, and Moldova (taken from Romania) completed the republican structure of the Soviet Union. Its territorial expansion also included the annexation of Karelia and Tuva, as autonomous republics within the RSFSR, and the incorporation of new territories in Western Ukraine and Western Byelorussia, extracted from Poland, in the 1939–44 period, and Kaliningrad, taken from Germany in 1945.[89]

The formation of the federal state of the Soviet Union was the result of a compromise following intense political and ideological debates during the revolutionary period.[90] Originally, the Bolshevik position denied the relevance of nationality as a significant criterion for the building of the new state, since class-based proletarian internationalism intended to supersede national differences between the working and exploited masses, manipulated into inter-ethnic confrontations by bourgeois imperialism, as demonstrated by World War I. But in January 1918 the urgency of finding military alliances in the civil war that followed the Bolshevik October coup convinced Lenin of the importance of support from nationalist forces outside Russia, particularly in Ukraine. The Third All-Russian Congress of Soviets in January 1918 adopted the "Declaration of the Rights of Working and Exploited People," outlining the conversion of the former Russian Empire into the "fraternal union of Soviet Republics of Russia freely meeting on a federal basis."[91] To this "internal federalization" of Russia, the Bolsheviks added the project for the "external federalization" of other

89   Singh (1982); Hill (1985); Kozlov (1988).
90   Carrere d'Encausse (1987).
91   Quoted by Singh (1982: 61).

nations in April 1918, explicitly calling to the Union the people of Poland, Ukraine, Crimea, Transcaucasia, Turkestan, Kirghiz, "and others." But the critical debate concerned the principle under which ethnic and national identity would be recognized in the new Soviet state. Lenin and Stalin opposed the views of the Bundists and other socialists who wanted national cultures recognized throughout the whole structure of the state, making the Soviet Union truly multicultural in its institutions. *They opposed to such a view the principle of territoriality as the basis for nationhood.*[92] Furthermore, ethnic/national rights were to be institutionalized under the form of Union Republics, Autonomous Republics, and Autonomous Regions. The result was a complete encapsulation of the national question into the multilayered structure of the Soviet state: identities were recognized only as far as they could be marshalled within the institutions of governance. This was considered to be the expression of the principle of democratic centralism in reconciling the unitary project of the Soviet state with the recognition of the diversity of its territorial subjects.[93] Thus, the Soviet Union was constructed around the principle of a double identity: ethnic/national identities (including Russian) and Soviet identity as the foundation of the new culture of a new society.

Beyond ideology, the territorial principle of Soviet federalism was the application of a daring geopolitical strategy aimed at spreading communism throughout the world. A.M. Salmin has proposed an interesting model for interpreting the Leninist–Stalinist strategy underlying Soviet federalism.[94] The Soviet Union, in this view, was a centralized but flexible institutional system whose structure should remain open and adaptive to receive new members who would add to the system as the cause of socialism inexorably advanced in the world. This is why the Soviet Constitution of 1924 established the right of republics not only to enter the Union, but also to secede from it, making such decisions sovereign and reversible. History showed how difficult the application of such a right to secede became in the practice of the Soviet state. Yet, it was this principle, inherited from the early revolutionary debates and reproduced in the 1936 and 1977 Constitutions, that provided the legal/institutional basis for the separatist movements during the Gorbachev era, thus taking revolutionary ideology at its word and reversing, and ultimately dismantling, the odd construction of Soviet federalism.[95]

92 Suny (1993: 110ff).
93 Rezun (1992).
94 Salmin (1992).
95 On the relationship between the national–territorial principle of Soviet federalism and the process of disintegration of the Soviet Union, see the insightful analysis of Granberg (1993b). For a recollection of the events, see Smith (1992).

In the geopolitical model proposed by Salmin, which seems to fit with the historical evidence on the origins of the Soviet state,[96] five concentric circles were designed as both security areas and waves of expansion of the Soviet state as the standard-bearer of world communism. The first was Russia and its satellite autonomous republics, organized in the RSFSR. This was considered to be the core of Soviet power, to the point that, paradoxically, it was the only republic of the USSR not to have specific Communist party organizations, the only one without a president of the Republican Supreme Soviet, and the one with the least developed republican state institutions. In other words, the RSFSR was the reserved domain of the CPSU. Significantly, the RSFSR did not have land boundaries with the potentially aggressive capitalist world. Around this core of Soviet power, a protective second circle was formed by the Union republics, formally equal in rights to the RSFSR. Since several RSFSR autonomous republics (for example, Chechnya) were as non-Russian as some of the Union republics, it would seem that the actual criterion for their inclusion in one or other formation was precisely the fact that the Union republics had boundaries in direct contact with the outside world, thus acting as a territorial glacis for security purposes. The third circle was formed by the "people's democracies," outside the Soviet Union but under direct Soviet control, both militarily and territorially. Originally, this was the case for Khoresm and Bukhara (later dispatched between Uzbekistan and Turkmenia), Mongolia, and Tannu-Tura. In the 1940s, the People's Democracies of Eastern Europe also played such a role. The fourth circle was represented by the vassal states of pro-Soviet orientation (eventually this category was formed by countries such as Cuba, Vietnam, and North Korea); China was never really considered to be in such a category in spite of the triumph of communism: indeed, it was soon to be seen as a geopolitical threat. Finally, a fifth circle was formed by the international communist movement and its allies around the world, as embryos of the expansion of the Soviet state to the entire planet when historical conditions would precipitate the inexorable demise of capitalism.[97]

This constant tension between the a-historical, class-based universalism of communist utopia and the geopolitical interest of supporting ethnic/national identities as potential territorial allies determined the schizophrenia of Soviet policy toward the national question.

On the one hand, national cultures and languages were spurred, and in some cases reconstructed, in the union republics, autonomous

96   Suny (1993: 110ff).
97   Conquest (1967); Singh (1982); Mace (1983); Carrere d'Encausse (1987); Suny (1993).

republics, and ethnically based territories (*krai*). Nativization (*korenizatsiya*) policies were supported by Lenin and Stalin until the 1930s, encouraging the use of native languages and customs, implementing "affirmative action," pro-minority recruitment and promotion policies in the state and party apparatuses in the republics, and fostering the development of endogenous political and cultural elites in the republican institutions.[98] Although these policies suffered the backlash of anti-nationalist repression during the collectivization years, under Khrushchev and Brezhnev they were revived and led to the consolidation of powerful national/ethnic elites in the republics. Khrushchev, himself a Ukrainian, went so far in the non-Russian bias of Soviet federalism as to decide suddenly in 1954 on the transfer of the Crimea, a historically Russian territory, to Ukraine, reportedly after a night of heavy drinking on the eve of the Ukrainian national day. Furthermore, in the central Asian and Caucasian republics, during the Brezhnev period, traditional ethnic networks of patronage combined with party affiliation to establish a tight system that linked *nomenklatura*, clientelism, and the shadow economy in a hierarchical chain of personal loyalties that extended all the way up to the Central Committee in Moscow, a system that Helene Carrere d'Encausse calls "Mafiocracy."[99] Thus, when in December 1986 Gorbachev tried to clean up the corrupt party apparatus in Kazakhstan, the removal of a long-time Brezhnev protégé (Brezhnev himself started his career as party chief in Kazakhstan), the Kazakh Dinmukhammed Kunaev, and his replacement by a Russian as secretary of the party, provoked massive riots in Alma Ata in defense of ethnic, Kazakh rights.[100]

The greatest paradox of this policy toward nationalities was that Russian culture and national traditions were oppressed by the Soviet state.[101] Russian traditions, religious symbols, and Russian folk were persecuted or ignored, depending upon the needs of communist politics at each point in time. Redistribution of economic resources took place in a reverse sense to what a "Russian imperialism" would have dictated: Russia was the net loser in inter-republican exchanges,[102] a situation that has continued into the post-communist era (see table 1.5). If we refer to Salmin's geopolitical theory of the Soviet state, the system operated as if the preservation of communist power in Russia

98   Suny (1993: ch. 3).
99   Carrere d'Encausse (1991: ch. 2).
100 Wright (1989: 40–5, 71–4); Carrere d'Encausse (1991).
101 Suny (1993); Galina Starovoitova, Lecture at the Center for Slavic and Eastern European Studies, University of California at Berkeley, February 23, 1994, Emma Kiselyova's notes.
102 See, among other works by Alexander Granberg, Granberg and Spehl (1989) and Granberg (1993a).

Table 1.5 Balance of inter-republican exchange of products and resources, 1987

| Republic | Output balance (billions of rubles) | | Full balance | |
	Direct	Full	Fixed assets (billions of rubles)	Labor resources (million person-years)
Russia	3.65	−4.53	15.70	−0.78
Ukraine and Moldova	2.19	10.30	8.61	0.87
Byelorussia	3.14	7.89	1.33	0.42
Kazakhstan	−5.43	−15.01	−17.50	−0.87
Central Asia	−5.80	−13.41	20.04	−0.89
Transcaucasia	3.20	7.78	2.48	0.57
Baltic republics	−0.96	−0.39	−3.22	−0.05
Total	0.00	−7.37	−12.63	−0.74

Source: Granberg (1993a)

was dependent on the ability of the party to lure into the system other nations, not only subduing them through repression, but also co-opting their allegiance by providing resources and rights in excess of what Russian citizens were given. This does not exclude, of course, ethnic discrimination in major institutions of the state, for instance in the army and in the KGB, whose commanders were overwhelmingly Russian; or the policy of russification in the language, in the media, in culture, and science.[103] Yet, overall, Russian nationalism was generally repressed (except during the war when the assault of Nazi troops provoked Stalin into resurrecting Alexander Nevsky) as much as the cultural identity of the non-Russian subjected nations. As a consequence of this, when the relaxation of controls in Gorbachev's *glasnost* allowed nationalism to emerge, Russian nationalism was not only one of the most popularly supported but was actually the one that was decisive in dismantling the Soviet Union, in alliance with democratic nationalist movements in the Baltic republics. In contrast, in spite of their strong ethnic/national specificity, the Muslim republics of central Asia were the last bastion of Soviet communism, and only converted to independentism toward the end of the process. This was because the political elites of these republics were under direct patronage from

103   Rezun (1992).

Table 1.6 Ethnic composition of Russia's autonomous republics, 1989

Republic	Area (thousands of km²)	Percentage population share	
		Titular group	Russians
Bashkir	144	21.9	39.3
Buryat	351	24.0	70.0
Chechen-Ingush	19	70.7	23.1
Chuvash	18	67.8	26.7
Dagestan	50	27.5 (Avars)	9.2
Kabardino-Balkar	13	57.6	31.9
Kalmyk	76	45.4	37.7
Karelian	172	10.0	73.6
Komi	416	23.3	57.7
Mari	23	43.3	47.5
Mordva	26	32.5	60.8
North Ossetian	8	53.0	29.9
Tatar	68	48.5	43.3
Tuva	171	64.3	32.0
Udmurt	42	30.9	58.9
Yakut	3103	33.4	50.3

Source: Shaw (1993: 532)

Moscow, and their resources were highly dependent upon the politically motivated redistribution process within the Soviet state.[104]

On the other hand, autonomous nationalist expressions were harshly repressed, particularly during the 1930s, when Stalin decided to break the back of all potential opposition to his program of accelerated industrialization and building of military power at whatever cost. The leading Ukrainian national communist, Mykola Skypnyk committed suicide in 1933, after realizing that the dreams of national emancipation within the Soviet Union had been another illusion in the long list of the Bolshevik revolution's unfulfilled promises.[105] The Baltic republics and Moldova were cynically annexed in 1940 on the basis of the 1939 Ribbentrop–Molotov pact, and national expressions in these areas were severely curtailed until the 1980s.[106] Furthermore, ethnic and national groups that were not trusted in their loyalty were submitted to massive deportation away from their original territories, and their autonomous republics abolished: such was the case for Crimean Tat-ars, Volga Germans, for Metsketyans, Chechens, Ingushi, Balkars, Karachai, Kalmyks.[107] Also, millions of Ukrainians, Estonians, Latvians,

104 Carrere d'Encausse (1991).
105 Mace (1983).
106 Simon (1991).
107 Nekrich (1978).

and Lithuanians suspected of collaboration with the enemy during World War II suffered a similar fate. Anti-Semitism was a permanent feature of the Soviet state and permeated down to every single mechanism of political and professional promotion.[108] In addition, the policy of industrialization and settlement in the eastern regions led to the emigration (induced by the Soviet state) of millions of Russians into other republics, in which they became a sizeable minority, or even the largest ethnic group (as in Kazakhstan) while still being represented in the state by the native elites of each republic (see table 1.6). At the end of the Soviet Union, about 60 million citizens were living outside their native land.[109] This largely artificial federal construction was more a system of cooptation of local/regional elites than a recognition of national rights. The real power was always in the hands of the CPSU, and the party was hierarchically organized throughout the Soviet territory, directly conveying orders from Moscow to the party organization in each republic, autonomous republic or *oblast*.[110] Furthermore, by mixing different national populations on such a large scale, and over a long period of time, a new Soviet identity did emerge, made up not just of ideology, but of family ties, friendships, and work relationships.

Thus, the Soviet state recognized national identity, with the odd exception of Russian identity, but it simultaneously defined identity in institutions organized on the basis of territoriality, while national populations were mixed all over the Soviet Union. At the same time, it practiced ethnic discrimination and forbade autonomous nationalist expressions outside the sphere of Communist power. This contradictory policy created a highly unstable political construction that lasted only as long as systemic repression could be enforced with the help of national Communist political elites which had their vested interests in the Soviet federal state. But by channeling identity into national/ethnic self-definition as the only admissible alternative expression to the dominant socialist ideology, the dynamics of the Soviet state created the conditions for the challenge to its rule. The political mobilization of nationally-based republics, including Russia, against the superstructure of the a-national federal state was the lever that actually brought about the collapse of the Soviet Union.

The creation of a new, Soviet people (*sovetskii narod*) as an entity culturally distinct from each historic nationality was still too fragile to stand the assault of civil societies against the Soviet state. Paradoxically, this fragility was due to a large extent to the Communist

108 Pinkus (1988).
109 Suny (1993).
110 Gerner and Hedlund (1989).

emphasis on the rights of national cultures and institutions, as defined within the framework of the Soviet state. And this emphasis was directly motivated by the geopolitical interests of the CPSU, as the vanguard of a communist movement aiming at world power. Because people were allowed self-definition on the basis of their primary, national/ethnic identity, the ideological void created by the failure of Marxism–Leninism simplified the terms of the cultural debate into the opposition between subdued cynicism and rediscovered nationalism. While the nationalist fault produced only minor tremors under the iron hand of unabashed Communist authority, as soon as the pressure was released by the political expediency of the restructuring process, its shock waves wrecked the foundations of the Soviet state.

The Last *Perestroika*[111]

In April 1983, about six months after Brezhnev's death, a closed seminar, organized in Novosibirsk by the Sociology Department of the Institute of Economics and Industrial Engineering of the Soviet Academy of Sciences, brought together 120 participants from 17 cities to discuss a daring report that denounced "the substantial lagging of production relations in the Soviet society behind the development of its productive forces."[112] The "Novosibirsk Report," intended to be ex-

111   This section, and the one following, are mainly based on fieldwork, interviews and personal observation by myself and my Russian collaborators in Russia, as mentioned above, during the period 1989–96. Among relevant personalities interviewed were: A. Aganbegyan, T. Zaslavskaya, N. Shatalin, G. Yazov, B. Orlov, N. Khandruyev, Y. Afanasiev, G. Burbulis, Y. Gaidar, A. Shokhin, A. Golovkov, and several high-ranking officials of the Soviet Council of Ministers (1990, 1991), and of the Government of the Russian Federation (1991, 1992). A preliminary synthesis of these observations can be found in Castells (1992). Information on the political structure of the Soviet Union and of the political process between 1990 and 1993, based on Russian sources and interviews with political actors, is given in Castells, Shkaratan and Kolomietz (1993). (There is a Russian language version of the same report: Russian Sociological Association, Moscow.) Specific bibliographical references are given only when applicable to an argument or event mentioned in the text. I have not considered it necessary to provide specific references for reports in the Russian press of events and facts that are by now public knowledge. There are, in English, a number of excellent journalists' accounts of the process of reform and political conflict during the last decade of the Soviet Union. Two of the best are Kaiser (1991); and Pulitzer Prize Winner David Remnick (1993).

112   *Survey* (1984). The real story of the Novosibirsk Report differs from what was reported in the media, and accepted by the scholarly community. The generally acknowledged author of the report, sociologist Tatyana I. Zaslavskaya, wrote to Emma Kiselyova and myself to convey her own account of the origins and uses of the Novosibirsk Report. It did not originate in a meeting of the economic section of the Central Committee of the CPSU, as has been reported. Nor did the Central Committee ever discuss the document as such. The report was prepared for discussion in an academic meeting at the Institute of Economics and Industrial Engineering in Novosibirsk. Its distribution was forbidden, and it was stamped as

clusively for confidential use, was mysteriously leaked to *The Washington Post* which published it in August 1983. The impact of such a report *abroad* prompted Gorbachev, still not in full power, to read it and discuss it informally in the higher circles of the party. The report had been prepared under the direction of sociologist Tatyana Zaslavskaya at the Novosibirsk Institute. The director of the Institute at the time was one of the leading Soviet economists, Abel Aganbegyan. Only two years later, Aganbegyan became the top economic adviser of the newly appointed Secretary General Mikhail Gorbachev. Tatyana Zaslavskaya, as director of the first serious public opinion research institute in Moscow, was often consulted by Gorbachev, until her data started to show the decline of Gorbachev's popularity in 1988.

It is generally considered that the theses presented in the Novosibirsk document directly inspired Gorbachev's report to the 27th Congress of the CPSU on February 23, 1986. In his report the Secretary General called into question the predominance of "administrative methods" in the management of a complex economy, ushering in what appeared to be the most ambitious *perestroika* in Russian history.

Gorbachev's *perestroika* was born of Andropov's efforts to steer the Communist party ship out of the stagnant waters of the last Brezhnev years.[113] As KGB chief from 1967, Andropov had enough information to know that the shadow economy had spread all over the system to the point of disorganizing the command economy, bringing corruption to the highest levels of the state, namely to Brezhnev's family. Work discipline had broken down, ideological indoctrination was met with massive cynicism, political dissidence was rising, and the war in Afghanistan was revealing how the technology of Soviet armed forces lagged behind in conventional, electronic-based warfare. Andropov succeeded in obtaining the support of a younger generation of Soviet leaders who had grown up in post-Stalinist society, and were

---

a "restricted use document," each copy numbered for the exclusive use of participants at the meeting. During the meeting in Novosibirsk two of the copies disappeared. The KGB immediately tried to recover the copies, searching for them over the whole Institute, and confiscating all copies from the participants at the meeting, as well as the original manuscript of the report. Tatyana Zaslavskaya could not keep a single copy of her own report, and only received it in 1989 as a personal gift from the BBC in London. According to Zaslavskaya, Gorbachev read the report only after its publication in the West in August 1983. It seems plausible that he used some of the ideas in the elaboration of his own reformist strategy, as early as October 1984, in a Central Committee meeting on the management of the economy. Several observers trace back some key elements of Gorbachev's crucial report to the 27th Party Congress in February 1986 to the themes developed by Zaslavskaya in the Novosibirsk document. However, Zaslavskaya herself is much more skeptical concerning her intellectual influence on Gorbachev and on the Soviet leadership.

113   For a documented analysis of the transition in the Soviet leadership from Brezhnev to Gorbachev, see Breslauer (1990).

ready to modernize the country, to open it up to the world, ending the siege mentality that still prevailed among the Politburo's old guard.

Thus, the systemic contradictions, outlined in the preceding sections of this study, built up toward a critical point of potential breakdown. But the cautious Soviet leadership was not willing to take risks. As is often the case in history, structural matters do not affect historical processes until they align with the personal interests of social and political actors. In fact, these new actors were able to organize themselves in the CPSU around Andropov only because Brezhnev's designated successor, Andrei Kirilenko, was disabled by arteriosclerosis. In spite of his brief tenure (15 months between his election as Secretary General and his death), and his ailing health during these months, Andropov played a critical role in paving the way for Gorbachev's reforms: by appointing him as his deputy, and by purging the party and creating a network of reformers on whom Gorbachev could later capitalize.[114] These reformers were hardly liberals. Leading members of the group were Yegor Ligachev, the ideologist who went on to lead the resistance to Gorbachev during *perestroika*, and Nikolai Ryzhkov, who later, as Gorbachev's Prime Minister, defended the command economy against the liberal proposals of Shatalin, Yavlinsky, and other pro-market economists. Andropov's original blueprints for reform focused on restoring order, honesty, and discipline, both in the party and at the workplace, by means of a strong, clean government. Indeed, when Gorbachev was finally elected in March 1985, after the last stand of the old guard in the short-lived appointment of Chernenko, his first version of *perestroika* closely echoed Andropov's themes. The two main stated objectives of his policies were: technological modernization, starting with the machine-tools industry, and the restoration of labor discipline by calling on the responsibility of workers and by launching a decisive anti-alcohol campaign.

It soon became evident that the correction of failures in the Soviet system, as described in the Novosibirsk Report, required a major overhaul of the institutions and of domestic and foreign policy.[115] It was the historic merit of Gorbachev to have fully realized this need and to dare to take up the challenge, convinced as he was that the solidity of the Communist party, in whose fundamental principles he never ceased to believe, could endure the pain of restructuring so that a new, healthy, socialist Soviet Union could emerge from the process. In the 1986 27th Congress of the CPSU he articulated the series of policies that will remain in history as Gorbachev's *perestroika*.[116]

---

114 An excellent report on the power struggles in the CPSU's Politburo after Brezhnev's death can be found in Walker (1986: 24ff.); see also Mitchell (1990).
115 See Aslund (1989).
116 See the series edited by Aganbegyan (1988–90).

The last Communist *perestroika*, as its predecessors in Soviet and Russian history, was a topdown process, without any participation by the civil society in its inception and early implementation. It was not a response to pressures from below or from outside the system. It was aimed at rectifying internal failures from within the system, while keeping unscathed its fundamental principles: the Communist party monopoly of power, the command economy, and the superpower status of a unitary Soviet state.

In its strictest sense, Gorbachev's *perestroika* included a number of policies personally decided by Gorbachev, aimed at restructuring Soviet communism, between February 1986 (27th Congress) and September–November 1990, when Gorbachev rejected the "500 days plan" of transition to the market economy, and ceded to the pressures of the CPSU's Central Committee by appointing a conservative government which all but stalled the reforms and eventually engineered the August 1991 coup against Gorbachev himself.

Perestroika had four main distinct, yet interrelated, dimensions: (a) disarmament, release of the Soviet Empire in Eastern Europe, and end to the Cold War; (b)economic reform; (c) gradual liberalization of public opinion, media, and cultural expressions (the so-called *glasnost*); and (d) controlled democratization and decentralization of the political system. Significantly enough, nationalist demands within the Soviet Union were not on the agenda, until the Nagorno-Karabagh conflict, mobilization in the Baltic republics, and the 1989 Tbilisi massacre forced Gorbachev to deal with the issues involved.

The end of the Cold War will remain in history as Gorbachev's fundamental contribution to humankind. Without his personal decision to take the West at its word, and to overcome the resistance of Soviet hawks in the security establishment, it is unlikely that the process of disarmament and the partial dismantling of Soviet and American nuclear arsenals would have gone as far as they have, in spite of limitations and delays in the process. Furthermore, Gorbachev's initiative was decisive in the crumbling of communist regimes in Eastern Europe, since he even threatened (behind the scenes) the use of Soviet troops to thwart the Stasi's intention of shooting at demonstrations in Leipzig. To relinquish control over Eastern Europe was Gorbachev's masterful move to make disarmament and truly peaceful coexistence with the West possible. Both processes were indispensable in order to attack the problems of the Soviet economy and to link it up with the world economy, as was Gorbachev's ultimate design. Only if the burden of the gigantic military effort could be removed from the Soviet state could human and economic resources be reoriented toward technological modernization, production of consumer goods, and improvement in the living standards of the population, thus finding new sources of legitimacy for the Soviet system.

Yet, economic reforms proved to be difficult, even taking into account the promise of future disarmament.[117] The conversion of military enterprises proved so cumbersome that it is still unfulfilled after several years of post-Communist regime in Russia. World oil prices fell in 1986, contributing to lagging productivity and falling production in the Siberian oil and gas fields, so that the hard-currency cushion, which for about a decade had spared the Soviet Union from major economic shortages, started to dwindle, increasing the difficulty of the transition. The dramatic nuclear accident at Chernobyl in April 1986 showed that the technological failure of Soviet industrialism had reached a dangerous level, and, in fact, helped liberalization by providing Gorbachev with additional arguments to shake up state bureaucracy. Yet, the most serious obstacles to economic reform came from the Soviet state, and even from the ranks of Gorbachev's reformers themselves. While there was agreement on the gradual movement toward the introduction of semi-market mechanisms in some sectors (mainly in housing and in services), neither Gorbachev nor his economic advisers really envisaged accepting the private property of land and means of production, liberalizing prices throughout the economy, freeing credit from direct Gosbank control, or dismantling the core of the planned economy. Had they tried these reforms, as in the "500 days plan" elaborated by Shatalin and Yavlinsky in the summer of 1990, they would have faced the staunch opposition of the Soviet state apparatus and of the Communist party leadership. Indeed, this is exactly what happened when they hinted at such a possibility in the summer of 1990. At the root of the difficulties inherent in *perestroika* lay Gorbachev's personal and political contradiction in trying to reform the system by using the Communist party, while moving in a direction that would ultimately undermine the power of the Communist party itself. The "stop-and-go" policies that derived from such half-hearted reform literally disorganized the Soviet economy, provoking massive shortages and inflation. Inflation fueled speculation and illegal stockpiling, providing the ground for an even greater sprawling of the shadow economy in all areas of activity. From its subsidiary role, as a profitable parasite of the command economy, the shadow economy took over entire sectors of trade and distribution of goods and services, so that for a long time, and even more after the end of Communism, the former shadow economy, with its cohort of criminal mafias and corrupt officials, became the predominant organizational form of profit-

117   See Aganbegyan (1989).

making economic activity in the Soviet Union, and in its successor societies.[118] The takeover of the most dynamic economic sectors by the shadow economy further disorganized the formerly planned economy, plunging the Soviet economy into chaos and hyperinflation by 1990.

Gorbachev was not a visionary idealist, but a pragmatic leader, a veteran, skillful party politician, who had confronted the endemic problems of Soviet agriculture in his native Stavropol province. He was self-assured about his capacity to maneuver, convince, coopt, buy off, and, when necessary, repress his political adversaries, as circumstances fitted to his design. His *perestroika* became both radicalized and paralyzed because he sincerely believed that he could perfect the system without fundamentally antagonizing the social interests that supported Soviet communism. In this sense, he was at the same time sociologically naïve and politically arrogant. If he had paid closer attention to the sociological analysis implicit in Zaslavskaya's document, he would have had a clearer vision of the social groups on which he could have relied, and of those that would ultimately oppose any significant attempt to ground the system on a different logic, whether political democracy or market economy. In the final analysis, the structure of society largely determines the fate of political projects. This is why it is relevant to remember at this point in the discussion what was the basic social structure underlying the power system in the Soviet statist society. Four major interest groups represented the essence of Soviet social power:[119]

1   The communist ideologists, linked to the defense of Marxist–Leninist values and of their dominance on social habits and institutions. These were the doctrinaire leaders of the Communist party (headed by Ligachev during the *perestroika* years), but also included power-holders in the cultural and media apparatuses of the Soviet Union, from the press, television and radio, to the Academy of Sciences and universities, including also official artists and writers.

2   The power elite of the state apparatus, interested in the continuation of its monopoly of power in the Soviet state, a source of extraordinary privileges to the point of representing a caste, rather than a class. This power elite was itself subdivided into at least four major categories which obviously do not exhaust the complex structure of the Soviet state:
    (a)   The core political apparatus of the CPSU, which constituted

the source of the *nomenklatura*, the actual ruling class of the Soviet Union. As it is known, the term *nomenklatura* has a precise meaning: it was the list of positions in the state and in the party, for which it was necessary to have the explicit agreement of the relevant party committee on the name of each person to be appointed; in the strictest, and most relevant sense, the top of the *nomenklatura* (literally thousands of positions) required explicit agreement by the Central Committee of the CPSU. This was the fundamental mechanism through which the Communist party controlled the Soviet state for seven decades.

(b) The second, distinct elite group of the state apparatus was formed by Gosplan officers, who single-handedly managed the entire Soviet economy and gave instructions to the relevant ministries and administrative units. Gossnab, and to some extent Gosbank, executives, should also be included in this category.

(c) A third group was formed by the commanders of the armed forces. Although they were always submitted to the party authority (particularly after their decimation by Stalin in the 1930s), they represented an increasingly autonomous group as the army grew in complexity, and became more reliant on technology and intelligence. They increasingly exercised their power of veto, and could not be counted on without serious consultation in the last decade of the Soviet Union, as the 1991 plotters learned too late.[120]

(d) Last, but not least, KGB and Interior Ministry special forces continued to play an important, and relatively autonomous, role in the Soviet state, trying to embody the interests of the state beyond the variations of political rivalry within the party. It should be remembered that the contemporary KGB was created after Stalin's death, in March 1954, after the alliance of the party leadership and the armed forces suppressed an attempted coup by Beria and the MVD (the former political police) with whom the army always kept quarrel because of the memories of the 1930s' terror. Thus, in spite of obvious continuities, the KGB of the 1980s was not the direct historical heir of Dzerzhinsky and Beria, but a more professional force, still dependent on the CPSU but more focused on the power and stability of the Soviet state than on the ideological purity of its communist construction.[121] This explains the paradoxical support of the KGB for the last round of reforms, from Andropov to Gorbachev, and its resistance to the 1991 coup, in spite of the active participation of Kryuchkov, the KGB chief.

120 On the Soviet armed forces, see Taibo (1993a).
121 Andrew and Gordievsky (1990).

3   A third group at the roots of Soviet power was formed by the industrial managers of large state enterprises, particularly in two major sectors: the military–industrial complex,[122] and the oil and gas industry.[123] This group, while professionally competent, and interested in technological modernization, was fundamentally opposed to the move toward the market, to the demilitarization of the economy, and to releasing control over foreign trade. Because of their economic, social, and political power in the enterprises and in key cities and regions around the country, the mobilization of this power elite against the reforms was decisive in blocking Gorbachev's efforts in the Central Committee of the CPSU, which in 1990 had come under the control of this group.[124]

4   Finally, another extremely important interest group was organized throughout the structure of the Soviet state. This was the network formed between the *nomenklatura* and the "bosses" of the shadow economy. In fact, this group was not different from those named above in terms of the persons involved. Yet their structural position in the Soviet power system was different: their power source came from their connection to the shadow economy. This group was opposed to the dismantling of the planned economy as it could only prosper in the cracks of this economy. However, once the command economy became disorganized, the shadow economy, deeply connected to the communist *nomenklatura*, took advantage of the situation, transforming the whole economy into a gigantic speculative mechanism. Because a shadow economy thrives particularly well in times of economic chaos, the quasi-criminal leaders of the shadow economy, later transformed into wild proto-capitalism, were and are a major destabilizing factor during *perestroika* and its aftermath.[125]

This was, in a nutshell, the set of powerful interest groups that Gorbachev was up against to reform communism without abolishing

122   See Castells and Natalushko (1993).
123   See Kuleshov and Castells (1993). (The original research report is in Russian and can be consulted at the Institute of Economics and Industrial Engineering, Russian Academy of Sciences, Siberian Branch, Novosibirsk, 1993). See also Kiselyova et al. (1996).
124   The group that controlled the Central Committee of the CPSU in the Fall of 1990, who blocked the reforms, and whose initiatives paved the way for the preparation of the coup, was led by Lukyanov, chair of the Supreme Soviet of the USSR; Guidaspov, Leningrad's Party Secretary; Masljukov, Velitchko, and Laverov, leaders of military–industrial enterprises; and Baklanov, Secretary of the Military Commission of the Central Committee. Baklanov was considered to have played a decisive role in the preparation of the coup and he was one of the members of the "State of Emergency Committee" that seized power on August 19, 1991 (information from interviews with Russian political observers).
125   See Handelman (1995).

the privileges generated by the system. He scored an easy victory against the ideologists. When systems reach crisis point, mechanisms for legitimating the values of the system can go the same way they came in, as long as new forms of cultural domination are generated and then embedded in the material interests of the dominant elites. Ligachev and the Nina Andreyevas of the Soviet Union became the perfect target against whom to size up the progress of reform. The army was a more potent force to reckon with, since it is never easy for the military to accept a decline in power, particularly when it goes hand in hand with the shock of realizing that entire units cannot be repatriated to the motherland because they would lack housing and basic facilities. Yet, Gorbachev won their acquiescence to disarmament by building on their understanding of the need to regroup and re-equip after losing the technological race in conventional weapons. Marshal Ogarkov, Chief of the General Staff, was dismissed in September 1984 a year after he had publicly claimed the need for higher military budgets to update the technology of Soviet military equipment, whose inferiority had been exposed in the 1982 Bekaa Valley air massacre of Syrian jets by the Israeli Air Force. Yet, his message was received, and Gorbachev, in fact, increased the military budget, even in the middle of the harshest economic times. Gorbachev's military plans were not too different from those of the American administration: they aimed at reducing costs over time, dismantling a useless plethora of redundant nuclear missiles, while elevating the professional and technological quality of the Soviet armed forces to the level of a superpower not aiming at nuclear holocaust. This strategy was, in fact, supported by both the armed forces and the KGB which, therefore, were not in principle opposed to the reforms, provided that two limits were not transgressed: the territorial integrity of the Soviet state; and the control of the military–industrial complex by the Ministry of Defense. Thus, while Gorbachev seemed convinced of the support of the army and security forces, these two non-negotiable conditions were decisively damaging for Gorbachev's reforms because, in practice, they meant that nationalism had to be repressed (regardless of Gorbachev's personal views), and that the core of industry could not operate under market rules.

Between 1987 and 1990, the party *nomenklatura*, the top state bureaucracy, the military–industrial complex, the oil generals, and the bosses of the shadow economy effectively resisted Gorbachev's reforms, conceding ideological battles, but retrenching themselves in the structure of the party and of the state bureaucracy. Gorbachev's decrees gradually became paper tigers, as had so often been the case in the history of Russian *perestroikas*.

But Gorbachev was a fighter. He decided not to follow Khrushchev

in his historic defeat, and counted on the support of the new generation of Communist leaders, up against the Soviet gerontocracy, on the
sympathy of the West, on the disarray of the state bureaucracy, and
on the neutrality of the army and security forces toward political infighting. Thus, to overcome the resistance of interest groups that had
become a political obstacle to *perestroika*, while still believing in the
future of socialism and in a reformed Communist party as its instrument, he appealed to civil society to mobilize in support of his reforms: *uskorenie* led to *perestroika* and *perestroika* became dependent
on *glasnost*, opening the way for democratization.[126] So doing, he inadvertently triggered a process that ultimately doomed the Communist party, the Soviet state, and his own hold on power. Yet, while for
the majority of the Soviet people Gorbachev was the last Communist
chief of state, and for the Communist minority he was the traitor who
ruined Lenin's heritage, for history Gorbachev will remain the hero
who changed the world by destroying the Soviet empire, although he
did it without knowing it and without wanting it.

Nationalism, Democracy, and the Disintegration of the Soviet State

The liberalization of politics and the mass media, decided upon by
Gorbachev to involve civil society in support of his reforms, resulted
in widespread social mobilization on a variety of themes. The recu-
peration of historical memory, stimulated by an increasingly assertive
Soviet press and television, brought into the open public opinion,
ideologies, and values from a suddenly freed society, often in confused
expression, but with a shared rejection of all sorts of official truths.
Between 1987 and 1991, in a social whirlwind of increasing intensity,
intellectuals denounced the system, workers went on strike for their
demands and their rights, ecologists exposed environmental catastrophes, human rights groups staged their protests, the Memorial Movement reconstructed the horrors of Stalinism, and voters used every
opportunity in parliamentary and local elections to reject official candidates from the Communist party, thus delegitimizing the established
power structure.

Yet, the most powerful mobilizations, and the direct challenge to
the Soviet state came from nationalist movements.[127] In February 1988,
the massacre of Armenians by Azeris in Sumgait revived the latent

126   See the excellent journalist's report on the influence of the media in the disintegration
of the Soviet Union in Shane (1994).
127   Carrere d'Encausse (1991).

conflict in the Armenian enclave of Nagorno-Karabagh in Azerbaijan, a conflict that degenerated into open warfare and forced the intervention of the Soviet army and the direct administration of the territory from Moscow. Inter-ethnic tensions in the Caucasus exploded into the open, after decades of forced suppression and artificial integration. In 1989, hundreds of people were killed in the Ferghana Valley, in Uzbekistan, in rioting between Uzbeks and Metsketyans. On April 9, 1989, a massive, peaceful demonstration of Georgian nationalists in Tbilisi was repressed with poison gas, killing 23 people, and prompting an investigation from Moscow. Also in early 1989, the Moldavian National Front began a campaign for the independence of the republic and its eventual reintegration into Romania.

However, the most powerful and uncompromising nationalist mobilization came from the Baltic republics. In August 1988, the publication of the 1939 secret treaty between Stalin and Hitler to annex the Baltic republics led to massive demonstrations in the three republics and to the formation of popular fronts in each of them. Thereafter, the Estonian Parliament voted to change its time zone, shifting it from Moscow time to Finland time. Lithuania started issuing its own passports. In August 1989, to protest against the fiftieth anniversary of the Ribbentrop–Molotov pact, two million people formed a human chain stretching over the territories of the three republics. In the spring of 1989, the Supreme Soviets of the three republics declared their sovereignty, and their right to overrule legislation from Moscow, triggering an open confrontation with the Soviet leadership which responded with an embargo of supplies to Lithuania.

Significantly, the Muslim republics of central Asia and the Caucasus did not rebel against the Soviet state, although Islamism was on the rise, particularly among intellectual elites. Conflicts in the Caucasus and central Asia predominantly took the form of inter-ethnic confrontation and political civil wars within the republics (as in Georgia) or between republics (for example, Azerbaijan versus Armenia).

Nationalism was not only the expression of collective ethnic identity. It was the predominant form of democratic movement throughout the Soviet Union, and particularly in Russia. The "democratic movement" that led the process of political mobilization in the main urban centers of the Soviet Union was never an organized front, nor was "Democratic Russia," the popular movement founded by Yuri Afanasiev and other intellectuals, a party. There were dozens of proto-parties of all political tendencies, but by and large the movement was profoundly anti-party, given the historical experience of highly structured organizations. The distrust of formalized ideologies and party politics led socio-political movements, especially in Russia, but also in

Ukraine, in Armenia, and in the Baltic republics, to structure themselves loosely around two signs of identity: on the one hand, the negation of Soviet communism in whatever form, whether restructured or not; on the other hand, the affirmation of a collective primary identity, whose broadest expression was national identity, the only historical memory to which people could refer after the vacuum created by Marxism–Leninism and its subsequent demise. In Russia, this renewed nationalism found a particularly strong echo among the people as a reaction to the anti-Russian nationalism of other republics. Thus, as has often been the case in history, various nationalisms fed each other. This is why Yeltsin, against all the odds, became the only Russian political leader with massive popular support and trust, in spite of (and probably because of) all the efforts of Gorbachev and the CPSU to destroy his image and his reputation. Gennadi Burbulis, Yeltsin's main political adviser in the 1988–92 period, tried to explain, in one of our conversations in 1991, the deep-seated reasons for Yeltsin's appeal to the Russian people. It is worth while to quote him directly:

> What Western observers do not understand is that, after 70 years of Stalinist terror and of suppression of all independent thinking, Russian society is deeply irrational. And societies that have been reduced to irrationality mobilize primarily around myths. This myth in contemporary Russia is named Yeltsin. This is why he is the only true force of the democratic movement.[128]

Indeed, in the critical demonstration of March 28, 1991 in Moscow, when the democratic movement definitively opposed Gorbachev and occupied the streets in spite of his prohibition, defying the presence of army troops, the hundreds of thousands of demonstrators shouted just two rallying cries: "*Rossiya!*" and "Yeltsin!, Yeltsin!" The affirmation of the forgotten past, and the negation of the present symbolized by the man who could say "No!" and still survive, were the only clearly shared principles of a newly born civil society.

The connection between the democratic movement, the nationalist mobilization, and the process of dismantlement of Soviet power was paradoxically predetermined by the structure of the Soviet federal state. Because all the power was concentrated in the Central Committee of the CPSU and in the central institutions of the Soviet state (Congress of People's Deputies, Supreme Soviet of the USSR, Council of Ministers, and Presidency of the USSR), the process of democratization under Gorbachev took the form of allowing competing candidacies (but not free political association) for the soviets of cities, regions, and

128   Interview with Gennadi Burbulis, April 2, 1991.

republics, while keeping under tighter control the USSR Congress of People's Deputies, and the USSR Supreme Soviet. Between 1989 and 1991, a majority of the seats in the local soviets of the main cities, and in the republican parliaments, went to candidates opposed to the official Communist candidates.

The hierarchical structure of the Soviet state seemed to limit the damage inflicted on the mechanisms of political control. Yet, the strategy, deliberately designed by political strategists of the democratic movement, and particularly those working with Yeltsin, was to consolidate power in the representative republican institutions, and then to use these institutions as a lever of opposition against the Soviet central state, claiming as much power as feasible for the republics. Thus, what appeared to be an autonomist or separatist movement was also a movement to break away from the discipline of the Soviet state, and ultimately to be freed from the control of the Communist party. This strategy explains why the key political battle in 1990–91 in Russia focused on increasing the power and autonomy of the Russian Federation, the only one not to have a president of its republican parliament. Thus, while Gorbachev thought he could claim victory when he won the majority of the popular vote in the referendum on a new Union Treaty on March 15, 1991, in fact the results of this referendum were the beginning of the end of the Soviet Union. Yeltsin's supporters were able to introduce in the ballot a question demanding direct popular election for the presidency of the Russian Federation, with a precise election date, June 12. The approval of this question by the electorate, thus automatically calling for such an election, was far more important than the approval given to the vague proposals of Gorbachev for a new federal state. When Yeltsin became the first Russian chief of state to be democratically elected a fundamental cleavage was created between the representative political structures of Russia and of other republics, and the increasingly isolated superstructure of the Soviet federal state. At this point, only massive, decisive repression could have turned the process back under control.

But the Soviet Communist party was not in a condition to launch repression. It had become divided, disconcerted, disorganized by Gorbachev's maneuvers, and by penetration into its ranks of the values and projects of a revived society. Under the impact of criticism from all quarters, the political *nomenklatura* lost its self-confidence.[129] For instance, the election of Yeltsin as chair of the Russian Parliament in March 1991 was only possible because an important faction of the

129   The loss of self-confidence by the party *nomenklatura* as a major factor in preventing an early reaction against Gorbachev's reforms was called to my attention by George Breslauer.

newly established Russian Communist party, led by Rutskoi, joined the democrats' camp against the nationalist-communist leadership of Polozkov, leader of the majority of the Russian Communist party, who was in open opposition to Gorbachev. In fact, the most influential group of the Central Committee of the CPSU, loosely articulated around Anatoly Lukyanov, chairman of the USSR Supreme Soviet (and a law school classmate of Gorbachev), had decided to draw the line against further reforms in the fall of 1990. The then appointed Pavlov government aimed at re-establishing the command economy. Police measures were taken to restore order in the cities and to curb nationalism, starting with the Baltic republics. But the brutal assault on the television station in Vilnius by Interior Ministry special forces in January 1991 prompted Gorbachev to ask for restraint and to halt the repression. By July 1991, Gorbachev was ready to establish a new Union Treaty without six of the 15 republics (the Baltic republics, Moldova, Georgia, and Armenia), and to grant extensive powers to the republics as the only way to save the Soviet Union. In his speech to the Central Committee on July 25, 1991, he also outlined an ideological program for abandoning Leninism and converting the party to democratic socialism. He won an easy victory. The real forces of the Central Committee, and the majority of the Soviet government, had already embarked on preparation of a coup against their Secretary General and President, after failing to control the process through standard institutional procedures that were no longer working because most of the republics, and particularly Russia, had broken loose from the control of the Soviet central state.

The circumstances of the August 1991 coup, the event that precipitated the disintegration of the Soviet Union, have not been fully exposed, and it is doubtful whether they will be in a long time, given the maze of political interests woven around the plot. On a superficial level, it seems surprising that a coup organized from the Central Committee of the CPSU with the full participation of the chief of the KGB, the Minister of the Interior, the Minister of Defense, the Vice-president of the USSR, and most of the Soviet government, could fail. And indeed, in spite of all the analysis presented here about the inevitability of the crisis of the Soviet Union, the 1991 coup could have succeeded if Yeltsin and a few thousand supporters had not stood up to it, openly risking their lives, counting on the presence of the media as their symbolic defense, and if, all over Russia and in some Soviet republics, people of all social sectors had not met in their workplaces and voted their support for Yeltsin by sending tens of thousands of telegrams to Moscow to make their position known. After seven decades of repression, people were still there, confused but ready to fight if necessary to defend their new-found freedom. The possible success of the coup in the short term would not necessarily have meant that the crisis of the Soviet Union could have been halted, given the process of decomposition of the whole system. Yet the crisis would have had another denouement, and history would have been different. What determined the coup's failure were two fundamental factors: the attitude of the KGB and the army; and a misunderstanding of the Communist leadership about their own country as a result of their growing isolation at the summit of the Soviet state. Key units of the security forces refused to cooperate: the elite KGB's Alpha unit refused to obey the order to attack the White House, and received support from key KGB commanders; the paratroopers under the command of General Pavel Grachev declared their loyalty to Gorbachev and Yeltsin; and, finally, the Air Force Commander, General Shaposhnikov, threatened the Minister of Defense that he would bomb the Kremlin. Surrender came within hours of this ultimatum. These decisions resulted from the fact that the army and the KGB had been transformed during the period of *perestroika*. It was not so much that they were active supporters of democracy, but that they had been in direct contact with the evolution of society at large, so that any decisive move against the established chain of command could divide the forces and open the way for civil war. No responsible commander would risk a civil war in an army equipped with a gigantic and diverse nuclear arsenal. In fact, the organizers of the *putsch* themselves were not ready to start a civil war. They were convinced that a show of force and the legal removal of Gorbachev, following the historical precedent of Khrushchev's successful ousting, would be enough to bring the country under control. They underestimated Yeltsin's determination, and they did not understand the new role of the media, and the extent to which the media were outside Communist control. They planned and executed a coup as if they were in the Soviet Union of the 1960s, probably the last time they had been in the street without bodyguards. When they discovered the new country that had grown up in the last quarter of the century, it was too late. Their fall became the fall of their party-state. Yet, the dismantling of the Communist state and, even more, the break up of the Soviet Union were not a historical necessity. They required deliberate political action in the following months, enacted by a small group of decisive revolutionaries, in the purest Leninist tradition. Yeltsin's strategists, led by Burbulis, the undisputed Machiavelli of the new democratic Russia, took to the limit the plan of separation between the socially rooted institutions of the republics and the by then isolated superstructure of the Soviet federal state. While Gorbachev was desperately trying to survive the dissolution of the Communist party, and to reform Soviet institutions, Yeltsin convinced the Ukrainian and Byelorussian Communist leaders, quickly reconverted to nationalism and independentism, to secede jointly from the Soviet Union. Their agreement in Belovezhskaya Pushcha on December 9, 1991 to dissolve the Soviet state, and to create a loose Commonwealth of Independent States as a mechanism to distribute the legacy of the defunct Soviet Union among the newly sovereign republics, signaled the end of one of the boldest and most damaging social experiments in human history. But the ease with which Yeltsin and his aides undertook the dismantlement process in only four months revealed the absolute decomposition of an overgrown state apparatus that had become uprooted from its own society.

The Scars of History, the Lessons for Theory, the Legacy for Society

The Soviet experiment marked decisively a twentieth century that, by and large, revolved around its development and consequences for the whole world. It cast a giant shadow not only over the geopolitics of states, but also over the imaginary constructions of social transformation. In spite of the horrors of Stalinism, the political left and social movements around the world looked to Soviet communism for a long time at least as a motive of hope, and very often as a source of inspiration and support, perceived through the distorting veil of capitalist propaganda. Few intellectuals of the generations born in the first half of the century escaped the fascination of the debate about Marxism, communism, and the construction of the Soviet Union. A large number of leading social scientists in the West have constructed their theories for, against, and in relation to the Soviet experience. Indeed, some of the most prominent intellectual critics of Soviet communism were influenced in their student years by Trotskyism, an ultra-Bolshevik ideology. That all this effort, all this human suffering and passion, all these ideas, all these dreams, could have vanished in such a short period of time, revealing the emptiness of the debate, is a stunning expression of our collective capacity to build political fantasies so powerful that they end up changing history, though in the opposite direction of intended historical projects. This is perhaps the most painful failure of the communist utopia: the abduction and distortion of the revolutionary dreams and hopes of so many people in Russia, and around the world, converting liberation into oppression, turning the project of a classless society into a caste-dominated state, and shifting from solidarity among exploited workers to complicity among *nomenklatura* apparatchiks on their way to becoming ringleaders of the world's shadow economy. On balance, and in spite of some positive elements in social policies in the post-Stalin era, the Soviet experiment brought considerable suffering to the peoples of the Soviet Union, and to the world at large. Russia could have industrialized and modernized otherwise, not without pain but without the human holocaust that took place during Stalin's period. Relative social equality, full employment, and a welfare state were accomplished by social-democratic regimes in neighboring, then poor, Scandinavia, without resorting to such extreme policies. The Nazi machine was defeated not by Stalin (who, in fact, had decimated and weakened the Red Army just before the war to impose his personal control) but by the secular Russian will against the foreign invader. The domination of the Comintern over a large segment of the world's revolutionary and socialist movements sterilized energies, stalled political projects, and led entire nations to dead ends. The division of Europe, and of the world, into military blocs enclosed a substantial part of the technological advances and economic growth of the post-World War II years in a senseless arms race. To be sure, the American (and to a lesser extent European) Cold War establishment bears equal responsibility for engaging in the confrontation, for developing and using nuclear weapons, and for building up a bipolar symmetry for the purpose of world domination.[130] However, without the coherence, strength, and threatening façade of Soviet power, Western societies and public opinion would hardly have accepted the expansion of their warfare states and the continuation of blatant colonial enterprises, as has been shown after the end of the Cold War. Furthermore, the building of a superpower without relying on a productive economy and an open society has proved to be unsustainable in the long run, thus ruining Russia, and the other Soviet republics, without much apparent benefit to their people, if we except job security, and some improvement of living conditions in the 1960–80 period: a period that is now idealized in Russia by many because of the desperate situation in which large segments of the population now find themselves in the wild transition to wild capitalism.

130 The history of the Cold War is full of events and anecdotes that reveal how the two military blocs kept feeding their own defensive paranoia beyond reasonable limits. An illustration of this mentality, too quickly forgotten, is the 1995 revelation of the mystery of Soviet submarines in Swedish waters. As some may remember, for more than two decades Swedish naval forces, supported by the Western Alliance, claimed that the country's maritime borders were repeatedly intruded upon by Soviet submarines, and they resorted to regular dropping of explosive depth-charges broadcast by television all over the world. Only in 1995 did Sweden confirm "an embarrassing fact: that its defense forces have been hunting minkies, not Russian submarines . . . New hydrophonic instruments introduced into the Swedish navy in 1992 showed that minkies could give off sound patterns similar to those of submarines" (*New York Times*, February 12, 1995, p. 8). As for the fate of the minkies, there is no reference in the report.

Yet, the most damaging historic irony was the mockery that the communist state made of the values of human solidarity in which three generations of Soviet citizens were educated. While most people sincerely believed in sharing difficulties, and in helping each other to build a better society, they gradually discovered, and finally realized, that their trust had been systematically abused by a caste of cynical bureaucrats. Once the truth was exposed, the moral injuries thus inflicted on the people of the Soviet Union are likely to unfold for a long time: the sense of life lost; human values at the roots of everyday efforts degraded. Cynicism and violence have become pervasive throughout society after the hopes, inspired by democracy in the aftermath of the Soviet collapse, quickly faded away. The successive failures of the Soviet experiment, of *perestroika*, and of democratic politics in the 1990s have brought ruin and despair to the lands of Russia and the former Soviet republics.

As for intellectuals, the most important political lesson to be learnt from the communist experiment is the fundamental distance that should be kept between theoretical blueprints and the historical development of political projects. To put it bluntly, all Utopias lead to Terror if there is a serious attempt at implementing them. Theories, and their inseparable ideological narratives, can be (and have been) useful tools for understanding, and thus for guiding collective action. But only as tools, always to be rectified and adjusted according to experience. Never as schemata to be reproduced, in their elegant coherence, in the imperfect yet wonderful world of human flesh. Because such attempts are at best cynical rationalizations of personal or group interests. At worst, when they are truly believed and enacted by their believers, such theoretical constructions become the source of political fundamentalism, always an undercurrent of dictatorship and terror. I am not arguing for a bland political landscape free of values and passions. Dreams and projects are the stuff of which social change is made. A purely rational, selfish subject, of the "free rider" type, would always stay at home, and let the work of historical change be done by "the others." The only problem with such an attitude (the best "economic rational choice") is that it assumes collective action from others. In other words, it is a form of historical parasitism. Fortunately, few societies in history have been constructed by parasites, precisely because they are too selfish to be involved. Societies are, and will always be, shaped by social actors, mobilized around interests, ideas and values, in an open, conflictive process. Social and political change is what ultimately determines the fate and structure of societies. Thus, what the Soviet experience shows is not the need for a non-political, value-free process of social transformation, but the necessary distance and tension between theoretical analysis, systems of representation of society, and actual political practice. Relatively successful political practice always muddles through the limits of history, not trying to progress by leaps and bounds, but adapting to the contours of social evolution and accepting the slow-motion process of transformation of human behavior. This argument has nothing to do with the distinction between reform and revolution. When material conditions and subjective consciousness are transformed in society at large to a point where institutions do not correspond with such conditions, a revolution (peaceful or not, or in between) is part of the normal process of historical evolution, as the case of South Africa shows. When vanguards, who are almost invariably intellectual vanguards, aim at accelerating the historical tempo beyond what societies can actually take, in order to satisfy both their desire for power and their theoretical doctrine, they may win and reshape society, but only on the condition of strangling souls and torturing bodies. Surviving intellectuals may then reflect, from the comfort of their libraries, upon the excesses of their distorted revolutionary dream. Yet, what it is crucial to learn as the main political lesson of the Soviet experience is that revolutions (or reforms) are too important and too costly in human lives to be left to dreams or, for that matter, to theories. It is up to the people, using whatever tools they may have in their reach, including theoretical and organizational tools, to find and walk the collective path of their individual lives. The artificial paradise of theoretically inspired politics should be buried for ever with the Soviet state. Because the most important lesson from the collapse of communism is the realization that there is no sense of history beyond the history we sense.

There are also important lessons to be drawn for social theory in general and for the theory of the information society in particular. The process of social change is shaped by the historical matrix of the society in which it takes place. Thus, the sources of statism's dynamics became at the same time its structural limitations and the triggers of contradictory processes within the system. The capture of society and the economy by the state allows for the full mobilization of human and material resources around the objectives of power and ideology. Yet, this effort is economically wasteful because it has no built-in constraints in the use and allocation of scarce resources. And it is socially sustainable only as long as civil society is either subdued by sheer coercion or reduced to a passive role of contributing to work and public service at the lowest possible level. Under statism, as soon as society becomes active, it also becomes unpredictable in its relationship to the state. The state itself is weakened by its inability to mobilize its subjects, who refuse their cooperation, either through resistance or withdrawal.

Soviet statism faced a particularly difficult task in managing its relationship to economy and society in the historical context of the transition to informationalism. To the inherent wasteful tendencies of the command economy, and to the limits imposed on society by the structural priority given to military power, were added the pressures of adapting to the specific demands of informationalism. Paradoxically, a system built under the banner of the development of productive forces could not master the most important technological revolution in human history. This is because the characteristics of informationalism, the symbiotic interaction between socially determined processing of information and material production, became incompatible with the monopoly of information by the state, and with the closing of technology within the boundaries of warfare. At the level of organizations, the structural logic of vertical bureaucracies was made obsolete by the informational trend toward flexible networks, much as happened in the West. But, unlike in the West, the vertical command chain was at the core of the system, making the transformation of large corporations into the new forms of networked business organizations much more difficult. Furthermore, Soviet managers and bureaucrats did discover flexibility and networking as an organizational form. But they applied it to the development of the shadow economy, thus undermining the control capacity of the command economy from the inside, increasing the distance between the institutional organization of the Soviet system and the functional demands of the real economy.

Moreover, the information society is not the superstructure of a new technological paradigm. It is based on the historical tension between the material power of abstract information processing and society's search for meaningful cultural identity. On both counts, statism seems to be unable to grasp the new history. Not only does it suffocate the capacity for technological innovation, but it appropriates and redefines historically rooted identities in order to dissolve them into the all-important process of power-making. Ultimately, statism becomes powerless in a world where society's capacity to constantly renew information and information-embodying technology are the fundamental sources of economic and military power. And statism is also weakened, and ultimately destroyed, by its incapacity to generate legitimacy on the basis of identity. The abstraction of state power on behalf of a rapidly fading ideological construction cannot endure the test of time against the double challenge of historical traditions and individual desires.

Yet, in spite of these fundamental structural contradictions, Soviet statism did not collapse under the assault of social movements born of these contradictions. An important contribution of the Soviet experience to a general theory of social change is that, under certain conditions, social systems can disappear as a result of their own pitfalls without being decisively battered by consciously mobilized social actors. Such conditions seem to be the historical work of the state in destroying the foundations of civil society. This is not to say that the mosaic of societies that formed the Soviet Union was not capable of political insurgency, social revolt, or even revolutionary mobilization. Indeed, the nationalist mobilization of the Baltic republics, or the massive democratic demonstrations in Moscow and Leningrad in the spring of 1991, showed the existence of an active, politically conscious segment of the urban population lurching to overcome the Soviet state. Yet, not only was there little political organization, but, more importantly, there was no consistent, positive social movement projecting alternative views of politics and society. In its best expression, the Russian democratic movement toward the end of the Soviet Union was a free-speech movement, mainly characterized by the recovery of society's ability to declare and speak out. In its mainstream manifestation, the Russian democratic movement was a collective denial of the experience that society had lived through, without further affirmation of values other than the confused reconstruction of an historical, national identity. When the obvious enemy (Soviet communism) disintegrated, when the material difficulties of the transition led to the deterioration of daily life, and when the gray reality of the meager heritage gained after seven decades of daily struggle settled in the minds of the ex-Soviet people, the absence of a collective project, beyond the fact of being "ex," spread political confusion, and fostered wild competition in a race for individual survival throughout society.

The consequences of a major social change resulting from the disintegration of a system, rather than from the construction of an alternative project, can be felt in the painful legacy that Russia and the ex-Soviet societies have received from Soviet statism, and from the pitfalls of *perestroika* policies. The economy was wrecked, to the unbearable pain of the people, by speculative maneuvers for the benefit of the *nomenklatura*; by irresponsible advice on abstract free-market policies by the International Monetary Fund, some Western advisers, and politically inexperienced Russian economists, who suddenly found themselves in the posts of high command; and by the paralysis of the democratic state as a result of byzantine quarrels between political factions dominated by personal ambitions. The criminal economy grew to proportions never witnessed in a major industrial country, linking up with the world's criminal economy, and becoming a fundamental factor to be reckoned with, both in Russia and in the international scene. Short-sighted policies from the United States, in fact aimed at finishing off the Russian Bear in world politics, triggered nationalist reactions, threatening to fuel again the arms race and international tension. Nationalist pressures within the army, political maneuvers in Yeltsin's Kremlin, and criminal interests in power positions, led to the catastrophic adventure of war in Chechn'ya. The democrats in power became lost between their novice faith in the power of the market and their Machiavellian strategies tailored for the backrooms of Moscow's political establishment but rather ignorant of the basic condition of a traumatized population, spread around the huge territory of an increasingly disarticulated country.

The most enduring legacy of Soviet statism will be the destruction of civil society after decades of systematic negation of its existence. Reduced to networks of primary identity and individual survival, Russian people, and the people of the ex-Soviet societies, will have to muddle through the reconstruction of their collective identity, in the midst of a world where the flows of power and money are trying to render piecemeal the emerging economic and social institutions before they come into being, in order to swallow them in their global networks. Nowhere is the ongoing struggle between global economic flows and cultural identity more important than in the wasteland created by the collapse of Soviet statism on the historical edge of the information society.

2

The Rise of the Fourth World: Informational Capitalism, Poverty, and Social Exclusion

The rise of informationalism at the turn of the millennium is intertwined with rising inequality and social exclusion throughout the world. In this chapter I shall try to explain why and how this is so, while displaying some snapshots of the new faces of human suffering. The process of capitalist restructuring, with its hardened logic of economic competitiveness, has much to do with it. But new technological and organizational conditions of the Information Age, as analyzed in this book, provide a new, powerful twist to the old pattern of profit-seeking taking over soul-searching.

However, there is contradictory evidence, fueling an ideologically charged debate, on the actual plight of people around the world. After all, the last quarter of the twentieth century saw access to development, industrialization, and consumption for tens of millions of Chinese, Koreans, Indians, Malaysians, Thais, Indonesians, Chileans, Brazilians, Mexicans, Argentinians, and smaller numbers in a variety of countries – even allowing for the reversal of fortune for some of these millions as a consequence of the Asian financial crisis of 1997–8, and its aftershocks in other areas of the world. The bulk of the population in Western Europe still enjoys the highest living standards in the world, and in the world's history. And in the United States, while average real wages for male workers stagnated or declined for over two decades, until 1996, with the exception of the top of the scale of college graduates, the massive incorporation of women into paid labor, relatively closing their wage gap with men, has maintained decent standards of living, overall, on the condition of being stable enough to keep a two-wage household, and agreeing to put up with increased working time. Health, education, and income statistics around the world show, on average, considerable improvement over historical standards.[1] In fact, for the population as a whole, only the former Soviet Union, after the collapse of statism, and Sub-Saharan Africa, after its marginalization from capitalism, have experienced a decline in living conditions, and for some countries in vital statistics, in the past ten years (although most of Latin America regressed in the 1980s). Yet, as Stephen Gould entitled a wonderful article years ago, "the median isn't the message."[2] Even without entering into a full discussion of the meaning of the quality of life, including the environmental consequences of the latest round of industrialization, the apparently mixed record of development at the dawn of the Information Age conveys ideologically manipulated bewilderment in the absence of analytical clarity.

This is why it is necessary, in assessing the social dynamics of informationalism, to establish a distinction between several processes of social differentiation: on the one hand, *inequality, polarization, poverty*, and *misery* all pertain to the domain of relationships of distribution/consumption or differential appropriation of the wealth generated by collective effort. On the other hand, *individualization of work, over-exploitation of workers, social exclusion*, and *perverse integration* are characteristic of four specific processes *vis-à-vis* relations of production.[3]

Inequality refers to the differential appropriation of wealth (income and assets) by different individuals and social groups, relative to each other. *Polarization* is a specific process of inequality that occurs when both the top and the bottom of the scale of income or wealth distribution grow faster than the middle, thus shrinking the middle, and sharpening social differences between two extreme segments of the population. *Poverty* is an institutionally defined norm concerning a level of resources below which it is not possible to reach the living standards considered to be the minimum norm in a given society at a given time (usually, a level of income per a given number of members of household, as defined by governments or authoritative institutions). *Misery*, a term I propose, refers to what social statisticians call "extreme poverty," that is the bottom of the distribution of income/assets, or what some experts conceptualize as "deprivation," introducing a wider range

---

1   UNDP (1996).
2   Gould (1985).
3   For an informed discussion on analyzing poverty and social exclusion in a comparative perspective, see Rodgers et al. (1995); Mingione (1996).

of social/economic disadvantages. In the United States, for instance, extreme poverty refers to those households whose income falls below 50 percent of the income that defines the poverty line. It is obvious that all these definitions (with powerful effects in categorizing populations, and defining social policies and resource allocation) are statistically relative and culturally defined, besides being politically manipulated. Yet, they at least allow us to be precise about what we say when describing/analyzing social differentiation under informational capitalism.

The second set of processes, and their categorization, pertains to the analysis of relations of production. Thus, when observers criticize "precarious" labor relations, they are usually referring to the process of individualization of work, and to its induced instability on employment patterns. Or else the discourse on social exclusion denotes the observed tendency to permanently exclude from formal labor markets certain categories of the population. These processes do have fundamental consequences for inequality, polarization, poverty, and misery. But the two planes must be analytically and empirically differentiated in order to establish their causal relationships, thus paving the way for understanding the dynamics of social differentiation, exploitation, and exclusion in the network society.

By *individualization of labor* I mean the process by which labor contribution to production is defined specifically for each worker, and for each of his/her contributions, either under the form of self-employment or under individually contracted, largely unregulated, salaried labor. I developed, empirically, the argument about the diffusion of this form of labor arrangement in volume I, chapter 4. I simply add here a reminder that individualization of labor is the overwhelming practice in the urban informal economy that has become the predominant form of employment in most developing countries, as well as in certain labor markets of advanced economies.[4]

I use the term *over-exploitation*[5] to indicate working arrangements that allow capital to systematically withhold payment/resource allocation, or impose harsher working conditions, on certain types of workers, below what is the norm/regulation in a given formal labor market in a given time and space. This refers to discrimination against

---

4 Portes et al. (1989).
5 I use the term "over-exploitation" to distinguish it from the concept of exploitation in the Marxian tradition, that, in strict Marxist economics, would be applicable to all salaried labor. Since this categorization would imply accepting the labor theory of value, a matter of belief rather than of research, I prefer to bypass the debate altogether, but avoid creating further confusion by using "exploitation," as I would like to do for cases of systematic discrimination such as the ones I am referring to in my categorization.

immigrants, minorities, women, young people, children, or other categories of discriminated workers, as tolerated, or sanctioned, by regulatory agencies. A particularly meaningful trend in this context is the resurgence of child paid labor throughout the world, in conditions of extreme exploitation, defenselessness, and abuse, reversing the historical pattern of social protection of children existing under late industrial capitalism, as well as in industrial statism and traditional agricultural societies.[6]

Social exclusion is a concept proposed by the social policy think-tanks of the European Union's Commission, and adopted by the United Nation's International Labour Office.[7] According to the European Commission's Observatory on National Policies to Combat Social Exclusion, it refers to "the social rights of citizens . . . to a certain basic standard of living and to participation in the major social and occupational opportunities of the society."[8] Trying to be more precise, I define *social exclusion as the process by which certain individuals and groups are systemically barred from access to positions that would enable them to an autonomous livelihood within the social standards framed by institutions and values in a given context.*[9] Under normal circumstances, in informational capitalism, *such a position is usually associated with the possibility of access to relatively regular, paid labor, for at least one member of a stable household.* Social exclusion is, in fact, the process that disfranchises a person as labor in the context of capitalism. In countries with a well-developed welfare state, inclusion may also encompass generous compensations in case of long-term unemployment or disability, although these conditions are increasingly exceptional. I would consider among the socially excluded the mass of people on long-term welfare assistance under institutionally punitive conditions, such as is the case in the United States. To be sure, among the English gentry, and among the oil sheiks, there are still a few independently wealthy individuals who could not care less about being demoted to non-labor: I do not consider them to be socially excluded.

Social exclusion is a process, not a condition. Thus, its boundaries

---

6　ILO (1996).
7　Rodgers et al. (1995).
8　Room (1992: 14).
9　By "autonomy," in this context, I mean the average margin of individual autonomy/social heteronomy as constructed by society. It is obvious that a worker, or even a self-employed person, is not autonomous *vis-à-vis* his/her employer, or network of clients. I refer to social conditions that represent the social norm, in contrast with people's inability to organize their own lives even under the constraints of social structure, because of their lack of access to resources that social structure mandates as necessary to construct their limited autonomy. This discussion of socially constrained autonomy is what underlies the conceptualization of inclusion/exclusion as the differential expression of people's social rights.

shift, and who is excluded and included may vary over time, depending on education, demographic characteristics, social prejudices, business practices, and public policies. Furthermore, although the lack of regular work as a source of income is ultimately the key mechanism in social exclusion, how and why individuals and groups are placed under structural difficulty/impossibility to provide for themselves follows a wide array of avenues of destitution. It is not only a matter of lacking skills or not being able to find a job. It may be that illness strikes in a society without health coverage for a substantial proportion of its members (for example, the United States). Or else drug addiction or alcoholism destroys humanity in a person. Or the culture of prisons and the stigma of being an ex-convict closes ways out of crime on return to freedom. Or the injuries of mental illness, or of a nervous breakdown, placing a person between the alternatives of psychiatric repression and irresponsible de-institutionalization, paralyze the soul and cancel the will. Or, more simply, functional illiteracy, illegal status, inability to pay the rent, thus inducing homelessness, or sheer bad luck with a boss or a cop, trigger a chain of events that sends a person (and his/her family very often) drifting toward the outer regions of society, inhabited by the wreckage of failed humanity.

Moreover, the process of social exclusion in the network society concerns both people and territories. So that, under certain conditions, entire countries, regions, cities, and neighborhoods become excluded, embracing in this exclusion most, or all, of their populations. This is different from the traditional process of spatial segregation, as I shall try to show when examining the new features of American inner-city ghettos. Under the new, dominant logic of the space of flows (volume I, chapter 6), areas that are non-valuable from the perspective of informational capitalism, and that do not have significant political interest for the powers that be, are bypassed by flows of wealth and information, and ultimately deprived of the basic technological infrastructure that allows us to communicate, innovate, produce, consume, and even live, in today's world. This process induces an extremely uneven geography of social/territorial exclusion and inclusion, which disables large segments of people while linking up trans-territorially, through information technology, whatever and whoever may offer value in the global networks accumulating wealth, information, and power.

The process of social exclusion, and the insufficiency of remedial policies of social integration, lead to a fourth, key process characterizing some specific forms of relations of production in informational capitalism: I call it *perverse integration*. It refers to the labor process in the criminal economy. By criminal economy, I mean income-generating activities that are normatively declared to be crime, and accordingly prosecuted, in a given institutional context. There is no value judgment in the labeling, not because I condone drug trafficking, but because I do not condone either a number of institutionally respectable activities that inflict tremendous damage on people's lives. Yet, what a given society considers to be criminal is so, and it has substantial consequences for whoever engages in such activities. As I will argue in chapter 3, informational capitalism is characterized by the formation of a global criminal economy, and by its growing interdependence with the formal economy and political institutions. Segments of the socially excluded population, along with individuals who choose far more profitable, if risky, ways to make a living, constitute an increasingly populated underworld which is becoming an essential feature of social dynamics in most of the planet.

There are systemic relationships between informational capitalism, capitalist restructuring, trends in the relationships of production, and new trends in the relationships of distribution. Or, in a nutshell, between the dynamics of the network society, inequality, and social exclusion. I shall try to advance some hypotheses on the nature and shape of these relationships. But rather than proposing a formal, theoretical matrix, I shall survey the interaction between these processes, and their social outcomes, by focusing on three empirical matters, from which I will try to distill some analytical conclusions. I shall focus on the process of social exclusion of almost an entire continent, Sub-Saharan Africa, and of most of its 500 million people. I shall report on the spread and deepening of urban poverty in the country that boasts the leading economy, and the most advanced technology in the world, the United States. And I shall consider a different view of the process of global development and underdevelopment: the view of children. Beforehand, let me briefly overview the state of the world concerning inequality, poverty, and social exclusion.

Toward a Polarized World? A Global Overview

"Divergence in output per person across countries is perhaps *the* dominant feature of modern economic history. The ratio of per capita income in the richest versus the poorest country [between 1870 and 1989] has increased by a factor of 6 and the standard deviation of GDP per capita has increased between 60 and 100 percent" writes Pritchett, summarizing the findings of his econometric study for the World Bank.[10] In much of the world, this geographical disparity in the

10   Pritchett (1995: 2–3).

Table 2.1 GDP per capita in a 55-country sample

Country	GDP/capita (in 1990 US$)			Index of GDP/capita (USA = 100)			Change in GDP/capita index (Numerical change)		Change in GDP/capita index (% change)	
	1950	1973	1992	1950	1973	1992	1950–73	1973–92	1950–73	1973–92
USA	9,573	16,607	21,558	100	100	100	0	0	0	0
Japan	1,873	11,017	19,425	20	66	90	47	24	239	36
16 Western European countries										
Austria	3,731	11,308	17,160	39	68	80	29	12	75	17
Belgium	5,346	11,905	17,165	56	72	80	16	8	28	11
Denmark	6,683	13,416	18,293	70	81	85	11	4	16	5
Finland	4,131	10,768	14,646	43	65	68	22	3	50	5
France	5,221	12,940	17,959	55	78	83	23	5	43	7
Germany	4,281	13,152	19,351	45	79	90	34	11	77	13
Greece	1,951	7,779	10,314	20	47	48	26	1	130	2
Ireland	3,518	7,023	11,711	37	42	54	6	12	15	28
Italy	3,425	10,409	16,229	36	63	75	27	13	75	20
Netherlands	5,850	12,763	16,898	61	77	78	16	2	26	2
Norway	4,969	10,229	17,543	52	62	81	10	20	19	32
Portugal	2,132	7,568	11,130	22	46	52	23	6	105	13
Spain	2,397	8,739	12,498	25	53	58	28	5	110	10
Sweden	6,738	13,494	16,927	70	81	79	11	–3	15	–3
Switzerland	8,939	17,953	21,036	93	108	98	15	–11	16	–10
UK	6,847	11,992	15,738	72	72	73	1	1	1	1
Average	4,760	11,340	15,912	50	68	74	19	6	37	8

3 Western offshoots										
Australia	7,218	12,485	16,237	75	75	75	0	0	0	0
Canada	7,047	13,644	18,159	74	82	84	9	2	12	3
New Zealand	8,495	12,575	13,947	89	76	65	-13	-11	-15	-15
Average	7,587	12,901	16,114	79	78	75	-2	-3	-2	-4
7 East European countries										
Bulgaria	1,651	5,284	4,054	17	32	19	15	-13	84	-41
Czechoslovakia	3,501	7,036	6,845	37	42	32	6	-11	16	-25
Hungary	2,480	5,596	5,638	26	34	26	8	-8	30	-22
Poland	2,447	5,334	4,726	26	32	22	7	-10	26	-32
Romania	1,182	3,477	2,565	12	21	12	9	-9	70	-43
USSR	2,834	6,058	4,671	30	36	22	7	-15	23	-41
Yugoslavia	1,546	4,237	3,887	16	26	18	9	-7	58	-29
Average	2,234	5,289	4,627	23	32	21	9	-10	36	-33
7 Latin American countries										
Argentina	4,987	7,970	7,616	52	48	35	-4	-13	-8	-26
Brazil	1,673	3,913	4,637	17	24	22	6	-2	35	-9
Chile	3,827	5,028	7,238	40	30	34	-10	3	-24	11
Colombia	2,089	3,539	5,025	22	21	23	-1	2	-2	9
Mexico	2,085	4,189	5,112	22	25	24	3	-2	16	-6
Peru	2,263	3,953	2,854	24	24	13	0	-11	1	-44
Venezuela	7,424	10,717	9,163	78	65	43	-13	-22	-17	-34
Average	3,478	5,616	5,949	36	34	28	-3	-6	-7	-18

Table 2.1 (contd)

Country	GDP/capita (in 1990 US$)			Index of GDP/capita (USA = 100)			Change in GDP/capita index (Numerical change)		Change in GDP/capita index (% change)	
	1950	1973	1992	1950	1973	1992	1950–73	1973–92	1950–73	1973–92
10 Asian countries										
Bangladesh	551	478	720	6	3	3	−3	0	−50	16
Burma	393	589	748	4	4	3	−1	0	−14	−2
China	614	1,186	3,098	6	7	14	1	7	11	101
India	597	853	1,348	6	5	6	−1	1	−18	22
Indonesia	874	1,538	2,749	9	9	13	0	3	1	38
Pakistan	650	981	1,642	7	6	8	−1	2	−13	29
Philippines	1,293	1,956	2,213	14	12	10	−2	−2	−13	−13
South Korea	876	2,840	10,010	9	17	46	8	29	87	172
Taiwan	922	3,669	11,590	10	22	54	12	32	129	143
Thailand	848	1,750	4,694	9	11	22	2	11	19	107
Average	762	1,584	3,881	8	10	18	2	8	20	89
10 African countries										
Côte d'Ivoire	859	1,727	1,134	9	10	5	1	−5	16	−49
Egypt	517	947	1,927	5	6	9	0	3	6	57
Ethiopia	277	412	300	3	2	1	0	−1	−14	−44
Ghana	1,193	1,260	1,007	12	8	5	−5	−3	−39	−38
Kenya	609	947	1,055	6	6	5	−1	−1	−10	−14
Morocco	1,611	1,651	2,327	17	10	11	−7	1	−41	9
Nigeria	547	1,120	1,152	6	7	5	1	−1	18	−21
South Africa	2,251	3,844	3,451	24	23	16	0	−7	−2	−31
Tanzania	427	655	601	4	4	3	−1	−1	−12	−29
Zaïre	636	757	353	7	5	2	−2	−3	−31	−64
Average	893	1,332	1,331	9	8	6	−1	−2	−14	−23

Source: Maddison (1995), calculated from table 1–3

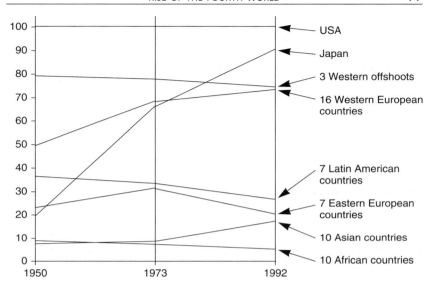

Figure 2.1 GDP per capita index in a 55-country sample (USA = 100)
Source: elaborated from table 2.1

creation/appropriation of wealth has increased in the past two decades, while the differential between OECD countries and the rest of
the planet, representing the overwhelming proportion of the population, is still abysmal. Thus, using the historical economic statistics elaborated by Maddison,[11] Benner and I have elaborated table 2.1,
represented graphically in figure 2.1, displaying the evolution of GDP
per capita index for a group of selected countries, ranked by the relative value of their index *vis-à-vis* the United States, between 1950,
1973, and 1992. Japan has succeeded in almost catching up in the
past four decades, while Western Europe has improved its relative
position, but still trails the US by a considerable margin. During the
1973–92 period, the sample of Latin American, African, and Eastern
European countries studied by Maddison have fallen behind even further. As for ten Asian countries, including the economic miracles of
South Korea, China, and Taiwan, they have substantially improved
their relative position, but in absolute levels, in 1992, they were still
poorer than any other region of the world except Africa, representing,
as a whole, only 18 percent of the US level of wealth, although this is
mainly due to China's population.

11   Maddison (1995).

However, if the distribution of wealth between countries continues to diverge, overall the average living conditions of the world's population, as measured by the United Nations Human Development Index, have improved steadily over the past three decades. This is due, primarily, to better educational opportunities, and improved health standards, which translate into a dramatic increase in life expectancy, which in developing countries went up from 46 years in the 1960s to 62 years in 1993, and to 64.4 years in 1997, particularly for women.[12]

The evolution of income inequality presents a different profile if we take a global view, or if we look at its evolution within specific countries in a comparative perspective. In a global approach, there has been, over the past three decades, increasing inequality and polarization in the distribution of wealth. According to UNDP's 1996/1999 Human Development Reports, in 1993 only US$5 trillion of the US$23 trillion global GDP were from the developing countries even if they accounted for nearly 80 percent of total population. The poorest 20 percent of the world's people have seen their share of global income decline from 2.3 percent to 1.4 percent in the past 30 years. Meanwhile, the share of the richest 20 percent has risen from 70 percent to 85 percent. The ratio of the income of the 20 percent richest people in the world over the poorest 20 percent increased – from 30 : 1 in 1960 to 74 : 1 in 1997. In 1994 the assets of the world's 358 billionaires (in US dollars) exceeded the combined annual incomes of countries with 45 percent of the world's population. The concentration of wealth at the very top accelerated in the second half of the 1990s: the net worth of the world's 200 richest people increased from US$440 billion to more than US$1 trillion between 1994 and 1998. Thus, in 1998, the assets of the three richest people in the world were more than the combined GNP of the 48 least developed countries, comprising 600 million people.[13] The gap in per capita income between the industrial and the developing worlds tripled, from US$5,700 in 1960 to US$15,000 in 1993.[14] "Between 1960 and 1991, all but the richest quintile [of the world's people] saw their income share fall, so that by 1991 more than 85 percent of the world's population received only 15 percent of its income – yet another indication of an even more polarized world."[15]

On the other hand, there is considerable disparity in the evolution of *intra-country inequality* in different areas of the world. In the past two decades, income inequality has increased in the United States,[16]

12   UNDP (1996: 18–19).
13   UNDP (1999: 37).
14   UNDP (1996: 2–3).
15   UNDP (1996: 13).
16   Fischer et al. (1996).

Table 2.2   Change in income inequality after 1979 in OECD countries

		Annual change in Gini coefficient[1]	
Country	Period	Relative (%)	Absolute (point change)
United Kingdom	1979–95	1.80	0.22
Sweden	1979–94	1.68	0.38
Denmark	1981–90	1.20	–
Australia	1981–89	1.16	0.34
Netherlands	1979–94	1.07	0.25
Japan	1979–93	0.84	0.25
United States	1979–95	0.79	0.35
Germany[2]	1979–95	0.50	0.13
France	1979–89	0.40	0.12
Norway	1979–92	0.22	0.05
Canada	1979–95	−0.02	0.00
Finland	1979–94	−0.10	−0.02
Italy	1980–91	−0.64	−0.58

[1] Measured as the relative change in the Gini coefficient, where growth reflects more inequality.
[2] Western Germany.
Source: Gottschalk and Smeeding (1997) elaborated by Mishel et al. (1999: 374)

United Kingdom,[17] Brazil, Argentina, Venezuela, Bolivia, Peru, Thailand, and Russia;[18] and, in the 1980s, in Japan,[19] Canada, Sweden, Australia, Germany,[20] and in Mexico,[21] just to cite a few relevant countries. But income inequality *decreased* in the 1960–90 period in India, Malaysia, Hong Kong, Singapore, Taiwan, and South Korea.[22] Also, according to data elaborated by Deininger and Squire, if we compare the level of income inequality, measured by Gini coefficient, by major regions of the world, between the 1990s and the 1970s, in 1990 it was much higher in Eastern Europe, somewhat higher in Latin America, but lower in all other regions, when analyzed at a highly aggregate level.[23] The Gini coefficient, remained for Latin America as a whole at about 0.58 throughout the 1990s, thus reflecting the highest level of inequality among major regions in the world.[24]

Yet, while allowing for a certain range of variation of trends in different countries, table 2.1 shows a predominant trend toward increas-

17   Townsend (1993).
18   UNDP (1996).
19   Bauer and Mason (1992).
20   Green et al. (1992).
21   Skezely (1995).
22   UNDP (1996).
23   Deininger and Squire (1996: 584).
24   UNDP (1999: 39).

ing inequality, as measured by the annual change in Gini coefficient, for most OECD countries between the late 1970s and the mid-1990s. The United Kingdom is the country where inequality increased the fastest. But what is particularly striking is that the two other countries with rapidly increasing inequality are Sweden and Denmark, which were until recently egalitarian societies. If we add Japan to the same category of fast-growing inequality in societies with low levels of inequality, this observation would suggest the hypothesis of a structural trend toward increasing inequality in the network society. On the other hand, Finland, a very advanced network society, did not follow the trend of its Scandinavian neighbors, and Italy significantly reduced inequality. If Spanish and Portuguese data were included in the table they would show a pattern of stable, moderate inequality. Transition economies in Eastern Europe and the CIS experienced, in the 1990s, the fastest rise in inequality ever. By the end of the twentieth century, in Russia the income share of the richer 20 percent was 11 times that of the poorer 20 percent.[25]

If the evolution of intra-country inequality varies, *what appears to be a global phenomenon (albeit with some important exceptions, particularly China) is the growth of poverty, and particularly of extreme poverty*. Indeed, the acceleration of uneven development, and the simultaneous inclusion and exclusion of people in the growth process, which I consider to be a feature of informational capitalism, translates into polarization, and the spread of misery among a growing number of people. Thus, according to UNDP:

> Since 1980, there has been a dramatic surge in economic growth in some 15 countries, bringing rapidly rising incomes to many of their 1.5 billion people, more than a quarter of the world's population. Over much of this period, however, economic decline or stagnation has affected 100 countries, reducing the incomes of 1.6 billion people, again more than a quarter of the world's population. In 70 of these countries average incomes are less than they were in 1980 – and in 43 countries less than they were in 1970. [Furthermore], during 1970–85 global GNP increased by 40 percent, yet the number of poor increased by 17 percent. While 200 million people saw their per capita incomes fall during 1965–80, more than one billion people did in 1980–93.[26]

In the mid-1990s, taking as the extreme poverty line a consumption equivalent to one US dollar a day, 1.3 billion people, accounting for 33 percent of the developing world's population, were in misery. Of these poor people, 550 million lived in South Asia, 215 million in Sub-

25   UNDP (1999: 36).
26   UNDP (1996: 1–2)

Saharan Africa, and 150 million in Latin America.[27] In a similar estimate, using the one dollar a day dividing line for extreme poverty, ILO estimated that the percentage of the population below this line increased from 53.5 percent in 1985 to 54.4 percent in 1990 in Sub-Saharan Africa; from 23 percent to 27.8 percent in Latin America; and decreased from 61.1 percent to 59 percent in South Asia, and from 15.7 percent to 14.7 percent in East/South-East Asia (without China). According to UNDP, between 1987 and 1993 the number of people with incomes of less than one dollar a day increased by 100 million to reach 1.3 billion. If we consider the level of income of less than two dollars a day, another billion people should be added. Thus, at the turn of the millennium well over one third of humankind was living at subsistence or below subsistence level. In addition to income poverty, other dimensions of poverty are even more striking: in the mid-1990s about 840 million people were illiterate, more than 1.2 billion lacked access to safe water, 800 million lacked access to health services, and more than 800 million suffered hunger. Nearly a third of the people in the least developed countries – mainly in Sub-Saharan Africa – were not expected to survive to the age of 40. Women and children suffer most from poverty: 160 million children under five were malnourished, and the maternal mortality rate was about 500 women per 100,000 live births.[28] The largest concentration of poverty was, by far, in the rural areas: in 1990, the proportion of poor among the rural population was 66 percent in Brazil, 72 percent in Peru, 43 percent in Mexico, 49 percent in India, and 54 percent in the Philippines.[29] As for Russia, the CIS countries, and Eastern Europe, a report issued by the World Bank in April 1999 calculated that there were 147 million people living below the poverty line of four dollars a day. The equivalent figure for 1989 was 14 million.

On the other hand, some countries, and particularly China and Chile, reduced substantially their poverty level during the 1990s. In the case of China this was due to high economic growth, coupled with rural–urban migration. In the case of Chile it was the result of deliberate policies by the first Chilean democratic administration, after Pinochet's "miracle" had reduced to poverty about 43 percent of the Chilean population.[30] Thus structural trends notwithstanding, poverty is also a function of public policies. The issue is that during the 1980s and 1990s most governments gave priority to techno-economic restructuring over social welfare. As a result, poverty also increased during the

27   UNDP (1996: 27).
28   ILO (1995: table 13).
29   ILO (1994).
30   UNDP – Chile (1998).

1980s and early 1990s in most developed countries. The number of families below the poverty line increased by 60 percent in the UK, and by 40 percent in The Netherlands. Overall, by the mid-1990s, there were over 100 million people below the poverty level in industrialized countries, including five million homeless people.[31]

To the structural persistence of poverty in all areas of the world must be added the sudden inducement of poverty by economic crises linked to volatility in global financial markets. Thus, the Asian crisis of 1997–8, plunged into poverty in Indonesia an additional 40 million people, or 20 percent of the population, and brought below the poverty level 5.5 million people in Korea and 6.7 million in Thailand. Indeed, while markets and exports may recover in a relatively short time (about two years in most Asian economies affected by the 1997–8 crisis), employment, income, and social benefits are curtailed for a much longer period. An analysis of over 300 economic crises in more than 80 counties since 1973 showed that output growth recovered to the level prior to the crisis in one year on average. But real wage growth took about four years to recover and employment growth five years. Income distribution worsened on average for three years, improving over pre-crisis levels by the fifth year.[32] And this is counting on the fact that, during this three to five year period, there is no further crisis.

Thus, overall, *the ascent of informational, global capitalism is indeed characterized by simultaneous economic development and underdevelopment, social inclusion and social exclusion*, in a process very roughly reflected in comparative statistics. There is polarization in the distribution of wealth at the global level, differential evolution of intra-country income inequality, albeit with a predominantly upward trend toward increasing inequality, and substantial growth of poverty and misery in the world at large and in most – but not all – countries, both developed and developing. However, the patterns of social exclusion, and the factors accounting for them, require a qualitative analysis of the processes by which they are induced.

The De-humanization of Africa[33]

The rise of informational/global capitalism in the last quarter of the twentieth century coincided with the collapse of Africa's economies,

31   UNDP (1997: 24; 1999: 37).
32   UNDP (1999: 40).
33   The analysis presented here is exclusively concerned with Sub-Saharan Africa, excepting South Africa and Botswana, as they are both special cases. Throughout this chapter, when writing on Africa, I shall be referring to this socio-economic unit, as defined by inter-

the disintegration of many of its states, and the breakdown of most of its societies. As a result, famines, epidemics, violence, civil wars, massacres, mass exodus, and social and political chaos are, in this turn of the millennium, salient features of the land that nurtured the birth of Lucy, perhaps the shared grandmother of humankind. I argue that structural, social causality underlies this historical coincidence. And I shall try, in the following pages, to show the complex interplay between economy, technology, society, and politics in the making of a process that denies humanity to African people, as well as to all of us in our inner selves.

Marginalization and selective integration of Sub-Saharan Africa in the informational-global economy

In the last two decades of the twentieth century, while a dynamic, global economy was constituted in much of the world, Sub-Saharan Africa experienced a substantial deterioration in its relative position in trade, investment, production, and consumption *vis-à-vis* all other areas of the world, while its per capita GDP declined during the period 1980–95 (table 2.3). In the early 1990s, the combined export earnings of its 45 countries, with about 500 million people, amounted to just 36 billion in current US dollars, down from 50 billion in 1980. This figure represents less than half of Hong Kong's exports in the same period. In a historical perspective, from 1870 to 1970, during Africa's incorporation into the capitalist economy, under colonial domination, African exports grew rapidly, and their share of developing countries' exports increased. In 1950, Africa accounted for over 3 percent of world exports; in 1990, for about 1.1 percent.[34] In 1980, Africa was the destination of 3.1 percent of world exports; in 1995, of just 1.5 percent. World imports from Africa declined from 3.7 percent in 1980 to 1.4 percent in 1995.[35]

Furthermore, African exports have remained confined to primary commodities (92 percent of all exports), and particularly to agricul-

---

national institutions, minus Botswana and South Africa. I will deal with South Africa in the concluding pages of this section by analyzing its potential role in the overall development of the region. I will not deal with Botswana because its heavy specialization in diamond mining and exports (second largest producer in the world after Russia), and its interpenetration with South Africa's economy, invalidate comparison with the conditions in the rest of the region. However, I would like to point out that, after growing at a stunning annual average of 13 percent in real GDP since its independence (1966), Botswana also faced serious problems of unemployment and poverty in the 1990s. Interested readers should see Hope (1996).
34   Svedberg (1993).
35   UN (1996: 318–19).

Table 2.3 Per capita GDP of developing economies, 1980–96

	Annual rate of growth of per capita GDP (%)				Per capita GDP (1988 dollars)			
	1981–90	1991–95	1995[a]	1996[b]	1980	1990	1995[a]	1996[b]
Developing economies	1.0	2.9	3.3	4.0	770	858	988	1,028
Latin America	-0.9	0.8	-0.9	0.75	2,148	2,008	2,092	2,106
Africa	-0.9	-1.3	0.0	1.5	721	700	657	667
West Asia	-5.3	-0.6	0.4	0.25	5,736	3,423	3,328	3,335
South-East Asia	3.9	4.0	5.0	6.0	460	674	817	865
China	7.5	10.2	9.1	8.0	202	411	664	716
Least developed countries	-0.5	-0.9	0.4	1.75	261	249	238	243

[a] Preliminary estimate.
[b] Forecast.
Source: UN/DESIPA

Table 2.4 Value of exports from world, less-developed countries, and Sub-Saharan Africa, 1950–90

Region	1950	1960	1970	1980	1990
	Billions of current dollars				
World	60.7	129.1	315.1	2,002.0	3,415.3
LDCs	18.9	28.3	57.9	573.3	738.0
SSA	2.0	3.8	8.0	49.4	36.8
	Share of LDCs (%)				
World exports	31.1	21.9	18.4	28.6	21.6
	Share of SSA (%)				
World exports	3.3	2.9	2.5	2.5	1.1
LDC exports	10.6	13.4	13.8	8.6	5.0

LDCs, less-developed countries; SSA, Sub-Saharan Africa.
Source: UNCTAD 1979, 1989 and 1991, table 1.1; elaborated by Simon et al. (1995)

tural exports (about 76 percent of export earnings in 1989–90). There is also an increased concentration of these agricultural exports in a few crops, such as coffee and cocoa, which accounted for 40 percent of export earnings in 1989–90. The ratio of manufactured goods exports to total exports fell from 7.8 percent in 1965 to 5.9 percent in 1985, while it rose from 3 percent to 8.2 percent in West Asia, from 28.3 percent to 58.5 percent in South/South-East Asia, and from 5.2 percent to 18.6 percent in Latin America.[36] Since the prices of primary commodities have been depressed since the mid-1970s, the deterioration in the terms of trade, as a result of the structure of exports, makes it extremely difficult for Africa to grow on the basis of an outward orientation of its economies. Indeed, according to Simon et al., adjustment policies, inspired by the IMF/World Bank to improve export performance, have actually increased dependence on primary commodities such as cotton and copper, thus undermining the efforts of some countries to diversify their economies to make them less vulnerable to the long-term deterioration of prices of primary commodities *vis-à-vis* higher value added goods and services.[37] Overall, the terms of trade deteriorated substantially for most African countries between 1985 and 1994 (see tables 2.4–2.7).

On the other hand, weak domestic markets have been unable to sustain import-substitution industrialization, and even agricultural production for domestic markets. Between 1965 and 1989, the ratio of total manufacturing value added to GDP did not rise above 11

36   Riddell (1993: 222–3).
37   Simon et al. (1995).

Table 2.5 Structure of exports (percentage share), 1990

Region	Fuels, minerals and metals	Other primary commodities	Machinery and transport equipment	Other manufacturing	Textiles and clothing
Sub-Saharan Africa	63	29	1	7	1
East Asia and Pacific	13	18	22	47	19
South Asia	6	24	5	65	33
Europe	9	16	27	47	16
Middle East and North Africa	75	12	1	15	4
Latin America and Caribbean	38	29	11	21	3
Low and middle-income countries	31	20	15	35	12
Low-income countries	27	20	9	45	21

Percentages are of respective regions' exports; data weighted by size of flows; all SSA classified as low income except: (a) lower-middle-income: Zimbabwe, Senegal, Côte d'Ivoire, Cameroon, Congo, Botswana, Angola, Namibia; (b) upper-middle-income: South Africa, Gabon; low-income includes India and China.
Source: World Bank (1992) *World Development Report 1992*; elaborated by Simon et al. (1995)

Table 2.6 Percentage share of Sub-Saharan Africa in world exports of major product categories

Product category	Share of product category in world exports		Sub-Saharan Africa's share of world exports		Share of product category in SSA exports	
	1970	1988	1970	1988	1970	1988
Crude oil (SITC 331)	5.3	6.0	6.5	6.9	14.0	34.5
Non-oil products (SITC 0–9 less 331)	94.7	94.0	2.2	0.8	86.0	65.5
Primary commodities[a] (non oil)	25.9	16.3	7.0	3.7	73.8	50.4
Agricultural commodities	7.0	2.8	6.3	3.6	12.3	8.2
Minerals and ores	7.5	3.8	9.7	4.2	30.0	14.6
18 IPC commodities[b]	9.1	4.3	16.1	10.0	59.1	35.6

[a] Standard International Trade Classification (SITC) 0, 1, 2–(233, 244, 266, 267), 4, 68 and item 522.56.
[b] What UNCTAD labels the Integrated Programme Commodities (IPC) (which supposedly are of greatest importance to developing countries): bananas, cocoa, coffee, cotton, and cotton yarn, hard fibers and products, jute and jute manufactures, bovine meat, rubber, sugar, tea, tropical timber, vegetable oils and oilseeds, bauxite, copper, iron ore, manganese, phosphates and tin. SSA, Sub-Saharan Africa.
Sources: Derived on the basis of data from UNCTAD 1984, 1986, 1988, and 1989: various tables; UNCTAD 1980: tables 1.1 and 1.2; elaborated by Simon et al. (1995)

percent, compared with an increase from 20 to 30 percent for all developing countries.[38] Agricultural production has lagged behind the 3 percent annual population growth rate. Thus, since the early 1980s, food imports have risen by about 10 percent per annum.[39] Table 2.8 shows that Africa's economy has consistently grown at a lower rate than any other area in the world in agriculture, industry, and services since 1973. Particularly noticeable is the collapse of industry in the 1980s, after a hefty growth in the 1960s, and a moderate increase in the 1970s. It appears that Africa's industrialization went into crisis at exactly the time when technological renewal and export-oriented industrialization characterized most of the world, including other developing countries.

Under these conditions, the survival of most African economies has

38 Riddell (1993: 22–3).
39 Simon et al. (1995: 22).

Table 2.7   Terms of trade of selected African countries, 1985–94

Country	Terms of trade (1987=100)	
	1985	1994
Burkina Faso	103	103
Burundi	133	52
Cameroon	113	79
Chad	99	103
Congo	150	93
Côte d'Ivoire	109	81
Ethiopia	119	74
Gambia (The)	137	111
Kenya	124	80
Madagascar	124	82
Malawi	99	87
Mali	100	103
Mozambique	113	124
Niger	91	101
Nigeria	167	86
Rwanda	136	75
Senegal	107	107
Sierra Leone	109	89
Tanzania	126	83
Togo	139	90
Uganda	149	58
Zimbabwe	100	84

Source: IBRD (1996), table 3, p. 192

come to depend on international aid and foreign borrowing. Aid, mainly from governments, but also from humanitarian donors, has become an essential feature of Africa's political economy. In 1990, Africa received 30 percent of all aid funding in the world. In 1994, international aid represented 12.4 percent of GNP in Africa, compared with 1.1 percent for low and middle-income countries as a whole.[40] In a number of countries, it actually accounts for a substantial share of GNP (for example, 65.7 percent in Mozambique, 45.9 percent in Somalia).[41]

In the 1980s there was a massive influx of foreign loans (most of it from governments and international institutions, or endorsed by such institutions) to rescue the collapsing African economies. As a result, Africa has become the most indebted area in the world. As a percent-

40   IBRD (1996).
41   Simon et al. (1995).

Table 2.8 Sectoral growth rates (average annual percentage change of value added), 1965–89

Country group	Agriculture			Industry			Services		
	1965–73	*1973–80*	*1980–89*	*1965–73*	*1973–80*	*1980–89*	*1965–73*	*1973–80*	*1980–89*
Low-income economies	2.9	1.8	4.3	10.7	7.0	8.7	6.3	5.3	6.1
Middle-income economies	3.2	3.0	2.7	8.0	4.0	3.2	7.6	6.3	3.1
Severely indebted middle-income economies	3.1	3.6	2.7	6.8	5.4	1.0	7.2	5.4	1.7
Sub-Saharan Africa	2.2	–0.3	1.8	13.9	4.2	–0.2	4.1	3.1	1.5
East Asia	3.2	2.5	5.3	12.7	9.2	10.3	10.5	7.3	7.9
South Asia	3.1	2.2	2.7	3.9	5.6	7.2	4.0	5.3	6.1
Latin America and the Caribbean	3.0	3.7	2.5	6.8	5.1	1.1	7.3	5.4	1.7

Figures in italics in the 1980–89 columns are not for the full decade.
Source: World Bank (1990) *World Development Report 1990*, p. 162; elaborated by Simon et al. (1995)

age of GNP, total external debt has risen from 30.6 percent in 1980 to 78.7 percent in 1994;[42] and as a percentage of the value of exports, it went up from 97 percent in 1980 to 324 percent in 1990.[43]

Since it is generally acknowledged that such a debt cannot be repayed, government creditors, and international institutions, have used this financial dependence to impose adjustment policies on African countries, exchanging their subservience against partial condonement of the debt, or renegotiation of payments servicing the debt. I shall discuss later the actual impact of these adjustment policies in the specific context of Africa's political economy.

Foreign direct investment is bypassing Africa at a time when it is growing substantially all over the world. According to Collier,

> while direct private investment into developing countries has increased enormously over the past decade, to around US$200 billion per annum, the share going to Africa has shrunk to negligible proportions: current estimates are that less than 1 percent of this flow is going to Sub-Saharan Africa. Even this level is falling: the absolute amount in 1992 was less in real terms than the inflow in 1985, the nadir of the economic crisis for much of the continent.[44]

Simon et al. also report that foreign direct investment in Africa declined consistently in both absolute and relative terms in the 1980s and early 1990s, representing in 1992 just about 6 percent of total foreign direct investment (FDI) in developing countries. While Africa represented 4 percent of UK worldwide net industrial FDI in the mid-1970s, its share went down to 0.5 percent in 1986.[45]

The reasons for this marginalization of Africa in the global economy are the subject of heated debate among experts, as well as among political leaders. Paul Collier has suggested a multi-causal interpretation, supported by the results of his survey of 150 foreign business executives in Eastern Africa.[46] It can be summarized under three headings: an unreliable institutional environment; lack of production and communications infrastructure, as well as of human capital; and erroneous economic policies which penalize exports and investment for the sake of local businesses favored by their association with state bureaucracy. Altogether, investing in Africa is a highly risky venture, which discourages even the most daring capitalists. Being unable to compete in the new global economy, most African countries represent

42   IBRD (1996).
43   Simon et al. (1995: 25).
44   Collier (1995: 542).
45   Simon et al. (1995: 28).
46   Collier (1995).

small domestic markets that do not provide the basis for endogenous capital accumulation.

However, not all of Africa is marginalized from the global networks. Valuable resources, such as oil, gold, diamonds, and metals, continue to be exported, inducing substantial economic growth in Botswana, and providing considerable earnings to other countries, such as Nigeria. The problem is the use of earnings from these resources, as well as of international aid funds received by governments.[47] The small, but affluent, bureaucratic class in many countries displays a high level of consumption of expensive imported goods, including Western food products and international fashion wear.[48] Capital flows from African countries to personal accounts and profitable international investment throughout the world, for the exclusive benefit of a few wealthy individuals, provide evidence of substantial private accumulation that is not reinvested in the country where the wealth is generated.[49] So, there is a selective integration of small segments of African capital, affluent markets, and profitable exports into the global networks of capital, goods, and services, while most of the economy, and the overwhelming majority of the population, are left to their own fate, between bare subsistence and violent pillage.[50]

Furthermore, while African businesses can hardly compete in the global economy, the existing linkages to this economy have deeply penetrated Africa's traditional sectors. Thus, subsistence agriculture and food production for local markets have plunged into a crisis, in most countries, as a result of the conversion to export-oriented agriculture and specialized cash crops, in a desperate attempt to sell into international markets.[51] Thus, what is marginal globally is still central in Africa, and actually contributes to disorganizing traditional economic forms.[52] In this sense, Africa is not external to the global economy. Instead, it is disarticulated by its fragmented incorporation into the global economy through linkages such as a limited amount of commodity exports, speculative appropriation of valuable resources, financial transfers abroad, and parasitic consumption of imported goods.

The consequence of this process of disinvestment throughout Africa, at the precise historical moment when the information technology revolution has transformed the infrastructure of production,

47   Yansane (1996).
48   Ekholm-Friedman (1993).
49   Jackson and Rosberg (1994); Collier (1995).
50   Blomstrom and Lundhal (1993); Simon et al. (1995).
51   Jamal (1995).
52   Callaghy and Ravenhill (1993).

management, and communications elsewhere, has been the de-linking of African firms and labor from the workings of the new economy characterizing most of the world, while linking up African elites to the global networks of wealth, power, information, and communication.

Africa's technological apartheid at the dawn of the Information Age

Information technology, and the ability to use it and adapt it, is the critical factor in generating and accessing wealth, power, and knowledge in our time (see volume I, chapters 2 and 3). Africa (with the fundamental exception of South Africa) is, for the time being, excluded from the information technology revolution, if we except a few nodes of finance and international management directly connected to global networks while bypassing African economies and societies.

Not only is Africa, by far, the least computerized region of the world, but it does not have the minimum infrastructure required to make use of computers, thus making nonsense of many of the efforts to provide electronic equipment to countries and organizations.[53] Indeed, before moving into electronics, Africa first needs a reliable electricity supply: between 1971 and 1993 the commercial use of energy in Africa rose from only 251 kilowatts per capita to 288 kilowatts per capita, while in developing countries as a whole, consumption more than doubled, from 255 kW to 536 kW per capita. This compares with a consumption of 4,589 kW per capita in 1991 for industrial countries.[54] Furthermore, the critical aspect of computer use in the Information Age is its networking capability, which relies on telecommunications infrastructure and network connectivity. Africa's telecommunications are meagre, compared with current world standards. There are more telephone lines in Manhattan or in Tokyo than in the whole of Sub-Saharan Africa. In 1991, there was one telephone line per 100 people in Africa, compared to 2.3 for all developing countries, and 37.2 for industrial countries. In 1994, Africa accounted for only about 2 percent of world telephone lines.[55] Some of the obstacles to developing telecommunications come from government bureaucracies, and stem from their policy of keeping a monopoly for their national companies, thus slowing down their modernization. Permission is required from national telephone operators to install any telephone device. Import of telecommunications equipment is expensive, and uncertain, as it is

53 Odedra et al. (1993); Jensen (1995); Heeks (1996).
54 UNDP (1996: 183).
55 Hall (1995); Jensen (1995); UNDP (1996:167).

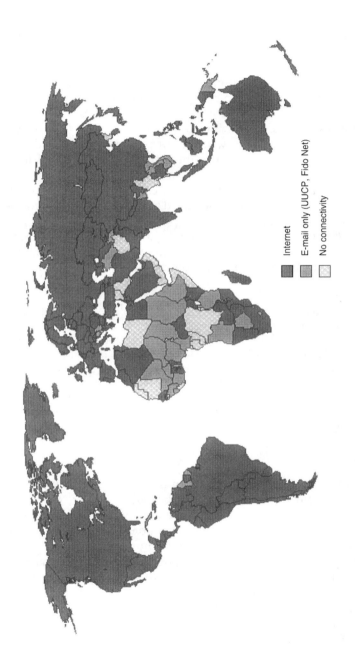

Figure 2.2 International connectivity

Source: copyright © 1995 Larry Landweber and the Internet Society

Internet

E-mail only (UUCP, Fido Net)

No connectivity

often "lost" in customs.[56] The Organization of African Unity established the Pan African Telecommunications Union to coordinate telecommunications policy in Africa, but the decision to locate the office
in Zaïre, at Mobutu's insistence, limited its effectiveness, since Zaïre
has one of the poorest telecommunications networks. Connection to
the Internet is very limited because of insufficient international band-
width, and lack of connectivity between African countries. Half of the
African countries had no connection to the Internet in 1995, and Africa remains, by and large, the switched-off region of the world (see
figure 2.2). However, what is significant is that, in 1996, 22 African
capitals had full Internet connectivity, but in only one country (Senegal) was Internet access possible outside the capital city.[57] Thus, while
some directional centers are being connected to the Internet, their countries remain switched off.

If the physical infrastructure is lagging behind, the human skills to
operate information technology remain totally inadequate. An acute
observer of Africa's information technology, Mayuri Odedra, writes
that

> Sub-Saharan Africa lacks computer skills in all areas, including systems
> analysis, programming, maintenance and consulting, and at all opera-
> tional levels, from basic use to management. Most countries lack the
> educational and training facilities needed to help people acquire the proper
> skills. The few training centers that do exist have not been able to keep
> up with demand. Only a handful of countries, such as Nigeria, Malawi,
> and Zimbabwe have universities that offer computer science degrees. The
> programs available in the other countries are mainly diplomas and cer-
> tificates. As a result of unskilled and untrained personnel, user organiza-
> tions are forced to hire expatriate staff, who in turn lack knowledge about
> local organizations and thus design poor systems.[58]

Most computing work is aimed at routine data processing, with
little computer-aided decision-making. The public sector, the overwhelming force in African economies, proceeds with "blind computerization," induced by the ideology of modernization and/or by
financial enticements by foreign computer companies, without actually using installed computer power to process relevant information.
Regulations often impose centralized acquisition of computer equipment by the public sector, and tax private firms to discourage independent imports. The limited computerization of Africa has become

56　Adam (1996).
57　Jensen (1995).
58　Odedra et al. (1993: 1–2).

another source of money-making for bureaucrats, without linkage to the needs of the economy or of public service.[59] In the 1980s, half of the computers introduced into Africa were aid-donated, most of them technologically obsolete, so that experts consider that Africa has become the dumping ground for a mass of equipment made obsolete by a fast-moving technological revolution. As for the private computer market, it is dominated by multinationals which generally ensure that they carry out the maintenance. Most of the systems are bought off the shelf, leading to some local knowledge of how to operate, but not of how to program or repair, the systems. The few indigenous software houses are only capable of undertaking small programming jobs.[60]

Technological dependency and technological underdevelopment, in a period of accelerated technological change in the rest of the world, make it literally impossible for Africa to compete internationally either in manufacturing or in advanced services. Other activities that also rely on efficient information processing, such as the promising tourist industry, come under the control of international tour operators and travel agencies, which take the lion's share of the tourists' share of lions, by controlling market information. Even agricultural and mineral exports, constituting the bulk of Africa's exports, are increasingly dependent on the management of information of international operations, as well as on electronic equipment and chemical/biotechnological inputs for advanced agricultural production. Because of the inability of African countries to produce/use advanced technological equipment and know-how, their balance of trade becomes unsustainable, as the added value of technology-intensive goods and services continues to increase *vis-à-vis* the value of raw materials and agricultural products, limiting their capacity to import inputs necessary to keep their commodity production systems in operation. It follows a downward spiral of competitiveness, as Africa becomes increasingly marginalized in the informational/global economy by each leap forward in technological change. The disinformation of Africa at the dawn of the Information Age may be the most lasting wound inflicted on this continent by new patterns of dependency, aggravated by the policies of the predatory state.

The predatory state

There seems to be a convergence in the views of a growing number of Africanists on the destructive role of African nation-states on their

---

59 Bates (1988: 352).
60 Woherem (1994); Heeks (1996).

economies and societies. Frimpong-Ansah, a former governor of Ghana's central bank, considers that capital constraint is not the obstacle to development. What is critical is the institutional capacity to mobilize savings, and this was eroded in Africa from the mid-1970s because of the misuse of capital by the "vampire state," that is, a state entirely patrimonialized by political elites for their own personal profit.[61] From a different perspective, one of the most respected Africanists, Basil Davidson, thinks that "Africa's crisis of society derives from many upsets and conflicts, but the root of the problem is different from these . . . Primarily, this is a crisis of institutions. Which institutions? We have to be concerned here with the nationalism that produced the nation-states of newly independent Africa after the colonial period: with the nationalism that became nation-statism."[62] Fatton argues that the "predatory rule" characterizing most African states results from a process of individualization of ruling classes: "Their members tend to be mercenaries, as their hold on positions of privilege and power is at the mercy of the capricious decisions of an ultimate leader."[63] This seems to apply to bloody dictatorial rules, such as that of Mobutu in Zaïre or of "Emperor" Bokassa in the Central African Republic, as well as to benevolent pseudo-democracies, such as Houphouet-Boigny's regime in the Ivory Coast. As Colin Leys writes: "Few theorists of any of these persuasions [Marxists, dependency theorists] expected the post-colonial states of all ideological stripes to be corrupt, rapacious, insufficient, and unstable, as they have almost all been."[64]

Jean-François Bayart interprets Africa's plight as the result of a long-term historical trajectory dominated by "the politics of the belly" practiced by elites with no other strategy than reaping the riches of their countries, and of their countries' international linkages.[65] He proposes a typology of mechanisms of private appropriation of resources using positions of power in the state:

- Access to resources of "extraversion" (international connections), including diplomatic and military resources, as well as cultural resources, and Western know-how.
- Jobs in the public sector, which provide a regular salary, a fundamental asset, regardless of its amount.
- Positions of predation, using power to extract goods, cash or labor:

61   Frimpong-Ansah (1991).
62   Davidson (1992: 10).
63   Fatton (1992: 20).
64   Leys (1994: 41).
65   Bayart (1989).

"In the countryside at least, most of the administrative and political cadres act this way."[66]

- Prebends obtained without violence or the threat of it, by being receptive to a variety of bribes and donations from various interests, constituting a widespread "state informal economy." Most technical or administrative decisions involving potential beneficiaries carry a price tag for the interested parties. Bayart cites the case of a regional commissar of the rich province of Shaba in Zaïre, in 1974, who received a monthly salary of US$2,000, complemented by about US$100,000 a month from prebends.[67]

- Links to foreign trade and investment are crucial sources of private accumulation, as custom duties and protectionist regulations offer the opportunity to circumvent them in exchange for a contribution to the chain of bureaucrats in charge of enforcing them.

- International development aid, including food aid, is channeled through private interests, and only reaches the needy, or the targeted development program, if ever, after substantial discount by government agencies, and their personnel, in charge of its distribution and implementation.

- State officials, and political elites at large, use some of this wealth to buy property, and invest in agriculture and transport businesses in their countries, constantly scanning opportunities for profitable, short-term investments, and helping each other to collectively control whatever source of profit appears in the country. However, a substantial amount of this private wealth is deposited in foreign bank accounts, representing a significant proportion of capital accumulated in each country. As Houphouet-Boigny, the (god)father of the Ivory Coast, put it "Who in the world would not deposit part of his goods in Switzerland?"[68] Mobutu's personal fortune in 1984, also deposited in foreign banks and invested abroad, was estimated at US$ 4 billion, roughly equivalent to Zaïre's total foreign debt.[69] By 1993, while Zaïre was in the process of disintegration, Mobutu's fortune outside the country was estimated to have increased to about US$10 billion.[70]

Lewis, on the basis of his analysis of Nigeria, introduces an interesting distinction between *prebendalism* and *predation*.[71] "Prebendalism"

66 Bayart (1989: 76).
67 Bayart (1989: 78).
68 Cited by Bayart (1989: 101).
69 Sandbrook (1985: 91).
70 Kempster (1993).
71 Lewis (1996).

is not essentially different from political patronage and systematic government corruption as practiced in most countries of the world. He argues, convincingly, that it was only in the late 1980s and early 1990s in Nigeria, under the Babangida regime, that the politics of predation became dominant, diffusing a model of "Zaïreanization" of the military-dominated state oligarchy. Although Lewis does not extend his analysis beyond Nigeria, it seems plausible, on the basis of information on other countries,[72] that this transition to predatory rule took place only in a later stage of Africa's crisis, with a different time of onset depending on each country. This is in contrast to Bayart's historical reconstruction that affirms the continuity of Africa's pillage by its own political elites from the pre-colonial period. In contrast to prebendalism, predatory rule is characterized by the concentration of power at the top, and the personalization of networks of delegation of this power. It is enforced by ruthless repression. Economic inducements to government personnel, and generalized corruption and bribery, become the way of life in government. This pattern of behavior leads to the erosion of political institutions as stable systems, being replaced by close-knit circles of personal and ethnic loyalties: the entire state is informalized, while power, and power networks, are personalized. While it is arguable whether predation was already the rule in precolonial times, or in the early period of African nationalism after independence (Bayart thinks the fomer, but he is challenged by Davidson, Leys, Lewis, and Fatton, among others), what matters, to understand current processes of social exclusion, is that the predatory model, and not just prebendalism, seems to characterize most African states at the turn of the millennium, with the exception of South Africa and a few other possible cases.

Three major consequences follow from this exercise of predatory rule, characteristic of most African states. First, whatever resources, from international or domestic sources, arrive into these state-dominated economies are processed according to a logic of personalized accumulation, largely disconnected from the country's economy. What does not make sense from the point of view of the country's economic development and political stability makes a lot of sense from the point of view of its rulers. Secondly, access to state power is equivalent to accessing wealth, and the sources of future wealth. It follows a pattern of violent confrontation, and unstable alliances between different political factions competing for the opportunity to practice pillage, ultimately resulting in the instability of state institutions and in the decisive

---

72   Fatton (1992); Nzongola-Ntalaja (1993); Leys (1994); Kaiser (1996); *The Economist* (1996a).

role played by the military in most African states. Thirdly, political support is built around clientelistic networks which link the power-holders with segments of the population. Because the overwhelming share of wealth existing in the country is in the hands of the political/military elite and state bureaucrats, people must pay allegiance to the chain of patronage to be included in the distribution of jobs, services, and petty favors at all levels of the state, from internationally oriented agencies to local government benevolence. Under such a patronage system, various elites, at different levels of government, ultimately connected to the top of state power, engage in complex calculations and strategies: how to maximize support, and consolidate clienteles, while minimizing the amount of resources necessary to obtain this support. A mixture of criteria, encompassing ethnicity, territoriality, and economics, contribute to form networks of variable geometry that constitute the real-life politics in most of Africa.

While detailed empirical analyses are beyond the scope of this chapter, I shall illustrate the dynamics of African predatory states with a brief reference to the two largest countries, Zaïre (in 1997, Congo) and Nigeria.

Zaïre: the personal appropriation of the state

Zaïre became, at least before 1997 (and perhaps, renamed as Congo, beyond this date) the epitome of predatory politics, as well as a warning of the consequences of social and political disintegration, as well as of human catastrophes (epidemics, pillage, massacres, civil wars), resulting from these politics.[73] The Zaïrean state was organized around the personal dictatorship of Sergeant Mobutu, supported by France, Belgium, and the United States in the context of Cold War politics. Norman Kempster, a *Los Angeles Times* staff writer, summarized, in 1993, Mobutu's trajectory as follows:

> Mobutu is a former sergeant in Belgium's colonial army who seized power with US and Western backing in 1965, ending a chaotic rivalry between pro-Communist and anti-Communist factions. For three decades, he put his vast country, the second largest in Sub-Saharan Africa at the disposal of the CIA and other Western agencies, which used it as a staging base for activities throughout the continent. In exchange, he enjoyed a free hand at home, diverting for his use billions of dollars from Zaïre's mineral wealth while leaving most Zaïreans in poverty.[74]

---

73 Sandbrook (1985); Bayart (1989); Davidson (1992); Noble (1992); Kempster (1993); Press (1993); Leys (1994); French (1995); Weiss (1995); McKinley (1996).
74 Kempster (1993: 7).

Mobutu relied on a very simple system of power. He controlled the only operational unit of the army, the presidential guard, and divided politics, government, and army positions among different ethnic groups. He patronized all of them, but also encouraged their violent confrontation.[75] He concentrated on controlling mining business, particularly cobalt, industrial diamonds, and copper, using government companies, in association with foreign investors, for his own benefit. The "Zaïreanization" of foreign companies also put all valuable assets in the country into the hands of the bureaucracy and the military. He disinvested in social services and infrastructure, focusing on operating a few profitable ventures, and exporting earnings abroad. He encouraged the entire army staff, and government agencies, to proceed in the same way. Thus, Bayart reports how the Zaïrean Air Force engaged in pirate air transportation, then in smuggling, and ultimately in the selling of spare parts of the aircraft, until all planes became useless.[76] This made it possible for Mobutu to request additional aircraft equipment from his Western allies. Lack of control over local and provincial governments led to the practical disintegration of the Zaïrean state, with most localities, including Kinshasa, becoming out of control of central government. Army mutinies, followed by indiscriminate pillage, as in September 1991, led to the exodus of foreign residents, and ultimately to the retrenchment of Mobutu in his native town of Gbadolite, in Equateur Province, kept off limits by his private army, although the dictator spent much of his time in his various mansions in Switzerland, France, Spain, and Portugal. Provincial governments, left to themselves, followed the leader's example in many instances, using their power to abuse and steal from their own subjects, starting with the least powerful ethnic groups. Ultimately, the rapacity of some provincial governments was fatal for the whole enterprise, when, in 1996, the government of Kivu, in Eastern Zaïre, moved to expropriate the lands of the Banyamulenge, a Tutsi minority that had been settled in this area for centuries, ordering them to leave the region. The subsequent rebellion of the Banyamulenge and other ethnic groups, led by a veteran revolutionary, Laurent Kabila, routed in a few months the gangs of thugs posing as the Zaïrean army, and exposed the fiction of the Zaïrean state leading to the end of Mobutu's regime in 1997.[77] It took only a few months for the new Congo to fall into a new round of civil war and inter-ethnic strife, as Kabila turned against his former allies, and various African states intervened in the war to support their

75   Press (1993).
76   Bayart (1989: 235–7).
77   McKinley (1996); *The Economist* (1996c); French (1997).

surrogate forces in the struggle for the control of Congo's riches. The consequences of this three-decade long pillage of one of the richest countries in Africa by its own rulers and their associates, with the open complicity of Western powers, are dramatic and long lasting, for Zaïre/Congo, for Africa, and for the world. For Zaïre/Congo: because its entire communications, transportation, and production infrastructure has collapsed, deteriorating considerably below its level at the time of independence, while Zaïre/Congo's people have suffered massive malnutrition, and have been kept in illiteracy, and misery, losing in the process much of their subsistence agriculture. For Africa: because the disarticulation of one of its largest economies, at the very core of the continent, has blocked effective regional integration. Besides, the "Zaïrean model" acted as a magnetic example for other elites in the continent. It was personally promoted by Mobutu, who, as a privileged partner of the West, played an important role in the Organization of African Unity, and in Africa's political scene. For the world: because Zaïre/Congo has become a pre-eminent source of deadly "epidemics of dereliction," including the Ebola virus, whose potential for calamity may well impact upon the twenty-first century's livelihood. Furthermore, the indirect contribution of the West, and particularly of France, to the private appropriation of Zaïre by a military/bureaucratic clique removed much of the credibility for future policies of international cooperation in the minds of some of the best Africans. The disintegration of the Zaïrean state in the form inherited from Mobutu marked the limits of predatory rule, underscoring its historical association with the politics of the Cold War and post-colonial domination patterns. Yet, the post-Mobutu experience showed that this model, while originated by the superpowers' confrontation in Africa, outlasted its historical origin. Indeed, the experience of Nigeria seems to indicate that the predatory state has deeper structural and historical roots, linked both to Africa's colonial past and to its evolving pattern of selective linkages with the global economy.

Nigeria: oil, ethnicity, and military predation

The fate of Nigeria, accounting for about one-fifth of the total population of Sub-Saharan Africa, is likely to condition the future of Africa. If so, prospects are bleak. The economy of Nigeria revolves around the state, and state control over oil revenues, which account for 95 percent of Nigerian exports, and 80 percent of government revenues. The politics and structure of the state are organized by and around the military, which has controlled the government for 26 of the 35 years of independence, canceling elections and imposing its will when necessary, as in the 1993 coup led by General Sani Abacha.[78] The appropriation of oil wealth, exploited in consortium between the Nigerian National Petroleum Corporation and multinational oil companies, is at the source of ethnic, territorial and factional struggles which have destabilized the Nigerian state since the 1966–70 civil war. Political struggles oppose factions organized around three axes: North (controlling the army) against the South (producing the oil); rivalries between the three major ethnic groups: the Hausa-Fulani (usually in control of armed forces' general staff), the Yoruba, and the Igbo; and opposition between these main ethnic groups and the 374 minority ethnic groups that, together, constitute the majority of the population but are excluded from power. Out of 30 states of Nigeria's federation, only four states in the Niger delta (Rivers, Delta, Edo, and Akwa-Ibom) produce virtually all the oil. They are home to ethnic minority groups, particularly the Ogoni, by and large excluded from the riches of their land. The Ogoni's opposition, and the ensuing ferocious repression by the military regime, were dramatically underscored in 1995 when Sane-Wiwa, and several other Ogoni leaders, were executed by the Abacha regime to put down social unrest in the oil-producing areas, and to suppress environmental denouncements by the Ogoni against the destruction of their land by the methods used in oil exploration and production, thus prompting international outcry.

The Nigerian state, an arbitrary colonial construction, was, at its origin, alien to the large majority of its constituencies. Thus, its leaders used the control of resources to build enough support to maintain their power. As Herbst writes:

> Clientelism as it is practiced in Nigeria should not be seen merely as theft by individuals seeking to raid the coffers of the state . . . Rather, the distribution of state offices is legitimated by a set of political norms according to which the appropriation of such offices is not just an act of individual greed or ambition but concurrently the satisfaction of the short-term objectives of a subset of the population.[79]

Who is included in this subset, and how large it is, determine the dynamics of Nigerian politics and access to resources that are, indirectly or directly, in the hands of the state. These patronage relationships expanded substantially with oil revenues, particularly in the 1970s, and with the "oil boomlet" of 1990–91. To reduce the threat of ethnic opposition from excluded groups, the federal government,

78   *The Economist* (1993); Forrest (1993); Agbese (1996); Herbst (1996); Ikporukpo (1996); Lewis (1996).
79   Herbst (1996: 157).

under military control, increased the number of states from 12 to 19, then to 30, to enhance cross-ethnic state clientelism and to multiply the extent of government bureaucracies, and consequently of jobs, sinecures, and channels to government resources and rent-generating positions. Under pressure from international financial institutions and foreign companies and governments, there were, however, some attempts at stabilizing the Nigerian economy, bringing into line its productive sectors with global trade and investment. The most notable effort was in the first half of General Babangida's regime (1985–93), which partially deregulated the economy, dismantled the monopoly of marketing boards for agricultural exports, and restrained monetary supply and government debt for a short period. These efforts were undertaken without curtailing the privileges of the dominant, Northern military elite, at the expense of Southern states and ethnic minorities. When, in 1990, an attempt at a military coup by young officers, claiming support from Southern regions, almost succeeded, the regime, after a bloody repression, decided to stabilize its power by sharing wealth among a broader spectrum of Nigeria's ruling classes. Yet, to share the pie without diminishing its enjoyment, the pie had to be bigger, that is, more wealth had to be extracted from the public revenues. The result was, in the late 1980s and early 1990s, the shift from "prebendalism" to "predatory rule," following Lewis's analysis, and the extension of the realm of income-generating activities, by using the control of the state, to a whole array of illicit deals, including international drug trafficking, money laundering, and smuggling networks.[80] The use of the adjustment program, supported and financed by international institutions, for the private use of Nigeria's power-holders is summarized by Lewis in the following terms:

> In sum, the government managed the adjustment programme through a mixture of domestic political orchestration, compensatory measures, and coercion. For elites, the state provided special access to nascent markets and illegal activities, and manipulated key policies to provide the opportune rents . . . Faced with growing political contention, looming personal insecurity, and a fortuitous appearance of new revenues, the President [Babangida] engaged in increasingly reckless economic management. This involved a massive diversion of public resources, abdication of basic fiscal and monetary controls, and expansion of the illicit economy.[81]

With personal insecurity rampant and economic and legal institutions breaking down, legal foreign investment and trade stalled. The

80 Lewis (1996: 97–9).
81 Lewis (1996: 91).

regime tried to find a political issue through electoral mobilization around the competition between various members of the business elite in the 1993 election. Then, Babangida annulled the election, social protest mounted, including a general strike that affected oil transport, and regional factionalism threatened a new round of disintegration of the state. At this point, the army intervened again, establishing a new authoritarian rule, under General Abacha. The new dictator de-linked Nigeria's monetary flows from the international economy by re-evaluating the naira, decreeing negative interest rates, and reinforcing protectionism. This created anew the basis for personal accumulation of those in positions of control, while inducing capital flight, undermining legal exports, and favoring smuggling. The country was left with

> a legacy of weak central government, fractious ethnic competition, and centralised revenues that have sharply politicised economic management . . . Nigeria's political economy increasingly embodied the characteristics of such autocratic regimes as Mobutu Sese Seko's Zaïre, Haiti under Jean-Claude Duvalier, or the Somoza dynasty's Nicaragua. A transition was soon apparent from decentralised clientelist rule, or prebendalism, to purely avaricious dictatorship or predation.[82]

As for the Nigerian people, not despite but because of the oil boom and its political consequences, they were poorer in 1995 than at independence, their per capita income having declined by 22 percent between 1973 (date of increase in world oil prices) and 1987 (date of economic adjustment programme).[83]

Thus, nation-states in most of Africa have become, to a large extent, predators of their own societies, constituting a formidable obstacle not only to development but to survival and civility. Indeed, because of the extraordinary benefits resulting from control of states, various factions, closer to cliques and gangs than to parties and social groupings, have engaged in atrocious civil wars, sometimes on the basis of ethnic, territorial, and religious cleavages. There has followed the displacement of millions of people around the continent, the disruption of subsistence agricultural production, the uprooting of human settlements, the breaking down of social order, and, in a number of cases (Zaïre, Liberia, Sierra Leone, Somalia, among others), the disappearance of the nation-state for all practical purposes.

Why so? Why have nation-states in Africa come to be predatory? Is there an historical continuity, specific to the social structure of much

82 Lewis (1996: 102–3).
83 Herbst (1996: 159).

of the continent, before, during, and after colonization, as Bayart suggests? Or, on the contrary, is it the result of the lasting wounds of colonialism and the perverse legacy of the political institutions invented and imposed by the Berlin Treaty, as Davidson proposes? Is the state's exteriority to African societies the result of an ethnic puzzle, reproducing ancestral inter-ethnic struggles, as the media often interpret? Why did the nation-state become predatory in Africa, while it emerged as a developmental agency in the Asian Pacific? Are the processes of state formation truly independent of the forms of Africa's incorporation (or lack of incorporation) into the new global economy, as argued by many critics of the dependency theory school? These are fundamental questions that require a careful, if tentative, answer.

Ethnic identity, economic globalization, and state formation in Africa

The plight of Africa is often attributed, particularly in the media, to inter-ethnic hostility. Indeed, in the 1990s, ethnic strife exploded all over the continent, leading in some cases to massacres and attempted genocides. Ethnicity matters a lot, in Africa, as everywhere else. Yet, the relationships between ethnicity, society, the state, and the economy are too complex to be reducible to "tribal" conflicts. It is precisely this complex web of relationships, and its transformation in the past two decades, that lies at the root of the predatory state.

If ethnicity matters, the ethnic differences that are at the forefront of Africa's political scene today are politically constructed, rather than culturally rooted. From contrasting theoretical perspectives, Africanists as different as Bayart, Davidson, Lemarchand, and Adekanye, among others, converge toward a similar conclusion.[84] As Bayart writes:

> Most situations where the structuring of the political arena seems to be enunciated in terms of ethnicity relate to identities which did not exist a century ago or, at least, were then not as clearly defined . . . The colonisers conceptualised indistinct human landscapes which they had occupied as specific identities, constructed in their imagination on the model of a bargain basement nation-state. With its Jacobin and prefectoral origins, the French Administration had an avowedly territorial concept of the state, British indirect rule, by contrast, being much more culturalist. Aside from such nuances, it was along these lines that the colonial regime was organised and that it aimed to order reality. To achieve this it used coercion, by an authoritarian policy of forced settlement, by controlling migratory movements, by more or less artificially fixing

84 Bayart (1989); Davidson (1992, 1994); Lemarchand (1994a, b); Adekanye (1995).

ethnic details through birth certificates and identity cards. *But the contemporary force of ethnic consciousness comes much more from its appropriation by local people, circumscribing the allocation of the state's resources.*[85]

Davidson anchors this ethnic classification of subjugated territories in the ideologically prejudiced, political-bureaucratic logic of colonial administrations:

Europeans had supposed that Africans lived in "tribes" – a word of no certain meaning – and that "tribal loyalties" were the only, and primitive, stuff of African politics. Colonial rule had worked on the assumption, dividing Africans into tribes even when these "tribes" had to be invented. But appearances were misleading. What rapidly developed was not the politics of tribalism, but something different and more divisive. This was the politics of clientelism. What tribalism had supposed was that each tribe recognized a common interest represented by common spokespersons, and there was thus the possibility of a "tribal unity" produced by agreement between "tribal representatives". But clientelism – the "Tammany Hall" approach – almost at once led to a dogfight for the spoils of political power.[86]

This redefinition of ethnic identity by colonial powers mirrored the structure of the colonial state, in a way that would reverberate in the long term for independent nation-states. First of all, states were made up arbitrarily, following the boundaries of conquest, uncertain maps of colonial geographers, and diplomatic maneuvers in the 1884–5 conference that led to the Berlin Treaty.[87] Furthermore, the functioning of the colonial state, largely reproduced in the post-independence period, followed the distinction in levels of a "bifurcated state," as conceptualized by Mahmood Mamdani in his brilliant analysis of state formation.[88] On the one hand there was the legal state, as a racialized entity, under the control of Europeans; on the other hand was the customary power of native power structures, as an ethnic/tribal identity. The unity of the former and the fragmentation of the latter were essential mechanisms of control under colonial administrations which usually dedicated scarce resources in personnel and equipment to maximize net gains in their ventures (Germany, for instance, had only five civil officers, and 24 military officers in Rwanda in 1914). Who was a member of which unit was decided administratively, in an effort of

85   Bayart (1989: 51, my italic).
86   Davidson (1992: 206–7).
87   Davidson (1992); Lindqvist (1996).
88   Mamdani (1996).

simplification that translated into assigning identities in ID cards, sometimes based on criteria of physical appearance according to summary classifications by physical anthropologists. Yet, once the structure of tribal chiefs was established, the customary state became a fundamental source of control over land and labor, so that belonging to a certain tribe was the only acknowledged channel to access resources, and the only recognized avenue of intermediation *vis-à-vis* the legal/modern state that was the connection with the vast resources of the outside world, the international system of wealth and power. After independence, Africa's nationalist elites simply occupied the same structures of the legal/modern state which, therefore, were de-racialized. Yet, they kept in place the fragmented, ethnicized customary state. If and when the distribution of resources became difficult because of both growing scarcity in the country and the growing rapacity of the elites, a choice was made in favor of the ethnicized constituencies that were best represented in the legal state and/or those who, on the basis of their larger numbers or their control of the military, came to power. Ethnicity became the main avenue to access the state's control over resources. But it was the state, and its elites, that shaped and reshaped ethnic identity and allegiance, not the other way around. According to Bayart:

> In Africa, ethnicity is almost never absent from politics, yet at the same time it does not provide its basic fabric . . . In the context of the contemporary state, ethnicity exists mainly as an agent of accumulation, both of wealth and political power. Tribalism is thus perceived as a political force in itself, as a channel through which competition for the acquisition of wealth, power, and status is expressed.[89]

Indeed, in many areas, and particularly in the Great Lakes region, this process of ethnic definition by the power structure, as a way of channeling/limiting access to resources, seems to have pre-dated colonial rule.[90] At this point in the analysis, its complexity could be made somewhat clearer by a brief empirical illustration. For obvious reasons of actuality at this turn of the millennium, I have selected the violent confrontation between Tutsis and Hutus in Rwanda, Burundi, and beyond (eastern Zaïre, southern Uganda). As this is a well-known subject, on which exists a vast literature,[91] I will exclusively focus on a few matters that are relevant to the broader analysis of Africa's contemporary crises.

To start with, the "objective" distinction between Tutsis and Hutus

89   Bayart (1989: 55).
90   Mamdani (1996); Lemarchand (1970).
91   Lemarchand (1970; 1993, 1994a, b); Newbury (1988); Adekanye (1995); Mamdani (1996).

is much less clear than is usually thought. As the leading Western expert on the matter, René Lemarchand, writes:

> As has repeatedly been emphasized, Hutu and Tutsi speak the same language – Kirundi in Burundi, Kinyarwanda in Rwanda – share the same customs, and lived in relative harmony side by side with each other for centuries before the advent of colonial rule. Contrary to the image projected by the media, the patterns of exclusion brought to light during and after independence cannot be reduced to "deep-seated, ancestral enmities". Although pre-colonial Rwanda was unquestionably more rigidly stratified than Burundi, and hence more vulnerable to Hutu-led revolutions, the key to an understanding of their contrasting political fortunes lies in the uneven rhythms at which processes of ethnic mobilization were set in motion in the years immediately preceding independence . . . In both instances it is the interplay between ethnic realities and their subjective reconstruction (or manipulation) by political entrepreneurs that lies at the root of the Hutu–Tutsi conflict.[92]

Even physical differences (the tall, lighter-skinned Tutsis, the stocky, darker-skinned Hutus) have been over-emphasized, among other things because of frequent inter-ethnic marriages and family formation. Thus, Mamdani reports that, during the 1994 massacres of Tutsis by the murderous Intrahamwe Hutu militia, identity was often checked through ID cards, and Tutsi wives were denounced and sent to their deaths by their Hutu husbands, fearful of appearing as traitors.[93] Besides, it is often forgotten that thousands of moderate Hutus were murdered along with the hundreds of thousands of Tutsis, underscoring the social and political cleavages behind a calculated strategy of extermination. Let me remind you of the overall story in a nutshell, trying then to sort out the analytical lessons.

In pre-colonial times, the state built in the lands that would become Rwanda and Burundi was under the control of a pastoralist/warrior aristocracy, defining itself as Tutsis. Peasants (Hutu) (as well as bushmen, Batwa) were, by and large, excluded from the state and from power positions, almost entirely in Rwanda, less so in Burundi. However, accumulation of wealth (mainly cattle) would allow a Hutu family to move into the upper echelons of society (a process named Kwihutura), thus becoming Tutsi: so much for biological/cultural determination of ethnicity! As Mamdani writes:

> It is clear that we are talking of a political distinction, one that divided the subject from the non-subject population, and not a socio-economic

92   Lemarchand (1994a: 588).
93   Mamdani (1996).

distinction, between exploiters and exploited or rich and poor . . . The Batutsi developed a political identity – they formed a distinct social category, marked by marriage and ethnic taboos, says Mafeje – a self-consciousness of being distinguished from the subject population. Thus the mere fact of some physical difference – often the nose, less often the height – could become symbolic of a great political difference.[94]

The colonial state – German first, Belgian afterwards – considerably sharpened and mobilized this political/ethnic cleavage, by giving the Tutsis full control over the customary state (even in areas that were before in the hands of the Hutu majority), and by providing them with access to education, resources, and administrative jobs, thus creating a Tutsi native state as a subordinate appendix to the colonial, Belgian state: a process not so different from the one that took place in Zanzibar, when British rulers established an Arab Sultanate to administer the native population. Under Belgian rule even the Kwihutura was abolished, and the system became a caste-like society. As could be expected, the process of independence, and its ensuing political mobilization, freed the explosive energy accumulated by the exclusion from all spheres of power of the Hutu majority (about 84 percent of the population). However, the political outcomes were different in Rwanda and Burundi. In Rwanda, the 1959 Hutu revolution led to Hutu majority rule, to pogroms and mass killings of Tutsis, and to the exile of a significant number of Tutsis, both to Burundi and to Uganda. In Burundi, a constitutional monarchy around the prestigious figure of Prince Rwagasore, seemed to be able to organize ethnic coexistence around a national state. However, the assassination of the prince in 1961, and the failed Hutu coup attempt of 1965, allowed the Tutsi-dominated military to seize control of the country, making it a republic, and institutionalizing political marginalization of the Hutu, whose insurgency was repressed in a bloodbath: in 1972, the Tutsi army massacred over 100,000 Hutus in Burundi. Again, in 1988, massacres of thousands of Tutsis by Hutu peasants around Ntega/Marangara were responded to by the massacre of tens of thousands of Hutu civilians by the Tutsi army. In 1990, the invasion of Rwanda by Rwandan Tutsi exiles from Uganda (where they had participated in the victorious guerrilla war against Milton Obote) led to a civil war that, as is general knowledge, triggered the 1994 massacres when Hutu militia and the presidential guard went on the rampage, supposedly in retaliation for the killing of President Habyarimana when a missile hit his plane in circumstances still obscure. The attempted genocide of Tutsis involved not only the Rwandan army and militia, but large segments

94   Mamdani (1996: 10).

of the Hutu civilian population, in every neighborhood and every village: it was a decentralized, mass-participated holocaust. Thus, the military victory of the Tutsi-dominated Rwandan Patriotic Front triggered an exile of millions, whose exodus to Zaïre, and its subsequent partial return to Rwanda by the end of 1996, may well have contributed to the full political destabilization of Central Africa. Meanwhile, in Burundi, the 1993 elections permitted for the first time a democratically elected Hutu president, Melchior Ndadye, to come to power. But only three months later he was assassinated by Tutsi military officers, triggering a new round of reciprocal massacres, the exodus of hundreds of thousands of Hutus, and a civil war, which was aggravated by a Tutsi military coup in July 1996, prompting a trade embargo to Burundi from its neighboring states.

After decades of mutual political exclusion, and repeated massacres, mainly organized around ethnic lines, it would be foolish to deny that there are Tutsi and Hutu identities, to the point that a majority rule, in a democratic polity, seems to be out of the question.[95] This situation seems to open the way for the establishment of Tutsi or Hutu ruthless domination, a protracted civil war, or the redrawing of political boundaries. Yet, what this dramatic experience seems to show is that the sharpening of ethnic differences, and the crystallization of ethnicity in social status and political power, came from the historical dynamics of the social basis of the state, colonial first, independent nation-state later. It also shows the incapacity of ethnically constituted political elites to transcend the definition inherited from the past, since they used their ethnicity as the rallying flag to seize state power or to resist it. In so doing, they made a plural, democratic state nonviable, as citizenship and ethnicity are contradictory principles of democratic political legitimacy. Furthermore, the memory of extermination, made fresh by atrocious repetition of the worst nightmares on both sides, marked in blood the ethnic boundaries of power as violence. From then on, ethnicity overtook politics, after having been shaped, and hardened, by the politics of the state. It is this complex interaction between ethnicity and the state, under the dominance of state logic, that we must have in mind to understand African politics, and beyond it, Africa's tragedy.

However, if the state is ethnicized, it is scarcely nationalized. Indeed, one of the key features explaining why a developmental state emerged in the Asian Pacific, as well as, with lesser fortune, in Latin America, and not in Africa, is the weakness of the nation in the African nation-state. Not that nationalism was absent from Africa's scene:

95   Mamdani (1996).

after all, nationalist movements were the driving force to achieve independence, and, in the late 1950s and early 1960s, a fierce brand of nationalist leader (Sekou Ture, N'krumah, Kenyatta, Lumumba) shook the world, inspiring the promise of African renaissance. But they received a meager national heritage from colonialism, as the cultural/ethnic/historical/geographical/economic puzzle of Africa's political map confined, by and large, African nationalism to the educated elite of the legal/modern state, and to the small urban business class. As Davidson, in line with many other Africanists, writes: "An analysis of Africa's trouble has also to be an inquiry into the process – the process largely of nationalism – that has crystallized the division of Africa's many hundreds of peoples and cultures into a few dozen nation-states, each claiming sovereignty against the others, and then all of them sorely in trouble."[96] The lack of a national basis for these new African nation-states, a basis that in other latitudes was usually made up of shared geography, history, and culture (see volume II, chapter 1), is a fundamental difference between Africa and the Asian Pacific, with the exception of Indonesia, in the differential fate of their developmental processes (see chapter 4). It is true that two other elements (widespread literacy and a relatively high level of education in East Asia, and geopolitical support from the US and the openness of its market to Asian Pacific countries) were equally important in facilitating a successful outward-looking development strategy in the Pacific. But Africa provided primary education on a large scale quite rapidly, at least in the urban centers, and France and Britain continued to "help" their former colonies, allowing access to markets in the former metropolises. The crucial difference was the ability of Asian Pacific countries to mobilize their nations, under authoritarian rule, around a developmental goal, on the basis of strong national/cultural identity, and the politics of survival (see chapter 4). The weak social basis of the nationalist project considerably debilitated African states, both *vis-à-vis* their diverse ethnic constituencies and *vis-à-vis* foreign states competing for influence over Africa in the framework of the Cold War.

Africa, in the first three decades of its independence, has been the object of repeated interventions by foreign troops, and military advisers, from Western powers (particularly France, Belgium, Portugal, and white South Africa, but also the US, UK, Israel, and Spain), as well as from the Soviet Union, Cuba, and Libya, thus making much of Africa a hot war battleground. The splitting of political factions, states, and regions in different geopolitical alignments contributed to the destabilization and militarization of African states, to the unbearable

96   Davidson (1992: 13).

burden of gigantic defense budgets, and left the heritage of a formidable arsenal of military hardware, most of it in unreliable hands.[97]
The short history of African nation-states, built on historically shaky
ground, undermined nations and nationalism as a basis for legitimacy,
and as a relevant unit for development.

There is another, fundamental element to be added to the equation
explaining Africa's contemporary crisis. *This is the linkage between
the ethnic politics of the [weak nation]-state, on the one hand, and the
political economy of Africa in the past three decades, on the other
hand.* Without reference to this connection, it is easy to descend to
quasi-racist statements about the innately perverse nature of African
politics. Colin Leys argues, and I concur, that Africa's crisis cannot be
understood, including the role played by the state, without reference
to economic history. For a number of reasons, which he hypothesizes,
including the low development of productive forces, and the predominance of the household production system until the end of colonialism, "the timing of Africa's original incorporation in the world capitalist
system, combined with the extreme backwardness of its precolonial
economies and the limitations of subsequent colonial policy, prevented
most of the continent from starting at all on the key transition to self-
sustaining capital accumulation after independence."[98] I will briefly
elaborate on this insight in my own terms.[99]

In historical sequence, in the 1960s Africa "got off to a bad start."[100]
In the 1970s, in the context of world capitalism's crisis and restructuring, its development model collapsed, needing, by the end of the decade, a bail out from foreign lenders and international institutions. In
the 1980s, the burden of the debt and the structural adjustment programs, imposed as a condition for international lending, disarticulated
economies, impoverished societies, and destabilized states. It triggered,
in the 1990s, the incorporation of some minuscule sectors of some
countries into global capitalism, as well as the chaotic de-linking of
most people and most territories from the global economy. What were
the reasons for these successive developments? In the 1960s, policies
oriented toward agricultural exports and autarkic industrialization
contributed to destroying the local peasant economy, and much of the
subsistence basis of the population. Domestic markets were too narrow to sustain large-scale industrialization. International economic
exchanges were still dominated by neo-colonial interests. In the 1970s,

---

97   de Waal (1996).
98   Leys (1994: 45).
99   For relevant data, see Sarkar and Singer (1991); Blomstrom and Lundhal (1993);
Riddell (1995); Yansane (1996); *The Economist* (1996a).
100 Dumont (1964).

technological backwardness, managerial inefficiency, and the persistence of post-colonial constraints (for example, the Franc zone in ex-French Africa) made it impossible to compete in international markets, while the deterioration of terms of trade made imports increasingly difficult precisely when the modern sector needed new technology and the population needed to import food. Indebtedness without criteria or control (much of it was used in stepped-up defense spending, industrial "white elephants," and conspicuous consumption; for example, the construction of Yamassoukro, Houphouet-Boigny's dream capital in his native village) led to bankruptcy in most of Africa. Structural adjustment programs, advised/imposed by the International Monetary Fund and the World Bank, aggravated social conditions while failing by and large to make the economies dynamic. They focused on downsizing the state and stimulating primary commodity exports. This latter goal, in general terms, is a losing bet in today's technological and economic environment; and in specific terms an unrealistic proposition when confronted with persistent agricultural protectionism in OECD markets.[101] While islands of economic efficiency have indeed emerged in some countries, including some large, competitive African companies (for example, Ghana's Ashanti Goldfields), material and human resources have been wasted and, as documented above, the African economy as a whole was in substantially worse shape in the 1990s than it had been in the 1960s, both in production and in consumption.

The massive shrinkage of resources, resulting from the economic crisis and adjustment policies of the 1980s, dramatically affected the political dynamics of nation-states, built on the capacity of the state elites to distribute to different clienteles, usually ethnically or territorially defined, and still keep enough for themselves. Three consequences followed from this shrinkage:

1   As international aid and foreign lending became a fundamental source of income, states engaged in the *political economy of begging*, thus developing a vested interest in human catastrophes that would gain international attention and generate charitable resources. This strategy was particularly important when the end of the Cold War dried up financial and military transfers from foreign powers to their African vassal states.

2   As resources from the formal, modern sector of the economy became scarcer, political leaders, military officers, bureaucrats and local businessmen alike engaged in *large-scale illicit trade*, includ-

101   Adepoju (1993); Adekanye (1995); Simon et al. (1995).

ing joint ventures with various partners in the global criminal economy (see chapter 3).

3   As resources decreased and the population's needs increased, *choices had to be made between different clienteles, usually in favor of the most reliable ethnic or regional groups* (that is, those closer to the dominant factions of the elite). Some factions, losing out in state power, resorted to political intrigue or military force, either to obtain their share or simply to appropriate the whole system of political control over resources. In their struggle for power they sought the support of those ethnic or regional groups that had been excluded by the state from a share of resources.

As factionalism increased, and national armies split, the distinction between banditry and violent political opposition became increasingly blurred. Since ethnic and regional affiliations became the only identifiable sources of membership and loyalty, violence trickled down to the population at large, so that neighbors, co-workers, and compatriots suddenly became, first, competitors for survival, then enemies, and, in the last resort, potential killers or victims. Institutional disintegration, widespread violence, and civil war further disorganized the economy, and triggered massive movements of population, escaping to uncertain safety.

Furthermore, people also learned the downgraded version of the political economy of begging, as their condition as refugees might, just might, entitle them to survival under the various flags of the United Nations, governments, and NGOs. In the end, by the mid-1990s, not only was Africa increasingly marginalized from the global/informational economy, but in much of the continent nation-states were disintegrating, and people, uprooted and harassed, were regrouping in communes of survival, under a variety of labels, depending on the anthropologist's taste.

Africa's plight

The deliberate attempt by international financial institutions to take Africa out of the 1980s' debt crisis by homogenizing the conditions of trade and investment in Africa with the rules of the new global economy ended in a considerable fiasco, according to the evaluation of a number of observers and international agencies.[102] A study of the impact of structural adjustments in Africa, elaborated by the United Nations Population Fund, summarizes its findings in the following manner:

102   Adepoju (1993); Ravenhill (1993); Hutchful (1995); Loxley (1995); Riddell (1995).

There is consensus among the authors of this volume that, in the countries surveyed, one does not find a strong association between adjustment policies and economic performance. There are strong indications that adjustment policies may not be able to guarantee that African countries will overcome the effects of external shocks even in the long run, unless there is a more favourable external environment. In many African countries pursuing structural adjustment, what progress there is has been confined to nominal growth in GDP without any transformation of the structure of the economy. Ghana [the show case of the World Bank's evaluation], for example, achieved an average annual growth rate of 5 percent over 1984–88. But manufacturing capacity utilization has remained low, at 35 percent in 1988. In Nigeria it was just 38 percent in 1986–87. In most countries covered in this study, small and medium enterprises have been marginalized by the exchange rate and trade liberalization measures. High domestic interest rates, resulting from restrictive monetary and credit policies, created disruptive business climates. Industrial closures were rampant, four out of ten banks were shut down in Cameroon, whilst in many countries marketing boards for major commodities were scrapped. Although agriculture grew modestly in these countries, production of food stuffs declined. In Ghana, production of cereal fell by 7 percent and starchy staples by 39 percent between 1984 and 1988. Other countries had similar experiences. Although export earnings generally increased, imports also rose, intensifying the balance of payments crisis . . . A United Nations-organized conference concluded that "adjustment measures have been implemented at high human costs and sacrifices and are rending the fabric of African society."[103]

The social, economic, and political cost of this failed attempt at globalizing African economies, without informationalizing its societies, can be shown along three main lines of argument, and one over-arching consequence: the growing dereliction of a majority of Africa's people.

First, formal urban labor markets stopped absorbing labor, generating a substantial increase in unemployment and underemployment, which translated into a higher incidence of poverty levels. An ILO study on the evolution of labor markets in Africa, focusing on six French-speaking countries,[104] found a statistical relationship between employment status and incidence of poverty. In Sub-Saharan Africa as a whole, the urban unemployment rate doubled between 1975 and 1990, rising from 10 to 20 percent. Employment in the modern sector, and especially in the public sector, stagnated or declined. In 14 countries, salaried employment grew by an annual average of 3 percent in

103   Adepoju (1993: 3–4).
104   Lachaud (1994).

1975–80, but only by 1 percent in the first half of the 1980s, way below what was needed to absorb labor increases from population growth and rural–urban migration. The informal sector of employment, growing at 6.7 percent per year, became the refuge for surplus labor. Most labor in African cities is now in the categories of "irregular," "marginal self-employment," and "non-protected salaried worker", all leading to lower incomes, lack of protection, and a high incidence of poverty. For the population as a whole, in 1985, 47 percent of Africans lived below the poverty level, as compared to 33 percent for developing countries as a whole. The number of destitute persons in Africa increased by two-thirds between 1975 and 1985, and Africa was, according to projections in the 1990s, the only region of the world where poverty levels were set to increase.[105]

Secondly, African agricultural production per capita, and particularly food production, has declined substantially in the past decade (see figure 2.3), making many countries vulnerable to famine and epidemics when droughts, war, or other catastrophes strike. Agricultural crisis seems to be the result of a combination of excessive focus on export-oriented production and of ill-advised transition to technologies or product lines inappropriate to a country's ecological and economic conditions.[106] For instance, in West Africa, foreign forestry companies pushed for replacing acacias with non-indigenous trees, only to reverse the process a few years later when it became clear that acacias needed less water and less attention, besides helping to feed goats and sheep during the dry season. Or, in another illustration of inappropriate technological change, at Lake Turkana, in East Africa, Norwegian experts organized a program of conversion of Turkana cattlemen into producers of more marketable fish products, such as tilapia and perch. However, the cost of the equipment for chilling the fish was so high that production/distribution costs were higher than the fish price in accessible markets. Not being able to turn back to cattle-raising, 20,000 nomadic Turkana became dependent on food aid from donor agencies.[107] The difficulty of penetrating international markets for a small range of African agricultural products, and the transformation of government policies toward agriculture during the 1980s, made farming highly unpredictable. Thus, many farmers turned to short-term, survival strategies of cultivation, instead of investing in a long-term conversion to export-oriented, commercial agriculture, thus undermining their future chance of being internationally competitive.[108]

105   Adepoju (1993).
106   Jamal (1995).
107   *The Economist* (1996a).
108   Berry (1993: 270–71).

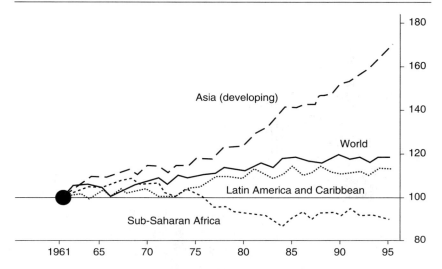

Figure 2.3 Food production per person (1961 = 100) (Sub-Saharan Africa excludes South Africa)
Source: compiled by *The Economist* (September 7, 1996) from figures from the Food and Agriculture Organization

The third major trend in the social and economic evolution of Africa is the disorganization of production and livelihood induced by the disintegration of the state. The pattern of violence, pillage, civil wars, banditry, and massacres, which struck the large majority of African countries in the 1980s and 1990s, has thrown out of their towns and villages millions of people, ruined the economy of regions and countries, and reduced to shambles much of the institutional capacity to manage crises and reconstruct the material bases of life.[109]

Urban poverty, the crisis of agriculture, particularly of subsistence agriculture, institutional collapse, widespread violence, and massive population movements have combined to significantly deteriorate the living conditions of the majority of the African population in the past decade, as documented by the United Nations 1996 Human Development Report. Poverty, migration, and social disorganization have also contributed to creating the conditions for devastating epidemics that threaten the extermination of a substantial proportion of Africans, as well as the potential spread of diseases to the rest of the world. It should be emphasized that it is not only the conditions of hygiene and nutrition under which most Africans live that are the source of

109   Leys (1994); Adekanye (1995); Kaiser (1996).

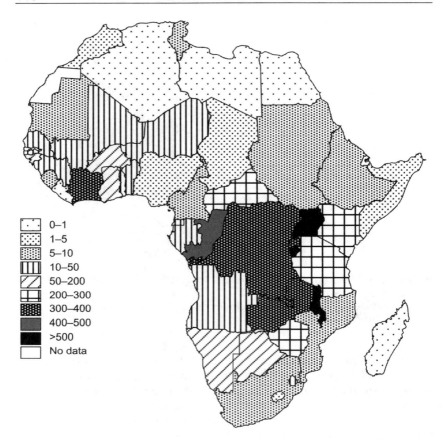

Figure 2.4 AIDS cases per million in Africa, 1990
Sources: WHO Epidemiological Record; WorldAIDS, 1990 and 1991, elaborated by
Barnett and Blaikie (1992)

diseases and epidemics, but the lack of adequate health care and education greatly contribute to the diffusion of disease.

A dramatic case in point is the AIDS epidemic.[110] While the first HIV infections were reported in Africa in the early 1980s, by the mid-1990s, Sub-Saharan Africa accounted for about 60 percent of the estimated 17 million HIV-positive people in the world (see figure 2.4).[111]

110   Barnett and Blaikie (1992); Hope (1995); Philipson and Posner (1995); Boahene (1996); Kamali et al. (1996).
111   Boahene (1996).

Table 2.9 Estimated HI seroprevalence for adults (15–49 years) for cities and rural areas in selected African countries, c.1987

| Country | HIV seroprevalence (%) | | Population infected with HIV (000s) |
	Cities	Rural	
Uganda	24.1	12.3	894.3
Rwanda	20.1	2.2	81.5
Zambia	17.2	–	205.2
Congo	10.2	–	46.5
Côte d'Ivoire	10.0	1.3	183.0
Malawi	9.5	4.2	142.5
Central African Republic	7.8	3.7	54.3
Zaïre	7.1	0.5	281.8
Ghana	4.7	–	98.7
Burundi	4.3	–	15.0
Tanzania	3.6	0.7	96.6
Zimbabwe	3.2	0.0	30.9
Kenya	2.7	0.2	44.5
Cameroon	1.1	0.6	33.2
Mozambique	1.0	0.6	43.5
Sudan	0.3	–	6.8
Nigeria	0.1	0.0	8.1
Swaziland	0.0	–	0.0
Total infected persons, all African countries (incl. others not listed)			2,497.6
Total African population infected, 1987(%)			0.9

Source: Over (1990), reported by Barnett and Blaikie (1992)

In countries such as Uganda, Rwanda, and Zambia, between 17 and 24 percent of the urban population were infected by about 1987 (see table 2.9). In general, this proportion has certainly increased in recent years in most countries, with some exceptions (Gabon). AIDS is now considered to be the leading cause of death in Uganda, and a major cause in other countries. Because AIDS in Africa is transmitted through heterosexual contact in 80 percent of cases, women are particularly at risk, given their sexual subservience to men, and men's increased promiscuity at a time of migration and uprooting. About 4.5 million women are estimated to be HIV-positive. Their patriarchal submission limits their access to information and resources for prevention, and decreases their access to treatment for AIDS-related infections. Studies have shown that women are less likely to visit a hospital, die of HIV/AIDS at a younger age, and are more likely to stay with their spouses when the latter are diagnosed as HIV-positive than the other way round.[112] Thus, a large number of women of reproductive age are HIV-positive. Over the next 10–25 years, the impact of AIDS on child survival is projected to be more severe than the impact of the disease on the overall population. AIDS is expected to cause more deaths in children in Sub-Saharan Africa than either malaria or measles. Child and infant mortality rates, which were projected to decrease by 35–40 percent in the next decade, are now expected to remain the same, or even increase, because of AIDS. Child orphans are becoming a massive problem. The prediction was that an estimated 10 million uninfected children would lose one or two parents to the AIDS epidemic by the year 2000. Extended family systems are breaking down under the pressure of this wave of orphans.

The size and speed of diffusion of the AIDS epidemic in Africa are induced by social and economic conditions. As a leading expert on the matter, Kempe Ronald Hope writes: "Without a doubt, poverty and economic distress in the African countries have contributed greatly to the rapid spread of HIV and AIDS."[113] Lack of adequate health care, low levels of education, insanitary living conditions, limited access to basic services, rapid urbanization, unemployment, and poverty are related phenomena, and they are all factors associated with HIV infection. Access to health care in Africa is extremely limited. Data for 1988–91 indicate that the population per doctor in Sub-Saharan Africa was 18,488, compared with 5,767 for all developing countries, and 344 for industrial countries.[114] Poverty limits access to information about prevention, as well as access to preventive methods. Agricultural crisis, famine, and wars have forced migration and disorganized families, communities, and social networks. Men who have migrated to urban areas, and periodically return to their communities of origin, are major carriers of HIV, spreading the virus through prostitutes, and diffusing it throughout trucking routes. Poor people who contract HIV tend to develop AIDS much faster than those of higher socio-economic status.

The potential spread of the AIDS epidemic from Africa to other regions of the world represents a more serious risk than is usually acknowledged. South Africa provides striking evidence in this regard. While it is a country that borders areas where the epidemics began in the 1980s, and its black population was left for a long time in poor social and health conditions, South Africa's level of economic and institutional development is much higher than that of the rest of Africa.

112   Boahene (1996).
113   Hope (1995: 82).
114   UNDP (1996).

Yet, in the 1990s, the AIDS epidemic became rampant in South Africa, reproducing the patterns and the speed of diffusion experienced in neighboring countries a decade earlier. Certain groups, such as prostitutes and migrant laborers, are estimated to be infected in a 10–30 percent range. Among women of child-bearing age, estimates of HIV infection for the whole country are as high as 4.7 percent, with a higher incidence in some areas, such as Kwa/Zulu Natal. At current rates of diffusion, models of the future spread of HIV/AIDs estimate that, by the year 2010, 27 percent of the South African population will have been infected. More optimistic models, assuming a 40 percent reduction in the number of sexual partners, and a 20 percent increase in effective condom use, still project, for the same date, that 8 percent of the total population will have been infected.[115]

If Africa's plight is ignored or played down, it is unlikely to remain confined within its geographical boundaries. Both humankind and our sense of humanity will be threatened. Global apartheid is a cynic's illusion in the Information Age.

Africa's hope? The South African connection

Is Sub-Saharan Africa condemned to social exclusion in the new global economy, at least in the foreseeable future? This is a fundamental issue, but one that exceeds the limits of this chapter, and the purpose of this book, which is concerned with analysis rather than with policy or forecasting. However, on strictly empirical grounds, the end of apartheid in South Africa, and the potential linkage between a democratic, black-majority ruled South Africa and African countries, at least those in eastern/southern Africa, allows us to examine the hypothesis of the incorporation of Africa into global capitalism under new, more favorable conditions via the South African connection. Because of the implications for an overall analysis of the conditions reproducing or modifying social exclusion in the global economy, I will briefly examine this matter before moving out of Africa.

South Africa is clearly different from the rest of Sub-Saharan Africa. It has a much higher level of industrialization, a more diversified economy, and it plays a more significant role in the global economy than the rest of the continent. It is neither a low-wage dependent economy, nor a higher-skilled, competitive emerging economy. In fact, it combines aspects of both, and in some ways the processes of simultaneous inclusion and exclusion are more obvious and glaring in South Africa than in many other countries. The political environment is chang-

115 Campbell and Williams (1996).

ing rapidly in the post-election, democratic period, and the economy is being helped by rapid reincorporation into the global economy after several decades of relative isolation, due both to sanctions and to high tariff barriers from South Africa's policies of import substitution industrialization.

South Africa accounts for 44 percent of the total GDP of all Sub-Saharan Africa, and 52 percent of its industrial output. It uses 64 percent of the electricity consumed in Sub-Saharan Africa. In 1993, real GDP per capita for Sub-Saharan Africa (including South Africa) was US$1,288, while for South Africa alone it was 3,127. There are nine times more telephone lines per capita in South Africa than in Sub-Saharan Africa.

The Johannesburg Stock Exchange is the tenth largest (by market capitalization) in the world. Yet the banking and financial system is dominated by four large commercial banks and has primarily serviced the major industrial sectors. Few funds have been available for small-scale entrepreneurs. At least since the discovery of diamonds in the nineteenth century, South Africa has played a role in the global economy. Mining was crucial in the overall development of the country in the twentieth century, providing a growth engine for capital accumulation. Despite recent decline, gold mining is still the core of South Africa's mining complex, constituting about 70 percent of mining exports and employment, and 80 percent of revenue.[116] Yet most of South Africa's gold reserves have been exhausted. Over the past century, over 45 thousand tonnes of gold have been removed, constituting over two-thirds of the original resource base, and the 20 thousand tonnes remaining tend to be deep and low grade. Other strategic mining and mineral-processing industries include iron, steel, zinc, tin, ferroalloys, manganese, copper, silver, aluminum and platinum. Mining still accounts for 71 percent of total foreign exchange earnings, though just over half of GDP comes from services and nearly a quarter from manufacturing.[117] The mining industry, more than any other industry, was dependent on the apartheid system because of its reliance on migrant and compound labor.

Manufacturing industry grew substantially in the 1960s, but began to slow in the 1970s and stagnated entirely in the 1980s. Manufacturing output growth in the 1970s averaged 5.3 percent per year.[118] But between 1980 and 1985, manufacturing output actually declined by 1.2 percent, and growth between 1985 and 1991 was only 0.7 percent, while employment in manufacturing actually declined by 1.4

116   MERG (1993).
117   *The Economist* (1995).
118   ISP (1995: 6).

percent.[119] South Africa's manufacturing sector is characterized by the classic problems of import substitution industrialization, with a strong capacity in consumer goods production, and a certain amount of heavy industry linked to the mining and mineral-processing industries, but an absence of capital goods and many intermediate goods. However, South Africa is linked to the informational/global economy. It has the highest number of Internet hosts, for instance, of any non-OECD country.[120] Yet growth in technological capability is limited by a fragmented institutional environment and lack of effective government support. Business expenditure in R&D declined some 27 percent from 1983–4 to 1989–90 and there is a strong reliance on acquisition of technology from abroad, primarily through license agreements. R&D is significantly less than in other rapidly growing countries.[121] In 1993, at least, "there was little evidence that such technology transfer is accompanied by programmes of training to ensure effective assimilation."[122]

Overall employment has been on a downward trend since the mid-1970s, with falls in employment in agriculture, transport, mining, and manufacturing. If there had not been substantial growth in public sector employment in the period 1986–90, total employment growth would have been negative in that period. From 1989 to 1992, total employment in the non-agricultural sectors of the economy declined by 4.8 percent, equivalent to the loss of about 286,000 jobs, with positive growth only in the public sector. Total private sector employment declined by 7.8 percent during this period. The proportion of the labor force employed in the formal economy in 1989 ranged from 61 percent in the Johannesburg/Pretoria area to only 22 percent in the poorest regions. While no reliable figures for unemployment exist, it is clear that a large and rapidly increasing gap exists between the number of people requiring employment and the capacity of the formal economy to provide employment. Real wage growth for African workers was negative in the period 1986–90. For African workers in the lowest educational and occupational categories, real wages between 1975 and 1985 declined at a rate of 3 percent per year.[123] The official unemployment rate was estimated at 32.6 percent by the Central Statistical Service in 1994, but the absence – relative to other African countries – of opportunities for earnings and subsistence from the land, and hence of a rural safety net, underlines the problem of mass unemployment. Unemployment is especially serious among the young; 64 percent of the

119   MERG (1993: 239).
120   Network Wizards (1996).
121   Industrial Strategy Project (1995: 239).
122   MERG (1993: 232).
123   MERG (1993: 149–50).

economically active population between the ages of 16 and 24 (about one million young people) were jobless in 1995.

Thus, many South Africans depend for survival on the informal economy, although estimates of their number vary. The Central Statistical Service estimated in 1990 that 2.7 million people, or 24 percent of the labor force, were active in the informal economy. This may be a significant understatement of informal economic activity, however. For instance, in a 1990 survey of residents of Alexandra township, a major township in the Johannesburg area, 48 percent of residents reported that they were self-employed, worked at home, or worked elsewhere in the township.[124] South Africa's informal economy is primarily an economy of bare survival. Approximately 70 percent of all informal enterprises involve street selling, primarily of food, clothing, and curios.[125] Only an estimated 15–20 percent involve some form of manufacturing enterprise, and sub-contracting seems to be much less common in the informal sector in South Africa than elsewhere. The reason for the low incidence of manufacturing in informal enterprises is explained not only by the apartheid policies that hindered black urbanization and prohibited blacks from becoming entrepreneurs, but also by the fact that blacks were systematically deprived of access to education, skills and the experience essential for the emergence of dynamic entrepreneurship, and especially informational skills. The South African economy also has high levels of concentration of capital and oligopolistic control.[126]

South Africa has an extremely unequal income distribution, by some measures the most unequal distribution in the world. It has a Gini coefficient of 0.65, compared with 0.61 for Brazil, 0.50 for Mexico, and 0.48 for Malaysia, and coefficients of 0.41 or less for the advanced industrialized countries. The bottom 20 percent of income-earners capture a mere 1.5 percent of national income, while the wealthiest 10 percent of households receive fully 50 percent of national income. Between 36 and 53 percent of South Africans are estimated to live below the poverty line. Poverty is overwhelmingly concentrated in the African and coloured population: 95 percent of the poor are African, and 65 percent of Africans are poor, compared with 33 percent of the coloured population, 2.5 percent of Asians and 0.7 percent of whites.[127]

Racial differences are still a major factor in inequality, despite an increase in the black middle class. For example, the October 1994

124 Greater Alexandra/Sandton UDP Report (1990), cited by Benner (1994).
125 Riley (1993).
126 Rogerson (1993); Manning (1993); Manning and Mashigo (1994).
127 South African Government (1996a).

household survey of the Central Statistical Service found that only 2 percent of black men were employed in top management, compared with 11 percent of white men. Of this top management, 51 percent of black men earned over R2,000 (roughly US$500) a month, compared with 89 percent of white men who earned over R2,000 a month. Some 51 percent of black men were employed as "elementary workers" or "operators and assemblers," compared with 36 percent of white men.[128]

Thus, South Africa's economy and society are less buoyant than they look in comparison with its continental environment, constituted by the poorest countries in the world. Yet we must also consider South Africa's economic relations with its neighbors. The frontline states around Africa suffered a great deal during the anti-apartheid struggle, as South Africa waged a total war for control of the region and punished neighboring countries for their support of the African National Congress. Despite efforts at developing alternative transport routes and diversifying their trade relations, most southern African states remained heavily dependent on their relationship with South Africa throughout the 1980s. Starting in the early 1990s, the focus shifted toward an evaluation of the extent to which South Africa could become a "growth engine" for the whole region. The entire southern Africa region is integrated via South Africa, with most transport routes running through South Africa, and with many of the surrounding countries part of an extended migrant labor force for South African industries. For example, a total of 45 percent of the mining workforce in 1994 of 368,463 workers were foreign workers. This represents a decline from a peak in 1974 when 77 percent of all mine workers were foreign. Estimates of the number of undocumented people in South Africa from neighboring countries range widely. The South African police services estimate the number to be between 5.5 million and 8 million people. The Human Sciences Research Council calculated a similar figure of between 5 and 8 million.[129]

The unevenness of the relationship between South Africa and its neighbors is clear. The 11 countries of southern Africa have a combined population of 130 million people, but over 40 million of these live in South Africa. South Africa alone accounts for 80 percent of the entire area's GDP. South Africans are, on average, 36 times richer than Mozambicans. South African exports to the region are eight times bigger than the traffic in the other direction. There are, however, talks of regional integration as a free trade bloc. Efforts are underway to rebuild railways devastated by the war in Mozambique and to rebuild

128 South African Government (1996b).
129 South African Government (1996a).

Mozambique's ports to handle exports from Zimbabwe, Botswana, and Zambia. However, looking at the differential economic structure between South Africa and its neighbors, two observations bear considerable significance: (a) all economies, including South Africa, are by and large commodity dependent in their export earnings; and (b) with the exception of South Africa's minuscule satellites, Botswana and Lesotho, there is little manufacturing capacity that could provide an export base for the large South African market. Indeed, trade data reveal that South African companies take over most of the limited import market capacity of neighboring countries.

Thus, in strictly economic terms, there is little complementarity between South Africa and its African environment. If anything, there will be competition in some key industries, such as global tourism. South Africa does not have the manufacturing and technological base to represent by itself a substantial center of accumulation on a scale large enough to propel development in its wake. Indeed, it has substantial social and economic problems that will require employment policies oriented toward its citizen population, with potentially disastrous consequences for migrants from other countries, whose remittances are a critical source of hard currency for the neighboring economies. The real problem for South Africa is how to avoid being pushed aside itself from the harsh competition in the new global economy, once its economy is open. Thus, regional cooperation programs may help the development of a transportation and technological infrastructure in the neighboring countries; and some spillover from South Africa into southern Africa (for instance, investing in mining resources and in tourism) will certainly alleviate extreme conditions of poverty, as is already the case in Namibia, Botswana, and Mozambique. However, the vision of a new South Africa becoming the engine of development for much of the continent, through its multilayered incorporation into the global economy (in an African version of the "flying geese" pattern so much liked by Japanese strategists), seems, at close examination, utterly unrealistic. If the political fate of South Africa is indeed linked to its African identity, its developmental path continues to diverge from its ravaged neighbors – unless the end of the gold rush, a lagging technological capability, and increasing social and ethnic tensions push South Africa toward the abyss of social exclusion from which the African National Congress fought so bravely to escape.

Out of Africa or back to Africa? The politics and economics of self-reliance

Anthropologist Ida Susser, returning from her field trip in the Kalahari Desert in Namibia in 1996, reports that the lives of farmers and farm laborers go on, surviving in the interstices of the state. Their meager subsistence is covered on a day-to-day basis. There are no apparent signs of social disintegration and mass starvation: there is poverty, but not destitution.[130] They may not be representative of the diversity of subsistence economies that still allow survival for a sizeable proportion of Africans around the continent. Yet could these subsistence economies, and the traditional communities with which they are associated, constitute a refuge against the whirlwind of destruction and disintegration that blows across Africa? In fact, a growing number of voices in the intellectual and political world of Africa, or among those concerned with Africa, call for a reconstruction of African societies on the basis of self-reliance.[131] It would not imply remaining attached to primitive economies and to traditional societies, but to build from the bottom up, gaining access to modernity through a different path, fundamentally rejecting the values and goals predominant in today's global capitalism. Strong arguments for this position can be found in the current experiences of technological/economic marginalization of Africa, the rise of the predatory state, and the failure of IMF/World Bank-inspired adjustment policies, both in economic and in social terms. An alternative model of development, one that would in fact be more socially and environmentally sustainable, is not a utopia, and there is an abundance of realistic, technically sound proposals for self-reliant development models in a number of countries, as well as strategies for Africa-centered regional cooperation. In most cases, they assume the necessary partial de-linking of African economies from global networks of capital accumulation, given the consequences of current asymmetrical linkages, as presented in this chapter. However, there is a fundamental obstacle to the implementation of strategies of self-reliance: the interests and values of the majority of Africa's political elites and their networks of patronage. I have shown how and why what is a human tragedy for most Africans continues to represent a source of wealth and privilege for the elites. This perverted political system has been historically produced, and is structurally maintained by the European/American powers, and by the fragmented incorporation of Africa into global capitalist networks. It is precisely

130 Susser, personal communication (1996).
131 Davidson (1992, 1994); Aina (1993); Wa Mutharika (1995).

this selective articulation of elites and valuable assets, together with the social exclusion of most people and the economic devaluation of most natural resources, that is specific to the newest expression of Africa's tragedy.

Thus, the de-linking of Africa in its own terms would take a revolution, in the oldest, political meaning of this word – an unlikely event in the foreseeable future, considering the ethnic fragmentation of the population, and the people's devastating experience *vis-à-vis* most of their leaders and saviors. Yet the writing is on the wall if we refer to historical experience, according to which there is no oppression that is not met with resistance. As for the social and political outcomes of this resistance, uncertainty and experimentation are the only possible assessments, as the process of change muddles through the collective experience of rage, conflict, struggle, hope, failure, and compromise.

The New American Dilemma: Inequality, Urban Poverty, and Social Exclusion in the Information Age

The United States features the largest and most technologically advanced economy in the world. It is the society that first experienced the structural and organizational transformations characteristic of the network society, at the dawn of the Information Age. But it is also a society that displayed, in the last two decades of the twentieth century, a substantial increase in social inequality, polarization, poverty, and misery. To be sure, America is a highly specific society, with an historical pattern of racial discrimination, with a peculiar urban form – the inner city – and with a deep-seated, ideological and political reluctance to government regulation and to the welfare state. None the less, its experience with social inequality and social exclusion, in the formative stage of the network society, may be a sign of the times to come in other areas of the world as well, and particularly in Europe, for two main reasons. First, the dominant ideology and politics of most capitalist countries emphasize deregulation of markets, and flexibility of management, in a sort of "recapitalization of capitalism" that closely echoes many of the strategies, policies, and management decisions experienced in America in the 1980s and 1990s.[132] Secondly, and perhaps more decisively, the growing integration of capital, markets, and firms, in a shared global economy, makes it extremely difficult for some countries to depart sharply from the institutional/

132   Brown and Crompton (1994); Hutton (1996).

macroeconomic environment of other areas – particularly if one of these "other areas" is as large and as central to the global economy as the United States. For European or Japanese firms, capital, and labor markets to operate under different rules, and with higher production costs, than firms based in the United States, one of two conditions has to be met. Their markets, including their capital and services markets, have to be protected. Or else productivity has to be higher than in America. But we know that the productivity of American labor, while lagging in productivity growth in the past two decades, is among the highest in the world in comparative terms, slightly trailing France and Germany, and equal to that of The Netherlands and Belgium, yet well above the average of OECD countries. As for market protection, while it is still largely the case for Japan, new trade pacts, and increasing mobility of capital, are paving the way for a relative equalization of labor conditions across OECD countries. Thus, while each society will reckon with its own problems according to its social structure and political process, what happens in America regarding inequality, poverty, and social exclusion may be taken as a probable structural outcome of trends embedded in informational capitalism when market forces remain largely unchecked. Indeed, comparative studies show similar trends (but different levels) in the growth of poverty and inequality in Western Europe and the United States, particularly in the United Kingdom.[133] While sharp inequality between the upper and lower levels of society is a universal trend, it is particularly blatant in the United States.

To ground the discussion of the social implications of informational capitalism in advanced societies, I shall proceed with an empirical survey, as succinct as possible, of the evolution of inequality, poverty, and social exclusion in America during the past two decades, assessing these trends within the framework of categories proposed at the outset of this chapter.

Dual America

In the 1990s, American capitalism seemed to have succeeded in becoming a most profitable system, under the conditions of restructuring, informationalism, and globalization.[134] After-tax profit rates at business-cycle peaks went up from 4.7 percent in 1973 to 5.1 percent in 1979, stabilized in the 1980s and then went up to 7 percent in

133   Funken and Cooper (1995); Hutton (1996).
134   The main source of data for this section on "Dual America" are the excellent studies by Mishel et al. (1996, 1999), which provide their own insightful elaboration of reliable statistics. Unless otherwise indicated, data cited in the text are from this source.

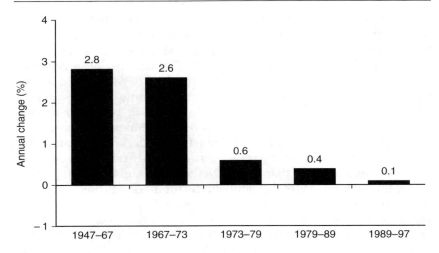

Figure 2.5   Annual growth of median family income in US, 1947–97
Source: US Bureau of the Census, 1998

1995. Stock market values reached, in 1999, their highest historical level, with the Dow Jones index jumping at one point over the 11,000 mark. Although stocks do go up and down, unless there is a catastrophic collapse of financial markets (always a possibility), the average plateau of the Dow Jones index seems to be established at an increasingly high level. Not only is capital rewarded, capitalist managers are also doing well. Counting in 1995 dollars, average total pay for chief executive officers (CEOs) in major US companies in the US went up from $1,269,000 a year in 1973 to $3,180,000 in 1989, and to $4,367,000 in 1995. The ratio of total CEO pay to total worker pay climbed from 44.8 times more in 1973 to 172.5 times more in 1995. In 1999, the richest 1 percent of households earned an average $515,600 in after–tax income, up from $243,700 in 1977.[135]

At the same time, median family income grew by an annual 0.6 percent in the 1970s, 0.4 percent in the 1980s, and by a meager 0.1 percent in the 1990s (see figure 2.5). This is particularly the result of a decline in real average weekly earnings for production and non-supervisory workers that went from $479.44 in 1973 to $395.37 in 1995. Some 80 percent of American households, or 217 million people, saw their share of national income decline, from 56 percent in 1977 to under 50 percent in 1999.

135   Bureau of the US Census, 1999.

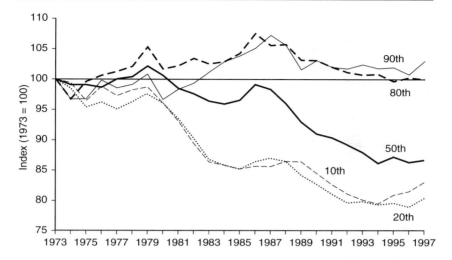

Figure 2.6a Real hourly wages for men by wage percentile in US, 1973–97
Source: Mishel et al. (1999: 133)

In Golden California, in the midst of the 1990s' boom, the median hourly wage for all workers declined by 1 percent between 1993 and 1998, and for men the decline was of 5 percent.[136] Indeed, in the US as a whole, most families could cope only if and when two members were contributing to the household budget, as the median percentage contribution of working wives grew from around 26 percent of family income in 1979 to 32 percent in 1992, so that household structure becomes a major source of income difference between families. The decline of hourly wages for men was particularly concentrated among the lowest paid workers, while the highest paid (top percentile) were the only group that did not experience a decline (figure 2.6a). Yet even the most educated groups of male workers, on average, experienced a decline in real wages for most of the 1980s and 1990s: thus college-educated men with 1–5 years of experience saw their hourly wages decline by 10.7 percent in 1979–95. However, in 1996–9, wages for male college graduates increased somewhat, although in a very un-even pattern depending on the industry where they were employed. Yet, on average, the increase was modest. For instance, in California, the Mecca of the new economy, between 1993 and 1998, average hourly wages for male college graduates increased by only 0.9 percent, and

136   Benner et al. (1999).

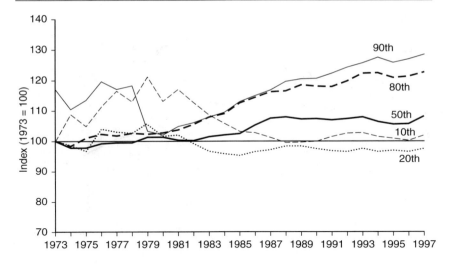

Figure 2.6b   Real hourly wages for women by wage percentile in US, 1973–97
Source: Mishel et al. (1999: 134)

for those with an advanced college degree, by 0.8 percent. In contrast, many women have seen their wages increase, substantially for the experienced group, in this period (figure 2.6b). In California, college-educated women saw their hourly wages soar by 6.1 percent between 1993 and 1998. But, overall, in the United States, women's median hourly wage in 1989–97 increased only by $0.08. So, while the gender gap in hourly wages was slightly reduced, from 66.4 percent in 1989 to 66.9 percent in 1997, most of this reduction was due to male wage decline.

The average decline in income has affected differentially the upper, middle, and lower strata. Social inequality, as measured by the Gini coefficient, rose from 0.399 in 1967 to 0.450 in 1995. Furthermore, inequality has taken the shape of polarization: in 1979–97 the richer families increased their average annual income the fastest, while the poorer ones saw their income decline (see figure 2.7). As a result of this process, in 1999, 1 percent of households with the highest income accounted for 12.9 percent of total income, after having increased their after-tax income by 119.7 percent between 1977 and 1999. The top fifth accounted for 50.4 percent of total income, up from 44.2 percent in 1977. While the lowest fifth accounted for just 4.2 percent of all income, having seen their after-tax income plunge by 12 percent between 1977 and 1999 (see table 2.10)

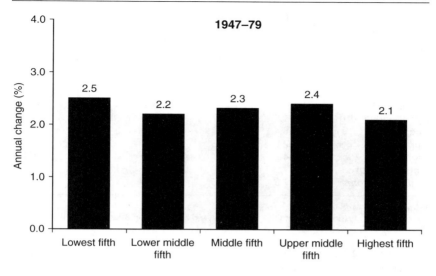

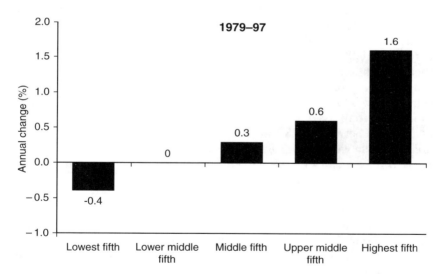

Figure 2.7 Average annual change in family income in US, 1947–97
Source: US Bureau of the Census (various years); analysis by Mishel et al. (1999: 52)

Table 2.10 Income inequality in the United States, 1977–99

	Share of all income (%)[1]		Average after-tax income (estimated) ($)		Change
Income group	1977	1999	1977	1999	(%)
Lowest fifth	5.7	4.2	10,000	8,800	−12.0
Lower middle fifth	11.5	9.7	22,100	20,000	−9.5
Middle fifth	16.4	14.7	32,400	31,400	−3.1
Upper middle fifth	22.8	21.3	42,600	45,100	+5.9
Highest fifth	44.2	50.4	74,000	102,300	+38.2
1 percent with highest income	7.3	12.9	234,700	515,600	+119.7

[1] Figures do not add to 100 due to rounding.
Source: US Congressional Budget Office data analyzed by Center on Budget and Policy Priorities

According to Wolff's calculations,[137] a similar concentration and polarization exists in the distribution of wealth (households assets minus debts) and in its evolution in 1983–97. In 1997 the top 1 percent of households accounted for 39.1 percent of total wealth, up from 33.8 percent in 1983. On the other hand, the bottom four-fifths of households account for only 15.7 percent of total wealth, down from 18.7 percent in 1983. The rise in value of the stock market probably further contributed to concentration of wealth in 1995–7, since the share of the top 1 percent increased from 37.6 percent in 1995 to 39.1 percent in 1997. On the other hand, the lowest fifth of households had more debt than assets both in 1983 and in 1997. Calculating in rates of change, between 1989 and 1997 the top fifth of households increased their wealth by 1.8 percent, while the bottom four-fifths decreased their wealth by 0.8 percent.[138] So, there is not only increasing inequality, but also increasing polarization.

In 1997–9, there was some improvement for the bottom 10 percent of wage earners, as their wages increased by 10 percent, way above the overall average. While business circles used this as evidence of a trickle down of benefits from the "new economy," in fact, the main cause for the improvement was a government decision – the rise of the legal minimum wage in 1996. At any rate, this 10 percent hike amounted to 60 cents an hour, and still left the level of real wages for the lowest 10 percent of workers well below their level in 1979.

Poverty has also increased. The percentage of persons whose income is below the poverty line increased from 11.1 percent in 1973 to

137   Wolff (1994); Mishel et al. (1999).
138   Mishel et al. (1999: 262).

13.3 percent in 1997, that is, over 35 million Americans, two-thirds of whom are white, including a substantial proportion in rural areas. Misery, or extreme poverty, has expanded even faster. Defining this category as those poor persons with incomes below 50 percent of the poverty level (in 1994, $7,571 annual income for a family of four), they accounted for almost 30 percent of all poor in 1975, and they reached 41 percent of all poor in 1997, which is about 14.6 million Americans.

The causes of increasing inequality, polarization, poverty, and misery in informational America are the subject of raging debate, and I do not pretend to settle the question in a few paragraphs. I can, however, suggest some hypotheses relating to the main line of argument in this book. To cut a long story short, I think that empirical evidence supports an interpretation that links the growth of inequality and poverty in America in the 1990s to six interrelated processes: (a) the shift from an industrial to an informational economy, with structural transformation in the sectoral composition of the labor force; (b) the premium placed by the informational economy on a high level of education, coupled with growing inequality in access to good quality, public education; (c) the impact of globalization of industrial production, labor, and markets, inducing processes of deindustrialization; (d) individualization and networking of the labor process; (e) the growing immigrant component of the labor force, under conditions of discrimination; and (f) the incorporation of women into paid labor in the informational economy, under conditions of patriarchal discrimination, and with the added economic burden resulting from the crisis of the patriarchal family. To these structural processes, I must add the sociopolitical factors that, by ensuring the domination of unrestricted market forces, accentuate the logic of inequality.[139]

How do these mechanisms operate to induce increasing inequality and poverty? First of all, there is an increasing disparity in the dynamism of the economy between its "new economy" sector, and its traditional sector (see volume 1, chapter 2). According to calculations by *Business Week* in September 1999, in the period 1994–9, when the "new economy" began to blossom, average real wages in the industries of this new economy increased by 11 percent compared with 3 percent for the rest of the economy.[140] Furthermore, calculating the evolution of real wages between 1988 and 1999, they were down by 4.5 percent in "traditional economy" industries. For an index of 100 in 1988, the index value of real wages in the new economy in 1999

---

139   Brown and Crompton (1994); Navarro (1997).
140   *Business Week* (1999a: 92–100).

went up to 112, while for the "old economy" it went down to 95.5. The key is that, by this definition, the workforce of the new economy comprised 19 million workers in 1999, while the old economy still employed 91 million workers. The two macro-sectors feature major differences in productivity, profits, and employment growth. Because new economy firms need workers, they are ready to pay high wages, particularly for the highly educated workers who are crucial for innovation and competition. On the other hand, traditional industries do not have the profit margins, or the expectation of growth in the value of their stocks, to compensate workers, regardless of their skills level. Indeed, they usually try to clamp down on wages or reduce costs by trimming their labor force, in a downward spiral of competing by cost-cutting rather than by spurring innovation and productivity. Because a much larger proportion of the labor force is trapped in the old economy, the value-generating capacity of the new, informational economy is concentrated in a relatively small sector of employment, thus disproportionately appropriating the fruits of productivity. Those who work in the new economy accumulate enough income to invest in the stock market, thus further benefiting from economic growth. It may be possible that over time, given the higher growth rate of employment in the new economy, and the diffusion of the best technology and best management practices throughout the economy, a much larger segment of the population will benefit from current processes of wealth generation. Yet, inequality induced by the disparity between the two sectors in the initial stage tends to reproduce itself, as lower income and education lead to lower chances of prospering in a knowledge-based economy. In the last resort, structural pockets of poverty are constituted among the sectors of the population who do not fit the profile of the information worker.

Secondly, education becomes the critical resource to add value to one's labor in the new economy. In 1979, the average college graduate earned 38 percent more than the average high-school graduate. In 1999, the difference was 71 percent. Furthermore, education is not the same as schooling. The knowledge-based economy requires general analytical skills and a capacity to understand and innovate, which can only be satisfied in upgraded educational institutions. Low-income groups, immigrants, and minorities have significantly lower chances of access to quality education, both at the secondary level and in college.[141] Thus, the greater the role of education in occupational advancement, the greater the likelihood of increasing inequality, in the absence of compensatory education policies. Since the projections are that in 2050

141   Carnoy (1994); Lemann (1999).

about 50 percent of the US population will be made up of members of ethnic minorities, unless current trends are corrected a sharp socio-ethnic divide may develop.

Thirdly, globalization has led to the partial deindustrialization of America as a result of the geographical shift (not disappearance) of industrial production to other areas of the world. Thus, globalization does reduce traditional manufacturing jobs – the kind of semi-skilled, decently paid jobs that constituted the backbone of working America. The key issue here has been the dismantling of the economic and organizational basis of organized labor, thus weakening labor unions and depriving workers of their instrument of collective defense. After all, it was the existence of strong labor unions that explains why manufacturing jobs were better paid than service jobs at equivalent levels of skill. The rate of unionization in the US in 1999 was down to 13.9 percent of the labor force, and an increasing share of unionized workers are concentrated in the public sector. There is ample evidence of the positive relationship between union membership and wages, particularly in areas of high union density, as is the case in the public sector. Between 1985 and 1999, the average wage for non-union workers declined by 6 percent, while for union workers it declined by only 3 percent.[142]

The fourth mechanism, the individualization of work, and the concomitant transformation of firms under the form of the network enterprise, is the most important factor inducing inequality (see volume I, chapters 3 and 4). This is, on the one hand, because workers, as a group, are placed in highly specific working conditions for each one of them – and thus are left to their individual fates. Thus, in the key area of expansion of the networked economy, California, from 1993 to 1997, large businesses lost 277,443 jobs, while firms with fewer than 100 employees created over 1.3 million net new jobs,with firms of fewer than 20 workers accounting for 65 percent of this growth. This was a powerful display of entrepreneurialism, but the consequences for workers were dire: employees of firms of 1,000 or more workers earn, on average, 39 percent more than employees of small firms, over 68 percent are covered by pension plans, in contrast to only 13.2 percent in the small businesses, and 78.4 percent have health insurance, compared with 30 percent of workers in small firms. In addition, job tenure is twice as long in large firms than in firms with fewer than 25 employees.[143]

On the other hand, the individualized bargaining process between

142 Benner et al. (1999).
143 Benner et al. (1999: 31).

employers and workers leads to an extraordinary diversity of labor arrangements and puts a decisive premium on workers who have unique skills, yet makes many other workers easily replaceable. Furthermore, by denying life-long career patterns, the successful worker today may become the discarded worker tomorrow, so that, overall, only those workers who are consistently at the top of the ladder, for a long enough period, can accumulate assets. Membership of this privileged minority has to do with a high level of education. But it does not follow that education will provide the solution, either for individuals or for social equality. It is a necessary, but not sufficient, condition to prosper in the informational economy. Data show that, on average, male college graduates also saw their real wages stagnate in the first half of the 1990s, and increased only moderately during the boom of the late 1990s. The increasing earnings gap between college-educated and non-college-educated workers is mainly due to the sharp decline of wages for the less educated. The highly rewarded workers constitute a different group, hardly captured in traditional statistical categories. They are those workers/performers/entrepreneurs who, for whatever reason, provide an edge to business in their specific field of activity: sometimes it has more to do with image-making than with substance. This embodying of value-added induces an increasing disparity between a few, highly paid entrepreneurs/workers/collaborators/consultants, and a growing mass of individuals who, because they are individuals, must usually accept the lowest common denominator of what the market offers them. Such a disparity induces an increasingly skewed distribution of incomes and assets.

Fifthly, growing immigration, under conditions of structural discrimination, leads to lower wages for the immigrants in the first place. Thus, while immigration is a significant, positive contribution to overall economic growth, it contributes to inequality since most immigrants are paid below market rates, particularly if they are undocumented. In California, a 1999 study by the Public Policy Institute of California found that immigration appeared to be responsible for about one-quarter of the increase in inequality. Indeed, the study showed that immigration and education accounted for 44 percent of the increase in inequality during the 1990s.[144]

Finally, the massive incorporation of women into the informational economy has been critical in allowing the economy to operate efficiently at a much lower cost. While the wages of educated women have gone up substantially in America (particularly for white women), they are still, on average, about 67 percent of those of their equivalent

144   Reed (1999).

male workers. So, overall, the share of wages on total GDP declined in the last two decades of the twentieth century. It does not follow that women constitute the success story of workers in the informational economy. Indeed, the crisis of the patriarchal family (partly related to women's growing economic autonomy) has had punitive effects on most people, but particularly on women, and single mothers. Indeed, studies by Eggebeen and Lichter, Lerman, and Rodgers show the close connection between changing family structure and increasing poverty for women and their children.[145] Lerman estimates that the trend away from marriage toward single-parent households accounted for almost half the increase in child income inequality and for the entire rise in child poverty rates between 1971 and 1989.[146]

The poverty rate of persons not living in families grew by 2.2 percent in 1989–94 to reach 21.5 percent of this group, accounting for 14.5 percent of all persons. As for female-headed families, their poverty rate also increased by 2.2 percent in the same period, to reach, in 1994, 38.6 percent of all female-headed families. As a result, between 1973 and 1993, the number of white children living in poverty increased by 52.6 percent, for Hispanic children by 116 percent, and for black children by 26.9 percent.[147] Overall, 19.9 percent of American children were living in poverty in 1997, while the proportion for black children was 37.2 percent. The proportion increases for children under six (22 percent and 40.2 percent, respectively)

What characterizes the so-called "new poverty" is that it widely affects working people and families, who simply cannot maintain a livelihood on the basis of their earnings. As shown in figure 2.8, the share of workers earning poverty-level wages increased substantially for men, between 1973 and 1997, while decreasing for women, so that by 1997, 28.6 percent of American workers were earning poverty-level wages, up from 23.7 percent in 1973. One of the most striking faces of this new poverty is homelessness, which skyrocketed in the 1980s in American cities, and continued at a high level in the 1990s. Estimates of the homeless population varied widely. The 1994 Clinton Administration's "Priority: Home!" report estimated that the number of homeless in the second half of the 1980s was somewhere between 5 and 9 million people, and that about 7 percent of American adults had been homeless at some point in their lives. This estimate was probably exaggerated, but the most important point is that a large proportion, and the fastest growing segment, of the homeless population comprises families with children. Indeed, they represent the majority in some cities, such as New

145   Eggebeen and Lichter (1991); Lerman(1996); Rodgers (1996).
146   Lerman (1996).
147   Cook and Brown (1994).

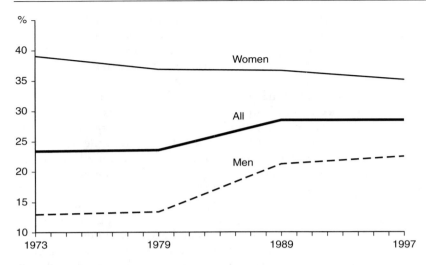

Figure 2.8   Percentage of workers earning poverty-level wages in US, 1973–97
Source: Mishel et al. (1999: 137)

York, where, in the early 1990s, families made up about three-quarters of the homeless.[148] The issue is that once poverty becomes shaped as misery and social exclusion – when life is on the street – stigma sets in, and the destruction of personality and social networks deepens the situation of distress.[149] This is how the set of relationships between dominant trends of informational capitalism, inequality, and poverty ultimately lead to the process of social exclusion, as epitomized in the dereliction of life in America's inner-city ghettos.

The inner-city ghetto as a system of social exclusion

The daily injuries of life in the ghetto constitute one of the oldest, and most poignant, American social problems. For decades, the urban social crisis, epitomized in inner-city areas segregated by race and class, has been the focus of an array of public policies, as well as of heated political debates, besides providing the ground for a distinguished research tradition in urban sociology.[150] And yet, at the turn of the millennium, inner-city ghettos, particularly black ghettos, but also some

148   Da Costa Nunez (1996: 3–8).
149   Susser (1996).
150   Drake and Cayton (1945).

Latino ghettos, such as the one in East Los Angeles, concentrate the worst expressions of inequality, discrimination, human misery, and social crisis precisely at the time of the rise of informationalism in America. Indeed, it can be argued that the social, economic, and housing conditions in most inner-city ghettos have considerably worsened over the past three decades, in spite (or because?) of a sustained effort in urban social programs and welfare policies.[151] I propose the hypothesis, along with William J. Wilson and other social scientists,[152] that there is a systemic relationship between the structural transformations I have analyzed as characteristic of the new, network society and the growing dereliction of the ghetto: the constitution of an informational/global economy, under the conditions of capitalist restructuring; the crisis of the nation-state, with one of its main manifestations in the crisis of the welfare state; the demise of the patriarchal family without being replaced by an alternative form of conviviality and socialization; the emergence of a global, yet decentralized, criminal economy, penetrating society and institutions at all levels, and taking over certain territories from which to operate; and the process of political alienation, and communal retrenchment, among the large segments of the population that are poor and feel disfranchised. Racial discrimination and spatial segregation are still major factors in the formation/reinforcement of ghettos as systems of social exclusion. But their effects take new meaning, and become increasingly devastating, under the conditions of informationalism – for reasons that I shall try to spell out in the following paragraphs.

To do so, I will rely on the powerful, empirically grounded analysis proposed by William J. Wilson in his 1996 book *When Work Disappears*. However, while I find his interpretation convincing in its main thrust, I will recast it in my own terms, both to link up with the theory presented in this book, and to avoid making Wilson responsible for my own reading of his findings. I shall also use other sources when necessary.

The formation of large ghetto areas in the inner cities of metropolitan America is the result of a series of well-known processes.[153] Mechanization of Southern agriculture and the mobilization of an industrial labor force, during and after World War II, led to massive migration of black laborers who concentrated in the neighborhoods left vacant by the suburbanization process stimulated by federal housing and transportation policies. Massive displacement by the federal urban renewal

151   Jones (1992); Massey and Denton (1993); Gans (1995); Van Kempen and Marcuse (1996).
152   Wilson (1987, 1996); Wacquant (1993, 1996); Susser (1996).
153   Castells (1977: 379–427).

program to preserve the business and cultural centers in the metropolitan cores further increased the concentration of blacks and other minorities in the most dilapidated neighborhoods. The location of public housing projects contributed to segregation. Slum landlordism and residential abandonment accelerated the process of escape from poor inner-city areas for whoever had the opportunity. The organization of schooling on the basis of residential location, in a decentralized system that split cities from suburbs, concentrated disadvantaged children in an under-funded, under-staffed public school system in the inner city, which soon deteriorated. The perversion of the Jeffersonian tradition of local self-governance led to fiscal disparity between needs and resources, with suburbs enjoying higher resources and cities suffering greater needs. This is the pattern of formation of the classic American ghetto, whose social inequities triggered social revolts and political protests in the 1960s. The social policies that responded to grassroots pressure reduced institutional discrimination, somewhat empowered African-American political elites, and helped individual upward mobility for the most educated African-Americans, most of whom moved out of the inner city. Yet the residents of ghettos saw their condition dramatically deteriorate over the next quarter of the century. Why so?

Wilson anchors his interpretation, and I concur, in the transformation of work and employment under the conditions of informationalization and globalization of the economy. Not that new technologies induce unemployment: I showed in volume I, chapter 4 that both the empirical record and analytical insights reject the simplistic assumption of machines phasing out work and workers on a grand scale. Indeed, around the world, there is an unprecedented expansion of paid labor via the massive incorporation of women into the labor force, and the displacement of agricultural workers toward manufacturing, services, and the urban informal economy. It is precisely this globalization of manufacturing, and outsourcing of production in lower-cost areas, that greatly contributes to the elimination of those jobs that are costlier to perform in America, but not skilled enough to require location in a highly industrialized environment. Informationalization spurs job growth in the higher tier of skills in America, while globalization offshores low-skilled manufacturing jobs to newly industrializing countries.[154] Thus, in America, there is indeed a substantial reduction of manufacturing jobs, and particularly of low-skilled jobs, precisely the kind of jobs that brought black migrants into the urban areas and constituted the stable, hard core of their employment. Many of the

154   Carnoy et al. (1997).

new jobs of the informational economy require higher education and verbal/relational skills that inner-city public schools rarely provide. Besides, new manufacturing, and an increasing proportion of service jobs, have become suburbanized, decreasing accessibility for inner-city residents. Thus, there is a growing mismatch between the profile of many new jobs and the profile of poor blacks living in the inner city.[155]

Nevertheless, there are other sources of low-paid jobs, particularly in social services and in the public sector. Thanks to affirmative action policies, these are, indeed, the main employment opportunities for inner-city women, including black women.[156] Low-educated black men, however, are less likely to obtain these jobs. Furthermore, the shrinkage of public employment, following the retrenchment of social services in the past two decades, has reduced the availability of public jobs, and increased educational requirements for applicants.

There are also menial jobs in low-skill service activities (for example, janitorial services, food services, informal construction, repair and maintenance). Why black men do not easily get these jobs is less clear in Wilson's analysis. In my view, racial discrimination could be a reason. But Wilson does not find supportive evidence for it, emphasizing instead, for instance, that black employers are also reluctant to hire inner-city black men. Wilson hints at two possible factors. On one hand, comparison with the much better performance of Mexican immigrants in the labor market for low-skill service activities seems to result from the willingness of Mexicans, and other immigrant groups, to accept low pay and hard work, under discriminatory conditions which are imposed upon them because of their vulnerability, often linked to their undocumented status. Thus, it would seem that the standards of work and pay that many poor blacks set for themselves, often resulting in complaints and dissatisfaction while performing a job, backfires in the perception of their prospective employers, inducing the notion of inner-city black males as being "difficult workers." Furthermore, new service jobs often require relational abilities that seem to be lacking among poor blacks, particularly among men, thus undermining their chances of employment. I would consider widespread racism among the population at large, particularly aimed at blacks, as an important factor, if not the only one, in the greater difficulty experienced in relating to a black employee outside a context of black-majority clientele.[157] Thus, although it may be true that deteriorating schools do not prepare the low-skilled labor force for relational

155   Kasarda (1990, 1995).
156   Carnoy (1994).
157   West (1993).

and informational activities in the new service economy, this new handicap may interact with an older source of exclusion, namely the racial barriers that bias social interaction. I would also add that the crisis of family life, and the instability of living and working patterns in the ghetto, strongly interact with the difficulty for black men, particularly young black men, of fitting into the pattern of social acceptability and work ethic that still underlies hiring decisions in many businesses. Finally, poverty and the family crisis in the black ghetto lead to an impoverishment of social networks, thus diminishing the chances of finding a job via personal connections. This, as Wilson argues, and as Alejandro Portes and his collaborators have demonstrated,[158] is in sharp contrast to the experience of Mexican and Latino immigrants/minorities, whose stronger family structure and broad social networks provide considerable support in job referrals and information.

As a result of these mutually reinforcing trends, formal work by and large disappears, particularly for men, and even more so for young men, in black ghetto areas. Wilson emphasizes that, in addition to high rates of unemployment in these areas, particularly among young people, there is a considerable number of adults who have dropped out of the labor force, and are not even looking for a job. He cites findings of his studies on Woodlawn and Oakland (two poor neighborhoods on Chicago's South Side) where, in 1990, only 37 percent and 23 percent respectively of adults were working in a given week.[159] Furthermore, most poor men are also excluded from the programs of the urban welfare state.[160]

It does not follow that most adults are inactive or without access to sources of income. The informal economy, and particularly the criminal economy, become prevalent in many poor neighborhoods, which become the shopfloor of these activities, and increasingly influence the habits and culture of segments of their population. The explosion of crack cocaine's traffic and consumption in the black ghettos in the 1980s was a turning point for many communities.[161] Gangs became important forms of youth organization and patterns of behavior.[162] Guns are, at the same time, working tools, signs of self-esteem, and motives for peers' respect.[163] The widespread presence of guns calls for more guns, as everybody rushes to self-defense, particularly after the police gave up serious law enforcement in a number of poor

158 Portes (1995); Wilson (1996).
159 Wilson (1996: 23).
160 Susser (1993).
161 Bourgois and Dunlap (1993); Bourgois (1995).
162 Sanchez Jankowski (1991).
163 Wilson (1996).

neighborhoods.[164] Economic transactions in these inner-city areas often become marked by the criminal economy, as a source of work and income, as demand-generating activities, and as the operational unit for protection/taxation in the informal economy. Economic competition is often played out through violence, thus further destroying community life, and increasingly identifying gangs with surviving social networks, with the crucial exception of community-based churches. As Hagedorn writes, concluding his insightful study of Milwaukee's gangs:

> The story of the people and folks in Milwaukee is a story of contemporary urban America. The male and female gang members we studied have struggled to become productive and happy adults, only to watch their economic security snatched away by forces over which they had no control. Young women mainly held on to traditional gender roles and tried to raise their families under more trying conditions. What the future holds for them is uncertain ... The more reckless men, on the other hand, predictably responded to the loss of legitimate jobs by "going for the gold" in the drug economy. Their response was predictable because the values they held and their cultural understanding of them is familiar to us all – they wanted their piece of the pie. The fundamental tenets of the American Dream are alive and well on the corners of our central cities.[165]

The crisis of the ghetto goes beyond the issue of formal unemployment versus informal/criminal employment. It affects the patterns of family formation in the context of the crisis of patriarchalism that I analyzed in volume II, chapter 4. Trends toward increasing single parenthood and births out of wedlock are by no means exclusively linked to poverty or to African-American culture. Indeed, in 1993, in America, 27 percent of all children under the age of 18 were living with a single parent, 21 percent of white children, 32 percent of Hispanic children, and 57 percent of black children. Between 1980 and 1992, the rate of births out of wedlock increased by 9 percent for blacks, but by a staggering 94 percent for whites.[166] This differential growth is due, partly, to the traditionally high rate of incidence of births out of marriage among African-Americans. Indeed, the crisis of the black family has been a critical argument of sociologists and social policy-makers for a long time. Yet, it could also be argued that, instead of seeing it as a symptom of social deviance, it could reflect a pioneering effort by black women to take control of their own lives, without begging men's

---

164 Susser (1995).
165 Hagedorn and Macon (1998: 208).
166 Wilson (1996: 87).

lagging responsibility. Whatever the historical/cultural reasons for the weakness of the patriarchal family among urban African-Americans, this pattern, seen in historical perspective, seems to be a forerunner of the times to come for many Americans, as well as for many people in the world (see volume II, chapter 4).

A number of factors, identified by Wilson, seem to concur toward the single female-centeredness of a majority of families with children in poor black neighborhoods. First, there is the lack of employment opportunities for young black males, leading to uncertainty in their income, and thus undermining their ability to make commitments. I would also add that, given the high likelihood of imprisonment, injury, or even death among ghetto youth, in some cases it could actually be considered a responsible attitude not to set up a family, whose future care is at best uncertain. Secondly, Wilson documents, on the basis of his team's ethnographic studies, an extraordinary degree of distrust, and even hostility, between young women and men in the black neighborhoods that were studied. My only caveat on this most important observation is that similar studies among middle-class whites in large metropolitan areas may yield similar results. The difference, however, is in the coherent attitude of many young African-American women in deciding not to marry, and to have babies out of wedlock. This decision, Wilson hints, in line with Drake and Cayton's classic study of the black ghetto,[167] may be related to the lack of economic rewards and expectation of social mobility linked to marriage, in contrast with marriage patterns in the white middle class. With no apparent economic and social benefits from the marriage, and with a long-standing distrust of men's commitment, poor young black women have little incentive to marry, and to have to cope with men's problems in addition to their own. Thus, while in 1993, 9 percent of American children were living with a never-married parent, the proportion for black children was 31 percent, but it was even higher for poor blacks. According to Wilson's data, in Chicago's inner-city neighborhoods, almost 60 percent of black adults aged 18–44 years have never been married, and among black parents living in high-poverty areas, only 15.6 percent are married.[168] Why do black women, and particularly very young women, still choose to have children? It seems to be, primarily, a matter of self-esteem, of gaining respect, of becoming someone in their social environment, besides having someone of their own and a tangible goal in life. While most teenage pregnancies are the byproduct of love/sex without further thinking, the decision to keep

167 Drake and Cayton (1945).
168 Wilson (1996: 89).

the baby is usually associated with assuming womanhood, in contrast with the scarce chance of receiving education or a rewarding job under the conditions of ghetto life.[169] There seems to be little evidence to support the conservative argument according to which welfare provisions to help single mothers and their children offer an incentive to single motherhood.[170] However, once women have children on their own, fundamentally for personal reasons, it becomes increasingly difficult for them to leave the welfare trap.[171] This is because the kind of jobs they can access are so poorly paid that they cannot match the cost of child care, transportation, housing, and health care (usually not provided by most of their employers) with their wage. Thus, as difficult as it is to survive on welfare, it becomes a better option than working, particularly when health care for the children is taken into consideration. The deep cuts in welfare to single mothers with children mandated from January 1997 are likely to have devastating effects on poor women and their children, and assure the further deterioration of social life in poor neighborhoods.

With many young men out of jobs and out of families, often reduced to the opportunities provided by the criminal economy, work ethics and job patterns hardly fit the expectations of prospective employers, thus providing a material basis to reinforce prejudicial attitudes toward employing inner-city black men, ultimately sealing their fate. Thus, there is a link between joblessness and poverty for black men, but the link is specified by racial discrimination and by their rage against this discrimination.

Spatial structure interacts decisively with the economic, social, and cultural processes I have described. Urban segregation is reinforced by the increasing separation between the logic of the space of flows and the logic of the space of places I have identified as characteristic of the network society (volume I, chapter 6). The ghetto as a place has become increasingly confined in its poverty and marginality.[172] A decisive factor in this sense has been the upward mobility of a significant proportion of black urban families which, helped by politics, education, affirmative action programs, and their own effort, has earned them their place in mainstream society. In their vast majority, they left the inner city to save their children from a system that was reproducing social exclusion and stigma. Yet, by saving themselves individually, they left behind, trapped in the crumbling structures of the ghetto, most of the one-third of poor blacks (and over 40 percent of black

169   Plotnick (1990).
170   Wilson (1996: 94–5).
171   Susser and Kreniske (1987).
172   Wacquant (1996).

children) that now form the most destitute segment of the American population. Furthermore, the emergence of the space of flows, using telecommunications and transportation to link up valuable places in a non-contiguous pattern, has allowed the reconfiguration of metropolitan areas around selective connections of strategically located activities, bypassing undesirable areas, left to themselves. Suburbanization first, ex-urban sprawl later, and the formation of "Edge City"'s peripheral nodes (see volume I, chapter 6) allowed the metropolitan world to exclude entirely inner-city ghettos from their function and meaning, disassociating space and society along the lines of urban dualism and social exclusion.[173] The spatial confinement of poor blacks replicated their growing exclusion from the formal labor market, diminished their educational opportunities, dilapidated their housing and urban environment, left their neighborhoods under the threat of criminal gangs, and, because of their symbolic association with crime, violence, and drugs, delegitimized their political options. American inner-city ghettos, and particularly the black ghetto, has become part of the earthly hell being built to punish the dangerous classes of the undeserving poor. And because a large proportion of black children are growing up in these neighborhoods, America is systemically reproducing its deepest pattern of social exclusion, inter-racial hostility, and interpersonal violence.

When the underclass goes to hell

The ultimate expression of social exclusion is the physical and institutional confinement of a segment of society either in prison or under the supervision of the justice system, in probation and parole. America has the dubious distinction of being the country with the highest percentage of prison population in the world. The fastest growth of incarceration rates took place from 1980, a sharp increase *vis-à-vis* historical tendencies (see figure 2.9). On January 1, 1996, there were almost 1.6 million inmates in prisons and jails (local, state, and federal), and an additional 3.8 million people on probation and parole, giving a total of 5.4 million, representing 2.8 percent of all adults, under correctional supervision. This number has almost tripled since 1980, growing at an average annual rate of 7.4 percent (see figure 2.10). The proportion of inmates to general population in 1996 was 600 inmates per 100,000 US residents, a rate that has nearly doubled in ten years. Federal prisons in 1996 were operating at 26 percent over their capacity, and state

173   Mollenkopf and Castells (1991).
174   Department of Justice (1996); Gilliard and Beck (1996).

Figure 2.9 Incarceration rates in US, 1850–1991

Sources: Margaret Werner Cahalan, *Historical Corrections Statistics, 1850–1984* (Rockville, MD: Westat, 1986); Bureau of Justice Statistics, *Sourcebook of Criminal Justice Statistics, 1991* (Washington, DC: US Department of Justice, 1992); Bureau of Justice Statistics, *Prisoners in 1991* (Washington, DC: US Department of Justice, 1992), elaborated by Gilliard and Beck (1996)

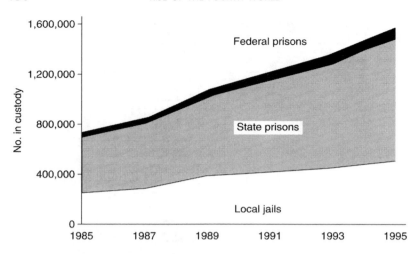

Figure 2.10   Number of inmates held in state or federal prisons or in local jails in US, 1985–95 (figures include prisoners in custody, prisoners in local jails because of prison overcrowding, and prisoners supervised elsewhere, such as in treatment centers. Counts for 1994 and 1995 exclude persons who were supervised outside a jail. Total of people in custody of state, federal, or local jurisdictions per 100,000 US residents)
Source: Bulletin of the US Bureau of Justice Statistics, August 1996

prisons at between 14 and 25 percent over capacity.[174]

This prison population is socially and ethnically biased: in 1991, 53 percent of inmates were black, and 46 percent white, the proportion of blacks continuing to climb in the 1990s. Hispanics made up 13 percent of the prison population, and 14 percent of the jail population. Blacks also accounted for 40 percent of Death Row inmates. The ratio of incarceration rates of blacks *vis-à-vis* whites in 1990 was 6.44. Evidence shows that this is largely due to discrimination in sentencing, and preventive imprisonment, rather than because of the frequency or characteristics of the crimes committed.[175] As for adults on parole, in 1995, 49 percent were black, and 21 percent Hispanic.[176]

Let us look at the evolution of the incarceration system in a close up of California, the state that holds the distinction of having the largest prison population in the United States.[177] The number of prisoners in

175   Tonry (1995).
176   Department of Justice (1996).
177   Hewitt et al. (1994); Koetting and Schiraldi (1994); Schiraldi (1994); Connolly et al. (1996).

the state increased fourfold between 1980 and 1991. The total rate of incarceration in the mid-1990s was 626 per 100,000 people, which was nearly double that of South Africa or Russia. The incarceration rate for whites was 215 per 100,000, but for blacks it was 1,951 per 100,000. In 1990s' California, about four in ten young African-American men were under some form of criminal justice control. These figures are particularly striking when compared with those for African-Americans in college education. In the early 1990s, 27,707 African-American students attended a four-year public university course in California, while 44,792 were in prison. The California Department of Corrections reported in 1996 that its prisons were operating at 194 percent capacity, and estimated that 24 new prisons would have to be built by 2005 to keep pace with the rate of incarceration. Projections were for the occupancy rate to reach 256 percent of capacity by 1996. The system was entirely geared toward punishment, and presumed deterrence. Rehabilitation as a goal of imprisonment was removed from the California Penal Code in 1977.[178]

Irwin, Austin, Tonry, Welch, and Mergenhagen,[179] among others, have carefully established the profile of the prison population, the reasons for their incarceration, and the social consequences of their imprisonment. They found that the majority of offenders are non-violent. Indeed, in 1990, 28 percent of those sent to prison were admitted for parole violation, in two-thirds of the cases for technical violations of the parole, without committing a crime. For the 68 percent who received a court sentence, about 70 percent were sentenced for non-violent crimes (burglary, drugs possession or trafficking, robbery, public order offenses). In 1993, 26 percent of inmates were in prison for drug-related offenses, up from 8 percent in 1980, while the percentage of those imprisoned for violent offenses (including robbery) dropped from 57 to 45 percent.[180] In their survey, Irwin and Austin found that most crimes were "much pettier than the popular images promoted by those who sensationalize the crime issue . . . Our inner cities actually contain a growing number of young men, mostly non-white, who become involved in unskilled, petty crime because of no avenues to a viable, satisfying conventional life."[181] Indeed, 64 percent of inmates lack a formal high school education, and most of them are "uneducated, unskilled (at crime as well as other pursuits), and highly disorganized

178   Connolly et al. (1996).
179   Irwin (1985); Irwin and Austin (1994); Tonry (1995); Welch (1994, 1995); Mergenhagen (1996).
180   Mergenhagen (1996).
181   Irwin and Austin (1994; 59–60).
182   Irwin and Austin (1994: 143).

persons."[182] There has been a rapid increase in the number of juveniles dealt with in the criminal justice system: 600,000 in 1991, of which 100,000 were in prisons or juvenile detention facilities. Women are only 6 percent of prisoners, but their proportion is sharply up, from 4 percent in 1980; 6 percent of them come to prison pregnant. Most inmates are parents: 78 percent of women and 64 percent of men have children under 18. This, apparently, makes very good business for telephone companies, as inmates call collect to stay in touch with their children, so that, according to a report by *The Wall Street Journal*, a single prison telephone can gross as much as $15,000 a year. Furthermore, jails are dangerous places, plagued by drug consumption and violence, ruled by gangs, sometimes related to prison guards. Health is a major issue. One-third of state prison inmates participate in drug-treatment programs. And almost 3 percent of state prison inmates are HIV-positive or sick with AIDS. The incidence of tuberculosis is four times higher than for the population at large, and about one-quarter of inmates have some type of clinical psychiatric problem.[183]

The prison society reproduces, and furthers, the culture of criminality, so that those who end up in prison see their chances of social integration substantially decreased, both because of social stigma and because of their inner injuries. In Irwin and Austin's words, "prisons have become true human warehouses – often highly crowded, violent, and cruel."[184] This, at a very high cost for taxpayers: about $39,000 a year per inmate. As in the old saying of criminologists: it costs more to send a young man to jail than to Yale. The state of California in the 1990s spends as much money on its prisons as its education system (about 9 percent of the state budget on each).

A number of studies has shown the small impact of punishment on the actual incidence of crime.[185] In the words of Robert Gangi, director of the Correctional Association of New York: "building more prisons to address crime is like building more graveyards to address a fatal disease."[186] Yet the mass punishment of social deviance does have a substantial effect, well beyond its instrumental value as a crime deterrent: it marks the boundaries of social exclusion in terms that blame the excluded for their plight, delegitimize their potential rebellion, and confine social problems into a customized hell. The making of a sizeable proportion of the underclass's young men into a dangerous class could well be the most striking expression of the new American dilemma in the Information Age.

183   Mergenhagen (1996).
184   Irwin and Austin (1994: 144).
185   Roberts (1994); Lynch and Paterson (1995).
186   Cited by Smolowe (1994: 55).

Globalization, Over-exploitation, and Social Exclusion: the View from the Children

If any doubts were left about the fact that the main labor issue in the Information Age is not the end of work but the condition of workers, they are definitively settled by the explosion of low-paid child labor in the past decade. According to the report released by the International Labour Office in November 1996,[187] about 250 million children between the ages of 5 and 14 were working for pay in developing countries, of which 120 million were working full time. These estimates, based on an improved methodology – and counting children aged 5–10 years for the first time – doubled previous estimates. Some 153 million of these child workers were in Asia, 80 million in Africa, and 17.5 million in Latin America. However, Africa has the highest incidence of child labor, at around 40 percent of children aged 5–14. A 1995 ILO survey of child labor in Ghana, India, Indonesia, and Senegal found that 25 percent of all children between 5 and 14 years of age had engaged in economic activity, and that around 33 percent did not attend school. The ILO also reports, without quantifying, a significant growth in child labor in Eastern European and Asian countries in the transition to a market economy.[188] While the overwhelming majority of child workers are in the developing world, the phenomenon is also on the rise in advanced capitalist countries, particularly in the United States, where fast-food outlets prosper on the basis of teenage work, and other businesses – for example, commercial candy sales – are following apace. In 1992, the US Department of Labor registered 19,443 offenses against child labor laws, twice the level of 1980. Besides the main culprit, the fast-food industry, other cases reported concerned immigrant children working illegally in garment factories in Manhattan, in construction works in the Bronx, or on farms in Texas, California, and Florida. The National Safe Workplace Institute estimates that every year 300 children are killed and 70,000 injured on the job. Dumaine, citing experts, attributes the rise in child labor in America to the deterioration of working-class life conditions, and to increased undocumented immigration.[189] Lavalette found a similar expansion of child labor in Britain. He cites studies according to which, for school children aged 13–16 years, 80 percent of girls and 69 percent of boys had some form of employment; in Birmingham, a survey of 1,827 school students aged 10–16 found that 43.7 percent

187   ILO (1996)
188   ILO (1996: 7–8).
189   Dumaine (1993).

were working in some way, or had had a job in the recent past.[190] He states that "the existing studies of children's part-time jobs in advanced economies, though limited in number, all suggest that child employment is an extensive activity, carried out for little reward and performed in poor working conditions."[191] Out of reach of statistical observation, large numbers of children, both in developed and developing countries, are involved in income-generating activities linked to the criminal economy, particularly in drug traffic, petty thefts, and organized begging.[192] Much of the proliferation of street children is linked to these activities. Thus, studies in Brazil, whose cities, and particularly Rio de Janeiro, have been highlighted as the most striking example of thousands of children living in the street, show that, in fact, most of them return to their poor homes at the end of the day, bringing their meager gains to the family. A 1989 survey of street children in Rio found that those living by themselves on the streets, without their families, accounted for only 14.6 percent of street children, among whom 80 percent were drug addicts. Another 13.6 percent were homeless, but shared street life with their families; 21.4 percent were in the family home and worked in the streets under the control of their family. The majority (50.5 percent) had contact with their families, but worked in the streets independently, and occasionally slept there. Yet all categories shared a high risk of violence and death, often at the hands of "vigilantes" and policemen, engaging in "street cleanups."[193] Pedrazzini and Sanchez report a similar situation among the "malandros" (bad boys) of Caracas.[194]

According to the ILO, child labor is present in a whole array of activities, many of them highly hazardous.[195] Besides the well-known case of rugs and carpet weaving, an export industry that in India and Pakistan utilizes child labor on a large scale, child workers are reported in the brassware industry of India; in the brick-making factories of Pakistan; in Muro-ami fishing (involving deep-sea diving) in South-East Asia; in the pesticide-poisoned plantations of Sri Lanka; in toxic fume-filled repair shops and woodwork shops in Egypt, the Philippines, and Turkey; in small-scale mines in Africa, Asia, and Latin America; and in millions of homes, as domestic workers, frequently exposed to abuse. Thus, around 5 million children are employed as domestic workers in Indonesia, and half a million in Sri Lanka. In

190 Lavalette (1994: 29-31).
191 Lavalette (1994: 1).
192 Hallinan (1994); Pedrazzini and Sanchez (1996).
193 Rizzini (1994).
194 Pedrazzini and Sanchez (1996).
195 ILO (1996).

Venezuela, 60 percent of the girls working between 10 and 14 years of age are in domestic work. A substantial proportion of child domestic workers are very young: 24 percent in Bangladesh, and 26 percent in Venezuela, were less than 10 years old. These domestic workers work as much as 10–15 hours a day, and studies report what the ILO describes as "alarming evidence of physical, mental, and sexual abuse of adolescents and young women working as domestics."[196]

The rapid growth of global tourism, an industry currently employing about 7 percent of the total global workforce, is also a major source of child labor around the world.[197] Because it is a labor-intensive industry, seasonal and irregular in its activity, it is highly conducive to the employment of flexible, cheap labor, thus to child labor. Types of jobs include bell boys, waitresses, maids, collectors of fares in public taxis, masseuses, receptionists, "hospitality" workers, ball boys, caddies, messengers, servers of tea and snacks, minders of deck-chairs and ponies on the beach and so on. Pay is extremely low: a study in Acapulco, Mexico, reported by Black, found that children of 7–12 years of age were employed as drink servers with no pay other than tips and a small commission per drink served.[198] This seems to be consistent with reports from other countries.

In some instances, child labor is involved in gruesome activities. Thus, in poverty-stricken, civil-war torn Kabul, in 1996, many children engaged, for the benefit of their families, in profitable robbing and smuggling of human bones. They obtained the bones from graveyards, mixed them (to disguise their origin) with bones from dogs, cows, and horses, and sold them to middlemen who ship them to Pakistan, where they are used for making cooking oil, soap, chicken feed, and buttons. A child in this trade made about 12 dollars a month, three times the salary of a civil servant in Taliban-dominated Afghanistan.[199]

A particularly exploitative type of child labor is bonded labor. As the 1996 ILO report writes: "Slavery is not dead. Societies are loath to admit to still harbouring it but, as can be surmised from cases reported to the ILO, numerous children are trapped in slavery in many parts of the world. Of all working children, surely these are the most imperiled."[200] Thus, according to a 1994 study of the US Department of Labor:

196   ILO (1996: 15).
197   Black (1995).
198   Black (1995).
199   *The New York Times Magazine*, January 12, 1997: 30–2
200   ILO (1996: 15).

in India, where conservative estimates of adult and child bonded laborers start at 3 million, debt bondage occurs when a person needing a loan and having no security to offer, pledges his/her labor, or that of someone under his/her control, as a security for the loan . . . There are increasing reports of child bonded laborers in both the service and manufacturing sectors in India . . . In some countries, recruiters comb the countryside paying for parents to recruit their children for work in factories. For example, in Thailand, many child workers come from poverty-stricken parts of the northeast regions, having been sold by their parents, or made part of a debt bondage arrangement. Unscrupulous "employment agencies" often negotiate the transaction and deliver children to industries, like shrimp peeling, or prostitution. In the Philippines, two separate raids on a sardine canning factory found children, as young as 11, filling cans with sliced fish to repay the debt to the labor recruiter.[201]

This report is filled with case studies from a variety of countries documenting child bondage. Another US Department of Labor report provides ample evidence of child forced and bonded labor in commercial agriculture, as well as the damaging consequences of their early-age exposure to chemical fertilizers and pesticides.[202]

Why this surge in child labor? In the first place, it results from the simultaneous deepening of poverty and globalization of economic activity. The crisis of subsistence economies and the impoverishment of large segments of the population, as documented above, force families, and their children, into all kinds of survival strategies: no time for schooling, the family needs as many income-earners as possible, and it needs them right now. Families, pushed by necessity, sometimes offer their children to bonded labor, or send them into the streets. Studies have shown the influence of large-size families on child labor: the higher the number of children, the more the likelihood of a family triage between those sent to school and into the streets. However, the same studies also show that the effect of family size on child labor is sharply reduced in countries or regions with more developed social welfare policies.[203]

On the other hand, the globalization of economic activities provides the opportunity for substantial gain by employing children, counting on the difference between the cost of a child laborer in developing countries and the price of goods and services in affluent markets. This is clearly the case in the international tourist industry. The luxurious services that middle-income tourists can afford in many "tropical

201 US Department of Labor (1994: 19).
202 US Department of Labor (1995).
203 Grootaert and Kanbur (1995).

paradises" rely to a large extent on the over-exploitation of local labor, including many children, as documented by Black.[204] Yet, the 1996 report by the ILO argues that labor costs are not necessarily the main determinants for hiring children. In India, for instance, savings from child labor seem to account for only 5 percent of the final price of bangles, and between 5 and 10 percent for carpets. Why then hire children? According to the report, "the answer lies in *where* the gains from using child labor occur. In the carpet industry, for example, it is the loom owners who supervise the weaving who benefit directly. Many in number, they are usually poor, small contractors who work to a very slim profit margin and who can as much as double their meagre income by utilizing child workers."[205] Thus, *it is the networking between small producers, and larger firms, exporting to affluent markets, often through the intermediation of wholesale merchants and large department stores in these markets, that explains both the flexibility and the profitability of the industry.* A 1994 US Labor Department study also found that, while most child workers were not directly working in export-oriented firms, the spread of sub-contracting networks and of home-based production in many countries was incorporating children into export industries. For instance, a study of a sample of seamstresses in the garment industry in Latin America found that 80 percent of them were women working at home. Of those, 34 percent had their children help, and, for those working 50 hours a week, 40 percent had their children as helpers. In another example, the majority of workers in export-oriented Mexico's *maquiladoras* are young women, of 14–20 years of age; it is thought that among them there are also some who are younger than 14.[206]

However, the most important factor in employing children seems to be their *defenselessness*, leading to the relatively easy imposition of minimal pay and atrocious working conditions. As the ILO report states:

> Since the children do not have irreplaceable skills and are often not much less costly than adults, a major important explanation for hiring seems to be non-economic. There are many non-pecuniary reasons but the most important seems to be the fact that children are less aware of their rights, less troublesome and more willing to take orders and to do monotonous work without complaining, more trustworthy, less likely to steal, and less likely to be absent from work. Children's lower absentee rate is especially valuable for employers in informal sector industries

204 Black (1995).
205 ILO (1996: 19).
206 US Department of Labor (1994: 19).

where workers are employed on a daily, casual basis and a full contingent of workers must therefore be found each day.[207]

Children as ready-to-use, disposable labor are the last frontier of renewed over-exploitation under networked, global capitalism. Or are they?

The sexual exploitation of children

My question is indeed rhetorical. There is much worse in the current plight of many children: they have become sexual commodities in a large-scale industry, organized internationally through the use of advanced technology, and by taking advantage of the globalization of tourism and images. The World Congress Against Commercial Sexual Exploitation of Children, which took place in Stockholm on August 27–31, 1996, put together an impressive set of documents providing evidence of the extent of this exploitation, of its rapid diffusion, and of the causes underlying the phenomenon.[208] Statistics cannot be precise on this matter, but reliable empirical estimates point toward the importance of the problem, and toward its fast growth, frequently associated with the globalization of tourism, and with the perverse search for sexual enjoyment beyond standardized sex consumption.[209] In Thailand, the hot spot of the global sex industry, the Center for Protection of Children's Rights, a well-established, non-governmental organization, estimates that as many as 800,000 children are in prostitution, with HIV infection being pervasive among them. Indeed, virginity is a well-paid merchandise, and sex without condoms is highly priced. A 1991 survey of *India Today* puts the number of child prostitutes in India somewhere between 400,000 and 500,000. In Sri Lanka, estimates range around 20,000. In the tiny Dominican Republic, over 25,000 minors were in prostitution. Another study counted 3,000 minors working as prostitutes in Bogota. Beyer estimates that Brazil has about 200,000 adolescent prostitutes, and Peru about half a million.[210] But the problem is not confined to developing countries by any means. The Council of Europe estimated that in Paris, in 1988, 5,000 boys and 3,000 girls were working as prostitutes on the streets; the Defence of the Child International evaluated at 1,000 the number of child prostitutes in The Netherlands in 1990; and a 1996 study presented to the World Congress indicated substantial growth of child

207   ILO (1996: 20).
208   World Congress (1996).
209   *Christian Science Monitor* (1996).
210   Beyer (1996).

prostitution among Russian, Polish, Romanian, Hungarian, and Czech children.[211] In Belgium, one of the largest political demonstrations ever took place in Brussels on October 20, 1996 to protest against the government cover-up of the implications of the murder of four little girls, apparently linked to a child prostitution ring in which leading politicians may have been involved.[212]

One of the fastest growing markets for child prostitution is in the United States and Canada, where, in 1996, estimates varied widely between 100,000 and 300,000 child prostitutes.[213] Some areas of the country are targeted. For instance, New York pimps like to recruit their sex slaves in Kansas and Florida. Pimps move children from city to city to keep them in unfamiliar surroundings; they keep them locked up, and give them no money. How do children end up in this situation? According to a report from the US Department of Labor, reasons may vary:

> Parents knowingly sell children to recruiters to augment family income, recruiters make false promises, children are kidnapped, or they run away and are lured into prostitution to survive on the streets . . . No matter what the cause, the outcome is the same. A large and profitable industry is willing to sexually exploit children to satisfy a demand for child prostitutes. The children are generally scarred for life – which may be short, since occupational hazards such as AIDS and other sexually transmitted diseases, or brutal physical abuse, often kill them.[214]

Related to prostitution, but as a distinct segment of the booming child sex industry, is child pornography. Technology is a major factor in spurring this industry. Camcorders, VCRs, home editing desks, and computer graphics have all moved the child porn industry into the home, making it difficult to police. The Internet has opened up new channels of information for those seeking access to children for sex. In some instances, computerized information systems have been operated from prison by incarcerated pedophiles. Thus, an impoverished, deindustrialized town in Northern Minnesota found their children specifically targeted in the records confiscated by police of a pedophile network operated from prison by inmates. Because pornographic images and video clips can be uploaded and downloaded almost anonymously, a global network of child pornography has developed, in a wholly decentralized manner, and with few possibilities for law en-

---

211 World Congress (1996).
212 *The Economist* (1996b); Trueheart(1996).
213 Clayton (1996); Flores (1996).
214 US Department of Labor (1995: 11).

forcement.[215] Indeed, on-line child pornography is a major argument for establishing censorship of the Internet. It is easier to blame the messenger than to question the sources of the message; that is, to ask why our informational society engages in this activity on such a large scale. Major producers and distributors of child pornography (much of which concerns boys rather than girls) are legal firms located in permissive environments in high-technology societies, such as Japan, Denmark, Holland, and Sweden.[216]

Various analyses of the reasons for this staggering rise in a global industry of child sex (distinct from traditional sexual abuse of children throughout history) converge toward a set of factors. First is the globalization of markets for everything, and from everywhere to everywhere, whether it be organized sex tours or audiovisual distribution of pornographic material worldwide. Anonymity, guaranteed either by the electronic home or by exotic travel, helps break the barrier of fear for the masses of perverts who live among us. The escape into further transgression to find sexual excitement in a society of normalized sexuality (see volume II, chapter 4) fuels the demand for new emotions, particularly among affluent segments of bored professionals.

On the supply side, poverty and the crisis of the family provide the raw material. The link up between supply and demand is often made by the global criminal networks that control much prostitution throughout the world, and are always striving to find new, more profitable product lines and markets. Specifically, South-East Asian child prostitution networks buy children in the poorest rural areas of Thailand, Cambodia, the Philippines, and other countries, to feed their distribution networks in Asia, particularly targeting the international tourist hubs, and Japan, in cooperation with the *Yakuza*. Bangkok, Manila, and Osaka are internationally notorious places for child prostitution. In 1998, Honduras became a favorite destination for American pedophiles, conveniently informed of the contact addresses in Tegucigalpa via the Internet. Finally, as the 1996 World Congress document stated, media interest in child pornography and prostitution can unintentionally fuel demand, and the ease of access of information both opens up supply routes and increases demand.

Thus, the network society devours itself, as it consumes/destroys enough of its own children to lose the sense of continuity of life across generations, so denying the future of humans as a humane species.

215 World Congress (1996).
216 Healy (1996).

The killing of children: war massacres and child soldiers

There is still more to report in this negation of ourselves. At this turn of the millennium, in countries around the world, particularly (but not only, by any means) in the most devastated region, Africa, millions of children have been or are being killed by war. And tens of thousands of children have been or are being transformed into fighting/dying animals to feed the bloody, senseless, slow wars that haunt the planet. According to the 1996 UNICEF report on the *State of the World's Children*,[217] mainly devoted to the issue of the impact of war on children, during the past decade, as a direct effect of war, in this post-Cold War world, 2 million children were killed, between 4 and 5 million were disabled, over 1 million were orphaned or separated from their parents, 12 million were left homeless, and over 10 million were psychologically traumatized. The increasing proportion of children among the victims of war is due to the character of these new, forgotten wars, once the affluent world decided to live in peace (see volume I, chapter 7). As the UNICEF report states:

> Rather than being set-piece battles between contending armies, these are much more complex affairs – struggles between the military and civilians, or between contending groups of armed civilians. They are likely to be fought in villages and suburban streets as anywhere else. In this case, the enemy camp is all around, and distinctions between combatant and non combatant melt away in the suspicions and confrontations of daily strife.[218]

But children are also brought into these wars as soldiers, in growing numbers. Cohn and Goodwin Gill have researched this matter in depth.[219] They document the extent to which hundreds of thousands of children have been recruited into the regular armies of states (such as Iran or Bosnia), into rebel militia, and into gangs of bandits. In some instances, children were simply sent to die in the minefields. In other cases, as in Mozambique's RENAMO anti-government guerrillas, or in Cambodia's Khmer Rouge, they tortured children for a period to make them fierce warriors, albeit mentally damaged. In all cases, children join, or are forced to join, these courageous military leaders, out of a lack of alternatives. Poverty, displacement, separation from their families, ideological or religious manipulation, all play

217 Bellamy (1996).
218 Bellamy (1996: 14).
219 Cohn and Goodwin Gill (1994).

a role.[220] In some cases, such as among the rebels of Eastern Zaïre in 1996, children are made to believe that they have magic powers and cannot die. In others, the feeling of power, of instilling fear, of "becoming a man," or a warrior, are powerful drives to entice a child. In all cases, children seem to be ferocious fighters, ready to kill, willing to die, with little awareness of the actual borderline between war and play, life and death. With new weapons technology providing extraordinary fire power in light, portable arms, these armies of kids are capable of inflicting tremendous casualties. To each other. For those who survive, in the words of Cohn and Goodwin Gill, "children who have participated in hostilities are often marked for life, mentally, morally, and physically."[221]

Why children are wasted

So, what does informational capitalism have to do with this horror? Haven't children, after all, been abused, alas, throughout history? Yes and no. It is true that children have been historically victimized, often by their own families; that they have been submitted to physical, psychological, and sexual abuse by the powers that be in all historical periods; and that the rise of the industrial era also witnessed the massive use of child labor in mines and factories, often in conditions close to bondage. And, since children are people, the form in which societies have treated childhood inflicts lasting moral wounds on the human condition. But, I argue, there is something different in this beginning of the Information Age: there is a systemic link between the *current*, unchecked characteristics of informational capitalism and the destruction of lives in a large segment of the world's children.

What is different is that we are witnessing a dramatic reversal of social conquests and children's rights obtained by social reform in mature industrial societies in the wake of large-scale deregulation and the bypassing of governments by global networks. What is different is the disintegration of traditional societies throughout the world, exposing children to the unprotected lands of mega-cities' slums. What is different is children in Pakistan weaving carpets for worldwide export via networks of suppliers to large department stores in affluent markets. What is new is mass, global tourism organized around pedophilia. What is new is electronic child pornography on the net, worldwide. What is new is the disintegration of patriarchalism, without being replaced by a system of protection of children provided

220   Drogin (1995).
221   Cohn and Goodwin Gill (1994: 4).

either by new families or the state. And what is new is the weakening of institutions of support for children's rights, such as labor unions or the politics of social reform, to be replaced by moral admonitions to family values which often blame the victims for their plight. Furthermore, informational capitalism is not an entity. It is a specific social structure, with its rules and its dynamics, which, through the processes documented in this chapter, are systemically related to children's over-exploitation and abuse, unless deliberate policies and strategies counter these trends.

At the roots of children's exploitation are the mechanisms generating poverty and social exclusion throughout the world, from Sub-Saharan Africa to the United States of America. With children in poverty, and with entire countries, regions, and neighborhoods excluded from relevant circuits of wealth, power, and information, the crumbling of family structures breaks the last barrier of defense for children. In some countries, like Zaïre, Cambodia, or Venezuela, misery overwhelms families, in rural areas as in shanty towns, so that children are sold for survival, are sent to the streets to help out, or end up running away from the hell of their homes into the hell of their non-existence. In other societies, the historical crisis of patriarchalism brings down the traditional nuclear family without replacing it, making women and children pay for it. This is why almost 22 percent of American children live in poverty, the worst child poverty rate in the industrialized world. This is also why, according to the documented analyses of Rodgers and of Lerman, there is a close relationship between changing family structure and the increase in women and child poverty in the United States.[222] Whoever challenges patriarchalism does it at her risk. And at her children's risk. A 1996 report from the US Department of Health and Human Services estimated that child abuse and neglect in the United States doubled between 1986 and 1993, growing from 1.4 million children affected to over 2.8 million in 1993. The number of children who were seriously injured quadrupled from 143,000 to 570,000. Children from the lowest income families were 18 times more likely to be sexually abused, almost 56 times more likely to be educationally neglected, and 22 times more likely to be seriously injured from maltreatment. Meanwhile, the percentage of cases investigated sharply declined.[223]

The supply of children provided by this weakened family structure, and by this impoverished childhood, is met, on the demand side, by the processes of globalization, business networking, criminalization

---

222 Lerman (1996); Rodgers (1996).
223 Sedlak and Broadhurst (1996).

of a segment of the economy, and advanced communication technologies, to which I have specifically referred in the analyses presented above. To both sets of supply and demand factors, we must add, as sources of children's over-exploitation, exclusion, and destruction, the disintegration of states and societies, and the massive uprooting of populations by war, famine, epidemics, and banditry.

There is something else, in the fragmented culture of our societies, that helps, and even rationalizes, the wasting of children's lives. Among the children themselves there is the diffusion of what Pedrazzini and Sanchez, on the basis of their fieldwork in the streets of Caracas, have labeled "the culture of urgency."[224] This is the idea that there is no future, and no roots, only the present. And the present is made up of instants, of each instant. So, life has to be lived as if each instant were the last one, with no other reference than the explosive fulfillment of individualized hyperconsumption. This constant, fearless challenge to explore life beyond its present dereliction keeps destitute children going: for a little while, until facing utter destruction.

On the side of society at large, the crumbling of social institutions, behind the façade of repetitive formulas on the virtues of a traditional family that, by and large, has ceased to exist, leaves individuals, and particularly men, alone with their desires of transgression, with their power surges, with their endless search for consumption, characterized by an immediate gratification pattern. Why then not prey on the most defenseless members of society?

And on the side of the economy, when global markets of everything from everywhere to everywhere become possible, the ultimate commodification drive, the one affecting our own kind, does not seem to contradict the strictest rule of a sheer market logic as the only guide for relationships among people, bypassing values and institutions of society. I am certainly not proposing the notion that informational capitalism is made up of a mob of pimps and child abusers. Conservative, capitalist elites are certainly fond of family values, and major corporations fund and support child defense causes. However, there is a structural link between unrestricted market logic in a global, networked economy, empowered by advanced information technologies, and the phenomena I have described in this chapter. Indeed, it is frequent to find in the economic development field, experts' views accepting, and supporting, the spread of child labor, as a rational market response which, under certain conditions, will yield benefits to countries and families. The main reason why children are wasted is because, in the Information Age, social trends are extraordinarily

224   Pedrazzini and Sanchez (1996).

amplified by society's new technological/organizational capacity, while institutions of social control are bypassed by global networks of information and capital. And since we are all inhabited, at the same time, by humanity's angels and devils, whenever and wherever our dark side takes over it triggers the release of unprecedented, destructive power.

Conclusion: the Black Holes of Informational Capitalism

I have tried to show in this chapter the complex set of linkages between the characteristics of informational capitalism and the rise of inequality, social polarization, poverty, and misery in most of the world. Informationalism does create a sharp divide between valuable and non-valuable people and locales. Globalization proceeds selectively, including and excluding segments of economies and societies in and out of the networks of information, wealth, and power that characterize the new, dominant system. Individualization of work leaves workers to each one of themselves, to bargain their fate *vis-à-vis* constantly changing market forces. The crisis of the nation-state, and of the institutions of civil society constructed around it during the industrial era, undermines institutional capacity to correct social imbalances derived from unrestricted market logic. At the limit, as in some African or Latin American states, the state, emptied of representativeness, becomes a predator of its own people. New information technologies tool this global whirlwind of accumulation of wealth and diffusion of poverty.

But there is more than inequality and poverty in this process of social restructuring. There is also exclusion of people and territories which, from the perspective of dominant interests in global, informational capitalism, shift to a position of structural irrelevance. This widespread, multiform process of social exclusion leads to the constitution of what I call, taking the liberty of a cosmic metaphor, the *black holes of informational capitalism*. These are regions of society from which, statistically speaking, there is no escape from the pain and destruction inflicted on the human condition for those who, in one way or another, enter these social landscapes. This is unless there is a change in the laws that govern the universe of informational capitalism, since, unlike cosmic forces, purposive human action *can* change the rules of social structure, including those inducing social exclusion.

These black holes concentrate in their density all the destructive energy that affects humanity from multiple sources. How people, and locales, enter these black holes is less important than what happens

afterwards; that is, the reproduction of social exclusion, and the inflic-
tion of additional injuries to those who are already excluded. For instance, Timmer et al. have shown the diversity of paths toward
homelessness in American cities.[225] The homeless population of the
1990s was composed of a mixture of "old homeless," classic skid-
row types, or de-institutionalized mentally ill persons, and of newer
characters, such as "welfare moms," young families left behind by
deindustrialization and restructuring, tenants evicted by gentrification,
runaway teenagers, migrants without a home, and battered women,
escaping from men. Yet once they are in the street, the black hole of
homelessness, as a stigma, and as a world of violence and abuse, acts
upon the homeless indiscriminately, damning them to destitution if
their life goes on in the street for some time. For instance, Ida Susser
has shown the impact of shelters' regulations for the New York homeless on the separation of women from their children in a process that
often triggers the wasting of children, in the sense made explicit in the
preceding pages.[226]

In another instance, less often cited, functional illiteracy triggers
mechanisms of unemployability, poverty, and, ultimately, social exclusion in a society that increasingly relies on some minimum capacity
to decode language. This functional disability is much more widespread
in advanced societies than is generally acknowledged. Thus, in 1988,
a national literacy survey by the US Education Department found that
21–23 percent of a representative national sample – therefore, about
40–44 million adults in America – had blatantly insufficient levels of
reading and writing in English, as well as of elementary arithmetic.
Two-thirds of them had never completed secondary education. One-
quarter of them comprised immigrants in the process of learning English, which still leaves over 30 million native Americans functionally
illiterate. An additional 25–28 percent demonstrated abilities of what
the study called level 2, a very narrow level of understanding that
included an ability to receive written instructions, but did not extend
to abilities such as writing a letter to explain an error in a credit card
statement, or to plan meetings by using bus or flight schedules. Functional illiteracy is a fundamental obstacle to integration in the formal
labor market, at whatever level, and it is strongly correlated with low-
wage employment and poverty: nearly half of the lowest level in the
literacy scale were living in poverty. Likewise, the majority of the prison
population in the US is functionally illiterate.[227] Drug addiction, men-

225   Timmer et al. (1994).
226   Susser (1991, 1993, 1996).
227   Kirsch et al. (1993); Newman et al. (1993).

tal illness, delinquency, incarceration, and illegality are also avenues toward specific conditions of dereliction, increasing the likelihood of irreversibly stumbling away from the socially sanctioned right to live. They all have one attribute in common: poverty, from which they originate or to where they lead.

These black holes often communicate with each other, while being *socially/culturally* out of communication with the universe of mainstream society. They are, however, economically connected to some specific markets (for example, through the criminal economy of drugs and prostitution), and bureaucratically related to the state (to the agencies set up for their containment, such as police and welfare). Drugs, illness (for example, AIDS), crime, prostitution, and violence are part of the same networks, each feature reinforcing the others (as in contracting HIV from sharing needles among drug addicts and/or through prostituted sex).[228]

Social exclusion is often expressed in spatial terms. The territorial confinement of systemically worthless populations, disconnected from networks of valuable functions and people, is indeed a major characteristic of the spatial logic of the network society, as I argued in volume I, chapter 6. In this chapter, I have documented the spatial logic of social exclusion with an overview of the marginalization of Sub-Saharan Africa, and with reference to American inner-city ghettos. But there are many other instances of such a territorially shaped exclusion in the uneven geography of informational capitalism. Not the least striking is the fate of most Pacific islands, tropical paradises living in abject poverty and experiencing social disintegration induced by tourism, in the midst of a Pacific region transformed in the powerhouse of global capitalism.[229] Likewise, why people enter black holes, why and how territories become excluded or included, is dependent on specific events that "lock in" trajectories of marginality. It may be a rapacious dictator, as in Zaïre; or a police decision to abandon certain neighborhoods to drug traffickers; or "red lining" from housing lenders; or the exhaustion of mines or the devaluation of agricultural products on which a region was making a living. Whatever the reason, for these territories, and for the people trapped in them, a downward spiral of poverty, then dereliction, finally irrelevance, operates until or unless a countervailing force, including people's revolt against their condition, reverses the trend.

At this turn of the millennium, what used to be called the Second World (the statist universe) has disintegrated, incapable of mastering

228 Susser (1996).
229 Wallace (1995).

the forces of the Information Age. At the same time, the Third World has disappeared as a relevant entity, emptied of its geopolitical meaning, and extraordinarily diversified in its economic and social development. Yet, the First World has not become the all-embracing universe of neo-liberal mythology. Because a new world, the Fourth World, has emerged, made up of multiple black holes of social exclusion throughout the planet. The Fourth World comprises large areas of the globe, such as much of Sub-Saharan Africa, and impoverished rural areas of Latin America and Asia. But it is also present in literally every country, and every city, in this new geography of social exclusion. It is formed of American inner-city ghettos, Spanish enclaves of mass youth unemployment, French banlieues warehousing North Africans, Japanese Yoseba quarters, and Asian mega-cities' shanty towns. And it is populated by millions of homeless, incarcerated, prostituted, criminalized, brutalized, stigmatized, sick, and illiterate persons. They are the majority in some areas, the minority in others, and a tiny minority in a few privileged contexts. But, everywhere, they are growing in number, and increasing in visibility, as the selective triage of informational capitalism, and the political breakdown of the welfare state, intensify social exclusion. In the current historical context, the rise of the Fourth World is inseparable from the rise of informational global capitalism.

3

The Perverse Connection: the Global Criminal Economy

During the last few years, the international community has experienced an increasing number of political upheavals, geopolitical changes and technological restructuring. No doubt, organized transnational crime, a new dimension of more "traditional" forms of organized crime, has emerged as one of the most alarming of these challenges. Organized transnational crime, with the capacity to expand its activities and to target the security and the economies of countries, in particular developing ones and those in transition, represents one of the major threats that governments have to deal with in order to ensure their stability, the safety of their people, the preservation of the whole fabric of society, and the viability and further development of their economies.

United Nations, Economic and Social Council, 1994, p. 3

International criminal organizations have reached agreements and understanding to divide up geographical areas, develop new market strategies, work out forms of mutual assistance and the settlement of conflicts ... and this on a planetary level. We are faced with a genuine criminal counter-power, capable of imposing its will on legitimate states, of undermining institutions and forces of law and order, of upsetting delicate economic and financial equilibrium and destroying democratic life.

Anti-Mafia Commission of the Italian Parliament[1]

Crime is as old as humankind. Indeed, in the biblical account of our origins, our plight began with the illegal traffic of apples. But global

---

1   Report of the Anti-Mafia Commission of the Italian Parliament to the United Nations Assembly, March 20, 1990, cited by Sterling (1994: 66).

crime, the networking of powerful criminal organizations, and their associates, in shared activities throughout the planet, is a new phenomenon that profoundly affects international and national economies, politics, security, and, ultimately, societies at large. The Sicilian *Cosa Nostra* (and its associates, *La Camorra*, *Ndrangheta*, and *Sacra Corona Unita*), the American Mafia, the Colombian cartels, the Mexican cartels, the Nigerian criminal networks, the Japanese *Yakuza*, the Chinese Triads, the constellation of Russian *Mafiyas*, the Turkish heroin traffickers, the Jamaican Posses, and a myriad of regional and local criminal groupings in all countries, have come together in a global, diversified network, that permeates boundaries and links up ventures of all sorts. While drugs traffic is the most important segment of this worldwide industry, arms deals also represent a high-value market. In addition, is everything that receives added value precisely from its prohibition in a given institutional environment: smuggling of everything from everywhere to everywhere, including radioactive material, human organs, and illegal immigrants; prostitution; gambling; loan-sharking; kidnapping; racketeering and extortion; counterfeiting of goods, bank notes, financial documents, credit cards, and identity cards; killers for hire; traffic of sensitive information, technology, or art objects; international sales of stolen goods; or even dumping garbage illegally from one country into another (for example, US garbage smuggled into China in 1996). Extortion is also practiced on an international scale; for instance, by the *Yakuza* on Japanese corporations abroad. At the heart of the system, there is money laundering by the hundreds of billions (maybe trillions) of dollars. Complex financial schemes and international trade networks link up the criminal economy to the formal economy, thus deeply penetrating financial markets, and constituting a critical, volatile element in a fragile global economy. The economies *and politics* of many countries (such as Italy, Russia, the former Soviet Union republics, Colombia, Mexico, Bolivia, Peru, Ecuador, Paraguay, Panama, Venezuela, Turkey, Afghanistan, Burma, Thailand, but also Japan (see chapter 4), Taiwan, Hong Kong, and a multiplicity of small countries which include Luxembourg and Austria) cannot be understood without considering the dynamics of criminal networks present in their daily workings. The flexible connection of these criminal activities in international networks constitutes an essential feature of the new global economy, and of the social/political dynamics of the Information Age. There is general acknowledgment of the importance and reality of this phenomenon, and a wealth of evidence, mainly from well-documented journalists' reports, and the conferences of international organizations.[2] Yet, the phenomenon is largely ignored by social scientists, when it comes to understanding economies and societies, with the arguments that the data are not truly reliable, and that sensationalism taints interpretation. I take exception to these views. If a phenomenon is acknowledged as a fundamental dimension of our societies, indeed of the new, globalized system, we must use whatever evidence is available to explore the connection between these criminal activities and societies and economies at large.

Organizational Globalization of Crime, Cultural Identification of Criminals[3]

In the past two decades, criminal organizations have increasingly set up their operations transnationally, taking advantage of economic globalization and new communication and transportation technologies. Their strategy is to base their management and production functions in low-risk areas, where they have relative control of the institutional environment, while targeting as preferential markets those areas with the most affluent demand, so that higher prices can be charged. This is clearly the case for the drug cartels, whether it is cocaine in Colombia and the Andean region, or opium/heroin from the South-East Asian Golden Triangle, or from Afghanistan and Central Asia. But it is also

2   The most authoritative, international source on global crime is the documentation assembled by the Economic and Social Council of the United Nations on the occasion of the World Ministerial Conference on Organized Transnational Crime held in Naples November 21–23, 1994. I have used these materials extensively and wish to thank the people who provided them for me: Dr Gopinath, Director of the International Institute for Labour Studies of the ILO, in Geneva, and Mr Vetere, Chief of the Crime Prevention and Criminal Justice Branch of the United Nations, in Vienna. An excellent, documented overview of the expansion of global crime can be found in Sterling (1994). Although Sterling's work has been criticized for its sensationalism, I am not aware that the facts she reports, always backed by investigative reporting, and personal interviews, have been challenged. See also Martin and Romano (1992); Gootenberg (1999); and, although it is a bit old, Kelly (1986).
3   The source for data presented in this section, when not specifically cited, is the Background Report of the 1994 United Nations Conference on Organized Transnational Crime, given as United Nations, Economic and Social Council (UN-ESC), (1994). On the impact of organized crime in Europe, besides Sterling's (1994) perceptive analysis, see Roth and Frey (1995). On the Italian Mafia, see Colombo (1990); Santino and La Fiura (1990); Catanzaro (1991); Calvi (1992); Savona (1993); Tranfaglia (1992) and Arlacchi (1995). On the recent transformation of American Mafia, see Potter (1994), and, again, Sterling (1994). On the impact of global crime on American crime, see Kleinknecht (1996). On the Chinese Triads, see Booth (1991); Murray (1994); Chu (1996). On heroin traffic in/from the Burmese/Thai Golden Triangle, see Renard (1996). On the Japanese *Yakuza*, see Kaplan and Dubro (1986), and Seymour (1996). On Africa, see Fottorino (1991). On Russia and Latin America, see below. In addition, I have used a number of sources from press reports, published in America, Europe, and Russia, collected and analyzed by Emma Kiselyova. Sources for specific information used in this section are cited in the footnotes.

the essential mechanism in weapons trade or traffic in radioactive material. Using their relative impunity in Russia and the former Soviet Union republics during the transition period, criminal networks, both Russian/ex-Soviet and from all around the world, took control of a significant amount of military and nuclear supplies to be offered to the highest bidder in the chaotic post-Cold War international scene. This internationalization of criminal activities induces organized crime from different countries to establish strategic alliances to cooperate, rather than fight, on each other's turf, through subcontracting arrangements, and joint ventures, whose business practice closely follows the organizational logic of what I identified as "the network enterprise," characteristic of the Information Age (volume I, chapter 3). Furthermore, the bulk of the proceedings of these activities are by definition globalized through their laundering via global financial markets.

Estimates of profits and financial flows originating in the criminal economy vary wildly and are not fully reliable. Yet they are indicative of the staggering size of the phenomenon we are describing. The 1994 United Nations Conference on Global Organized Crime estimated that global trade in drugs amounted to about US$500 billion a year; that is, it was larger than the global trade in oil.[4] Overall profits from all kinds of activities were put as high as US$750 billion a year.[5] Other estimates mention the figure of US$1 trillion a year in 1993, which was about the same size as the US federal budget at that time.[6] Sterling considers plausible the figure of US$500 billion as the likely global turnover of "narcodollars."[7] In 1999, the IMF ventured a very broad estimate of global money laundering in a range between 500 billion and 1.5 trillion dollars a year (or 5 percent of global GDP).[8] A substantial proportion of profits is laundered (with a commission for the launderers of between 15 and 25 percent of nominal dollars price), and about half of the laundered money, at least in the case of the Sicilian Mafia, is reinvested in legitimate activities.[9] This continuity between profits from criminal activities and their investment in legitimate activities makes it impossible to limit the economic impact of global crime to the former, since the latter play a major role in ensuring, and covering up, the overall dynamics of the system. Furthermore, enforcement of deals also combines the skillful manipulation of

4   UN-ESC (1994).
5   UN sources, reported by Cowell, (1994).
6   Washington-based National Strategy Information Center, reported by *Newsweek*, December 13, 1993.
7   Sterling (1994).
8   *The Economist* (1999a: 17).
9   Sterling (1994: 30).

legal procedures and financial systems in each country and internationally, with the selective use of violence, and widespread corruption of government officials, bankers, bureaucrats, and law-enforcement personnel.

At the sources of global crime, there are nationally, regionally, and ethnically rooted organizations, most of them with a long history, linked to the culture of specific countries and regions, with their ideology, their codes of honor, and their bonding mechanisms. These culturally based criminal organizations do not disappear in the new, global networks. On the contrary, their global networking allows traditional criminal organizations to survive, and prosper, by escaping the controls of a given state at a difficult time. Thus, the American Mafia, after considerably suffering from devastating strikes from the FBI in the 1980s, was revived in the 1990s by an influx of Sicilian Mafia, and by alliances with the Chinese Triads, the Russian *Mafiyas*, and a variety of ethnic mobs.[10]

The Sicilian Mafia is still one of the most powerful criminal organizations in the world, using its historical control over the South of Italy, and its deep penetration of the Italian state. Its links with the Italian Christian Democratic Party allowed the Mafia to extend its presence to the entire country, to link up with the banking system, and, through it, with the entire political and business elite of the country, even coming very close to the Vatican through the Banco Ambrosiano which appears to have been under Mafia influence. In 1987, an agreement between the Sicilian Mafia and the Medellin cartel opened the way to swap heroin from Asia/Europe for cocaine from Colombia. Thus, the Colombians could enter the heroin market in the United States, shared until then between the Sicilian and American Mafias and the Chinese Triads. While using the Sicilian infrastructure, Colombian cartels could distribute their cocaine in Europe, paying a share to the Sicilians.[11] This was only the best documented of a series of international moves by the Sicilian Mafia, which included the deep penetration of Germany's criminal markets, and major speculative takeovers of Soviet property and currency during the transition period (see below).

When the Italian state tried to regain its autonomy by confronting the Mafia, once the grip of the Christian Democrats and other traditional parties over the country was shaken in the early 1990s, the Mafia's reaction reached unprecedented brutality, including the killing of some leading figures in the anti-crime operations in Italy, most notably Judges Falcone and Borsalino. Popular reaction, exposure in

10   Kleinknecht (1996).
11   Sterling (1994).

the media, and the partial crumbling of corrupt Italian politics weakened considerably the power of the Mafia in Italy itself, with the capture and imprisonment of its bloody *capo di tutti capi* Toto Riina. Yet the increased internationalization of Mafia activities in the 1990s allowed a new round of prosperity for its members, even if they had to relinquish some (but not most) of their control over local societies and government institutions in Italy.

In this internationalization process, the Italian Mafia coincides with the Chinese Triads, currently one of the largest and best articulated networks of criminal organization in the world, numbering, in Hong Kong alone, some 160,000 members, divided between the 14k, the Sun Yee On, and the Wo Group. Another powerful network, the United Bamboo, is based in Taiwan. Like the Italian and American Mafias, the Triads are also rooted in history and ethnicity. They originated in southern China in the sixteenth century as a resistance movement against the Manchu invaders of the Qing dynasty. They fled China after the Communist revolution, and expanded throughout the world, particularly in the United States. The loss of their Hong Kong base in 1997 was anticipated ten years earlier with a large-scale movement toward internationalization, and diversification, using primarily Chinese illegal immigrants to the United States, Europe, and Canada, often smuggled into the country by the Triads, and in some cases kept under their control. The Place d'Italie in Paris, and San Francisco's old (around Grant Street) and new (around Clemens Street) Chinatowns, witness the proliferation of Chinese businesses some of which may serve as support, and money-laundering devices, to a wide array of criminal activities, the most prominent of which continues to be the traffic of heroin from the Golden Triangle, historically controlled by drug lords' armies, originally members of Chiang Kai-shek's military, and supported by the CIA during the Cold War.[12]

The Japanese *Yakuza* (the *Boryokudan*, that is "the violent ones") has a quasi-legal existence in Japan, and is openly present in a wide array of businesses and political activities (usually ultra-nationalistic political associations). The most important gangs are *Yamagachi-gumi*, with 26,000 members in 944 networked gangs; *Inagawa-kai*, with 8,600 members; and *Sumiyoshi-kai*, with over 7,000 members. They also originated in the protection networks created by disaffected *samurai* among the poor population of cities in the early stages of Japanese urbanization in the nineteenth century. As with the other organizations, protection turned into preying on their own members. For a long time, the Japanese *Yakuza* felt so secure at home that its interna-

12   Renard (1996).

tional activities were limited to smuggling weapons from the US into Japan, and to providing women sex slaves from other Asian countries to Japanese brothels and night clubs. Yet, they followed the globalization of Japanese corporations, and went into exporting to the United States their customary practice of blackmail and the extortion of corporations, intimidating Japanese executives abroad by sending in their *Sokaiya* (violent *provocateurs*). They also imitated Japanese firms by investing heavily in real estate, particularly in America, and by manipulating stocks in financial markets. To operate in the United States and Europe, they made a number of deals with the Sicilian and American Mafias, as well as with various Russian criminal groups.

The dramatic expansion of several Russian criminal networks has made headline news throughout the world since the early 1990s. Although some leaders of this underworld relate to the old Russian tradition of *vorovskoi mir* ("thieves' community" or "thieves' world"), organized crime in contemporary Russia and the ex-Soviet republics is the result of the chaotic, uncontrolled transition from statism to wild capitalism. Members of the Soviet *nomenklatura*, exceedingly entrepreneurial "capitalists" aspiring to become "end of millennium robber barons," and a myriad of ethnic mobs (with the Chechens as the most brutal and villified), constituted criminal networks in the wasteland created by the collapse of the Soviet Union. From there, they expanded throughout the world, linking up with organized crime everywhere, converging or competing, sharing profits with or killing each other, depending upon circumstances.[13]

Emerging from drug traffic in Latin America, the Medellin and Cali cartels in Colombia, the Tamaulipas, Tijuana, and Ciudad Juarez cartels in Mexico, and similar groups in almost every Latin American country, organized a network of production, management, and distribution activities that linked up agricultural production areas, chemical laboratories, storage facilities, and transportation systems for export to affluent markets. These cartels focused almost exclusively on drug traffic, originally cocaine, but later they added marijuana, heroin, and

13 In one of the most striking cases of linkages between internationalized Russian crime and Latin American drug traffickers, in March 1997 the US Drug Enforcement Administration in Miami arrested Ludwig Fainberg, a Russian immigrant, and Juan Almeida and Nelson Yester, two Cubans considered to be middlemen for Colombian drug cartels. According to the DEA, Fainberg, owner of a strip bar near Miami Airport, was negotiating the sale of a Soviet submarine, complete with its crew, headed by a former admiral of the Soviet navy, to smuggle cocaine into ports along the West Coast of the United States. In fact, these partners had already done business together in 1992, when two Russian helicopters were sold to the cartels. Fainberg, a former dentist in the Soviet Union, was also organizing shipments of cocaine into Russia, and designing new methods of drug transportation to be operated jointly by Russian and Colombian criminal organizations (see Adams, 1997; Navarro, 1997).

chemical drugs. They set up their enforcement units, and their autonomous money-laundering schemes. They also favored penetration of the police, the army, judicial and political systems, in a vast network of influence and corruption that changed Latin American politics, and will exercise its influence for years to come. By their very essence, these cartels (actually made up of a coordinated network of smaller producers, under the control of cartel leaders through violence, finance, and distribution capability) were internationalized from the outset. They aimed essentially at exports to the United States, later to Europe, then to the whole world. Their strategies were, in fact, a peculiar adaptation of IMF-inspired export-oriented, growth policies toward the actual ability of some Latin American regions to compete in the high-technology environment of the new global economy. They linked up with national/local crime organizations in America and Europe to distribute their merchandise. And they set up a vast financial and commercial empire of money-laundering operations that, more than any other criminal organization, deeply penetrated the global financial system. Colombian and Latin American drug traffickers, as their Sicilian, Chinese, Japanese, or Russian counterparts, are also deeply rooted in their national, cultural identity. Pablo Escobar, the leader of the Medellin cartel made famous his slogan: "I prefer a tomb in Colombia than a prison in the United States." He succeeded in fulfilling his wish. His attitude, and similar attitudes among Latin America's drug kingpins reflect an obvious opportunism, since they are confident of their relative control over judges, police, and the penal system in their own countries. But there is undoubtedly something else, a more specific cultural component in their stand against the United States, and in their attachment to their regions and nations, a theme on which I will elaborate below.

The nationally and ethnically based criminal organizations that I have cited are the most notorious, but they are not, by any means, the only ones in the global scene. Turkish organized crime (enjoying significant influence in Turkey's politics and law-enforcement agencies) is a major player in the traditional Balkan route that brings heroin into Europe, a route now used for all kinds of additional traffic. In the late 1990s the Albanian mafias asserted themselves as the dominant force in the traffic of illegal immigrants to Italy. They also played a definite geopolitical role in the Balkans, as they actively participated in financing and arming the Kosovo Liberation Army in 1998–9. Diversified Nigerian criminal networks have become a force to reckon with, not only in Nigeria and in Africa (where they subcontract their knowledge of the field to international cartels), but in the world arena, where they excel, for instance, in credit-card fraud. In every country, and in every region, gangs, and networks of gangs, are now aware of their chances of linking up with broader chains of activities in this underworld that has a dominant presence in many neighborhoods, cities, and regions and that has even been able to buy most of the assets of some small countries, such as the island nation of Aruba, off the Venezuelan coast.

From these local, national, and ethnic bases, rooted in identity, and relying on interpersonal relationships of trust/distrust (naturally enforced with machine guns), criminal organizations engage in a wide range of activities. Drug traffic is the paramount business, to the point that the legalization of drugs is probably the greatest threat that organized crime would have to confront. But they can rely on the political blindness, and misplaced morality, of societies that do not come to terms with the bottom line of the problem: demand drives supply. The source of drug addiction, and therefore of most crimes in the world, lies in the psychological injuries inflicted on people by everyday life in our societies. Therefore, there will be mass consumption of drugs, for the foreseeable future, regardless of repression. And global organized crime will find ways to supply this demand, making it a most profitable business, and the mother of most other crimes.

Yet, besides drug trafficking, the criminal economy has expanded its realm to an extraordinary diversity of operations, making it an increasingly diversified, and interconnected, global industry. The 1994 United Nations Conference on Transnational Crime listed the main activities in which this kind of organized crime is engaged, *in addition to drug traffic*:

(1)   *Weapons trafficking*   This is, of course, a multi-billion dollar business whose boundaries with the legal export of arms are not easy to determine. The critical matter in the business is the identity of the end-user, barred by international agreements or geopolitical considerations from receiving certain types of weapons. In some cases, these are states under an international embargo (such as Iran, Iraq, Libya, Bosnia, or Serbia). In other instances, they are guerrilla groups, or parties involved in a civil war. Still others are terrorist groups, and criminal organizations. The United States and the Soviet Union created the main supply of war weaponry in the world by providing it generously to various warring parties to influence them in their geopolitical games. After the end of the Cold War, weapons were left in often unreliable hands, which used their stocks to feed the market. Other deals originate in semi-legal exports from arms-producing countries, such as France, the UK, China, the Czech Republic, Spain, or Israel. For instance, in May 1996, 2,000 AK-47 assault rifles, illegally

imported from China, were seized in San Francisco in a sting operation, with a representative of China's main government-owned arms
company being involved in the transaction.[14] According to the UN
report: "Whoever the end user may be, however, black market arms
deals have three characteristics: they are a covert activity, a large part
of the cost is related to the surreptitious nature of the transaction, and
the return flow of money is laundered."[15]

(2) *Trafficking of nuclear material* This involves the smuggling
of nuclear weapons grade material, for eventual use in building these
weapons and/or blackmailing by threatening their use. The disintegration of the Soviet Union provided a major opportunity for supplying
this kind of material. Germany has been, in the 1990s, at the forefront
of this kind of traffic, as criminal networks from the former Warsaw
Pact countries have been smuggling nuclear material on behalf of international agents, sometimes in reckless ways, including carrying extremely radioactive items in the pockets of the smuggler.[16] According
to the public testimony by Hans-Ludwig Zachert, President of the German Federal Police, in 1992 there were 158 cases of illicit trade in
radioactive material; and, in 1993, 241 cases. In these two years there
was a total of 39 seizures, and in 1993 545 suspects were identified,
53 percent of whom were Germans, with the others being predominantly Czech, Polish, and Russian.[17] But the trade, while being supplied mainly from Eastern Europe, is international: on August 10, 1994,
German police seized 350 grams of enriched plutonium, and arrested
one Colombian and two Spaniards, although, in this case, reportedly,
the deal was a set-up by the German Intelligence Service.[18] Other seizures of nuclear material took place in Budapest and Prague. Experts
believe that Chinese nuclear stocks are also leaking some material into
criminal trade.[19] At the source of this traffic, however, lies the catastrophic situation in Russia's nuclear weapons industry. It employs
about 100,000 workers, who, in 1994, were paid (when they were
paid at all) salaries of US$113 a month, on average. They resorted to
strikes several times to call attention to their plight. In 1996, the director of the leading nuclear research institute related to the military nuclear complex in Russia committed suicide, out of despair. Under these
circumstances, the temptation is too great for at least a few of these
tens of thousands of workers, given the fact that the potential black-

14   *Time*, June 3, 1996.
15   UN-ESC (1994: 18).
16   Sterling (1994).
17   UN-ESC (1994: 18).
18   *Der Spiegel*, April, 4, 1995.
19   *Time*, August 1, 1994.

market price of a bomb-size amount of plutonium is in the range of hundreds of millions of dollars. Furthermore, the security conditions under which the dismantlement of Soviet bases outside Russia was conducted were very lax: in 1995, the Estonian government admitted that there had been a theft of radioactive material at the Padilski nuclear base.[20] In the Russian far east ports, radioactive wastes from nuclear submarines are piling up without proper storage facilities, not only representing a serious hazard, but inviting easy smuggling across a loosely guarded Eastern border.[21] The UN-ESC 1994 report concludes on this matter:

> It is clear that this trade has considerable potential for extortion, as well as for significant environmental damage, if only as a result of improper handling of the materials . . . The fact that nuclear materials are often procured from government-controlled organizations in the Russian Federation suggests the involvement of criminal organizations seeking profit. If they cannot obtain these profits in one way [by selling to a client], then it is only a small step to attempting to obtain them through some kind of nuclear blackmail. As nuclear disarmament continues, the availability of material is likely to increase rather than decrease.[22]

(3) *Smuggling of illegal immigrants* The combination of misery around the world, displacement of populations, and dynamism in the core economies pushes millions of people to emigrate. On the other hand, increased border controls, particularly in the affluent societies, try to stem the immigration flow. These contradictory trends provide an exceptional opportunity to criminal organizations to tap into an immense market: "coyote" traffic on a global scale.[23] The 1994 United Nations report cites reliable estimates that put the volume of illegal immigrant traffic from poor to richer countries at about one million people per year, about 20 percent of them being Chinese. This hardly accounts for about 700,000 undocumented immigrants who arrive every year in the United States by different means. In the late 1990s, in the European Union, illegal immigration increased to about 500,000 per year (see figure 3.1), and the Eastern European mafias were major players in organizing some of this traffic.[24] Thus, the actual number of illegal immigrants in the world must be much higher than the UN estimates. Criminally controlled illegal immigration is not only a source of profit from the payments of the would-be immigrants (for instance,

20 *Baltic Observer*, March 30–April 5, 1995.
21 *San Francisco Chronicle*, December 18, 1996.
22 UN-ESC (1994: 19).
23 "Coyote" is the nickname for smugglers of immigrants between Mexico and the US.
24 *The Economist* (1999b: 26–8).

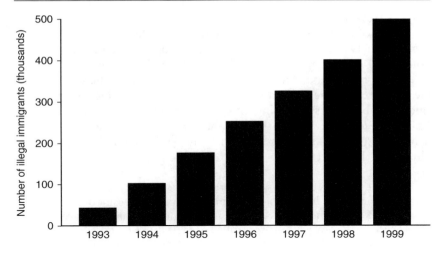

Figure 3.1 Illegal immigrants entering the European Union, 1993–9 (estimates)
Source: International Centre for Migration Policy Development, elaborated by *The Economist* (1999b: 26)

an estimated US$3.5 billion a year in Mexico and the Caribbean alone). It also keeps many of them in bondage for a long time to repay their debt with a high interest. It exposes them, as well, to fraud, abuse, violence, and death. Furthermore, by threatening to overwhelm channels of lawful immigration, it triggers a xenophobic backlash which, manipulated by demagogic politicians, is destroying cultural tolerance and feelings of solidarity in most countries.

(4) *Trafficking in women and children*   Global tourism has become closely linked with a global prostitution industry, particularly active in Asia, where it is often under the control of the Triads and the *Yakuza*. But it is also present in Europe, for instance in Italy, where Albanian mafias organized,in the late 1990s, a vast network of prostitution by trafficking in enslaved immigrant women, many of them from Albania, others from Eastern Europe and the Middle East. This illegal traffic of human beings increasingly affects children as well (see chapter 2). In addition to child abuse and exploitation, there is also a growing industry in child adoption, particularly in Latin America, with destination to the United States. In 1994, Central American babies were being sold for 20,000 dollars to adoption rings, in most cases (but not always) with their parents' consent. It is believed that this traffic has grown into a multi-million dollar business.

(5) *Trafficking in body parts*   According to the United Nations 1994 report, there have been confirmed reports of such trafficking in Argentina, Brazil, Honduras, Mexico, and Peru, largely with destination to German, Swiss, and Italian buyers. In Argentina, there have been examples of the removal of corneas of patients who were declared brain dead after fabricated brain scans. The problem seems to be serious in Russia, mainly because of thousands of unclaimed bodies in the morgues: it was reported in 1993 that one company in Moscow had extracted 700 major organs, kidneys, hearts and lungs, over 1,400 liver sections, 18,000 thymus organs, 2,000 eyes, and over 3,000 pairs of testicles, all destined for transplant to high-paying clients.[25] In 1999, the Russian press reported several cases in St Petersburg of killings suspected to be related to organs traffic. Also in 1999, the Japanese press reported cases of loan sharks demanding organs as repayment of overdue debts. The international conference on Commerce in Organs: Culture, Politics, and Bioethics of the Global Market, held at the University of California, Berkeley, on April 26–28, 1996, with the participation of leading academics and professionals from around the world, confirmed the importance of this expanding market. It also emphasized the thin line between criminal traffic and government-inspired trade. For instance, according to reports presented at this conference, the Chinese government seems to have routinely authorized the sale of body parts from people who have been executed, several hundreds of them every year, with the proceedings going, legally, into state coffers. Traffic seems to be particularly important in India and in Egypt, with destination to wealthy Middle Eastern patients. Most of these organs are voluntarily sold by people, either alive (one kidney, one eye), or by their families once they are dead. Yet, because of national and international legislation, the traffic is indeed illegal, and handled by smuggling networks, whose ultimate clients are, naturally, leading hospitals around the world. This is one of the links between global poverty and high technology. In November 1999, academics and human rights defenders met again in Berkeley, and established a permanent institution, "Organs Watch," to document, publicize, and eventually curtail cases of human organs traffic.

(6) *Money laundering*   The whole criminal system only makes business sense if the profits generated can be used and reinvested in the legal economy. This has become increasingly complicated given the staggering volume of these profits. This is why money laundering is the matrix of global crime, and its most direct connecting point to

25   *The Times*, November 18, 1993.

global capitalism. Money laundering[26] involves three stages. The first, and most delicate, requires the placement of cash into the financial system through banks or other financial institutions. In some instances, banks are located in countries with little control. Panama, Aruba, the Cayman Islands, the Bahamas, St Maertens, Vanuatu, but also Luxembourg and Austria (although in these two countries things are changing lately) are often cited in police reports as key entry points for dirty money into the financial system. In the leading economies, however, cash transactions over a certain sum (10,000 dollars in the US) must be reported. Thus, deposits operate through a large number of $9,999 (or less) transactions, a process called "smurfing." The second stage is "layering"; that is, separating funds from their source to avoid detection by future audits. What is critical here is the globalization of financial markets, and the availability of electronic transfer funds in seconds. Together with currency swaps, investments in different stocks, and use of some of this "dirty money" as collateral for loans from legitimate funds, the speed and diversity of transactions makes it extremely difficult to detect the origin of these funds. Evidence of this difficulty is the very small amount of funds seized in the main capitalist countries.[27] The third stage is "integration"; that is, the introduction of laundered capital into the legal economy, usually in real estate or stocks, and generally using the weakest entry points of the legal economy, in countries with no or little anti-money-laundering legislation. After this integration, criminally-generated profits join the whirlwind of global financial flows.[28]

The key to the success and expansion of global crime in the 1990s is the flexibility and versatility of their organization. *Networking is their form of operation*, both internally, in each criminal organization (for example, the Sicilian Mafia, the Cali cartel), and in relation to other criminal organizations. Distribution networks operate on the basis of autonomous local gangs, to which they supply goods and services, and from which they receive cash. Each major criminal organization has its own means of enforcing deals. Ruthless violence (including intimidation, torture, kidnapping of family members, killings) are, of course, part of the routine, often subcontracted to contract killers. But more important is the "security apparatus" of organized crime, the

26   The origin of the term "money laundering" comes from 1920s' Chicago, when one financier from the local Mafia bought a few automatic laundries where services could be paid for only in cash. Every evening, prior to declaring his daily earnings for tax purposes, he would add some "dirty" money to his "laundered" money (reported by *Literaturnaya Gazeta*, July 12, 1994).
27   Sterling (1994).
28   De Feo and Savona (1994).

network of law-enforcement agents, judges, and politicians, who are on the payroll. Once they enter this system, they are captive for life. While judicial tactics of plea bargains and crime witness-protection schemes have helped the repression of organized crime, particularly in America and Italy, the increasing ability of criminal leaders to find safe havens, and the global reach of killers-for-hire, are considerably limiting the effectiveness of the classic repression methods of 1950s' America and 1980s' Italy.

This need to escape police repression based on nation-states makes *strategic alliances between criminal networks* essential in their new mode of operation. No one organization can by itself link up throughout the globe. Moreover, it cannot extend its international reach without entering the traditional territory of another criminal power. This is why, in strictly business logic, criminal organizations respect each other, and find points of convergence across national boundaries and turfs. Most of the killings are intranational: Russians killing Russians, Sicilians killing Sicilians, the Medellin cartel and the Cali cartel members killing each other, precisely to control their local/national base from which they can operate comfortably. It is this combination of flexible networking between local turfs, rooted in tradition and identity, in a favorable institutional environment, and the global reach provided by strategic alliances, that explains the organizational strength of global crime. It makes it a fundamental actor in the economy and society of the Information Age. Nowhere is this global strategic role more evident than in the pillage of Russia during, and in the aftermath of, the transition from Soviet statism to wild proto-capitalism.

The Pillage of Russia[29]

Where does the mafia take its source from? This is simple, it begins with the common interests of politicians, business people, and gangsters. All others are hostages of this unholy alliance – all others means us.
Pavel Voshchanov, *Komsomolskaya Pravda*, p. 13

29 This section is based on various sources. First, an analysis of press reports, both from Russian and Western sources, carried out by Emma Kiselyova. I have not considered it necessary to cite all these reports, since they are public knowledge. Secondly, the fieldwork research I conducted in Russia in 1989–96, as referred to and presented in chapter 1 of this volume, and in chapter 2 of volume 1. Although my research was not directly concerned with organized crime, I constantly found its traces among the processes of economic and political change that I tried to investigate. Thirdly, I have used a few important books and articles on the subject. The best account in English of Russian organized crime is Handelman (1995). Sterling (1994) has some powerful sections on Russia in her book on global crime. Voshchanov (1995) and Goldman (1996) articulate compelling arguments on the interpretation of the sources of criminalization of the Russian economy.

The chaotic transition of the Soviet Union to the market economy created the conditions for the widespread penetration of business activities in Russia and the other republics by organized crime. It also induced the proliferation of criminal activities originating in and from Russia, and the ex-Soviet Union, such as the illegal traffic of weapons, nuclear materials, rare metals, oil, natural resources, and currency. International criminal organizations linked up with hundreds of networks of post-Soviet *Mafiyas*, many of them organized around ethnic lines (Chechens, Azeris, Georgians, and so on), to launder money, to acquire valuable property, and to take control of prosperous illegal and legal businesses. A 1994 report on organized crime by the Analytical Center for Social and Economic Politics of the Presidency of Russia estimated that virtually all small private businesses were paying tribute to criminal groups. As for larger private firms and commercial banks, it was reported that between 70 and 80 percent of them were also paying protection dues to criminal groups. These payments represented between 10 and 20 percent of capital turnover for these firms, an amount that was equivalent to over half of their profits.[30]

The situation did not seem to have improved in 1997. According to another *Izvestiya* report, it was estimated that about 41,000 industrial companies, 50 percent of banks, and 80 percent of joint ventures had criminal connections.[31] The report stated that the shadow economy, in all its manifestations, may account for as much as 40 percent of the Russian economy. Other observers, including Marshall Goldman, concur in estimating widespread penetration of business and government by organized crime.[32] The collapse of the taxation system is directly related to the payments of business to extortion organizations to solve their problems in the absence of a reliable state. Faced with the choice between an unresponsive administration and an effective, if ruthless, racketeering business, firms and people are growing accustomed to relying on the second, out of fear or convenience, or both.

In some cities (for example, Vladivostok), the local administration is highly conditioned in its functioning by its dubious connections. Furthermore, even if a given business is not related to organized crime, it operates in an environment in which the presence of criminal groups is pervasive, particularly in banking, import–export operations, trade in oil, and in rare and precious metals. The level of violence in the Russian business world in the mid-1990s was truly extraordinary: *Kommersant*, in 1996, was publishing a *daily* obituary section listing the businessmen killed in the line of duty. Contract killings became a

30   Reported by *Izvestiya*, January 26, 1994.
31   *Izvestiya*, February 18, 1997.
32   Goldman (1996).

way of life in the business world.[33] According to the Minister of the Interior, in 1995 about 450 contract killings were detected, and only 60 of them were solved by the police. Newly rich Russians were operating their Moscow businesses on line from their California mansions to escape the threats to them and their families, while still being daily involved in the wheelings and dealings that offered opportunities of making a fortune almost without parallel in the world. Enforcement of business deals, in an uncertain legal environment, was often carried on by intimidation, sometimes by killing. Organized crime was not usually satisfied with subcontracting violence or illegal operations for a price. They wanted, and usually obtained, a share of business, either in stocks or, more frequently, in cash, or else special favors, such as preferential loans or smuggling possibilities. In the private sector, businesses were paying "taxes" to criminal organizations instead of paying them to government. Indeed, the threat of denouncing a business's fiscal fraud to the government's tax inspectors was one of the extortion methods used by organized crime.

The widespread presence of international criminal cartels in Russia and the ex-Soviet republics was duly reciprocated by a dramatic expansion of post-Soviet criminal networks abroad, particularly in the United States and Germany. These criminal networks in America operated at a high level of financial and technological sophistication, usually organized by highly educated, young professionals, who did not hesitate in backing up their operations with extreme, but calculated, violence, often performed by ex-KGB officers, who found themselves a post-Cold War professional career.[34] Because of the strategic, economic, and political importance of Russia, and because of its large military and nuclear arsenal, its new, deep connection to global organized crime has become one of the most worrisome issues at this turn of the millennium, and a hot topic in geopolitical meetings around the world.[35]

How has this state of affairs come about? First of all, it must be said that this is *not* in historical continuity with past Russian experience, or with the underground economy of the Soviet Union, even though

33 Shargorodsky (1995).
34 Kleinknecht (1996); Kuznetsova (1996); Wallace (1996).
35 On the significance of Russian participation in global crime, see Ovchinsky (1993). On the persistence of criminal activity in Russia, a report by Interior Minister A. Kulikov of January 17, 1997, provided the following estimates: about 7 million crimes were committed in 1996, and about 2.62 million were reported. 29,700 murders and attempted murders were committed. More than 200 gangs were broken up by the police. Mr Kulikov acknowledged widespread corruption in his Ministry. The head of the Ministry's Technical and Military Supplies Administration, and 30 other officers were fired for embezzlement. About 10,000 Interior Ministry employees were brought to book in 1996, including 3,500 for criminal offenses.

people involved in criminal or illegal activities in the former system are certainly very active in the new criminal economy. But they have been joined by many other actors in the criminal scene, and the mechanisms of formation and growth of the new criminal economy are entirely different. Criminal organizations have existed in Russia for centuries.[36] The *vorovskoi mir* ("thieves' world"), usually run from the prisons by an elite of *vory v zakonye* ("thieves-in-law"), survived repression, and kept their distance *vis-à-vis* the Czarist and Soviet states. They were, however, severely punished under Stalin, and subsequently weakened by their internal divisions and killings, particularly during the so-called "Scab Wars" of the 1950s. They reappeared during *perestroika*, but they had to share and compete for the control of the streets and criminal trafficking with a proliferation of ethnic *Mafiyas*, and a legion of newcomers to the business. In the 1990s they were just a component of a much broader picture, whose centers of power and wealth originated during the transition years. Nor are contemporary Russian *Mafiyas* a continuation of the networks that used to control the underground economy that grew up during the Brezhnev period. The underground economy was not in the hands of criminals, but of the Communist *nomenklatura*. It added flexibility to an increasingly rigid command economy, while providing rewards (rents) for the gatekeepers of each bureaucratic hurdle. As I described in chapter 1, this underground economy included barter between enterprises, as well as illegal sales of goods and services at all levels of the economic system, under the supervision, and for the personal benefit, of a gigantic network of bureaucrats, usually associated with the Communist power structure. The existence of this underground economy was entirely linked to the command economy, and thus its networks could not survive the collapse of the Soviet state. While many of these *nomenklatura* profiteers used their accumulated wealth and influence to take up positions in the new criminal economy of post-Soviet Russia, the structure of this criminal economy, and its mechanisms of connection to business and government, were entirely new.

The new criminal networks were formed in the 1987–93 period for the sake of proceeding with the pillage of Russia, and they consolidated their intertwining with the business world and the political system throughout the 1990s.[37] In trying to analyze this extraordinary

---

36   Handelman (1995).
37   The designation of 1987–93 as the period of formation of contemporary Russian *Mafiyas* is not arbitrary. In 1987 Gorbachev authorized the creation of private businesses (mainly under the form of cooperatives) in the most confusing terms, and without a proper legal environment, thus inducing an embryonic proto-capitalism that often had to operate under unlawful protection schemes. In October 1993, Yeltsin used tanks to crush the rebellion of

development, I will propose a three-step explanation that I believe to be plausible in the light of available evidence.[38] I combine a structural interpretation, the identification of the actors involved in the uncontrolled appropriation of Soviet assets, and a description of the mechanisms used by these actors to accumulate wealth and power in a very short time.

The structural perspective

The economic chaos that resulted in the partial criminalization of business came, first of all, from a process of transition from a command economy to a market economy operated without institutions that could organize and regulate markets, and hampered by the collapse of state agencies, which became unable to control or repress developments. As Marshall Goldman writes:

> The break up of the Soviet Union was accompanied by the collapse of the economic infrastructure; Gosplan, the ministries, the wholesale operations – all simply disappeared. Eventually there was an institutional vacuum. On top of everything else, there was no accepted code of business behavior. Suddenly Russia found itself with the makings of a market but with no commercial code, no civil code, no effective bank system, no effective accounting system, no procedures for declaring bankruptcy. What was left over was not very helpful, especially the prevailing notion that it was perfectly appropriate to cheat the state.[39]

Under such conditions of institutional chaos, the accelerated transition to market mechanisms, including the liberalization of price controls, opened the way for a wild competition to grab state property by whatever means, often in association with criminal elements. As Goldman writes, "An argument can be made that to some extent the

---

the last Russian Parliament established during the Soviet era, actually ending the political transition. It was during this uncertain period, when nobody really knew who was in charge, except for the President himself, that organized crime set up its business networks, while many politicians positioned themselves in the generalized graft of Russian wealth. By the end of 1993, with a new Constitution, and a new, democratically elected Parliament, Russia entered into some kind of institutional normality. However, by this time, the intertwining of business, government, and crime had already been consolidated and became a feature of the new system.

38   See the sources cited in note 29 above. See, in addition, Bohlen (1993, 1994); Bonet (1993, 1994); Ovchinskyi (1993); Commission on Security and Cooperation in Europe (1994); Erlanger (1994a,b); Gamayunov (1994); *Izvestiya* (1994b,c); Podlesskikh and Tereshonok (1994); Savvateyeva (1994); *The Current Digest* (1994); Kuznetsova(1996); Bennett (1997).

39   Goldman (1996: 42).

Russian reformers made the Mafia movement worse than it needed to have been."[40]

This institutional chaos was made worse by the break up of the Soviet Union into 15 independent republics. Security agencies, and the armed forces, were disorganized; bureaucratic lines of command were blurred; legislation proliferated in disorder, while border controls were non-existent. Proto-capitalists and criminals moved around the different republics, picking up the most favorable environments, and still operating in the whole expanse of the ex-Soviet Union. Technological underdevelopment made it difficult to keep track of movements of capital, goods, and services in a huge territory. Local *Mafiyas* took control of local states, and established their own connection networks. The *Mafiyas*, and their business associates, jumped into the Information Age much faster than state bureaucracies. Controlling both the local nodes and the communication links, semi-criminal businesses bypassed most centralized controls still in place. They run the country through their own networks.

Identifying the actors

Who are the actors involved in the making of this wild process of accumulation, partly shaped by criminal interests? For one of the most respected observers of the Russian political scene, Pavel Voshchanov, the answer is unambiguous:

40   Goldman (1996: 40).The first government of democratic Russia, in 1992, was duly warned of the potential consequences of an accelerated transition to a market economy without previously setting up the institutions that would allow markets to operate properly. The international advisory committee to the Russian government that I chaired in 1992 (see explanation in chapter 1 of this volume, and in chapter 2 of volume I) delivered several notes and reports (which I still have), besides repeated verbal warnings, that indicated that markets required institutions and regulations, as demonstrated by the history of capitalist development in other countries. Burbulis told me in July 1992 that he agreed with our arguments but that "forces in the Kremlin" were in favor of a more pragmatic, less regulatory approach that would provide greater freedom of maneuver. Gaidar, supported by the IMF, believed firmly in the intrinsic capacity of market forces to remove obstacles by themselves, once prices were liberalized, and people could use their vouchers to acquire shares. In 1996, acknowledging *ex post facto* some of the problems of uncontrolled privatization, which our committee had foreseen from March 1992, he blamed "the Communists and their allies." I personally do not think that Gaidar, Burbulis, and other leaders of the first Yeltsin cabinet were corrupt in 1992. I believe the key point is that they had really no legal, political, or bureaucratic power to control the results of their decisions. Thus, they liberalized, unleashing economic forces, and they were bypassed and overwhelmed by all kinds of pressure groups located inside and outside the state. When the process of liberalization and privatization became a free-for-all fight, and state institutions could offer no guarantee, various *Mafiyas* stepped in, and took partial control of the process. This is an important lesson for history. When and where there is no regulation and control by the legitimate forces of the state, there will be ruthless control by the illegitimate forces of violent, private groups. Unfettered markets are tantamount to wild societies.

How was the criminal Russian state born? In a way it emerged after the August 1991 coup. At that time the new political elite was pondering perhaps the most important question – how to make the post-coup economic and political changes irreversible. Those officials were unanimous that they must have their own social basis – a class of owners. It had to be rather large and be capable of supporting their patrons. The problem was to create this class starting from the point where all were roughly equal in terms of income and property . . . What was the major obstacle for the new nomenklatura at the Kremlin? It was the law. Any law was an obstacle as it, according to presidential aides in 1991, "hampered the progress of democracy."[41]

The strategic, political interests of reformers in power in 1991–2 induced a rapid process of liberalization and privatization that could create a large owners' class, with vested interests in the development of capitalism in Russia. Some of these reformers may, as well, have had it in mind to obtain personal benefit from their positions of power, as some eventually did in the following years. However, the most important point is that, inadvertently or not, they created the opportunity for those with the money and power to seize state property – that is, the whole of Russia. These would-be capitalists were, first of all, leading members of the Communist *nomenklatura* who had accumulated wealth, particularly during the *perestroika* years, by diverting state funds into personal bank accounts abroad. I was told by high-ranking members of the Yeltsin cabinet in 1992 that, when they came to power, the gold and hard currency reserves of the Soviet state were almost entirely gone, a report that was later confirmed by various sources, and publicly stated, among others, by Yegor Gaidar in 1996. This was in addition to the secret foreign accounts of the Communist party of the Soviet Union that simply vanished in the global financial flows. Altogether this may represent, in all likelihood, tens of billions of dollars. A fraction of this capital was quite enough to buy a considerable amount of property, enterprises, banks, goods and services, in Russia, particularly if the political influence still in the hands of the *nomenklatura*'s friends facilitated the purchase of state property. Only a few months after the end of the Soviet Union, gigantic financial empires, with a highly diversified range of investments, emerged in the Russian economy. Soon, these conglomerates found connections in the new political system, since the institutional vacuum required some form of *ad hoc* government support to prosper in an uncertain environment, periodically shaken by a flurry of decrees.

There were other actors actively participating in the wild develop-

41   Voshchanov (1995: 13).

ment of new Russian capitalism. Global organized crime, particularly the Sicilian Mafia and the Colombian cartels, seized the chance of Russian chaos to launder considerable sums of money, as well as mixing "dirty money" with counterfeited dollars by the billions.[42] Gaidar himself acknowledged in 1994 the existence of sizeable amounts of "dirty" money, laundered capital, and capital in the process of being laundered in Russia.[43] Having positioned themselves in Russia in the late 1980s and early 1990s, global criminal networks were able to take advantage of the privatization process, linking up with Russian organized crime, as well as inducing the development of new criminal organizations. They also linked up with the smuggling networks that sprung up around weapons depots, nuclear installations, oil fields, and precious and rare metals mines.[44]

When the institutional system broke down in 1991, and a disorderly market economy flourished at the street level, criminals of all kind, old and new, from various ethnic backgrounds, proliferated as parasites of whatever business, small or large, that emerged in Russia. Many nonprofit, tax-exempt organizations came under *Mafiya* influence, for instance, the National Sports Foundation, the Russian Fund for Invalids of the Afghanistan War, and the All-Russian Society for the Deaf. Even the Russian Orthodox Church went into tax-exempt business, probably under the protection of the *Mafiya*, importing cigarettes duty-free for humanitarian aid, and investing in oil-trading companies.[45] Because of the absence of effective state regulation and control, a symbiotic relationship was established between the growth of private business and its protection/extortion from criminal networks. This crime-penetrated business linked up with politicians at the local, provincial, and national levels, so that, ultimately, the three spheres (politics, business, crime) became intertwined. It does not mean that crime controls politics or that most businesses are criminal. It means, none the less, that business operates in an environment deeply penetrated by crime; that business needs the protection of political power; and that many politicians, in the 1990s, have amassed considerable fortunes through their business contacts.

Mechanisms of Accumulation

The mechanisms through which this kind of primitive capitalist accumulation in Russia has been performed are diverse: indeed, daring,

---

42 Sterling (1994).
43 Interview with Gaidar, *Trud*, February 10, 1994.
44 Beaty (1994); Handelman (1995); Gordon (1996).
45 *Business Week*, December 9, 1996; Specter (1996).

imaginative schemes are the daily staple of Russian capitalists and crooks. But the essential mechanism has been *the process of privatization*, conducted with no transparency, scarce control, and unreliable accounting. It was through uncontrolled privatization that all valuable assets in Russia were sold for ridiculous prices to whoever had the money and the power to control the transaction. This is how and why government officials, ex-*nomenklatura*, and organized crime, Russian and international, came together, willingly or unwillingly.

Just prior to the privatization process several mega-scams helped to destabilize economic institutions, and provided seed capital to engage in primitive accumulation of Russian assets. Claire Sterling has identified, and carefully documented, what is probably the largest of these scams in 1990–92, initiated by global criminal networks, particularly by the Sicilian Mafia, with the complicity of contacts in the Soviet government and, probably, of Western intelligence agencies as well. I refer to her account which lists a number of credible sources, citing names, places, dates, and figures.[46] In a nutshell, through a number of intermediaries posing as "international business men," criminal organizations and their contacts depreciated the ruble by buying billions of rubles in Russia at a large discount, with "dirty" dollars, and offering these rubles in the world market at a low price. Furthermore, they diffused rumors of even larger transactions, contributing to higher depreciation. Elements of the *nomenklatura* were interested in converting these worthless rubles into hard currency, both for their benefit and, in some cases, for increasing the currency reserves of the Soviet state. These transactions fueled capital flight from the Soviet Union during the last period of *perestroika*. It seems that state gold reserves were used as a guarantee of some of these transactions. The devaluation of the ruble made assets and commodities much cheaper in Russia. Criminal networks, speculative intermediaries, and *nomenklatura* bosses used the billions of rubles they had amassed, and a few millions of dollars, to buy and smuggle oil, weapons, raw materials, rare and precious metals. They also invested in real estate, hotels, and restaurants. And they bought large packages of privatization vouchers from private citizens who did not know what to do with them, or were forced into selling. Once this speculative/criminal capital positioned itself in the economy it sought, and obtained, the support of the Soviet, then Russian, government for investment in the country, and for import/export activities. This investment, originally made out of laundered money and/or from funds embezzled from the state, therefore multiplied considerably. Since much legitimate foreign investment was

46   Sterling (1994: 169–243).

soon scared off from investing in Russia's insecure environment, Soviet and Russian legislation favoring foreign capital and trade worked largely in favor of para-criminal networks. Some of these scam creators were fully identified (Sterling cites Americans Leo Wanta and Marc Rich), but were never caught, and continued to run their businesses from their havens in other countries (Rich was based in Zug, Switzerland, in 1994). Sterling has evaluated the illicit smuggling of capital in 1992 at about US$20 billion, and the illicit outflow of oil and materials at another US$17 billion. This is several times the total foreign direct investment in Russia during the 1991–6 period. While Sterling's story has all the features of a fiction thriller, her documentation is serious enough to make it plausible, and the main thrust of her argument coincides with reports from other sources.[47] Furthermore, while I do not have factual evidence of my own, the picture of illegal deals and economic destabilization that I gathered during my fieldwork research in Russia in 1989–96, including interviews at the highest levels of Soviet and Russian government, does not contradict what Sterling, Handelman, Voshchanov, and many other observers, report.

Yet speculative maneuvers by global crime during the chaotic times of the Soviet collapse could not have sufficed to establish the intertwining of politics, business, and crime that characterizes the Russian scene in the 1990s. The dramatic errors made by Gorbachev first, in disorganizing the Soviet system without replacing it, and the Russian democrats later, in pushing for an accelerated transition to the market economy without social and institutional control, created the conditions for the takeover of one of the largest and naturally wealthiest countries in the world. It is this wild appropriation of wealth, enacted or tolerated by the powers that be, that explains the overwhelming presence of crime, not the other way around. But, unlike American "robber barons" who used all the means at their disposal to accumulate capital for investment, besides enriching themselves, wild Russian capitalism is deeply entrenched in global crime and in global financial networks. As soon as profits are generated, they are sent into the anonymous whirlwind of global finance, from which only a portion is reinvested, once conveniently laundered, into the rewarding, but risky, Russian economy.

In August 1999, *The New York Times* brought to international attention a sophisticated scheme for the illegal transfer of capital from Russia through the Bank of New York, via the intermediation of a series of shadow companies, based in Britain, Switzerland, the US,

---

47   Sterling's (1994) argument coincides with other sources as cited in the notes to this chapter.

and several offshore locations. Estimates of the amounts involved were in the tens of billions of dollars. Because of the size of the transfers, it soon became clear that the Russian mafias alone could not have been the source of this capital, in spite of the involvement in some of these operations of Mr Mogilevich, an Israeli citizen and a notorious boss of the Eastern European mafias, formerly based in Budapest. As the affair unfolded over the following months, the European press, and the Russian press, reported extensively on a vast network of interests converging toward tax fraud and the illegal export of staggering sums from Russia. It was suggested that a significant share of IMF loans to Russia was being diverted, and transferred out of Russia by bankers and government officials, with the knowledge of very high-level Russian authorities. Reports in the *Corriere della Sera* directly implicated the manager of the Kremlin estate and the family of President Yeltsin in the scheme. *The Times* of London (November 7, 1999) documented the illegal transfer of funds from Russia to the United States via British banks, and charged that the destination of this money was to pay bribes to American officials in Washington, DC. As information and counter-information became political ammunition in Russia, and in the world at large, it was increasingly difficult to disentangle facts, fabrication, and manipulation, let alone to prove anything in this increasingly important, and exceedingly obscure affair. For the sake of clarity, I will suggest the following. First, at the root of the illegal export of capital is the absurd and obscure regulation of the Russian government concerning capital controls and business taxation, and the thoroughly arbitrary implementation of these rules. Thus, legitimate businesses in Russia, particularly in the finance industry and the export business, have to resort to extraordinary measures to be able to function: this includes keeping payments for legitimate export operations abroad and investing their profits internationally to escape the constraints of the Russian bureaucracy. It may be illegal, but this is not, in itself, a Mafia-related operation. Second, tax-evasion schemes have to find their way out of the country. Third, proceedings from unduly appropriated funds in and around the government also need an exit. Fourth, government officials at various levels of the administration cover up these schemes for both illegal export of capital and illicit income generation, receiving in exchange their share, and joining the club of capital exporters. Fifth, it is likely that some criminal organizations helped to set up the networks of illegal capital circulation, using them as well to launder their own revenues. Sixth, a network of intermediaries, both in Russia and in the West, developed a complex system of shadow companies, and financial institutions, most of them in the gray zone of international commerce, to siphon off

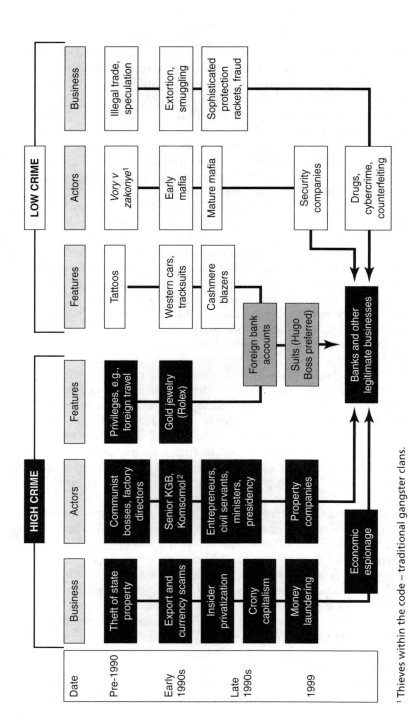

¹ Thieves within the code – traditional gangster clans.
² Communist Party Youth League.

Chart 3.1   The evolution of illegal and criminal networks in Russia
Source: Control Risk, *The Economist* (1999a)

Russian capital from various origins, and profit from their gray business. Finally, the Bank of New York, and other respectable financial institutions, simply take the money, no questions asked: in fact, rewarding their Russian-born employees for their lucrative business connections – particularly when the money is in the order of tens of billions of dollars. At that point, the money is free from constraints, and some of it can even be re-invested in Russia, as foreign capital, under new, more favorable conditions. Therefore, what the media call the Russian mafia is only a small fraction of the vast network of illegal operations through which, ultimately, much of the wealth of the country (and, perhaps, a share of international aid) is appropriated by a few individuals, and ultimately transferred to the global financial networks, in cooperation (knowingly or not) with major Western banks and financial institutions.[48]

In August 1999, *The Economist*, after investigating the evolution of the Russian shadow economy during the 1990s, proposed a chart summarizing the transformation of this economy from low-crime activities, conducted by marginal individuals and ethnic mafias, to high-crime activities that intensified along the privatization process, under the umbrella of the state, and (my addition) with the knowledge of Western governments and institutions which chose to condone corruption as long as Russia remained politically subdued under its pro-Western leadership (see chart 3.1). Thus, the pillage of Russia goes on, as a source of easy profits, and as a platform for international criminal and illegal activities, whose proceedings are diffused in the global financial networks.

Russian society, in its vast majority, is excluded from the Information Age at this turn of the millennium. But its crime-infested capitalism is fully immersed in the global flows of wealth and power that it has been able to access by perverting the hopes of Russian democracy.[49]

Narcotrafico, Development, and Dependency in Latin America[50]

The extraordinary growth of the drug traffic industry since the 1970s has transformed the economics and politics of Latin America. Classic

48   For a summary of this affair, and chronology of events up to November 1999, a synthetic source, in Russian, can be found in the Russian political news web site (http://www.polit.ru/stones.html). For information from Western sources, see Bonner and O'Brien (1999) and *The Economist* (1999a).
49   Castells and Kiselyova (1998).
50   One of the best political-economic analyses of drug traffic in Latin America, although centered on Colombia, is Thoumi (1994). On the international structure of the drug industry in Latin America see Arnedy (1990); Tokatlian and Bagley (1990); Del Olmo (1991);

paradigms of dependency and development have to be rethought to include, as a fundamental feature, the characteristics of the drugs industry, and its deep penetration of state institutions and social organization. The industry is mainly centered around the production, processing, and export of coca and cocaine. However, in the 1990s heroin became an increasingly important component, and marijuana, particularly in Mexico, recovered some of the significance it had in the late 1960s and early 1970s. Around powerful criminal networks built from drug traffic, other criminal activities (particularly money laundering, smuggling, arms traffic, immigrants traffic, international prostitution, and kidnapping) are being organized, thus constituting a complex, criminal world, whose highly decentralized structure permeates, and marks, all Latin American societies. Several major features characterize *narcotrafico*'s industry.

(1) It is *demand driven and export oriented*. Its original, and still most important, market is the United States. However, Western Europe and affluent Asia are fast becoming important markets as well. As an illustration of the bottom-line economics of the cocaine industry, in 1991 the cost of producing one kilogram of cocaine in Colombia (including the cost of production of coca paste received from other countries) was estimated at US$750; its price for export from Colombia was about US$2,000; wholesale price for the same kilogram in Miami was US$15,000; and in the streets of American cities, sold by the gram, once conveniently "cut" with other ingredients, its value could reach up to US$135,000.[51] Transportation and distribution costs, and protection of these distribution systems, are obviously linked to its illegality, and to its sustained demand in the United States.

Simposio Internacional (1991); Laserna (1991); and Bastias (1993). On the effects of coca production and cocaine traffic on national and regional economies, see Laserna (1995, 1996). To understand the psychology, social context, and political implications of drug traffic, probably the most inspiring document is the extraordinary report by Gabriel Garcia Marquez *Noticia de un secuestro* (1996). On the cultural dimensions of the world of drug traffic see De Bernieres (1991); Prolongeau (1992); and Salazar and Jaramillo (1992). On the links between the drug industry and US–Latin American relations, see the classic book by Scott and Marshall (1991). On Bolivia, see Laserna (1995) and Pasquini and De Miguel (1995). On Ecuador, Bagley et al. (1991). On Venezuela, Azocar Alcala (1994). On Mexico, Mejia Prieto (1988); Garcia (1991); and chapter 5 of volume II. On Peru, Turbino (1992); and Pardo Segovia (1995). A major source of information and ideas on the political economy of drug traffic in Latin America has been Roberto Laserna, Professor of Economics at the Universidad Mayor de San Simon, in Cochabamba. Our intellectual interaction for more than 15 years has decisively shaped my thinking on this matter, although he bears no responsibility for my possible mistakes. Also, my stays in La Paz and Cochabamba in 1985, then in 1998, including a most interesting visit to the Chapare in 1985, by then one of the centers of coca cultivation in Latin America, were essential in my understanding of the drug industry.
51   Thoumi (1994: 295).

(2) *The industry is fully internationalized, with a changing division of labor between different locations.* Again focusing on cocaine, coca leaves are, and have been, cultivated and safely consumed for thousands of years in the Andean region.[52] At the turn of the century, Colombia produced about 40 percent of coca leaves in the world, Bolivia and Peru together about another 40 percent, with the rest shared mainly between Ecuador, Venezuela, and, more recently, Brazil and Mexico. Transformation of coca leaves into coca paste, and, lately, into a base of coca, usually takes place in the cultivating countries, although at some distance from the fields to avoid detection. For instance, when in 1985 I visited the then main coca-producing center in Bolivia, the Chapare, in Cochabamba province, coca paste was produced at about 100 km from Chapare, in villages of the valleys surrounding the city of Cochabamba, from where coca paste was carried on the backs of porters to clandestine landing strips in the forest. From there, as well as from Alto Huallaga, the main producing area in Peru, coca paste and coca base were/are flown into Colombia, where the main centers of the industry have consolidated their control since the late 1970s. In spite of repression, Colombia remains the main center for refining and advanced processing of cocaine. It also harbors management and commercial centers, from which is organized the most delicate operation: transportation into the affluent markets, particularly in the United States. In addition, in the late 1990s, after the Peruvian and Bolivian governments, after demands from the US Drug Enforcement Administration (DEA), stepped up pressure on coca cultivators, Colombia also became a major cultivation center. This is because the existence of vast areas of the country, out of the control of the Colombian government, makes it possible for peasants to cultivate coca leaves with a lower risk of suppression than in other countries.

After primitive smuggling by human carriers in the early stages of the industry, the main form of transportation to the US is now by small planes flown from the Caribbean. This method was first organized by leading trafficker Carlos Lehder who bought an islet, Norman's Cay, in the Bahamas, and lent its landing strip to other exporters, thus constituting a basis for cooperation – a flexible cartel – between exporters. But many other ways were and are used, as seizures by customs officers increased: commercial airlines, cargo ships, personal couriers, cocaine hidden in legally exported merchandise (construction materials, glass panels, fruits, cans, clothing, and so on), as well as, particularly in the 1990s, land transportation across the Mexico–US border. Thus, Mexican drug cartels developed strongly in the 1990s,

---

52   Laserna (1996); Gootenberg (1999).

first as intermediaries for the Colombians, then on their own, adding heroin, amphetamines, and marijuana to the cocaine they carried as partners of the Colombians.

In many instances, the method of transportation is straightforward: bribing customs officers of one or several countries. In other cases, it is more imaginative: for instance, in 1999, persuading the wife of the US colonel in charge of the US military operations in Colombia to mail six packages to New York City from the American Embassy in Colombia.[53] Long routes, such as to Europe or Asia, depend mainly on cargo ships, unloaded by smaller boats near the coast: this is the case in Galicia, Spain, one of the main entry points into Europe, in historical continuity with cigarette smuggling networks in Galicia. Networks of distribution in the United States tend to be controlled by Colombians, or their associates, often Mexican, using networks of immigrants from their national (or even regional) origin: trust-bonded networks. In Europe and Asia, Colombian cartels provide the merchandise, and leave the criminal organizations in charge of each territory to control distribution. Guayaquil plays a major role for sea shipments to the US. Venezuela is a staging point for air shipments to Europe.

Other critical inputs for the industry are chemical precursors, mainly imported from Switzerland, Germany, and the United States, but increasingly supplied by the Latin American chemical industry, particularly in Argentina and Brazil. Brazil, where a limited amount of coca is cultivated, has also joined the processing industry, as Colombian laboratories came under increasing pressure from the US DEA. While the geographical pattern of *narcotrafico* is evolving and extending its reach, it has maintained remarkable stability in its internal hierarchy, as the Colombian "cartels" have been able to maintain their domination, for reasons and with mechanisms that I will present below.

The three most important *transformations of this international division of labor of the drug industry at the turn of the century* are: (a) the emergence of Mexico as a quasi-autonomous export center, benefiting from its proximity to the United States; (b) the strategic alliances between Colombian cartels and criminal organizations around the world, particularly with the Sicilian Mafia, the American Mafia, and the Russian criminal networks; (c) the widespread use of new communication technology, particularly mobile phones and portable computers, to communicate, and keep track of transactions, thus increasing the flexibility and complexity of the industry.

(3)   The *critical component of the entire drugs industry is the money-laundering system.* It is also under the control of the main traffickers

53   McFadden (1999).

from Colombia and Mexico, but it is performed by specialized agents whose main locations are in the banks and financial institutions of Colombia, Venezuela, Panama, and Florida. The financial institutions in various small Caribbean countries, such as the Cayman Islands, Turcos y Caicos, Aruba, and the Bahamas, played an essential role as entry points of money laundering in the 1980s, but their exposure, and the small size of their financial systems, have diminished their role in global money laundering, although they still provide safe savings accounts for traffickers' personal finances.

(4) The whole set of transactions relies on *enforcement by an extraordinary level of violence*. All major criminal organizations have established their own networks of killers (for example, the Colombian *sicarios*), some of them highly specialized and professional. Many others, by the thousands, are in charge of policing and terrorizing entire cities, either as members of the organization or as subcontractors. Besides their enforcement function, these networks of killers are also instruments for competition, and for protection, when organizations fight each other for the control of a given market, or dispute the terms of profit-sharing. Indeed, as Thoumi observes, this high level of violence acts as a decisive "entry barrier" for would-be competitors in the industry.[54] Unless they have the resources, and the drive, to take the risk, they will simply be eliminated before they can position themselves in the market.

(5) *The industry needs the corruption and penetration of its institutional environment to operate at all points in the system.* Drug traffickers have to corrupt and/or intimidate local and national authorities, police, customs, judges, politicians, bankers, chemists, transportation workers, journalists, media owners, and businessmen. For most of these people, the alternative between obtaining considerable amounts of money or seeing their families terrorized is too powerful to be resisted. In the absence of a decisive affirmation of state power, *narcotrafico*'s networks take control of as many people and organizations as they need in their environment. True, a frontal assault against the state, as the one launched by Pablo Escobar and the Medellin cartel in Colombia in 1984–93, usually brings doom on the criminals. However, the Medellin tactics were extreme, and very much linked to the personality of its leaders, Rodriguez Gacha "el Mexicano," killed in 1989, and Pablo Escobar, deeply resentful against a government that had declared him to be a political outcast. The Cali cartel, as ruthless and violent as Medellin's, developed a more subtle strategy of penetration

54 Thoumi (1994).

of the state, buying instead of killing, while reserving the killings for its Medellin rivals, and for low-level personnel who could be easily brought into subservience. As a result of this strategy, when the leaders of the Cali cartel, Miguel and Gilberto Rodriguez Orejuela, were finally apprehended, and brought to justice, in January 1997, they were sentenced to what, most likely, would amount to about three or four years in prison. Systematic corruption of the state, and extreme violence as a way of life, are essential components of the *narcotrafico* industry.

What are the economic consequences of the drugs industry for Latin America?

There is no doubt that the criminal economy represents a sizeable, and most dynamic, segment of Latin American economies at this turn of the millennium. Moreover, unlike traditional patterns of international-ization of production and trade in Latin America, this is a Latin American controlled, export-oriented industry, with proven global competitiveness. Even if, in the future, chemical drugs substitute for the real thing, the Colombian-based networks have the system in place to continue their pre-eminence in the market, including the R&D ac-tivities they finance for new product design and transportation tech-nology. The main market is still in the United States, with its stable, sizeable demand for drug consumption. As a consequence of its addic-tion, the US suffers an extraordinary burden of crime, social disinte-gration and police/judiciary/penitentiary costs, whose main origin lies in the criminalization of drugs and drugs traffic. Heroin from Asia also plays a part, and American and Sicilian Mafias, as well as homegrown gangs in many American cities, are significant in the crime scene. Yet, Latin American-based drugs traffic is an essential com-ponent of American crime, to the point that US policy toward Latin America is dominated by the obsession to fight drugs traffic at the point of supply. This is an impossible task, but one that has entirely transformed US–Latin American relations from old-fashioned imperi-alism to hysterical pursuit of a vanishing enemy which, in its repeated escapes, damages political systems.

If *narcotrafico* has reversed the pattern of dependency is it develop-mental? Debate rages on the matter. A leading Latin American econo-mist on the political economy of drugs traffic, Francisco Thoumi, thinks it is not. Others, like Sarmiento, link Colombian growth to foreign remittances, and investment, generated by drugs traffic.[55] Still others,

55   Sarmiento (1990).

such as Laserna, take an intermediate position, evaluating coca/cocaine's economic impact depending on which kind of development we are assessing, from which segment of the industry, and where it takes place.[56] I tend to concur with him. Areas of cultivation – in Bolivia, Peru, Ecuador, Colombia – improve their income, but not their living conditions. This is because the precariousness of the production blocks permanent investment in these settlements. These are frontier towns, always on the run, ready to be dismantled in one location, to start again 100 km deeper into the rain forest. What I saw in Chapare, in 1985, at the peak of its production boom, were poor huts, with no sanitary conditions, no water, scarce electricity, no schools, no health care, few women, and even fewer children. But I also saw, in a place with just 3 km of paved road, a proliferation of Mercedes and BMWs, an abundance of Japanese consumer electronics, and an unplugged IBM PC whose owner proudly told me that it was going to be the key to the education of his children. Most of the money generated in Chapare (about US$20,000 a year for a family of coca cultivators, collecting four crops a year) was changed for pesos in the streets, to buy a truck and build a house back in the village. A share of the money was deposited in banks in Cochabamba, from which this capital would be laundered through La Paz, the Caribbean, and Miami. Even Cochabamba did not display much wealth in 1985, except for half a dozen freshly built mansions. However, during a second visit, in 1998, I saw many more mansions in Cochabamba, and much greater conspicuous consumption, as if the "narco-bourgeoisie" were feeling safer and more respectable. La Paz, and the Bolivian economy as a whole, has benefited to a greater extent. As Peru did, somewhat: a share of its stunning capital investment in 1992–6 may have originated in the criminal economy. But peasants in Alto Huallaga, a region largely under the control of Sendero Luminoso guerrillas – allied to narcotraffickers – did not seem to have gained much advantage from this boom. Colombians appropriated a much larger share of the profits, even if the largest proportion was certainly recycled in the global financial markets for the profit of a small, criminally based business elite. But there was, from the mid-1980s, a significant boom of construction, real-estate development, and investment in Colombia. In spite of the devastation of narco-terrorism, and of political instability, in 1995, the Bogota metropolitan area experienced an annual GDP growth of about 12 percent. During my most surrealist dinner with the Mayor of Medellin, in Bogota in December 1994, he laid out his grandiose plans for new development in the city, bridging into the twenty-first century.

56 Laserna (1995, 1996).

To be sure, this wave of investment in the mid-1990s cannot be rigorously traced back to criminal origins. Yet, given the prudent distance of regular foreign capital from the Colombian scene, it is plausible that some of this investment, and even more, the proliferation of intermediaries who are managing investment in construction, agriculture, industry, and advanced services in Colombia, can be related to a recycling of drugs traffic profits into legitimate business. Thus, Bogota, and Colombia, seem to have benefited economically from their central position in profitable drugs traffic, although the benefits of this trade have been partially offset by the destruction wrought by terrorism, by the climate of violence, and by the political instability generated by contradictory pressures from drug traffickers and from the US government. Indeed, in the late 1990s, with Colombian drug traffickers under increased pressure from both the government and US agencies, and with violence and guerrilla war spreading in Colombia, the Colombian economy went into a serious recession, underscoring the structural instability of an economy addicted to narco-capital.

Why Colombia?[57]

The dominance in the global cocaine industry of the Colombian cartels/networks, occupying for the first time a hegemonic position in a major sector of the global economy, besides coffee exports, is linked to *cultural and institutional characteristics*. A brief reminder of how an export-oriented drugs traffic industry developed in Colombia, under Colombian control, will allow me to introduce a major theme of my interpretation of global crime: *the importance of cultural identity in the constitution, functioning, and strategies of criminal networks*.

Export-oriented drugs traffic in Colombia began in the late 1960s

57 A documented social history of drug traffic in Colombia is Betancourt and Garcia (1994). A good journalistic account is Castillo (1991). For analyses of economic impacts in Colombia, see Sarmiento (1990); L.F.Sarmiento (1991); Kalmanovitz (1993); and Thoumi (1994). For social analyses of Colombian criminal subcultures and their relationship to everyday life, see Prolongeau (1992) and Salazar and Jaramillo (1992). For reports and analyses of the Medellin cartel, the most documented of cocaine-related criminal organizations, and on its wars with the Cali cartel see Veloza (1988); De Bernieres (1991); Gomez and Giraldo (1992); and Strong (1995). On the links between *narcotrafico* and paramilitary organizations in Colombia, with emphasis on Boyaca, see Medina Gallego (1990). For additional information, see also Camacho Guizado (1988); Perez Gomez (1988); and Arrieta et al. (1990). Again, the reading of Garcia Marquez's *Noticia de un secuestro* (1996) is the most illuminating source for understanding the interaction between *narcotrafico* and Colombian society. I also formed my analysis, and gathered information, during visits to Bogota in 1992, 1994, and 1999. I had the privilege of conversations and meetings with a number of colleagues and friends, whose names I prefer not to mention in a display of caution that is probably excessive. I do want, however, to express to all of them, and particularly to E.H., my deepest, if silent, gratitude.

and early 1970s in the Atlantic Coast area of La Guajira, trading in marijuana cultivated in the sierras near Santa Marta (the famous "Santa Marta Gold" variety of marijuana). Social historians in Colombia report that the discovery of the potential of marijuana came from the enthusiasm shown for Colombian marijuana by young Americans sent to Colombia in the 1960s by the US Peace Corps. The American Mafia, linked to Colombia from Panama, organized the traffic in cooperation with a loose set of networks in La Guajira, around Barranquilla, an area that for centuries was a land of pirates, end of the world immigrants, and smugglers. They came to be known as the *Marimberos* in the new prosperous era of the 1970s. It did not last. Marijuana was too bulky to transport, and the low price–volume ratio made it uncompetitive when faced with tougher controls by US customs. The US marijuana market began to be supplied by the United States. Humboldt County, in northern California, soon surpassed Colombia as a marijuana producer. US-induced repression of marijuana culture and traffic in Mexico and Colombia accentuated the shift of most production sites to within the US (for example, the Appalachian region) until the 1990s, when the control of Mexican cartels over large sections of the Mexican state made it possible to return to marijuana production for export across the border.

The networks that had been created around Colombia's marijuana exports survived to some extent. Panama-based American mafiosi mixed up Colombia with Bolivia (sic), and asked their Colombian contacts about the chances of switching to cocaine. Some entrepreneurial Colombians, in the smuggling business, seized the opportunity. They could also cultivate coca, but, more importantly, they could take over the incipient traffic being developed in Bolivia, Ecuador, Peru, and Chile. One of them was a former student leader from Medellin, Pablo Escobar, who was making a killing in trafficking stolen tombstones, and who had already learned how to escape judicial repression by bribery and murder. He benefited from a favorable business environment.

Medellin, the capital of Antioquia, had traditionally been the seedbed of Colombia's entrepreneurialism, the equivalent of Sao Paulo in Brazil. In the 1970s, its traditional textile industry was in a shambles as a result of international competition from synthetic fibers. So was the other major entrepreneurial center of Colombia, Cali, the capital of the Valle del Cauca, whose sugar industry was struck by the new sugar quotas established in international trade. A third region, Boyaca, in the center of the country, was also undergoing turmoil because of a crisis in emerald mining and smuggling, its basic staple. These three areas became the centers of drug-traffic networks around cocaine.

Boyaca, led by a bloody, populist leader, Rodriguez Gacha, joined the Medellin group, led by Pablo Escobar and the Ochoa family. Cali constituted its own network, and more often than not engaged in a ferocious war against the Medellin group. The Cali group, led by the brothers Rodriguez Orejuela, came from the upper-middle class of Cali, and never challenged the power of the traditional Colombian oligarchy, which has always controlled business, prestige, wealth, land, government, and the two parties *Conservador* and *Liberal*. These oligarchs still found a way of pitching *Liberales* against *Conservadores* in the most murderous civil war in Latin America, *La Violencia* of the 1950s, suggesting a pattern of violence that would become the trademark of Colombian criminal networks.

In contrast, the Medellin group, coming from the lower-middle class, had to settle its class differences with the local elite, in a culture where only wealth provides respect. They were also highly politicized, to the point that Pablo Escobar and a close political ally were elected to the Colombian Congress in 1982, only to be expelled thereafter when the US Embassy intervened. Also, the relationship between the two cartels and the marginal sections of the population were sharply different. Escobar financed a low-income housing program and social services for the poor in Medellin, and built significant social support among shanty-town dwellers. He even tried to defend the "human rights" of his youth gangs against the obvious abuses of the national police. The Cali cartel, on the other hand, practiced "social cleaning"; that is, randomly killing hundreds, maybe thousands, of *"desechables"* (discardables), who, in the drug traffickers' view, included the homeless, prostitutes, street children, beggars, petty thieves, and homosexuals. This practice is unfortunately carried on at this very moment in Bogota by paramilitary units, and upper-class-inspired "hunting parties," which bring terror to the city at night.

Yet, all drug-trafficking groups built up their military skills in the same killers' network: the MAS (*Muerte a Secuestradores*), which was created in 1981 in response to the kidnapping of Martha Nieves de Ochoa (from Medellin's Ochoa family) by the leftist guerrillas of M-19. Ms Ochoa was freed, after negotiations, but killings, by the hundreds, went on for years: drug traffickers continued to send the message that they were strong enough, and determined enough, not to let anyone impose anything on them.

Yet, regardless of their violent divergences, and their contrasting tactics, both the Medellin and Cali groups hoped for their full integration into Colombian society. Repeatedly, they proposed to various presidents to pay off the Colombian foreign debt in cash (for different amounts, always in billions of dollars, at different times), and reinvest their capital in Colombia, thus becoming legitimate businessmen. It was not an impossible dream. But it was, indeed, a dream because the US government decided to draw the line, and use all means available to prevent drug traffickers making Colombia into a safe house. Thus, the main issue was the extradition of drug traffickers to the United States, a measure that the US succeeded in obtaining during the 1980s. But this was also the reason why the Medellin cartel launched a frontal assault against the Colombian state, on behalf of the *"Extraditables"* to reverse the law. It lost the battle, but won the war. After years of the most violent urban terrorism ever witnessed in Latin America, the Medellin cartel's leadership was decimated, and Pablo Escobar was gunned down on a Medellin roof in December 1993. Yet, in 1992, the new Colombian Constitution prohibited extradition of nationals. However, yielding to pressure from the US, the extradition procedure was re-instated in 1998.

The attachment of drug traffickers to their country, and to their regions of origin, goes beyond strategic calculation. They were/are deeply rooted in their cultures, traditions, and regional societies. Not only have they shared their wealth with their cities, and invested a significant amount (but not most) of their fortune in their country, but they have also revived local cultures, rebuilt rural life, strongly affirmed their religious feelings, and their beliefs in local saints and miracles, supported musical folklore (and were rewarded with laudatory songs from Colombian bards), made Colombian football teams (traditionally poor) the pride of the nation, and revitalized the dormant economies and social scenes of Medellin and Cali – until bombs and machine guns disturbed their joy. The funeral of Pablo Escobar was a homage to him by the city, and particularly by the poor of the city: many considered him to have been their benefactor. Thousands gathered, chanting slogans against the government, praying, singing, crying, and saluting.

Why Colombia? Because of the original combination of dormant networks of drug traffic linking up to the United States, an existing entrepreneurial class marginalized by the failed industrialization of Latin America, and the strong rooting of the relatively educated, upwardly mobile smugglers into their cultures and local societies. This serendipitous formula, however, built on a tradition, and took advantage of a very favorable institutional environment. The tradition was the violence that has characterized Colombia throughout its history, and particularly in the 1950s. The *sicarios* of the 1980s were a reincarnation of the *pajaros* ("birds" = killers) that worked for both liberals and conservatives all over rural Colombia during *La Violencia*. And the Colombian drug traffickers took advantage of the perennial crisis of legitimacy and control of the Colombian state. Colombia is the only state in South America where, at the turn of the millennium, sizeable areas of the country escape government control. Communist guerrillas, such as the *Fuerzas Armadas Revolucionarias Colombianas*, and other smaller groups, such as *Ejercito de Liberacion Nacional*, have controlled areas of the Colombian countryside, forests, and mountains, for the past half a century. In the 1980s, Rodriguez Gacha and Carlos Lehder organized "anti-communist free territories" in central Colombia, freely exercising their terror, with the tolerance of the army. The Colombian state has been, even more than other Latin American states, both captured by a narrow oligarchy, and deeply penetrated by corruption. When courageous leaders, such as Luis Carlos Galan, tried to reverse this course, they were simply murdered (in his case by Pablo Escobar's *sicarios*). Paramilitary groups, linked to elements in the police and the armed forces, have imposed their ferocious diktat over moderates in government, often going on a rampage of killings of elected officials, union leaders, community activists, intellectuals, and left-wing militants. And organized crime had its say in government well before cocaine traffic became significant in Colombia. Thus, Thoumi's hypothesis that points to the weakness of the Colombian state as a critical factor in fostering Colombia's pre-eminence in global cocaine traffic seems plausible.[58] It also suggests a broader trend. If large but weak states (such as Colombia) facilitate the location of command and control centers of global criminal networks, the power of these criminal centers is likely to overwhelm these states even further. It follows a downward spiral where, ultimately, criminal organizations may control some states: not by following the violent confrontation of the Medellin type of tactics, but by combining bribery, intimidation, the financing of politics, and the affirmation of cultural identity with skillful international business management. Colombia, then Mexico, then Russia, then Thailand, then Nigeria, then Albania, then . . .

Globalization and identity interact in the criminal economy of Latin America. They organize the perverse connection that redefines development and dependency in historically unforeseen ways.

The Impact of Global Crime on Economy, Politics, and Culture

Money laundering, and its derivatives, have become a significant and

58   Thoumi (1994).

troubling component of global financial flows and stock markets. The size of these capitals, while unknown, is likely to be considerable. But more important is their mobility. To avoid tracking, capital originating in the criminal economy shifts constantly from financial institution to financial institution, from currency to currency, from stock to stock, from investment in real estate to investment in entertainment. Because of its volatility, and its willingness to take high risks, criminal capital follows, and amplifies, speculative turbulences in financial markets. Thus, it has become an important source of destabilization of international finance and capital markets.

Criminal activity has also a powerful direct effect on a number of national economies. In some cases, the size of its capital overwhelms the economy of small countries. In other cases, such as Colombia, Peru, Bolivia, and Nigeria, it represents an amount sizeable enough to condition macroeconomic processes, becoming decisive in specific regions or sectors. Still in other countries, such as Russia and Italy, its penetration of business and institutions transforms the economic environment, making it unpredictable, and favoring investment strategies focused on short-term returns. Even in economies as large and solid as Japan, financial crises can be triggered by criminal maneuvers, as was the case in 1995 of the savings and loans defaults, for hundreds of billions of dollars, as a result of bad loans forced on some bankers by the *Yakuza*. The distorting effects of the unseen criminal economy on monetary policies, and on economic policies at large, make it even more difficult to control nationally based economic processes in a globalized economy, one component of which has no official existence.

The impact of crime on state institutions and politics is even greater. State sovereignty, already battered by the processes of globalization and identification, is directly threatened by flexible networks of crime that bypass controls, and assume a level of risk that no other organizations are capable of absorbing (see volume II, chapter 5). The technological and organizational opportunity to set up global networks has transformed, and empowered, organized crime. For a long time, its fundamental strategy was to penetrate national and local state institutions in its home country, in order to protect its activities. The Sicilian Mafia, the Japanese *Yakuza*, the Hong Kong-based, or Taiwan-based, or Bangkok-based Triads, the Colombian cartels relied on their capacity to build over time a deep connection with segments of national and regional states, both with bureaucrats and with politicians. This is still an important element in the operational procedures of organized crime: it can only survive on the basis of corruption and intimidation of state personnel and, sometimes, of state institutions. However, in recent times, globalization has added a decisive twist to the institutional strategy of organized crime. Safe, or relatively safe, houses have been found around the planet: small (Aruba), medium (Colombia), large (Mexico) or extra-large (Russia), among many others. Besides, the high mobility and extreme flexibility of the networks makes it possible to evade national regulations and the rigid procedures of international police cooperation. Thus, the consolidation of the European Union has handed organized crime a wonderful opportunity to take advantage of contradictions between national legislations and of the reluctance of most police forces to relinquish their independence. Thus, Germany has become a major operational center for the Sicilian Mafia, Galicia is a major staging point for the Colombian cartels, and The Netherlands harbors important nodes of heroin traffic of the Chinese Triads.[59] When pressure from the state, and from international forces (usually US intelligence agencies), becomes excessive in a given country, even in a region that was "safe" for organized crime (for example, the significant repression of crime in Sicily in 1995–6, or in Medellin and Cali in 1994–6), the flexibility of the network allows it to shift its organizational geometry, moving supply bases, altering transportation routes, and finding new places of residence for their bosses, increasingly in respectable countries, such as Switzerland, Spain, and Austria. As for the real thing, that is the money, it circulates safely in the flows of computerized financial transactions, managed from offshore banking bases that direct its swirling in time and space.

Furthermore, escaping police control through networking and globalization allows organized crime to keep its grip on its national bases. For instance, in the mid-1990s, while the Colombian cartels (particularly Medellin) suffered serious blows, Colombian drug traffickers survived by modifying their organization and decentralizing their structure. In fact, they were never a hierarchical, consolidated cartel, but a loose association of exporters, including, in Cali, for instance, over 200 independent organizations. Thus, when some leaders become too inconvenient (as, for example, Rodriguez Gacha or Escobar), or are eliminated, these networks find new arrangements, new power relationships, and new, albeit unstable, forms of cooperation. By emphasizing local flexibility and international complexity, the criminal economy adapts itself to the desperate control attempts by rigid, nationally bound state institutions, that, for the time being, know they are losing the battle. With it, they are also losing an essential component of state sovereignty *and legitimacy*: its ability to impose law and order.

---

59   Sterling (1994); Roth and Frey (1995); *The Economist* (1999b).

In a desperate reaction to the growing power of organized crime, democratic states, in self-defense, resort to measures that curtail, and will curtail, democratic liberties. Furthermore, since immigrant networks are often used by organized crime to penetrate societies, the excessive, and unjust, association between immigration and crime triggers xenophobic feelings in public opinion, undermining the tolerance and capacity of coexistence that our increasingly multi-ethnic societies desperately need. With the nation-state under siege, and with national societies and economies already insecure from their intertwining with transnational networks of capital and people, the growing influence of global crime may induce a substantial retrenchment of democratic rights, values, and institutions.

The state is not only being bypassed from outside by organized crime. It is disintegrating from within. Besides the ability of criminals to bribe and/or intimidate police, judges, and government officials, there is a more insidious and devastating penetration: *the corruption of democratic politics*. The increasingly important financial needs of political candidates and parties create a golden opportunity for organized crime to offer support in critical moments of political campaigns. Any movement in this direction will haunt the politician for ever. Furthermore, the domination of the democratic process by scandal politics, character assassination, and image-making also offers organized crime a privileged terrain of political influence (see volume II, chapter 6). By luring politicians into sex, drugs, and money, or fabricating allegations as necessary, organized crime has created a wide network of intelligence and extortion, which traffics influence against silence. In the 1990s, the politics of many countries, not only in Latin America, have been dominated by scandals and crises induced by the direct or indirect connection between organized crime and politics. But in addition to these known, or suspected, cases of political corruption, the pervasiveness of scandal politics suggests the possibility that organized crime has discretely positioned itself in the world of politics and media in a number of countries, for instance in Japan (*Yakuza*),[60] and Italy (Sicilian Mafia).

---

60 To mention just one example of penetration of government by organized crime in Japan, let me summarize a report from a reliable Japanese magazine. On January 3, 1997, former Minister of Defense of the Japanese government, Keisuke Nakanishi, still a leading politician of the Shinshinto party, was attacked and slightly injured at Haneda Airport by two members of the *Yakuza*. The attack seemed to have been motivated by a dispute between the *Yakuza* and the ex-Minister about his behavior while securing a large loan from a bank to a developer for the benefit of the *Yakuza*. During the transaction, about 200 million yen disappeared, and the *Yakuza* was using intimidation to recover the money. Mr Nakanishi was suspected of engaging in various joint business ventures with *Yakuza* groups during his tenure as Minister of Defense (from *Shukan Shincho*, January 16, 1997).

The influence of global crime also reaches the *cultural realm* in more subtle ways. On the one hand, cultural identity nurtures most of these criminal networks, and provides the codes and bonding that build trust and communication within each network. This complicity does not preclude violence against their own kind. On the contrary, most violence is within the network. Yet there is a broader level of sharing and understanding in the criminal organization, that builds on history, culture, and tradition, and generates its own legitimizing ideology. This has been documented in numerous studies of the Sicilian and American Mafias, since their resistance to French occupation in the eighteenth century, and among the Chinese Triads, which originated in southern resistance to northern invaders, and then developed as a brotherhood in foreign lands. In my brief description of the Colombian cartels I have given a glimpse of their deep rooting in regional culture, and in their rural past, which they tried to revive. As for Russian crime, which is probably the most cosmopolitan in its projection, it is also embedded in Russian culture and institutions. In fact, the more organized crime becomes global, the more its most important components emphasize their cultural identity, so as not to disappear in the whirlwind of the space of flows. In so doing, they preserve their ethnic, cultural, and, where possible, territorial bases. This is their strength. Criminal networks are probably in advance of multinational corporations in their decisive ability to combine cultural identity and global business.

However, the main cultural impact of global crime networks on societies at large, beyond the expression of their own cultural identity, is in *the new culture they induce.* In many contexts, daring, successful criminals have become role models for a young generation that does not see an easy way out of poverty, and certainly no chance of enjoying consumption and live adventure. From Russia to Colombia, observers emphasize the fascination of local youth for the mafiosi. In a world of exclusion, and in the midst of a crisis of political legitimacy, the boundary between protest, patterns of immediate gratification, adventure, and crime becomes increasingly blurred. Perhaps Garcia Marquez, better than anyone else, has captured the "culture of urgency" of young killers in the world of organized crime. In his nonfiction book *Noticia de un secuestro* (1996), he describes the fatalism and negativism of young killers. For them, there is no hope in society, and everything, particularly politics and politicians, is rotten. Life itself has no meaning, and their life has no future. They know they will die soon. So, only the moment counts, immediate consumption, good clothing, good life, on the run, together with the satisfaction of inducing fear, of feeling powerful with their guns. Just one supreme value:

their families, and in particular their mother, for whom they would do anything. And their religious beliefs, particularly for specific saints that would help in bad moments. In striking literary terms, Garcia Marquez recounts the phenomenon that many social scientists around the world have observed: young criminals are caught between their enthusiasm for life and the realization of their limits. Thus, they compress life into a few instants, to live it fully, and then disappear. For those brief moments of existence, the breaking of the rules, and the feeling of empowerment, compensates for the monotone display of a longer, but miserable life. Their values are, to a large extent, shared by many other youngsters, albeit in less extreme forms.[61]

The diffusion of the culture of organized crime is reinforced by the pervasiveness of the everyday life of the criminal world in the media. People around the world are probably more acquainted with the media version of the working conditions and psyche of "hit men" and drug traffickers than with the dynamics of financial markets where people invest their money. The collective fascination of the entire planet with action movies where the protagonists are the players in organized crime cannot be explained just by the repressed urge for violence in our psychological make up. It may well indicate the cultural breakdown of traditional moral order, and the implicit recognition of a new society, made up of communal identity and unruly competition, of which global crime is a condensed expression.

61   Souza Minayo et al. (1999); Waiselfisz (1999).

4

Development and Crisis in the Asian Pacific: Globalization and the State[1]

The Changing Fortunes of the Asian Pacific[2]

Before July 2, 1997 the Asian Pacific was considered, rightly, to be the world's success story of economic development and technological modernization of the past half-century. Indeed, between 1965 and 1996, average annual growth of GNP in real terms for the world at large was 3.1 percent. In contrast, in the Asian Pacific, China grew at an annual average rate of 8.5 percent, Hong Kong at 7.5 percent, South Korea at 8.9 percent, Singapore at 8.3 percent, Thailand at 7.3 percent, Indonesia at 6.7 percent, Malaysia at 6.8 percent, the Philippines at 3.5 percent, and Japan at 4.5 percent. In 1950, Asia accounted for just 19 percent of the world's income; in 1996, its share reached 33

1 This chapter was substantially revised in the fall of 1999 to introduce new material and analyses, taking into account the 1997–8 Asian crisis and its implications for states and societies in the Asian Pacific, as well as for the global economy.
2 The data on the Asian crisis, for all countries, for 1996–8 have been obtained from standard business publications, particularly from *Far Eastern Economic Review*, *Business Week*, *The Economist*, *The Wall Street Journal*, *The Financial Times*, and *The International Herald Tribune*, as well as from sources on the Internet. Given that all these sources are in the public domain, I do not consider it necessary to provide specific references for each figure cited here. See also Jomo (1999) and Henderson (1999). Several colleagues provided valuable ideas and information. I would particularly like to thank Chu-Joe Hsia of the National Taiwan University; Jeffrey Henderson of the University of Manchester; You-tien Hsing of the University of British Columbia; Jong-Cheol Kim of the University of California, Berkeley; and Jeffrey Sachs of Harvard University.

percent. In the span of about three decades the Asian Pacific had become the major center of capital accumulation in the planet, the largest manufacturing producer, the most competitive trading region, one of the two leading centers of information technology innovation and production (the other was the US), and the fastest growing market. And, in a development full of implications, the hottest destination for global capital investment in emerging markets: during the 1990s Asian developing countries received a capital inflow estimated at over 420 billion US dollars. Together with China's rise as a world power, and with Japan's technological and financial might, it looked as though a geo-economic tectonic shift was in the making, ushering in the Pacific Era. Then, in a few months, in 1997 and 1998, entire economies collapsed (Indonesia, South Korea), others went into a deep recession (Malaysia, Thailand, Hong Kong, the Philippines), and the leading economy, Japan, the second largest in the world, was shaken by financial bankruptcies, prompting the international downgrading of Japanese bonds and stocks. Ultimately, the Japanese economy went into a recession as well. Taiwan and Singapore suffered much less, although they experienced moderate currency devaluation. Taiwan's growth slowed down, and Singapore declined slightly, for the first time, in 1998. China seemed to absorb the shock at the onset of the crisis, and was the only country which contributed to stabilizing the region. The differential behavior of the economies of China, Taiwan, and Singapore in the midst of the global turmoil of 1997 and 1998 is a most significant observation that may provide some clues for the explanation of the crisis and its aftermath. I will interpret the meaning of this observation at the end of the chapter.

In early 1999, the Asian economies seemed to bounce back from the crisis. Led by a government-induced revival of the Japanese economy, which increased its imports from Asian countries by 13 percent, after a 10 percent drop in imports in 1998, the Asian Pacific resumed growth. Exports, helped by devaluation of most currencies, were again the engine of economic recovery. Stock exchanges in the region went up sharply until July 1999: equity prices increased in the first half of 1999 by 60 percent in South Korea, Malaysia, and Indonesia. Yet, the second half of 1999 saw a substantial slow down of economic growth in all countries, except Japan. While China kept growing at around 7 percent, it was mainly due to government spending, pumping money into an economy on the edge of deflation. Foreign lending in the Asian Pacific (minus Japan) had a negative balance of 50 billion dollars in 1998, and another negative balance of 26 billion in 1999, in contrast to the positive balance of 110 billion in 1996 before the crisis. Projections were similarly negative for 2000. Indeed, in 1998, according to

Business Week (October 18, 1999), foreign debt issuers in East Asia had to write off debts with a value of 300 billion dollars. Portfolio investment in Asia also declined sharply between 1996 and 2000. Thus, overall, the post-crisis situation was characterized by economic instability and financial market volatility. The Asian Pacific entered indeed a new era with the new millennium. Yet, it was not the Pacific era, but an era of uncertainty and economic restructuring, as a new set of relationships between economies, societies, and state institutions emerged in the aftermath of the crisis.

A consideration of the causes and characteristics of the 1997–8 Asian crisis may help us to understand the specific process of integration of Asia in global capitalism, and thus the new features of global capitalism itself. There is, of course, a raging debate between economists on this matter, a debate whose detailed presentation would take us too far away from the central, analytical focus of this chapter. Besides, because this Asian crisis was not a single event, and its consequences continue to unfold, in a continuing process, any empirical evaluation of its contours will be outdated by the time you read these lines. Thus, I will concentrate on what is of general analytical value in interpreting the Asian crisis in the framework of the long-term process of Asian development, focusing on what I believe to be the central factor in this process: the evolving relationship between globalization and the state.

The Asian crisis was, at its source, a financial crisis, prompted by a currency crisis. After the devaluation of the Thai baht on July 2, 1997, most currencies in the region, with the exception of the not fully convertible yuan, began tumbling (the Indonesian rupiah, for instance, lost 80 percent of its value against the dollar in one year, although the six-month mark was much worse: −250 percent). The devaluation of currencies made it impossible for local banks to repay their short-term debt to foreign lenders, since they were operating in currencies that were until then pegged to the dollar. When governments acted, in most cases under IMF pressure, to raise interest rates in order to defend the currency, they put added pressure upon insolvent banks, and firms, and they ultimately stalled their economies by drying up capital sources. Furthermore, it has been convincingly argued, by leading economists such as Jeffrey Sachs, that the intervention of the IMF considerably aggravated the crisis.[3] Indeed, when the major issue at stake was the lack of credibility of a given currency, it was crucial to restore confidence in it. Instead, the IMF's alarming statements concerning the economies in crisis, and the unreliability of their banks and financial institutions, amplified the financial panic, prompting both international

3   Sachs (1998).

and domestic investors to withdraw their money, and cut off new lending. Therefore, currencies slid further, and bankruptcies were suffered by thousands of firms. Instability in Asian financial markets prompted speculative movements that diffused throughout the region's currency markets. When, on October 23, 1997, the Hong Kong dollar, a symbol of stability, came under sustained attack, the territory's economy was seriously undermined, with property values plunging by 40 percent between mid-1997 and mid-1998, wiping out 140 billion US dollars of Hong Kong's wealth. While China's determination to defend Hong Kong's financial system stabilized the currency for some time, the Hong Kong crisis was the turning point which alerted global investors to the dangers of Asian emerging markets. The most indebted economy, South Korea, the eleventh largest economy of the world at the time, actually collapsed. By the end of 1997, South Korea had to declare itself bankrupt, and surrender its economic sovereignty to the IMF in exchange for a 58 billion US dollar bail-out, the largest ever in the IMF's history. The austerity measures introduced in South Korea, and in the region at large, sent most Asian Pacific economies into a recession in 1998, except for China, and Taiwan.

Thus, at the root of the Asian crisis was the loss of investor trust and the sudden lack of credibility of Asian currencies and securities in global financial markets. What triggered the crisis was the brutal reversal in capital flows: the five most damaged economies (South Korea, Thailand, Indonesia, Malaysia, and the Philippines) posted a capital inflow of $93 billion in 1996, which became a capital outflow of $12 billion in 1997 – a swing of $105 billion. But what was the cause of this credibility crisis? Some economists, such as Krugman and the IMF's Fischer, point to the economic weaknesses of Asian economies: for example, current account deficits, secluded financial systems, overvalued currencies, excessive short-term indebtedness, and the use of inflated real estate as loan collateral. Other economists, such as Sachs and Stiglitz, point, on the contrary, to the fundamentally sound features of most Asian economies: for example, budget surpluses, low inflation, high saving rates, export-oriented economies – all the features that are the usual staple of good developing economics. Indeed, this is what global investors used to think. Furthermore, there were considerable differences between the macroeconomic data and industrial mix of the various economies that, ultimately, shared the crisis; while other economies, particularly Taiwan, China, and to some extent Singapore, did weather the storm, avoiding a recession. So, on the one hand, there was an external source to the crisis, linked to the dynamics of global financial markets. On the other hand, economic diversity and institutional specificity led to very different outcomes in the impact of the crisis and its aftermath.[4] Let us consider these two observations, in sequence.

First of all, the external dimension of the crisis: why and how the globalization of finance affected the financial stability of a number of countries. Some elements of the Asian economies (such as politically regulated banking practices and lack of accounting transparency) were worrisome for prudent capitalist investment. But these had been well-known features for years, and they did not deter massive foreign investment, both direct and in securities. Why, suddenly, in 1997 did this confidence vanish in a few months? How, in the investors' perception, did government protection mutate into crony capitalism and financial flexibility into irresponsible lending? One major reason for the instability of Asian finance seems to have been the excessively large volume of foreign lending, much of it short term. It had reached such a dimension that, as Jeffrey Sachs suggested, investors understood that if every investor stopped lending, countries such as Thailand, Indonesia, and South Korea would default. Thus, as soon as concerns emerged on the overvaluation of certain currencies (the baht, the won, in particular), there was a race among investors to take out their money before others did. It became a self-fulfilling prophecy. When real-estate prices collapsed as a result of economic uncertainty, most of the assets guaranteeing outstanding loans vanished. And government support became non-viable when confronted with the scale of assistance needed by numerous banks and corporations, all at the same time. Then, global agencies deepened the crisis. Private rating agencies, such as Moody's and Standard & Poor, sounded the alarm by downgrading entire countries – South Korea, for instance – a downgrading that extends automatically to all financial firms and corporations operating from the downgraded country (the so-called "sovereign ceiling doctrine"). Thus, inflows of foreign investment came to a halt, except for bargain price acquisition of domestic fledgling firms, particularly in the financial industry. On the other hand, IMF-imposed policies saved much of the money of foreign investors at the price of worsening the credibility crisis, and stagnating the domestic economies by making it even more difficult for firms to repay the loans, thus extending bankruptcy. The weakest economies, such as Indonesia, literally collapsed, giving rise to widespread deindustrialization and reverse migration to the countryside. There followed substantial social unrest: sometimes chaotic, turning to ethnic/religious hatred; sometimes beneficial for social and political change (for example, the end of Suharto's dictatorship; economic reform and strengthening of

4   Henderson (1998a).

democracy in South Korea, under Kim Dae-Jung; political change in Thailand).

There is another factor which must be taken into consideration to account for the timing and characteristics of the Asian crisis. This is the crisis of Japan itself during most of the 1990s, which was a major factor in the inability of the region to react to the disruption provoked by volatile capital flows. Had Japan been able to lend capital, absorb imports, and reorganize financial markets, the Asian crisis would have been limited to a temporary turmoil. But, in fact, Japan had been suffering a structural crisis of its development model since the early 1990s. Furthermore, for some time the Japanese state indulged in self-denial, with the result that Japan, instead of being a rampart against the crisis in Asia, itself suffered seriously from the impact of financial collapse throughout the region. The shaky condition of Japanese banks and financial institutions became exposed, and the economy went into a recession, after years of stagnation, until Japan finally engaged in a process of economic reform that yielded some results in 1998–9. I will return later in the chapter to the specific crisis in Japan, and its relationship to the Asian crisis as a whole.

This interpretation of the Asian crisis must, however, be placed in the framework of a broader analysis, in line with the theory of informational, global capitalism proposed throughout this book. I argue that the main reason why global financial markets overwhelmed the stability of Asian national economies was because, by the mid-1990s, global financial flows had penetrated these economies so deeply that they had become addicted to massive short-term borrowing, a practice that made economies extremely vulnerable to any sudden reversal of investment flows. Speculative maneuvering was certainly a factor in the demise of a number of currencies. Yet we should not equate speculation with the supposed action of a few sinister characters conspiring in a corporate room. Rather, I understand by speculation profit-making strategies by investors of all kinds, including hedge fund firms, as well as institutional investors, linking up anonymously via computer networks to create financial advantage on a runaway currency or on a fledgling stock market – thus decisively amplifying market trends.

Yet, why did global financial flows acquire such an overwhelming role in Asian economies? It seems that two main factors were at work: first, the success of these economies, and their prospects for high economic growth; secondly, the weakness of their financial institutions, entirely dependent on the state. Foreign investors were obtaining returns substantially higher than in the US or European markets – with no questions asked. Since Asian governments had, for a long time, fully backed their banks and financial institutions (in the case of Hong

Kong, the main backer was, paradoxically, the PRC government, as shown in the 1997 crisis), the expectation was that, if anything went wrong, it would be covered by governments. So, what have become the general complaints of global investors (lack of legal regulation, government interference) were the very reasons that prompted unprecedented capital investment in Asia in the first place.

There is still another important question to be asked: why were Asian financial institutions, banks, and securities firms so shaky? Why did the mechanisms of financial steering that had allowed governments to create the most extraordinary process of economic growth in Asian history become ineffectual in managing global lending and investment? My view is that, throughout the process of fast development, between the early 1960s and late 1980s, Asian economies were protected by their states from the whirlwind of global financial markets – and even, to some extent, from global trade competition – while, on the other hand, Asian firms sheltered in their economies were becoming global players in trade and investment. When the scale of these economies, the size of these firms, and their interconnection with global capitalist networks led to a two-sided integration in the global economy, states could no longer protect or control movements of capital, goods, and services. Thus, they were bypassed by global economic flows, and were not in a position to regulate or command their economies under the pre-existing rules, made obsolete by their own success. With no protection from the state, Asian financial markets, and firms, were taken by global capital flows that made substantial profits, and then left these markets when their lack of transparency made them too risky. Calculated or not, it was, overall, and in most cases, a profitable operation for global investors (including globalized Asian capital), since the international bail-out of defaulted loans was mainly aimed to cover their losses. In addition, the busting of local firms became a welcome opportunity for foreign firms, particularly American and Western European, that could finally crack the financial industry in Asian countries, through acquisitions, and joint ventures, under very favorable conditions. In sum, the institutional system that was at the heart of the Asian miracle, the developmental state, became the obstacle for the new stage of global integration and capitalist development in the Asian economy. For Asian economies to fully join the global economy, not just as competitors and investors, but as markets and recipients of global investment, they had to come under the discipline of global financial markets. This implied their submission to standard market rules, enforced, when necessary, through bankruptcy, bad ratings, and subsequent IMF-style imposed policies. This was not the result of a capitalist plot, but the inexorable consequence of a shared, global, capitalist logic, enacted through the integration of financial and currency markets. The historic journey of the Asian developmental state succeeded in bringing poor, peripheral economies onto the high seas of informational capitalism. Then, upon reaching the stormy ocean of global financial networks, without a center, and without institutions, in most countries the developmental state sunk – a useless vessel, a captive of its anchoring in national shores. Economies and societies became gradually de-statized, while suddenly realizing the new tyranny of capital flows revealed by flashes of instructions on computer screens.

However, as Henderson has observed,[5] the pattern of development and crisis in the Asian Pacific varied greatly according to specific social, economic, and institutional environments. What happened in Japan, Korea, China, Singapore, Taiwan, Indonesia, or in any other country, was dependent upon the specific set of relationships between the state, economy, and society. Thus, we need to explain, at the same time, why each economy developed, why it suffered the crisis (or did not), and why the crisis affected, in varying degrees, countries with very different conditions. It is in the interplay of internal, social dynamics and external, financial flows, both mediated by the institutions of the state, that the explanation for the contradictory process of Asian Pacific development and crisis lies.

Thus, to understand the new historical stage of the Asian Pacific, and its relationship to the Information Age, I must retrace the social and institutional roots of its developmental saga, focusing on specific societies and developmental processes. Only after proceeding through a series of country-based analyses will I be able to return to the causes and consequences of the Asian crisis of 1997–8 to evaluate its potential outcome for the Pacific and for the world at large. Because societies are not global, but historically and culturally rooted, to proceed with the analysis of the rise of the Asian Pacific, I will summarize the historical journey of several societies over the past three decades. Because of the limits of my research capacity, I will have to omit from this observation some countries that are important for the understanding of the crisis, particularly Indonesia, Thailand, and Malaysia. However, I will try to integrate the analysis of their economic crises, in the context of the restructuring of the Asian Pacific, in the final section of this chapter. I will first focus on the process of development of the six lands that, together, constituted the core of the new Asian Pacific economy, and changed for ever the historical meaning of development. I will start with the decisive economy of the region – Japan – and will

5 Henderson (1998b).

continue with a study of the four Asian "tigers," ending with a summary view of the transformation of the Middle Kingdom, home to one-fifth of humankind.

Heisei's Japan: Developmental State versus Information Society[6]

Japan's defeat was inevitable. Japan lacked raw materials, was backward in science, and the character of the people have long been corrupted and blind. You should consider Japan's defeat as providential and as a divine judgment, and should work joyously to contribute to the reconstruction of our new fatherland. The Japanese people should be reborn. Having come to this conclusion, I am a happy man today [on the day of his execution].

Last letter from a medical officer of the Japanese Navy, executed in Guam in 1949.[7]

The process of economic growth, technological transformation, and social development achieved by Japan in the past half-century, emerging from the ashes of its crushed imperialistic ambitions, is nothing short of extraordinary. It has indeed changed the world, and our perception of world development, as it was able to combine growth with redistribution, raise real wages substantially, and reduce income inequality to one of the lowest levels in the world.[8] Furthermore, while Japanese social and environmental landscapes were deeply transformed, Japanese cultural identity was by and large preserved, in a powerful display of the historical feasibility of modernizing without Westernizing.[9] To be sure, these achievements required a strenuous effort from the entire Japanese society, with workers working many more hours

---

6 My analysis of Japanese society was mainly elaborated during my tenure as a visiting professor of sociology at Hitotsubashi University in 1995. I am particularly grateful to Professor Shujiro Yazawa, Dean of the Faculty of Social Sciences, both for his invitation, and for the most enlightening discussions we had, and continued to have later on. I am also indebted to the faculty and graduate students from various Japanese universities for their active participation and insightful input to my seminars at Hitotsubashi, and to my research assistant, Keisuke Hasegawa, who helped me with the analysis of Japanese material, and built a database on Japan's information society. Professor Kokichi Shoji, Chair of the Sociology Department at Tokyo University, generously provided me with a wealth of sociological studies on Japan, and shared with me his ideas on Japanese social transformation. Both Yazawa and Shoji have been sources of inspiration in my interpretation, but, naturally, they bear no responsibility for any of my statements or possible misunderstandings.
7 Quoted by Tsurumi (1970: 172).
8 Allen (1981); Tsuru (1993).
9 Reischauer (1988); Shoji (1991).

than their American and European counterparts, consuming much less, and saving/investing much more over a long period of time.[10] Japan was also paradoxically helped by the reforms imposed by the American occupation. Particularly important among these reforms were land reform, labor legislation, including the recognition of rights for organized labor, the prohibition of economic monopolies, leading to the dismantling of the *zaibatsu*, and new electoral laws that accorded women the right to vote. In addition, the military umbrella that the United States set up for Japan, in the context of the Cold War, freed the Japanese economy from the burden of military expenditures, and the Japanese state from foreign policy headaches that could have distracted it from its obsessive focus on production, technology, and exports. Yet, even taking into account this favorable context, the awesome process of development and structural transformation undergone by Japan can only be explained by the internal dynamics of Japanese society.

At the root of this dynamics was a project of affirmation of national identity, in historical continuity with 1868 *Ishin Meiji*. Japan was, and is, one of the most culturally and socially homogeneous societies in the world, albeit not as much as most Japanese think themselves, forgetting the millions of its residents who are Korean, Okinawan, and Ainu, as well as the culturally assimilated but socially excluded Burakumins. Its insular isolation for centuries reinforced this identity, which came under threat from Western colonialism's imposed opening to Western trade by the "black ships" of Commodore Perry in 1853. The reaction to this threat led to the Meiji Restoration, and to the accelerated modernization of the country in the following decades, as the only way to enable Japan to stand up to the Western challenge.[11] This is still the essential factor in understanding the social consensus and political legitimacy that have been the basis of Japan's developmental effort for more than a century. After the failure of both the democratic path to modernization during the Taisho period (1912–26), and of the militaristic, ultra-nationalist project in the second decade of Showa (1935–45), Japanese nationalism re-emerged in the form of a state-guided project of economic development oriented toward peaceful competition in the international economy.[12] An impoverished, defenseless country, entirely dependent in energy and natural resources, and confronted with self-doubt and, in progressive intellectual circles, with guilt and shame, Japan mobilized collectively: first to survive, then to compete, finally to assert itself by means of industrial produc-

10   Tsuru (1993).
11   Norman (1940).
12   Kato (1987); Beasley (1990).

tion, economic management, and technological innovation. This must be the starting point of any analysis of *Japanese development: it was the pursuit of national independence, and national power, by peaceful (economic) means*, in accordance with the 1947 Constitution, which renounced for ever war and armed forces. I will try to show the direct link between this nationalist project and the Japanese model of development that characterized both the hyper-growth period of 1956–73, and the bold techno-economic restructuring that successfully answered the challenges of the 1974 oil shock. However, the argument I put forward, in the context of my analysis of the emergence of the Pacific as a pivotal area for the twenty-first century, goes beyond a reassessment of this well-known experience of development. I suggest that *there is a fundamental crisis of the Japanese model of development in the* Heisei *period* (started on January 7, 1989), manifested during the 1990s in the instability of the political system, in sharp contrast to the preceding five decades; in the long recession that followed the bursting of the "bubble economy," and in the psychological confusion pervasive among significant sections of the youth, as dramatically revealed by the insurgency of *Aum Shinrikyo* (see volume II, chapter 3). I propose the hypothesis that *this multidimensional crisis results precisely from the success of the Japanese model of development, which induced new economic, social, and cultural forces that came to challenge the priority of the nationalist project, and therefore, the developmental state*. The conditions and forms of resolution of this crisis will deeply affect Japanese society, Japan's relations with the Pacific, and, ultimately, the fate of the whole Pacific area.

A social model of the Japanese developmental process[13]

It should be evident, after decades of research in the sociology of development, that processes of economic growth and structural trans-

---

13 In my opinion, the best political economic analysis on the origins and characteristics of Japanese development, from a Western perspective, is a little-known book by a distinguished English scholar, G.C. Allen (1981). Of course, the classic study on the formation and workings of the developmental state, and the one that invented the concept, is Chalmers Johnson's *MITI and the Japanese Miracle* (1982). For further elaboration of this perspective see a selection of his writings on Japan's political system in Johnson (1995). The best historical analysis of the emergence of Japan's modern state, starting with the Meiji Restoration, remains the one by Norman (1940). For a Japanese view of the process of economic development since the 1950s, see Tsuru (1993). On the cultural and psychological conditions under which the new developmental state emerged, see Tsurumi (1970). For a sweeping socio-political analysis of Japan's evolution in the period 1960–90, with emphasis on neo-nationalism, see Shoji (1991). For an analysis of Japanese social movements, see Yazawa (1997). For a study of cultural nationalism, see Yoshino (1992). If you want to indulge in

formation are embedded in institutions, oriented by culture, supported by social consensus, shaped by social conflict, fought over by politics, and guided by policies and strategies.[14] At the heart of the Japanese process of development, since the 1950s, is the nationalist project of the developmental state, enacted by the state bureaucracy on behalf of the nation.[15] In a nutshell, state bureaucracy has guided and coordinated Japanese corporations, organized in business networks (*keiretsu* and *kigyo shudan*), helping them through trade policy, technology policy, and credit, to compete successfully in the world economy. Trade surplus was recycled as financial surplus and, together with a high rate of domestic savings, allowed for non-inflationary expansion, making possible at the same time high rates of investment, rapidly rising real wages, and improvement in living standards. High rates of investment in R&D, and a focus on advanced manufacturing, enabled Japan to take a leading position in information technology industries at a time when their products and processes were becoming essential in the global economy. This economic performance relied on social stability and high labor productivity through management–labor cooperation, made possible by stable employment, and by seniority-based promotion, for the core labor force. Labor market flexibility was assured by part-time and contingent employment, usually made up of women, whose rate of participation in the labor force sky-rocketed. Overall social stability relied on three major factors: (a) people's commitment to rebuilding the nation; (b) access to consumption, and substantial improvement in living standards; and (c) a strong, stable patriarchal family, which reproduced traditional values, induced work

Western criticisms of Japanese society and politics (biased, in my opinion), you will find them in Van Wolferen (1989), and Harvey (1994). For a sympathetic Western perspective, see Reischauer (1988). For a theoretical interpretation of the Japanese state, see Kato (1984, 1987), and Taguchi and Kato (1985). An interesting chronicle of the internal dynamics of the Japanese state is Ikuta (1995). An excellent, up-to-date study of *Kanryo* (the Japanese bureaucracy) is Inoguchi (1995). An empirical analysis of Japanese political life can be found in Kishima (1991). For a study of Japanese political machines, including political corruption, see Schlesinger (1997). On Japanese neo-nationalism, see Watanabe (1996). On the condition of women, and women's mobilization in Japan see Ueno (1987); Gelb and Lief-Palley (1994); Shinotsuka (1994); and Yazawa (1995). On the Japanese family, see Seki (1987) and Totani and Yatazawa (1990). For an empirical view on Japanese schools, see Tsuneyoshi (1994). For a guided sociological bibliography of Japanese sources, see Shoji (1994). For Japanese business structure, industrial relations, work organization, labor markets, and employment practices, see my analysis in volume I, chapters 3 and 4. I will not repeat here references to sources used in these analyses, which can be found in volume I. Other sources used in my analysis in this section are cited in the footnotes to the text. Naturally, the overwhelming mass of potential sources on bibliography and data for the subjects covered in this section is not even touched. *I am referring only to those sources that I have directly used in my elaboration.*

14   Evans (1995).
15   Kato (1984); Taguchi and Kato (1985); Johnson (1995).

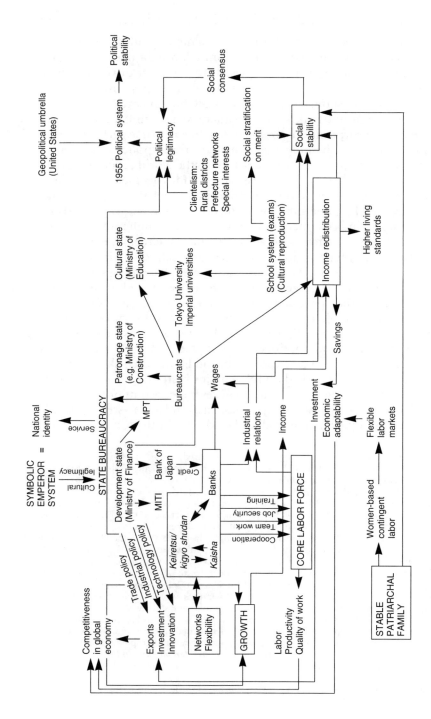

Chart 4.1 A social model of Japanese development, 1955–85

ethics, and provided personal security for its members, at the cost of keeping women under submission. Political stability was ensured by organizing a coalition of interests and patronage constituencies under the umbrella of the Liberal Democratic Party, which controlled the government until 1993, counting on the adamant support of the United States, regardless of widespread corruption practices. The developmental state, while building its specific legitimacy by delivering the promise of economic development, benefited, additionally, from a double source of legitimacy: from people's votes for the LDP, and from the "Symbolic Emperor system," which provided historical continuity with the roots of national identity. Chart 4.1 attempts a synthetic representation of the social/institutional logic underlying Japan's economic development. I will go into a brief elaboration to clarify this excessively condensed summary.

As in all processes of social mobilization, it is essential to identify the sources of legitimacy that allow the dominant actor in the process (in this case the Japanese state) to find support in society, and to bring business under its coordination. The origins of the state's legitimacy are to be found outside the bureaucracy, in the so-called "Symbolic Emperor system" (*Shocho Tennosei*), and, since the 1947 Constitution, to a lesser extent, in the democratically elected political system. I say to a lesser extent because the government, while constitutionally elected, was dependent for almost five decades on "*Nagatacho* politics"; that is, the coalition of interests, factions, and patronage networks organized around the Liberal Democratic Party, rigged by corruption, and hardly valued in the eyes of most people. The guidance of the development process came essentially from an efficient, usually clean, state bureaucracy, which ensured the stability of policy-making, bridging over the quarrels between different factions of the LDP, formed of a miscellaneous coalition of interests, ideologies, and personalities.[16] Although formally dependent on the government, the state bureaucracy built its legitimacy on the values of an updated Symbolic Emperor system. Masao Maruyama wrote in 1946 a classic of Japanese political science, which is still considered to be the most insightful analysis of the Symbolic Emperor system, and of its role in Japanese culture and politics. According to his analysis, "In Japan we are faced with a situation in which national sovereignty involves both spiritual authority and political power. The standard according to which the nation's actions are judged as right or wrong lies within itself (that is in the 'national polity')."[17] This is because

16   Inoguchi (1995); Schlesinger (1997).
17   Maruyama (1963: 8).

whereas in the West national power after the Reformation was based on formal, external sovereignty, the Japanese state [after Meiji] never came to the point of drawing a distinction between the external and internal spheres and of recognizing that its authority was valid only for the former . . . Accordingly, until the day in 1946 when the divinity of the Emperor was formally denied in an Imperial Rescript, there was in principle no basis in Japan for freedom of belief. Since the nation includes in its "national polity" all the internal values of truth, morality, and beauty, neither scholarship nor art could exist apart from these national values . . . It was precisely when the success motive joined forces with nationalism that modern Japan was able to embark on its "rush towards progress." Yet, at the same time it was this very combination that led to Japan's decay. For the logic according to which private affairs cannot be morally justified within themselves but must always be identified with national affairs, has a converse implication: private interests endlessly infiltrate into national concerns.[18]

The social logic of what would become corporatist Japan, or Japan Inc. in the labeling of its critics, is implicit in Maruyama's analysis of political culture. After the humiliating defeat of the ultra-nationalist project, a revamped Symbolic Emperor system ensured historical continuity and political legitimacy for a bureaucracy that went on to reconstruct the country, and, in the process, discovered pragmatically how to create a strong, modern Japan by taking on the world economy. G.C. Allen and Chalmers Johnson have provided convincing empirical analyses of the rise of the Japanese developmental state, and its critical role in guiding strategically the nation's economic growth, at least between 1955 and 1985.[19] The dominating agency in this bureaucracy is the Ministry of Finance, which controls the purse, and thus has the material power of decision-making. Its two main instruments are the legendary MITI (Ministry of International Trade and Industry) and the Bank of Japan, since credit, export/import allocations, and support for technological development are the essential tools through which state bureaucracy is able to coordinate, help, organize competition, and, sometimes, subdue Japanese business. Additionally, other infrastructure-oriented ministries, particularly the Ministry of Posts and Telecommunications (MPT), from the 1980s onwards, were also critical in providing the material conditions of production, and in selectively organizing the diffusion of technology. In parallel, and sometimes in conflict, other ministries performed different functions, according to their specific field of competence. Thus, the Ministry of Education had the care of preserving cultural identity, and organizing

18   Maruyama (1963: 6–7).
19   Allen (1981); Johnson (1982, 1995).

an orderly system of stratification and social mobility by enforcing a hierarchical, rigid examination system, which punctuated the entire lives of Japanese children and young people, and thus encapsulated all families into the ideology and rituals of meritocracy. Other ministries performed more political functions. Thus, the Ministry of Construction, the Ministry of Agriculture, and the Ministry of Transport seem to have played a major role in channeling private funds into the political campaigns of the LDP, and into securing local clienteles by distributing government funds to receptive local and provincial governments.[20] The coherence of the state bureaucracy, including that of the branches belonging to the developmental state, should not be over-emphasized. As all states, the Japanese state is also torn by internal conflicts, and contradictory interests, as various bureaucracies vie to establish their position in the power game. For instance, the MPT's role was not limited to infrastructure and technology, since its control of the largest source of savings, through the postal savings system, gave it the power decisively to intervene in financial markets, and into government funding of public and private investments. Furthermore, while, in general terms, the state bureaucracy was largely autonomous of the political elites, and less influenced by interest groups, there was considerable cross-breeding between politicians and bureaucrats, as ministerial posts served as power bases for various political factions, adding complexity to the system. However, cultural homogeneity, and a shared belief in the superior interests of the nation, still symbolically embodied in the Emperor system, were assured through strict control of recruitment sources for the top bureaucracy, from institutions carefully monitored by the Ministry of Education. Key elements in this recruitment were (and still are) the University of Tokyo, particularly its Faculty of Law, and the imperial universities which, together with a few elite private universities, supply practically all the members of the top bureaucracy. This social cohesion at the top permeates throughout society, since only about 1 percent of these recruits make it to the top of the state bureaucracy. The others, in the later stages of their career, "descend from heaven," taking positions as corporate executives, political leaders, or heads of para-public foundations in charge of structuring and guiding civil society. Thus, the cultural glue of the bureaucratic class diffuses by the circulation of elites between different spheres of social and economic life, ensuring the communication of ideas, the negotiation of interests, and the reproduction of ideology.

The mechanisms inducive to economic growth, designed and imple-

20   Ikuta (1995); Johnson (1995).

mented by this nationalist bureaucracy, have been exposed in a flurry of monographs on the "Japanese miracle": an all-out export orientation, on the basis of outstanding competitiveness, made possible by substantial increases in labor productivity, by the quality of work, and by protection of domestic markets; abundance of capital, on the basis of a high savings rate, and short-term lending to the banks of *keiretsu* by the Bank of Japan, at a low interest rate; sustained effort in technological development with government-sponsored programs of technology acquisition, and technological innovation; emphasis on manufacturing; industrial policy, shifting from low-technology to medium-technology, then to high-technology industries, following the evolution of technology, of world demand, and of the productive capacity of Japanese industries. MITI, after clearing its programs with the Ministry of Finance, played a substantial role in strategic planning, and in helping, guiding, and supporting Japanese business networks, particularly in trade policy, in technology policy, and in industrial policy, deciding the sectors of priority for investment. Its decisions were not always successful, nor were they necessarily followed. For instance, the much-publicized Fifth Generation Computers Program in the 1980s was a fiasco. And most of the 26 Technopoles induced by MITI's Technopolis Program in prefectures around the country in the 1980s and 1990s, when and if successful, were agglomerations of branch plants rather than mini-Silicon Valleys, as MITI intended in its original vision. Yet, over time, more often than not, MITI's strategic planners were on target, and Japanese industries were able to move with remarkable speed from low value added to high value added products and processes, overtaking Europe first, and the United States later, in most key industries, from automobiles to semiconductors, until the technological/managerial counter-offensive of American companies in the 1990s put them ahead of Japanese competitors in the higher tier of microcomputers, software, microelectronics, telecommunications, biotechnology, and in the decisive, new industry developed around the Internet. Yet, Japanese firms continue to dominate consumer electronics, memory chips, and semiconductors equipment manufacturing, and hold very strong competitive positions in a whole range of advanced manufacturing industries, with the important exceptions of pharmaceuticals and chemicals. And it would be ill advised to discount their future competitiveness in Internet-related technologies and business.

The effectiveness of administrative guidance was decisively helped by the networking structure of Japanese business, which I presented in some detail in volume I, chapter 3. By coordinating a few players, and by keeping competition between corporate networks at the top, the

state bureaucrats were able to reach out to the entire economic structure without resorting to the self-destructive procedure of centralized
planning. The Japanese model is a critical experience in showing how
strategic, selective state intervention can make a market economy more
productive, and more competitive, thus rejecting ideological claims
about the inherent superior efficiency of *laissez-faire* economics.

But none of the above could have worked without full cooperation
between management and labor, the source of productivity, stability,
and long-range strategic investment, which were the ultimate determinants of Japanese competitiveness. Trade protectionism was widely
practiced by Latin American economies, some of them very large, without ever being able to emerge as major players in high value added,
global markets. It was labor's involvement at the shop-floor level, and
the social peace enjoyed by Japanese business, that provided, early on,
a decisive edge to the Japanese economy. This was particularly important in ensuring the Japanese transition to information-technology
based manufacturing and services, requiring the full mobilization of
labor's thinking capacity to make the best out of new technologies.
But labor's involvement and cooperation with firms cannot be attributed to ethno-cultural idiosyncrasy. The strong cultural specificity of
Japanese workers did not prevent them from mobilizing, striking, and
organizing a militant labor movement when they had the freedom to
do so, in the 1920s and early 1930s, and then again in the late 1940s
and 1950s.[21] These struggles led to a series of labor and social policy
reforms in the 1950s. On the basis of these reforms, around 1960
a new system of labor policy and industrial relations was set up by
Japanese business and government. It was built around four major
features. The first was a commitment by companies to long-term employment for the core labor force of large firms, either in the firm or in
other firms of the *keiretsu*; in exchange, Japanese workers would also
commit themselves to remain in the same firm for the duration of their
working lives. The second was the seniority system for promotion,
thus removing management's discretionary power to reward/punish
workers, therefore dividing them through individual competition; this
seniority system allowed for predictability in workers' life patterns.
The third feature was the cooperative system of working practices,
including a flat organizational hierarchy in supervisory work in factories and offices, the formation of work teams and quality control
circles, and widespread use of workers' initiative in improving the efficiency and quality of the production process. The fourth factor was
the company-based organization of labor unions, which identified the

21   Yazawa (1997).

interests of union leaders and members with the interests of the firm. There were/are Japanese labor federations, and there is also collective bargaining of sorts at the national level for some sectors, preceded by symbolic mobilization (such as the ritual "spring offensives") in order to assert organized labor's potential. Yet, by and large, through firm-specific unionism, workers' participation at the shop-floor level, and joint commitment from management and labor to the well-being of the national economy, Japanese capitalism has enjoyed better industrial relations than any other market economy.

These labor practices were essential for the implementation of mechanisms that are usually associated with successful Japanese management practices, as I argued in my analysis of Japanese labor and working arrangements in volume I, chapters 3 and 4. Thus, the "just in time" system to eliminate inventories can only function in the absence of work stoppages, derived from a smooth system of industrial relations. The development and diffusion of "tacit knowledge" by workers which, according to Nonaka and Takeuchi's influential analysis is at the source of the "knowledge-generating company,"[22] is only possible if workers have incentives to invest their unique expertise, their insider knowledge of the company's production system, in the success of the firm to which they belong. In sum, labor productivity and quality of work, fundamental sources of Japanese competitiveness, were based on a system of working cooperation and industrial relations that was made possible by substantial gains for labor, including generous company benefits, and long-term commitment to keep jobs, even during downturns of the business cycle. It is also true, however, that some cultural elements, such as the search for Wa (harmony) in working relations, the communal spirit of teamwork, and the national mobilization to rebuild Japan, and to make it a strong, respected nation, also contributed to the consolidation of the social pact achieved between business, labor, and government around 1960.

None the less, this cooperative dimension of labor relations is only part of the story of Japanese labor markets. Following the empirical analysis that I presented in volume I, chapter 4, flexibility of labor markets was assured by much more flexible labor practices, and fewer workers' rights, in small firms, in traditional sectors (such as retail trade), and for part-time workers in large firms. Much of this part-time and contingent employment was, and increasingly is, the lot of women, particularly of married women, who return to work after rearing children in their early years. The expanding women's labor market (currently reaching about 50 percent of adult women) is the key to

22   Nonaka and Takeuchi (1994).

flexibility and adaptability of labor markets, ensuring the stability of the core labor force, as the source of labor productivity, while still allowing firms to cushion themselves during recessions by firing contingent workers. In other industrialized countries there is a similar segmentation of labor markets, leading to an equally segmented social structure, thus to inequality and poverty. The true miracle of Japanese society is that this class segmentation is cancelled by the strength of the Japanese patriarchal family, which reunites within the family stable male workers and contingent female workers, so that social cleavages are dissolved in the unity of the family. This is particularly significant when we consider the high level of education of Japanese women, which means that this contingent labor is not less skilled, but simply less valued.

Patriarchalism is an essential ingredient of the Japanese developmental model. And not only for economic reasons. The patriarchal family has survived accelerated industrialization and modernization as a stable unit of personal stability and cultural reproduction. Rates of divorce, while increasing, are way below those in other advanced industrialized countries, except Italy and Spain (see volume II, chapter 3). Almost two-thirds of elderly Japanese were living with their adult children in 1980, and the majority still do, even if the proportion has declined rapidly in the past 30 years. Children are, by and large, kept under strict parental discipline, and the culture of shame is still a major determinant of their behavior. Women fulfill all their roles with little sign of widespread rebellion, to a large extent because most Japanese husbands, unlike in America, have honored their patriarchal commitments, usually not indulging in the pursuit of personal happiness outside family rules (see volume II, chapter 3). When necessary the state comes in to add a little institutional twist, rewarding patriarchalism. For instance, the Japanese tax code makes it nonsensical for women to add too much money beyond part-time wages because the double-income household tax bracket becomes punitively high. The contribution of educated, hyper-active women to Japanese flexible labor markets, stable families and traditional culture is a critical component of the entire social and economic balance of Japan. And perhaps the weakest link in the Japanese model, if comparative experience is of any value.

Cultural reproduction is also assured by the state, particularly through the Ministry of Education, which closely supervises educational programs from pre-schools to leading universities. Emphasis is placed on traditional culture, and on a hierarchical, complex examination system which determines the occupational fate of each Japanese person, most often very early in his or her life. Strict discipline is the rule, as exemplified in a tragic incident in 1990 when a schoolgirl was killed when trapped by the sliding gate installed by the school to keep out pupils arriving late for class. This stratified, cultural homogeneity is essential in ensuring cooperation, communication, and a sense of belonging in a communal/national culture, while acknowledging social differences and respecting everybody's relative place. The combined pressure of a strong patriarchal family from below, and of a strong Ministry of Education from above, smooths cultural reproduction, and exiles alternative values to radical challenges outside the system, thus marginalizing rebellion.

On the basis of rising standards of living, industrial cooperation, orderly reproduction of traditional values, and social mobilization on behalf of the nation, political stability was assured by a makeshift coalition of personalities, interest groups, and clienteles, hastily assembled under the name of the Liberal Democratic Party, in the wake of American occupation. The LDP was (much like the Italian Christian Democrats, built by the Vatican and the United States to resist communism and socialism) an unstable coalition of political factions, each one with its "capo" (the most powerful of whom was Kakuei Tanaka), around whom a web of interests, complicities, machinations, silences, and debts was weaved for five decades. Benefiting from American complacency (a fundamental matter for Japanese business, which needed a US-trusted interlocutor to assure critical access to American markets and supplies), the LDP's factions perfected the art of political intermediation. They exchanged votes for money, money for favors, favors for positions, positions for patronage, then patronage for votes, and so on. They constantly quarreled about control of resources in this patronage system, but always united around their common good. They were periodically rocked by scandals, particularly after the 1976 "Lockheed affair," which prompted the resignation of Prime Minister Tanaka, and showed the possibility of political revelations in the media, an event similar to the impact of Nixon's Watergate on US politics. As analyzed in volume II, chapter 6, political corruption was, in Japan as in most other countries, linked to the financing of political campaigns, and of political factions, adding also a little tip for the party's fundraisers. As mentioned above, the Ministries of Construction, Agriculture, and Transport seem to have been privileged mechanisms for channeling state funds to favored private companies, in exchange for which, companies funded the LDP's activities and leaders, and local bosses delivered votes.[23] But this was certainly not the only source of political funding. Furthermore, open links between the

23   Ikuta (1995); Johnson (1995); Schlesinger (1997).

Yakuza and LDP leaders (including Prime Ministers) have been repeatedly exposed in the Japanese media.

Beyond political corruption, traditional patronage systems ensured widespread support for LDP candidates in rural districts and less-developed provinces. Electoral law over-represented these districts in Parliament, thus making it extremely difficult to challenge the LDP's repeated success. It worked. For almost five decades, for all its limitations, the LDP system ensured political stability in Japan, keeping conflicts within "the family," and letting the populace enjoy their hard-earned prosperity while becoming increasingly cynical about all politicians. However, this system was only able to survive, in spite of its limited legitimacy, because a higher authority, the Symbolic Emperor system, remained a moral guarantee for the Japanese people, and because a cast of enlightened despots took care of the affairs of the state, bringing business and workers together in the rebuilding of the nation.

This was the social model of development that stunned the world, scared America, and sent European governments running for the cover of the European Union. It was coherent, powerful, brilliant indeed. It was also short-lived by historical standards, as it reached its zenith in the mid-1980s, and entered into an open, structural crisis around the early years of the *Heisei* period.

Declining sun: the crisis of the Japanese model of development

From the mid-1980s Japan went gradually into a structural crisis, expressed in different dimensions of the economic, social, and political landscape. While in 1999 the Japanese economy seemed to be on its way to recovery, most of the problems underlying the crisis were unsolved, by and large, so that the restructuring of Japan was still unfolding at the turn of the century. The 1990s' crisis manifested itself in a series of apparently unrelated events, whose interconnected logic I hope to be able to show at the end of my analysis.

Let us focus first on the financial crisis that seems to be at the forefront of Japan's structural crisis.[24] Boiling down the complexity of the financial crisis to its essence, the main problem was the staggering amount of bad loans accumulated by Japanese banks, estimated in 1998 at about 80 trillion yen, equivalent to 12 percent of Japan's GDP.

24   The analysis of the Japanese financial crisis in the 1996–8 period is based on reports in the business press, as cited in note 2. For useful overviews, see *The Economist* (1997); Eisenstodt (1998); and the intriguing scenarios of Nakame International Economic Research, Nikkei, and Global Business Network (1998).

Foreign experts, assessing the situation of Japanese banks in 1998, considered that only two of the top 19 banks had an adequate capitalization to cover their potential losses. The most blatant case was that of one of the largest banks in the world, the Long Term Credit Bank, in which the government intervened in the fall of 1998, after it became in default for over US$7 billion, before being sold to a financial group organized around Ripplewood Holdings, an American fund management firm. Among the banks in a desperate situation were Fuji Bank, with $17 billion in bad loans, Sakura Bank, with another $11 billion in potential losses, and Nippon Credit, $1.5 billion in debt, all of which were variously nationalized, restructured and merged, or, in some cases, liquidated, in 1998–9. The near-default situation of Japanese banks depreciated the value of their stocks and made it prohibitively expensive for them to access international credit. Accordingly, surviving banks drastically restricted their lending, thus drying up credit for the economy. In 1998, for the first time since the 1970s' oil crisis, Japan's economy shrunk.

The key question is: why were there so many bad loans, and why was their potential default ignored for such a long time? The answer lies in the contradictions built into the model of Japanese development, aggravated by the growing exposure of Japanese financial institutions to global financial markets. Let me explain. Japan's high growth relied on a government-backed financial system geared toward ensuring security for both savers and banks, while providing low-interest, easy credit for firms. For a long time, Japanese financial institutions operated in relative isolation from international capital flows, and under regulations and policy guidelines set and interpreted by the Ministry of Finance. The stock market was not a major source of finance, and did not provide an attractive investment for savings. High saving rates were critical to fuel investment without inflation. But the intermediation between savings and investments was channeled through deposits in the post office, in banks, and in savings and loans. In 1997, the share of deposits over GDP was 92.5 percent in Japan, compared with 34 percent in the US. So, banks and savings institutions were loaded with cash, eager to lend it. Banks were linked to a *keiretsu*, and thus were obliged in their lending practices to preferred customers. In return, they were covered by the overall *keiretsu* structure. The government took care that no bank would go bankrupt. Loans were collateralized by property and shares. So, with low risk, and low interest rates, banks had a vested interest in high-volume lending, rather than in profit margins. As easy money propelled the economy, both internationally and domestically, high rates of growth seemed to assure the repayment of loans, providing more cash for future loans.

Besides, real-estate prices sky-rocketed, particularly in Tokyo, and Osaka, providing more collateral value for an endless expansion of money-lending. The reasons for this overvaluation of land and real estate were twofold. On the one hand, rapid accumulation of capital in Japan, which was, mainly, the result of continuing trade surplus, made funds available for investment in real estate, pushing up land prices. On the other hand, the unplanned, chaotic nature of Japanese urbanization, in sharp contrast with the careful strategic planning of production and technology, induced a wild real-estate market.[25] Fast economic growth concentrated population and activities in dense urban areas, in a country already obsessed with the scarcity of usable land. Land prices increased dramatically because of mechanisms of political patronage which provided a special bonus to a large number of small landholders, many of them in the rural periphery of metropolitan areas. As an illustration, between 1983 and 1988 average prices of residential and commercial land rose, respectively, by 119 percent and 203 percent in the Tokyo area.[26] Real-estate speculation by petty landlords was helped by major financial firms, which benefited most from it. Local governments were assured of revenues, and of political support, precisely by not planning, and not providing housing alternatives, letting the market decide, making landowners, and banks, artificially rich in inflated real-estate values. At the same time, people aspiring to home ownership had to increase their savings, thus providing additional money to banks and financial institutions. In a related development, the stock market, also fueled by the proceeds of Japanese exports, multiplied its value, thus inducing additional lending, supposedly secured by inflated stock assets. As long as the system worked, based on competitiveness abroad, high earnings from exports, high saving rates, and inflated values at home, the financial system fueled its own expansion. Indeed, business consultants from around the world flocked to Tokyo to study, and praise, the miracle of a financial system able to self-generate value, while spurring industrial and trade competitiveness. By 1990, eight of the ten largest banks in the world, measured by the volume of their deposits, were Japanese.

There was also another, hidden, dimension to the practice of easy lending: the biased access to credit. Banks were obliged to lend to firms, individuals, or organizations that had a privileged access to the bank, regardless of the soundness of the investment or the risk of the loan. There were (are?) four main sources of this "preferred borrower" pattern. The first was the firms of the bank's *keiretsu*, so that lending

25 Machimura (1994).
26 Fukui (1992: 217).

policy was part of a broader corporate policy. Second was the advice, direct or indirect, of the Ministry of Finance concerning a particular loan deemed to be of interest to the Japanese economy. The third was the yielding of the bank (or savings and loans institution) to pressures from firms connected to the *Yakuza* (see above, chapter 3). The fourth was the financing of political parties, usually the government party, the LDP, or support for some of their personnel. After all, in return, banks were shielded from bad fortune precisely by the ultimate protection of the government, their *keiretsu*, and the banking industry at large. The circle was closed. With financial markets, individual investors, and consumers having little influence over the banking system, Japanese finance worked as a text-book case of state-capitalist corporatism. Banks had little autonomy: they were mainly an instrument for capturing savings and allocating them to targets decided by the entangled web of Japan Inc., to serve the national interest of Japan, and the personal interest of its representatives.

As long as it lasted, this system was highly dynamic, and reasonably efficient in fulfilling its own goals. But when it reversed itself, shifting from value creation to value destruction, it shattered the Japanese economy. Three sets of factors were critical in the demise of this financial system. First, the real-estate and stockmarket bubble burst in 1991. Secondly, the exposure of Japanese financial institutions to global financial markets made it increasingly difficult to follow Japanese customary financial practices. Thirdly, the government lost much of its capacity to cover bank debt and potential default. Let us examine these three developments in some detail.

First, the bubble burst because all bubbles do eventually. It is called the business cycle. But there were specific, aggravating circumstances in the Japanese case. An overheated economy pushed the yen's exchange rate upwards, undermining Japanese trade competitiveness. But a strong yen, and a buoyant stock market, induced corporations to enter financial investment and lent large sums, both internationally and domestically. Real-estate prices finally came down because of the structural incapacity of housing demand to absorb price increases and because of overcapacity in the office-building market. Stock markets followed the drop, destabilizing Japan's financial system, which was based on the risky assumption of a continuous, high-flying pattern. Fearful of inflation, the government put the brakes on the economy, inducing a recession in the early 1990s. The sharp decline of the stock market, together with the real-estate collapse, erased by 1996 most of the value artificially generated in the 1980s (see figure 4.1). For the first time in four decades, Japan's economy became stagnant, and only recovered in the mid-1990s, stimulated by government spending, al-

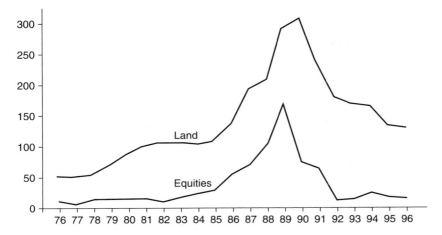

Figure 4.1   Japan's values in equities and land in billions of yen, 1976–96 (unrealized profits total value)
Source: The Economist (1997: 4)

beit growing at a slow pace.[27] But this recovery was short-lived. Financial instability forced banks to tighten their lending practices. So, in spite of the government's effort to lower interest rates, which hit historic low levels in 1998 at around 1 percent, the economy was squeezed of money, halting growth. In 1997 and 1998, Japan slid into sharp downturn.

Yet the most serious problem affecting Japanese finance came from its growing exposure to global financial markets. Three main issues should be considered in this regard. First, faced with a stagnant Japanese economy, and with a booming Asian Pacific market, Japanese banks and financial institutions lent heavily in these emerging markets. They reproduced the same lending practices that they used at home: they lent short term, in large volume, to preferred customers, regardless of their solvency, under the double guarantee of major local corporations and governments. They took overvalued real-estate property as collateral for many of their loans. In so doing, they exposed their Asian lending to the same risks as their Japanese loans. When the Asian real-estate bubble burst, many loans lost their collateral, inducing their default. When the stock market collapsed in Thailand, Indonesia, Malaysia, the Philippines, South Korea, and Hong Kong, domestic firms which guaranteed the loans became unable to repay

27   *Asahi Shimbun* (1995).

them. When local currencies plunged, Japanese banks were unable to recover their dollar, or yen, denominated loans. And when they turned to Asian governments, including their expensively acquired "friends" in government, asking them to honor their commitments, governments simply could not do it. Governments were faced with a mountain of financial debts which became due at the same time. So, looking for salvation in the Asian markets, Japanese financial institutions largely contributed to exporting their crisis, which eventually came home to roost.

Secondly, when Japanese financial firms became global players, it was more difficult for them to continue with insider trading and borderline business practices that had been customary at home. This is not because they went into a "cleaner environment." In fact, there are numerous examples of questionable, risky, and even illegal practices in Western financial institutions. US and European governments and banking industries have had their share of having to bail out banks and financial institutions that would have collapsed, and provoked financial panic, without decisive government action, often using taxpayers' money. The bailing out of savings and loans associations in the US in the 1980s (at the staggering cost of $250 billion), the closing of BCCI in Luxembourg, the salvaging of Crédit Lyonnais in France (covering a financial hole of US$100 million), and the 1998 rescue of Long Term Capital Management in New York (a $4 billion bail out), are illustrations of a widespread pattern of risky financial practices in the global economy. The problem for Japanese banks and securities firms was that they did not have a precise grasp of the rules of the game abroad. In other words, they did not have the same inside knowledge and networks of contracts, globally, that they enjoyed in Japan. Moreover, unlike in Japan, they could not count on the complicity of governments in the main financial markets around the world. By the time they learned the global rules, the hard way, it was too late for many of the banks and securities firms. Among others, Sanwa Bank was penalized in the United States; Nomura Securities was hit by scandal and huge losses in Japan and the US; and Yamaichi Securities, one of the largest firms in the world, was forced into bankruptcy in 1997.

Furthermore, by fully embracing global financial markets, Japanese banks and securities firms joined the growing legion of apparently mighty, yet powerless, financial groups. In other words, while accumulating, and investing, huge volumes of capital, they had little control of events that shape, and reshape, financial markets. So, Japanese firms were exposed to the same risks as others around the world. But there were two factors which became sources of higher risk for Japanese firms. First, they had built a financial pyramid, counting on repayment of risky loans, on the basis of high, sustained growth. Any downturn could cause a chain effect of financial losses, given the short-term horizon of a substantial part of their lending. Secondly, there is what I call the "weak giant paradox." Contrary to what common sense might dictate, the larger a financial institution in the current system of global finance, the more vulnerable it is to crisis. This is because size determines the extent of involvement around the world. The higher the volume of capital requiring return, the larger the scope and the scale of operation in which the financial institution has to be involved in order to ensure average profits. Global financial markets are interdependent, and turbulence in any node of these financial networks diffuses to other markets, for reasons largely independent of economic fundamentals. Thus, the larger the exposure of investments from a firm, the higher the probability of suffering a loss somewhere – or, simultaneously, multiple losses. Conversely, the probability of earning a profit, in successful markets, also increases with size. But since profits and losses are not predictable in time and space, volatility of returns on investment will increase with size and complexity of the financial firm. Thus, for a given level of risk, the larger the firm, and the larger the extent of its globalization, the higher will be the volatility of its financial yields. Hedge funds were supposed to be an answer to this paradox. Instead, they have become the most adventurous sources of investment patterns. Usually, hedge fund firms bet on alternative scenarios of a financial asset not to diminish risk, but to earn extra profits on the relative discrepancies in time and space between the two sides of the bet. Thus, ultimately, hedge funds increase financial volatility, rather than preventing it. In this context, when giant Japanese banks, loaded with cash from Japanese corporations' trade surpluses, went global, they became increasingly vulnerable to the instability of financial markets, accelerated by the speed of electronic transactions (see volume I, chapter 2).

The third major development inducing the crisis of the Japanese financial system was the declining capacity of the Japanese government to cover the losses of financial institutions. This was due to several reasons. Losses grew in volume and size to such a level that public funds came up increasingly short of what was needed, particularly when losses took place at the same time because of the ripple effect of financial pyramids. Trying to stimulate the economy out of stagnation, the Ministry of Finance lowered interest rates, depriving banks of additional revenue. Besides, available public funds were assigned to public works investment, reducing the financial margin of maneuver to bail out banks with taxpayers' money. Yet, the most important factor in accounting for the government's dwindling capacity to revamp the financial system was its political weakness. As I will discuss below, the end of the LDP's dominance of Japanese politics meant that decision-making had to be made accountable to opposition parties. When scandal after scandal wrecked public trust, the government lost the power to help financial friends in trouble behind the scene. Furthermore, the crisis of confidence affected, for the first time, the Japanese bureaucracy, particularly the formerly all-powerful Finance Ministry. In 1997–8, all calls for reform from the opposition began with the demand to set up an independent financial agency, separate from the Ministry of Finance, to oversee financial reform. Thus, the political weakness of both the LDP and the bureaucracy contributed to the crisis of the old financial system. And the deepening of the crisis contributed to weakening the government even further, thus making it increasingly difficult to refloat banks without political accountability.

Finally, the three factors I have analyzed – namely, the reversal of the business cycle, the contradictions inherent in the globalization of finance, and the crisis of political management – reinforced each other throughout the 1990s, spiraling the overall banking crisis out of control. While the government rushed to protect investors, irreversible damage was done to the credibility of Japanese financial institutions. The partial deregulation of financial transactions, allowing easier movement of capital flows, allowed for capital flight from Japan, bringing down the yen, and thus further increasing capital outflows. Since Japanese savers/investors will enjoy in the near future easier access to international mutual investment funds, and since interest rates are higher in foreign markets, the possibility of a hollowing out of Japan's finance loomed on the horizon.

Faced with the collapse of stocks and real-estate prices at home, and unable to claim the large sums that they had lent in Japan and in Asia without sufficient guarantees, Japanese banks and financial firms called the government to their rescue. The government obliged, in 1997, with a package of more than US$60 billion dollars, then with an additional infusion of US$570 billion in 1998, to which were added in 1999 another US$72 billion, just for the Daiwa Bank group. Some banks were nationalized or taken over, then sold, and most of them restructured and/or merged. Several major mergers, induced by the government, created giant banks/financial groups in 1999: DKB, IBJ, and Fuji Bank, with joint assets of 141 trillion yen, making it the world's biggest bank, in terms of assets; Sumitomo and Sakura Bank, with 98.7 trillion yen; Tokai and Asahi Bank, with 66.3 trillion yen, possibly to be joined by Daiwa Bank. The most important feature of these mergers is that they operated across different *keiretsu*, potentially ending the dependency of banks on their *keiretsu* obligations. This trend also brought together banks, insurance companies, and financial institutions. After this restructuring, adding the Bank of Tokyo/Mitsubishi, and the Sanwa group, Japan's financial industry became organized around just five major groups. The government assumed a substantial share of the banks' bad loans. By the end of 1999, the stock market rewarded the banks' restructuring efforts, as the big banks' shares increased their value by 60 times over previous forecasts of earnings per share for 1999. Since the government did not have the cash to pay for the bail-out, at the same time that it was increasing spending to stimulate the economy it borrowed the money. So, the price the government, and the country, had to pay to save Japanese banks was to accept a staggering budget deficit (10 percent of GDP), and an unprecedented level of national debt (at about 140 percent of GDP), that will come to haunt the Japanese economy in the twenty-first century. The temporary settlement of the financial crisis in Japan did not solve, however, the deep-seated problems of the Japanese economy. It was the overall model of economic development that was being called into question.

Indeed, globalization also transformed the model of industrial development. In the mid-1980s, fears of protectionism from America and Europe, as well as the strong yen, and high costs of operating in Japan, finally pushed Japanese corporations toward global decentralization, relatively weakening Japan's manufacturing basis.[28] The first moves were to Asia, in search of lower production costs, and more favorable platforms to export to the advanced economies.[29] But by the late 1980s it accelerated, with the transfer of entire production units, comprising R&D centers together with factories and commercial establishments, to Japan's main markets, particularly in the United States, the United Kingdom, and Germany.[30] Asian countries also became a market and not just a production base. MITI tried to counter this migration of Japanese capital and technology by developing the Technopolis Program, in cooperation with the prefectures of less-developed provinces, to lure high-technology companies to a regional decentralization strategy as opposed to offshoring.[31] Kyushu greatly benefited from the Technopolis Program, partly because of the interest of foreign electronic companies in locating in the Japanese market. Japanese firms also decentralized some of their branch plants, while keeping their essential talent and high-level operations in the Tokyo–Yokohama milieu of innovation. Yet, the offshoring movement of manufacturing, commercial, and financial activities involved incom-

28 Aoyama (1996).
29 Ozawa (1996).
30 Aoyama (1996).
31 Castells and Hall (1994)

parably higher volumes of investment. Some of this offshoring aimed at producing at lower costs and shipping products back to Japan, so that a substantial part of Japan's trade with Asia is, in fact, back and forth shipping of Japanese production networks in Asia. But most of it, as empirically shown by Aoyama, in her Berkeley doctoral dissertation on the international location strategies of Japanese consumer electronics firms,[32] amounts to a true globalization of Japanese companies beyond the shores of Japan. The trend expanded in the late 1990s, pushed by fears of protectionism, and by the need to secure specific market knowledge, to access technology (in the case of the US), to tap labour markets (skilled, as well as unskilled), and to diversify export platforms. Overall, there has been a growing trend toward dissociation between Japanese multinationals and Japan's national economy. The most important consequence of this trend is that MITI, and the developmental state system, have lost much of their clout, and even influence, over Japanese corporations. This is not only because they are much bigger, and consider themselves strong enough to decide their own strategies, but also because they are global, and belong to global networks, so that their interests, as firms and groups of firms, are increasingly diversified, and require different strategies for different countries, different sectors, and different product lines.[33] To be sure, most of their assets are still in Japan (albeit in a decreasing proportion), and there is probably a higher cultural/geographical loyalty among Japanese companies toward their country than other companies of similar global reach. It is also still true that the Japanese state adopts policies favorable to its firms, as the US government does (for example, the support of the Department of Defense for the mega-merger between Boeing and McDonnell Douglas in 1996 to counter competition from Airbus). But, in contrast to the 1960s or 1970s, MITI no longer has direct influence over Japanese corporations; nor do these corporations decide their strategies primarily within the framework of Japan's economic interest. The decoupling of systemic interaction between the developmental state and Japanese-based multinational networks introduces a new dynamic to Japan, and to the world at large.

Among the key elements of this new dynamic are the following. It is doubtful whether, exposed to conditions of global competition in a multilayered locational structure, Japanese companies can maintain the system of tenured employment for their core labor force. In 1999, unemployment increased, albeit at a moderate level of about 4.6 percent. But most new jobs created were part-time. Japanese corpora-

32   Aoyama (1996).
33   Imai (1990).

tions were phasing out a large number of their less well performing subsidiary firms, thus closing down the honorable exit for workers and managers who become redundant in the main company. Manufacturing was particularly hard hit by lay-offs. The gradual weakening of the stable employment system, and the expansion of contingent labor, are undermining Japanese institutions of stable industrial relations. It is also doubtful whether Fortress Japan can be kept for long under the new rules of the World Trade Organization, as the serious frictions in trade negotiations with the US administration seem to indicate. Japanese attempts to multilateralize trade negotiations, to avoid direct confrontation with the US, may in fact heighten tensions, since the European Union is in the way to strengthen its competitive position. The over-exposure of Japanese financial investments throughout the world to the uncertainties of global flows makes it increasingly difficult for Japanese banks to fulfill their intra-*keiretsu* obligations. The constant swirl of financial flows in and out of the Japanese economy limits the impact of monetary controls by the Bank of Japan, so that the Finance Ministry is no longer able to determine interest rates, the cornerstone of Japanese industrial finance policy. Deregulation of telecommunications, media, and utilities is proceeding slowly but surely, opening up opportunities for investment from a variety of sources, including foreign sources.[34] While the restructuring of Japanese finance restored some level of stability, the newly restructured Japanese banks became entangled in the networks of global finance, and had to play by the rules of the global game, rather than follow the advice of government bureaucracy. Furthermore, the most potent factor behind the rise of the Nikkei stocks index in 1999, signaling the recovery of the Japanese economy, was the massive inflow of foreign investment in Japanese stocks (about 125 billion dollars in 1999). In 1999, 15 percent of Tokyo's stock exchange value was in the hands of foreign investors, in contrast to 5 percent a decade earlier. As the experience of other Asian countries shows, the downside of this bonanza is the volatility of the market, when and if capital flows reverse course. Thus, post-crisis financial markets have linked Japan deeply to the movements of global capital, undermining the autonomy of the Japanese state.

Moreover, in 1998, the G7 group, the US government, and the International Monetary Fund felt Japan to be so weak that they were not afraid to prescribe to the Japanese government economic policies which they deemed necessary to overcome the crisis that threatened the global economy as a whole. While Japan adamantly refused to be

34 Khan and Yoshihara (1994).

advised by foreigners, these pressures were a factor in deciding several key measures in Japan, particularly those concerning financial reform and fiscal policy.

In sum, the system of administrative guidance that characterized Japan's miracle is in the process of disintegration, particularly because of the inability of the government to keep the financial system under control under the conditions of globalization of financial markets. There remains a series of cultural/institutional obstacles to the opening of Japanese markets, such as bureaucratic red-tape, the internal discipline of business networks, and the cultural nationalist habit of buying/consuming Japanese. The imposing state machinery set up over the past half-century is still there to guide/help/support Japanese business. It is a well-known rule of bureaucratic life that the instrument creates the function: MITI will always find something to do. There is, none the less, a fundamental transformation in the overall pattern of development, as companies try to identify Japan's interests with their interests (in plural), instead of serving the national interest, in line with Maruyama's prediction.

There is a more fundamental change in the making. As Sumiko Yazawa, Chizuko Ueno, and other researchers have argued,[35] on the basis of empirical studies, Japanese women are increasingly mobilizing, both at the grassroots level, and in the political system, particularly in local politics, in parallel with their massive entry into the labor force. While explicit feminism is still limited in its expression, women's struggles and women's rights have come to the forefront in a growing number of local communities. The media focus on these activities is amplifying their impact, opening the way for a challenge to the current status of women as second-class workers and politically subdued subjects. When, and if, the women's movement expands, permeating into the private sphere of the patriarchal family, the whole Japanese social structure will come under stress because of the interconnection of patriarchalism with the entire institutional system. And there are scattered, but significant, signs that these challenges are emerging. In 1999, divorce rates were sharply up in Japan, women were marrying at a later age, and growing gestures of professional and personal independence across the spectrum of Japanese everyday life provided anecdotal evidence of an ongoing transformation in Japan's patriarchal relationships.[36] In the last resort, economic crisis and social change in Japan combined to induce a fundamental political crisis, potentially opening the way for a new model of relationship between the state and civil society.

35 Ueno (1987); Yazawa (1995).
36 Yazawa et al. (1992); Iwao (1993); Yazawa (1995).

The end of "Nagatacho *politics*"

The crisis of the Japanese model of development was compounded in the 1990s by the crisis of its political system. The crisis was ushered in by the loss of the 1993 election by the LDP, and the formation of a coalition government formed between new parties, splitting from the LDP, and the Socialists. Two years later, the game was changed, with the LDP returning to government in coalition with the Socialists. And in 1996 a new election brought in a minority LDP government with parliamentary support from small parties, including a reduced Socialist party. The composition of parliament made clear, however, that new coalitions would form and dissolve, ushering in an era of instability in Japanese politics. Indeed, in July 1998, the LDP was crushed in the elections to the upper house of parliament, winning only 44 of the 126 seats contested. The election saw the rise of Naoto Kan, leader of the opposition Democratic party, who became the most popular politician in Japan. In a significant development, the Communist party, conducting an active, grassroots campaign, tripled the number of its seats. As a result of this electoral rebuke, the prime minister, and leader of the LDP, Hashimoto, resigned. He was replaced by an experienced, consensus-builder, party *apparatchik*, Keizo Obuchi, in a desperate attempt by the LDP to fight the centrifugal forces that were threatening to disintegrate the party. Yet, while Obuchi surprised many critics with his determination in pushing for economic reforms, few observers were giving the LDP much chance to remain in control of government after the next election. Indeed, at the turn of the century, the LDP seemed to be increasingly dependent on its alliance with the Buddhist-inspired coalition Komeito, a loose cannon in the political arena.

This political crisis is more important for what it reveals than because of its direct social consequences.[37] Indeed, it could be argued that no real change in the political personnel took place in 1993–9 since the Socialists lost considerable support, and the main reason that the LDP lost control of the government was that several of its factions left the LDP to create new parties. In some cases, the acrimonious intra-party fighting has made future coalitions between the LDP and ex-LDP groups difficult, notably in the case of Ichiro Ozawa's *Jiyu* party. Yet, the crisis is deeper than it looks. I will follow Shoji's suggestion that the "big change" came as a consequence of an accumulation of "small changes," foremost among which was a transformation in Japanese people's lifestyle.[38]

37 Ikuta (1995); Johnson (1995); Schlesinger (1997).
38 Shoji (1995); Smith (1997).

The gradual fragmentation of the LDP was facilitated by the end of the geopolitical state of emergency, under which the national unity of pro-American forces was paramount, both for Japanese business and social elites, and for American interests.[39] Furthermore, the open recognition of trade tensions with America showed that old-fashioned LDP politics were no longer instrumental in taming America's reluctance to acknowledge a new economic superpower. The diversification of Japan's national interests, in line with the globalization of its economy, and with the crisis in its finances, opened up the debate on policies and strategies, requiring the constitution of a truly competitive political system, beyond the coalition of caretakers that were rubber-stamping the policies of the bureaucrats of the developmental state. The full urbanization of Japan undermined traditional patronage networks. To acknowledge the new electoral map, a political reform redrew electoral districts in 1994–5, and combined single-constituency representation with a national vote in the election of the parliament. The public disgust with the systemic political corruption put politicians on the defensive, so that several of them tried a new departure, presenting themselves as regenerated political leaders. The opening up of political competition, and the relinquishing of loyalties in the LDP family, created opportunities for political jockeying, with personalities, political clubs, and special interests engaging in political marketing, and entering a new field of competitive politics. In the process, the LDP's dirty laundry was further exposed by increasingly daring, autonomous media, thus undermining the reconstruction of the coalition and spurring centrifugal forces. This is why most Japanese and foreign observers consider that the era of LDP domination is over.[40] What is next is a much more difficult prediction, since the Socialists are disintegrating even faster than the LDP, and local personalities, such as Tokyo's independent Governor Aoshima, elected in 1995 on an anti-corporate platform, quickly ran out of steam without stable popular support or a convincing program. It may well be that this era of "transitional politics" will not be transitional at all: that is, that the "party system" will be replaced by a "political market," dependent on media exposure and support from public opinion. Systemic political instability will follow, eliminating the convenient cushion of political parties between people's discontent and the heights of the state bureaucracy, acting on behalf of the Symbolic Emperor system. The loss of power of the Ministry of Finance during the 1997–8 financial crisis, and the distrust of business, opposition politicians, and people in gen-

39   Curtis (1993).
40   Curtis (1993); Johnson (1995); Schlesinger (1997).

eral *vis-à-vis* the formerly untouchable bureaucracy, signaled the end of a cycle for the Japanese state. Not that the bureaucracy is out of power. In fact, it is probably the only coherent, stable power system left in Japan today. Yet its authority is challenged from so many quarters that it has become another node, if an essential one, in the entangled web of Japanese decision-making. From this direct confrontation between the aspirations of a new Japanese society and the old structures of historical legitimacy a more fundamental political crisis could result, affecting the heart of the Japanese national identity.

Some elements of this deeper social and political crisis surfaced in mid-1990s' Japan. On the one hand, there was a limited revival of social movements that have been dormant, by and large, since the political and cultural defeat of radical student movements in the 1960s. These incipient forms of social protest focus, primarily, on environmental and anti-nuclear issues, on women's causes, and on community and regional revitalization.[41] Often, they connect to local politics, for instance in successfully supporting populist candidates in municipal elections (as in Tokyo's and Osaka's 1995 municipal elections), or rejecting the building of nuclear power plants by popular referendum, as in the town of Maki, in August 1996. On the other hand, an increasingly confused society, particularly in its younger sections, having grown up in affluence, becomes deprived of meaningful values, as the traditional structures of familial patriarchalism and bureaucratic indoctrination lose their grip in a culture filled with information flows from diverse sources. A mixture of ritualistic Japanese traditions, American icons, and high-tech consumption fills the vacuum in social dynamics, cultural challenges, or personal dreams of a society that has finished its assigned task: to make Japan secure, rich, and respected within 50 years. Now, after their hard labor, the Japanese find the tunnel at the end of the light, as increasingly abstract, new technocratic challenges are proposed by a developmental state that has outlived the state of emergency. Or, even worse, financial crisis and the impact of globalization has plunged Japan into stagnation, prompting economic restructuring, and undermining stable employment, after decades of strenuous effort to be prosperous, secure, and independent. According to sociological studies, most people just want to enjoy the quiet consumption of the good life, meaning less *karoshi*, more vacation, better housing, better cities, and a life without exams;[42] while young people, bursting with the energy of their increasingly liberated passions, search for ways of experimentation. It is from these dark

41 Hasegawa (1994); Smith (1997); Yazawa (1997).
42 Shoji (1994, 1995).

alleys, visited during such explorations, that symptoms of destructive revolt have surged, as epitomized by *Aum Shinrikyo* (see volume II, chapter 3). *Aum* was not, and will not remain, an isolated incident because the cracks in the mirror of Japanese society, revealed by Asahara and his followers, seem to originate in the fundamental contradiction emerging in *Heisei*'s Japan: the incompatibility between the developmental state – the actor of Japanese development and guarantor of Japanese identity – and the information society that this state decisively helped to bring to life.

Hatten Hokka *and* Johoka Shakai: *a contradictory relationship*[43]

The concept of "information society" (*Johoka Shakai*) is, in fact, a Japanese invention, exported to the West in 1978 by Simon Nora and Alain Minc in the title of their report to the French Prime Minister.[44] It was proposed for the first time in 1963 by Tadao Umesao in an article on an evolutionary theory of society based on the density of "information industries." The article was the object of debate in the January 1964 issue of the journal *Hoso Asahi*, whose editors, introducing the debate, used the term *Johoka Shakai* for the first time. It was popularized a few years later by Japanese futurologists, particularly Masuda and Hayashi. However, the reason that the information society became a major theme for prospective policy and strategic thinking was its adoption as the central issue of the Information Industry Section of MITI's Industrial Structure Council in 1967. Having reached the limits of the extensive model of development, based on traditional manufacturing, MITI was in search of new mobilizing goals for the nation, with the emphasis on finding industrial sectors that would be less polluting, and that could hold a competitive edge against the emerging

---

43   This analysis of the Japanese information society is partly based on the database compiled and elaborated in 1995 by my assistant Keisuke Hasegawa, Department of Sociology, Hitotsubashi University. A prior overview of literature and data on Japan's information society was prepared by my assistant Yuko Aoyama, in 1990–94 in Berkeley, University of California, Department of City and Regional Planning. Additional information came from our study with Peter Hall on Japanese Technopoles (Castells and Hall, 1994), and from interviews I conducted in Japan in 1989 and in 1995. A major source of statistical data concerning the diffusion of information technologies in Japan is Ministry of Posts and Telecommunications (1995). See also Japan Information Processing Development Center (1994); Wakabayashi (1994); and InfoCom Research (1995). For a Western perspective on Japanese competitiveness in information technology industries, somewhat outdated by the mid-1990s in his statement of the "Japanese conquest," see the excellent overview by Forester (1993). For some glimpses of the discussion of analytical issues of social transformations linked to the informationalization of Japan, see Ito (1980, 1991, 1993, 1994a,b); Kazuhiro (1990); Watanuki (1990); and Sakaiya (1991).
44   Ito (1991).

Asian competitors producing at lower costs. Information technology industries were the obvious candidates, according to the document issued by the Council in 1969: "Tasks for Johoka – Report on the Development of Information Processing Industries."

This report was remarkable on two grounds: on the one hand, it foresaw the essential role of electronics in the new stage of global competition; on the other hand, it extended the concept of informationalism to the overall economy and society, calling for a profound transformation of Japan through the diffusion of information technology. Indeed, this new mode of development fitted very well with Japan's project of specializing in intelligence-intensive production and exports, and moving away from resource-consuming and energy-intensive industries, in which Japan was at a clear disadvantage because of its poor natural endowment. The oil crisis of 1973 underscored the accuracy of this diagnosis, propelling Japan in an all-out race to become the world leader in information technology. It almost succeeded: it came in second, after the United States, after an extraordinary competitive effort for over three decades.[45] In parallel with design, produce, and export information technology products, Japan also embarked on a rapid diffusion of new technologies in factories and offices of the corporate sector of the economy. Most of the world's factory robots are in Japan. Micro-electronics-based numerical control machines became a Japanese domain, and were widely used in Japanese factories earlier than in the rest of the world. VCRs, TV sets, video games, video cameras, and consumer electronics in general became a Japanese monopoly until the other Asian producers started to compete at the low-end of the industry. Karaoke machines dotted the vast majority of Japanese bars and entertainment centers. Government agencies, homes, and schools were much slower to access information technologies. None the less, Japan's technological modernization proceeded faster than the rest of the world, with the major exception of the United States. With the help of Keisuke Hasegawa, I have constructed some indicators of comparative levels and development of "informationalization" in Japan, the US, and the UK, in 1985 and 1992 (latest available statistics at the time of my study in 1995). According to our data (which I consider unnecessary to reprint here since they are widely available in Japanese statistical yearbooks), Japan still lagged behind the US, while being ahead of the UK, but its progression was very fast (although slower than the US in personal electronic equipment, such as home computers and mobile telephones).

Together with the production and diffusion of information technol-

45   Forester (1993).

ogy machines, Japan built a new mythology around a futurological view of the information society, which actually tried to replace social thinking and political projects with images of a computerized/ telecommunicated society, to which were added some humanistic, pseudo-philosophical platitudes. A flurry of foundations, publications, seminars, and international conferences provided the apparatus of the new ideology, according to which the technological revolution would solve the future of Japan and, in passing, of the world as well. The developmental state (*Hatten Hokka* in Japanese) found a new gold mine of strategic initiatives: each ministry competed in creating technology-oriented programs which, in their respective areas of competence, aimed at transforming Japan by setting up the infrastructure of the information society.[46] Then, MITI launched the Technopolis Program, whose target was to mass-produce Silicon Valleys and, in the process, to patronize regional prefectures, strengthening MITI's political position in the Information Age. The Ministry of Posts and Telecommunications asserted its privileged role in telecommunications and, among other initiatives, launched its Teletopia Program, to install interactive media in 63 model cities. The Ministry of Construction countered with its own Intelligent Cities Program, using its control of rights of way to install optical fiber networks, and its control of public works to construct smart buildings, office and residential complexes. The Japan Regional Development Corporation created the Science City of Tsukuba, and obtained from the national government the establishment of a new university, and the location in Tsukuba of 40 national research institutes, with emphasis on agricultural and biological research. Powerful prefectures developed programs of their own, so that most of Japan became involved in building the material basis of the new information society, as promised by an army of futurologists, led by retired top bureaucrats and executives heading a whole array of think-tank foundations. The problem was that, in the meantime, Japanese society evolved toward its culturally/historically specific model of the information society, and this came into contradiction not only with the technocratic blueprints of an abstract social model, but with the institutional and political interests of its procreators. Furthermore, after Japan bet its entire technological and economic development on the informational paradigm, the logic of the state came into contradiction with the full blossoming of this paradigm. Let me explain.

An information society is not a society that uses information technology. It is the specific social structure, associated with, but not de-

46   Castells and Hall (1994).

termined by, the rise of the informational paradigm. The first volume of this book tried to present both the structural features and historic/cultural variations of this society which, in order to propose a more sociological characterization, I call the *network society*. Most of its features characterized Japan in the 1990s, albeit with Japanese characteristics. These features of the network society entered into contradiction with the institutions and logic of the Japanese state as historically constituted in the past half-century. I shall explain why and how.

First, the globalization of Japanese corporations, and financial markets, as mentioned above, undermined the influence of the developmental state, and exposed its bureaucratic, paralyzing dimension, which becomes a handicap in a world of variable geometry where freedom of maneuver and adaptability are critical for survival in a relentless, competitive race.

Second, the wave of deregulation and privatization, in the world and in Japan, forced the Japanese government gradually, but surely, to loosen its grip on telecommunications, the media, the utilities, construction work, and a number of other areas, thus losing many of its ways to control the economy, and to steer the country.

Third, the weakness of Japanese science limited Japanese ability to improve existing technology, to make it better and cheaper, once Japanese companies reached the cutting edge of technological innovation. The success of American electronic companies to reverse the tide of Japanese competition in the 1990s, as well as the limited progress of Japanese firms in biotechnology and software, stem from this lagging behind in basic science and research training. The explanation for this gap between Japanese ability to adapt technology and to generate science-based technology lies in institutional, not cultural, factors, notwithstanding quasi-racist generalizations about Japanese innate capacities/incapacities. It lies, essentially, in the bureaucratic character of the Japanese university system, and in the examination-oriented, outdated pedagogic system, focused on assuring cultural reproduction rather than on stimulating intellectual innovation. As is known, universities are instructed not to work for corporations, professors are civil servants, usually forbidden to do business, graduate schools are weak, doctoral programs are geared toward in-house promotion, and endogamy is the rule in the recruitment of faculty, thus discouraging investment in time and resources studying abroad. Moreover, women are blatantly discriminated against in their academic careers, thus wasting an extraordinary potential for scientific innovation and quality teaching. Universities are degree-granting bureaucracies, primarily aimed at cultural reproduction and social selection, not centers of innovation and training for autonomous thinking. These facts are widely acknowledged by state institutions, but not easily remedied because their correction would contradict the fundamental mission embodied by the Ministry of Education: the preservation of Japanese identity, the transmission of traditional values, and the reproduction of meritocratic stratification. To open the system up to individual competition, autonomous thinking, variation of programs depending on market demands, and foreign influence would be tantamount to dismantling the bastion of *nihonjiron* (ideology of Japanese uniqueness). Let me be clear: I am not arguing that Japanese identity is contradictory to the information society, although, like any cultural identity, it will necessarily be modified by the course of history. My point is that the Japanese educational system, the source of production of the subjects of the information society, in its current structure and goals, is incapable of generating the critical mass of researchers and research programs on which business can rely to innovate in the new fields of industrial, technological, and cultural development, in spite of the astronomical number of engineering graduates. And because the imitation game at which Japanese firms excelled in the 1960s–1980s is now practiced by a plurality of competitors around the world, Japanese companies cannot rely any longer on Japanese institutions and Japanese-trained scientists and engineers to keep up with competition in the high tier of information-based industries. The Japanese government seemed to acknowledge this fact when, in August 1996, it approved a special plan to advance the effort in science and technology, investing US$155 billion over five years for programs to be conducted in 100 national universities and private schools.[47] Yet, unless there is a fundamental reform of educational institutions, additional funding would simply mean more, better-trained, bureaucratically minded graduates, in bureaucratically organized research centers, which would be decreasingly able to interact with the increasingly interactive universe of global research. The worldwide explosive development of the Internet in the late 1990s, both in business and in society at large, further exposed Japan's technological flaws, as a result of the lack of individual entrepreneurialism, and as the fall out from erroneous forecasting by a government bureaucracy that thought the information society would be based upon supercomputers rather than on computer-mediated communication.

A fourth institutional limit to the flexibility requirements of the network society concerns the potential calling into question of the system of long-term employment tenure for the core labor force. This system was not just the result of bargaining between capital and labor. It

47   "Japan's blast-off in science," *Business Week*, September 2, 1996.

came about in a situation of emergency and national mobilization for development called upon by the state. The growing interdependence of Japanese business with business practices around the world, and particularly in the Asian Pacific, characterized by labor flexibility, makes the preservation of the *choki koyo* system increasingly difficult (see volume I, chapter 4). This system is at the heart of social stability on three dimensions: the system of industrial relations; the legitimacy of the state, whose paternalism guarantees long-term security; and the patriarchal family, because only the assurance of stability of employment for the patriarch allows flexibility for women, as it makes it less risky for women to keep their double role as homemakers and temporary workers without building their own, independent future. Job insecurity, if it diffuses beyond the current trends of employment instability among young workers, will be particularly dramatic in Japan because most social benefits depend on the employing company.

Fifth, the culture of real virtuality (see volume I, chapter 5) is diffusing fast in Japan. Multimedia, video games, karaoke, cable television, and, lately, computer-mediated communication are the new frontier of Japanese social life, particularly for the younger generations.[48] What characterizes the culture of real virtuality is the mixing of themes, messages, images, and identities in a potentially interactive hypertext. As a result of the simultaneous globalization and individualization of this culture, specific Japanese identities will merge and/or interact with this text, and be open to a variety of cultural expressions. What will be the outcome for Japanese identity? A superficial observer would notice the apparent Americanization of Japanese youth culture (from Rap to sports icons). Yet, a closer look reveals specific adaptations of these images into a twenty-first century Japanese way of being. Whatever it is, it is not traditional Japanese identity. Nor is it an updated version of Japanese culture. It is something else: a kaleidoscope of messages and icons from various cultural sources, including Japan's own, brewed and consumed in Japan and by Japanese, but never again in isolation from global alleys of the virtual hypertext. In this sense, the emphasis of traditional cultural apparatuses on enforcing loyalty to unique Japanese values enters into contradiction with the cultural environment in which the new generations are growing up. It follows cacophony rather than high fidelity.

Sixth, the new avenues of identity-based social mobilization, around the defense of territorial community, gender, and the environment, directly contradict the myth of Japanese social homogeneity, and the image of a supreme national community represented by the state bu-

---

48   Dentsu Institute for Human Studies (1994).

reaucracy. True, the majority of Japanese are still cultural nationalists and express a clear feeling of cultural superiority *vis-à-vis* other cultures in the world, according to Shoji's surveys.[49] But the embryos of social movements, emerging in Japan in the 1990s, take exception to this image of national unity, and put forward their differential interests, not against the nation, but claiming diversity within the nation. This perspective directly contradicts the indissoluble unity of the national polity on which the Symbolic Emperor system is based.

Seventh, the information society created in Japan over the past 20 years is an active, autonomous, assertive civil society, which has grown increasingly critical of a corrupt, inefficient political system, and rejects the routinization of the political debate.[50] This society requires a dynamic, open political system, able to process the fundamental debates emerging in Japan around what life should be after the end of the siege, and, consequently, beyond the siege mentality. Because the "1955 political system" was a control mechanism somewhat cosmetically added to the developmental state, it lacks the legitimacy and the capacity to transform itself into the citizens' *agora* of the Information Age.[51] Thus, the demise of the political system's legitimacy directly exposes the developmental state to the claims and challenges of *Johoka Shakai*. This confrontation dominates, and will dominate, Japan.

Finally, at the turn of the century, there were multiple signs that Japan's network society was developing along unforeseen lines, in spite of all the obstacles mentioned above.[52] The Internet was developing fast: about 23 million Japanese were using the Internet in 1999–2000. This made possible horizontal, free communication, which was soon utilized to voice criticism from consumers and citizens, and to link up with the world. PC sales also increased sharply (by 80 percent in 1999), powering young professionals with access to information-processing capacity and e-mail communication. E-commerce became a viable industry, bypassing established companies. Individual entrepreneurship became an option to part-time, contingent employment, and to long waiting in line on the corporate ladder, for thousands of young graduates who were no longer ready to accept the pecking order of traditional Japanese firms. The potential freeing up of $430 billion in postal savings deposits by 2001 offered the possibility of a huge reservoir of capital to invest in promising new ventures, a perspective that could revolutionize the Japanese economy. The simultaneous crisis of stable job careers, and the opening up of individual mobility avenues, seri-

49 Shoji (1994).
50 Shoji (1995); Smith (1997); Yazawa (1997).
51 Inoguchi (1995).
52 *Business Week* (1999b).

ously undermined the deferred gratification pattern on which social behavior was predicated. Women asserted their rights in increasing numbers, and with new-found determination. The traditional Japanese family came under threat, together with the Japanese traditional corporation, and with them the Japanese developmental state.

Thus, for MITI's strategic planners, if they are still around, the future is now. And, as is always the case in history, it looks messier than was forecast in their blueprints because it is filled with the actual needs, claims, fears, and dreams of the Japanese people.

Japan and the Pacific

The proof that the Symbolic Emperor system is alive and well in Japan is the, otherwise incomprehensible, stubborn refusal of Japanese political elites to apologize to their Asian neighbors for Japan's aggression and war crimes in the 1930s and 1940s. Had Germany adopted such an attitude, there would be no European Union today. And because Japan chose a different road, *rooted in its institutions of cultural nationalism*,[53] there will be no Pacific institutions of political integration, which are and will be consistently rejected by the Chinese, the Koreans, and the Russians (also a Pacific country).

On the other hand, there is a growing economic interdependence in the Asian Pacific, and a set of interests largely built around Japanese companies' production networks in Asia. Furthermore, Japan's dependence for energy and raw materials, its geographical proximity, and the expansion of Asian markets, create powerful incentives for peaceful cooperation and exchange, in a process that could lead, eventually, to enhanced Pacific cooperation. Nevertheless, the very institutions that propelled Japan, and the other Asian Pacific countries, toward the global economy and the information society are the main obstacles for further cooperation beyond the tense sharing of economic interests. This is because, both for Japan and the Asian Pacific countries, the engine of the development process has been the nationalist project at the heart of their respective developmental states. Therefore, only the superseding of the nationalist developmental state, in Japan and elsewhere, could create the conditions for new identities, new institutions, and new historical trajectories.

53 Watanabe (1996).

Beheading the Dragon? Four Asian Tigers with a Dragon Head, and their Civil Societies[54]

The development of Japan, and its challenge to the West, came as only half an historical surprise. After all, Japan had industrialized since the late nineteenth century, and was able to build a formidable industrial and military machine in the 1930s. What really rang alarm bells around the orderly world of domination by cultures of European ancestry (naturally including Russia) was the rise of the four East Asian "tigers": South Korea, Taiwan, Singapore, and Hong Kong. That these barren territories, with their economies devastated by war and geopolitics, with no domestic markets or natural or energy resources, without industrial tradition or technological basis, were able to transform themselves in three decades into the most competitive producers and exporters in the world sent a clear signal that the new, global economy was paced and structured by new rules of the game – rules that these "tigers" seemed to have learned faster, and mastered better, than older industrialized countries. Among these rules was the ability to assimilate, use, and enhance new information technologies, both in products and in processes, and the strategic capacity to foresee the potential of new technologies, thus focusing on the technological overhaul of the countries' industries, management, and labor. Thus, analysis of the development process of the four "tigers" sheds light on the new relationships between technology, economy, state, and society, characterizing the transition to the informational, global economy. Furthermore, the Asian economic crisis that began in 1997 had very different impacts and manifestations in each one of the four "tigers." South Korea's economy, the largest of the four, collapsed, defaulting on its international debt payments on November 21, 1997. From October

54   This analysis largely relies on fieldwork, readings, and personal experience during my teaching, lecturing, and researching in Hong Kong (University of Hong Kong, 1983, 1987), Singapore (National University of Singapore, 1987, 1989), South Korea (Korean Research Institute of Human Settlements, and Seoul National University, 1988), and Taiwan (National Taiwan University, 1989). For my analysis of Hong Kong and Singapore, see Castells et al. (1990), which should be considered as a generic reference for sources on Hong Kong and Singapore, up to 1990 in order not to repeat here the bibliography contained in this monograph. I also wish to acknowledge the help and ideas of Professors Chu-Joe Hsia and You-tien Hsing about Taiwan, and from Professor Ju-Chool Kim about South Korea. Additional sources directly used in this section include: Lethbridge (1978); Amsdem (1979, 1985, 1989, 1992); Lau (1982); Lim (1982); Chua (1985); Gold (1986); Deyo (1987a); Krause et al. (1987); Kim (1987); White (1988); Winckler and Greenhalgh (1988); Robinson (1991); Sigur (1994); Evans (1995). I would also like to mention an interesting, prospective, little-known contribution by a young Korean researcher who died soon after finishing his book: Ahn (1994). Other materials consulted are specifically referred to in the footnotes of the text.

1997 onwards, Hong Kong suffered a dramatic drop in the value of its stocks, and real estate, as mentioned above. Repercussions of the crisis in Singapore were in spite of a moderate depreciation of the Singapore dollar, and negative growth in 1998. And Taiwan seemed to withstand the crisis.

For the analytical purpose of this book, the differential response to the crisis among the four "tigers" offers a great opportunity for understanding the nature of the crisis itself. Thus, after observing and interpreting the process of development of the four "tigers" in a comparative approach, I will extend this comparative analysis to the interpretation of their crisis. I shall also attempt in this section to move beyond the analysis of processes of development, and crisis, to interpret the social and political contradictions triggered by these processes, inducing the transition to informational societies, and their integration into the global economy. Indeed, while the role of the developmental state (the "dragon" of my story) was critical in fostering, guiding, and ensuring economic growth and technological modernization for about three decades, in the 1990s civil society and corporate business grew increasingly uneasy about the suffocating presence of the state. And the globalization of the economy contradicted the nationalization of society. As a result, new social and political conditions were created in three of the four countries, with the fourth one, Singapore, transforming itself into an extraordinary experiment of a cybernetic, global node. It is in the evolving interaction between development, crisis, state, and society that we may find the explanation for the different forms of incorporation of these Asian societies in the global economy, and for their specific paths of social change.

Understanding Asian development

The understanding of social processes that, between 1960 and 1990, led to the spectacular economic growth and modernization of these four countries, albeit at the price of high social costs and political repression, remains obscured by the passion of ideological debate. This is because the performance of these economies challenges the conventional wisdom of both dogmatic dependency analysis and neo-classical economics in the field of development theory.[55] Against the prevailing left-wing view, according to which economic development cannot take place for dependent societies under capitalism, the four Asian "tigers" sustained the highest rate of GNP growth in the world for about three decades, and won substantial shares of world markets,

55   Amsdem (1979); Evans (1995).

transforming in the process their economic structure and their social fabric. Furthermore, while exploitation and oppression were integral parts of the development process (as they were in European industrialization), economic growth was coupled with substantial improvement in living conditions (in wages, health, education, and housing). In addition, income inequality decreased in the 1960s, stabilized in the 1970s, and, although slightly increasing in the 1980s, was still lower in the mid-1980s than in the 1950s, and lower than in the US, the UK, France, and Spain. True, this economic and social transformation took place in a context of political and ideological repression. But most developing societies in the world were under similar repressive conditions, while still being unable to overcome their obstacles to development, largely inherited from their colonial or semi-colonial past. Only the "tigers" could successfully break with that past, thus inspiring emulation in the rest of the Asian countries that, in the 1990s, seem to be following a similar path, albeit under different conditions, and with somewhat different policies, precisely because the development of the "tigers" changed the context in which they were operating, establishing the new Pacific connection to the global economy.

On the other hand, the economic success of the Asian "tigers" has been used to support the ideological discourse of some free-market economists and politicians who found, in their reconstructed version of Asian development, the lost paradise of neo-liberalism. And yet, any serious, unbiased observer of the Asian Pacific scene knows that systematic state intervention in the economy, as well as the state's strategic guidance of national firms and multinational corporations located in the country's territory, were fundamental factors in ensuring the transition of industrializing economies to each of the stages they were reaching in their developmental process.[56] As in Japan, the "developmental state" lies at the core of the experience of newly industrialized economies.[57] There is widespread acknowledgment of this fact concerning Singapore, South Korea, and Taiwan. On the basis of a stream of less well-known studies, including my own, I shall argue that this was also the case for Hong Kong.[58] But arguing that the state was the driving force in the economic development of these countries raises more questions than it answers for development theory. Because, given the widespread, and generally inefficient, state intervention in other developing economies, we must reconstruct the complex set of relationships between the state, society, and economy in the Asian

56   Deyo (1987a); Appelbaum and Henderson (1992).
57   Johnson (1987).
58   Castells et al. (1990).

Pacific to understand the specific social conditions explaining the successful outcome of the developmental process. I shall try to provide such an explanation, focusing first on the specific process of each country, then trying to raise analytical questions, and to answer them, in a comparative perspective. The sequence of presentation follows an order from the highest to the lowest level of state intervention: Singapore, South Korea, Taiwan, and Hong Kong.

Singapore: state nation-building via multinational corporations

In econometric terms, the analysis of Yuan Tsao, on sources of growth in Singapore for the 1965–84 period, shows the input of capital to be the main contributing factor, with labor input also having a positive effect, while total factor productivity had a negligible contribution.[59]

Concerning labor, in 1966 Singapore had an unemployment rate of 9 percent, with a labor participation rate of 42.3 percent. By 1983, the unemployment rate had gone down to 3 percent, with a labor force participation of 63 percent, mainly thanks to the massive incorporation of women into the labor force. Education of workers substantially improved, with mandatory English in schools, and the expansion of vocational training. Immigration was severely limited to avoid the location of low-wage activities, and to privilege Singapore citizens. Undocumented immigration was harshly repressed.

The critical factor, however, was the massive inflow of capital, from two main sources: (a) direct foreign investment which oscillated between 10 and 20 percent of GDP, during the 1970s; and (b) an exceptional rate of growth of gross national savings which reached 42 percent of GDP in the mid-1980s, the highest savings rate in the world. For the overall period 1966–85, gross national savings represented over 74 percent of total gross domestic capital formation. Much of it was generated by the public sector (46 percent), mainly through the Central Provident Fund, a government-controlled social security scheme designed to impose savings on the population. The government invested most, but not all, of these savings, much of it in social and physical infrastructure, some in public corporations (over 500 public companies in Singapore in the 1980s). Government also invested abroad, in stocks, and real estate, to decrease the vulnerability of government revenues *vis-à-vis* the cycles of Singapore's economy. Additionally, about one-quarter of total government revenue was kept in a government development fund to stabilize the economy, and allow for

59   Tsao (1986: 17–65).

strategic government expenditures. This reserve provided the government with a substantial instrument to ensure monetary stability and to control inflation.

The government's fiscal prudence left the responsibility for investment and economic growth to foreign direct investment. The Singapore government decided from the moment of its independence, in 1965, that its impoverished, tiny territory could prosper only by offering itself as an export platform to multinational corporations.[60] Still, the central factor in Singapore's development process was the role of government to provide the necessary incentives to attract foreign capital, and to reach out to investors through the creation of an Economic Development Board (EDB), which did strategic planning on the future direction of the international economy. Among critical factors attracting investment to Singapore, mainly in manufacturing in the first stage, were: a favorable business environment, including low labor costs; social peace, after the repression and dismantling of independent trade unions in the early 1960s; an educated labor force, largely English-speaking; business-friendly social and environmental legislation; excellent transportation and communications infrastructure; a supply of industrial land, fully equipped, including the possibility of "turn-key" factories built by the government; an advantageous inflation differential; stable fiscal policy; and political stability.[61]

The Singapore government was essential in making industrial diversification possible, as well as in upgrading the technical level of production operations performed in Singapore, enhancing the value of Singapore's products over time. Singapore shifted gradually from traditional services (regional trade) to manufacturing (mainly electronics assembly), then to advanced services (offshore finance, communications, business services). It moved from low-skill assembly manufacturing to advanced manufacturing products and processes, including R&D and wafer fabrication in micro-electronics; and from an economy dominated by maritime trade and petroleum refining to a highly diversified industrial structure, including machinery, electronics, transport equipment, producer services, and international finance. The government was largely responsible for this upgrading by creating the technological and educational infrastructure (including some of the best telecommunications and air transportation infrastructure in the world); by providing the real estate, the information systems, and the loosely regulated environment in which new, international business services could prosper; and by upgrading labor through a

60   Deyo (1981).
61   Chen (1983).

series of bold measures, including a deliberate, sharp increase of wages in 1979–82 to squeeze out companies looking for unskilled, cheap labor, after Singapore's economy had passed the survival stage. Efficient government management and political stability, ensured through ruthless domination and social integration mechanisms, gave the multinationals reason to believe that Singapore was the safest haven in a troubled world. It was, except for intellectuals, independent journalists, political dissidents, unruly teenagers, undocumented immigrants, pregnant legal immigrants, smokers, drug addicts, and litter louts. Public housing of increasingly decent quality, most of it in planned, green, residential estates, fully equipped with amenities, was provided for 87 percent of the population, first as rented housing, then in ownership. In addition, heavily subsidized public health, public education, and mass transit, combined with rising real wages, and declining income inequality, dramatically improved the living conditions of the whole population: Singapore in the 1990s has a much higher per capita income than Britain. This material prosperity helped to pacify the social and inter-ethnic unrest that characterized Singapore in the 1950s and early 1960s. A sophisticated state security apparatus took discreet care of the few dissenters, and insulated Singapore from the influence of "non-Asian values." The restructuring process undertaken by Singapore in the early 1980s in order to upgrade its educational and technological basis led to a short economic recession in 1985–6. But the Lion City emerged from it leaner and meaner, as the government embarked on economic liberalization and internationalization, gradually transforming Singapore into the technological, financial, and business services center of South-East Asia, in close competition with Kuala Lumpur.

In the 1990s, when middle-skilled manufacturing product lines, such as computer disk drives, started to move out of Singapore, toward lower-cost production sites in South-East Asia, the government launched a major effort to anchor micro-electronics production in Singapore, to make sure that the manufacturing contribution to GDP would not fall below 25 percent, coherent with its strategic conviction that manufacturing matters to the wealth of the country. It aimed at high-value manufacturing – that is, R&D and wafer production of advanced chips. Since the Singapore government was now rich, it invested by itself in micro-electronics production. Government-owned Chartered Semiconductor Manufacturing built two plants in Singapore, for a total investment of US$1.1 billion, and was planning, in 1996, to build four more plants. The government also formed a joint venture with Texas Instruments, Canon and Hewlett Packard to build another two plants, with an investment of US$1.6 billion; and yet an additional joint venture with Hitachi and Nippon Steel to build another semiconductors plant for about US$1 billion. SGS–Thomson, counting on government support in training and tax subsidies, decided to expand its chip-making plant in Singapore with a new investment of US$710 million dollars by 1998. Altogether, Singapore's semiconductors industry was positioned to overtake, in quantity and quality, the micro-electronics production of any European country by the year 2000.

Furthermore, the fast growth of economies in the region, particularly of Thailand, Malaysia, and Indonesia, helped Singapore to climb up the ladder of informationalism, and to become one of the hubs of the global economy. It was not only growing fast, but transforming the quality of its growth, as companies around the world chose Singapore as their preferred base of operation for management and investment in the midst of the most dynamic economic region in the planet.

Thus, coming out of a devastated economy in the mid-1960s, forcibly cut off from its Malaysian hinterland in 1965, and abandoned as entrepôt and military base by a retreating British Empire in 1968, Singapore, against all the odds, established itself as the showcase of the new developmental process, building a national identity on the basis of multinational investment, attracted and protected by a developmental city-state.

South Korea: the state production of oligopolistic capitalism

American intervention in Korea was fundamental in creating the basis for a modern economy, in 1948–60, through land reform, military support for South Korea, and massive financial aid that allowed the reconstruction and survival of the country after one of the bloodiest wars in recent history. Yet, South Korea's fast developmental process started only under the Park Chung Hee regime, established by the military coup of May 1961, and institutionalized as the Third Republic by the rigged election of October 1963.

On the basis of military, financial, and political support from the United States – a support determined by the meaning of the 38th parallel as the Berlin Wall of Asia – the South Korean military, and its political arm, the Democratic Republican Party, undertook the construction of a powerful economy as the foundation for its nationalist project. In the initial stages of development, the state assumed an entrepreneurial role via public corporations and government investments. Thus, in the period 1963–79, purchases by government and public corporations amounted to an annual average of almost 38 percent of gross domestic capital formation. The Park regime, however, heavily influenced by the Japanese model, aimed at creating an industrial structure based on large Korean companies, organized as conglomerates. To do so, it set up strong protectionist measures to preserve domestic markets. Yet, given the limited purchasing power of the domestic market, the government decided to sustain an all-out export strategy based on manufacturing. Using its control of the banking system, and of export-import licences, the state pushed Korean companies to merge, in the form of large, vertical networks (the *chaebol*), similar to the Japanese *keiretsu* but without financial independence (see volume I, chapter 3). By 1977, Korean firms employing over 500 workers, while representing only 2.2 percent of firms, accounted for 44 percent of the labor force. The government established an Economic Planning Board which designed and implemented a series of five-year economic plans. It guided Korean companies toward sectors considered strategic for the national economy, either in terms of building self-reliance or in fostering competitiveness in the world economy. Thus, South Korea methodically walked the path of industrial development, investing sequentially in textiles, petrochemicals, ship-building, steel, electrical machinery, consumer electronics, and (in the 1980s) in automobiles, personal computers, and micro-electronics (with some spectacular successes in this latter industry, including endogenous capacity to design and produce 256k chips earlier than Western Europe).[62] Often, some of the strategic decisions by state's agencies were grossly misguided, leading to economic setbacks.[63] But the government was there to absorb the losses, reconvert factories, and secure new loans.[64]

As in the case of Singapore, but on a much larger scale, the critical role of the state was to attract capital and to control and mobilize labor to make the formation and growth of *chaebol* possible during the 1960s and 1970s. A critical share of capital was of foreign origin, but with a crucial difference from the Singapore experience. The nationalism of the Korean government led to the rejection of the excessive presence of foreign multinational corporations, out of fear of their influence on society and politics. Thus, capital influx into South Korea mainly took the form of loans, guaranteed by the government under the sponsorship of the United States. Public loans, mainly from international institutions, such as the World Bank, were provided to the government to build a productive infrastructure. Private loans were channeled by the government to Korean companies, according to their compliance with the government's strategic plans. Foreign capital thus

62 Lee (1988).
63 Johnson (1987).
64 Lim and Yang (1987).

accounted for 30 percent of all gross domestic capital formation between 1962 and 1979. The ratio of foreign debt to GNP rose to over 26 percent in 1978, making South Korea one of the world's most indebted economies by the early 1980s. Yet, debt service as a proportion of exports was not excessive, and, in fact, declined from 19.4 percent in 1970 to 10.5 percent at the end of the decade. Indeed, the ratio of foreign trade (exports and imports) to GNP jumped from 22.7 percent in 1963 to 72.7 percent in 1979. The experience of South Korea indicates that indebtedness *per se* is not an obstacle to development: it is the proper use of the loans that determines the economic outcome. South Korea, in contrast to some Latin American military regimes (for example, Argentina), used the loans to build infrastructure and support exports. Its freedom of maneuver was guaranteed by the US footing the huge defense bill of the South Korean government, in compensation for being the Asian bulwark against communism.

Only in the 1970s, when the foundations of the South Korean economy were solidly established under the tight control of the *chaebol*, guided by the state, did the government actively seek direct foreign investment. But, even then, severe restrictions were imposed on foreign companies: foreign equity holding was limited to a maximum of 50 percent, forcing foreigners into joint ventures with Korean firms, except in Export Processing Zones insulated from the Korean market. The government was also very selective in allowing foreign investment, looking particularly for companies that could facilitate some technology transfer. Japanese companies invested in textiles, electrical machinery, and electronics. American companies established their presence mainly in petroleum and chemicals. Yet overall foreign investment remained limited, accounting in 1978 for only 19 percent of South Korean exports, and for 16 percent of total manufacturing output.

The state also organized the submissive incorporation of labor into the new industrial economy, under the principle of producing first, redistributing later. Korean labor, educated and hard working, was, as in the rest of East Asia, a critical factor in the developmental process. However, its mode of incorporation was much more repressive in Korea than in other societies.[65] The concentration of workers in large factories organized by quasi-military management favored the emergence of militant trade unionism. Yet independent workers' unions were forbidden, strikes were brutally repressed, and working and living conditions, in the factory and in the home, were kept to a minimum for a long period. Such a repressive attitude led to the formation

65 Deyo (1987b).

of the most militant labor movement in Asia, as the frequency and violence of strikes in the 1980s and 1990s came to demonstrate. Keeping the growth of wages at a substantially lower level than productivity growth was a cornerstone of government economic policy.

Living conditions did improve, however, for the population at large as well as for industrial workers because of the impressive performance of the economy, under the impulse of export-led industrialization. For instance, during the critical developmental period 1972–9, government revenues increased at a stunning annual rate of 94.7 percent, the top 46 *chaebol* collected an annual increase in value added of 22.8 percent, and real wages grew at an annual rate of 9.8 percent. The proportion of the population below the poverty line declined from 41 percent in 1965 to 15 percent in 1975. And while income inequality worsened in the 1970s, overall, South Korea still displayed, in the 1980s, a more equitable income distribution than the United States.

Finally, an emphasis on science and technology, and the upgrading of products and process in Korean industry, have been the obsession of the South Korean state since the 1960s. It created and staffed a series of specialized R&D institutes, linking them to industry under the guidance of the Ministry of Science and Technology. South Korea is the industrializing country that has most rapidly climbed the technological ladder in the new international division of labor.[66] For instance, between 1970 and 1986, South Korean engineering exports grew at an average annual rate of 39 percent, far exceeding the performance of Japan, at 20 percent. In the 1990s, Korean micro-electronics, consumer electronics, and computer industries have become serious competitors of Japanese and American companies, far outstripping European firms in winning world market share in electronics.

South Korea was rightly dubbed by Alice Amsdem "Asia's next economic giant": it increased its share of world domestic production by 345 percent between 1965 and 1986.[67] The four leading South Korean *chaebol*, Samsung, Lucky Gold Star, Daewoo, and Hyundai, were, in the 1990s, among the world's 50 largest conglomerates. They are now investors with a global reach, penetrating markets in America, Europe, Asia, and Latin America, both with their exports and their direct investment. European and American regions fight each other to attract Korean investment. In 1996 the French government tried to sell for 1 franc its ailing "national champion," Thomson, to a consortium led by Daewoo, only to retreat from the deal after the announcement prompted nationalist outrage in France.

66 Ernst and O'Connor (1992).
67 Amsdem (1989).

At the roots of such an extraordinary rise from the ashes of a destroyed and divided country, in about only three decades, lies the nationalist project of a developmental state that deliberately sought the creation of major Korean companies able to become global players in the world economy. It achieved its goal by using foreign loans, American military support, and the ruthless exploitation of Korean labor.

Taiwan: flexible capitalism under the guidance of an inflexible state

Even by the high standards of Asian Pacific development, Taiwan is probably *the* success story, in terms of the combination of a sustained high rate of growth (annual average of 8.7 percent in 1953–82, and of 6.9 percent in 1965–86), increase in world share of GDP (multiplied by a factor of 3.6 in 1965–86), increase in share of world exports (2 percent in 1986, above all other newly industrialized countries, including South Korea), increase in the share of world manufacturing output (multiplied by a factor of 6.8 in 1965–86, as compared to South Korea's 3.6). And this within the context of an income distribution less unequal than any other country, except for Scandinavia and Japan, with inequality declining rapidly during the growth process: Gini coefficient of 0.558 in 1953, and of 0.303 in 1980, well below that of the US or Western European average, although inequality increased somewhat during the 1980s.[68] There were also substantial improvements in the conditions of health, education, and general living standards.[69]

Taiwanese growth was largely accomplished through productivity and competitiveness generated by a flexible production system,[70] put into practice in Taiwan before American academics discovered it in northern Italy. The flexibility concerns both the industrial structure itself, and its overall adaptability to changing conditions of the world economy, under the guidance of a strong state, supported and advised in the initial stages of development by the US Agency for International Development (AID). Throughout the process of development the model of economic growth changed quite dramatically, from an import-substitution emphasis in the 1950s, to export-oriented industrialization in the 1960s (the take-off period), to what Thomas Gold calls "export-oriented import substitution" during the 1970s and 1980s (that is, the deepening of the industrial base to feed exports of manufactured goods).[71] In the 1980s, as Taiwan became an economic power in

68   Kuo (1983).
69   Gold (1986).
70   Greenhalgh (1988).
71   Gold (1986).

its own right, Taiwanese companies took on the world market, internationalizing their production and investments both in Asia (particularly in China) and in the OECD countries (particularly in the United States).[72]

At each of these four stages in the process, we observe a different industrial structure that evolves and superimposes upon itself without major crises. But in all instances two features are critical for the understanding of the process: (a) the Kuomintang (KMT) state was at the center of the structure; and (b) the structure is a network, made up of relationships between firms; between firms and the state; between firms and the world market through trading companies (mainly Japanese), and worldwide commercial intermediaries (see volume I, chapter 3).

During the 1950s, the KMT state, with massive economic aid and military protection from the US, undertook the reform of the economy, after bringing society under its total control by means of the bloody repression of 1947–50 and the "white terror" of the 1950s. An American-inspired land reform destroyed the landowning class and created a large population of small farmers who, with state support, increased agricultural productivity substantially. Agricultural productivity was the first source of surplus accumulation. It generated capital for investment, and freed labor for work in the urban–industrial sector. The government forced farmers into unequal exchange with the industrial economy by controlling credit and fertilizers, and organizing a barter system that exchanged agricultural inputs for rice. With the control of the banks (generally government-owned), and of import licenses, the state geared the Taiwanese economy toward import substitution industrialization, forming an incipient capitalist structure in an entirely protected market. It also provided, with the support of USAID, the necessary industrial and communications infrastructure, and emphasized the education of the labor force. To implement these strategies, several government agencies were established, and four-year plans were elaborated.

By the end of the 1950s, the domestic market had exhausted its demand potential to stimulate growth. Following, again, the advice of US experts, the KMT state embarked on an ambitious program of economic restructuring, this time following an outward orientation. In 1960, the 19-point "Program of Economic and Financial Reform" liberalized trade controls, stimulated exports, and designed a strategy to attract foreign investment. Taiwan was the first country to create an Export Processing Zone, in Kaoshiung. In 1964, General Instruments pioneered electronics assembly offshoring in Taiwan. Japanese

72   Hsing (1997a).

medium-sized companies quickly moved to benefit from low wages, lack of environmental controls, educated labor, and government support. Yet the nucleus of Taiwanese industrial structure was home grown. It was made of a large number of small and medium firms, set up with family savings and cooperative savings networks (the famous *huis*), and supported when necessary with government bank credits. Most of these firms started in the rural fringes of metropolitan areas, where families shared work on the land and in industrial shops at the same time. For instance, in 1989, I visited a rural–industrial area of Chang-hua county, near Taichung, where networks of small firms were supplying about 50 percent of the world's umbrellas. The Taiwanese state attracted foreign investment as a way of obtaining capital and access to international markets. But foreign corporations were linked through subcontracting arrangements to a wide network of small firms that provided a substantial base for industrial production. In fact, with the exception of electronics, direct foreign investment did not, and does not, represent a major component of Taiwan's economy. For instance, in 1981, direct capital stock of foreign companies in Taiwan represented only 2 percent of GNP, employment in foreign firms was about 4.8 percent of total employment, their output about 13.9 percent of total output, and their exports only 25.6 percent of total exports.[73] Access to world markets was initially facilitated by Japanese trading companies and by buyers of American department stores looking for direct supplies from Taiwanese firms.

Thus, the outward orientation of the economy did not imply control of it by multinationals (as in Singapore), nor the formation of large national conglomerates (as in Korea), although a number of industrial groups did grow up under the auspices of the state, and in the 1990s there were several very large, fully internationalized Taiwanese companies. But most of Taiwan's development was enacted by a flexible combination of decentralized networks of family-based Taiwanese firms, acting as subcontractors for foreign manufacturers located in Taiwan, and as suppliers of international commercial networks, usually linked through intermediaries. This is how "Made in Taiwan" merchandise penetrated the whole realm of our everyday life.

In spite of the importance of Taiwan's medium and small firms in winning competitiveness through flexibility, the role of the state in the development process cannot be overlooked, at least until the mid-1980s. It was the central actor in guiding and coordinating the process of industrialization, in setting up the necessary infrastructure, in attracting foreign capital, in deciding priorities for strategic investment, and

73   Purcell (1989: 81).

imposing its conditions when necessary. For instance, the first attempt to start automobile production in Taiwan failed when the government rejected the conditions requested by Toyota.

As in the case of the other "tigers," a critical factor in enhancing economic productivity was the high yield of labor through a combination of low wages, decent education, hard work, and social peace. The social control of labor in Taiwan was achieved, first, by establishing the precedent of unrestrained repression of any challenge to state authority. But, in addition to repression, a number of factors contributed decisively to diffuse conflict and to quell workers' demands. The state did provide a safety net in the form of subsidized health and education, but not housing. Housing cooperatives, helped by government banks, played a role in delaying the housing crisis that finally came into the open in the late 1980s, triggering active urban social movements. However, the most important factor in keeping social peace was the industrial structure itself, made up of thousands of small companies, many of which were based on family members and primary social networks, sometimes linked to part-time agricultural activity. In multinational corporations, the bulk of the unskilled labor force, as in other Asian societies, were young women who were subjected to the double patriarchalism of family and factory. While this began to change with the growth of a powerful feminist movement in Taiwan in the 1990s (see volume II, chapter 3), the gendering of the labor force was an important factor in ensuring social peace during the critical period of industrial take-off.

From the mid-1970s onward, to fight the threat of protectionism in world markets, and to counter the threat of international isolation after the diplomatic recognition of China by the United States, the KMT state engaged in a process of upgrading and modernizing industry, particularly in high-technology manufacturing. This effort included the launching of Taiwan's micro-electronics, personal computer, and computer peripheral industries, and the building of one of the most successful technology parks in Asia: Hsinchu, near Taipei.[74] A number of Taiwanese companies became major suppliers to large electronics firms such as DEC and IBM, while others, linked up in networks, set up shop in Silicon Valley, and other US locations, and thrived on their own.[75] Other industrial sectors, such as garments and textiles, were advised by the government to raise the quality and value of their products to circumvent import restriction quotas in foreign markets, usually calculated by volume.

74 Castells and Hall (1994).
75 Ernst and O'Connor (1992).

By the mid-1980s Taiwan had become a mature, diversified economy, with a solid footing in world markets, and the largest currency reserves in the world. Taiwanese firms felt strong enough to take on China, investing through Hong Kong, and becoming a key player in the Chinese economic miracle (see below). Because of rising wages and the increasing organization of workers in Taiwan, together with the tightening of quotas *vis-à-vis* Taiwanese-originated exports, the largest Taiwanese companies proceeded to offshore production in China and South-East Asia. For instance, Taiwan is currently the world's largest exporter of shoes, but a large proportion of Taiwanese firms' production actually takes place in China.[76] However, this consolidation of Taiwan's firms in international markets, combined with the growth of a civil society, led to an increasing rejection of KMT's grip, resulting in a transformation of the Taiwanese state when Teng Hui Lee, a native Taiwanese, assumed the presidency in January 1988. The process of development begun by KMT to regain new legitimacy in Taiwan, and, across the Taiwan strait, in China itself, created a complex industrial economy, and an affluent, educated society, which made the KMT state obsolete.

Hong Kong model versus Hong Kong reality: small business in a world economy, and the colonial version of the welfare state

Hong Kong remains the historical reference for the advocates of unfettered capitalism. While the prominent role of the state in the hypergrowth economies of Japan, South Korea, Singapore, and Taiwan is too obvious to be denied, Hong Kong, with its early take-off in the 1950s, and its apparent *laissez-faire* brand of capitalism, embodies the dreams of stateless capitalism, supported by the Hong Kong government's explicit policy of "positive non-intervention." Thus, the Hong Kong model may well survive the crisis of 1997. It was, as the saying goes, a society built in a borrowed place, on borrowed time. And, yet, a careful analysis of Hong Kong's economic development since the mid-1950s reveals the decisive role of the state in creating conditions for growth and competitiveness, albeit in a more subtle, indirect, but no less important, mode of intervention than the ways followed by the other three "tigers."[77]

Let us first review certain facts. In the free-market paradise of Hong Kong, all land (with the exception of communal village land of the

76   Hsing (1997a).
77   Leung et al. (1980); Youngson (1982); Schiffer (1983); Castells et al. (1990).

New Territories) was Crown land, which the government leased, not sold, over the years, in a land market entirely manipulated by government control in order to increase public revenue. This land policy also allowed the government to subsidize its public housing projects (land was provided at no cost), as well as government-developed industrial estates, and factories with flats, which played a substantial role in housing small manufacturing firms in the first stage of industrialization. Furthermore, during the critical years of economic take-off (1949–80), while GDP grew by an impressive factor of 13, real government expenditure grew by 26 times, and government social expenditures (including housing, education, health, and social welfare) grew by an astounding 72 times. Thus, government expenditure as a proportion of GDP reached 20.3 percent in 1980. Government share of total capital formation grew during the 1960s and 1970s, from 13.6 percent in 1966 to 23.4 percent in 1983, before declining to around 16 percent in the late 1980s.[78]

Government regulation was more important than is usually acknowledged. It was, for instance, significant in the banking industry, after a series of financial scandals in the early 1980s threatened to wreck Hong Kong's markets.[79] But what was really crucial was the role played by government in creating the conditions for competitiveness of Hong Kong's economy in world markets. I shall summarize the argument.

The classic econometric study by Edward K.Y. Chen on the sources of economic growth in Hong Kong for the period 1955–74 showed that capital and labor inputs played in Hong Kong, as in Singapore, a much greater role than in advanced industrial economies.[80] He also identified exports and international trade as the leading causes of Hong Kong's growth. This interpretation was confirmed, and expanded, in the careful statistical analysis of Tsong-Biau Lin, Victor Mok, and Yin-Ping Ho on the close relationship between exports of manufacturing goods and economic growth.[81] This was hardly a surprising finding, but still constituted an observation full of meaning, particularly from the vantage point of the 1990s, when the rise of Hong Kong as a financial and advanced services center somehow obscures the original sources of the Territory's prosperity. Their study showed that exports were concentrated over time in the same few industries – textiles, garments, footwear, plastics, consumer electronics – in a different pattern from that observed in the other three "tigers." The expansion of exports was mainly due to what Lin et al. have called "changes due to

78   Ho (1979); Youngson (1982); Castells et al. (1990).
79   Ghose (1987).
80   Chen (1979).
81   Lin et al. (1980).

differential commodity composition";[82] that is, changes of product line and in the value of the products within the same industry. In this sense, *what was fundamental was the flexibility of Hong Kong manufacturers to adapt quickly and effectively to the demand of world markets within the same industries.*

We still need to explain the competitiveness of these industries besides their ability to adapt to demand. Another econometric study by E.K.Y. Chen provided the clue: *the critical explanatory variable in Hong Kong's growth equation was the differential between Hong Kong's relative prices and the level of income in the United States, the main market for Hong Kong's exports.*[83] Since the level of prices for manufactures in Hong Kong was mainly determined by wage levels in labor-intensive industries, it was the ability of Hong Kong firms to keep wage increases well below the increase in US income, while still assuring an efficient, skilled, healthy, and motivated labor force, that provided the ground base for the expansion of manufactured exports, and thus for economic growth. Thus, *flexibility of manufacturing, and competitive prices on the basis of relatively low production costs, were the main factors explaining Hong Kong's growth.* But the "explanatory variables" are themselves the result of a specific industrial structure and of a given institutional environment that made the flexibility and competitiveness of the economy possible.

On one hand, *flexibility was the result of an industrial structure characterized by small business*: more than 90 percent of manufacturing firms in Hong Kong in 1981 employed fewer than 50 workers, and large firms (over 100 workers) accounted for only 22.5 percent of manufacturing contribution to GDP. Since 90 percent of manufactured goods were exported, we may assume that small businesses were equally significant in exports, although there are no available data to show it directly. We do know, however, that foreign manufacturers accounted for a small proportion of Hong Kong's manufacturing exports (10.9 percent in 1974, 13.6 percent in 1984). In fact, the average size of manufacturing establishments in Hong Kong decreased over time: from an average of 52.5 workers per establishment in 1951 to 20 in 1981. The mystery lies in how these small firms were able to link up with the world market. Unlike Taiwan, foreign trading companies were not important in Hong Kong. There were, indeed, the traditionally established British trading "Hongs" (such as the legendary Jardine Matheson or Swire groups, whose personas populated James Clavell's novels), but their role in manufacturing exports was rather small. Ac-

82   Lin et al. (1980).
83   Chen (1980).

cording to a classic study by Victor Sit, about 75 percent of local exports were handled by local export/import firms.[84] The great majority of these small firms were small businesses themselves. There were more than 14,000 such firms in Hong Kong in 1977. It was only in the 1980s that large department stores from the United States, Japan, and Western Europe set up their own offices in Hong Kong to place orders with local firms. Thus, the basic industrial structure of Hong Kong consisted of networks of small firms, networking and subcontracting among themselves on an *ad hoc* basis, following the orders channeled by small firms specializing in export/import. Such a flexible structure, originating from the initial nucleus of 21 Shanghainese industrialists who relocated to Hong Kong after the Chinese revolution, with their know-how and small family savings, became an effective business tool for adapting to rapidly changing demand in an expanding world market.

But how were these small businesses able to obtain information about the world market, to upgrade their production, to improve their machinery, to increase their productivity? The Hong Kong government played a significant, albeit not decisive, role in this matter. First, it organized the distribution of export quotas allowed under the MultiFiber Agreement among different firms in the textile industry, thus shaping the production networks under the guidance of the Industry Department. Secondly, it established (in the 1960s) several information and training centers, such as the Hong Kong Productivity Center, engaged in training programs and consulting and technology services; and the Hong Kong Trade Development Council, with offices around the world to promote exports, and to disseminate information among Hong Kong's firms. Other services, such as the Hong Kong Credit Insurance Corporation, served to cover some of the risks incurred by exporters. In the late 1970s, when the need for restructuring and upgrading of Hong Kong's economy became necessary to answer the challenge of protectionism in core markets, the government appointed a Committee on Industrial Diversification, which elaborated a strategic plan for Hong Kong's new stage of industrialization, a plan that was implemented by and large during the 1980s.

The fundamental contribution, however, of Hong Kong's government to the flexibility and competitiveness of small business was its widespread intervention in the realm of collective consumption. The key element in this intervention was a large public housing program, the second largest in the capitalist world, in terms of the proportion of the population housed in it: about 45 percent in the 1980s. Although

84   Sit (1982).

the first estates were of appalling quality, they improved over time, with the building of several large new towns, fully equipped with urban amenities. In the late 1980s, the government undertook the upgrading of the program, demolishing and rehabilitating old structures, and building new housing for displaced tenants. In addition, a comprehensive system of public education, public health, subsidized mass transport, social services, and subsidized foodstuffs was put into place over the years, amounting to a major subsidy of indirect wages for the labor force. Schiffer calculated the impact of non-market forces on household blue-collar expenditures in 1973–4: on average it amounted to a 50.2 percent subsidy of total expenditures for each household.[85] Yu and Li estimated a transfer-in-kind to the average public housing tenant equivalent to 70 percent of household income.[86] Thus, public housing and the special brand of welfare state that emerged in Hong Kong subsidized workers, and allowed them to work long hours without putting too much pressure on their employers, most of whom had little margin to afford salary increases. By shifting onto the government's shoulders much of the responsibility for workers' well-being, small business could concentrate on competitive pricing, shrinking and expanding their labor force according to the variations of demand.

Hong Kong's colonial welfare state did perform two other important functions directly related to the competitiveness of the economy. First, it made possible industrial peace for a long period, a matter of some consequence given the historical tradition of social struggle (often overlooked) among Hong Kong's working class, an underlying current that surfaced with rampaging violence in the urban riots of 1956, 1966, and 1967.[87] Secondly, it created a safety net for low-risk entrepreneurialism that characterized the small business scene in Hong Kong. In fact, small businesses in Hong Kong, as everywhere else, had a high failure rate: on average, an entrepreneur succeeded only after seven attempts.[88] But most businesses were started by workers who betted their small savings, and relied on family support, and on the safety net of public housing and subsidized public amenities to take their chance. If and when their entrepreneurial dreams were busted, they were able to land softly in this safety net, to regroup, and try again.

Thus, social stability and subsidized collective consumption were critical for moderating the pressure of direct wages on business, for

85   Schiffer (1983).
86   Yu and Li (1985).
87   Hong Kong Government (1967); Endacott and Birch (1978); Chesneaux (1982); Chan et al. (1986).
88   Sit (1982).

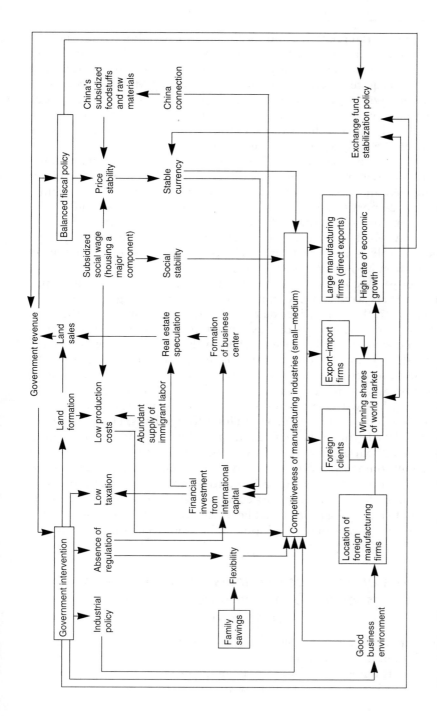

Chart 4.2 The structure and process of economic development in Hong Kong, 1950–85

stable industrial relations, and for the creation of a burgeoning nest of small- and medium-sized entrepreneurs who were, indeed, the driving force of Hong Kong's development, but under social and institutional conditions quite different from those imagined by Milton Friedman in his fiction writing about the Hong Kong economy. Chart 4.2 provides a synthetic view of the set of relationships that, according to my research and sources, characterized Hong Kong's development process between the early 1950s and the mid-1980s.

After the conclusion of the 1984 Sino-British agreement on the transfer of sovereignty at the historically established date of 1997, Hong Kong went into a new model of development, pushed at the same time by new competitive pressures from the world economy, and by the imminent transformation of its institutional environment. Its new economy relied on three major strategic moves. First, Hong Kong deepened its role in manufacturing exports by decentralizing most of its production into the Pearl River delta across the border (see volume I, chapter 6). According to estimates, 10, or 6, or no fewer than 5 million workers were engaged in manufacturing for Hong Kong firms in and around the Pearl River delta, in Guandong province, in the mid-1990s. Secondly, Hong Kong expanded its role as international business center that had been established in the 1980s, taking advantage of its flexible financial regulations, its excellent communications and business infrastructure, and its networks of connections. Thirdly, Hong Kong became, as it had been in history, but this time on a much larger scale, the link with China, and with the Chinese miracle. Most investment in China circulates through Hong Kong. Thus, Hong Kong anticipated its destiny by becoming indispensable to China's incorporation into the global economy, and by betting on its ability to adapt to a new environment, and to thrive in a potentially Chinese-dominated Pacific century. Yet, for Hong Kong to be able to sell itself, to China and to the world, it relies on its economic growth performance of the past half-century – a process that belies the so-called Hong Kong model, but suggests a wealth of developmental lessons to be learned from the Hong Kong reality.

The breeding of the tigers: commonalities and dissimilarities in their process of economic development

In the preceding pages I have tried to summarize the underlying political/economic logic specific to the development process in each of the four lands under consideration. To make progress in the path of theorizing their experience, I will now attempt to think comparatively, by focusing on both the commonalities and the dissimilarities between the four processes, as clues to understanding the social and institutional conditions inducing development in the global economy.

Let us start with the *differential factors*, those that clearly differ in each case, and therefore cannot be considered to be critical elements in the development process. The most important dissimilarity is the industrial structure of each country. In particular, we should reject the "new international division of labor" thesis, according to which new industrialization "in the periphery" is mainly due to productive decentralization from multinational corporations from "the core." Multinationals are fundamental to Singapore, but they played a secondary role in Taiwan's industrialization, and they were, and still are, minor players in South Korea and Hong Kong (although in Hong Kong multinational *financial* corporations became an important factor from the mid-1980s). As mentioned above, the industrial structure of Singapore is characterized by the direct linkage between multinational corporations and the state, including a number of significant state-owned, or state-participated-in, corporations. The South Korean economy was/ is centered around the Korean *chaebol*, nurtured, supported and guided by the state; indeed, in the mid-1990s, the four largest *chaebol* still accounted for 84 percent of Korea's output. Taiwan blends a flexible structure of small- and medium-sized, family business networks; a few large, national firms; and a significant, but minority, presence of foreign firms, either large (American) or medium (Japanese). Hong Kong's economic growth, until the mid-1980s, was mainly engineered by local manufacturing firms, most of them small and medium, supported by a benevolent, colonial state, which provided the productive infrastructure, subsidized collective consumption, and ventured into a subtle form of industrial policy. Therefore, there is no relationship between a given industrial structure and economic growth.

Nor is the sectoral specialization of the economies a common feature. It was not the concentration of industrial effort on textiles or on electronics that explained competitiveness, since South Korea, and Taiwan to a lesser extent, gradually diversified their activities into a variety of sectors. Singapore began with petroleum and electronics (mainly semiconductors), and went on to deepen its electronics specialization (adding computer disk drives, of which it became the main world producer in the 1980s, and then advanced micro-electronics in the 1990s), but reaching out to a whole range of advanced services, finance, and trade activities. Hong Kong, on the other hand, deepened and upgraded its early specialization in five sectors: textiles, garments, plastics, footwear, and consumer electronics, adding, like Singapore, a buoyant advanced services industry. So, the only common feature of the four development processes is the adaptability and flexibility of firms and policies in dealing with world market demand. But this flexibility was performed either by a simultaneous presence in several sectors (Taiwan), or by a succession of priority sectors (as in South Korea), or by upgrading the traditional sectors (as in Hong Kong). Competitiveness does not seem to result from "picking the winners" but from learning how to win.

The existence of a welfare state of sorts, through subsidized collective consumption, was a decisive element in the development of city-states – Hong Kong and Singapore – but was clearly not so in South Korea, where the state did not take care of workers' needs and only the *chaebol* introduced some elements of "repressive paternalism," such as company housing. Nor was it the case in Taiwan, where the state aimed at reducing income inequality, and assured education, but let the market provide the basic goods for the population, trusting the trickle-down effect from economic growth.

Last but not least, the myth of social peace as a major component of the development process in East Asia does not stand up to observation. Singapore became stable only after massive state repression, and the outlawing of the independent, majority trade union movement in the early 1960s. Taiwan was tensely pacified only after the execution of an estimated 10,000–20,000 Taiwanese resisting KMT's occupation, and the widespread "white terror" of the 1950s. Besides, social conflicts in Taiwan started to develop again after the 1977 Chung Li riot, and social movements of all kinds proliferated in the late 1980s, without endangering economic dynamism. Hong Kong had, for a long time, a relatively high degree of unionization in its workforce, and the largest labor federation was controlled by PRC's Communists. Hong Kong's "social peace" was repeatedly shattered by the riots of 1956, 1966, and 1967, the last one followed by several months of protest, including bombings. Since the late 1970s, powerful community movements in Hong Kong have created the foundation of what is today an active "democracy movement," which raises serious concerns among the authorities, both in Hong Kong and in Beijing. South Korea went from the 1960 student uprising that toppled Syngman Rhee to an endless succession of student demonstrations, workers' struggles (most of them subdued and ignored), and citizens' and workers' insurrections, most notably the 1980 Kwangju uprising that was repressed by the dictatorship of Chun Doo Hwan, resulting in the killing of possibly 2,000 people. Korean social movements and political protest brought down the military regime in 1987, and opened the door for democracy. Political turmoil, and workers' daily resistance and powerful strikes, challenged the authoritarianism of the *chaebol*, but did not undermine South Korea's growth, which continued to proceed at a brisk pace in the 1990s, with annual rates of growth oscillating between 5 and 9 percent in 1991-6.

Thus, while the search for social stability, and the partial achievement of this goal, was a fundamental element in the development policy of the four countries, it was not a given of the society. Quite the opposite: all four societies began their development process with volatile social and political situations, so that important segments of society had to be repressed, tamed, and later integrated, in order to keep a minimum order under which the economy could grow. And when social movements appeared again on the surface, economic development adapted to social tensions, and the four countries were able to keep growth and redistribution, together with democratic liberalization, except in Singapore. Social stability was not a prerequisite for development, but an always uncertain result of it.

I also find commonalities in my observation of Asian development. Without them, we could not think about a recurrent pattern that would shed light on our understanding of new historical processes of development. The first common factor concerns the *existence of an emergency situation in the society*, as a result of major tensions and conflicts, both national and geopolitical. It is obvious in the cases of South Korea and Taiwan. It should also be recalled that Hong Kong dramatically changed in 1949 as a consequence of the Chinese revolution, losing most of its traditional role as an entrepôt for China trade, thus being forced into manufacturing exports as a way to survive without being a burden on the Crown's budget. Indeed, it was its role *vis-à-vis* China, together with its economic success, that prevented Hong Kong from joining the decolonization process, since neither the United Kingdom nor China could accept its independence. This was also the case for Singapore, first prevented by British troops from being annexed by Indonesia, then expelled from the Federation of Malaysia in 1965, and abandoned to its fate by Britain in 1965-8, then saved politically and economically because of its support for the American effort in the Vietnam War. The critical geopolitical element in East Asia, in contrast with Latin America, was that the US perceived much of Asia as being in danger of being taken over by communists and their allies, and in fact there were elements to support this perception. Strategic considerations overshadowed all other calculations for US policy in the region, giving considerable freedom of maneuver to Asian states in the running of their economies, on the condition that they would remain "vassal states" of the United States in terms of foreign policy and repression of domestic communism, a condition to which they gladly agreed. If there is a fundamental common thread to the policies of the four "tigers" (including Hong

Kong) it is that, at the origin of their process of development, we find *policies dictated by the politics of survival.*

Another consequence of this context, dominated by the Asian Cold War, was the importance of American and British support for these governments and for their economies. American aid was the major element in the reconstruction and orientation of the economies of South Korea and Taiwan during the second-half of the 1950s. Although Hong Kong contributed more to Britain than Britain did to Hong Kong, some crucial functions, like defense, remained on British shoulders. And, most importantly, Hong Kong was allowed to export to the Commonwealth, and received strong support from the UK in securing export quotas that were decisive for its early penetration of world markets. While Singapore did not receive much foreign aid, the economy got its jump-start from profitable oil and ship-repairing commerce with the American military in Vietnam during the 1960s. Geopolitics provided the ground for the politics of survival to become successful developmental policies.

A second major common factor is that all four development processes were based on an *outward orientation of the economy, and, more specifically, on their success in exporting manufactured goods,* particularly targeting the US market. It is true that for both South Korea and Taiwan import-substitution policies were essential to establish an industrial base at the outset of the development process. Yet, their high growth came only when, starting from their protected domestic markets, they succeeded in exporting. In this sense, the explosion of world trade in the 1960s, and the process of formation of a new, global economy, seem to have been the indispensable habitat of the Asian "tigers."

A third common factor is the *absence of a rural, landowning class,* non-existent in Hong Kong and Singapore, and obliterated (or transformed into industrialists) in South Korea and Taiwan by the American-inspired land reforms of the 1950s. The existence of a powerful landowning class is an obstacle to development because of the usually speculative character of their investments, and because of their reluctance to embark on processes of modernization that would jeopardize their social and cultural domination. It seems that this was one of the obstacles to the Indonesian development process, until the internationalization of its economy in the 1980s, under the aegis of the state, bypassed the interests of traditional rural/financial oligarchies.[89]

A fourth common factor in the development of the four countries was the *availability of educated labor, able to reskill itself during the*

89   Yoshihara (1988).

process of industrial upgrading, with high productivity and a level of wages that was low by international standards. Labor was kept, by and large, under control, in terms of work discipline, and labor demands, with the exception of South Korean labor in large factories in the late 1980s. Disciplined, efficient, relatively cheap labor was a fundamental element in Asian development. But this discipline and effectiveness did not come from the supposedly submissive nature of Asian labor (plainly a racist statement) nor, in more sophisticated vein, from Confucianism. Confucianism does explain the high value placed on education, and therefore the high quality of labor once the state provides the conditions for access to education. But Confucianism does not explain subordination since, in Confucian philosophy, authority must be legitimate, and exercised in legitimate ways, or else it should be resisted. Indeed, the long history of popular uprisings in China, as well as the tradition of revolutionary working-class movements in Shanghai and Canton, contradicts such ill-informed, ideological statements.[90] As mentioned above, in all four countries labor discipline was imposed first by repression. But in all cases there were also, subsequently, powerful elements of social integration that explain why a historically rebellious population ultimately accommodated to the exploitative conditions that characterized working and living conditions for most people for most of the development period. Paramount among the integrative factors was the actual betterment of workers' living standards. What was a low wage for an American or a Japanese worker was a fortune for the industrial labor force of poor East Asian countries. Furthermore, data show a decrease in income inequality in the first stage of development, and a dramatic rise in real wages over three decades. Besides, in the case of Hong Kong and Singapore, a peculiar version of the welfare state, materially organized around public housing projects and new towns, was essential in both improving living conditions and establishing the state's social control and political legitimacy. In the case of Taiwan, the integration of rural and urban life in the same families, and the vitality of social networks, provided, at the same time, the safety net to resist the shocks of fast industrialization and the peer-group social-control mechanisms to discourage workers from challenging the system. Thus, through a combination of state repression, state integration, economic improvement, and social network protection and control, an increasingly educated labor force (much of which was made up of women) found it in its best interests to fulfill the expectations of a system that was as dynamic as it was ruthless. Only when the survival stage was passed did

90   Chesneaux (1982); Chan et al. (1986).

spontaneous social resistance start to take shape in a labor movement, and political alternatives, particularly in South Korea.

A fifth common factor in East Asian industrialization was the *ability of these economies to adapt to the informational paradigm and to the changing pattern of the global economy*, climbing the ladder of development through technological upgrading, market expansion, and economic diversification. What is particularly remarkable (as in the case of Japan, which provided the role model for development, except in Hong Kong) is their understanding of the critical role played by R&D and high-technology sectors of the new global economy. Their emphasis on science and technology (stronger in South Korea and Taiwan, but also present in the city-states) was decided and implemented by the state, but it was welcomed and internalized by industrial firms. The four countries, over three decades, made the transition into the advanced productive structures of the informational economy, albeit still keeping many low-tech activities, as was also the case in the US.

It was this ability to shift from one level of development to another, and from peripheral incorporation into the global economy into a more dynamic, competitive positioning, in higher-value generating activities, that led to sustained growth, in contrast with the short-lived bursts of growth that characterized most Latin American economies.[91]

Behind most of the critical factors common to the experiences of the four East Asian "tigers" is what seems to be the most significant of all commonalities: *the role of the state in the development process*. The production of high-quality labor and its subsequent control, the strategic guidance through the hazardous seas of the world economy, the ability to lead the economy in the transition to informationalism and globalization, the process of diversification, the creation of a science and technology base, and its diffusion in the industrial system – these are all critical policies whose success determined the feasibility of the development process.

Policies are, of course, the outcome of politics, enacted by the state. Behind the economic performance of Asian "tigers" breathes the dragon of the developmental state.

The developmental state in East Asian industrialization: on the concept of the developmental state

If the characterization of East Asian industrialization I have presented in the preceding pages is plausible, then understanding this develop-

91   Fajnzylber (1983).

ment experience requires a sociological analysis of the formation and intervention of the developmental state in these countries. But, first, I need to define the precise meaning of developmental state, which I have already used in my analysis of Japan. I take it from Chalmers Johnson's conceptualization, and I do not disagree with the meaning given to it by Johnson, Peter Evans, Alice Amsdem, and other scholars in the field of development theory. I think, however, it would be useful to provide my own definition, as I understand it, on the basis of my analysis of East Asian "tigers," although it can be used in other contexts.

A state is developmental when it establishes as its principle of legitimacy its ability to promote and sustain development, understanding by development the combination of steady high rates of economic growth and structural change in the productive system, both domestically and in its relationship to the international economy. This definition needs, however, to specify the meaning of "legitimacy" in a given historical context. Many political scientists remain prisoner to an ethnocentric conception of legitimacy, related to the democratic state. Under this conception, the state is legitimate when it establishes hegemony or consensus *vis-à-vis* the civil society. Yet, this particular form of legitimacy presupposes acceptance by the state itself of its submission to the principle of representation of society as it is. But we know that states that have tried over history to break away from the existing order did not recognize civil-society-as-it-was as the source of their legitimacy. And yet, they were not pure apparatuses of naked power, as has been the case with defensive military dictatorships in many instances. The clearest examples are revolutionary states, particularly those emerging from communist revolutions or national liberation movements. They have never pretended to be legitimate in terms of the acquiescence of their subjects, but in terms of the historical project they embodied, as *avant-gardes* of the classes and nations that were not yet fully aware of their destiny and interests. The obvious, and significant, political and ideological differences between communist and revolutionary states and the right-wing dictatorships of East Asia have, in my opinion, led to the overlooking of some fundamental similarities that go beyond formal resemblances to the heart of the logic of the state: the legitimacy principle holding together the apparatus, and structuring and organizing the codes and the principles for accessing power and for exercising it. In other words, the legitimacy principle may be exercised on behalf of society (the democratic state) or on behalf of a societal project. When the state substitutes itself for society in the definition of societal goals, when such a societal project involves a fundamental transformation of the social order (regardless of our value judgment on the matter), I refer to it as a revolutionary state. *When the societal project respects the broader parameters of social order (for example, global capitalism), but aims at fundamental transformations of the economic order (regardless of the interests or desires of the civil society), I propose the hypothesis that we are in the presence of the developmental state.* The historical expression of this societal project generally takes the form (and was the case in most East Asian experience) of the building, or rebuilding, of national identity, affirming the national presence of a given society, or a given culture, in the world. Sometimes this national affirmation does not even coincide with the territory under the political control of the developmental state: for example, the Kuomintang state speaking on behalf of the "Republic of China," behind the safe refuge provided by the US Seventh Fleet.

Thus, ultimately, *for the developmental state, economic development is not a goal but a means.* To become competitive in the world economy, for all Asian "tigers," was first their way of surviving, both as a state and as a society. Secondly, it also became their only way of asserting their national interests in the world – that is, to break away from a situation of dependency, even at the price of becoming an unconditional frontline for the United States. I propose the idea that the developmental state effects the transition from a political subject "in itself" to a political apparatus "for itself" by affirming the only legitimacy principle that does not seem to be threatening for the international powers overseeing its destiny: economic development.

The rise of the developmental state: from the politics of survival to the process of nation-building

The East Asian developmental state was born of the need for survival, and then it grew on the basis of a nationalist project, affirming cultural/political identity in the world scene. *Survival came first.*

Singapore was a non-entity at the outset of its independence in 1965. An abandoned military outpost of the crumbled British Empire, a bankrupt entrepôt economy cut off from its ties with Indonesia, an integral part of Malaysia expelled from the Federation of Malaysia against its will, and a pluri-ethnic society subjected to the pressure of its Malay environment and torn by internal, violent ethnic and religious strife between the Chinese majority and the Muslim Malay and Hindu Tamil minorities, it could have easily become another Sri Lanka. The first concern of Lee Kwan Yew's People's Action Party (PAP), which led the anti-colonial struggle against the British, was to hold Singapore together and to make it viable, while fighting off what was perceived as the menace from guerrillas of the Malaysian Communist Party, led by Chinese, and supported by the PRC.

South Korea had just survived an all-out assault from communist North Korea, and barely escaped being caught in the middle of a nuclear war between MacArthur's imperial fantasies and the victorious Chinese People's Liberation Army. In 1953, the country was in a shambles, the nation divided, and Syngman Rhee's First Republic was but a superstructure for the United States to build a strong defensive line, based on a new, war-hardened, South Korean army, on the northern Asian frontier between communism and the Free World.

Taiwan was not yet Taiwan. It was an impoverished and terrorized island that had become the last bastion of the vanquished Kuomintang armies, kept in reserve by the United States as a potential threat, and as a political standpoint against the rising power of the PRC. In fact, it was the communist invasion of South Korea that brought the United States to the decision to draw the line in the Taiwan Strait, a decision that saved the KMT and allowed it to live its ideological fantasy of reconstructing the Republic of China from Taiwan Province, a fantasy not shared by Chinese capitalists, most of whom emigrated elsewhere.

Hong Kong was rapidly becoming an anachronism after the Chinese revolution and the embargo on China imposed by the United Nations on the occasion of the Korean War. With its entrepôt commerce with China downgraded to smuggling, it was on its way to being the last colony of a fading empire. Fundamental doubts about China's willingness to let it live outside Chinese control, as well as political fears that either the Labour party or British public opinion would include the Territory in the next round of decolonization, kept Hong Kong wondering about its fate, while wave upon wave of Chinese immigrants/refugees were making the colony into their own trap, escaping either from revolution or misery.

The first reflex of state apparatuses that later became developmental (PAP state in Singapore, the Park Regime in South Korea, the KMT in Taiwan, and the colonial state in Hong Kong) was to ensure the physical, social, and institutional viability of the societies they came to be in charge of. In the process, they constructed and consolidated their own identity as political apparatuses. However, according to the hypothesis I am proposing, they shaped their states around the developmental principle of legitimacy on the basis of specific political projects that had, in each case, specific political actors, all of which were created in rupture with the societies they were about to control and lead.

In Singapore, the PAP did lead the anti-colonialist struggle, but it did so in the 1950s in close alliance with the left-wing movement (including the left-wing labor unions), and even with the communists, until the events of the early 1960s convinced Singapore's national leader, Lee Kwan Yew, that he had to repress the left (which he did ruthlessly) to affirm an autonomous political project aimed at transforming Singapore from a colonial outpost into a modern nation.[92] The PAP was, in fact, organized along Leninist lines, with tight mechanisms of social control and social mobilization, centralized forms of party power, and direct guidance of the economy through a well-trained, well-paid, usually clean, state technocracy. The social policies of the PAP, including public housing and community services, aimed at blending into one national culture the complex pluri-ethnic structure of Singapore, while the emphasis on Confucianism and on Mandarin literacy among the Chinese deliberately sought to break up the subcultures organized around dialects spoken by Chinese networks of various regional origins. Economic development was the means to achieve both goals of making Singapore a viable country and of building it as a new nation.

In Taiwan, once the KMT had to accept the reality of having lost China, it tried to convert Taiwan into a showcase of what a reformed KMT could do for China and the Chinese people, after acknowledging the disastrous economic management and the damage that their unrestrained corruption had done to their political control over China.[93] A quasi-Leninist party, explicitly organized around the principles of democratic centralism, the KMT attempted to reform itself, made its adherence to Sun Yat-Sen's "three principles of the people" official ideology, and derived from it its policies of land reform, reduction of inequality, and emphasis on education. The critical matter for the consolidation of KMT power in Taiwan was its ability to assure the island's growing prosperity. The KMT considered the success of its developmental project to be critical in obtaining the support of Chinese all over the world for its future challenge to communist power on the mainland. In fact, the Chinese "open-door policy" of the 1980s was partly an answer to the impact of Taiwan's economic miracle, not only among the informed Chinese population, but among the Chinese leadership itself.

The origins of the Park Regime in South Korea can also be traced back to the emergence of a new political actor, breaking away both from the colonial order and from the corrupt, inefficient Rhee regime that had seen the remnants of the pro-Japanese commercial bourgeoisie prosper through the state redistribution of US aid, while the country continued to suffer from the devastation of war.[94] Although the 1961

92   Chua (1985).
93   Gold (1986).
94   Cole and Lyman (1971); Lim (1982).

coup toppled the short-lived civilian government of John Chang, issued from student-led rebellion against Syngman Rhee, the ideology
and practice of military plotters went beyond a simple law-and-order
reflex. The leaders of the coup were young, nationalist, military officers of low rank, with the exception of Major General Park, who was
trained in Japan and had served in the Japanese Army in Manchuria.
The South Korean military was an entirely new institution, whose organization and growth was obviously linked to the Korean War. It
grew from 100,000 in 1950 to 600,000 in 1961, making it one of the
most numerous, well-trained, and more professional armies in the
world. Given the military interest of the US in Korea, most of the
effort of modernization and support was focused on the armed forces.
Thus, the army's professional training and organizational capacity
seems to have been above the rest of South Korean society in the 1960s,
if we except a small group of students, and an even smaller intelligentsia. Thus, in the presence of the disintegration of the state, economy,
and society, the military officers who seized power in 1961–3 appear
to have been close to the "Nasserite" brand of nationalist military
regimes. Lacking a social basis, and feeling uncertain of the support of
the United States toward the national projection of Korea beyond its
geopolitical function, the Park Regime conceived the developmental
strategy as an instrument of rebuilding the Korean nation, and of winning degrees of political freedom.

But what about Hong Kong? How did the half-hearted, more subtle
brand of Hong Kong's semi-developmental state come into being? How
could a colonial government identify itself with the destiny of the
colony? If the traditional Hongs and the new entrepreneurs cared only
about their business, if the British old-timers mainly dreamed about
their retirement in Surrey, and the Chinese industrialists about their
green (residence) cards in California, how could a collective political
actor emerge in Hong Kong to make it into a thriving city-state projecting itself in the world economy? Let us examine the question in
historical close-up.

Institutional power in Hong Kong, during the entire development
process, was concentrated in the hands of the colonial governor, appointed by Westminster. Once appointed, however, the Governor was
almost entirely autonomous in deciding domestic Hong Kong policies.[95] From 1957, the Hong Kong budget did not require formal approval from London. Thus, the Colony was run as an autonomous
state, centered on the Governor and a series of appointed Committees,
headed by Secretaries, also appointed by the Governor. This executive

95   Miners (1986).

branch of government relied on the support of a number of legislative and advisory bodies made up of official and unofficial members, most of them also appointed by the government until the political reforms of the 1980s. These institutions were served by a numerous, well-trained, and efficient government public service, numbering 166,000 civil servants in the 1980s. However, behind this formal structure of power, the empirical study by Miron Mushkat, the historical–anthropological monograph of Henry Lethbridge, and a number of other studies,[96] including my own fieldwork, reveal a different, fascinating story about the real power structure of Hong Kong. The core of this power structure seems to have been in the hands of what Mushkat calls the "administrative class," a small, select group of civil servants who, until the 1970s, were recruited overwhelmingly in Britain by the Colonial Civil Service, out of the best British universities, and generally from Oxford and Cambridge. Between 1842 and 1941 there were only 85 "cadets" (as they were called until 1960) of the Hong Kong Colonial Civil Service. Even after the huge expansion of personnel in the 1970s, including the massive recruitment of Chinese, there were only 398 "general grade administrative officers."[97] It was this administrative class, with strong social and ideological cohesion, shared professional interests and cultural values, that seems to have controlled power within the Hong Kong state for most of the history of the Colony. They exercised power while keeping in mind the interests of the business elite, but only to the extent that business would assure the economic prosperity of Hong Kong, on which the power, income, prestige, and ideological self-legitimation of the administrative class depended. Their interest in relation to the future of Hong Kong was twofold: to maintain the Colony in the midst of the turmoil of decolonization and the threatening stands of the British Labour party; and to show the world that the Colonial Service, on behalf of what was left of the tradition of the British Empire, was more able than any other political institution (including the new independent national states) to ensure the prosperity of the new Asian world, including to a large extent the well-being of its people, in a paternalistic attitude that evokes the historical precedent of "enlightened despotism." Although my ethnographic material on the subject is too unsystematic to be conclusive, it did convince me that the dedication and effectiveness of the elite Colonial Civil Service of Hong Kong was tantamount to the last hurrah of the British Empire. The "Hong Kong cadets" aimed at building Hong Kong's prosperity as an ideological

96   Lethbridge (1970); Mushkat (1982); Kwan and Chan (1986).
97   Scott and Burns (1984).

monument to the historic memory of the lost Empire, while also taking care of their retirement years, in England.

Thus, under different forms specific to each society, the developmental state in the newly industrialized Asian countries seems to have been the instrument of nation (or city) building (or rebuilding) processes enacted by political actors largely autonomous of their societies. However, it was only because these political actors were able both to mobilize and to control their civil societies that they could implement their developmental strategy.

The state and civil society in the restructuring of East Asia: how the developmental state succeeded in the development process

To identify the main actors of the development process in the Asian Pacific (the developmental states) does not solve the fundamental issue of why they were able to succeed, if by success we understand the achievement of their vision of economic development. To identify the factors explaining their success I must address three questions: (a) the relationship between Asian developmental states and other states in the international system; (b) the internal logic of developmental states; and (c) the relationship between developmental states and their societies.

First, it is important to remember that the first stages of East Asian industrialization were extraordinarily favored by the geopolitical context in which these economies took shape: the Asian Cold War and the full support of the United States for these regimes, and, in the case of Hong Kong, the support of Britain. However, we must reject the leftist oversimplification of seeing these states as "puppets of American imperialism": in fact, these states did show their autonomy by fostering their own nation-building projects. To understand their historical specificity, I propose the concept of "vassal state" for this particular political form. By *vassal state*, using the analogy with feudalism, *I understand a state that is largely autonomous in the conduct of its policies, once it has abided by the specific contribution it has to make to its "sovereign state."* Thus, the states of the Asian tigers were not "dependent states" in the sense in which dependent societies and dependent states are defined by the structural–historical theory of dependency. These are states with very limited autonomy *vis-à-vis* the overall geopolitical system to which they belong, in exchange for which they receive protection along with a significant degree of autonomy in the conduct of their domestic affairs. I propose the notion that Taiwan, at least until the early 1970s, and South Korea, at least until

1987, were vassal states of the United States, while Hong Kong was all along a vassal city-state (rather than a colony) of the UK. As for Singapore, it was a semi-vassal state of the United States, from the Vietnam War, including some curious linkages such as the organizing and training of its military by the Israelis. This "vassal" condition created a security umbrella, relieved much of the burden of the defense budget of these countries, and played a role in the critical initial stages in facilitating access to world markets.

The second element explaining the success of the developmental strategy was *the construction of an efficient, technocratic, state apparatus.* This has little to do with the traditional distinction between corrupt bureaucracies and clean bureaucracies. Corruption was widespread in South Korea, significant in Taiwan, present in Hong Kong, and more limited, but not absent, in Singapore. And, yet, the four states were able to operate with a high level of efficiency, served by well-trained civil servants, and organized on flexible lines that changed according to the needs of each stage of development. In functional terms, corruption is only an obstacle to efficiency when it prevents the bureaucracy from fulfilling its assigned task. And it is only an obstacle to legitimacy if there is a democratic state, accountable to a civil society that expects public service to prevail over private interests. In South Korea, for instance, corruption was the pay-off exacted by military officers and party officials from Korean industrialists in exchange for running the country toward developmental aims that created huge benefits for these state-sponsored industrialists. Overall, these states were more technocratic than bureaucratic, since their apparatuses were set up to implement a strategic, historical project, and not only (but also) to reap the benefits of dictatorship.

Yet, the fundamental element in the ability of developmental states to fulfill their project was *their political capacity to impose and internalize their logic on their societies.* The autonomy of developmental states, and their ability to implement their project with few concessions to society's demands, must be explained in empirical, historical terms, without calling upon the metaphysics of Confucianism.

The first explanation is a simple one: repression. The Kuomintang began to establish its hold on the island by the widespread massacres of May 9, 1947. It went on to set up a ruthless political control apparatus which, for the next three decades, arrested, tortured, and killed political dissenters, whether from right or left, all lumped under the communist label. The PAP in Singapore liquidated all serious political opposition in the period 1961–5, banning the main trade union, and arresting leaders of the opposition Barisan Socialists, which led to the expulsion of the PAP from membership of the Socialist International.

Later, it often used the British Colonial Internal Security Act, allowing the government to detain without charge for an indefinite period anyone suspected of "subversion." Hong Kong used British troops to quell the riots of 1956, 1966, and 1967, and kept a very large and efficient police force of over 20,000, which did not hesitate to deport on the spot to China any dissident considered a threat to public order. South Korea, under the aegis of one of the most effective, and brutal, police forces in the world (the Korean CIA), arrested, tortured, imprisoned, and killed dissidents, while forbidding all independent union activity and most independent political activity until the demise of the authoritarian regime in the late 1980s.

Most Third World countries, however, practice similar repressive policies, without much success either in containing protest or, even less, in mobilizing their societies on the path to development. Thus, other factors must have accounted for the organizational capacity demonstrated by the East Asian developmental states *vis-à-vis* their societies.

An important element was that *the traditional, dominant social classes were either destroyed, disorganized, or made subordinate to the state*, with the partial exception of Hong Kong. Land reforms in Korea and Taiwan, and the absence of a non-colonial bourgeoisie in Singapore, destroyed the traditional oligarchy in these societies. What was left of the commercial–industrial bourgeoisie was made an appendage of the developmental strategy decided by the state. With no domestic base from which to accumulate, the role of the state as gatekeeper to the world economy made any local capitalist entirely dependent on import–export licenses and government-sponsored credit. In Singapore, the multinationals quickly understood that the Lion City could be a tropical paradise for them only on the condition of "not messing up" with the government. In Hong Kong, as usual, a more complex pattern developed. The bourgeoisie, both traditional (the British Hongs), and newcomers (the Shanghainese industrialists), were co-opted via a number of government committees. The Chinese bourgeoisie was left to run its own business on the condition of reporting to the government and abiding by its instructions. The Jockey Club socially "glued" the political and business elites together, but under the clear leadership of the "cadets." And a significant number of high-ranking government officials retired to become representatives of Hong Kong business associations, thus establishing an informal and effective channel of communication between government and business, in a harmonious division of labor, generally led by government's enlightened technocracy.[98]

98 Lethbridge (1978); King and Lee (1981); Scott (1987); Castells et al. (1990).

As for the working class, the four states devised strategies of integration to complement repression and, if possible, to substitute for it in the long run. All four states counted on economic growth and the improvement of living standards, including access to education and health, to keep workers content. In fact, the strategy was effective for most of the period. In addition to improving living conditions, there were policies explicitly designed for social integration. Taiwan emphasized reduction in income inequality. Both Hong Kong and Singapore created an Asian version of the British welfare state, centered around public housing and social services. Public housing estates played a fundamental role in social integration. In the case of Hong Kong, tenancy in public housing was the *de facto* citizenship accorded to a largely immigrant working class. In the case of Singapore, social engineering through the public housing/new towns program was essential in diffusing inter-ethnic tensions in everyday life.[99] South Korea practiced a much harsher policy toward the working class, and as a result had to confront what is today one of the most militant labor movements in Asia. Yet, the extraordinary improvement in living conditions, the emergence of an affluent middle class, and the particularly strong persistence of patriarchalism in the family allowed South Korea to keep labor conflicts under control until the 1980s. Thus, the developmental states were fully aware of the need to integrate their societies to the extent that this integration remained compatible with economic conditions necessary to be competitive in the world economy. They were not just repressive dictatorships. Their project consisted of a double-edged plowshare that they did not hesitate to transform into a sword when required.

However, the process of development they succeeded in implementing not only transformed the economy but completely changed the society. A new, more assertive capitalist class, ready to take on the world, emerged in the 1980s, increasingly confident that it no longer needed a state of technocrats, racketeers, and political police. A new, consumer-oriented, educated, liberal middle class decided that life was all too good to be sacrificed for the historical project of an artificially invented nation. And new, more conscious, better organized social movements, workers, students, citizens, women, environmentalists, appeared to be ready to raise questions about the conditions, goals, and sharing of development. The success of developmental states in East Asia ultimately led to the demise of their apparatuses and to the fading of their messianic dreams. The societies they helped to engender through sweat and tears are indeed industrialized, modern so-

99   Castells et al. (1990).

cieties. But, at the turn of the millennium, their actual historical projects are being shaped by their citizens, now in the open ground of history making.

Divergent paths: Asian "tigers" in the economic crisis[100]

The economic crisis of the late 1990s was felt very differently in the four lands we are analyzing. South Korea's economy collapsed. Hong Kong, between October 1997 and June 1998, lost about US$300 billion in the value of stocks and property: roughly the equivalent of all deposits in local banks. In 1998 Hong Kong's economy suffered its first recession in three decades. Singapore experienced a moderate downturn, declining by about 1 percent in 1998. Taiwan continued to grow in 1998 at a good pace, at around 5 percent. Although both Singapore's and Taiwan's economies suffered the impact of the Asian crisis, to understand their greater resilience to the crisis may open the way to comprehending future paths of development in the twenty-first century.

There was a sharp difference in the origins of the crisis in Hong Kong and in South Korea. In Hong Kong, the collapse of the property market, and its impact on stocks, played a decisive role in the financial crisis. In South Korea, it was the crisis of profitability of the large *chaebol* that prompted their risky borrowing from foreign funds, inducing the default of their debt payments. In both cases, however, speculative attacks on their currencies by global capital sources, acting on the opportunity provided by a shaky financial system, amplified the crisis. To simplify the analysis, I will contrast Hong Kong with Singapore, then South Korea with Taiwan.

In Hong Kong, real-estate values in the private market sky-rocketed during the 1990s. Between 1990 and 1996, the price of housing multiplied fourfold. This was partly due to a clause in the 1984 agreement between the UK and the PRC, under which auctions of government land would be limited to 50 hectares per year, unless otherwise authorized by the PRC. Thus, land supply shrunk, while demand on land increased at a fast pace, as a result of the boom in financial and business services in Hong Kong. The Hong Kong government benefited from rising land prices. As I showed above, land revenues were

100   This section is intellectually indebted to the contributions of Jeffrey Henderson, Chu-Joe Hsia, You-tien Hsing, and Jong-Cheol Kim, though all responsibility for errors of interpretation is mine. For analytical developments and sources of information, see Dolven (1998); Dornbusch (1998); Henderson (1998a, b); Henderson et al. (1998); Kim (1998); Stiglitz (1998); Thompson (1998).

a major source of income for the government – indeed, the substitute for tax revenue. Furthermore, in the 1990s Hong Kong transformed its economy from manufacturing to services. Instead of upgrading technologically, Hong Kong manufacturers opted for cutting costs by shifting production across the border, and investing in business services, financial markets, and real estate. They were joined by overseas Chinese investors, who made Hong Kong one of their main bases of operation, as well as their preferred stock market. There followed an extraordinary revaluation of stocks and property, which attracted short-term, speculative capital from around the world. Hong Kong lacked proper financial regulation, and the currency board system, established to keep the exchange rate stable, limited the government's capacity to act on monetary policy. Thus, the October 1997 run on the Hong Kong dollar undermined investors' confidence. Only the determination of the PRC to defend the Hong Kong currency kept it pegged to the US dollar. But the cost was staggering. High interest rates, and loss of investor confidence, led to a plunge in both the property market and the stock market. In the summer of 1998, the Hong Kong government tried to play cat and mouse with speculative financial flows, buying and selling Hong Kong stocks without warning, just to inflict punitive losses on speculators and discourage their moves. It was a desperate strategy, tantamount to using a bucket to contain a financial *tsunami*. After losing over 10 billion dollars, the Hong Kong government stopped the fight, and let the PRC take full responsibility for its currency. Having transformed itself into a financial and services economy, and losing competitiveness *vis-à-vis* its neighbors because of its stubborn refusal to devalue, Hong Kong learnt the meaning of recession.

Meanwhile, Singapore, the other city-state, followed a very different path in the 1990s, a path that eventually allowed it to absorb much of the shock of the crisis. Property values were kept under control, by and large. The much larger proportion of the population in public housing (87 percent) limited the impact of speculation on real-estate prices, since land, as in Hong Kong, was in the public domain. But, unlike in Hong Kong, land revenues had a limited role in government finance, so the government had little interest in pursuing the risky adventure of becoming itself a speculative landholder. Instead, the government continued to rely on the flow of funding accumulated in the Central Provident Fund, as well as on the proceeds of the vast, and mostly profitable, public enterprise sector. Indeed, in 1998, the government and government-related business were generating about 60 percent of Singapore's GDP.

Furthermore, while Singapore became a major financial hub and an advanced service economy, it made a point of remaining a leading manufacturing center as well. Manufacturing was, essentially, a multinational operation, but, as shown above in this chapter, it received steady support from government policies. The Singapore government designed a strategy of technological upgrading for Singapore-based companies so that the 25 percent of total employment in manufacturing would translate into a higher share of manufacturing in GDP because of the high value-added of manufactured products. With stronger regulations than Hong Kong in the financial markets (particularly after the collapse of Barings Bank in Singapore), tighter control on property values, a strong, productive public sector, and opportunities for profitable investment in manufacturing and business services, Singapore did not suffer the same speculative attacks as Malaysia or Hong Kong. To be sure, the strong connection between Singapore and the surrounding South-East Asian economies induced a downturn in its economic growth and a mild recession in 1998. The continuation of the Asian crisis still could inflict considerable pain on its economy. Yet, the strength and decisiveness of the Singaporean state, and its strong links with multinational manufacturing companies, proved to be better assets to weather the crisis than Hong Kong's free-wheeling financial markets, and orthodox economic policies, under the conditions of the new global economy.

South Korea and Taiwan are very different from the city-states. They both depend, fundamentally, on the competitiveness of their manufacturing industries. But their industrial structures are very different: large, vertically integrated *chaebol* in the case of South Korea; flexible, entrepreneurial small and medium companies, some of which grew considerably in scale through their competitiveness, in the case of Taiwan. State control was also different: the South Korean state was deeply involved with the *chaebol*, and entirely controlled their finance during the period of high growth. The Taiwanese state, instead, provided decisive support in technology, infrastructure, and trade policy, as presented above, but let firms decide their own strategies for themselves. Besides, while the Taiwanese state owned, or participated in, the major banks of Taiwan, it rarely used bank lending as an instrument of industrial policy. Instead, entrepreneurial start-ups in 1990s' Taiwan relied on the well-provided venture capital market which channeled domestic savings into productive investment. The differential trajectories of the two countries during the crisis highlight the importance of these differences.

The South Korean crisis started with the bankruptcy, in January 1997, of one of the large *chaebol*, Hanbo, which specialized in the steel and construction industries. In the following months, a number of other *chaebol*, all among the 30 largest, followed suit in declaring themselves bankrupt: Sammi, Jinnro, Daenong, Kia, Sangbangul, Haitai. By September 1997, defaulted loans and bankruptcies came to represent 32 trillion won; that is, about 7.5 percent of GDP. The subsequent decline in stock prices, and the downgrading of South Korean securities by international rating agencies, led to a stampede of foreign debtors, who called in their loans. Capital flight followed. After spending most of its reserves defending the currency, the South Korean government gave up, and the won collapsed. On November 21, 1997, the South Korean government declared insolvency in international payments, and asked for help from the IMF in exchange for surrendering its economic sovereignty. Thus, the financial crisis and the currency crisis were prompted by the bankruptcy of large South Korean corporations, which, not long before, had been among the fiercest competitors in the global economy.

Three factors seem to have been decisive in their demise. First, South Korean manufacturers had lost competitiveness substantially since the early 1990s, particularly in the US market. South Korean companies were producing at too high a cost to compete with the lower tier of new Asian producers, while not being able to match the technological level of Japanese, American, or even Taiwanese companies. This trend was particularly visible in semiconductors, where the relative dominance of Korean companies in memory chips (40 percent of the world market) was being eroded by more flexible and innovative Taiwanese firms (Acer, Powerchip, Windbond) which had taken about 9 percent of the world market by the end of 1998. The automobile company Kia suffered a major fiasco in its export strategy. The reaction of Korean *chaebol*, which had been accustomed to push through their own way, counting on the all-out support of the state, was to borrow, and invest, to increase their competitiveness. But the South Korean state, and the global economy, had changed by the early 1990s. Under Kim Young Sam's administration, the Economic Planning Board was moved to the Ministry of Finance and lost its strategic capacity to guide the economy. The financial system was deregulated, making direct access by the *chaebol* to foreign lending possible. Financial transactions were now mediated not by the state, but by loosely regulated South Korean banks. Japanese financial firms, unable to obtain high interest rates at home, were happy to lend to the *chaebol*, always counting on the customary protection of the South Korean state. Thus, the debt/equity ratio of South Korean firms sky-rocketed, sending the financial system on a risky path.

The third, and decisive, factor in triggering the crisis was the changing attitude of the South Korean state. This time, it did not bail out the *chaebol.* The resulting default of several *chaebol* precipitated the crisis of confidence among foreign debtors that prompted the overall financial crisis. But why did the state not prevent the bankruptcies by intervening earlier? First, the largest *chaebol* had become global players, quite independent of the state. The *chaebol* took advantage of financial deregulation to tap into a much larger, global source of credit than the one formerly provided by state-controlled banks. Secondly, the South Korean state, in the democratic context, had become accountable to society at large, so that its margin of maneuver was limited. The close links between the *chaebol* and the political class continued during the democratic regime, but it was a clientelistic relationship, rather than a systemic feature of the state. Various political factions had their own connections with specific *chaebol*, thus entering the game of supporting their cronies, rather than preserving the state/*chaebol* system as a whole. In other words, there was a change from corporatist state capitalism to corrupt government practices on behalf of specific business interests. Lack of regulation, and loose government control of the financial system, rather than excessive government intervention, were critical factors which allowed the financial crisis to ruin the economy.

Thus, the South Korean crisis may have been induced by the inability of the *chaebol* to continue to grow and compete in the global economy without the support of the developmental state. The South Korean developmental state could not deliver the same level of support as it had in the past. This was, on the one hand, because social mobilization and political democracy had imposed limits on the use of state resources for the exclusive benefit of *chaebol*; on the other hand, because the integration of the South Korean economy in the global economy, and the deregulation of financial markets and currency controls under pressure from the US, had removed essential policy tools from the hands of the state. The global whirlwind of speculative financial flows filled the gap thus created between the needs of the *chaebol* and the limited capacity of the state, providing easy money to South Korean firms. But short-term, high-risk lending is the kind of money that is recalled at the first sign of potential default.

To sum up, the South Korean crisis resulted from the cumulative effect of the following factors: a crisis in the profitability of large South Korean export manufacturers; the weakness of financial institutions in South Korea, exploited by speculative, high-risk foreign moneylenders, particularly Japanese; and the substantial limitation of the state's developmental capacity which resulted from new controls established by a democratic society and from international (namely, US) pressure pushing toward the liberalization of trade and finance.

In contrast, the Taiwanese state played a secondary role in the growing competitiveness of Taiwanese firms during the 1990s. Networks of these firms, in Taiwan, in Asia, and in the United States (particularly in Silicon Valley), found their own way out of the semiconductor slump. Indeed, they took on South Korean and Japanese competitors, winning market share in memory chips, in personal computers, in LCD screens, in software products. Taiwan's vast foreign currency reserves, the largest in the world, discouraged most speculative attacks. However, the currency was devalued by 6.5 percent, supposedly in a political ploy to bring down the yuan, thus taking the Chinese economy off track. But markets pushed the NT upward later on, in a clear indication of the basic soundness of the Taiwanese economy. Indeed, while Taiwan did suffer from the crisis because of the loss of substantial export markets in Asia, it was spared most of the financial turmoil. Its property market played a minor role in capital accumulation. Its banking system was largely de-linked from export manufacturers, which had their own funding sources. And the value of stocks in the stock market was mainly determined by the profitability of the companies traded in it. Taiwan thus offers a good example to appreciate the difference between suffering the impact of an external crisis and a home-grown crisis resulting from domestic economic and institutional flaws. The Taiwanese developmental state became weaker in the 1990s, as in the case of South Korea, because it had to reckon with democratic politics and an active civil society. It considerably downplayed its *dirigisme*. But because of its entrepreneurial flexibility, Taiwanese business did not need the state any longer. Relying on the competitiveness of its manufacturers, and on their domestic capital market, Taiwan's economy was not taken over by uncontrollable financial flows of global origin. Thus, financial turmoil did not ruin the economy, although it did jeopardize Taiwan's projected "March to the South," aimed at expanding investment and trade in South-East Asia.

Overall, no clear-cut pattern is emerging on the sources of the crisis in the four "tigers" since each case seems to be different. But we can say that the presence of the developmental state, and excessive interventionism, did not induce the crisis since Singapore provides evidence of effective state intervention which limited the impact of the crisis, while Hong Kong's deregulated environment and currency board policy, following orthodox economic prescriptions, led to a devastating destruction of financial value. Indeed, it would seem that, in the case of South Korea, it was the disorderly withdrawal of the developmental state from economic management, and its loose regulation of the banking system, that precipitated the crisis. So, it was not state intervention that caused the crisis, but the inconsistency of this intervention. Both the "soft landing" of Taiwan's *dirigisme* and the continuation of state control in Singapore avoided the pitfalls produced by the chaotic withdrawal of the state in South Korea and erratic government intervention in Hong Kong.

A second observation is that manufacturing competitiveness, in Taiwan and Singapore, continued to be at the root of their relatively solid economic performance, while the deindustrialization of Hong Kong, and the loss of competitiveness of the South Korean *chaebol*, weakened their economies. An advanced service economy still needs a solid link to a dynamic manufacturing sector – postindustrialist myths notwithstanding. Lastly, the destabilizing role of short-term movements by global financial flows remains the most important source of the crisis. But economies are further exposed to their destructive influence when they bring down their domestic regulations and become addicted to easy money. Institutional weaknesses are critical factors in the differential resistance of national economies to the disruptive effects of global finance. These institutional weaknesses can be traced back, in the last resort, to the crisis of the state. And the crisis of the developmental state seems to be a function of the changing patterns of relationship between state and society.

Democracy, identity, and development in East Asia in the 1990s

On August 26, 1996, former South Korean dictator and president General Chun Do Hwan was sentenced to death in Seoul for his participation in the 1979 coup, and his responsibility for the 1980 Kwangju massacre of pro-democracy demonstrators. His successor, and former protégé, Roh Tae Woo, who presided over South Korea's transition to democracy, received a 22-year minimum jail term. By this highly symbolic gesture, Korean democracy, under President Kim Young Sam, was asserting itself against the authoritarian state. Not only was the military dictatorship on trial: the corrupt linkage between the authoritarian regime and South Korean business was condemned as well. The heads of eight *chaebol* received prison sentences for bribing former president Roh. The sentences were suspended, but the trial was a break with the past.

An even greater break took place when, in December 1997, Kim Dae Jung, the undisputed leader of the South Korean radical democratic opposition, was elected president. The fact that he came to preside over an economy in shambles was equally symbolic. The South Korean developmental state had failed, both in its economic performance and in its political control. Kim Dae Jung, in a highly symbolic gesture, pardoned the former dictator, Chun Do Hwan, the man who had sentenced him to death. Democracy was strong enough to make gestures of national reconciliation, paving the way for the eventual reunification with the North in a future democratic nationalist project. But the rebuilding of this political project – breaking with the authoritarian developmental state – required an attack on the corrupt roots of South Korean politics. In September 1998, the public prosecutor accused the former government's Grand National Party of using tax collectors to extract from the *chaebol* 6 million dollars for its electoral campaign. President Kim Dae Jung asked the party to apologize for its "tax theft," prompting a new political crisis. Furthermore, in August 1999, President Kim Dae Jung brokered the break up of one of the largest *chaebol*, and perhaps the most symbolic of Korean development: Daewoo, employing over 2.5 million workers. To avoid its uncontrolled bankruptcy, as a result of a US$50 billion debt, the hundreds of firms of the *chaebol* were separated, and sold independently, with only the automobile company and the trading company being allowed to keep the brand name. The event signaled the new limits to the traditional domination of the *chaebol* over Korean politics and economy.

So, in a sequence of events in the 1990s, South Korean politics shifted its center of gravity from the remnants of military bureaucracy to a new democratic, political elite, rooted in the professional middle class. This transformation of politics, and of the state, could not have taken place without the transformation of civil society under the impulse of social movements.

On December 27, 1996, hundreds of thousands of Korean workers went on a general strike that, under various forms, lasted several weeks. They were protesting against a new law proposed by President Kim Young Sam, and approved by the government's parliamentary majority, which made it easier for Korean companies to dismiss workers, in an adaptation, according to proponents of the law, to the flexibility of labor markets required by new global competition. Workers were also protesting against the lack of legal recognition of the main confederation of trade unions. After weeks of strikes, demonstrations, and repeated clashes with police, the trade unions, with the support of public opinion and the political opposition, obtained the recognition of their union, as well as some concessions in labor legislation. Subsequently, labor unions grew in influence, in spite of the economic crisis. But, faced with the collapse of the South Korean economy, in 1998 they agreed to a social pact with business and government, so that President Kim Dae Jung could have a chance to manage the country toward recovery.

Four elements combined to transform the relationship between state, society, and the economy in South Korea, after 1987, when Chun ceded to pressures from democratic quarters to engage in a process of controlled liberalization. The first factor in bringing down the military regime was the increased assertiveness of civil society, in which powerful social movements were spreading. There was the traditionally militant student movement. But radical students had been isolated from society at large in their many years of struggle against the regime. By the late 1980s, they were joined by a revitalized labor movement, springing from hundreds of wild-cat strikes that shook up South Korea's repressive control of its working class. The strikes and demonstrations of December 1996 and January 1997 were a display of strength by the trade unions that made it clear that workers had shattered the domination exercised by government and business over labor. Community movements, particularly for housing and against urban renewal, often supported by churches, mobilized large sections of a predominantly urban society in Korea. And an educated, prosperous middle class aspired to live a "normal life" in a "normal country." Altogether, they contributed to changing the political landscape.

A second factor was the increasing distance of the Korean *chaebol* from the state, as they became global companies, diversified their interests, and resented the imposition of government policies. A third factor was international pressure, particularly from the United States, to stabilize a democratic South Korea, whose defense against North Korea would be acceptable on political grounds, when the disappearance of tension with the USSR undermined the geopolitical rationale of the US military commitment. The 1988 Olympic Games symbolized the opening of the new Republic of Korea to the world.

The fourth factor is less known but, in my opinion, was, and is, fundamental to understanding South Korea's political dynamics: the regionalization of politics. Surprising as it may seem in such an ethnically homogeneous nation, and in a geographically small country, regional identity is a critical factor in Korean politics, and the failure of the military regime to meld these identities into the nationalist project doomed its efforts for political control. For instance, in the first democratic parliamentary elections of 1988, Kim Young Sam's party took 15 out of 16 seats in his native Pusan province, and performed strongly in nearby South Kyungsang. His rival in the democratic opposition, Kim Dae Jung, took 31 out of 32 seats in his own regional base, North and South Cholla provinces. And "the third Kim," Kim Jong Pil, dominated in South Chungchung. As for the military-sponsored party, the DJP, it won overwhelmingly in Roh's home province, North Kyungsang. Only Seoul/Inchon, with its metropolitan population formed by waves of migration, appeared to have a diversified political constituency. In the 1997 presidential election, Kim Dae Jung's victory was based, again, on his overwhelming dominance in Cholla. But, in this election, Kim Dae Jung was able to marshal broad support in Seoul/Inchon, particularly because of the middle-class sector's discontent with the persistence of corruption under Kim Young Sam. This fractioning of South Korean politics on the basis of regional identity favored the organization of opposition to the military regime, on the basis of trusted, popular regional leaders, thus undermining military control, as soon as plural political expression was tolerated. Yet, on the other hand, it was also a weakening factor for the democratic opposition because of the division that it implied, thus undermining the electoral chances of democrats to defeat the government party. In fact, the stalemate was only overcome in the 1990s, when Kim Young Sam, in a brilliant, but risky, political maneuver, joined forces with Roh Tae Woo, thus being able to succeed Roh as president, in exchange for providing democratic legitimacy to the remnants of pro-military politicians. Yet, the fragmentation of regional identity continues to be a major factor in both mobilization and instability in South Korea. In my personal conversations with Kim Young Sam, at his home in Seoul in 1988, when he still embodied the ideals of a section of the democratic opposition, he pointed out to me what seems to be the critical goal in reorienting Korea's divisive politics. In his view, it was essential to take the nationalist project away from the non-democratic military and put it into the hand of the democrats. Only then could Korean regional identity be subsumed into a strong Korean national identity. But such democratic nationalism had to fulfill an essential task: Korean reunification. Korean reunification has indeed been the motto of democratic movements in Korea for a long time, and Korean democracy in the 1990s is still dominated by the debates on how to proceed in this direction – not an easy project because North Korean communism is more deeply entrenched in the country than, say, East German communism was. Yet, Korean democratic leaders, Kim Dae Jung, as well as Kim Young Sam, were convinced that reunification was essential to build a strong Korea for the twenty-first century, a Korea strong enough to survive the formidable challenge presented by the parallel rise of Japan and China to the summits of world power and influence, and stable enough to continue to be the home base for newly globalized Korean corporations. Thus, the rebuilding of the project of nationalist identity on democratic grounds is essential in the dismantling of the former developmental state, once the legitimacy principle shifted from developmental nationalism to citizen-based nationalism.

Identity is also crucial in the orientations and debates of Taiwan's democratic politics in the 1990s. Taiwan society has always suffered a problem of blurred identity, of what Taiwanese scholar Chu-joe Hsia calls "the orphan syndrome." The KMT and the Chinese Communist party agreed on only one thing: that Taiwan was not Taiwan, but a province of China. But since this was not its reality, for the past half-century, after being a Japanese colony for most of the previous half-century, Taiwan's people did not belong to anything. Matters were made worse by the fundamental split, in Taiwan, between Mainlanders and Taiwanese, and by the further split, among Taiwanese, between native Taiwanese, Fujien, and Hakka. Thus, even if, from an ethnic point of view, they were all Han Chinese, there was a sharp social/cultural divide among Taiwan's population, a division that permeated all levels of the state, as KMT leadership was firmly in the hands of Mainlanders until Chiang Ching Kuo's death in 1988. With the lifting of martial law in 1987 (significantly, the same year that South Korean democratization began), an effort was made to establish Taiwan's political system on Taiwan's new historical reality. In 1990, Teng Hui Lee, a Taiwanese-born, highly educated, KMT leader, was elected president. He presided over the democratization of Taiwan, and aimed at asserting Taiwan's autonomous existence in the international arena, negotiating Taiwan's economic and industrial power into its right to existence. A significant section of the democratic opposition went further: the leading opposition party, the Democratic Progressive Party (DPP), created in 1986, made Taiwan's independence its over-arching goal. China strongly opposed both moves and threatened military action if Taiwan went all the way toward becoming an independent country. The United States came, again, to the rescue of Taiwan, but within certain limits. That is, Taiwan had to behave, and remain in political limbo as long as China kept a cooperative attitude toward the United States. Thus, Taiwan in the 1990s went back to the beginning of its peculiar history: having been born out of the geopolitical strategy of the US *vis-à-vis* China, it remains, by and large, entirely dependent on US–China relations for the foreseeable future. The problem is that, in the meantime, there are 20 million people living on an island that has become an economic power house, fully networked into the global economy, and whose investments in China have played a significant role in the development of southern China's new capitalism. Taiwan's civil society sprung powerfully in the 1990s, with very active community movements, an environmental movement, student movement, women, gay, and lesbian movements (see volume II, chapter 3), somewhat revitalized labor unions, and an informed and educated public opinion, served by independent, influential media. The convergence of these social movements, and the search for a national and *local identity*, led the independence party, the DPP, to victory in Taipei's municipal elections of 1995. The newly elected mayor, Chen Shui-pien, found widespread people's support for his slogan: "A citizens' city." National politics, however, remained dominated by the KMT, as President Lee was re-elected until the twenty-first century, mainly from the people's concern that electing pro-independence leaders would provoke China, while Lee was assertive enough to be personally targeted as a foe by the Chinese government. Furthermore, in 1999, a KMT candidate was elected as Mayor of Taipei, taking advantage of the poor performance of the first democratic administration. But this was a very different KMT from the one that set up a bloody dictatorship on the island 50 years before. The KMT at the turn of the century is searching for a new legitimacy, both international and domestic, trying, for instance, to link up with community movements to set up mechanisms of participatory democracy. By contrast, the independence movement is increasingly split between its fundamentalist wing, striving for independence and national identity, and its social movement wing, aiming at democracy and social change, without entering the geopolitical debate. There is, however, convergence of opinions on the need to shrink, or even dismantle, the developmental state. Taiwan's business networks, both from large or small businesses, have now found their niches in the global or Asian economy. State economic guidance is generally considered a hindrance. Demands from Taiwan's civil society to the government concern consumption and the quality of life, rather than production and technology. And the search for identity increasingly shifts from the public to the private, from nation to family and the individual, from the impossible Taiwanese cultural identity to the daily personal identity of Chinese people who have struggled, survived, and lived in the barren island where they have ended up by the shifts of history.

Hong Kong's future is even more deeply woven in historical ambiguity. It is now part of China. But it will always be a very special part of China. This is, on the one hand, because it will continue to play the role that it has played for many years: the main link between China and the international economy, as well as China's capitalist business school and testing ground. But it is also, on the other hand, because, throughout the 1980s, Hong Kong became an active, civil society, where community movements, and a large, well-educated middle class, openly expressed their democratic values. Tens of thousands of professionals left Hong Kong for their havens in the United States, UK, Australia, and Canada. Additional tens of thousands hold resident cards or passports from foreign countries, and commute between their profitable jobs in Hong Kong and their families' new residences in Vancouver or Perth. But Hong Kong people are in Hong Kong. And businesses – local and multinational – are tied to Hong Kong because Hong Kong is still, and will continue to be, a major node of the global economy, even after its devastating real-estate and financial crisis. The future of Hong Kong people is less than certain, but their identity is sure. They are an essential component of the new China, a China made of transnational networks of business and regional societies, managed by, and interacted with, a complex web of national/provincial/local governments. And they will share, as well, China's uncertain future.

The last "tiger" of our story, Singapore, baffles me, as everybody else. Unlike the three other countries, no civil society has really developed in Singapore in the 1990s, and the state seems to be as powerful and active as ever, in spite of statements to the contrary. This applies to authoritarian politics, and the control of information, as much as to the steering and monitoring of Singapore's development. The state continues to work in close contact with multinational corporations, as was the case 30 years ago, but, having become rich, it also now uses its own resources to invest in companies, either by itself or in joint ventures. Per capita income in Singapore now exceeds the average of the European Union. The city-state works smoothly in a fully planned metropolitan system. The island is the first country to be entirely wired with optic fiber, and is poised to become the first smoking-free and drug-free country (drug traffickers are sentenced to death, and often executed). The city is clean: littering the streets is penalized with heavy fines, and with community work performed in green uniforms, with the culprits exposed in the media. Political and cultural dissent is kept to a minimum, without the need to resort to extreme repression. There is formal democracy, and token opposition. When an opposition leader denounces government abuses, he is sued in court by the corresponding government official, and the court takes care that the daring critic is heavily fined or jailed. There is effective management of inter-ethnic tensions. And there is relatively peaceful coexistence with its surrounding Muslim world, although the whole population continues to be organized in armed militia, and the Singaporean Air Force is on a constant state of alert to proceed with retaliatory bombing of large cities just minutes away in their flight plans. The towering figure of Lee Kwan Yew, while no longer Prime Minister, continues to permeate Singapore's political culture and institutions. He succeeded in inventing a society out of nowhere, and making it the historical proof of the superiority of "Asian values," a project probably dreamed in his Oxford years, as a nationalist without a nation.[101] In fact, he rediscov-

---

101   Chua (1998).

ered Victorian England, with its cult of moral virtues, its obsession with cleanliness, its abhorrence of the undeserving poor, its belief in education, and in the natural superiority of the few highly educated. He added a high-tech twist, actually funding studies to establish a scientific basis for the biological superiority of certain groups. Not on a racial basis, but on a class basis. His beliefs directly shaped Singapore's policies. For instance, college-educated women in Singapore received, in the 1980s, special allowances from the state to give birth to as many children as possible, as well as family leave to educate their children, while working-class women (Chinese or Malay) were taxed for having too many children. The aim was to improve the quality of the Singaporean population by increasing the proportion of children born to educated families. The whole of Singapore is based on the simple principle of survival of the fittest. The ultimate goal of state policies is to enable Singapore to survive, and win, against the implacable competition of the global economy, in an interdependent world, by means of technology, social engineering, cultural cohesiveness, self-selection of the human stock, and ruthless political determination. The PAP implemented this project, and continues to do so, in accordance with the principles of Leninism that Lee Kwan Yew knew, and appreciated, in his resistance years as a labor lawyer in the anti-colonialist movement. And, indeed, it is probably the only true Leninist project that has survived, outlasting its original matrix. Singapore represents the merger of the revolutionary state with the developmental state in the building of legitimacy, in its control of society, and in its maneuvering in the economy. It may also prefigure a successful model for the twenty-first century: a model that is being sought, consciously, by the Chinese Communist state, pursuing the developmental goals of a nationalist project.

While most of the Asian "tigers," and their newly industrializing neighbors, with the exception of Singapore, seem to be in the process of beheading the dragon of the developmental state, a much larger dragon (remember dragons are beneficial creatures in Chinese mythology) has emerged from its millennial isolation to take on the world, and, for good or bad, surely change it for ever.

Chinese Developmental Nationalism with Socialist Characteristics[102]

The policy of taking economic construction as the key link must never be changed; the reform and open-door policy must never be altered. The party's basic line must not be shaken for 100 years. We must properly draw the lesson from the former Soviet Union and handle well the relationships between the party centre and localities. We must uphold the leadership of the CCP. The CCP's status as the ruling party must never be challenged.

Deng Xiaoping, 1994[103]

China's Socialist modernization drive, the practice of the reform and open-door policy, and new developments in the world situation [must be synthesized by the party] so as to develop Marxism while adhering to it.

Jiang Zemin, 1990 [104]

---

102   My analysis of China relies on two main sources of first-hand observation. First were my own visits and fieldwork in China during the 1980s. Particularly important for my understanding of Chinese reforms was the fieldwork I conducted in 1987, together with Martin Carnoy and Patrizio Bianchi, to study technology policy and economic modernization at the invitation of the State Council's Institute of Technology and International Economy. We interviewed Chinese government officials, managers of Chinese factories, managers of American and European companies, and local and provincial representatives, in Beijing, Shanghai, Guangzhou, and Shenzhen. For a summary of our study, see Bianchi et al. (1988). Things have changed in China since then. This is why I relied extensively on a second source of direct observation: the fieldwork conducted between 1992 and 1997, all over China, but particularly in Guandong, Fujian, Shanghai, and Beijing, by Professor You-tien Hsing, from the University of British Columbia, who graciously provided me with extensive notes and documentation from her fieldwork, and followed this up with extensive personal conversations and e-mail communications on the matter. I am truly indebted to her for this critical help. However, the responsibility for this analysis is exclusively mine, and she should not be held accountable for my errors and excesses. For a partial view of her own analysis, see Hsing (1997, 1999). I have also consulted a number of sources on Chinese developments in the 1990s, just a minute sample of a vast literature. An excellent overview of events can be found in Lam (1995). Useful journalistic, economic appraisals can be found in *The Economist*, August 17, 1996, and in Overhalt (1993). A comprehensive historical account is Spence (1990). A classic work on Chinese social and political relations under communism is Walder (1986), followed up for the more recent period in Walder (1995). On overseas Chinese business networks, besides Hsing (1997a, b), see *Business Week*, November 29, 1993 (special report of "Asia's Wealth"); Clifford (1994); and Ong and Nonini (1997). On central–local relations in China, see Hao and Zhimin (1994). On *guanxi* and informal networks, see Yang (1994). On Chinese fiscal policies and central–local relations, see Wong et al. (1995). On democracy movements, see Lin (1994); and Walder (1992). For specific, selected bibliography, both in Chinese and English, on the characteristics of the new Chinese capitalism, see Hsing (1997a). And for those intellectuals who fantasized 30 years ago about the Cultural Revolution, I advise reading the documents collected and translated by Walder and Gong (1993). Additional sources consulted in writing this section are: Granick (1990); Nathan (1990); White (1991); Mackie (1992); Bowles and White (1993); Cheung(1994); Naughton (1995); Yabuki (1995); and Li (1996).

103   Speech while touring Qingdao, probably his last public political instructions, quoted in Lam (1995: 386).

104   Quoted by Lam (1995: 12).

Who are the biggest beneficiaries of the current policy? Careerists and capitalist-style politicians. The people are hurting badly. Chairman Mao's country will be destroyed by this people. From Confucius to Sun Yat-sen there has been a great deal of historical continuity in the development of our nation. History will condemn those who deny this. Allowing only admiration, and forbidding any mention of actual problems and difficulties, indicates a big cover-up of shortcomings and errors.

Mao Yingxing, 1970[105]

The new Chinese revolution

The Middle Kingdom, breaking with a millennial pattern of absolute or relative isolation, and deliberately incorporating itself into the rest of the world, has changed the world's history. Less than two decades after the beginning of the "open-door policy," China's economic growth, the fastest in the planet over the last two decades of the twentieth century, and its competitiveness in international trade, have stunned governments and firms alike, arousing contradictory feelings. On the one hand, the promise of adding a market of 1.2 billion people, even at a fraction of the level of the West's solvent demand, may well diffuse any crisis of overproduction for a long time, thus solidifying the rise of global capitalism into the twenty-first century. From a broader point of view, the growing interaction with human-kind's oldest civilization, with its extraordinary cultural tradition, is certain to enhance spiritual enrichment and reciprocal learning. Yet, on the other hand, the emergence of China as a major economic and military power, the persistence of the Communist party's control over society, and the unyielding attitude of the Chinese government toward international and domestic objections on human rights and political democracy, have triggered, particularly in Asia, but also in other countries, such as the United States, serious concerns about a potential, new Cold War, which would loom dangerously into the twenty-first century. Alternatively, some observers also fear a period of chaos and civil confrontation in China if the Asian economic crisis finally brings down the Chinese economy, and if poverty and unemployment fuel social protests and link up with political challenges. But, whatever the views and feelings on China's transformation in the 1990s, I believe that many of them reflect a profound misunderstanding of the social and political characteristics of Chinese development, thus giving rise to misleading inferences concerning the future of its economy, politics

---

105   A woman teacher in Jingning County, Guasu Province, who was executed on April 14, 1970, accused of being an "active counter-revolutionary" by the Department of Public Security, quoted in Walder and Gong (1993: 77). These words were from her last letter.

and international relations. Within the limits of this section, I shall try to suggest an alternative hypothesis that is based on a premise.

The premise: *China's modernization and international opening up is, and was, a deliberate state policy, designed and controlled, so far, by the leadership of the Communist party.* This was the work of Deng Xiaoping, after emerging victorious from his struggles against Maoists in the late 1970s, and against liberal reformers in the late 1980s. Jiang Zemin continued Deng's centrist, cautious policy, asserting his leadership after Deng's death without any significant challenge, or internal conflict within the party. Consequently, the motivations, orientations, and developments of the open-door policy have to be understood from the perspective of a specific political project, elaborated and implemented on the basis of the interests of the Communist party, as self-declared representative of the interests of the people and of the nation. Furthermore, in order to understand these interests, it is essential to recall that the *Chinese revolution was, primarily, a nationalist revolution with socialist characteristics.* It was the Japanese invasion, and the inept resistance of a corrupt, unpopular Kuomintang regime, that paved the way for the influence and growth of the People's Liberation Army, the backbone of Chinese communist power, and the stronghold of Mao's charismatic leadership. And it was the decisive participation of Chinese communists in World War II against Japan, in the context of the Western–Soviet alliance in that effort, that created the political and military conditions for their final run against KMT armies, routed in 1945–9 in spite of American support. Mao's ideology, and the Communist party's practice, never considered the Chinese revolution to be a socialist one: it was a "democratic revolution," based on a strategy of class alliances against "imperialism and its lackeys." It relied on the mobilization of poor peasants against the corrupt urban world of the compradore bourgeoisie. The "proletarian vanguard" was almost absent from this revolution, among other reasons because there was a very small proportion of industrial proletarians in sparsely industrialized China. While the categorization of Marxist–Leninist terminology clearly fails to apprehend the complexities of class structure and political ideology of twentieth-century China, it is a good indicator, none the less, of the predominantly nationalist rationale of the Chinese revolution. It was the defense of a humiliated China against foreign powers, including the brotherly Soviet Union, that rallied significant support around Chinese communists, together with an agrarian reform that reinforced the village structure, and eliminated the hated landowners, rather than persecuting kulaks. Agrarianism and nationalism were the two "marching legs" of the Chinese revolution. But the brain, the engine, and the gun were embodied in the Communist party. And because it was (and is) communist, that is Leninist, it imprinted "socialist" characteristics on Chinese revolutionary nationalism throughout the whole process of construction of a new state, a new economy, and a new society. Paramount among them, as in the Soviet Union, was the control of the party over the economy by a central planning system, and over society by an extensive ideological apparatus that ensured the dominance of Marxist–Leninist ideology and kept tight control over information and communication. The political system as well was molded in the Leninist–Stalinist tradition, with the party controlling all levels and branches of government institutions, including the army through the network of political commissars. At the heart of the power system was (and is) the Central Military Commission of the Central Committee of the party. The chairmanship of this Commission was the only position that Mao always held, the last one that Deng relinquished in 1989, and the one held by Jiang Zemin in 1997. For Chinese communists, then as now, "power lies in the barrel of the gun." But the party was also a powerful, decentralized political machine, present in every village, neighbor-hood, and production unit throughout the country, forming an immense, hierarchical net that, for the first time in history, actually controlled China to the smallest corner. And this is not just ancient history: in 1998, the 54-million member Chinese Communist party (CCP) was alive and well, and its local leaders and cadres were enjoying the highest level of power and influence, if not popularity, in their districts. This is a fundamental reality that conditions, and shapes, the evolution of China. At the top of the power system, as in all communist regimes – with no historical exceptions, except for brief interregnum periods – there was an extreme personalization of leadership, in fact a personality cult. After Mao Zedong's Thought, in the 1990s it was the time for Deng Xiaoping's Thought (even if Deng himself politely refused the term), as the People's Liberation Army was mandatorily engaged in reading and commenting on Deng's Selected Works. Discussions of the historical continuity of personalized leadership in China ("the new Emperors") do not seem especially significant, since this is a communist characteristic as much as a Chinese characteristic. The extreme personalization of leadership in Chinese communism lends political voluntarism a powerful hand. Whatever is decided by the leader becomes a material force by the chain of command that reverberates throughout society and the centers of power. This is the only way we can explain the extraordinary destructive adventures of the Great Leap Forward, and of the Great Proletarian Cultural Revolution, decided and directed by Mao Zedong, against the will of the party's collective leadership, to the point that *his* "revolutionary guards," with the backing of the PLA, went on a rampage mainly aimed at Communist party cadres and organizations. That the CCP survived its own suicidal tendencies (that is Maoism) shows a political strength far greater than that of any other communist experience. But Maoism was not a folly (although many of its acts were). It actually expressed one answer to the fundamental problem of the Chinese revolution: how to make China strong, and independent, while preserving Communist power, in a world dominated by superpowers, and where technological and economic development were proceeding apace on the opposite shores of the China Sea. Deng's and Liu Shao-shi's answer, since the 1950s, was accelerated industrialization, economic growth, and technological modernization, along the lines of the Soviet model, the only model available to Chinese Communists at that time. Mao's own answer was self-reliance, emphasis on ideology, preservation of ruralism, and decentralized, guerrilla warfare ("people's war") to resist any invader, while relying on nuclear armament as a deterrent of last resort (although at one point, at the height of the Cultural Revolution, Mao talked seriously about constructing socialism on the nuclear ruins of capitalism). In the middle, Zhu En-Lai obtained an agreement from the warring factions to steer a centrist course, preserving China's technological–military complex, as the necessary guarantee of its national independence. As a result, this technological–military complex remained relatively undisturbed by the political turmoil of the 1960s and 1970s. When, after the defeat of the "Gang of Four," Deng Xiaoping, who had survived the Cultural Revolution sweeping the streets of his native Chungking, returned to power, he went back to his basic idea that economic prosperity, and technological modernization were the fundamental pillars of Chinese power and independence. Furthermore, after the disastrous impact of the Cultural Revolution on people's lives and minds, not only did the independence of China have to be preserved, but the legitimacy of the Communist party had to be restored. After such a murderous ideological orgy, only the immediate improvement of living conditions, the diffusion of property rights, and the prospects of a better life in their lifetime, could rally the Chinese again around a revamped Communist regime. As Deng would state to the 13th Central Committee years later, in 1990: "If the economy improves, other policies could succeed and the Chinese people's faith in socialism will be enhanced. If not, socialism not only in China but in the rest of the world will be endangered."[106] But, in 1978, the Soviet Union was China's enemy and the Soviet economic model was clearly ailing, while, all around

106   Quoted in Lam (1995: 5).

China, the Asian Pacific and particularly the ethnically Chinese economies were growing and modernizing at the fastest pace in history. Thus,
the dramatic turn-round taken by the Central Committee, at Deng's
initiative, on a cold December day in Beijing in 1978, was aimed at
ensuring China's entry into the capitalist global economy and into the
informational paradigm (even if the proponents of the open-door policy
and of the "four modernizations" policy would not recognize these
words), using the lessons from the Asian "tigers" (called "dragons" in
China). However, this new developmental path should proceed in a
way that would preserve "socialism;" that is, the power, control, and
influence of the Communist party, as the representative of the Chinese
people. In this sense, it was not fundamentally different from what
Gorbachev would try to do in the Soviet Union only seven years later.
But, unlike Gorbachev, who was too arrogant to imagine he could
fail, the Chinese leadership understood that to release the Communist
grip over society in a period of rapid economic, and therefore social,
change, could derail the process toward "capitalism with Chinese
characteristics," thus putting them out of business. Deng, and his
entourage, were rightly obsessed with this idea, and the fate of
Gorbachev, and of the Soviet Union, fully confirmed their diagnosis,
at least in their view. This is why the "Singapore model" was, and is,
so popular among Chinese Communist leaders. The idea of a fully
fledged economic and technological development process without yielding to the pressures of civil society, and keeping the capacity to
maneuver in the global arena firmly in the hands of the state, appeals
strongly to a party whose ultimate *raison d'être* is the assertion of
China as a world power, if possible coupled with the preservation of
Communist mythology. Yet, the experience of tiny Singapore can hardly
be extrapolated to a country that accounts for 20 percent of humankind. And the Soviet experience of communist-controlled transition to
capitalism ended in disaster. This is why Chinese communists navi-
gate, with extreme caution and pragmatism, in uncharted historical
waters. And this is why the actual process of transformation in China
does not follow Deng's tentative blueprint of the early 1980s, but results from *ad hoc* decisions from a plurality of actors, and from the
interests, compromises, conflicts, and alliances triggered and revealed
by economic reform policies.

    To sum up, China's economic development and technological mod-
ernization, within the framework of the new global economy, were
(are) pursued by the Chinese communist leadership both as an indispensable tool for national power, and as a new legitimacy principle
for the Communist party. In this sense, Chinese communism in the
early twenty-first century represents the historical merger of the de-

velopmental state and the revolutionary state. But, in order to fulfill this strategic aim, the Communist party, led in the 1990s by Deng Xiaoping, Jiang Zemin and Zhu Rongji, had to reckon with a series of formidable problems: the form of integration in the global economy; the controlled decentralization of state power; the management of so-cial contradictions triggered by rural exodus and social inequality; the repression of political democracy; the control of an emerging civil so-ciety; and the balancing of power and influence among the power elite, keeping ideologues at bay without risking excessive factionalism in the army and in the party. I shall briefly elaborate on these various issues, building my argument toward an over-arching hypothesis: *that this complex act of balance is being accomplished, with reasonable, but not certain, chances of future success, by intertwining regional developmental states with a nationalist project of China as a great power, able to liberate itself for ever from the foreign devils.* Capital-ism, and the uncertain fate of democracy, are but means to that funda-mental goal, even if, in the process, the power elite considerably benefits from the new sources of wealth and prestige.

Guanxi *capitalism? China in the global economy*

China's integration into the global economy began on a false note in the early 1980s: the Special Economic Zones policy, creating four Export Processing Zones, facing Hong Kong, Macau, and Taiwan, and aimed at offering cheap labor and land, tax breaks, and social discipline to foreign investors, particularly multinational corporations, to be used as export platforms. The zones were designed to be physi-cally, and legally, separated from the rest of Chinese territory, so that socialism would not be contaminated. Chinese workers would be shipped to these zones, but other Chinese citizens would be excluded from these areas. In this scheme, Special Economic Zones would at-tract foreign capital and technology, generate revenue, and provide valuable expertise for China. The underlying project was tantamount to creating four, then many, new Chinese dragons, but this time under the control of the Chinese government, and for the benefit of China as a whole. It did not work. In my conversations on these matters with middle-level Chinese officials in 1987 I understood their fundamental mistake: they had read, and believed, the "new international division of labor theory," proposed by some Western Marxists, and they were eager to offer multinational corporations a fraction of Chinese labor to be exploited – at the price, mainly, of technology transfer. Yet, as I explained to them at the time, multinational corporations had no in-terest in going into China, with all its political unknowns and poor infrastructure, in search of cheap labor and tax breaks, when they could obtain similar conditions in a wide range of developing countries, under much more favorable political circumstances. What multinational corporations wanted was to penetrate the Chinese market, planting seeds of investment toward its future expansion. But, for this, they needed access to China at large, beyond the restrained Special Economic Zones; they needed to import their own supplies, without or with few excise duties; and they needed freedom to create their own network of suppliers and distributors. In a word: they needed to enter China's economy, not just to use Chinese labor and land for exporting purposes. But their obvious business requests spelled trouble for the prudent Chinese leaders. On the one hand, they had to protect the interests of the state-owned companies, which would be displaced by the competition of foreign firms in China. On the other hand, what China really needed was to export manufactured goods and import technology and know-how, not just simply let foreign producers take over China's industry, and foreign products overrun Chinese markets. Thus, while the Chinese government formally opened much of China's urban–industrial regions to foreign investment and trade, under the 14 Coastal Cities policy, restrictions and red-tape made sure that the process would be under government control. Multinational corporations reacted by restraining investment, withholding technology, and negotiating market shares directly with the government. In my interviews with American and European companies in Shanghai and Beijing in 1987, they described their operations as an industrial island in an ocean of technological and economic backwardness, some of them importing as much as 90 percent of the inputs they needed to manufacture their products. None was making a profit. All were trading capital investment and transfer of old technology for presence in China, in the hope of future opportunities. Things have changed since then, and the production of Japanese, American, and European companies has substantially increased, particularly through high-technology markets for government orders, and through regional markets protected by provincial governments (for example, Volkswagen in Shanghai, German beer in Shendang). Some symbolic agreements, such as the US$1 billion investment by General Motors in 1994, reflect the government's determination to lure foreign investors. Yet, at least until the mid-1990s, multinational corporations, and Western and Japanese investments, were not the main linkage between China and the global economy. Indeed, as table 4.1 shows, between 1979 and 1992, of the US$116.4 billion pledged for investment in China, 71.7 percent came from Hong Kong and Taiwan, 7 percent from the US, and 5.8 percent from Japan. Individual European countries' share of investment

Table 4.1 Contracted foreign investment in China by source, 1979–92 (US$ million, percentage shares in brackets)

	1979–90	1991	1992	1979–92
National total	45,244	12,422	58,736	116,402
	(100)	(100)	(100)	(100)
Hong Kong	26,480	7,531	40,502	74,513
	(58.5)	(60.6)	(69.0)	(64.0)
Taiwan	2,000	1,392	5,548	8,968
	(4.4)	(11.2)	(9.4)	(7.7)
US	4,476	555	3,142	8,163
	(9.9)	(4.5)	(5.3)	(7.0)
Japan	3,662	886	2,200	6,748
	(8.1)	(7.1)	(3.7)	(5.8)

Between 1979 and 1989, the total value of pledged (contracted) FDI in China was US$ 32.37 billion, the actual (realized) was US$ 15.61 billion, 48% of the total pledged FDI. If we use 48% as the percentage of the actual FDI in total pledged FDI, the national total of realized FDI in China between 1979 and 1992 is about US$ 56 billion.
Source: Sung (1994: 50).

was even lower. Similarly, only a fraction of China's imports originate in OECD countries. On the other hand, not counting weapons sales, a substantial proportion of Chinese exports (either from Chinese firms or from joint-venture companies located in China) are exported to Western Europe and the United States. Indeed, the United States seems to be in danger of running a trade deficit with China larger than it has with any other country. But the new competitiveness of China did not come from its inefficient state enterprises, nor, for the most part, from its still infant private business sector. It was organized around investment, know-how, and world market expertise from overseas Chinese investors which, in cooperation with a special kind of institutional partner (see below), constituted the fundamental link between China and the global economy in the 1980s and 1990s.

The ethnic connection of China's global integration is indeed an extraordinary story, full of practical and theoretical implications. But it must be told, as You-tien Hsing has done,[107] without the romanticizing and anecdotal evidence that characterizes much of the cottage-industry research generated on the "Chinese business networks" operating in the "China circle." These ethnic business networks are essential to contemporary Chinese development, but they came to life in China by taking advantage of the opportunity provided by the open-door policy. Investment in China was risky, but could yield very high profits in a largely untapped market, with negligible labor costs, on

107   Hsing (1999).

the condition of knowing how to operate in a complex environment. Chinese investors from Hong Kong and Taiwan used the opening to decentralize their production, particularly in the Pearl River Delta, and in other areas of southern China, when higher production costs at home, and a reduction of their export quotas threatened their competitive position. To minimize risks, they used their *guanxi* (relationship) networks, particularly looking for people who were from the same place of origin (*tong-xiang*), their relatives or friends, or for dialect-group acquaintances. The building of the necessary infrastructure to support international connections (hotels, business services, airports, roads, property development) created an immediate market for large Hong Kong-based firms, which went into this kind of investment very early in the process of economic reform (I enjoyed an international hotel developed by Hong Kong's business in Guangzhou as early as 1983). As analyzed in volume I, chapter 6, the mega-region Hong Kong – Shenzhen – Guangzhou – Zhuhai – Macau – Pearl River Delta, comprising about 60 million people, had become an economic unit by the early 1990s, constituting one of the potential global nodes of the twenty-first century. To answer in kind, Shanghai, with the support of the Beijing political elite, largely dominated by the "Shanghai group," launched in the early 1990s the new enterprise zone of Pudong, poised to become the major financial and advanced services center of China.

Once the investment networks from Hong Kong and Taiwan were established, by the late 1980s, capital flowed from all over the globe, much of it from overseas Chinese, from Singapore, Bangkok, Penang, Kuala Lumpur, Jakarta, California, New York, Canada, and Australia. The statistical pre-eminence of Hong Kong is, in fact, a mirage. It reflects the management of plural sources of investment by Hong Kong-based Chinese firms. It should be interpreted as "global capital." But this "global capital," which can be, and is, from any source, from Japanese banks to money launderers, is administered, and to a large extent controlled, by Chinese business networks, more often than not based on family relationships, and inter-linked among themselves, in spite of fierce rivalry in specific markets and projects. Why does Chinese business have an advantage over other foreign investors, and why does it not risk as much as Western or Japanese investors in the uncertain conditions of proto-capitalist China? I have grown skeptical of cultural explanations about insider knowledge and personal connections. After all, reading Yang's excellent anthropological account of rural *renqing* and urban *guanxi* practices in contemporary China,[108] I do not see any substantial difference from my knowledge of similar

108   Yang (1994).

practices in Latin America. And yet, US investors have dominated Latin American economies for decades, and Mexico, one of the most *guanxi*-oriented countries that I know, benefited in the 1990s from a flurry of direct international investment without much need of Mexican mediation, while Mexican business networks continued to export their savings abroad, instead of investing in Mexico. In the case of China, overseas Chinese business networks are indeed the main intermediaries between global capital, including overseas Chinese capital, and China's markets and producing/exporting sites. But the reason is not that they and their southern China partners both like steamed cod. It is because *China's multiple link to the global economy is local, that is, it is performed through the connection between overseas Chinese business and local and provincial governments in China*, the *sui generis* capitalist class that Hsing calls the "bureaucratic entrepreneurs."[109]

China's regional developmental states and the bureaucratic (capitalist) entrepreneurs

To overcome ideological resistances to economic reform from the CCP and PLA's high-ranking cadres, Deng sought the support of local and provincial governments from the outset of reform. To short-circuit the power of the conservatives, concentrated in the Beijing headquarters, and in the northern provinces, he proclaimed the principle of *yindizhiyi* ("to each locality according to its own characteristics"), proceeding during the 1980s to a considerable fiscal decentralization: the center's share of GDP declined from 37 percent in 1978 to 19 percent in 1992, and the center's share of total tax revenue amounted to only 35 percent in 1993.[110] He particularly courted Guandong and Shanghai, China's historical links to foreign trade and investment. In 1992, he went on his famous *nanxun* (imperial tour) of the south, encouraging Guandong, in particular, to overtake the Asian Pacific dragons, by accelerating its growth rate and its opening to the international economy. "Only development," he argued, "passes the test of reason."[111] Guandong, Shanghai, but also most other provinces, and localities, took Deng at his word, and asserted their economic autonomy, both in fiscal matters and in credit policy, to finance its own infrastructure, create new businesses, and attract foreign investors. The overheating of the economy, and consequent inflationary surges, in 1988, 1992, and 1993, led the central government to tighten controls,

109   Hsing (1999).
110   Lam (1995: 88).
111   Quoted by Lam (1995: 132).

and to reverse fiscal decentralization by instituting, in 1993, a dual tax system, under which the central government would keep its own source of revenue. Provincial governments, with Guandong leading the charge, used their new political and economic muscle to resist new revenue-sharing schemes. But their drive for autonomy (at the source of their new wealth) was mainly implemented not by subtracting resources from the center but by creating new sources of revenue for themselves, using precisely their new freedom of maneuver. If Deng wanted to infuse collective entrepreneurialism (probably too much sophistication for the pragmatist he was) he succeeded. Provincial and local governments in China (which I include under a "regional" label, for the sake of simplicity) invested in new market-oriented businesses, often in joint ventures with foreign investors, and became the source of "private" capitalist accumulation, as collective entrepreneurs who shared the benefits of their enterprises. In 1993, state enterprises ("wholly people's owned firms") accounted for 48.4 percent of the total value of industrial production; private ownership (including foreign-participated business) for only 13.4 percent; while "collective enterprises" (that is, businesses with participation of specific government administrations, most of them regional and private investors) represented 38.2 percent of the total, and growing.[112] Furthermore, industrial production was not the main sector of investment for regional governments, and their foreign partners, most frequently overseas Chinese. Property development was the entry point for these foreign investors: it was less risky, offered immediate pay-offs in a country that became, in its coastal areas, an instant, gigantic construction site, and provided a solid footing into local networks. Besides, control over their own land was an undisputed resource for local/provincial governments. Finance was also a critical sector for the strengthening of provincial autonomy and the introduction of capitalist economic management. A bold financial experiment was initiated, again, by Guandong government as early as 1981. The Guandong Branch of the People's Bank gained the autonomy to use a specific amount of capital and to issue short- and medium-term loans.[113] The establishment of the province's own financial institution, the shareholding Guandong Development Bank, was approved and incorporated in 1988. Then, Guandong was also allowed to develop a stock and security market, set up foreign exchange adjustment centers, and handle foreign exchange account business. The province was also able to obtain foreign borrowing and to issue its own bonds abroad, subject to central ap-

112   Lam (1995: 94–5).
113   Cheung (1994: 26–39).

proval. When the central government imposed fiscal austerity in 1994, Guangzhou's municipal government began to raise funds from international financial markets, either through foreign partners of joint ventures in Guangzhou, or through the municipal government-owned Guangzhou International Trust and Investment Corporation, and Yuexiu Enterprise in Hong Kong.[114] Between June and November 1994, in the midst of national austerity measures, six foreign banks in Guangzhou provided US$380 million in loans to local enterprises.[115] In addition to borrowing from abroad, Guandong also attracted capital from other provinces in China. Thus, while many regions were suffering from austerity measures, in the mid-1990s, cities and counties in the Pearl River Delta continued with their expansion plans, running a budget two to five times higher than allowed by government's central plans, and financing it with bonds and loans. In the midst of the controversy over the overheating of the economy, the mayor of Dongguan, a Pearl River Delta city, proclaimed: "How the Pearl River Delta could catch up with the four East Asian dragons if we take cautious steps?"[116] Guandong's local government attracted capital by offering exceptionally high interest rates (18–20 percent; that is, eight points higher than in Sichuan or Hunan provinces), under the principle of "water flows to low lands, people move to high places, and money goes to profits," in a display of the rapid assimilation of capitalist principles by Chinese slogan makers.[117] It is only thanks to this access to outside financial resources that Guandong, Shanghai, and other fast-growing areas in China have been able to short-circuit economic controls from the central planning system. This system is still in place, but its main role is to subsidize an unproductive state sector, and assure enough revenue collection to provide for the center's priorities. Among these priorities are technology and military investments, and the self-reproduction of the state and party apparatuses.

Through these, and similar processes, *a new capitalist class has emerged in China, mainly constituted of "bureaucratic entrepreneurs;" that is, by individuals (more often than not members of the Communist party) whose access to resources stems from their control of government institutions and finances.* Using these resources, they invest in business on behalf of the government institutions they represent, either by themselves, in association with other bureaucracies, or, increasingly, linking up with foreign investors. These mixed enterprises are the core of China's new capitalism. It is a highly decentralized

114   Lu (1994a).
115   Lu (1994b).
116   Quoted by Lu (1993).
117   Quoted by Hsing (1997).

capitalism because it follows the contours of provincial and local alliances, and of the business networks to which they connect: a capitalism that is oligopolistic in local markets, and competitive at the national
and international levels. And it is a capitalism that knows that it has
to generate enough surplus to pay its share (formally or informally) to
higher levels of government, not directly involved in business, and to
indispensable participants in the local/provincial enterprises, such as
high-ranking military officers and party cadres whose protection is
necessary to shrug off the planned economy.

This process of "bureaucratic capitalist development" was, by the
mid-1990s, under the supervision of the state. However, as the market
economy spread, it became increasingly difficult to exercise political
control, without creating chaos, for three main reasons: first, because
the centers of capital accumulation were mainly in the hands of this
constellation of provincial/local enterprises, directly linked to foreign
markets and financial sources. The second reason refers to the rapid
growth of thousands of *gumin* ("stocks-crazed speculators") who, using information technology to trade in the Bourses of Beijing, Shanghai, and Shenzhen, from anywhere in China, were channeling savings
and bypassing government controls. And the third, and fundamental,
reason is that the new power equilibrium in China has taken the form
of a complex pattern of interdependence between the center and the
regions, interconnected by the party and by the army. Any decisive
attempt by the center to curtail the regions' economic autonomy, particularly *vis-à-vis* the rich provinces, could not only derail economic
reforms (fundamentally based on provincial government capitalism),
but call into question the fragile status quo reached in the reformed
Communist state, under the twin banners of China's national power
and of Deng's slogan: "It's glorious to be rich."

Weathering the storm? China in the Asian economic crisis

By the end of 1999, China was still on a path of economic growth, at
about 7 percent. However, growth was largely dependent on massive
government spending, aimed at stimulating an economy that was in a
deflationary state, with prices falling for the twenty-third consecutive
month in the fall of 1999. Exports declined by about 5 percent, and
trade surplus dropped by over 60 percent in 1999. None the less, the
trade surplus still was at US$8 billion, and foreign currency reserves
stood at US$150 billion. A low government debt (at about 10 percent
of GDP) allowed an expanding budget to finance a reflationary government policy. Yet, the economic future was uncertain, as China's

development is largely dependent upon the overall performance of the Asian Pacific. Moreover, in spite of its initial success in defending the yuan against speculative attack, by the time you read this it is possible that China will have devalued its currency. The still pending, and important, question is by how much.

And yet, overall, during the crisis of 1997–8, China asserted its economic power and kept relative stability by resisting the destructive assault of financial flows, and by preventing a fall into recession. The Chinese government even felt strong enough to save the Hong Kong dollar from devaluation. The PRC's determination, backed by its US$140 billion in hard currency reserves, allowed Hong Kong's currency board system to survive, at least for a while. China had very good reasons to support Hong Kong's economy, in addition to the fact that the territory is now fully part of China. China's government, and banks, are the largest landholders, and among the largest stockholders, in Hong Kong, so they tried to limit their losses. But even more important is the fact that Hong Kong is the main source of foreign investment in China, most of it from overseas Chinese business, processed through Hong Kong firms. To stabilize Hong Kong it was essential to link up international investors with China's market at a time when China had to counter the trends of capital outflow. To preserve stable exchange rates for both the Hong Kong dollar and the yuan China was ready to sacrifice some of its trade competitiveness, as exports from its Asian competitors became substantially cheaper as a result of the devaluation of their currencies. China suffered on two grounds: export growth declined considerably, falling from a 22 percent growth rate in 1997 to about 5 percent in 1998. And capital outflows, as in other Asian countries, sky-rocketed: US$20 billion moved out in 1997, and a much larger sum in 1998, as investors feared the devaluation of the yuan. And yet, the Chinese economy suffered, overall, much less impact from the crisis than the rest of the Pacific. To understand why this was so has extremely important analytical implications, even if a new, home-grown crisis ultimately hits China hard.

The main factor explaining China's relative capacity to absorb the shock of the 1997–8 crisis was its limited integration in the global economy, particularly in terms of its financial markets. The yuan, in 1998, was not fully convertible, so it was much better protected from speculative attack than currencies traded in the open market. The banking system in China was, in 1997–8, in as much trouble as the one in Japan. Banks were at least US$240 billion in bad debt and most of them were insolvent. Other reports, from Standard & Poor, put bad bank loans at about 60 percent of China's GDP. However, the government was backing the banks, only forcing bankruptcy under controlled circumstances; and, because of tight controls on foreign lending, Chinese banks were not strangled by short-term foreign debt, the source of most of the financial crisis in the rest of Asia. In spite of the fact that some banks borrowed foreign money through Hong Kong-based banks, the Hong Kong "bumper" prevented in China the kind of financial panic that struck Indonesia and South Korea. Thus, government control of the links between the Chinese financial system and global markets provided a cushion to resist the wild movements of financial flows around the world.

A second factor which helped to keep China on the development path was government management of the pace of integration in international trade. In spite of China's push to become a member of the World Trade Organization, with its implications for open trade policy, in 1998 China compensated for its declining exports by restrictions on imports, thus maintaining a healthy current balance. To stop the flow of cheap, low-end products from Asian competitors into its market, China resorted to red tape, and to currency controls on import companies, to favor local production. But in the critical sector of high technology, and high-value manufactured goods, China was able to control imports because of the good technological level of its advanced manufacturing industries. Indeed, while much has been written on the obsolescence of the state enterprise sector, some of these state-controlled companies, particularly in telecommunications, have been able to improve their productivity, and technological quality, winning market share from their foreign competitors in China, even on those product lines that are manufactured in China by foreign companies. Relying on state-controlled companies, such as Huawei, Datang, and Great Dragon, Chinese companies have increased their share of the Chinese telecommunications market from 10 percent in 1995 to about 55 percent in 1998. While government support in some contracts, particularly at the provincial level, has helped Chinese manufacturers, industry observers consider that the high quality and hard work of low-wage, innovative Chinese engineers, and the R&D effort of Chinese local manufacturers, have been the most important factors in gaining competitiveness over foreign firms.[118] A similar trend is perceived in the automobile industry, in which sales of the Alto, produced in China by an all-Chinese company, Norinco, have taken on imports of foreign cars. Thus, the ability to upgrade, protect, and expand its manufacturing industry, geared primarily toward the domestic market, has been a key factor in China's avoiding a dramatic slump, at least during this crisis.

118   *The Economist* (1998: 64–6).

Yet, none of these circumstances would have pulled China out of a potential recession had it not been for government economic policies. Zhu Rongji, prime minister since March 1998, and the architect of the anti-inflation program of the 1990s, understood, well before the International Monetary Fund did, that the real problem faced by Asia was deflation, not government spending. Thus, instead of putting the brakes on the economy, and implementing austerity policies, as the IMF was forcing Indonesia, Thailand, and South Korea to do, the Chinese government embarked on an ambitious plan of government spending, most of it on infrastructure and housing. To pay for it, the government counted on mobilizing the estimated US$560 billion savings deposited in state-run commercial banks. To use the banks as intermediaries, the government first used US$32 billion to refloat the banks, and allow them to go back into the lending business, so stimulating the economy. Thus, what seems to have been at the root of China's initial success in weathering the financial crisis was Keynesianism on a grand scale, shielded from disruptive financial flows and guided by government through currency controls and managed trade policy. Major problems remain unsolved, on which I will elaborate below, and it is not certain by any means that China can continue to be "a little bit global" and "a little bit capitalist," while preserving Communist leadership and strong government intervention in the economy. Yet, the first results of the Chinese experience in handling the crisis, in contrast with what has happened in other "emerging markets" in the world, seem to support the argument concerning the decisive role of the state in managing the impacts of globalization.

Democracy, development, and nationalism in the new China

Observers of the new China often start their forecasts from the implicit assumption of the necessary association between development and democracy. Thus, their prognosis is for either the gradual erosion or the sudden overrun of Communist power, as the new urban middle classes grow, and a stronger, influential civil society comes to life. At present, available information does not support this view. The network of Communist party organizations is firmly in control of most voluntary associations and expressions of civic life. The party overwhelms *shimin shehui* (civil society). There is openness and diversity in the media, but within the margins of political correctness. There are new electronic media, but even foreign satellite broadcasting companies, such as Murdoch's Star TV, practice self-restraint as regards Chinese politics to avoid losing a giant market. The Internet is in China,

but China is the only country in the world which is having some success in controlling web sites and hook ups, although at the cost of
impoverishing its collective access to the worldwide net. As for the
middle class, it is too busy making money and consuming it, thus vin-
dicating Deng's vulgar economicist approach to the new stage of the
revolution. Furthermore, since access to government institutions, and
to party-controlled resources, is critical to be in business, and since
opportunities are plenty, there is little interest in dismantling the system, or opening it up, while everybody is dedicated to their personal
"primitive accumulation." This is why *guanxi* is so important, but so
dependent on the existence of a formal system of planned economy,
whose daily bypassing provides a major source of rent for its gatekeepers. The emerging market system in China develops by using competitive advantages obtained by positioning in the cracks of the still
predominant command economy. Thus, with little incentive to undermine communist control, and considerable risk in trying to do so, the
new urban middle class, while disliking the state, can shrug off its
dislike as long as its families keep prospering.

To be sure, there are many democrats in China, particularly among
the intelligentsia and students. And, in such a large country, it is easy
to count them by the hundreds of thousands, mostly concentrated in
the major metropolitan areas. But Tian An Men did teach some lessons. On the one hand, it showed the determination of the Communist state not to lose control of the transition process. On the other
hand, it also showed, although it is usually not acknowledged, that
the student movement could go as far as it did because of the relative
tolerance (if not encouragement) provided by Zhao Ziyang, fully engaged in his struggle against the left of the party. Who manipulated
whom (for instance, were the students, instead, manipulated by the
left to provoke a law and order reaction leading to the demise of Zhao
Ziyang and to counter-reform?) we will probably never know. But
what became clear was that the movement was limited, lacked widespread popular support, and was entirely dependent for its fate on
internal struggles in the CCP.

Thus, the ability of autonomous civil society to expand, and for
political democracy to develop, will depend, essentially, on how able
the CCP is to keep its unity, and how well the Chinese state manages
conflicts between different levels of government, and between different provinces vying for economic gains. A key element in the treatment of both issues is the strength, unity, and orientation of the People's
Liberation Army. Probably, Deng's main political legacy will be his
skillful maneuvering in the minefield of military command during his
last years. In the early 1990s he essentially proceeded, successfully,

with four key operations. First, he eliminated opposition from leftists, ideologues, and non-reliable officers at the top, particularly by dismissing General Yang Shangkung, vice-chairman of the Central Military Commission, together with his brother and 300 other officers, suspected of organizing a leftist network, in 1992. Secondly, he moved on to appointing pro-reform officers in the highest positions, while adopting a conciliatory attitude toward the traditional left in the army, as long as they would not plot against their new commanders. He also gave greater representation to the Army in the party's leading organs: in the 14th Congress of the CCP in 1992, the army's representation in the Central Committee went up from 18 to 22 percent, and a professional officer, General Liu Huaquing, was given a permanent seat in the Politburo. Thirdly, with the support of army commanders, Deng moved to put greater emphasis on professionalism and technology, to create what he labeled "an elite corps with Chinese characteristics." The PLA, like the Soviet army, had been greatly impressed by the performance of high-tech weapons and of the Western airforce in the Gulf War, undermining the position of those officers who were still emphasizing people's war tactics based on ideological motivation. As a result, the army decided to support economic and technological modernization which appeared to be indispensable to bring Chinese forces up to the level of twenty-first century warfare. Last but not least, Deng and Jiang made sure that the PLA fully participated in China's economic bonanza. Military factories were given the opportunity of targeting the civilian market, which they did with considerable success, counting on tariff protection against foreign imports. Individual officers were appointed to state companies, and to state supervising agencies, and were allowed to receive profits from their commercial activities. Provincial governments seconded this policy, so that thousands of military officers ended up on the boards of new "collective businesses," and became integrated into the new class of bureaucratic entrepreneurs. Furthermore, since officers on active duty could not dedicate themselves entirely to business, their sons and daughters were given the opportunity, both in China and in Hong Kong, so that a vast network of family interests linked up with overseas business networks, bureaucratic entrepreneurs, party leaders, PLA leaders, and their families, thus constituting China's dominant class in an inseparable web of political positions and business interests. In fact, the conversion of the PLA from the bastion of the left to a pro-business institution went too far for the political interests of the Chinese state. In 1998, Jiang Zemin issued several directives to limit the involvement of high-ranking officers in business because the army was losing discipline, and military readiness, given the excessive dedication of many officers to their business ventures. Yet, overall, the army continued to be a significant part of the new, profitable state capitalist economy in China. Thus, with party and army unity largely assured by their new economic bonds, and with society under control, the Chinese communist state seemed to be poised for a gradual transition to an economy and a polity that would respond to the interests of these elites in the context of China's integration into the global economy.

At the turn of the millennium, however, China had to face a number of difficult problems, whose effective resolution will condition its future, as well as the fate of the Pacific in the twenty-first century. None of them relates to democracy, which is a Western concern, rather than a real issue for most of China. But a democratic movement could indeed spur from the social conflicts generated around some of these issues. I have been able to identify at least four such problems. Perhaps the most immediate is the massive rural exodus provoked by the modernization and privatization of agriculture, which is estimated to have affected about 300 million peasants during the 1990s. A fraction of them are being absorbed into the small towns being developed by the Chinese government to stand the shock. Others are being employed in the new urban economy, and in the factories and shops scattered in semi-rural areas. Many of them (perhaps as many as 50 million) seem to be in the category of "floating urban population," wandering around Chinese cities looking for work and shelter. This mass of uprooted migrants can hardly be assimilated to the notion of a "civil society." They are unorganized, lack cultural and political resources to represent an articulate force of opposition. But they are an extraordinarily volatile element, whose potential rage could destabilize the whole process of transition to a market economy, should they come into contact with messianic leaders or with splintering factions of the Communist party.

A second major problem refers to the existence of bitter interprovincial conflicts. For reasons mentioned above, the opposition between the center and provinces, particularly with the rich provinces of the south and of coastal China, seem to be intelligently cushioned by the co-optation of provincial leaders (most notably from Shanghai) to the Beijing government, and by the freedom given by the center to the provinces to prosper on their own in the international economy. With the CCP and the PLA structuring their interests around central government and provincial institutions, the sharp conflicts that do exist between the center and the coastal provinces seem to have proper channels for their treatment. Besides, unlike in the former Soviet Union, the ethnic/national factor, in spite of Tibetan resistance and Muslim unrest, does not represent a major source of contradiction because Han Chinese constitute about 94 percent of the population. So, outside Tibet, Xinjiang, and Inner Mongolia, the ethnic basis for national or regional resistance to the center is very weak. However, there is intense rivalry and fierce competition between provinces, particularly pitching the poor regions of inland China against the rich coastal provinces that participate fully in the market economy and international exchange. In 1996, the Ministry of Civil Affairs revealed that over 1,000 disputes, and some "bloody fights," had taken place between provinces and regions concerning the definition of their territorial borders. Using their autonomy, some provinces ban the sale of products from other provinces within their borders, and follow tax, credit and industrial policies of their own. Since the political clout of provinces still largely depends on their influence in Beijing, their infighting is exported into the central apparatuses of party and government, with potential destabilizing tendencies. For instance, Shanghai's current dominance in the Beijing government is strongly resented in Guandong. The incorporation of Hong Kong seems to be reinforcing this tension, since the economic might of the mega-region Hong Kong/Guandong does not have commensurate political influence in Beijing. Furthermore, as regional disparities increase dramatically between the poor, subsidized regions and the self-sufficient market-oriented regions, the ideological conflicts about the extent and perdurability of the command economy and of the socialist safety net are taking, and will increasingly take, a regional connotation. The potential regional conflicts emerging in China will not look like the break up of the Soviet Union, but, rather, there will be regionalism with Chinese characteristics, perhaps threatening to degenerate into a new period of warring states, as the one that took place, among Han Chinese, for about 200 years, 24 centuries ago.

The third major problem confronting China is how to move toward a market economy while avoiding mass unemployment and the dismantling of the safety net. There are two main issues in this regard. The first is the privatization of housing. On the one hand, this is the government's secret weapon to stimulate the Chinese economy, by mobilizing the large, untapped mass of private savings, into a gigantic housing mortgage market. On the other hand, the largest section of the urban population does not have the means to access the new property market. Thus, displacement, urban segregation, and massive homelessness could be the consequence of fast-paced housing privatization. This is why the "big bang" of the privatization program announced for July 1998 was postponed indefinitely in order to proceed cautiously city by city.[119]

119   Po (forthcoming).

The second major issue which slows down Chinese economic reforms is the low productivity, and low profitability, of many (but not all, as I pointed out above) of the state enterprises, which survive on subsidies, and still employ the largest section of the industrial workforce. The problem is compounded by the fact that large state enterprises, as well as government administrations, are critical for all spheres of life for Chinese workers, from housing to health plans, from kindergartens to vacations. Privatization has proceeded apace, but most state enterprises find no buyers, and the government keeps financing them. For how long? All indications are that Chinese Communists are determined not to make the same mistakes as their European counterparts. While listening to Western economists on the handling of the international sector of the economy, they seem poised to ensure a long period of transition based on subsidizing the public sector and the welfare state, as the basis for their own power and legitimacy. For this, keeping the central planning system, as a system of accounting and management of the public sector, is crucial, thus justifying the function, and jobs, of millions of government employees who depend on them for their living. Therefore, the new Chinese economy is developing through the juxtaposition of three sectors: a public sector, insulated from market competition; an internationally oriented sector, geared toward foreign investment and trade; and a domestic market-oriented, capitalist sector, mainly built around bureaucratic entrepreneurs. The connections and passages between the three sectors is assured by the party's business networks, the so-called "red capitalists." Yet the complexity of the system, and the number of potential conflicts of interest, opens the door for acute power struggles. For instance, in 1999, the Finance Ministry understood that to prevent a banking crisis it had to reduce the number of "bad loans" provided by the banks to unprofitable state enterprises. To that end, it created an asset management company, China Cinda, managed by American-trained financial engineers. Cinda embarked on an ambitious program of debt-for-equity swaps on behalf of the large government banks, assuming some of their bad debt, and exchanging this debt for shares in the debtor companies. Then Cinda designed restructuring plans for each company, including lay-offs for thousands of workers, to cut costs and increase profitability. In spite of a number of painful restructuring experiments, Cinda was restrained in its hard-line approach to management by the China Securities Regulatory Commission whose approval was necessary for any restructuring. Thus, the progress of privatization, and of profit-oriented strategies, was highly dependent on political considerations, and conflicting views between the political authorities involved in the implementation of economic reform.

The fourth problem is of a different character, but I consider it critical for the feasibility of the "Singapore model," which Chinese Communist leaders seem to be seeking to implement. Indeed, it was, as I tried to argue in chapter 1, a major factor in the disintegration of the Soviet Union. It refers to technology, and particularly to information technology. If China's economy is going to compete in the global area, and if China's state is going to project its military might, a strong technological base is essential. China does not yet possess it. It certainly did not when I had the opportunity to evaluate it, even superficially, in 1987.[120] However, recent information suggests that China has made substantial progress in the past decade, particularly in telecommunications and personal computers, as mentioned above. Yet, the speed of technological change is such that China will have to step up its technological upgrading *vis-à-vis* the United States, Japan, the Asian "tigers," and multinational corporations around the world. Yes, China can put satellites in orbit, and has remarkable scientific teams. It is also a nuclear power, with missile-launching capability, including, probably, a limited stock of ICBMs. Yet satellite-launching is mainly a business practiced by other medium-tech countries, such as India; most science seems to develop in isolation from industry; and the ability to blow up part of the planet is a military deterrent of last resort, but not an indication of the technological capacity to project conventional warfare power. The question is, as it was for the Soviet Union, whether the current technological revolution, based on information technology, can be developed in a closed society, in which endogenous technology is secluded in the national security system, where commercial applications are dependent on foreign licensing or imitation, and, most fundamentally, where individuals, private business, and society at large, cannot appropriate technology and develop its uses and its potential; for instance, by freely accessing the Internet. I think not, and the experience of the Soviet Union seems to prove it, albeit it must be conceded that other important factors played a role in the Soviet crisis, and that Chinese communists have the benefit of hindsight with the Soviet experience. Chinese leaders think they can manage the contradiction by acquiring technology from abroad, by buying machines, by obtaining licenses, by technology transfer from foreign companies, and by sending their own scientists and engineers for training abroad. In my exchanges with some of their experts on this matter in 1987, and in our study of their technology policy, I realized that Chinese officials had an outdated, industrialist notion of what technology is. They still thought that technology was machines, and that

120   Bianchi et al. (1988).

with the scientific and technical excellence of Chinese professionals, they could handle everything if they just had the proper machinery. Hence their emphasis on licensing, on importing machinery, and on seeking the location of technologically advanced multinationals which would have a demonstrable effect on China's industrial structure. This is simply wrong, although this is not the place to lecture you on what technology is today. In the informational paradigm, the uses of technology cannot be separated from technology itself. The machines can easily be bought everywhere, except for specific military hardware. What is essential is to know what to do with them, how to program, reprogram, and interact, in a largely serendipitous process that requires an open, uncensored network of interaction and feedback. The essential technology is in our brains and experience. China continues to send students and professionals abroad, as the most effective means of building its technological potential. But, as faculty members of major universities around the world know, most of these bright young Chinese scientists and engineers are not truly welcome back home, suffocated by a bureaucratic system of science, by low-level uses of technology, and a generally oppressive cultural atmosphere. Thus, after their training, they bureaucratize themselves, or go into more profitable business, or, in many cases, just stay in the West or get a good job in the thriving Pacific outside China. I will not go so far as to say that without democracy China cannot truly gain access to the information technology paradigm, so vital for its grand design: political processes cannot be reduced to simple statements. But, without some form of open society, it probably cannot, for reasons argued in volume I, and in chapter 1 of this volume. Yet, there seems to be some evidence of technological improvement in Chinese high-technology industries, particularly in telecommunications equipment. This is to a large extent due to technology transfer from multinational corporations, and from overseas Chinese companies, cooperating with technologically advanced state enterprises, and counting on the excellence of Chinese technological universities. The question is whether this technological upgrading can be sustained without fully fledged modernization of the overall manufacturing industry, and without the much broader exposure of Chinese universities to international exchanges.

The key issue in this regard is the development of the Internet, the backbone of the network economy, but also of the network society. Both aspects are inseparable. Because the Chinese government is fully aware of the potential political implications of free communication, it is torn between the need to allow new entrepreneurialism and the loss of control over information. Internet users increased fast in China, from 900,000 in 1997 to over 4 million at the end of 1999. But potential growth is much greater, attracting substantial foreign investment in Chinese Internet companies. In September 1999, Minister of Information Industry Wu Jichuan called for a halt to foreign investment in the Internet, as this investment violated a 1993 ban on foreign control of Chinese telecommunications. There is currently a sharp conflict inside the Chinese government concerning how, and how much, to allow the spread of the Internet and its foreign connection. To sum up, China is muddling through the contradiction of developing information technology in an information-controlled society. But this pragmatic policy will face a much greater challenge when Chinese companies need a higher level of technological innovation, one that cannot be satisfied by reverse engineering.

Thus, while democracy is not a dramatic issue in China, and while Deng's succession seems to be under control by an able Communist leadership led by Jiang Zemin and Zhu Rongji, the promise of party rule in the twenty-first century, and the viability of implementing the "Singapore model," are under question, given the widespread range of conflictive issues that have to be tackled at the turn of the millennium. A fundamental question refers to the potential form of expression of these social issues as social conflicts. Reflecting on Chinese history, I hypothesize that social conflicts in twenty-first century China may develop as identity-based mobilizations rather than as political movements aimed at the seizing of the state, in line with my overall analysis of the contradictory relationship between globalization and identity. Indeed, in 1999, this possibility seemed to be confirmed by an editorial in the Chinese Communist party newspaper, *People's Daily* of November 5, 1999, asserting that "We must be fully prepared, with powerful counter measures, for the bitterness and complexity of struggle against this evil force . . . This is a major political issue that concerns the future of the country, the future of its people, and the future of the great endeavor of reform and opening up and of socialist modernization."[121] This "evil force" that could threaten the entire course of socialist modernization in China is not capitalism or imperialism any longer. It is not the pro-democracy movement, either. It is an obscure cult, Falun Gong, practicing the old Chinese tradition of *qigong*, to enhance the body's vital energy, mixing it with elements of Buddhism and Taoism. This cult, led by Li Hongzhi, a former petty bureaucrat exiled in New York, was able to mobilize thousands of supporters in front of the government headquarters in Beijing, in several instances, simply demanding to be left in peace. With several million faithful, in China and around the world, loosely coordinated via the Internet by

121   *The New York Times* (November 5, 1999: A3)

Li Hongzhi, Falun Gong instilled more fear in the Chinese Communists than any other protest movement in the past. A number of factors seem to explain this apparently exaggerated reaction. The first is the difficulty of controlling and repressing the movement. Its size (at least 2 million followers according to the government), its loose, decentralized structure, yet ability to converge on a given point and time for specific protests, appear to be a challenge to a state used to fight, and obliterate, well-organized political and military forces, but disconcerted by a flexible, network structure, based on the autonomy of individuals and coordination of the purpose. Secondly, Falun Gong seems to have its main support base among middle-aged unemployed and retired people from urban areas in economically distressed provinces; that is, precisely those sectors of the population hard hit by the transition to capitalism. Some observers hypothesized that the expected health benefits of practicing *qigong* is not a marginal consideration for many people with health problems and without health benefits after losing their jobs. Thirdly, there is a long tradition in China of religious and quasi-religious movements, rising against foreign influence, and resisting the crisis of traditional institutions in key moments of historical transition, such as the Taiping rebellion of 1845–64 (see volume II, chapter 1). Given the acute historical awareness of Chinese political leaders, anything resembling these ghosts would certainly sound the alarm. And by launching a major campaign of propaganda and repression, the Chinese government called people's attention to the existence of these sources of opposition, perhaps amplifying the impact of Falun Gong in a political direction that was not necessarily intended by the movement.

If conflicts flare up, if China feels the political pressure of the outside world, and if domestic politics grows restless, it is highly likely that the Chinese state will seek to perpetuate itself in the form of uncompromising nationalism. With revolutionary legitimacy exhausted among the people for all practical purposes, if consumerism does not reach a broad enough segment of the population to ensure social stability, the regime will emphasize its nationalist identity, as the defender of China, and of Chinese people around the world, finally being able to stand up to the East, West, and North, imposing respect simultaneously on Japan, the US, and Russia. In 1996–9, sabre rattling in the China Sea, confronting Taiwan, Vietnam, and Japan on the sovereignty of several islets, and open threats to Taiwan, seemed to indicate that this is a possible path of political evolution for the Chinese regime. It may rely on considerable popular support. Nationalism runs strong in China at this turn of millennium. Students spontaneously demonstrated against Japan's arrogance with such enthusiasm in

August 1996 that the government had to step in to calm down the movement before it went out of control. Thus, after half a century of communism, China has come full circle to affirm itself as a nation and as a civilization rather than as an alternative social system, while sharing by and large the risks and riches of global capitalism. But this renewed Chinese nationalism displays marked socialist characteristics. And it projects itself in the Pacific and beyond, daring for the first time to take on the world as a major power.

Conclusion: Globalization and the State

Enough evidence has been presented in this chapter to support the argument that the developmental state has been the driving force in the extraordinary process of economic growth and technological modernization of the Asian Pacific in the past half-century. To the cases we have analyzed, others could be added. Malaysia was as developmental as Singapore, albeit weakened by its internal, potentially explosive, ethnic and religious contradictions. Indonesia, like Thailand, in the 1980s, was a quasi-developmental state. Certainly, Suharto's regime was based on the Suharto family's appropriation of a significant share of the country's wealth through their control of the military, the government, and the banking system. Suharto's personal dictatorship enabled him, and his cronies, to form an alliance with the multinational corporations (particularly the Japanese), and with the wealthy Chinese business community, to allow them to run the country's economy for a share of the profits. Yet, while the developmental strategy, in both Indonesia and Thailand, included, as an essential element, the personal enrichment of the rulers, the policies of the state focused on linking up the country with the global economy to industrialize and dynamize the national economy. These policies met with considerable success in terms of growth and modernization – albeit at a high social cost. After all, in the states of South Korea, Taiwan, and even Japan, systemic corruption was also present. And personal dictatorship was, for a long time, a central feature of the state in South Korea, Taiwan, and Singapore. Thus, with the exception of Marcos's Philippines (a predatory state), militaristic Myanmar, and war-torn Cambodia and Laos, the developmental state, in different degrees, and in various forms, was the main actor in the successful development process of the Asian Pacific.

Its own success led to its demise, with the exception (for the time being) of China and Singapore. The developmental state was based on the premise of a double-edged, relative autonomy. Relative autonomy *vis-à-vis* the global economy, making the country's firms competitive in the international realm, but controlling trade and financial flows. Relative autonomy *vis-à-vis* society, repressing or limiting democracy, and building legitimacy on the improvement of living standards rather than on citizen participation. All this under the banner of serving the nation, or even creating it, while serving the rulers themselves. On both grounds, the autonomy of the state was challenged by the outcome of the developmental process. Full integration into the global economy made it increasingly difficult for the state to control financial flows, trade, and, therefore, industrial policy. Firms nurtured by the state became global corporations, or global networks of firms. Financial institutions tapped the international financial markets on their own. Global investors found their direct line into the booming Asian economies, the new Wild East of unfettered capitalism. And, in the late 1990s, in Japan as well. The traditional mechanisms set up by the developmental state were made obsolete, but new rules and regulations, adapted to the globalization of financial markets, were not in place. We know that capitalism does not mean just free markets. Unfettered markets without reliable institutions and regulations are tantamount to pillage, speculation, abusive, private appropriation, and ultimately chaos, if the lessons of history are of any value. The institutional void created by the confused transition from the developmental state to a new, regulatory capitalist framework was quickly filled by global financial lenders, speculators, and their local cronies.

The success of the developmental state in modernizing the economy led, in most cases, to the emergence of a civil society, asserting itself against the authoritarian state. When social change and democracy fought their way through the political institutions, the margin of maneuver for the developmental state was reduced, so that it became increasingly unable to ensure, at the same time, the management of global competition and the rulers' personal prosperity. No one seemed to understand better the connection between preserving this dual autonomy and the survival of the developmental state than Malaysia's national leader, Mahathir Mohamad. His response to the crisis was three-pronged. First, to partly de-link Malaysia from the global economy by making the ringgit non-convertible, and establishing strict controls on financial exchanges, while still supporting the direct, productive investment of multinationals in Malaysia. Secondly, to crack down on civil society and democracy, firing his liberal-minded deputy and finance minister, Anwar Ibrahim, jailing him under ridiculous pretexts, and beating up people demonstrating their support for Anwar. Thirdly, he rallied Malaysian nationalism, and called upon religious identity, by denouncing global financial strategies as a new form of colonialism and of Western domination, probably, it was said, inspired by Jews, and certainly orchestrated by George Soros. While most of these gestures had predominantly symbolic value, they signaled the refusal of at least one developmental state to be brought down by the process of globalization that the development states had helped to create.[122] Malaysia paid the price for this semblance of independence. When the Malaysian government lifted the 10 percent exit tax on repatriated principal of foreign portfolio on September 1, 1999, cumulative net foreign portfolio investment plunged from 1.2 billion dollars in August to 178 million in September, as foreign capital left the Malaysian stock market.

It is important to draw some analytical lessons from the specific processes that enabled Taiwan, Singapore, and China to withstand the financial crisis of 1997–8 because these lessons may help to explain the conditions and perspectives of resumption of economic growth in the Pacific, at the turn of the century. Taiwan offers no mystery. The Taiwanese economy, by the mid-1990s, had already made the transition to flexible, entrepreneurial networks linked up around, and across, the Pacific, with markets and manufacturing networks. The state was strong enough to partly shield the banking system, but not strong enough to impose crony capitalism or to suffocate the emerging civil society. Thus, overall, Taiwan's firms, and the country as a whole, were fully integrated in the rules and procedures of advanced global capitalism, with the benefits and risks of full integration. Taiwan was, by and large, globalized.

Singapore was, and remains, the ultimate developmental state, clearly perfecting its Japanese blueprint. And, yet, its economy suffered only a slight downturn as a consequence of the overall decline in South-East Asia. And its society, while affluent and modernized, cannot be characterized as a civil society, in the Gramscian sense. State control over economy, and society, is still unabated. I consider it an exception. Because it is fully integrated in the global economy, its currency is convertible, it is a leading financial center, it is fully open to multinational corporations, and still the state keeps considerable control over the economy and over wild fluctuations in the financial markets. And while the potential for state policing of individuals and organizations is ever present, it is the people's self-inflicted withdrawal and censorship, rather than brute force, which rule Singapore. I do not know of any state or society in the world that comes even close to Singapore's experience. It may prefigure a future model of human civilization, exactly what Lee Kwan Yew wanted. If so, an in-depth study

122   Jomo (1999).

of Singapore as a laboratory for one possible social future for the twenty-first century becomes an essential task.

China is a different matter, even if Chinese leaders would like to adapt the Singapore model. For the time being, China demonstrates the possibility of benefiting from globalization while partly shielding the country's economy from uncontrollable global market forces. By limiting the convertibility of the yuan, and keeping tight control over financial flows, with a banking system under full government control, the Chinese government was able to spur the competitiveness of Chinese firms in export markets and attract foreign investment, lured by market size. Thus, China was able to sustain high rates of economic growth, acting on inflation or on deflation depending on the business cycle. The obvious backdrop to a strategy of controlling financial flows is the reluctance of global investors to lend/invest in China. So, over time, foreign investment, which was one of the major sources of China's hypergrowth in the 1990s, could dwindle, threatening to stall growth. There is, however, a major alternative source of financing: a high rate of domestic savings. And, for a share of these savings to be in hard currency, what is needed is export competitiveness in world markets. After all, it was precisely this formula, engineered by the developmental state, which spurred growth in the Asian Pacific countries before China joined, and surpassed, them. Thus, while the developmental state seems to be failing in most of the Asian Pacific, the Chinese developmental state, as a tool of nationalist affirmation and political legitimacy, could be on the rise. The size of China, its scientific potential, its deep connections with dynamic, overseas Chinese business networks, may provide breathing space for the largest of all dragons. It is possible to follow here a Gerschenkronian logic as I hypothesize that the comparative advantage of the Chinese developmental state comes partly from its late arrival to the global economy. Thus, over time, this advantage will fade away, forcing China to face the same contradictions as its more precocious neighbors. However, history is not a pre-scripted scenario. The very fact that China can still behave as a developmental state changes the context because China is not a small exception to the global rule, as Singapore could be. If China succeeds in managing globalization, and marshalling society, in its transition to the Information Age, it means that the developmental state is alive and well for at least one-fifth of humankind. And if nations and states around the world feel increasingly powerless *vis-à-vis* global financial markets, they may look for alternatives and find inspiration in the Chinese experience. But this, of course, is only one of several possible courses of action. It may well happen, instead, that China loses control of its economy, and a rapid sequence of alternative deflation and inflation wrecks the country, triggers social explosions, and induces political conflict. If so, the developmental state will have run its historic course, and global flows of capital and information may reign uncontested – unless a new form of state, the network state, potentially exemplified by the European Union, comes to the rescue of societies, enslaved by their economies. The relationship between globalization and the state, at the heart of development and crisis in the Asian Pacific, is the dominant political issue at the turn of the millennium.

5

The Unification of Europe: Globalization, Identity, and the Network State

The unification of Europe around the turn of the second millennium, when and if completed, will be one of the most important trends defining our new world.[1] It is important, first of all, because it will probably (but not surely) bring to an end the millennial war-making between major European powers, a recurrent practice that brought destruction and suffering to Europe, and in the Modern Age to the world, throughout the entire span of recorded history, peaking with extraordinary violence in the first half of the twentieth century. It is also important because a unified Europe, with its economic and technological might,

1   This chapter is intellectually indebted to my interaction with a number of Europeanists, both faculty and graduate students, at the University of California, Berkeley, where I chaired the Center for Western European Studies from 1994 to 1998. I am also grateful to the many European scholars and speakers (including government officials from different countries) who have visited the Center during these years. My discussion of information technology in relation to European economies and societies has been partly informed by exchanges with my colleagues in the European Commission's High Level Expert Group on the Information Society, on which I served during 1995–7. I thank Luc Soete, chair of the group, for facilitating these exchanges. I have benefited, as well, from my participation in a research program organized at Berkeley by the Center for German and European Studies, and by the Center for Slavic and Eastern European Studies, in 1995–8, on "Europe East and West: Challenges to National Sovereignty from Above and from Below." I thank the directors of this research program, Victoria Bonnell, and Gerald Feldman, for their kind invitation to join the effort. Last, but not least, my conversations with Alain Touraine, Felipe Gonzalez, Javier Solana, Carlos Alonso Zaldivar, Jordi Borja, Roberto Dorado, Peter Schulze, Peter Hall, Stephen Cohen, Martin Carnoy, and John Zysman, on the topics covered in this chapter, have shaped my thought, and considerably enriched my information.

and its cultural and political influence, together with the rise of the Pacific, will anchor the world power system in a polycentric structure, precluding the existence of any hegemonic superpower, in spite of the continuing military (and technological) pre-eminence of the United States. And, I argue, it is also significant as a source of institutional innovation that may yield some answers to the crisis of the nation-state. This is because, around the process of formation of the European Union, new forms of governance, and new institutions of government, are being created, at the European, national, regional, and local levels, inducing a new form of state that I propose to call *the network state*.

However, the actual content of this unification, and the actors involved in it, are still unclear, and will be so for some time. It is precisely this ambiguity that makes unification possible, while characterizing its process as a debate rather than as a blueprint. Indeed, European unification grew in the past half-century from the convergence of alternative visions and conflicting interests between nation-states, and between economic and social actors. The very notion of Europe, as based on a common identity, is highly questionable. The noted historian Josep Fontana has documented how European identity, throughout history, was always constructed against "the other," the barbarians of different kinds and different origins.[2] The current process of unification is not different in this sense, as it was made from a succession of *defensive political projects* around some common interests among the participating nation-states. Yet, Europe at the turn of the millennium is something else, and more complex. It results from the internal dynamics of the unification process, building on these defensive projects, then recently twisted, supported, and challenged by the two macro-trends that characterize the Information Age: the globalization of economy, technology, and communication; and the parallel affirmation of identity as the source of meaning. Because of the failure of the classic nation-state in articulating the response to these symmetrical, opposing challenges, European institutions are trying, just trying, to cope with both trends by using new forms and new processes, thereby attempting the construction of a new institutional system, the network state. This is the story I shall recount in this chapter, without having the opportunity, or harboring the intention, of presenting the whole economic and political complexity that surrounds the construction of the European Union, thus referring the interested reader to an abundant, well-informed literature on these matters.[3] My focus here is in

2   Fontana (1994).
3   Much of the information on which my analysis relies can be found in general newspapers and magazines, such as *El País, Le Monde, The New York Times, The Economist,* and

showing how the trends I have identified as critical in configuring the Information Age – globalization, identity, and the crisis of the nation-state – are shaping European unification, and thus the world of the twenty-first century.

European Unification as a Sequence of Defensive Reactions: a Half-century Perspective

The European Union resulted from three outbursts of political initiatives and institution-building aimed at defending the participating countries against three perceived series of threats in three historical moments: the 1950s, the 1980s, and the 1990s. In all three cases, *the goal was primarily political, and the means to reach this goal were, mainly, economic measures.*

In 1948, several hundreds of European leaders met in The Hague to discuss the prospects of European integration. Beyond ideological proclamations, and technocratic ambitions, the essential goal of European integration was to avoid a new war. For this, a permanent form of accommodation had to be found with Germany, in sharp contrast to Germany's humiliating condition following World War I which led to World War II. The accommodation had to be primarily between Germany and the other European continental power, France, and it had to be blessed by the United States, Europe's protector in the aftermath of a most destructive war. Furthermore, the Cold War, with its front line passing through Germany, called for an economically strong, politically stable Western Europe. NATO provided the necessary military umbrella, and the Marshall Plan helped to rebuild European economies, while paving the way for investment by American multinationals. But political institutions were required to stabilize relationships

---

Business Week. I find it unnecessary to provide specific references to widely known facts. Nor do I intend to provide the reader with a dense bibliography on a set of highly specialized matters concerning European integration. I shall simply mention a few sources that I have found useful in refreshing my memory, and stimulating my thinking on a subject that I have followed very closely for the past quarter of a century in France, and Spain. Probably one of the most intelligent, informed analyses of the subject can be found in Alonso Zaldivar (1996). For a perceptive overview, whose argument I largely share, see Orstrom Moller (1995). A major source of ideas is Keohane and Hoffman (1991b). A seminal article on the political dimensions of European integration is Waever (1995). On multiculturalism and the crisis of democracy in Europe, see Touraine (1997). Additional, useful readings are: Ruggie (1993); Sachwald (1994); Ansell and Parsons (1995); Bernardez (1995); Bidelux and Taylor (1996); Estefanía (1996, 1997); Hill (1996); Hirst and Thompson (1996); Parsons (1996); Pisani-Ferry (1996); Tragardh (1996); Zysman et al. (1996); Zysman and Weber (1997); Ekholm and Nurmio (1999). It is also refreshing to go back to the classic texts by Ernst Haas (1958a,b, 1964), where many of the current political debates are advanced in analytical terms.

among nation-states that had been historically constituted fighting each other, or seeking alliances for the next war. No wonder that the first move toward European integration was a common market in the coal and steel industries, which made autonomous national development impossible in the industries that, at that time, were strategically central to any future war effort. The European Coal and Steel Community (ECSC) was created in Paris, in April 1951, by West Germany, France, Italy, and the Benelux countries. The good results of this initiative led to the two Treaties of Rome of March 25, 1957, creating Euratom, to coordinate policy in nuclear energy, the new strategic industry, and the European Economic Community, oriented toward improving trade and investment among the six nations.

The rapid increase of economic integration on the continent brought to the forefront of the European debate competing visions of the integration process. The technocrats who originated the blueprint of a unified Europe, and particularly Jean Monnet, dreamed of a federal state. None of the nation-states truly believed in it or wanted it. However, the inertia of the European institutions led to the accumulation of considerable influence (if not power) in the hands of European bureaucracy, while Germany, constrained in its international role, saw the EEC as a convenient international platform. The accession of de Gaulle to the French presidency put the brakes on the process of the transfer of sovereignty, and emphasized the option that would come to be known as intergovernmental, that is, placing European-wide decisions in the hands of the council of heads of executive powers from each country. De Gaulle tried to add a new political objective to the EEC: to assert its independence *vis-à-vis* the United States. This is why France vetoed twice, in 1963 and in 1966, the British application to join the EEC, considering that Britain's close ties to the United States would jeopardize European autonomous initiatives. Indeed, Britain represented, and to some extent still represents, a third, different vision of European integration: the one focusing on the development of a free-trade area, without conceding any significant political sovereignty. When Britain finally joined the EEC (together with Ireland and Denmark), in 1973, after de Gaulle's departure, this economic vision of European integration became predominant for about a decade, downplaying the political dynamics, and in fact slowing down the pace of integration, since the negotiation of national economic interests consumed most of the energy, and budget, of the EEC. The 1973 and 1979 economic crises ushered in the era of euro-pessimism, when most European nations felt deprived of political power by the two superpowers, technologically outclassed by the development of the information technology revolution largely beyond European shores, and economically lagging behind not only the United States but also new Pacific competitors.

The inclusion of Greece, in 1981, and particularly that of Spain and Portugal in 1986, did add breathing space to the European economy (after all, Spain was at the time the eighth largest market economy in the world), and brought in some dynamic new players. But it also added depressed regions, and complicated negotiations in key areas, such as agriculture, fishing, labor legislation, and voting procedures. Yet it was the feeling that Europe could become an economic and technological colony of American and Japanese companies that led to the second major defensive reaction, represented by the Single European Act (SEA) of 1987, setting up steps toward the constitution of a truly unified market by 1992. Economic measures were combined with an emphasis on technology policy, in coordination with the European-wide Eureka program, created at the initiative of the French government, this time under Mitterrand, aimed at counteracting the American technological onslaught that came to be symbolized by the Star Wars program. Furthermore, with Mitterrand softening the French position against supranationality, and Spain (under Felipe Gonzalez) supporting Germany's emphasis on European institutions, broader powers were given to the European Commission; the European Council (representing heads of executives) obtained majority voting procedures in several key domains, and the European Parliament received some limited powers, beyond its previously symbolic role.

The reason why Spain became, probably, together with Germany, the most federalist country is also political: to be anchored in a strong, unified Europe would prevent the country, in the view of Spanish democrats, from returning to the demons of political authoritarianism and cultural isolationism, which have dominated Spanish history for most of the past 500 years. Under the double impulse of southern Europe becoming fully democratic, and France and Germany defending the techno-economic autonomy of Europe in the new global system, the EEC became the EC: the European Community. Once again, an economic measure, the establishment of a truly common market for capital, goods, services, and labor, was, essentially, a measure to further political integration, ceding parts of national sovereignty to ensure some degree of autonomy for the member states in the new global environment. When Thatcher tried to resist, retrenching Britain in outdated state-nationalism, it cost her her job. Most British political and economic elites had understood the opportunity represented by a unified Europe, and had decided to go along, while reserving the possibility of opting out of undesirable policies, such as (for the Conservatives) workers' social rights.

Just when Europe had decided on an accelerated pace of economic integration, and on a moderate pace of political supranationality, the overall geopolitical environment suddenly changed, on November 9, 1989, prompting another round of European construction, to respond to the new political issues arising on the continent. The unexpected unification of Germany had necessarily to affect deeply the unification of Europe, since the neutralization of geopolitical tensions between Germany and its European neighbors was the original goal of European integration. The new, unified Germany, with 80 million people, and 30 percent of the European Community's GNP, represented a decisive force in the European context. Furthermore, the end of the Cold War allowed Germany to be truly independent of the tutelage under which it had been kept for over four decades by the victors of World War II. Thus, it became imperative again, for the whole of Europe, to strengthen the economic and political ties between Germany and the rest of the continent, by reinforcing the European Community, and accommodating German interests within it. The essence of the negotiation amounted to fully integrating the German economy with the rest of Europe, by moving toward a single European currency, the euro, and an independent, European Central Bank. For Germany to sacrifice its hard-won solid deutschmark, and to overcome the resistance of the Bundesbank, three major compensations were necessary:

1 The European economies had to absorb the deflationary policies made necessary by the alignment of monetary policies on the needs and pace of the German economy, particularly after the political decision of setting up the exchange rate between Western and Eastern German currencies on the parity of one mark for one mark, a decision that triggered inflationary pressures in Germany.

2 The European institutions would be reinforced in their powers, moving toward a higher level of supranationality, thus overcoming traditional French resistance, and British rejection, to any project approaching federalism. Again, the push toward further European integration was the only way for Germany to start projecting its weight in the international scene without triggering fear and hostility from most European countries. What Japan has never been able to do – that is, to bury the specters of World War II – is being accomplished by Germany via its full participation in supranational, European institutions.

3 Germany requested an additional concession from the 12 EC members, supported by Britain for its own, different reasons: the enlargement of the EC toward the north and east. In the case of

Austria, Sweden, and Finland, the goal was to balance the European Community with richer countries, and more developed economies, to compensate for the inclusion of southern Europe, with its burden of poor regions. In the case of Eastern Europe, Germany was (and is) trying to share with the rest of Europe the need to stabilize, economically and politically, these unsettled countries, as a way of preventing future turmoil from spilling over into Germany, either through immigration, or through geopolitical conflicts. Thus, Germany could play its traditional role of a Central/ Eastern European power, without being suspected of reconstructing Bismarck's imperial dream.

In this regard, it is interesting to observe the persistence of historical perceptions of what a geopolitical threat is. Eastern European countries put all kinds of pressures on Germany to join the European Union, and on the US to join NATO, fundamentally for security reasons: to escape, for ever, from Russian influence. Germany supported their case also with the goal of establishing a territorial glacis between its Eastern border and Russia. And, yet, the terms under which these strategic aims are being discussed seem to be obsolete. First of all, the large-scale wars of the Information Age can be fought, and will be fought, essentially from the air, and through electronic communications and jamming of signals, making meaningless a few more minutes of flight for missiles or aircraft. Secondly, Russia does not seem to represent a security threat to the West, even counting on the resurgence of Russian nationalism, as a reaction to the subordination of the Yeltsin regime to Western influence during the 1990s. Indeed, except for its status as a nuclear superpower, the state of the Russian military, and the economic weakness of the country, do not allow Russian nationalism to project ambitions of geopolitical power in Europe for many years to come. And, yet, centuries of confrontation between Russian, German, and French military power in Eastern Europe, with ferocious battles fought in these lands, have left a mark that goes beyond the transformation of the actual conditions of geopolitical confrontation in Europe today. Because of the fear of Russian power (real or potential), and because of the instability of Russian institutions, Russia, one of the oldest European cultures, will not become a member of the European Union. Eastern European countries have been taken under the "protection" of NATO, and will be associated with the European Union, under forms that will vary for each country. The enlargement of the European Union to the East, which will probably be delayed until the middle of the first decade of the twenty-first century, will in fact create greater difficulties for effective integration in the EU. This is because of the vast disparity of economic and techno-logical conditions between ex-statist countries and even the poorest of the EU members. Furthermore, by pure game theory, the larger the number of members, the more complex the decision-making process, threatening to paralyze European institutions, thus reducing the European Union to a free-trade area, with a weak degree of political integration. This is, in fact, the main reason why Britain supports the process of enlargement: the larger and more diverse the membership, the lower the threat to national sovereignty. Hence, the paradox of seeing Germany (the most federalist country) and Britain (the most anti-federalist country) supporting enlargement for entirely different reasons. The main issues confronting European unification in the first decade of the twenty-first century relate to the arduous process of incorporation of Eastern Europe, which will begin with the inclusion in the EU of Poland, the Czech Republic, Hungary, Slovenia, and possibly Estonia, all countries whose economies are deeply penetrated by European investment (mainly German), and are largely dependent on exports to the EU. However, the mobility of labor will be restricted for some time, and political hurdles will remain concerning voting procedures and decision-making in the European Union. Ultimately, the enlargement of the EU toward the East will force a reform of its political institutions.

The Maastricht Treaty, signed in December 1991, and revised in the Intergovernmental Conference held in 1996–7, after the 1993 Danish and French referenda, and British parliamentary opposition, threatened to reject it, reflected the compromise between these different interests, and the ambiguity of the institutional formulas aimed at continuing with the process of integration without openly confronting the fundamental issue of supranationality. In essence, by deciding on the creation of the euro currency, of the European Monetary Institute, and the harmonization of fiscal policies, Maastricht made an irreversible commitment to a fully unified European economy, coming into existence in the first years of the third millennium. By reinforcing the decision-making power of European institutions, particularly by making it more difficult to form a blocking minority vote in the European Council, European-wide policies began to take precedence over national policies, in areas as varied as infrastructure, technology, research, education, environment, regional development, immigration, justice and police, in a process of political integration symbolized by the change of name from European Community to European Union.

However, in the late 1990s, foreign policy, security, and defense were not truly integrated as they have been, for a long time, areas of indecision and confusion in the European Union in spite of rhetorical proclamations of convergence. Yet, the war in Kosovo opened up an entirely new perspective. After the catastrophic management of the war in Bosnia by the European Union, NATO asserted itself as the fundamental security instrument of the European Union, in close alliance with the United States. The election of a Spanish Socialist leader, Javier Solana, to the post of General Secretary of NATO, symbolized this transformation of a Cold War alliance into the operative tool of political/military coordination of European (and United States) initiatives in the new geopolitical context – an evolution that seemed to sentence to oblivion the Gaullian dream of a Europe militarily and strategically independent *vis-à-vis* the United States. Britain and Germany never wanted this independence, and none of the European countries' electorates was/is ready to foot the bill, in taxes and military effort, to be a world power, thus making Europe dependent on the United States in strategic terms.

Thus, in 1999, while European countries finally succeeded in acting together against Yugoslavia, triggering NATO's first war, the US air force and navy assumed the largest share of the campaign. The use of satellite-based technology, and precision-guided munition, made European armies largely tributaries of US military technology. The war over Kosovo showed the dependence of the European Union on NATO as the indispensable military tool of its foreign policy. The paradox is that the full realization of such dependence prompted the European Union, in the aftermath of the war, to search for an autonomous, common defense and security policy. With Blair's Britain pushing for an European defense system, the Western European Union alliance was re-tooled toward new security arrangements; the European defense industry was boosted in 1999 by the merger of the defense divisions of Daimler–Chrysler and Lagardere–Matra to form a major defense company EADS (European Aeronautic, Defense, and Space); and a new post was created in the European Union system of governance to be in charge of articulating the European policy on security and defense. Significantly, the first appointee to this position was none other than Javier Solana, after quitting his post with NATO, thus symbolizing the continuity between the two security arrangements. Indeed, the emergence of an autonomous European defense policy does not mean a break with the United States.

However, the success of NATO in the Yugoslav War may have signaled its historic decline, as a new coordination between European armies could pave the way for European military autonomy. Such autonomy, however, would imply a growing defense budget for European countries, as well as a significant effort in defense R&D and technology. Overall, for technological and geopolitical reasons, this

European defense system will still operate in close coordination with the US but with a greater degree of political freedom. In fact, the decision-making process in NATO has already evolved toward negotiation, consultation, and networking among its members: during the 1999 war in Yugoslavia, the political leaders of the main participating countries were in a continuing process of consultation by daily video-conference, among themselves and with NATO's Secretary General and military commanders. The collective, negotiated character of this decision-making process was illustrated in one of the most dangerous episodes of the war: after the surprise occupation by Russian paratroopers of the Pristina airport, the US General Commander of NATO ordered the eviction of Russian soldiers by force. But the British officer commanding the troops in the field resisted the order, and had the order eventually overturned by the political leadership of NATO. The US general was rewarded with early retirement. What was inconceivable behavior in the old logic of the nation-state, namely refusing to take orders from the supreme allied commander in the midst of war, had become acceptable practice within the networks of shared decision-making that characterized NATO's action during the Yugoslav War. Technological superiority, and the willingness to use its taxpayers' money to pay for superpower status, made the US the indispensable partner of European defense policy – but no longer as a dictating power, as was the case during the Cold War, but as a key node in a complex network of strategic decision-making.

In terms of the European construction, for all its limits and contradictions, the Maastricht Treaty marked an irreversible process of economic and political integration in the European Union, a process by and large confirmed in December 1996 by the "stability (and growth) pact" reached in Dublin. On the other hand, British, Swedish, and Danish reluctance to go along with conceding sovereignty through the European single currency, together with the diversity of situation among the countries negotiating their future membership, led to "Europe *à la carte*"; that is, to different levels of integration depending upon countries and issues. This "variable geometry" of European construction,[4] for all its incoherence, is an essential instrument of the construction itself, as it prevents frontal conflicts among major partners, while allowing European institutions to muddle through the challenges presented by the two processes that, at the same time, further and oppose integration: economic globalization and cultural identity.

4 Pisani-Ferry (1995).

Globalization and European Integration

European integration is, at the same time, a reaction to the process of globalization and its most advanced expression. It is also the proof that the global economy is not an undifferentiated system made up of firms and capital flows, but a regionalized structure in which old national institutions and new supranational entities still play a major role in organizing economic competition, and in reaping, or spoiling, the benefits of it. However, it does not follow that globalization is just an ideology. As I argued in volume I, chapter 2, and in volume II, chapter 5, while most economic activity, and most jobs, in the world are national, regional, or even local, the core, strategic economic activities are globally integrated in the Information Age through electronically enacted networks of exchange of capital, commodities, and information. It is this global integration that induces and shapes the current process of European unification, on the basis of European institutions historically constituted around predominantly political goals.

The foremost dimension in the globalization process concerns financial markets and currency markets. They are truly global, with the potential of working as a unit in real time, through electronic flows, and the ability to bypass, or overwhelm, government controls. The central decision that anchors the unification of Europe was the creation of the euro in 1999–2002, and the phasing out of national currencies, with the possible exception of the British pound, which will be, in fact, either pegged to the euro or pegged to the US dollar. In the 1990s, it became imperative to keep a minimum degree of monetary and financial stability in the European economies, after two revealing experiences. One was the failed attempt, in the early 1980s, of the first Mitterrand administration in France to embark independently on an expansionary policy, only to be forced to three successive devaluations of the franc, and to impose for a decade, both by Socialist and Conservative administrations, the most stringent budgetary policy of the whole continent. The second experience took place in the two-stage crisis of the European monetary system in the fall of 1992, and in the summer of 1993, when the pound and the lira were forced out of the system, and the peseta and the escudo were forced to devalue, in spite of the large-scale commitment of several European central banks, including the Italian, the British, and the Spanish, whose interventions were swept away by the movement of about US$1 trillion in a week of October 1992 in the European currency markets. After such an experience it became clear that, within closely linked economies, the floating of exchange rates between their national currencies constituted a permanent temptation to induce capital market turbulences, since capital flows in the global financial markets were/are in relentless movement to maximize instant opportunities to enhance their return. In this context, the notion of speculation is simply misleading. What we are witnessing is not "speculation," but the domination of financial markets over all other investment opportunities in maximizing profits as a structural feature of the new global, informational economy. This does not mean that banks, or financial institutions, dominate industrial capital, an obsolete formulation that does not do justice to the intertwining of capital movements between different sectors in the networked economy, a theme that I will develop in the conclusion to this book.

The integration of capital markets, and the establishment of a single currency, require the homogenization of macro-economic conditions in the different European economies, including fiscal policies. Budgets may still vary according to national policies, but only by giving priority to some budget items over others within the constraints of similar fiscal prudence. Furthermore, the alignment of European economies on a given set of macro-economic parameters is but one step toward their alignment on international standards, at least *vis-à-vis* OECD countries. Indeed, the basic requirements established by the Maastricht Treaty, and made more precise by the Dublin "stability and growth pact" of December 1996, closely mirror the standard criteria imposed by the International Monetary Fund around the world: low budget deficit (less than 3 percent of GDP); relatively low public debt (no more than 60 percent of GDP); low inflation; low long-term interest rates; and stable exchange rate. The harmonization of European economies is inseparable from the harmonization of global macro-economic parameters, to be watched over, and imposed if necessary, by the G-7 annual meetings of the rich countries, and by the International Monetary Fund for the rest of the world. It is in this sense that we can truly speak of globalization of capital, and of the conditions of circulation of capital, not a small matter in a capitalist economy. Down the line, an attempt at stabilizing the exchange rate between the euro, the US dollar, and the yen is to be expected. And since the speed and volume of electronic exchanges in the currency markets will make it impossible to control highly destabilizing movements (as was the case in eurocurrency markets), the three dominant currencies will be likely to be pegged to each other in the future, thus eliminating economic national sovereignty for all practical purposes, although national pride will preclude the creation of a global currency, and technical obstacles will make a return to the gold standard unlikely.

There is a second, major dimension of globalization: information technology, at the heart of the productive capacity of economies and the military might of states. As I mentioned above, in the mid-1980s, the intensification of European integration came partly as a response to a perceived technological deficit *vis-à-vis* the United States and Japan. In fact, most European technology policy initiatives failed, with the extremely important exception of Airbus and the aeronautics industry in general, predicated more on a successful commercial strategy than on technological excellence. Yet, Europe in the 1980s and early 1990s lost step with US companies in the critical areas of micro-electronics and software, and with Japanese and Korean companies in micro-electronics and advanced consumer electronics (with the exception of Nokia). The policy of "national champions" deteriorated in a wasteful subsidy to oversized, inefficient companies, as the (failed) attempt by the French government to sell Thomson to a consortium led by Daewoo for 1 franc in 1996 dramatically underscored. The European Union's research programs (such as Esprit) were too removed from industrial R&D, and the universities that most benefited from them were not advanced enough to break through new technological paths. Eureka's efforts at stimulating innovative businesses were too limited, and too dependent on a series of bureaucratic rules in establishing multi-country partnership, actually to make a difference in the overall picture. Telecommunications was the fundamental area in which European companies (particularly Alcatel, Siemens, and Ericsson) had cutting-edge know-how, a powerful industrial base, and well-established market connections. However, their dependence on electronic components and computers also made European technological autonomy unthinkable. So that, by the late 1990s, no serious policy-maker or industrial strategist in Europe thought about European technological independence in the way that de Gaulle or Mitterrand would have suggested. But the terms of this debate have been made obsolete by the nature of information technology industries in the new, global economy. High technology firms are all dependent on global networks of technological and economic exchange. True, there are some oligopolies, such as Microsoft in PC software, or Intel in advanced micro-electronics. And consumer electronics, with its array of critical technologies, such as HDTV or liquid crystal display, are, by and large, a Japanese (and increasingly Korean) domain. Yet the acceleration of technological change, the need to link up to specific markets, and the strategy of hedging technological bets among different partners (see volume I, chapters 1 and 3) have induced a fully fledged networking of multinational corporations and medium-level firms, in a model of interpenetration of technology, production, and markets that I have defined as "the network enterprise." Thus, instead of opposing Ameri-

can and Japanese companies to European companies, the globalization of information technology results in the complete entangling of
research, R&D, production, and distribution between the advanced
areas, firms, and institutions of the United States, the Pacific, and the
European Union.

Information technology is now asymmetrically globalized, and the
relevance of European research centers, firms, and markets assures
that Europe is deeply integrated into the dominant technological networks. For instance, the key breakthrough in the diffusion of the
Internet, the invention of the technologies underlying the World Wide
Web, took place in Geneva's CERN laboratory in 1990; on the basis
of these technologies, researchers at the University of Illinois'
Supercomputer Center developed a new Web browser (Mosaic) in 1993;
and, finally, the technology was commercialized in 1994–5 in Silicon
Valley by Netscape, a new firm created around the University of Illinois' team (see volume I, chapter 1). In another instance of technological interdependence, in the next technological wave, genetic engineering,
Japan lags way behind; European laboratories are on the cutting edge
of cloning; and while R&D is most dynamic in the United States, some
of the advanced American research, and researchers, have been acquired by giant pharmaceutical companies in Switzerland, Germany,
and France. Mobile telephony was far more advanced in Europe than
in the US at the turn of the millennium because of the ability of European countries and firms to share standards and protocols. Nokia, a
Finnish company, seems to be consolidating its position as the world
leader in cellular telephony by combining home-grown research resources with a deep connection to US innovative technology firms.
France's software giant, Cap Gemini, had also secured a significant
market share in Europe in 1999, and was making substantial inroads
into the US market, mainly through the acquisition of American start-
up firms. Thus, while it is true that American-based information technology research and production continue to be more advanced than in
Europe (with some notable exceptions, such as Nokia and Ericsson),
access to new sources of knowledge and application is guaranteed to
European firms and institutions by the intertwining of information
technology networks, and European companies are rapidly catching
up in high technology industries, both in Europe, and in the global
market. In this sense, the fundamental productive base of Europe in
the Information Age is truly globalized.

The globalization of capital and information technology force us to
consider the classic subject of the integration of trade and investment
in a new perspective. A major theme of debate about Europe and globalization concerns the potential decline of European competitiveness

in a truly global market, under the double squeeze of US and Japanese technology from above, and the lower production costs of newly industrialized countries from below. Yet, in the 1990s, the European Union's balance of trade *vis-à-vis* the United States and, in the late 1990s, *vis-à-vis* Japan was just equilibrated, year in, year out. There was a deficit in relation to newly industrialized countries, but European imports from these countries were not large enough to induce an overall imbalance. How was this possible? How does Europe, as a whole, keep its competitive position, in spite of higher labor costs, inferior entrepreneurialism, the financial conservatism of firms, and lower level of technological innovation? Part of the answer concerns timing. Markets for goods and services are not truly globalized *yet*. Some traditional sectors, such as textiles or garments, have been hurt by competition from Asia and Latin America. But most European trade is within the European Union, and the lowering of tariffs in strategic sectors, such as automobiles or farm products, still has a long way to go, and will have to operate on a reciprocity basis, in application of the Uruguay Round GATT agreements. Another factor is that the technological and managerial re-tooling of European companies in the 1990s allowed European economies to match (in Germany) or even surpass (in France) American labor productivity, thus ensuring the basis for competitiveness in an open economy. As for the competition with Japan, its labor costs are in fact higher than in Europe, and Japanese firms in key sectors of information technology, such as software and Internet design, are far behind European companies.

But there is something more important: networking of trade and investment across national boundaries. Japanese, American, and Asian Pacific companies are investing and producing in Europe besides exporting from their various platforms. And European firms are producing in Asia and in the United States. As much as one-third of world trade seems to be intra-firm, or intra-network, movements of goods and services, thus largely invisible to trade statistics (see volume I, chapter 2). And European companies, when faced with decreasing competitiveness for exports from their European bases, tend to invest in America, the Asian Pacific, and Latin America, both to serve these markets and to export back to Europe from their offshore production sites, such as Singapore. Thus, in 1994–6, while German industrial companies sharply reduced their investments in Germany, they went on an investment spree around the world, particularly in Asia. For instance, in 1995, investment abroad by German companies almost doubled, reaching a record US$32 billion, while investment fell in Germany. Thus, it is the global movement of investment, and the constitution of trans-border production networks, both in manufacturing and services, that characterize the process of globalization, rather than the constitution of a single, global market.

While globalization characterized the movement of capital, technology, and productive investment in the Europe of the 1990s, the movement of labor is far more restricted. To be sure, citizens of the European Union have the feeling of being invaded by immigrants, but the actual trends are more complex, and require some empirical clarification, given the importance of the question for European identity.[5] Up to 1990, as I showed in volume I, chapter 4, the proportion of foreign population *legally recorded* in the European Union as a whole remained at a modest 4.5 percent, albeit with a substantial increase from its 3.1 percent level in 1982. Much of this increase was due to emigration into Germany, Italy, and Austria, while Britain and France saw their respective percentage of foreign residents fall slightly during the 1980s. The situation substantially changed in the 1990s, on four grounds. First, the opening up of borders in Russia, and Eastern Europe, prompted significant emigration from these areas. The catastrophic predictions by the European Commission of 25 million Russians flocking into Western Europe did not materialize. But over 400,000 ethnic Germans from Russia and Eastern Europe exercised their immigration and citizenship rights. Hundreds of thousands of other Eastern Europeans also emigrated, most of them heading for Germany and Austria. Secondly, the destabilization of the Balkans by the disintegration of Yugoslavia, and the subsequent nationalist reactions and ethnic wars, generated a large influx of refugees, particularly into Germany and Italy. Germany found itself in a paradoxical situation derived from its contradictory naturalization policy. On the one hand, the difficulties of obtaining German nationality keep millions of long-time residents, including many born in Germany, as foreigners in their own land; on the other hand, the compensatory policy of liberal asylum attracts hundreds of thousands of political and economic refugees. Together, these two trends contributed to a sharp increase in the proportion of foreigners in Germany, approaching 12 percent by the turn of the century, a foreign stock to which should be added illegal immigrants and naturalized ethnic Germans. Italy suffered the full shock of the disintegration of Albania, and shared the impact of the Balkan Wars. Thirdly, the opening of internal European borders, increased immigration into countries, such as Spain, Portugal, and Italy, that were in the frontline of impoverished African lands. Migrants had the option of staying in these countries or searching for better job opportunities farther north. This contributed to an unfore-

5   Massey et al. (1999).

seen sharp increase of immigration in southern Europe. Fourthly, when the European Union tightened up its border controls illegal immigration exploded. By 1999, it was estimated that the flow of illegal immigration in the European Union was about 500,000 per year. Eastern European mafias made traffic in human beings their most profitable trade, including the sale of hundreds of thousands of women as prostitutes for the enjoyment of the civilized men of the European Union. Together with the demographic pressure from the Mediterranean southern rim, Fortress Europe will face a dramatic challenge in the twenty-first century. But, unlike the United States, which faces a similar issue from south of Rio Grande but has always been a multicultural, multi-ethnic society, most Europeans of the European Union continue to long for a culturally and ethnically homogeneous society, which is now irreversibly gone with the global wind. This schizophrenia between self-image and the new demographic reality of Europe constitutes a key feature of cultural and political dynamics linked to the redefinition of European identity.[6]

There are two additional dimensions of globalization that directly affect the process of European unification, which I simply mention here for the sake of coherence of the argument, without repeating it, since their analysis can be found elsewhere in this book. On the one hand, the globalization and interdependence of communication media (see volume I, chapter 5, and volume II, chapter 5) create a European audiovisual space that fundamentally transforms European culture and information, in a process, by and large, independent of the nation-states. On the other hand, the rise of a global criminal economy (see chapter 3 of this volume) finds a wonderful opportunity to prosper in a half-integrated institutional system, such as the one currently characterizing the European Union. Indeed, national controls are easily by-passed by the new mobility of capital, people, and information, while European police controls are slow to develop, precisely because of the resistance of national bureaucracies to give up their monopoly of power, thus inducing an historical no man's land where crime, power, and money link with each other. However, in October 1999, the European Union Council of Ministers, at its meeting in Tampere, Finland, adopted a series of measures to step up the coordination of police functions, as well as preliminary steps toward a European judicial space. In so doing, European governments were giving themselves the means to fight global crime but, at the same time, were crossing a major boundary toward the sharing of their national sovereignty.

The shaping of European unification by this multidimensional glo-

---

6   Al–Sayyad and Castells (2000).

balization has profound and lasting consequences for European societies. Probably the most important one is the difficulty of preserving the European welfare state in its present form. This is because the mobility of capital, and the networking of production, create the conditions for investment to move around the world, and around Europe, to areas of lower labor costs, lower social benefits, and lesser environmental constraints. Thus, in the late 1990s, European firms, and particularly German firms, were investing heavily in Eastern European countries (but not in Russia or Ukraine), taking advantage of lower labor costs, and in anticipation of their integration into the European Union: in 1999, Western European investment in Poland, Hungary, the Czech Republic, Estonia, and Slovenia totaled US$11 billion, and the projections were for 20 percent annual growth.

The preservation of the European welfare state in its present form also faces growing difficulties because the search for flexibility in the labor market, and the process of relative disinvestment in the European Union, reduce the employment basis on which the fiscal stability of the welfare state relies. Without job creation, and without a relative equalization of social costs in the internationally networked system, it is difficult to see how a comprehensive welfare state can be maintained in Europe, under the conditions of relatively similar, or in some cases lower, productivity *vis-à-vis* other areas of production (for example, the United States). Indeed, the UK, under Thatcher and Major, embarked on a major retrenchment of the welfare state from the 1980s, and, in the late 1990s, Germany, France, Spain, and (to a lesser extent) Italy had at the top of their agenda the significant shrinkage of the welfare state. Sweden's revival seems to be largely derived from a combination of deep cuts in social spending, flexibilization of labor markets, and higher taxes to finance human capital investment. If the UK experience is of any value, not to speak of the United States, a significant increase in inequality, poverty, and social exclusion will follow. Ultimately, political legitimacy will be undermined, since the welfare state is one of its pillars.[7]

A similar process of relative equalization of working arrangements between European Union, Eastern European, and American/Asian economies is taking place in the labor markets, as the push for flexibility and networking, characteristic of informational capitalism, is clearly on in most European countries. The ability of The Netherlands to generate jobs, reducing the unemployment level below 5 percent in the 1990s, was largely based on part-time employment. According to a 1996 report from the German *Länder* of Bavaria and Saxony, it was

7 Castells (1996); Navarro (1996).

projected that by 2015 about 50 percent of German workers would not hold a stable, full-time job.[8] If such were to be the case, the entire European social fabric would be transformed. Martin Carnoy has identified similar trends toward labor-market flexibility in the whole of Europe.[9]

I do not imply, however, that these consequences of globalization on European integration, and on European societies, are inexorable. There is, as Alain Touraine argues, an ideology of globalization that considers it as a natural force, reducing societies to economies, economies to markets, and markets to financial flows.[10] This is simply a crude rationalization of strictly capitalist interests, often defended with more vehemence by neo-liberal ideologists than by capitalists themselves, since many firms have a worldview broad enough to understand their social responsibility, and the need to preserve social stability. But Alain Touraine also points out that, too often, the opposition to globalization in Europe, and particularly in France, is carried out by social actors who defend narrow, corporatist interests, linked to an obsolete public sector subsidized by the taxpayer, without gaining much benefit from it.[11] However, together with the corporatism of privileged sectors of workers, such as Air France pilots, there is a widespread popular reaction, in France, and elsewhere, against the shrinkage and potential dismantling of the welfare state, and against flexibility in the labor market at the expense of workers' stable lives, an opposition often expressed in terms of the people against the politicians, the nation against the European state.[12] While the sources of this opposition are, to a great extent, rooted in social and economic interests, they tend to express themselves in the language of nationalism, and in the defense of cultural identity against the impersonal forces of global markets and the diktats of Eurocrats. The French farmers who, led by Jose Bove, attacked MacDonalds' establishments in 1999 were explicitly, and simultaneously, defending French identity (symbolized by French cooking versus fast food), fighting US taxes against French gourmet imports, and defending European health against genetically modified food. The political debate and the social conflicts around the ways to control, and guide, the transformation of European societies throughout their gradual integration into an increasingly globalized economy cannot be reduced to the elementary opposition between a-historical neo-liberalism and archaic public bureaucratism. In its re-

8   Touraine (1996c).
9   Carnoy (2000).
10 Touraine (1996b).
11 Touraine (1996b,c).
12 Touraine et al. (1996).

ality, this debate is expressed in the language of the Information Age – that is, in the opposition between the power of flows and the power of identity.

Cultural Identity and European Unification

The whirlwind of globalization is triggering defensive reactions around the world, often organized around the principles of national and territorial identity (volume II, chapters 1 and 2). In Europe, this perceived threat materializes in the expanding powers of the European Union. Widespread citizen hostility to the process of unification is reinforced by the discourse of most political leaders presenting the European Union as the necessary adaptation to globalization, with the corollary of economic adjustment, flexibility of labor markets, and shrinkage of the welfare state, as the *sine qua non* conditions for the integration of each country in the European Union.[13] Thus, since the acceleration of the integration process coincided in the 1990s with rising unemployment, widespread job insecurity, and greater social inequality, significant sections of the European population tend to affirm their nations against their states, seen as captives of European supranationality. It is revealing that, with the partial exception of Britain, the political establishment of all countries, both on the center-right and on the center-left, are unquestionably pro-European, while most public opinions are sharply divided, at best.[14] Xenophobic reactions against increased immigration fuel nationalist politics, including, in some countries, such as Austria and Switzerland, the extremist brand of nationalist politics that European citizens seemed to have rejected for good.

> Debate over European integration is not a matter of *raison d'état* but rather a matter of *raison de nation*. Whether European integration is allowed to proceed will depend on the ability of nations to secure their own survival. A nation will only allow integration when it is secure that its national identity will not be threatened, that it may even be strengthened by its exposure to different identities. If a nation feels that it is only able to survive through a close correspondence with a state that is sovereign and independent, if it does not believe that the state can be integrated while its culture is reproduced, it will block further integration.[15]

13 Touraine (1996b).
14 Alonso Zaldivar (1996).
15 Waever (1995: 16).

This insecurity is enhanced by the growing multi-ethnicity and multiculturalism of European societies, which trigger racism and xenophobia as people affirm their identity both against a supranational state and against cultural diversification.[16] The utilization of this insecurity by political demagogues, such as Le Pen in France, or Haider in Austria, amplifies the expression of cultural nationalism throughout the political system and the mass media. The linkage, in the public mind, between crime, violence, terrorism, and ethnic minorities/foreigners/the other, leads to a dramatic surge in European xenophobia, just at the high point of European universalism. This is, in fact, in historical continuity with the previous unification of medieval Europe around Christianity – that is, an intolerant, religious boundary, exclusive of infidels, pagans, and heretics.[17]

There is an additional, fundamental source of people's distrust of European institutions: what has come to be labeled "the democratic deficit." Significant powers affecting the livelihood of citizens have been transferred to the European Union, mainly to the European Council and the Council of Ministers, representing European nation-states, and to the European Commission acting on their behalf. Essential economic policy decisions have even been placed under the control of the European Central Bank. Thus, the capacity of citizens to influence these decisions has been considerably reduced. Between the act of choosing, every four years, from two different options of government, and the daily management of a complex, pan-European system, there is so much distance that citizens feel definitively left out. There are practically no effective channels for citizen participation in the European institutions. The European Commission's crisis of legitimacy was made worse by the level of mismanagement and petty corruption revealed by a parliamentary investigation in 1999, leading to the resignation of the entire Commission. While the appointment of a respected Italian economist Romano Prodi as the new President of the Commission seemed to restore some level of credibility, the damage was already done. The fact that, in June 1999, Mr Bangeman, the European Commissioner in charge of telecommunications, could be hired as a future consultant by the Spanish Telefonica at a time when he was still officially in his post in the Commission, while formally not breaking the rules, was widely considered an indication of how rotten the Brussels bureaucracy had become. Moreover, as Borja pointedly writes, there are no "European conflicts."[18] Indeed, the democratic process is not

16   Wieviorka (1993).
17   Fontana (1994).
18   Borja (1996: 12).

only based on representation and consensus building, but on democratically enacted conflicts between different social actors vying for their specific interests. Besides farmers littering the streets of Brussels with their produce (still unhappy in spite of being entirely subsidized by all other Europeans and, indirectly, by most of the developing world), expressions of transnational collective mobilization aimed at European decision-making are negligible. The apprenticeship of European citizenship is absent, to a large extent because European institutions are usually happy to live in their secluded world of technocratic agencies and deal-making councils of ministers. For instance, the possibilities of using networks of computer-mediated communication for the dissemination of information and citizen participation had been all but ignored by the end of the century.[19] Thus, confronted with a decline in democracy and citizen participation, at a time of globalization of the economy and Europeanization of politics, citizens retrench in their countries, and increasingly affirm their nations. Nationalism, not federalism, is the concomitant development of European integration. And only if the European Union is able to handle, and accommodate, nationalism will it survive as a political construction. As Waever, based on Anthony Smith's insights, proposes, while European institutions may adopt the French version of national identity, built around political identity, European nations may be heading toward the adoption of the German version of national identity, based on a linguistically united *Volk*.[20] As paradoxical as it may sound, it is possible that only the institutional and social articulation of both identity principles can make possible the development of a European Union as something other than a common market.

But if nations, independently from the state, become the sources of identity-based legitimacy for the European construction, the issue arises of which nations. It seems relatively clear in the case of France: after the successful extermination of plural national identities by the French Revolution on behalf of the universal principle of democratic citizenship. When French people react against Europe they do so in the name of "La France," in terms that would be equally understood by General de Gaulle and the French Communists. For different reasons, it is also clear in Germany, where the ethnic purity of the nation, even among Kazakhstan's Germans, remains untainted by the millions of immigrants, and sons of immigrants, that may never be German, after the grassroots campaign successfully orchestrated by the Christian Democrats in 1999 against the naturalization law of the Social Democratic/

19   HLEGIS (1997).
20   Waever (1995: 23).

Green government. The greatest fear of Eurocrats is that in the event of a political crisis, the German constitutional court will rule against the European institutions, in application of the principle of *Superrevisionsinstanz*, that it affirmed in its landmark verdict of October 12, 1993.

The appeal to national identity is more complicated in other countries, based on pluri-national states, as is the case in Spain, in the United Kingdom, and Belgium. Would *Catalunya* or Scotland affirm its identity against the European institutions, or, on the contrary, in favor of the European Union, bypassing, rather than opposing, the Spanish or British governments?[21] Furthermore, the affirmation of a "Padania" identity in northern Italy has been superficially ridiculed because of the extravagant character of Bossi, the leader of the *Lega Nord*. And yet, while it is true that the foundation of this identity is essentially economic, and even more narrowly fiscal, it also has historical roots in the artificial integration of Italy in the late nineteenth century, and its dynamics may go well beyond the political anecdote. Not that Padania exists, but in linguistic, cultural, social, and political terms, it is highly doubtful whether Italy existed until well into the twentieth century, with the Mezzogiorno, even today, having very little in common with Lombardy, Piedmont, or Emilia-Romagna.[22] The retrenchment around the principle of national identity is strengthening the nation-states against the European Union in some countries, while reinforcing the European Union against the current nation-states in others.

The search for identity as an antidote to economic globalization and political disfranchisement also permeates below the level of the nation-state, adding new dynamism to regions and cities around Europe. As Orstrom Moller writes, the future European model may be made up of the articulation of economic internationalization and cultural decentralization.[23] Regional and local governments are currently playing a major role in revitalizing democracy, and opinion polls show a higher degree of citizen trust in these lower levels of government compared with national and supranational levels. Cities have become critical actors in establishing strategies of economic development, in negotiated interaction with internationalized firms. And both cities and regions have established European networks that coordinate initiatives, and learn from each other, putting into action a novel principle of cooperation and competition, whose practice we have described elsewhere.[24]

21   Keating (1995).
22   Ginsborg (1994).
23   Orstrom Moller (1995).
24   Borja and Castells (1997).

On the light side, an illustration of this double dynamic of local identity and European networking, which I consider to be extremely important, is the structuring of professional sports, such as football or basketball, in the past decade. As everybody knows, the local team is an essential rallying point for people's identity. While national competitions continue to be played, maximum attention is given to European competitions (of which there are three for football, for instance), so that the reward for teams in the national competition is to become "European," a goal that many teams can reach, in contrast with only a few three decades ago. At the same time, the opening of labor markets for European players, and the mass migration to Europe of players from other countries, means that a significant proportion of players in the local team are foreigners. The result is that people mobilize around the identity of their city, as represented by a group of largely foreign professional players competing in various European leagues. It is through this kind of basic life mechanisms that the real Europe is coming into existence – by sharing experience on the basis of meaningful, palpable identity. How, then, can unification proceed between the high winds of globalization and the warm hearth of locality?

The Institutionalization of Europe: the Network State

When we reflect on the contradictory visions and interests surrounding the unification of Europe, and we consider the lack of enthusiasm among citizens of most countries, it seems miraculous that the process of integration is as advanced as it is at the turn of the millennium. Part of the explanation for this unlikely success can be found in the fact that the European Union does not supplant the existing nation-states but, on the contrary, is a fundamental instrument for their survival on the condition of conceding shares of sovereignty in exchange for a greater say in world, and domestic, affairs in the age of globalization. But this convergence of interests still had to find an institutional expression to be operational. It found it in a complex, and changing, geometry of European institutions that combines the control of decision-making by national governments (the European Council, and its summit meetings every six months, the principle of a rotating presidency of the Council, the regular meetings of the Council of Ministers), the management of common European business by a eurotechnocracy, directed by the politically appointed European Commission, and the symbolic expressions of legitimacy in the European Parliament, the Court of Justice, and the Court of Auditors.

The relentless negotiations within this set of institutions, and between the national actors pursuing their strategies in the framework of these institutions, may look cumbersome and inefficient. Yet it is precisely this indeterminacy and this complexity that make it possible to accommodate in the European Union various interests and changing policies, not only from different countries, but from the different political orientations of parties elected to government. The process becomes even more complicated with the introduction of a single currency and with the process of enlargement. Some countries, like Britain and Denmark, may exercise their opt-out clause. Others will negotiate exceptions to the general rules. And, because of increasing disparity between the conditions of countries within the Union, voting procedures will change, depending on issues. On the one hand, a majority vote in the Council of Ministers will make it possible for large countries to go ahead with strategic decisions without being paralyzed by the specific interests of one country, or of a minority coalition. On the other hand, the price to be paid for this reinforcement of majority powers will be flexibility in the application of Union decisions to some countries in some areas and for some time. As Alonso Zaldivar writes, under this system the federal and confederal logics are not mutually exclusive:

> For instance, in matters of defense, police, and public spending, the confederal or intergovernmental [logic] could take precedence, while in monetary policy, trade, residence, and circulation of capital, goods, and people, the functioning of the Union would be closer to federalism or supranationality. Other matters, such as foreign policy, environment, taxes, and immigration would occupy an intermediate position. The future, enlarged European Union must be less uniform and more flexible ... It is possible that the organigram of such an institution will be closer to a network than to a tree, and political theory still does not have a simple term adequate to this kind of configuration, but this is not an obstacle to building it. However, it will not be enough that enlightened bureaucrats conceive this institution: it will also be necessary for the citizens to accept it.[25]

The key element in gradually establishing the European Union's legitimacy, without jeopardizing its policy-making capacity, is the ability of its institutions to link up with subnational levels of government – regional and local – by a deliberate extension of the subsidiarity principle, under which the Union institutions only take charge of decisions that lower levels of government, including nation-states, cannot assume effectively. The Committee of the Regions, an advisory

25   Alonso Zaldivar (1996: 352–3); my translation.

body composed of 222 members representing regional and local governments from all the countries of the Union, is the most direct institutional expression of this concern. The real process of relegitimization of Europe appears to be taking place in the burgeoning of local and regional initiatives, in economic development, as well as in cultural expressions, and social rights, which link up horizontally with each other, while also linking up with European programs directly or through their respective national governments.[26]

Reflecting on the growing complexity and flexibility of European political process, Keohane and Hoffman propose the notion that the European Union "is essentially organized as a network that involves the pooling and sharing of sovereignty rather than the transfer of sovereignty to a higher level."[27] This analysis, developed and theorized by Waever,[28] brings European unification closer to the characterization of institutional neo-medievalism; that is, a plurality of overlapping powers, along the lines suggested years ago by Hedley Bull, and echoed by a number of European analysts, such as Alain Minc.[29] Although historians may object to such a parallel, the image illustrates powerfully the new form of state epitomized by European institutions: *the network state. It is a state characterized by the sharing of authority (that is, in the last resort, the capacity to impose legitimized violence) along a network*. A network, by definition, has nodes, not a center. Nodes may be of different sizes, and may be linked by asymmetrical relationships in the network, so that the network state does not preclude the existence of political inequalities among its members. Indeed, all governmental institutions are not equal in the European network. Not only do national governments still concentrate much decision-making capacity, but there are important differences of power between nation-states, although the hierarchy of power varies in different dimensions: Germany is the hegemonic economic power, but Britain and France hold far greater military power, and at least equal technological capacity. And Spain controls the most precious service for many Europeans: their vacations. However, regardless of these asymmetries, the various nodes of the European network state are interdependent on each other, so that no node, even the most powerful, can ignore the others, even the smallest, in the decision-making process. If some political nodes do so, the whole system is called into question. This is the difference between a political network and a centered political structure.

Available evidence, and recent debates in political theory, seem to

26 Borja (1992).
27 Keohane and Hoffman (1991b: 13).
28 Waever (1995).
29 Bull (1977); Minc (1993).

suggest that the network state, with its geometrically variable sovereignty, is the response of political systems to the challenges of globalization. And the European Union may be the clearest manifestation to date of this emerging form of state, probably characteristic of the Information Age.

European Identity or European Project?

In the end, however, the unification of Europe will probably not be fulfilled only by skillful political engineering. In the context of democratic societies, Europe will only unify, at various degrees and under forms yet to emerge, if its citizens want it. On the basis of the exploration of social trends presented in the three volumes of this book, it is unlikely that this acceptance will take place exclusively on the basis of instrumental interests of managing globalization, particularly when this management will certainly hurt considerable sections of the population. If meaning is linked to identity, and if identity remains exclusively national, regional or local, European integration may not last beyond the limits of a common market, parallel to free-trade zones constituted in other areas of the world. European unification, in a long-term perspective, requires European identity.

However, the notion of European identity is problematic at best.[30] Because of the separation of Church and state, and the tepid religiosity of most Europeans, it cannot be built around Christianity, as was the case historically, even if the widespread anti-Muslim reaction signals the historical persistence of the Crusader spirit. It cannot be built around democracy: first, because democratic ideals are shared around the world; secondly, precisely because democracy is in crisis in its current dependency on the nation-state (see volume II, chapter 6). It will be difficult, and dramatic, to build it around ethnicity at a time when Europe is becoming increasingly diverse in ethnic terms. It is by definition impossible to build it on national identity, albeit if the preservation of national identity will be necessary for European unification to proceed. And it will not be easy to defend a European economic identity ("Fortress Europe") as core economic activities become globalized, and cross-border production networks articulate the European Union with the rest of the world, starting with Eastern Europe and South-East Asia. Do most people feel European – besides feeling French, Spanish, or Catalan – according to opinion polls? Yes.[31] Do they know

---

30 Al-Sayyad and Castells (2000).
31 *The Economist*, October 23, 1999.

what it means? In their majority, not. Do *you* know? Even with the euro in circulation in 2002, its extra-economic meaning will be lost unless there is a broader cultural transformation of European societies.

So, by and large, there is no European identity. But it could be built, not in contradiction, but complementary to national, regional, and local identities. It would take a process of social construction that I have identified, in volume II, as *project identity*; that is, a blueprint of social values and institutional goals that appeal to a majority of citizens without excluding anybody, in principle. That was what democracy, or the nation-state, historically represented at the dawn of the industrial era. What could be the content of such a European identity project in the Information Age? I have my preferences, as everybody else, but they should not interfere with our exploration of history in the making. What are the elements that *actually appear in the discourse, and practice, of social actors opposing globalization and disfranchisement without regressing to communalism?*[32] Liberty, equality, fraternity; the defense of the welfare state, of social solidarity, of stable employment, and of workers' rights; concern for universal human rights and the plight of the Fourth World; the reaffirmation of democracy, and its extension to citizen participation at the local and regional level; the vitality of historically/territorially rooted cultures, often expressed in language, not surrendering to the culture of real virtuality. Most European citizens would probably support these values. Their affirmation, for instance in the defense of the welfare state and stable employment against the pressures of globalization, would take extraordinary changes in the economy and in institutions. But this is precisely what an identity project is: not a utopian proclamation of dreams, but a struggle to impose alternative ways of economic development, sociability, and governance. There are embryos of a European project identity. And, probably, only if these embryos find political expression will the process of European unification ultimately be accomplished.

32   Touraine (1997).

Conclusion: Making Sense of our World

This means to say that scarcely
have we landed into life
than we come as if new-born;
let us not fill our mouths
with so many faltering names,
with so many sad formalities,
with so many pompous letters,
with so much of yours and mine,
with so much signing of papers.

I have in mind to confuse things,
unite them, make them new-born,
mix them up, undress them,
until all light in the world
has the oneness of the ocean,
a generous, vast wholeness,
a crackling, living fragrance.

> Pablo Neruda, fragment of "Too Many Names," *Estravagario*

This is the general conclusion of the three-volume book, *The Information Age: Economy, Society, and Culture*. I have tried to avoid repetition. For definition of theoretical concepts used in this conclusion (for example, informationalism, or relationships of production), please refer to the Prologue of the book in volume I. See also the conclusion of volume I for an elaboration of the concept of network society, and the conclusion of volume II for an analysis of the relationships between cultural identity, social movements, and politics.

Genesis of a New World[1]

A new world is taking shape at this turn of the millennium. It originated in the historical coincidence, around the late 1960s and mid-1970s, of three *independent* processes: the information technology revolution; the economic crisis of both capitalism and statism, and their subsequent restructuring; and the blooming of cultural social movements, such as libertarianism, human rights, feminism, and environmentalism. The interaction between these processes, and the reactions they triggered, brought into being a new dominant social structure, the network society; a new economy, the informational/global economy; and a new culture, the culture of real virtuality. The logic embedded in this economy, this society, and this culture underlies social action and institutions throughout an interdependent world.

A few, decisive features of this new world have been identified in the investigation presented in the three volumes of this book. The information technology revolution induced the emergence of informationalism, as the material foundation of a new society. Under informationalism, the generation of wealth, the exercise of power, and the creation of cultural codes came to depend on the technological capacity of societies and individuals, with information technology as the core of this capacity. Information technology became the indispensable tool for the effective implementation of processes of socioeconomic restructuring. Particularly important was its role in allowing the development of networking as a dynamic, self-expanding form of

1 In discussions in my seminars in recent years a recurrent question comes up so often that I think it would be useful to take it to the reader. It is the question of newness. What is new about all this? Why is this a new world? I do believe that there is a new world emerging at this turn of millennium. In the three volumes of this book I have tried to provide information and ideas in support of this statement. Chips and computers are new; ubiquitous, mobile telecommunications are new; genetic engineering is new; electronically integrated, global financial markets working in real time are new; an inter-linked capitalist economy embracing the whole planet, and not only some of its segments, is new; a majority of the urban labor force in knowledge and information processing in advanced economies is new; a majority of urban population in the planet is new; the demise of the Soviet Empire, the fading away of communism, and the end of the Cold War are new; the rise of the Asian Pacific as an equal partner in the global economy is new; the widespread challenge to patriarchalism is new; the universal consciousness on ecological preservation is new; and the emergence of a network society, based on a space of flows, and on timeless time, is historically new. *Yet this is not the point I want to make.* My main statement is that it does not really matter if you believe that this world, or any of its features, is new or not. My analysis stands by itself. This is our world, the world of the Information Age. And this is my analysis of this world, which must be understood, used, judged, by itself, by its capacity, or incapacity, to identify and explain the phenomena that we observe and experience, regardless of its newness. After all, if nothing is new under the sun, why bother to try to investigate, think, write, and read about it?

organization of human activity. This prevailing, networking logic transforms all domains of social and economic life.

The crisis of models of economic development for both capitalism and statism prompted their parallel restructuring from the mid-1970s onwards. In capitalist economies, firms and governments proceeded with a number of measures and policies that, together, led to a new form of capitalism. It is characterized by globalization of core economic activities, organizational flexibility, and greater power for management in its relation to labor. Competitive pressures, flexibility of work, and weakening of organized labor led to the retrenchment of the welfare state, the cornerstone of the social contract in the industrial era. New information technologies played a decisive role in facilitating the emergence of this rejuvenated, flexible capitalism, by providing the tools for networking, distant communication, storing/processing of information, coordinated individualization of work, and simultaneous concentration and decentralization of decision-making.

In this global, interdependent economy, new competitors, firms and countries came to claim an increasing share of production, trade, capital, and labor. The emergence of a powerful, competitive Pacific economy, and the new processes of industrialization and market expansion in various areas of the world, regardless of recurrent crises and systemic instability, broadened the scope and scale of the global economy, establishing a multicultural foundation of economic interdependence. Networks of capital, labor, information, and markets linked up, through technology, valuable functions, people, and localities around the world, while switching off from their networks those populations and territories deprived of value and interest for the dynamics of global capitalism. There followed the social exclusion and economic irrelevance of segments of societies, of areas of cities, of regions, and of entire countries, constituting what I call the "Fourth World." The desperate attempt by some of these social groups and territories to link up with the global economy, to escape marginality, led to what I call the "perverse connection," when organized crime around the world took advantage of their plight to foster the development of a global criminal economy. It aims at satisfying forbidden desire and supplying outlawed commodities to endless demand from affluent societies and individuals.

The restructuring of statism proved to be more difficult, particularly for the dominant statist society in the world, the Soviet Union, at the center of a broad network of statist countries and parties. Soviet statism proved incapable of assimilating informationalism, thus stalling economic growth and decisively weakening its military machine, the ultimate source of power in a statist regime. Their awareness of stagnation and decline led some Soviet leaders, from Andropov to

Gorbachev, to attempt a restructuring of the system. In order to overcome inertia and resistance from the party/state, reformist leadership opened up information and called upon civil society for support. The powerful expression of national/cultural identities, and the people's demands for democracy, could not be easily channeled into a prescripted reform program. The pressure of events, tactical errors, political incompetence, and the internal split of statist apparatuses led to the sudden collapse of Soviet Communism, in one of the most extraordinary events in political history. With it, the Soviet Empire crumbled also, while statist regimes in its global area of influence were decisively weakened. So ended, in what amounted to an instant by historical standards, the revolutionary experiment that dominated the twentieth century. This was also the end of the Cold War between capitalism and statism, which had divided the world, determined geopolitics, and haunted our lives for the past half-century.

In its communist incarnation, statism ended there, for all practical purposes, although China's brand of statism took a more complicated, subtle way toward its historical exit, as I tried to show in chapter 4 of this volume. For the sake of the coherence of the argument presented here, let me remind the reader that the Chinese state at the turn of the millennium, while fully controlled by the Communist party, is organized around China's incorporation into global capitalism, on the basis of a nationalist project represented by the state. This Chinese nationalism with socialist characteristics is quickly moving away from statism into global capitalism, while trying to find a way to adapt to informationalism, without an open society.

After the demise of statism as a system, capitalism thrives throughout the world, and it deepens its penetration of countries, cultures, and domains of life. In spite of a highly diversified social and cultural landscape, for the first time in history the whole planet is organized around a largely common set of economic rules. It is, however, a different kind of capitalism from the one formed during the Industrial Revolution, or the one that emerged from the 1930s Depression and World War II, under the form of economic Keynesianism and social welfarism. It is a hardened form of capitalism in its goals, but is incomparably more flexible than any of its predecessors in its means. It is informational capitalism, relying on innovation-induced productivity and globalization-oriented competitiveness to generate wealth, and to appropriate it selectively. It is, more than ever, embedded in culture and tooled by technology. But, this time, both culture and technology depend on the ability of knowledge and information to act upon knowledge and information, in a recurrent network of globally connected exchanges.

Societies, however, are not just the result of technological and eco-nomic transformation, nor can social change be limited to institutional crises and adaptations. At about the same time that these develop-ments started to take place in the late 1960s, powerful social move-ments exploded almost simultaneously all over the industrialized world, first in the United States and France, then in Italy, Germany, Spain, Japan, Brazil, Mexico, Czechoslovakia, with echoes and reactions in numerous other countries. As a participant in these social movements (I was an assistant professor of sociology at the Nanterre campus of the University of Paris in 1968), I bear witness to their libertarianism. While they often adopted Marxist ideological expressions in their mili-tant vanguards, they had little to do with Marxism or, for that matter, with the working class. They were essentially cultural movements, wanting to change life rather than seizing power. They intuitively knew that access to the institutions of state co-opts the movement, while the construction of a new, revolutionary state perverts the movement. Their ambitions encompassed a multidimensional reaction to arbitrary au-thority, a revolt against injustice, and a search for personal experi-mentation. While often enacted by students, they were not by any means student movements, since they permeated throughout society, particularly among young people, and their values reverberated in all spheres of life. Of course, they were politically defeated because, as most utopian movements in history, they never pretended to political victory. But they faded away with high historical productivity, with many of their ideas, and some of their dreams, germinating in societies and blossoming as cultural innovations, to which politicians and ideologues will have to relate for generations to come. From these movements sprang the ideas that would be the source of environmen-talism, of feminism, of the endless defense of human rights, of sexual liberation, of ethnic equality, and of grassroots democracy. The cul-tural movements of the 1960s and early 1970s, in their affirmation of individual autonomy against both capital and the state, placed a re-newed stress on the politics of identity. These ideas paved the way for the building of cultural communes in the 1990s, when the legitimacy crisis of institutions of the industrial era blurred the meaning of demo-cratic politics.

The social movements were not reactions to the economic crisis. Indeed, they surged in the late 1960s, in the heyday of sustained growth and full employment, as a critique of the "consumption society." While they induced some workers' strikes, as in France, and helped the pol-itical left, as in Italy, they were not a part of the right/left politics of the industrial era that had been organized around the class cleavages of capitalism. And while they coexisted, broadly speaking, with the information technology revolution, technology was largely absent from either the values or critiques of most movements, if we except some calls against de-humanizing machinism, and their opposition to nuclear power (an old technology in the Information Age). But if these social movements were primarily cultural, and independent of economic and technological transformations, they did have an impact on economy, technology, and ensuing restructuring processes. Their libertarian spirit considerably influenced the movement toward individualized, decentralized uses of technology. Their sharp separation from traditional labor politics contributed to the weakening of organized labor, thus facilitating capitalist restructuring. Their cultural openness stimulated technological experimentation with symbol manipulation, constituting a new world of imaginary representations that would evolve toward the culture of real virtuality. Their cosmopolitanism, and internationalism, set up the intellectual bases for an interdependent world. And their abhorrence of the state undermined the legitimacy of democratic rituals, in spite of the fact that some leaders of the movement went on to renew political institutions. Moreover, by refusing the orderly transmission of eternal codes and established values, such as patriarchalism, religious traditionalism, and nationalism, the 1960s' movements set the stage for a fundamental split in societies all over the world: on the one hand, active, culturally self-defined elites, constructing their own values on the basis of their experience; on the other hand, increasingly uncertain, insecure social groups, deprived of information, resources, and power, digging their trenches of resistance precisely around those eternal values that had been decried by the rebellious 1960s.

The revolution of technology, the restructuring of economy, and the critique of culture converged toward a historical redefinition of the relationships of production, power, and experience, on which societies are based.

A New Society

A new society emerges when and if a structural transformation can be observed in the relationships of production, in the relationships of power, and in the relationships of experience. These transformations lead to an equally substantial modification of social forms of space and time, and to the emergence of a new culture.

Information and analyses presented in the three volumes of this book provide a strong indication of such a multidimensional transformation in the last lapse of the second millennium. I shall synthesize the main features of transformation for each dimension, referring the reader to the respective chapters covering each subject for empirical materials that lend some credibility to the conclusions presented here.

Relationships of production have been transformed, both socially and technically. To be sure, they are capitalist, but of a historically different brand of capitalism, which I call informational capitalism. For the sake of clarity, I shall consider, in sequence, the new characteristics of the production process, of labor, and of capital. Then, the transformation of class relationships can be made visible.

Productivity and competitiveness are the commanding processes of the informational/global economy. Productivity essentially stems from innovation, competitiveness from flexibility. Thus, firms, regions, countries, economic units of all kinds, gear their production relationships to maximize innovation and flexibility. Information technology, and the cultural capacity to use it, are essential in the performance of the new production function. In addition, a new kind of organization and management, aiming at simultaneous adaptability and coordination, becomes the basis for the most effective operating system, exemplified by what I label the network enterprise.

Under this new system of production, labor is redefined in its role as producer, and sharply differentiated according to workers' characteristics. A major difference refers to what I call generic labor versus self-programmable labor. The critical quality in differentiating these two kinds of labor is education, and the capacity of accessing higher levels of education; that is, embodied knowledge and information. The concept of education must be distinguished from skills. Skills can be quickly made obsolete by technological and organizational change. Education (as distinct from the warehousing of children and students) is the process by which people, that is labor, acquire the capability constantly to redefine the necessary skills for a given task, and to access the sources for learning these skills. Whoever is educated, in the proper organizational environment, can reprogram him/herself toward the endlessly changing tasks of the production process. On the other hand, generic labor is assigned a given task, with no reprogramming capability, and it does not presuppose the embodiment of information and knowledge beyond the ability to receive and execute signals. These "human terminals" can, of course, be replaced by machines, or by any other body around the city, the country, or the world, depending on business decisions. While they are collectively indispensable to the production process, they are individually expendable, as value added by each one of them is a small fraction of what is generated by and for the organization. Machines, and generic labor from various origins and locations, cohabit the same subservient circuits of the production system.

Flexibility, enacted organizationally by the network enterprise, requires networkers, and flextimers, as well as a wide array of working arrangements, including self-employment and reciprocal subcontracting. The variable geometry of these working arrangements leads to the coordinated decentralization of work and to the individualization of labor.

The informational/global economy is capitalist; in fact, more so than any other economy in history. But capital is as transformed as labor is in this new economy. The rule is still production for the sake of profit, and for the private appropriation of profit, on the basis of property rights – which is the essence of capitalism. But how does this appropriation of profit take place? Who are the capitalists? Three different levels must be considered in answering this fundamental question. Only the third level is specific to informational capitalism.

The first level concerns *the holders of property rights*. These are, basically, of three kinds: (a) shareholders of companies, a group in which institutional, anonymous shareholders are increasingly predominant and whose investment and disinvestment decisions are often governed solely by short-term financial considerations; (b) family owners, still a relevant form of capitalism, particularly in the Asian Pacific; and (c) individual entrepreneurs, owners of their own means of production (their minds being their main asset), risk-takers, and proprietors of their own profit-making. This last category, which was fundamental to the origins of industrial capitalism and then became largely phased out by corporate industrialism, has made a remarkable comeback under informational capitalism, using the pre-eminence of innovation and flexibility as the essential features of the new production system.

The second level of capitalist forms refers to *the managerial class*; that is, the controllers of capital assets on behalf of shareholders. These managers, whose pre-eminence Berle and Means had already shown in the 1930s, still constitute the heart of capitalism under informationalism, particularly in multinational corporations. I see no reason not to include among them managers of state-owned companies who, for all practical purposes, follow the same logic, and share the same culture, minus the risk for losses underwritten by the taxpayer.

The third level in the process of appropriation of profits by capital is both an old story and a fundamental feature of the new informational capitalism. The reason lies in the nature of *global financial markets*. It is in these markets that profits from all sources ultimately converge in search of higher profits. Indeed, the margins of gain in the stock market, in the bond market, in the currency market, in futures, options, and derivatives, in financial markets at large, are, on average, considerably greater than in most direct investments, excepting a few instances of speculation. This is so not because of the nature of financial capital, the oldest form of capital in history. But because of the technological conditions under which it operates in informationalism. Namely its annihilation of space and time by electronic means. Its technological and informational ability relentlessly to scan the entire planet for investment opportunities, and to move from one option to another in a matter of seconds, brings capital into constant movement, merging in this movement capital from all origins, as in mutual funds investments. The programming and forecasting capabilities of financial management models make it possible to colonize the future, and the interstices of the future (that is, possible alternative scenarios), selling this "unreal estate" as property rights of the immaterial. Played by the rules, there is nothing evil about this global casino. After all, if cautious management and proper technology avoid dramatic crushes of the market, the losses of some fractions of capital are the wins of others, so that, over the long term, the market balances out and keeps a dynamic equilibrium. However, because of the differential between the amount of profits obtained from the production of goods and services, and the amount that can be obtained from financial investments, individual capitals of all kinds are, in fact, dependent on the fate of their investments in global financial markets, since capital can never remain idle. Thus, *global financial markets, and their networks of management, are the actual collective capitalist, the mother of all accumulations.* To say so is not to say that financial capital dominates industrial capital, an old dichotomy that simply does not fit the new economic reality. Indeed, in the past quarter of a century, firms around the world have, by and large, self-financed the majority of their investments with the proceeds of their trade. Banks do not control manufacturing firms, nor do they control themselves. Firms of all kinds, financial producers, manufacturing producers, agricultural producers, service producers, as well as governments and public institutions, use global financial networks as the depositories of their earnings and as their potential source of higher profits. It is in this specific form that *global financial networks are the nerve center of informational capitalism.* Their movements determine the value of stocks, bonds, and currencies, bringing doom or bonanza to savers, investors, firms, and countries. But these movements do not follow a market logic. The market is twisted, manipulated, and transformed, by a combination of computer-enacted strategic maneuvers, crowd psychology from multicultural sources, and unexpected turbulences, caused by greater and greater degrees of complexity in the interaction between capital flows on a global scale. While cutting-edge economists are trying to model this market behavior on the basis of game theory, their heroic efforts to find rational expectation patterns are immediately downloaded in the computers of financial wizards to obtain new competitive advantage from this knowledge by innovating on already known patterns of investment.

The consequences of these developments on *social class relationships* are as profound as they are complex. But before identifying them I need to distinguish between different meanings of class relationships. One approach focuses on social inequality in income and social status, along the lines of social stratification theory. From this perspective, the new system is characterized by *a tendency to increased social inequality and polarization*, namely the simultaneous growth of both the top and the bottom of the social scale. This results from three features: (a) a fundamental differentiation between self-programmable, highly productive labor, and generic, expendable labor; (b) the individualization of labor, which undermines its collective organization, thus abandoning the weakest sections of the workforce to their fate; and (c) under the impact of individualization of labor, globalization of economy, and delegitimation of the state, the gradual demise of the welfare state, so removing the safety net for people who cannot be individually well off. This tendency toward inequality and polarization is certainly not inexorable: it can be countered and prevented by deliberate public policies. But inequality and polarization are prescribed in the dynamics of informational capitalism, and will prevail unless conscious action is taken to countervail these tendencies.

A second meaning of class relationships refers to *social exclusion*. By this I mean the de-linking between people-as-people and people-as-workers/consumers in the dynamics of informational capitalism on a global scale. In chapter 2 of this volume, I tried to show the causes and consequences of this trend in a variety of situations. Under the new system of production, a considerable number of humans, probably in a growing proportion, are irrelevant, both as producers and consumers, from the perspective of the system's logic. I must emphasize, again, that this is not the same as saying that there is, or will be, mass unemployment. Comparative data show that, by and large, in all urban societies, most people and/or their families work for pay, even in poor neighborhoods and in poor countries. The question is: what kind of work for what kind of pay under what conditions? What is happening is that the mass of generic labor circulates in a variety of jobs, increasingly occasional jobs, with a great deal of discontinuity. So, millions of people are constantly in and out of paid work, often included in informal activities, and, in sizeable numbers, on the shop floor of the criminal economy. Furthermore, the loss of a stable relationship to employment, and the weak bargaining power of many workers, lead to a higher level of incidence of major crises in the life of their families: temporary job loss, personal crises, illness, drugs/alcohol addictions, loss of employability, loss of assets, loss of credit. Many of these crises connect with each other, inducing the downward spiral of social exclusion, toward what I have called the "black holes of informational capitalism," from which, statistically speaking, it is difficult to escape.

The borderline between social exclusion and daily survival is increasingly blurred for a growing number of people in all societies. Having lost much of the safety net, particularly for the new generations of the post-welfare state era, people who cannot follow the constant updating of skills, and fall behind in the competitive race, position themselves for the next round of "downsizing" of that shrinking middle that made the strength of advanced capitalist societies during the industrial era. Thus, processes of social exclusion do not only affect the "truly disadvantaged," but those individuals and social categories who build their lives on a constant struggle to escape falling down to a stigmatized underworld of downgraded labor and socially disabled people.

A third way of understanding new class relationships, this time in the Marxian tradition, is concerned with *who the producers are and who appropriates the products of their labor.* If innovation is the main source of productivity, knowledge and information are the essential materials of the new production process, and education is the key quality of labor, the new producers of informational capitalism are those knowledge generators and information processors whose contribution is most valuable to the firm, the region, and the national economy. But innovation does not happen in isolation. It is part of a system in which management of organizations, processing of knowledge and information, and production of goods and services are intertwined. So defined, this category of informational producers includes a very large group of managers, professionals, and technicians, who form a "collective worker"; that is, a producer unit made up of cooperation between a variety of inseparable individual workers. In OECD countries they may account for about one-third of the employed population. Most other workers may be in the category of generic labor, potentially replaceable by machines or by other members of the generic labor force. They need the producers to protect their bargaining power. But informational producers do not need them: this is a fundamental cleavage in informational capitalism, leading to the gradual dissolution of the remnants of class solidarity of the industrial society.

But who appropriates a share of informational producers' work? In one sense, nothing has changed *vis-à-vis* classic capitalism: their employers do; this is why they employ them in the first place. But, on the other hand, the mechanism of appropriation of surplus is far more complicated. First, employment relationships are tendentially individualized, meaning that each producer will receive a different deal. Secondly, an increasing proportion of producers control their own work process, and enter into specific, horizontal working relationships, so that, to a large extent, they become independent producers, submitted to market forces, but playing market strategies. Thirdly, their earnings often go into the whirlwind of global financial markets, fed precisely by the affluent section of the global population, so that they are also collective owners of collective capital, thus becoming dependent on the performance of capital markets. Under these conditions, we can hardly consider that there is a class contradiction between these networks of highly individualized producers and the collective capitalist of global financial networks. To be sure, there is frequent abuse and exploitation of individual producers, as well as of large masses of generic labor, by whoever is in charge of production processes. Yet, segmentation of labor, individualization of work, and diffusion of capital in the circuits of global finance have jointly induced the gradual fading away of the class structure of the industrial society. There are, and will be, powerful social conflicts, some of them enacted by workers and organized labor, from Korea to Spain. Yet, they are not the expression of class struggle but of interest groups' demands and/or of revolt against injustice.

The *truly fundamental social cleavages of the Information Age* are: first, the internal fragmentation of labor between informational producers and replaceable generic labor. Secondly, the social exclusion of a significant segment of society made up of discarded individuals whose value as workers/consumers is used up, and whose relevance as people is ignored. And, thirdly, the separation between the market logic of global networks of capital flows and the human experience of workers' lives.

Power relations are being transformed as well by the social processes that I have identified and analyzed in this book. The main transformation concerns the *crisis of the nation-state as a sovereign entity, and the related crisis of political democracy*, as constructed in the past two centuries. Since commands from the state cannot be fully enforced, and since some of its fundamental promises, embodied in the welfare state, cannot be kept, both its authority and its legitimacy are called into question. Because representative democracy is predicated on the notion of a sovereign body, the blurring of boundaries of sovereignty leads to uncertainty in the process of delegation of people's will. Globalization of capital, multilateralization of power institutions, and decentralization of authority to regional and local governments induce a new geometry of power, perhaps inducing a new form of state, the network state. Social actors, and citizens at large, maximize the chances of representation of their interests and values by playing out strategies in the networks of relationships between various institutions, at various levels of competence. Citizens of a given European region will have a better chance of defending their interests if they support their regional authorities against their national government, in alliance with the European Union. Or the other way around. Or else, none of the above; that is, by affirming local/regional autonomy against both the nation-state and supranational institutions. American malcontents may revile the federal government on behalf of the American nation. Or new Chinese business elites may push their interests by linking up with their provincial government, or with the still powerful national government, or with overseas Chinese networks. In other words, the new structure of power is dominated by a network geometry, in which power relationships are always specific to a given configuration of actors and institutions.

Under such conditions, informational politics, enacted primarily by symbol manipulation in the space of the media, fits well with this constantly changing world of power relationships. Strategic games, customized representation, and personalized leadership substitute for class constituencies, ideological mobilization, and party control, which were characteristic of politics in the industrial era.

As politics becomes a theater, and political institutions are bargaining agencies rather than sites of power, citizens around the world react defensively, voting to prevent harm from the state in place of entrusting it with their will. In a certain sense, *the political system is voided of power*, albeit not of influence.

Power, however, does not disappear. In an informational society, *it becomes inscribed, at a fundamental level, in the cultural codes through which people and institutions represent life and make decisions, including political decisions.* In a sense, power, while real, becomes immaterial. It is real because wherever and whenever it consolidates, it provides, for a time, individuals and organizations with the capacity to enforce their decisions regardless of consensus. But it is immaterial because such a capacity derives from the ability to frame life experience under categories that predispose to a given behavior and can then be presented as to favor a given leadership. For instance, if a population feels threatened by unidentifiable, multidimensional fear, the framing of such fears under the codes of immigration = race = poverty = welfare = crime = job loss = taxes = threat, provides an identifiable target, defines an US versus THEM, and favors those leaders who are most credible in supporting what is perceived to be a reasonable dose of racism and xenophobia. Or, in a very different example, if people equate quality of life with conservation of nature, and with their spiritual serenity, new political actors could emerge and new public policies could be implemented.

Cultural battles are the power battles of the Information Age. They are primarily fought in and by the media, but the media are not the power-holders. Power, as the capacity to impose behavior, lies in the networks of information exchange and symbol manipulation, which relate social actors, institutions, and cultural movements, through icons, spokespersons, and intellectual amplifiers. In the long run, it does not really matter who is in power because the distribution of political roles becomes widespread and rotating. There are no more stable power elites. There are however, *elites from power*; that is, elites formed during their usually brief power tenure, in which they take advantage of their privileged political position to gain a more permanent access to material resources and social connections. Culture as the source of power, and power as the source of capital, underlie the new social hierarchy of the Information Age.

The transformation of *relationships of experience* revolves primarily around *the crisis of patriarchalism*, at the root of a profound redefinition of family, gender relationships, sexuality, and, thus, personality. Both for structural reasons (linked to the informational economy), and because of the impact of social movements (feminism, women's struggles, and sexual liberation), patriarchal authority is challenged in most of the world, albeit under various forms and intensity depending upon cultural/institutional contexts. The future of the family is uncertain, but the future of patriarchalism is not: it can only survive under the protection of authoritarian states and religious fundamentalism. As the studies presented in volume II, chapter 4 show, in open societies the patriarchal family is in deep crisis, while new embryos of egalitarian families are still struggling against the old world of interests, prejudices, and fears. Networks of people (particularly for women) increasingly substitute for nuclear families as primary forms of emotional and material support. Individuals and their children follow a pattern of sequential family, and non-family, personal arrangements throughout their lives. And while there is a rapidly growing trend of fathers' involvement with their children, women – whether single or living with each other – and their children, are an increasingly prevalent form of reproduction of society, thus fundamentally modifying patterns of socialization. Admittedly, I am taking as my main point of reference the experience of the United States, and of most of Western Europe (with southern Europe being, to some extent, an exception in the European context). Yet, as I argued in volume II, it can be shown that women's struggles, whether or not avowedly feminist, are spreading throughout the world, thus undermining patriarchalism in the family, in the economy, and in the institutions of society. I consider it very likely that, with the spread of women's struggles, and with women's increasing awareness of their oppression, their collective challenge to the patriarchal order will generalize, inducing processes of crisis in traditional family structures. I do see signs of a recomposition of the family, as millions of men appear to be ready to give up their privileges and work together with women to find new forms of loving, sharing, and having children. Indeed, I believe that rebuilding families under egalitarian forms is the necessary foundation for rebuilding society from the bottom up. Families are more than ever the providers of psychological security and material well-being to people, in a world characterized by individualization of work, destructuring of civil society, and delegitimation of the state. Yet the transition to new forms of family implies a fundamental redefinition of gender relationships in society at large, and thus of sexuality. Because personality systems are shaped by family and sexuality, they are also in a state of flux. I characterized such a state as flexible personalities, able to engage endlessly in the reconstruction of the self, rather than to define the self through adaptation to what were once conventional social roles, which are no longer viable and which have thus ceased to make sense. *The most fundamental transformation of relationships of experience in the Information Age is their transition to a pattern of social interaction constructed, primarily, by the actual experience of the relationship.* Nowadays, people produce forms of sociability, rather than follow models of behavior.

Changes in relationships of production, power, and experience converge toward *the transformation of material foundations of social life, space, and time.* The space of flows of the Information Age dominates the space of places of people's cultures. Timeless time as the social tendency toward the annihilation of time by technology supersedes the clock time logic of the industrial era. Capital circulates, power rules, and electronic communication swirls through flows of exchanges between selected, distant locales, while fragmented experience remains confined to places. Technology compresses time to a few, random instants, thus de-sequencing society, and de-historicizing history. By secluding power in the space of flows, allowing capital to escape from time, and dissolving history in the culture of the ephemeral, the network society disembodies social relationships, introducing the culture of real virtuality. Let me explain.

Throughout history, cultures have been generated by people sharing space and time, under conditions determined by relationships of production, power, and experience, and modified by their projects, fighting each other to impose over society their values and goals. Thus, spatio-temporal configurations were critical for the meaning of each culture, and for their differential evolution. Under the informational paradigm, a new culture has emerged from the superseding of places and the annihilation of time by the space of flows and by timeless time: *the culture of real virtuality*. As presented in volume I, chapter 5, by real virtuality I mean a system in which reality itself (that is, people's material/symbolic existence) is fully immersed in a virtual image setting, in the world of make believe, in which symbols are not just metaphors, but comprise the actual experience. This is not the consequence of electronic media, although they are the indispensable instruments of expression in the new culture. The material basis that explains why real virtuality is able to take over people's imagination and systems of representation is their livelihood in the space of flows and in timeless time. On the one hand, dominant functions and values in society are organized in simultaneity without contiguity; that is, in flows of information that escape from the experience embodied in any locale. On the other hand, dominant values and interests are constructed without reference to either past or future, in the timeless landscape of computer networks and electronic media, where all expressions are either instantaneous, or without predictable sequencing. All expressions from all times and from all spaces are mixed in the same hypertext, constantly rearranged, and communicated at any time, anywhere, depending on the interests of senders and the moods of receivers. This virtuality is our reality because it is within the framework of these timeless, placeless, symbolic systems that we construct the categories, and evoke the images, that shape behavior, induce politics, nurture dreams, and trigger nightmares.

This is the new social structure of the Information Age, which I call *the network society* because it is made up of networks of production, power, and experience, which construct a culture of virtuality in the global flows that transcend time and space. Not all dimensions and institutions of society follow the logic of the network society, in the same way that industrial societies included for a long time many pre-industrial forms of human existence. But all societies in the Information Age are indeed penetrated, with different intensity, by the pervasive logic of the network society, whose dynamic expansion gradually absorbs and subdues pre-existing social forms.

The network society, as any other social structure, is not absent of contradictions, social conflicts, and challenges from alternative forms of social organization. But these challenges are induced by the characteristics of the network society, and, thus, they are sharply distinct from those of the industrial era. Accordingly, they are incarnated by different subjects, even though these subjects often work with historical materials provided by the values and organizations inherited from industrial capitalism and statism.

The understanding of our world requires the simultaneous analysis of the network society, and of its conflictive challenges. The historical law that where there is domination there is resistance continues to apply. But it requires an analytical effort to identify who the challengers are of the processes of domination enacted by the immaterial, yet powerful, flows of the network society.

The New Avenues of Social Change

According to observation, and as recorded in volume II, social challenges against patterns of domination in the network society generally take the form of constructing autonomous identities. These identities are external to the organizing principles of the network society. Against the worshipping of technology, the power of flows, and the logic of markets, they oppose their being, their beliefs, and their bequest. What is characteristic of social movements and cultural projects built around identities in the Information Age is that they do not originate within the institutions of civil society. They introduce, from the outset, an alternative social logic, distinct from the principles of performance around which dominant institutions of society are built. In the industrial era, the labor movement fought fiercely against capital. Capital and labor had, however, shared the goals and values of industrialization – productivity and material progress – each seeking to control its development and for a larger share of its harvest. In the end they reached a social pact. In the Information Age, the prevailing logic of dominant, global networks is so pervasive and so penetrating that the only way out of their domination appears to be out of these networks, and to reconstruct meaning on the basis of an entirely distinct system of values and beliefs. This is the case for communes of resistance identity I have identified. Religious fundamentalism does not reject technology, but puts it at the service of God's Law, to which all institutions and purposes must submit, without possible bargaining. Nationalism, localism, ethnic separatism, and cultural communes break up with society at large, and rebuild its institutions not from the bottom up, but from the inside out, the "who we are" versus those who do not belong.

Even proactive movements, which aim at transforming the overall pattern of social relationships among people, such as feminism, or among people and nature, such as environmentalism, start from the rejection of basic principles on which our societies are constructed: patriarchalism, productivism. Naturally, there are all kind of nuances in the practice of social movements, as I tried to make clear in volume II, but, quite fundamentally, their principles of self-definition, at the source of their existence, represent a break with institutionalized social logic. Should institutions of society, economy, and culture truly accept feminism and environmentalism, they would be essentially transformed. Using an old word, it would be a revolution.

The strength of identity-based social movements is their autonomy *vis-à-vis* the institutions of the state, the logic of capital, and the seduction of technology. It is hard to co-opt them, although certainly some of their participants may be co-opted. Even in defeat, their resistance and projects impact and change society, as I have been able to show in a number of selected cases, presented in volume II. Societies of the Information Age cannot be reduced to the structure and dynamics of the network society. Following my scanning of our world, it appears that our societies are constituted by the interaction between the "net" and the "self," between the network society and the power of identity.

Yet, the fundamental problem raised by processes of social change that are primarily external to the institutions and values of society, as it is, is that they may fragment rather than reconstitute society. Instead of transformed institutions, we would have communes of all sorts. Instead of social classes, we would witness the rise of tribes. And instead of conflictive interaction between the functions of the space of flows and the meaning of the space of places, we may observe the retrenchment of dominant global elites in immaterial palaces made out of communication networks and information flows. Meanwhile, people's experience would remain confined to multiple, segregated locales, subdued in their existence and fragmented in their consciousness. With no Winter Palace to be seized, outbursts of revolt may implode, transformed into everyday senseless violence.

The reconstruction of society's institutions by cultural social movements, bringing technology under the control of people's needs and desires, seems to require a long march from the communes built around resistance identity to the heights of new project identities, sprouting from the values nurtured in these communes.

Examples of such processes, as observed in contemporary social movements and politics, are the construction of new, egalitarian families; the widespread acceptance of the concept of sustainable development, building intergenerational solidarity into the new model of economic growth; and the universal mobilization in defense of human rights wherever the defense has to be taken up. For this transition to be undertaken, from resistance identity to project identity, a new politics will have to emerge. This will be a cultural politics that starts from the premise that informational politics is predominantly enacted in the space of media, and fights with symbols, yet connects to values and issues that spring from people's life experience in the Information Age.

Beyond this Millennium

Throughout the pages of this book I have adamantly refused to indulge in futurology, staying as close as possible to observation of what we know the Information Age brings to us, as constituted in the last lapse of the twentieth century. In concluding this book, however, with the reader's benevolence, I would like to elaborate, for the span of just a few paragraphs, on some trends that may configure society in the early twenty-first century. This is simply an attempt to bring a dynamic, prospective dimension to this synthesis of findings and hypotheses.

The information technology revolution will accentuate its transformative potential. The twenty-first century will be marked by the completion of a global information superhighway, and by mobile telecommunication and computing power, thus decentralizing and diffusing the power of information, delivering the promise of multimedia, and enhancing the joy of interactive communication. Electronic communication networks will constitute the backbone of our lives. In addition, it will be the century of the full flowering of the genetic revolution. For the first time, our species will penetrate the secrets of life, and will be able to perform substantial manipulations of living matter. While this will trigger a dramatic debate on the social and environmental consequences of this capacity, the possibilities open to us are truly extraordinary. Prudently used, the genetic revolution may heal, fight pollution, improve life, and save time and effort from survival, so as to give us the chance to explore the largely unknown frontier of spirituality. Yet, if we make the same mistakes as we made in the twentieth century, using technology and industrialization to massacre each other in atrocious wars, with our new technological power we may well end life on the planet. It turned out to be relatively easy to stop short of nuclear holocaust because of the centralized control of nuclear energy and weaponry. But new genetic technologies are pervasive, their mutating impacts not fully controllable, and their institutional control much more decentralized. To prevent the evil effects of biological revolution we need not only responsible governments, but a responsible, educated society. Which way we go will depend on society's institutions, on people's values, and on the consciousness and determination of new social actors to shape and control their own destiny. Let me briefly review these prospects by pinpointing some major developments in the economy, polity, and culture.

The maturing of the informational economy, and the diffusion and proper use of information technology as a system, will likely unleash the productivity potential of this technological revolution. This will be made visible by changes in statistical accounting, when twentieth-century categories and procedures, already manifestly inadequate, will be replaced by new concepts able to measure the new economy. There is no question that the twenty-first century will witness the rise of an extraordinarily productive system by historical standards. Human labor will produce more and better with considerably less effort. Mental work will replace physical effort in the most productive sectors of the economy. However, the sharing of this wealth will depend for individuals on their access to education and, for society as a whole, on social organization, politics, and policies.

The global economy will expand in the twenty-first century, using substantial increases in the power of telecommunications and information processing. It will penetrate all countries, all territories, all cultures, all communication flows, and all financial networks, relentlessly scanning the planet for new opportunities for profit-making. But it will do so selectively, linking valuable segments and discarding used up, or irrelevant, locales and people. The territorial unevenness of production will result in an extraordinary geography of differential value-making that will sharply contrast countries, regions, and metropolitan areas. Valuable locales and people will be found everywhere, even in Sub-Saharan Africa, as I have argued in this volume. But switched-off territories and people will also be found everywhere, albeit in different proportions. The planet is being segmented into clearly distinct spaces, defined by different time regimes.

From the excluded segments of humankind, two different reactions can be expected. On the one hand, there will be a sharp increase in the operation of what I call the "perverse connection," that is, playing the game of global capitalism with different rules. The global criminal economy, whose profile and dynamics I tried to identify in chapter 3 of this volume, will be a fundamental feature of the twenty-first century, and its economic, political, and cultural influence will penetrate all spheres of life. The question is not whether our societies will be able to eliminate the criminal networks, but, rather, whether criminal networks will not end up controlling a substantial share of our economy, of our institutions, and of our everyday life.

There is another reaction against social exclusion and economic irrelevance that I am convinced will play an essential role in the twenty-first century: the exclusion of the excluders by the excluded. Because the whole world is, and will increasingly be, intertwined in the basic structures of life, under the logic of the network society, opting out by people and countries will not be a peaceful withdrawal. It takes, and it will take, the form of fundamentalist affirmation of an alternative set of values and principles of existence, under which no coexistence is possible with the evil system that so deeply damages people's lives. As I write, in the streets of Kabul women are beaten for improper dress by the courageous warriors of the Taliban. This is not in accordance with the humanistic teachings of Islam. There is however, as analyzed in volume II, an explosion of fundamentalist movements that take up the Qū'ran, the Bible, or any holy text, to interpret it and use it, as a banner of their despair and a weapon of their rage. Fundamentalisms of different kinds and from different sources will represent the most daring, uncompromising challenge to one-sided domination of informational, global capitalism. Their potential access to weapons of mass extermination casts a giant shadow on the optimistic prospects of the Information Age.

Nation-states will survive, but not so their sovereignty. They will band together in multilateral networks, with a variable geometry of commitments, responsibilities, alliances, and subordinations. The most notable multilateral construction will be the European Union, bringing together the technological and economic resources of most, but not all, European countries: Russia is likely to be left out, out of the West's historical fears, and Switzerland needs to be off limits to keep its job as the world's banker. But the European Union, for the time being, does not embody a historical project of building a European society. It is, essentially, a defensive construction on behalf of European civilization to avoid becoming an economic colony of Asians and Americans. European nation-states will remain and will bargain endlessly for their individual interests within the framework of European institutions, which they will need but, in spite of their federalist rhetoric, neither Europeans nor their governments will cherish. Europe's unofficial anthem (Beethoven's "Hymn of Joy") is universal, but its German accent may become more marked.

The global economy will be governed by a set of multilateral institutions, networked among themselves. At the core of this network is the G7 countries club, perhaps with a few additional members, and its executive arms, the International Monetary Fund, and the World Bank, charged with regulation and intervention on behalf of the ground rules of global capitalism. Technocrats and bureaucrats of these, and similar, international economic institutions will add their own dose of neoliberal ideology and professional expertise in the implementation of their broad mandate. Informal gatherings, such as the Davos meetings, or their equivalents, will help to create the cultural/personal glue of the global elite.

Global geopolitics will also be managed by multilateralism, with the United Nations, and regional international institutions ASEAN, OEA, or OAU, playing an increasing role in the management of international or even national conflicts. They will increasingly use security alliances, such as NATO, in the enforcement of their decisions. When necessary, *ad hoc* international police forces will be created to intervene in trouble spots.

Global security matters will be likely to be dominated by three main issues, if the analyses contained in this book are proved correct. The first is the rising tension in the Pacific, as China asserts its global power, Japan goes into another round of national paranoia, and Korea, Indonesia, and India react to both. The second is the resurgence of Russian power, not only as a nuclear superpower, but as a stronger nation, no longer tolerating humiliation. The conditions under which post-Communist Russia will be or will not be brought into the multilateral system of global co-management will determine the future geometry of security alignments. The third security issue is probably the most decisive of all, and will be likely to condition safety for the world at large for a long period of time. It refers to the new forms of warfare that will be used by individuals, organizations, and states, strong in their convictions, weak in their military means, but able to access new technologies of destruction, as well as find the vulnerable spots of our societies. Criminal gangs may also resort to high-intensity confrontation when they see no other option, as Colombia experienced in the 1990s. Global or local terrorism is already considered a major threat worldwide at the turn of the millennium. But, I believe this is only a modest beginning. Increasing technological sophistication leads to two trends converging toward outright terror: on the one hand, a small determined group, well financed, and well informed, can devastate entire cities, or strike at nerve centers of our livelihood; on the other hand, the infrastructure of our everyday life, from energy to transportation to water supply, has become so complex, and so intertwined, that its vulnerability has increased exponentially. While new technologies help security systems, they also make our daily life more exposed. The price for increased protection will be to live within a system of electronic locks, alarms systems, and on-line police patrols. It will also mean to grow up in fear. It is probably not different from the experience of most children in history. It is also a measure of the relativity of human progress.

Geopolitics will also be increasingly dominated by a fundamental contradiction between the multilateralism of decision-making and the unilateralism of military implementation of these decisions. This is because, after the demise of the Soviet Union, and the technological backwardness of the new Russia, the United States is, and will be for the foreseeable future, the only military superpower. Thus, most security decisions will have to be either implemented or supported by the United States to be truly effective or credible. The European Union, for all its arrogant talk, gave a clear demonstration of its operational inability to act alone in the Balkans. Japan has forbidden itself to build an army, and the pacifist feeling in the country runs deeper than the support for ultra-nationalist provocations. Outside the OECD, only China and India may have enough technological and military might to access global power in the foreseeable future, but certainly not to match the United States or even Russia. So, excepting the unlikely hypothesis of an extraordinary Chinese military build up, for which China simply does not yet have the technological capacity, the world is left with one superpower, the United States. Under such conditions, various security alliances will have to rely on American forces. But the US is confronted with such deep domestic social problems that it will certainly not have the means, nor the political support, to exercise such a power if the security of its citizens is not under direct threat, as American presidents discovered several times in the 1990s. With the Cold War forgotten, and no credible equivalent "new Cold War" looming on the horizon, the only way America may keep its military status is to lend its forces to the global security system. And have other countries pay for it. This is the ultimate twist of multilateralism, and the most striking illustration of the lost sovereignty of the nation-state.

The state does not disappear, though. It is simply downsized in the Information Age. It proliferates under the form of local and regional governments, which dot the world with their projects, build up constituencies, and negotiate with national governments, multinational corporations, and international agencies. The era of globalization of the economy is also the era of localization of polity. What local and regional governments lack in power and resources, they make up in flexibility and networking. They are the only match, if any, to the dynamism of global networks of wealth and information.

As for people, they are, and will be, increasingly distant from the halls of power, and disaffected from the crumbling institutions of civil society. They will be individualized in their work and lives, constructing their own meaning on the basis of their own experience, and, if they are lucky, reconstructing their family, their rock in this swirling ocean of unknown flows and uncontrolled networks. When subjected to collective threats, they will build communal havens, whence prophets may proclaim the coming of new gods.

The twenty-first century will not be a dark age. Nor will it deliver to most people the bounties promised by the most extraordinary technological revolution in history. Rather, it may well be characterized by informed bewilderment.

What is to be Done?

Each time an intellectual has tried to answer this question, and seriously implement the answer, catastrophe has ensued. This was particularly the case with a certain Ulianov in 1902. Thus, while certainly not pretending to qualify for this comparison, I shall abstain from suggesting any cure for the ills of our world. But since I do feel concerned by what I have seen on my journey across this early landscape of the Information Age, I would like to explain my abstention, writing in the first person, but thinking of my generation and of my political culture.

I come from a time and a tradition, the political left of the industrial era, obsessed by the inscription on Marx's tomb at Highgate, his (and Engel's) eleventh thesis on Feuerbach. Transformative political action was the ultimate goal of a truly meaningful intellectual endeavor. I still believe that there is considerable generosity in this attitude, certainly less selfish than the orderly pursuit of bureaucratic academic careers, undisturbed by the labors of people around the world. And, on the whole, I do not think that a classification between right-wing and left-wing intellectuals and social scientists would yield significant differences in scholarly quality between the two groups. After all, conservative intellectuals also went into political action, as much as the left did, often with little tolerance for their foes. So, the issue is not that political commitment prevents, or distorts, intellectual creativity. Many of us have learned, over the years, to live with the tension, and the contradiction, between what we find and what we would like to happen. I consider social action and political projects to be essential in the betterment of a society that clearly needs change and hope. And I do hope that this book, by raising some questions and providing empirical and theoretical elements to treat them, may contribute to informed social action in the pursuit of social change. In this sense, I am not, and I do not want to be, a neutral, detached observer of the human drama.

However, I have seen so much misled sacrifice, so many dead ends induced by ideology, and such horrors provoked by artificial paradises of dogmatic politics that I want to convey a salutary reaction against trying to frame political practice in accordance with social theory, or, for that matter, with ideology. Theory and research, in general as well as in this book, should be considered as a means for understanding our world, and should be judged exclusively on their accuracy, rigor, and relevance. How these tools are used, and for what purpose, should be the exclusive prerogative of social actors themselves, in specific social contexts, and on behalf of their values and interests. No more meta-politics, no more "*maîtres à penser*," and no more intellectuals pretending to be so. The most fundamental political liberation is for people to free themselves from uncritical adherence to theoretical or ideological schemes, to construct their practice on the basis of their experience, while using whatever information or analysis is available to them, from a variety of sources. In the twentieth century, philosophers tried to change the world. In the twenty-first century, it is time for them to interpret it differently. Hence my circumspection, which is not indifference, about a world troubled by its own promise.

Finale

The promise of the Information Age is the unleashing of unprecedented productive capacity by the power of the mind. I think, therefore I produce. In so doing, we will have the leisure to experiment with spirituality, and the opportunity of reconciliation with nature, without sacrificing the material well-being of our children. The dream of the Enlightenment, that reason and science would solve the problems of humankind, is within reach. Yet there is an extraordinary gap between our technological overdevelopment and our social underdevelopment. Our economy, society, and culture are built on interests, values, institutions, and systems of representation that, by and large, limit collective creativity, confiscate the harvest of information technology, and deviate our energy into self-destructive confrontation. This state of affairs must not be. There is no eternal evil in human nature. There is nothing that cannot be changed by conscious, purposive social action, provided with information, and supported by legitimacy. If people are informed, active, and communicate throughout the world; if business assumes its social responsibility; if the media become the messengers, rather than the message; if political actors react against cynicism, and restore belief in democracy; if culture is reconstructed from experience; if humankind feels the solidarity of the species throughout the globe; if we assert intergenerational solidarity by living in harmony with nature; if we depart for the exploration of our inner self, having made peace among ourselves. If all this is made possible by our informed, conscious, shared decision, while there is still time, maybe then, we may, at last, be able to live and let live, love and be loved.

I have exhausted my words. Thus, I will borrow, for the last time, from Pablo Neruda:

Por mi parte y tu parte, cumplimos, compartimos esperanzas e inviernos;	*For my part and yours, we comply, we shared our hopes and winters;*
y fuimos heridos no solo por los enemigos mortales	*and we have been wounded not only by mortal enemies*
sino por mortales amigos (y esto pareció más amargo),	*but by mortal friends (that seemed all the more bitter),*
pero no me parece más dulce mi pan o mi libro entretanto;	*but bread does not seem to taste sweeter, nor my book, in the meantime;*
agregamos viviendo la cifra que falta al dolor,	*living, we supply the statistics that pain still lacks,*
y seguimos amando el amor y con nuestra directa conducta	*we go on loving love and in our blunt way*
enterramos a los mentirosos y vivimos con los verdaderos.	*we bury the liars and live among the truth-tellers.*

Summary of Contents of Volumes I and II

Throughout this third volume of *The Information Age: Economy, Society and Culture*, reference has been made to the themes presented in Volumes I and II. An outline of their contents is given below. The conclusion to this volume stands as a conclusion to the three-volume book.

References

Adam, Lishan (1996) "Africa on the line?" *Ceres: the FAO Review*, 158, March–April.

Adams, David (1997) "Russian Mafia in Miami: 'Redfellas' linked to plan to smuggle coke in a submarine", *San Francisco Examiner*, March 9: 3.

Adekanye, J. Bayo (1995) "Structural adjustment, democratization and rising ethnic tensions in Africa", *Development and Change*, 26 (2): 355–74.

Adepoju, Aderanti (ed.) (1993) *The Impact of Structural Adjustment on the Population of Africa: the Implications for Education, Health and Employment*, Portsmouth, NH:United Nations Population Fund and Heinemann.

Afanasiev, V.G. (1972) *Nauchno-teknicheskaya revolyutsiya, upravleniye, obrazovaniye*, Moscow: Nauka.

Agamirzian, Igor (1991) "Computing in the USSR", *Byte*, April, pp. 120–9.

Aganbegyan, Abel (1988) *The Economic Challenge of Perestroika*, Bloomington, Ind.: Indiana University Press.

—— (1988-90) *Perestroika Annual*, vols 1–3. Washington, DC: Brassey.

—— (1989) *Inside Perestroika: The Future of the Soviet Economy*, New York: Harper and Row.

Agbese, Pita Ogaba (1996) "The military as an obstacle to the democratization enterprise: towards an agenda for permanent military disengagement from politics in Nigeria", *Journal of Asian and African Studies*, 31 (1–2): 82–98.

Ahn, Seung-Joon (1994) *From State to Community. Rethinking South Korean Modernization*, Littleton, Colo.: Aigis

Aina, Tade Akin (1993) "Development theory and Africa's lost decade: critical reflections on Africa's crisis and current trends in development thinking and practice", in Margareta Von Troil (ed.), *Changing Paradigms in Development – South, East and West*, Uppsala: Nordiska Afrikainstitutet, pp. 11–26

Alexander, A.J. (1990) *The Conversion of the Soviet Defense Industry*, Santa Monica, CA: Rand Corporation.

Allen, G.C. (1981) *The Japanese Economy*, New York: St Martin's Press.

Alonso Zaldivar, Carlos (1996) "Variaciones sobre un mundo en cambio", Madrid: Alianza

Al-Sayyad, Nezar and Castells, Manuel (eds) (2000) *Multicultural Europe: Islam and European Identity*, New York: University Press of America.

Alvarez Gonzalez, Maria Isabel (1993) "La reconversion del complejo industrial-militar sovietico", unpublished thesis, Madrid: Universidad Autonoma de Madrid, Departamento de Estructura Economica.

Amman, R. and Cooper, J. (1986) *Technical Progress and Soviet Economic Development*, Oxford: Blackwell.

Amsdem, Alice (1979) "Taiwan's economic history: a case of etatisme and a challenge to dependency theory", *Modern China*, 5 (3): 341–80.

—— (1985) "The state and Taiwan's economic development", in Peter Evans et al. (eds), *Bringing the State Back In*, Cambridge: Cambridge University Press.

—— (1989) *Asia's Next Giant: South Korea and Late Industrialization*, New York: Oxford University Press.

—— (1992) "A theory of government intervention in late industrialization", in Louis Putterman and Dietrich Rueschemeyer (eds), *State and Market in Development: Synergy or Rivalry?*, Boulder, Colo.: Lynne Rienner.

Andrew, Christopher and Gordievsky, Oleg (1990) *KGB: the Inside Story of its Foreign Operation from Lenin to Gorbachev*, London: Hodder and Stoughton.

Anonymous (1984) "The Novosibirsk Report", April 1983, translated into English in *Survey*, 28 (1): 88–108.

Ansell, Christopher K. and Parsons, Craig (1995) *Organizational Trajectories of Administrative States: Britain, France, and the US Compared*, Berkeley: University of California, Center for Western European Studies, Working Paper.

Antonov-Ovseyenko, Anton (1981) *The Time of Stalin*, New York: Harper and Row.

Aoyama, Yuko (1996) "From Fortress Japan to global networks: the emergence of network multinationals among Japanese electronics industry in the 1990s", unpublished PhD thesis, Berkeley: University of California, Department of City and Regional Planning.

Appelbaum, Richard P. and Henderson, Jeffrey (eds) (1992) *States and Development in the Asian Pacific Rim*, London: Sage.

Arbex, Jorge (1993) *Narcotrafico: um jogo de poder nas Americas*, Sao Paulo: Editora Moderna.

Arlacchi, Pino (1995) "The Mafia, Cosa Nostra, and Italian institutions", in Salvatore Secchi (ed.), *Deconstructing Italy: Italy in the Nineties*, Berkeley: University of California, International and Area Studies Series.

Arnedy, B. Alejandro (1990) *El narcotrafico en America Latina: sus conexiones, hombres y rutas*, Cordoba: Marcos Lerner Editora.

Arrieta, Carlos G. et al. (eds) (1990) *Narcotrafico en Colombia: dimensiones politicas, economicas, juridicas e internacionales*, Bogota: TM Editores.

Asahi Shimbun (1995) *Japan Almanac 1995*, Tokyo: Asahi Shimbun Publishing Company.

Aslund, Anders (1989) *Gorbachev's Struggle for Economic Reform*, Ithaca, NY: Cornell University Press.

Audigier, P. (1989) "Le poids des depenses de defense sur l'économie sovietique", *Defense Nationale*, May.

Azocar Alcala, Gustavo (1994) *Los barones de la droga: la historia del narcotrafico en Venezuela*, Caracas: Alfadil Ediciones.

Bagley, Bruce, Bonilla, Adrian and Paez, Alexei (eds) (1991) *La economía politica del narcotrafico: el caso ecuatoriano*, Quito: FLACSO.

Barnett, Tony and Blaikie, Piers (1992) *AIDS in Africa: its Present and Future Impact*, London: Balhaven Press.

Bastias, Maria Veronica (1993) "El salario del miedo: narcotrafico en America Latina", Buenos Aires: SERPAJ-AL

Bates, R. (1988) "Governments and agricultural markets in Africa", in R. Bates (ed.), *Toward a Political Economy of Development: a Rational Choice Perspective*, Berkeley: University of California Press.

Bates, Timothy and Dunham, Constance (1993) "Asian-American success in self-employment", *Economic Development Quarterly*, 7(2) 199–214.

Bauer, John and Mason, Andrew (1992), "The distribution of income and wealth in Japan", *Review of Income and Wealth*, 38(4): 403–28.

Bayart, Jean-François (1989) *L'état en Afrique: la politique du ventre*, Paris: Librairie Artheme Fayard. (English trans., London: Longman, 1993).

Baydar, Nazli, Brooks-Gunn, Jeanne and Furstenberg, Frank (1993) "Early warning signs of functional illiteracy: predictors in childhood and adolescence", *Child Development*, 63(3).

Beasley, W.G. (1990) *The Rise of Modern Japan*, London: Weidenfeld and Nicolson.

Beaty, Jonathan (1994) "Russia's yard sale", *Time*, April 18: 52–5.

Bellamy, Carol (director) (1996) *The State of the World's Children 1996*, New York: Oxford University Press for UNICEF.

Benner, Christopher (1994) "South Africa's informal economy: reflections on institutional change and socio-economic transformation", unpublished research seminar paper for geography 253, Berkeley: University of California.

——, Brownstein, Bob and Dean, Amy (1999) *Walking the Lifelong Tightrope: Negotiating Work in the New Economy*, San Jose, CA: Working Partnerships USA/Washington, DC: Economic Policy Institute.

Bennett, Vanora (1997) "Interchangeable cops and robbers: Russian police moonlighting for organized crime", *San Francisco Chronicle*, April 7: 12.

Bergson, Abram (1978) *Productivity and the Social System: the USSR and the West*, Cambridge, MA: Harvard University Press.

Berliner, J.S. (1986) *The Innovation Decision in Soviet Industry*, Cambridge, MA: MIT Press.

Bernardez, Julio (1995) *Europa: entre el timo y el mito*, Madrid: Temas de Hoy.

Berry, Sara (1993) "Coping with confusion: African farmers' responses to economic instability in the 1970s and 1980s", in Callaghy and Ravenhill, (eds), pp. 248–78.

Berryman, Sue (1994) "The role of literacy in the wealth of individuals and nations", *NCAL Technical Report TR94-13*, Philadelphia: National Center for Adult Literacy.

Betancourt, Dario and Garcia, Martha L. (1994) *Contrabandistas, marimberos y mafiosos: historia social de la mafia colombiana (1965–1992)*, Bogota; TM Editores.

Beyer, Dorianne (1996) "Child prostitution in Latin America", in US Department of Labor, Bureau of International Labor Affairs, *Forced Labor: the Prostitution of Children, Symposium Proceedings*, Washington DC: US Department of Labor.

Bianchi, Patrizio, Carnoy, Martin and Castells, Manuel (1988) "Economic modernization and technology transfer in the People's Republic of China", Stanford: Stanford University, Center for Educational Research at Stanford, Research Monograph.

Bidelux, Robert and Taylor, Richard (eds) (1996) *European Integration and Disintegration: East and West*, London: Routledge.

Black, Maggie (1995) *In the Twilight Zone: Child Workers in the Hotel, Tourism, and Catering Industry*, Geneva: International Labour Office.

Blomstrom, Magnus and Lundhal, Mats (eds) (1993) *Economic Crisis in Africa: Perspectives and Policy Responses*, London: Routledge.

Blyakhman, L. and Shkaratan, O. (1977) *Man at Work: the Scientific and Technological Revolution, the Soviet Working Class and Intelligentsia*, Moscow: Progress.

Boahene, K. (1996) "The IXth International Conference on AIDS and STD in Africa", *AIDS Care*, 8(5): 609–16.

Bohlen, Celestine (1993) "The Kremlin's latest intrigue shows how real life imitates James Bond", *The New York Times*, November 23.

—— (1994) "Organized crime has Russia by the throat", *The New York Times*, October 13.

Bonet, Pilar (1993) "El laberinto ruso", *El País Semanal*, December 12.

—— (1994) "La mafia rusa desafia al gobierno de Yeltsin con el uso de cochesbomba", *El País*, June 9.

Bonner, Raymond and O'Brien, Timothy L. (1999) "Activity at bank raises suspicions of Russia mob tie," *The New York Times*, August 19: A1–A6.

Booth, Martin (1991) *The Triads: the Growing Global Threat from the Chinese Criminal Societies*, New York: St Martin's Press.

Borja, Jordi (1992) *Estrategias de desarrollo e internacionalizacion de las ciudades europeas: las redes de ciudades*, Report to the European Community, Directorate General XVI, Barcelona: Consultores Europeos Asociados.

—— (1996) "Ciudadanos europeos?", *El País*, October 31: 12.

—— and Castells, Manuel (1997) *Local and Global: the Management of Cities in the Information Age*, London: Earthscan.

Bourgois, P. (1995) "The political economy of resistance and self-destruction in the crack economy: an ethnographic perspective", *Annals of the New York Academy of Sciences*, 749: 97–118.

—— and Dunlap, E. (1993) "Exorcising sex-for-crack: an ethnographic perspective from Harlem", in P. Bourgois and E. Dunlap (eds), *Crack Pipe as*

Pimp: an Ethnographic Investigation of Sex-for-Crack Exchange, New York: Lexington.

Bowles, Paul and White, Gordon (1993) *The Political Economy of China's Financial Reforms*, Boulder, Colo.: Westview Press.

Breslauer, George W. (1990) "Soviet economic reforms since Stalin: ideology, politics, and learning", *Soviet Economy*, 6(3): 252–80.

Brown, Phillip and Crompton, Rosemary (eds) (1994) *Economic Restructuring and Social Exclusion*, London: UCL Press.

Bull, Hedley (1977) *The Anarchical Society: a Study of Order in World Politics*, London: Macmillan.

Business Week (1996) "Helping the Russian Mafia help itself", December 9: 58.

—— (1999a) "The prosperity gap", September 27: 92–100.

—— (1999b) "A new Japan? Special report", October 25.

Callaghy, Thomas (1993) "Political passions and economic interests: economic reform and political structure in Africa", in Thomas Callaghy and John Ravenhill (eds), pp. 463–519.

—— and Ravenhill, John (eds) (1993), *Hemmed In: Responses to Africa's Economic Decline*, New York: Columbia University Press.

Calvi, Maurizio (1992) *Figure di una battaglia: documenti e riflessioni sulla Mafia dopo l'assassinio di G. Falcone e P. Borsellino*, Bari: Edizioni Dedalo.

Camacho Guizado, Alvaro (1988) *Droga y sociedad en Colombia*, Bogota: CEREC/CIDSE-Universidad del Valle.

Campbell, C.M. and Williams, B.G. (1996) "Academic research and HIV/AIDS in South Africa", *South African Medical Journal*, 86(1): 55–63.

Carnoy, Martin (1994) *Faded Dreams*, New York: Cambridge University Press.

—— (2000) *Work, Family, and Community in the Information Age*, Cambridge, Mass.: Harvard University Press.

——, Castells, Manuel and Benner, Chris (1997) "What is happening to the US labor market?" Research report of the Russell Sage Foundation, New York.

Carrere d'Encausse, Helene (1978) *L'empire eclate*, Paris: Flammarion.

—— (1987) *Le grand defi: Bolcheviks et nations, 1917–30*, Paris: Flammarion.

—— (1991) *La fin de l'empire sovietique: le triomphe des nations*, Paris: Fayard.

Castells, Manuel (1977) *The Urban Question*, Cambridge, MA: MIT Press.

—— (1989) *The Informational City: Information Technology, Economic Restructuring, and the Urban-regional Process*, Oxford: Blackwell.

—— (1991) *La ciudad cientifica de Akademogorodok y su relacion con el desarrollo economico de Siberia*, Madrid: UAM/IUSNT, research report.

—— (1992) *La nueva revolucion rusa*, Madrid: Sistema.

—— (1996) "El futuro del Estado del Bienestar en la sociedad informacional", *Sistema*, March: 35–53.

—— and Hall, Peter (1994) *Technopoles of the World: the Making of 21st Century Industrial Complexes*, London: Routledge.

—— and Kiselyova, Emma (1998) "Russia as a network society", unpublished paper delivered at the International Conference on Russia at the

End of the Twentieth Century, organized by the Department of Slavic Studies, Stanford University, California, November.

—— and Nataluskho, Svetlana (1993) *La modernizacion tecnologica de las empresas de electronica y de telecomunicaciones en Rusia*, Madrid: UAM/IUSNT, research report.

——, Goh, Lee and Kwok, Reginald Y.W. (1990) *The Shek Kip Mei Syndrome: Economic Development and Public Housing in Hong Kong and Singapore*, London: Pion.

——, Shkaratan, Ovsei and Kolomietz, Viktor (1993) *El impacto del movimiento politico sobre las estructuras del poder en la Rusia postcomunista*, Madrid: UAM/IUSNT, research report.

Castillo, Fabio (1991) *La coca nostra*, Bogota: Editorial Documentos Periodisticos.

Catanzaro, Raimondo (1991) *Il delito come impresa: storia sociale della mafia*, Milan: Rizzoli.

Cave, Martin (1980) *Computers and Economic Planning: the Soviet Experience*, Cambridge: Cambridge University Press.

Chan, M.K. et al. (eds) (1986) *Dimensions of the Chinese and Hong Kong Labor Movement*, Hong Kong: Hong Kong Christian Industrial Committee.

Cheal, David (1996) *New Poverty: Families in Postmodern Society*, Westport CT: Greenwood Press.

Chen, Edward K.Y. (1979) *Hypergrowth in Asian Economies: A Comparative Analysis of Hong Kong, Japan, Korea, Singapore, and Taiwan*, London: Macmillan.

—— (1980) "The economic setting", in David Lethbridge (ed.), *The Business Environment of Hong Kong*, Hong Kong: Oxford University Press.

Chen, Peter S.J. (1983) *Singapore: Development Policies and Trends*, Singapore: Oxford University Press.

Cheru, Fantu (1992) *The Not So Brave New World: Problems and Prospects of Regional Integration in Post-Apartheid Southern Africa*, Johannesburg: South African Institute of International Affairs.

Chesneaux, Jean (1982) *The Chinese Labor Movement: 1919–1927*, Stanford: Stanford University Press.

Cheung, Peter (1994) "The case of Guandong in central-provincial relations", in Hao and Zhimin (eds), pp. 207–35.

Christian Science Monitor (1996) "Safeguarding the children", series of reports, August 22–September 16.

Chu, Yiu-Kong (1996) "International Triad movements: the threat of Chinese organized crime", London: Research Institute for the Study of Conflict and Terrorism, Conflict Studies Series, July/August.

Chua, Beng-Huat (1985) "Pragmatism and the People's Action Party in Singapore", *Southeast Asian Journal of Social Sciences*, 13 (2).

—— (1998) "Unmaking Asia: revenge of the real against the discursive", paper presented to the Conference on Problematising Asia, National Taiwan University, Taipei, July 3–16.

CIA, Directorate of Intelligence (1990a) *Measures of Soviet GNP in 1982 Prices*", Washington, DC: CIA.

—— (1990b) *Measuring Soviet GNP: Problems and Solutions. A Conference Report*, Washington, DC: CIA.

Clayton, Mark (1996) "In United States, Canada, new laws fail to curb demand for child sex", *Christian Science Monitor*, September 3: 11.

Clifford, Mark (1994) "Family ties: heir force", *Far Eastern Economic Review*, November 17: 78–86.

Cohen, Stephen (1974) *Bukharin and the Bolshevik Revolution*, New York: Alfred Knopf.

Cohn, Ilene and Goodwin Gill, Guy (1994) *Child Soldiers: the Roles of Children in Armed Conflict*, Oxford: Clarendon Press.

Cole, D. C. and Lyman, J.A. (1971) *Korean Development: the Interplay of Politics and Economics*, Cambridge, MA: Harvard University Press.

Collier, Paul (1995) "The marginalization of Africa", *International Labour Review*, 134(4–5): 541–57.

Colombo, Gherardo (1990) *Il riciclaggio: gli istrumenti guidiziari di controllo dei flussi monetari illeciti con le modifiche introdotte dalla nuova legge antimafia*, Milan: Giuffre Editore.

Commission on Security and Cooperation in Europe (1994) *Crime and corruption in Russia*, Briefing of the Commission, Implementation of the Helsinki Accord, Washington, DC: June.

Connolly, Kathleen, McDermid, Lea, Schiraldi, Vincent and Macallair, Dan (1996) *From Classrooms to Cell Blocks: How Prison Building Affects Higher Education and African American Enrollment*, San Francisco: Center on Juvenile and Criminal Justice.

Conquest, Robert (ed.) (1967) *Soviet Nationalities Policy in Practice*, New York: Praeger.

—— (1968) *The Great Terror*, New York: Oxford University Press.

—— (1986) *The Harvest of Sorrow*, New York: Oxford University Press.

Cook, John T. and Brown, J. Larry (1994) "Two Americas: comparisons of US child poverty in rural, inner city and suburban areas. A linear trend analysis to the year 2010", Medford, MA: Tufts University School of Nutrition, Center on Hunger, Poverty and Nutrition Policy, Working Paper No. CPP-092394.

Cooper, J. (1991) *The Soviet Defence Industry: Conversion and Reform*, London: Pinter.

da Costa Nunez, Ralph (1996) *The New Poverty: Homeless Families in America*, New York: Insight Books.

Cowell, Alan (1994) "138 nations confer on rise in global crime", *The New York Times*, November 22.

Curtis, Gerald L. (1993) *Japan's Political Transfigurations: Interpretation and Implications*, Washington, DC: Woodrow Wilson International Center for Scholars.

Davidson, Basil (1992) *The Black Man's Burden: Africa and the Crisis of the Nation-State*, New York: Times Books.

—— (1994) *A Search for Africa: History, Culture, Politics*, New York: Times Books.

De Bernieres, Louis (1991) *Senor Vivo and the Coca Lord*, New York: Morrow.

De Feo, Michael and Savona, Ernesto (1994) "Money trails: international money laundering trends and prevention/control policies", Background Paper presented at the International Conference on Preventing and Controlling Money-Laundering and the Use of the Proceeds of Crime: a Global Approach, Courmayeur, Italy, June, 18–20.

Deininger, Klaus and Squire, Lyn (1996) "A new data set measuring income inequality", *The World Bank Economic Review*, 10(3): 565–91.

Del Olmo, Rosa (1991) "La geopolitica del narcotrafico en America Latina", in *Simposio Internacional*: 29–68.

Del Vecchio, Rick (1994) "When children turn to violence", *San Francisco Chronicle*, May 11.

Dentsu Institute for Human Studies/DataFlow International (1994) *Media in Japan*, Tokyo: DataFlow International.

Desai, Padma (1987) *The Soviet Economy: Problems and Prospects*, Oxford: Blackwell.

—— (1989) *Perestroika in Perspective: the Design and Dilemmas of Soviet Reforms*, Princeton, NJ: Princeton University Press.

Deyo, Frederic (1981) *Dependent Development and Industrial Order: An Asian Case Study*, New York: Praeger.

—— (ed.) (1987a) *The Political Economy of East Asian Industrialism*, Ithaca, NY: Cornell University Press.

——(1987b) "State and labor: modes of political exclusion in East Asian development", in Deyo (ed.).

Dolven, Ben (1998) "Taiwan's trump", *Far Eastern Economic Review*, August, 6: 12–15.

Dornbusch, Robert (1998) "Asian crisis themes" (http://www/iie.com/news98-1.htm).

Doucette, Diane (1995) "The restructuring of the telecommunications industry in the former Soviet Union", unpublished PhD dissertation, Berkeley: University of California.

Drake, St Clair, and Cayton, Horace (1945) *Black Metropolis: a Study of Negro Life in a Northern City*, New York: Harcourt Brace Jovanovich, rev. edn 1962.

Drogin, Bob (1995) "Sending children to war", *Los Angeles Times*, March 26, A1–A14.

Dryakhlov, N.I. et al. (1972) *Nauchno-teknischeskaya revolyutsiya i obshchestvo*, Moscow: Nauka.

Dumaine, Brian (1993) "Illegal child labor comes back", *Fortune* 127(7), April 5.

Dumont, René (1964) *L'Afrique Noire est mal partie*, Paris: Editions du Seuil.

Eggebeen, David and Lichter, Daniel (1991) "Race, family structure, and changing poverty among American children", *American Sociological Review*, 56.

Ehringhaus, Carolyn Chase (1990) "Functional literacy assessment: issues of interpretation", *Adult Education Quarterly*, 40(4).

Eisenstodt, Gail (1998) "Japan's crash and rebirth", *World Link*, September/October: 12–16.

Ekholm, Peter and Nurmio, Aarne (1999) *Europe at the Crossroads: The Future of the EU?*, Helsinki: Sitra.

Ekholm-Friedman, Kajsa (1993) "Afro-Marxism and its disastrous effects on the economy: the Congolese case", in Blomstrom and Lundhal (eds), pp. 219–45.

Ellman, M. and Kontorovich, V. (eds) (1992) *The Disintegration of the Soviet Economic System*, London: Routledge.

Endacott, G.B. and Birch, A. (1978) *Hong Kong Eclipse*, Hong Kong: Oxford University Press.

Erlanger, Steven (1994a) "Russia's new dictatorship of crime", *The New York Times*, May 15.

—— (1994b) "A slaying puts Russian underworld on parade", *The New York Times*, April 14.

Ernst, Dieter and O'Connor, David C. (1992) *Competing in the Electronics Industry: the Experience of Newly Industrializing Economies*, Paris: OECD, Development Centre Studies.

Estefanía, Joaquin (1996) *La nueva economia: la globalizacion*, Madrid: Temas para el Debate.

—— (1997) "La paradoja insoportable", *El País Internacional*, April 14: 8.

Evans, Peter (1995) *Embedded Autonomy: States and Industrial Transformation*, Princeton, NJ: Princeton University Press.

Fainstein, Norman (1993) "Race, class and segregation: discourses about African Americans", *International Journal of Urban and Regional Research*, 17(3): 384–403.

—— and Fainstein, Susan (1996) "Urban regimes and black citizens: the economic and social impacts of black political incorporation in US cities, *International Journal of Urban and Regional Research*, 20(1): March.

Fajnzylber, Fernando (1983) *La industrializacion truncada de America Latina*, Mexico: Nueva Imagen.

Fatton Jr, Robert (1992) *Predatory Rule: State and Civil Society in Africa*, Boulder, Colo.: Lynne Rienner.

Fischer, Claude et al. (1996) *Inequality by Design*, Princeton, NJ: Princeton University Press.

Flores, Robert (1996) "Child prostitution in the United States", in US Department of Labor, Bureau of International Labor Affairs, *Forced Labor: the Prostitution of Children, Symposium Proceedings*, Washington DC: US Department of Labor.

Fontana, Josep (1994) *Europa ante el espejo*, Barcelona: Critica.

Forester, Tom (1993) *Silicon Samurai: How Japan Conquered the World's IT Industry*, Oxford: Blackwell.

Forrest, Tom (1993) *Politics and Economic Development in Nigeria*, Cambridge: Cambridge University Press.

Fortescue, Stephen (1986) *The Communist Party and Soviet Science*, Baltimore: The Johns Hopkins University Press.

Fottorino, Eric (1991) *La piste blanche: l'Afrique sous l'emprise de la drogue*, Paris: Balland.

French, Howard (1995) "Mobutu, Zaïre's 'guide', leads nation into chaos", *The New York Times*, June 10: 1.

—— (1997) "Yielding power, Mobutu flees capital: rebels prepare full take-over of Zaïre", *The New York Times*, May 17: 1.

Frimpong-Ansah, Jonathan H. (1991) *The Vampire State in Africa: the Political Economy of Decline in Ghana*, London: James Curley.

Fukui, Harushiro (1992) "The Japanese state and economic development: a profile of a nationalist-paternalist capitalist state", in Richard Appelbaum and Jeffrey Henderson (eds), *States and Development in the Asian Pacific Rim*, Newbury Park, CA: Sage, pp. 190–226.

Funken, Claus and Cooper, Penny (eds) (1995) *Old and New Poverty: the Challenge for Reform*, London: Rivers Oram Press.

Gamayunov, Igor (1994) "Oborotni", *Literaturnaya gazeta*, December 7: 13.

Gans, Herbert (1993) "From 'underclass' to 'undercaste': some observations about the future of the postindustrial economy and its major victims" *International Journal of Urban and Regional Research*, 17(3): 327–35.

—— (1995) *The War against the Poor: the Underclass and Antipoverty Policy*, New York: Basic Books.

Garcia, Miguel (1991) *Los barones de la cocaina*, Mexico, DF: Planeta.

Garcia Marquez, Gabriel (1996) *Noticia de un secuestro*, New York: Penguin.

Gelb, Joyce and Lief-Palley, Marian (eds) (1994) *Women of Japan and Korea: Continuity and Change*, Philadelphia: Temple University Press.

Gerner, Kristian and Hedlund, Stefan (1989) *Ideology and Rationality in the Soviet Model: a Legacy for Gorbachev*, London: Routledge.

Ghose, T.K. (1987) *The Banking System of Hong Kong*, Singapore: Butterworth.

Gilliard, Darrell K. and Beck, Allen J. (1996) "Prison and jail inmates, 1995", *Bulletin of the Bureau of Justice Statistics*, Washington, DC: US Department of Justice, August.

Ginsborg, Paul (ed.) (1994) *Stato dell'Italia*, Milan: Il Saggiatore/Bruno Mondadori.

Gold, Thomas (1986) *State and Society in the Taiwan Miracle*, Armonk, NY: M.E. Sharpe.

Goldman, Marshall I. (1983) *USSR in Crisis: the Failure of an Economic System*, New York: W.W. Norton.

—— (1987) *Gorbachev's Challenge: Economic Reform in the Age of High Technology*, New York: W.W. Norton.

—— (1996) "Why is the Mafia so dominant in Russia?", *Challenge*, January–February: 39–47.

Golland, E.B. (1991) *Nauchno-teknicheskii progress kak osnova uskorenia razvitia narodnogo khoziaistva*, Novosibirsk: Nauka.

Gomez, Ignacio and Giraldo, Juan Carlos (1992) *El retorno de Pablo Escobar*, Bogota: Editorial Oveja Negra.

Gootenberg, Paul (ed.) (1999) *Cocaine: Global Histories*, London: Routledge.

Gordon, Michael R. (1996) "Russia struggles in a long race to prevent an atomic theft", *The New York Times*, April 20: 1–4.

Gottschalk, Peter and Smeeding, Timothy M. (1997) "Empirical evidence on income inequality in industrialized countries", Luxembourg Income Study working paper, no. 154.

Gould, Stephen Jay (1985) "The median isn't the message", *Discover*, June: 40–2.

Granberg, Alexander (1993a) "The national and regional commodity markets in the USSR: trends and contradictions in the transition period", *Papers in Regional Science*, 72(1): 3–23.

—— (1993b) "Politika i uchenyy, kotoryy zanimayetsya ey po dolgu sluzhby", *EKO*, 4: 24–8.

—— and Spehl, H. (1989) "Regionale Wirstchaftspolitik in der UdSSR und der BRD", report to the Fourth Soviet–West German Seminar on Regional Development, Kiev, October 1–10.

Granick, David (1990) *Chinese State Enterprises: a Regional Property Rights Analysis*, Chicago: University of Chicago Press.

Green, Gordon et al. (1992) "International comparisons of earnings inequality for men in the 1980s", *Review of Income and Wealth*, 38(1): 1–15.

Greenhalgh, Susan (1988) "Families and networks in Taiwan's economic development", in Winckler and Greenhalgh (eds).

Grindle, Merilee S. (1996) *Challenging the State: Crisis and Innovation in Latin America and Africa*. Cambridge: Cambridge University Press.

Grootaert, Christiaan and Kanbur, Ravi (1995) "Child labor: a review", Washington, DC: World Bank policy research working paper no. 1454.

Grossman, Gregory (1977) "The second economy of the USSR", *Problems of Communism*, 26: 25–40.

—— (1989) "Informal personal incomes and outlays of the Soviet urban population", in Portes et al. (eds), pp. 150–72.

Gugliotta, Guy, and Leen, Jeff (1989) *Kings of Cocaine: inside the Medellin Cartel*, New York: Simon and Schuster.

Gustafson, Thane (1981) *Reform in Soviet Politics*, New York: Cambridge University Press.

Haas, Ernst B. (1958a) *The Uniting of Europe: Political, Social, and Economic Forces, 1950–57*, Stanford: Stanford University Press.

—— (1958b) "The challenge of regionalism", *International Organization*, 12(4): 440–58.

—— (1964) *Beyond the Nation-State: Functionalism and International Organization*, Stanford: Stanford University Press.

Hagedorn, John and Macon, Perry (1998) *People and Folks: Gangs, Crime, and the Underclass in a Rustbelt City*, Chicago: Lake View Press.

Hall, Tony (1995) "Let's get Africa's act together . . .", report on the UNESCO/ITU/UNECA African Regional Symposium on Telematics for Development, Addis Ababa, Ethiopia, May.

Hallinan, Joe (1994) "Angry children ready to explode", *San Francisco Examiner*, May 22.

Handelman, Stephen (1993) "The Russian *Mafiya*", *Foreign Affairs*, 73(2): 83–96.

—— (1995) *Comrade Criminal: Russia's New Mafiya*, New Haven: Yale University Press.

Hao, Jia and Zhimin, Lin (eds) (1994) *Changing Central–Local Relations in China: Reform and State Capacity*, Boulder, Colo.: Westview Press.

Harrison, Mark (1993) "Soviet economic growth since 1928: the alternative statistics of G.I. Khanin", *Europe–Asia Studies*, 45(1): 141–67.

Harvey, Robert (1994), *The Undefeated: the Rise, Fall and Rise of Greater Japan*, London: Macmillan.

Hasegawa, Koichi (1994) "A comparative study of social movements for a post-nuclear energy era in Japan and the United States", paper delivered at the 23rd World Congress of Sociology, Research Committee on Collective Behavior and Social Movements, Bielefeld, Germany, July 18–23.

Healy, Margaret (1996) "Child pornography: an international perspective", working document prepared for the World Congress against Commercial Sexual Exploitation of Children, Stockholm, Sweden, August 27–31.

Heeks, Richard (1996) *Building Software Industries in Africa*, downloaded from: http://www.sas.upenn.edu/African_Studies/Acad_Research/softw_heeks.htaml.

Henderson, Jeffrey (1998a) "Danger and opportunity in the Asian Pacific", in G. Thompson (ed.), *Economic Dynamism in the Asian Pacific*, London: Routledge, pp. 356–84.

—— (1998b) "Uneven crises: institutional foundations of East Asian economic turmoil", paper delivered at the Annual Conference of the Society for the Advancement of Socio-economics, Vienna, July, 13–16.

—— (1999) "Uneven crisis: institutional foundations of East Asian economic turmoil", *Economy and Society*, 28(3): 327–68.

——, Hama, Noriko, Eccleston, Bernie and Thompson, Grahame (1998) "Deciphering the East Asian crisis: a roundtable discussion", *Renewal*, 6(2).

Herbst, Jeffrey (1996) "Is Nigeria a viable state?" *The Washington Quarterly* 19(2) : 151–72.

Hewitt, Chet, Shorter, Andrea and Godfrey, Michael (1994) *Race and Incarceration in San Francisco, Two Years Later*, San Francisco: Center on Juvenile and Criminal Justice.

High Level Expert Group on the Information Society (HLEGIS) (1997) "The European information society", report to the European Commission: Brussels, European Commission, Directorate General V.

Hill, Christopher (ed.) (1996) *The Actors in European Foreign Policy*, London: Routledge.

Hill, Ronald J. (1985) *The Soviet Union: Politics, Economics and Society. From Lenin to Gorbachev*, London: Pinter.

Hirst, Paul and Thompson, Grahame (1996) *Globalization in Question*, Oxford: Blackwell.

Ho, H.C.Y. (1979) *The Fiscal System of Hong Kong*, London: Croom Helm.

Holzman, Franklyn D. (1976) *International Trade under Communism*, New York: Basic Books.

Hondagneu-Sotelo, Pierrette (1994) "Regulating the unregulated?: domestic workers' social networks", *Social Problems,* 41:(1).

Hong Kong Government (1967) *Kowloon Disturbances, 1966: Report of the Commission of Inquiry,* Hong Kong: Hong Kong Government.

Hope, Kempe Ronald (1995) "The socio-economic context of AIDS in Africa", *Journal of Asian and African Studies,* 30: 1–2.

—— (1996) "Growth, unemployment and poverty in Botswana", *Journal of Contemporary African Studies,* 14: 1.

Hsing, Youtien (1997) "Transnational networks of Chinese capitalists and development in local China", paper presented at the Bamboo Networks and Economic Growth in the Asia Pacific Region Research Workshop on the Work of Chinese Entrepreneur Networks, Vancouver, University of British Columbia, Institute of Asian Research, April 11–12 (unpublished in 1997).

—— (1999) *Making Capitalism in China: The Taiwan Connection,* New York: Oxford University Press.

Hutchful, Eboe (1995) "Why regimes adjust: the World Bank ponders its 'star pupil' ", *Canadian Journal of African Studies,* 29: 2.

Hutching, Raymond (1976) *Soviet Science, Technology, Design,* London: Oxford University Press.

Hutton, Will (1996) *The State We're In,* rev. edn, London: Vintage.

Ikporukpo, C.O. (1996) "Federalism, political power and the economic game: conflict over access to petroleum resources in Nigeria", *Environment and Planning C: Government and Policy,* 14: 159–77.

Ikuta, Tadahide (1995) *Kanryo: Japan's Hidden Government,* Tokyo: NHK.

Imai, Ken'ichi (1990) *Jouhon Network Shakai no Tenkai* [The development of the information network society], Tokyo: Tikuma Shobou.

Industrial Strategy Project (ISP) (1995) *Improving Manufacturing Performance in South Africa,* Cape Town/Ottawa: UCT Press and International Development Research Centre.

InfoCom Research (1995) *Information and Communications in Japan, 1995,* Tokyo: InfoCom Research.

Inoguchi, Takashi (1995) "Kanryo: the Japanese bureaucracy in history's eye", paper delivered at a conference on Crisis and Change in Japan Today, Seattle, October 20–21 (read in a revised version, supplied by the University of Tokyo, March 1996).

International Bank for Reconstruction and Development (IBRD) (1994) *Adjustment in Africa: Reforms, Results and the Road Ahead,* Oxford: Oxford University Press.

—— (1996) *World Development Report 1996: From Plan to Market,* Oxford: Oxford University Press.

International Labour Office (ILO) (1994) *World Labour Report 1994,* Geneva: ILO.

—— (1995) *World Employment Report 1995,* Geneva: ILO.

—— (1996) *Child Labour: Targeting the Intolerable,* Geneva: ILO.

Irusta Medrano, Gerardo (1992) *Narcotrafico: hablan los arrepentidos – personajes y hechos reales,* La Paz: CEDEC.

Irwin, John (1985) *The Jail: Managing the Underclass in American Society,*

Berkeley: University of California Press.

—— and Austin, James (1994) *It's about Time: America's Imprisonment Binge* Belmont, Ca: Wadsworth.

Ito, Youichi (1980) "The *Johoka Shakai* approach to the study of communication in Japan", *Keio Communication Review*, 1: 13-40.

—— (1991) "Birth of *Johoka Shakai* and *Johoka* concepts in Japan and their diffusion outside Japan", *Keio Communication Review*, 13: 3-12.

—— (1993) "How Japan modernised earlier and faster than other non-Western countries: an information sociology approach", *The Journal of Development Communication*, 4(2).

—— (1994a) "Why information now?", in Georgette Wang (ed.), *Treading Different Paths: Informationization in Asian Nations*, Norwood, NJ: Ablex.

—— (1994b) "Japan", in Georgette Wang (ed.), *Treading Different Paths: Informationization in Asian Nations*, Norwood, NJ: Ablex.

Iwao, Sumiko (1993) *The Japanese Woman*, New York: Free Press.

Izvestiya, (1994a) "Krestnye ottsy i inoplanetyane", January 27.

—— (1994b) "Rossiiskaya mafia sobiraet dos'ye na krupnykh chinovnikov i politikov", January 26: 1–2.

—— (1994c) "Ugolovnaya rossiya", October 18, 19: 1–2.

Jackson, Robert H. and Rosberg, Carl G. (1994) "The political economy of African personal rule" in David Apter, and Carl Rosberg (eds), *Political Development and the New Realism in Sub-Saharan Africa*, Charlottesville: University of Virginia Press.

Jamal, Vali (ed.) (1995) *Structural Adjustment and Rural Labour Markets in Africa*, New York: St Martin's Press for the ILO.

James, Jeffrey (1995) *The State, Technology and Industrialization in Africa*, New York: St Martin's Press.

Japan Information Processing Development Center (1994) *Informatization White Paper*, Tokyo: JIPDEC.

Jasny, N. (1961) *Soviet Industrialization, 1928–1952*, Chicago: University of Chicago Press.

Jazairy, Idriss et al. (1992) *The State of World Rural Poverty: an Inquiry into its Causes and Consequences*, New York: New York University Press.

Jensen, Leif (1991) "Secondary earner strategies and family poverty: immigrant–native differentials, 1960–1980", *International Migration Review*, 25: 1.

Jensen, Mike (1995) Draft discussion paper for UNESCO/ITU/UNECA African Regional Symposium on Telematics for Development in Addis Ababa, May, downloaded from http://www.idsc.gov.eg//aii/ddpf.htm#tele.

—— (1996) "Economic and technical issues in building Africa's information technologies", presentation to Conference on Africa and the New Information Technologies, Geneva, October 17–19.

Johnson, Chalmers (1982) *MITI and the Japanese Miracle*, Stanford: Stanford University Press.

—— (1987) "Political institutions and economic performance: the government–business relationship in Japan, South Korea, and Taiwan", in Deyo (ed.).

—— (1995) *Japan: Who Governs? The Rise of the Developmental State*, New York: W.W. Norton.

Johnson, D. Gale, and McConnell Brooks, Karen (1983) *Prospects for Soviet Agriculture in the 1980s*, Bloomington, Ind.: Indiana University Press.

Jomo, Kwame S. (1999) "International financial liberalisation and the crisis of East Asian development", Kuala Lumpur, University of Malaya, Faculty of Economics and Administration, unpublished paper.

Jones, J. (1992) *The Dispossessed: America's Underclasses from the Civil War to the Present*, New York: Basic Books.

Jowitt, Kenneth (1971) *Revolutionary Breakthroughs and National Development: the Case of Romania, 1944–65*, Berkeley: University of California Press.

Kaiser, Paul (1996) "Structural adjustment and the fragile nation: the demise of social unity in Tanzania", *Journal of Modern African Studies*, 34: 2.

Kaiser, Robert G. (1991) *Why Gorbachev Happened: his Triumphs and his Failures*, New York: Simon and Schuster.

Kaldor, Mary (1981) *The Baroque Arsenal*, New York: Hill and Wang.

Kalmanovitz, Salomon (1993) *Analisis macro-economico del narcotrafico en la economia colombiana*, Bogota: Universidad Nacional de Colombia, Facultad de Ciencias Economicas.

Kamali, A. et al. (1996) "The orphan problem: experience of a Sub-Saharan African rural population in the AIDS epidemic", *AIDS Care*, 8(5): 509–15.

Kaplan, David E. and Dubro, Alec (1986) *Yakuza: the Explosive Account of Japan's Criminal Underworld*, Menlo Park, Calif.: Addison-Wesley.

Kasarda, John D. (1990) "Urban industrial transition and the underclass", *Annals of the American Academy of Political and Social Science*, 501: 26–47.

—— (1995) "Industrial restructuring and the changing location of jobs", in Reynolds Farley (ed.), *State of the Union: America in the 1990s*, New York: Russell Sage Foundation.

Kassel, Simon and Campbell, Cathleen (1980) *The Soviet Academy of Sciences and Technological Development*, Santa Monica, CA: Rand Corporation.

Kato, Tetsuro (1984) "A preliminary note on the state in contemporary Japan", *Hitotsubashi Journal of Social Studies*, 16(1): 19–30.

—— (1987) "Der neoetatismus im heutigen Japan", *Prokla*, 66: 91–105.

Kazantsev, Sergei (1991) "Ozenka ekonomicheskogo effekta NTP v sisteme tsentralizovannogo upravleniya nauchno-tekhnicheskim progressom", in E. Golland, and T. Rybakova (eds), *Tekhnologicheskiyi progress i ekonomicheskoye razvitiye*, Novosibirsk: Nauka, pp. 162-74.

Kazuhiro, Imamura (1990) "The computer, interpersonal communication, and education in Japan", in Adriana Boscaro, Franco Gatti, and Massimo Raveri (eds), *Rethinking Japan*, Folkestone, Kent: pp. 97–106.

Keating, Michael (1995) *Nations against the State: the New Politics of Nationalism in Quebec, Catalonia, and Scotland*, New York: St Martin's Press.

Kelly, R.J. (ed.) (1986) *Organized Crime: a Global Perspective*, Totowa, NJ:

Rowman and Littlefield.

Kempster, Norman (1993) "US consider seizing vast wealth of Zaïre's Mobutu to force him out", *Los Angeles Times*, March 3.

Keohane, Robert O. and Hoffman, Stanley (1991a) "Institutional change in Europe in the 1980s", in Keohane and Hoffman (eds).

—— and —— (eds) (1991b) *The New European Community: Decision Making and Institutional Change*, Boulder, Colo.: Westview Press.

Khan, Sikander and Yoshihara, Hideki (1994) *Strategy and Performance of Foreign Companies in Japan*, Westport, CT: Quorum Books.

Khanin, G.I. (1988) "Ekonomicheskii rost: al'ternativnaya otsenka", *Kommunist* 17.

—— (1991a) *Dinamika ekonomicheskogo razvitiya SSSR*, Novosibirsk: Nauka.

—— (1991b) "Ekonomicheskii rost v SSSR v 80-e gody", *EKO*, 5.

Khazanov, Anatoly M. (1995) *After the USSR: Ethnicity, Nationalism and Politics in the Commonwealth of Independent States*, Madison: University of Wisconsin Press.

Kibria, Nazli (1994) "Household structure and family ideologies: the dynamics of immigrant economic adaptation among Vietnamese refugees", *Social Problems*, 41:1.

Kim, Jong-Cheol (1998) "Asian financial crisis in 1997: institutional incompatibility of the developmental state in global capitalism", unpublished seminar paper for Sociology 280V, Berkeley: University of California, Department of Sociology, May.

Kim, Kyong-Dong, (ed.) (1987) *Dependency Issues in Korean Development*, Seoul: Seoul National University Press.

Kim, Seung-Kuk (1987) "Class formation and labor process in Korea", in Kim (ed.).

King, Ambrose Y.C. and Lee, Rance P. (eds) (1981) *Social Life and Development in Hong Kong*, Hong Kong: Chinese University Press.

King, Roy (1994) "Russian prisons after perestroika: end of the gulag?" *British Journal of Criminology*, 34, special issue.

—— and Mike Maguire (1994) "Contexts of imprisonment: an international perspective", *British Journal of Criminology*, 34, special issue.

Kirsch, Irwin, Jungeblut, Ann, Jenkins, Lynn and Kolstad, Andrew (1993) *Adult Literacy in America: a First Look at the Results of the National Adult Literacy Survey*, Washington, DC: US Department of Education.

Kiselyova, Emma, Castells, Manuel and Granberg, Alexander (1996) *The Missing Link: Siberian Oil and Gas and the Pacific Economy*, Berkeley, CA: University of California, Institute of Urban and Regional Development, Research Monograph.

Kishima, Takako (1991) *Political Life in Japan: Democracy in a Reversible World*, Princeton, NJ: Princeton University Press.

Kleinknecht, William (1996) *The New Ethnic Mobs: the Changing Face of Organized Crime in America*, New York: The Free Press.

Koetting, Mark and Schiraldi, Vincent (1994) *Singapore West: the Incarceration of 200,000 Californians*, San Francisco: Center on Juvenile and Criminal Justice.

Kontorovich, V. (1988) "Lessons of the 1965 Soviet economic reform", *Soviet Studies*, 40, 2.

Kornai, Janos (1980) "Economics of shortage", Amsterdam: North-Holland
—— (1986) *Contradictions and Dilemmas: Studies on the Socialist Economy and Society*, Cambridge, MA: MIT Press.
—— (1990) *Vision and Reality, Market and State*, New York: Routledge.

Korowkin, Wladimir (1994) "Die wirtschaftsbeziehungen Russlands zu den Staaten der ehemaligen UdSSR", *Osteuropa*, 2 (February): 161–74.

Kozlov, Viktor (1988) *The Peoples of the Soviet Union*, Bloomington, Ind.: Indiana University Press.

Kozol, Jonathan (1985) *Illiterate America*, New York: Anchor Press.

Krause, Lawrence, Koh Ai Tee and Lee (Tsao) Yuan (1987) *The Singapore Economy Reconsidered*, Singapore: Institute of South-East Asian Studies.

Kuleshov, Valery and Castells, Manuel (directors) (1993) "Problemas socio-economicos del complejo de gas y petroleo en Siberia Occidental en el contexto del la reforma economica", Madrid: UAM/IUSNT, research report.

Kuo, Shirley W.Y. (1983) *The Taiwan Economy in Transition*, Boulder, Colo.: Westview Press.

Kuznetsova, N.F. (1996) "Konferenciya po problemam organizovannoi prestupnosti", *Gosudarstvo i Pravo*, 5: 130–37.

Kwan, Alex Y.H. and Chan, David K.K. (eds) (1986) *Hong Kong Society*, Hong Kong: Writers and Publishers Cooperative.

Lachaud, Jean-Pierre (1994) *The Labour Market in Africa*, Geneva: International Institute for Labour Studies.

Lam, Willy Wo-Lap (1995) *China after Deng Xiaoping: the Power Struggle in Beijing since Tiananmen*, Singapore: Wiley.

Lane, David (1990) *Soviet Society under Perestroika*, London: Unwin and Hyman.

Laserna, Roberto (ed.) (1991) *Economia politica de las drogas: lecturas Latinoamericanas*, Cochabamba: CERES/CLACSO.
—— (1995) "Coca cultivation, drug traffic and regional development in Cochabamba, Bolivia", unpublished PhD thesis, Berkeley: University of California.
—— (1996) *20 juicios y prejuicios sobre coca-cocaina*, La Paz: Clave Consultores.

Lau, Siu-kai (1982) *Society and Politics in Hong Kong*, Hong Kong: The Chinese University Press.

Lavalette, Michael (1994) *Child Employment in the Capitalist Labour Market*, Aldershot: Avebury.

Lee, Chong Ouk (1988) *Science and Technology Policy of Korea and Cooperation with the United States*, Seoul: Korea Advanced Institute of Science and Technology, Center for Science and Technology Policy.

Leitzel, Jim et al. (1995) "Mafiosi and Matrioshki: organized crime and Russian reform", *The Brooking Review*, winter: 26–9.

Lemann, Nicholas (1999) *The Big Test: the Secret History of American Merit-*

ocracy, New York: Farrar, Strauss and Giroux.

Lemarchand, René (1970) *Rwanda and Burundi*, London: Pall Mall.

—— (1993) "Burundi in comparative perspective: dimensions of ethnic strife", in John McGarry and Brendan O'Leary (eds), *The Politics of Ethnic Conflict Regulation: Case Studies of Protracted Ethnic Conflicts*, London and New York: Routledge.

—— (1994a) "Managing transition anarchies: Rwanda, Burundi, and South Africa in comparative perspective", *The Journal of Modern African Studies*, 32(4): 581–604.

—— (1994b) *Burundi: Ethnocide as Discourse and Practice*, New York: Woodrow Wilson Center Press and Cambridge University Press.

Lerman, Robert (1996) "The impact of changing US family structure on child poverty and income inequality", *Economica*, 63: S119–39.

Lethbridge, H. (1970) "Hong Kong cadets, 1862–1941", *Journal of the Hong Kong Branch of the Royal Asiatic Society*, 10: 35–56.

—— (1978) *Hong Kong: Stability and Change: a Collection of Essays*, Hong Kong: Oxford University Press.

Leung, Chi-keung et al. (1980) *Hong Kong: Dilemmas of Growth*, Hong Kong: University of Hong Kong, Centre of Asian Studies.

Lewin, Moshe (1988) *The Gorbachev Phenomenon: a Historical Interpretation*, Berkeley: University of California Press.

Lewis, Peter (1996) "From prebendalism to predation: the political economy of decline in Nigeria", *Journal of Modern African Studies* 34(1): 79–103.

Leys, Colin (1994) "Confronting the African tragedy", *New Left Review*, 204: 33–47.

Li, Linda Ch. (1996) "Power as non-zero sum: central-provincial relations over investment implementation, Guandong and Shanghai, 1978–93", Hong Kong: City University of Hong Kong, Department of Public and Social Administration, working paper 1996/2.

Lim, Hyun-Chin (1982) *Dependent Development in Korea: 1963–79*, Seoul: Seoul National University Press.

—— and Yang, Jonghoe (1987) "The state, local capitalists and multinationals: the changing nature of a triple alliance in Korea", in Kyong-Dong Kim (ed.), *Dependency Issues in Korean Development*, Seoul: Seoul National University Press: pp. 347–59.

Lin, Jing (1994) *The Opening of the Chinese Mind: Democratic Changes in China since 1978*, Westport, CT: Praeger.

Lin, Tsong-Biau, Mok, Victor and Ho, Yin-Ping (1980) *Manufactured Exports and Employment in Hong Kong*, Hong Kong: Chinese University Press.

Lindqvist, Sven (1996) *Exterminate All the Brutes*, New York: The New Press.

Loxley, John (1995) "A review of *Adjustment in Africa: Reforms, Results and the Road Ahead*", *Canadian Journal of African Studies*, 29: 2.

Lu, Jia (1993) "*Jingji guore wnti geshuo gehua* (Disagreement between the central and the provincial government on the problems of overheated economy)", *China Times Weekly*, 61, February 28–March 6: 44–5.

—— (1994a) "*Zhonggong yabuzhu difang haiwai juzhaifeng* (The Chinese communists cannot control the trend of local government's foreign borrowing)", *China Times Weekly*, 150, November 13–19: 6–9.

—— (1994b) "*Laozi jiufen juyou zhongguo tese* (Labor disputes have Chinese characteristics)", *China Times Weekly*, 116, March 20–6; 11–13.

Lynch, Michael J. and Paterson, E. Britt (eds) (1995) *Race and Criminal Justice: a Further Examination*, New York: Harrow and Heston.

McDonald, Douglas (1994) "Public imprisonment by private means: the re-emergence of private prisons and jails in the United States, the United Kingdom, and Australia", *British Journal of Criminology*, 34, special issue.

Mace, James E. (1983) *Communism and the Dilemmas of National Liberation: National Communism in Soviet Ukraine, 1918–33*, Cambridge, MA: Harvard Ukrainian Research Institute.

McFadden, Robert D. (1999) "US colonel's wife named in Bogota drug smuggling", *The New York Times*, August 7: A1.

Machimura, Takashi (1994) *Sekai Toshi Tokyo no Kozo* [The structural transformation of a global city: Tokyo], Tokyo: Tokyo University Press.

Mackie, J.A.C. (1992) "Overseas Chinese entrepreneurship", *Asian Pacific Economic Literature*, 6(1): 41–64.

McKinley, James C. (1996) "Old revolutionary is a new power to be reckoned with in Central Africa", *The New York Times*, November 27.

Maddison, Angus (1995) *Monitoring the World Economy, 1820–1992*, Paris: OECD Development Centre Studies.

Malleret, T. and Delaporte, Y. (1991) "La conversion des industries de defense de l'ex-URSS", *Le Courrier des Pays de l'Est*, November.

Mamdani, Mahmood (1996) "From conquest to consent as the basis of state formation: reflections on Rwanda", *New Left Review*, 216: 3–36.

Manning, Claudia (1993) "Subcontracting in the South African economy: a review of the evidence and an analysis of future prospects", paper prepared for the TASKGRO Workshop, May 21–3.

—— and Mashigo, Angela Pinky (1994) "Manufacturing in South African microenterprises", *IDS Bulletin*, 25(1).

Marrese, Michael and Vanous, Jan (1983) *Soviet Subsidization of Trade with Eastern Europe: a Soviet Perspective*, Berkeley: University of California, Institute of International Studies.

Martin, John M. and Romano, Anne T. (1992) *Multinational Crime*, London: Sage.

Maruyama, Masao (1963) *Thought and Behaviour in Modern Japanese Politics* (ed. Ivan Morris), London: Oxford University Press.

Massey, Douglas S. and Denton, Nancy A. (1993) *American Apartheid: Segregation and the Making of the Underclass*, Cambridge, Ma: Harvard University Press.

——, Grow, Andrew and Shibuya, Kumiko (1994) "Migration, segregation and the geographic concentration of poverty" *American Sociological Review*, 59: 425–45.

Massey, Douglas S. et al. (1999) *Worlds in Motion: Understanding International Migration at the End of the Millennium*, Oxford: Clarendon Press/Oxford University Press.

Medina Gallego, Carlos (1990) *Autodefensas, paramilitares y narcotrafico en Colombia*, Bogota: Editorial Documentos Periodisticos.

Mejia Prieto, Jorge (1988) *México y el narcotráfico*, Mexico, DF: Editorial Universo.

Menshikov, Stanislas (1990) *Catastrophe or Catharsis? The Soviet Economy Today*, Moscow and London: Inter-Verso.

MERG (Macro-Economic Working Group) (1993) *Making Democracy Work: a Framework for Macroeconomic Policy in South Africa*, Belleville, South Africa: Center for Development Studies.

Mergenhagen, Paula (1996) "The prison population bomb", *American Demographics*, 18(2): 36–40.

Minc, Alain (1993) *Le nouveau Moyen Age*, Paris: Gallimard.

Miners, N.J. (1986) *The Government and Politics of Hong Kong*, Hong Kong: Oxford University Press.

Mingione, Enzo (1993) "The new urban poverty and the underclass: introduction", *International Journal of Urban and Regional Research*, 17(3).

—— (ed.) (1996) *Urban Poverty and the Underclass*, Oxford: Blackwell.

—— and Morlicchio, Enrica (1993) "New forms of urban poverty in Italy: risk path models in the north and south", *International Journal of Urban and Regional Research*, 17(3).

Mishel, Lawrence, Bernstein, Jared and Schmitt, John (1996) *The State of Working America, 1996–97*, Washington, DC: Economic Policy Institute.

——, —— and —— (1999) *The State of Working America 1998/99*, Ithaca and London: Cornell University Press/Economic Policy Institute.

Mita Barrientos, Fernando (1994) *El fenomeno del narcotrafico*, La Paz: AVF Producciones.

Mitchell, R. Judson (1990) *Getting to the Top in the USSR: Cyclical Patterns in the Leadership Succession Process*, Stanford, CA: Hoover Institution Press.

Mollenkopf, John and Castells, Manuel (eds) (1991) *Dual City: Restructuring New York*, New York: Russell Sage.

Morris, Martina, Bernhardt, Annette and Handcock, Mark (1994) "Economic inequality: new methods for new trends", *American Sociological Review*, 59: 205–19.

Motyl, Alexander M. (1987) *Will the Non-Russians Rebel? State, Ethnicity, and Stability in the USSR*, Ithaca, NY: Cornell University Press.

Muntarbhorn, Vitit (1996) "International perspectives and child prostitution in Asia", in US Department of Labor, Bureau of International Labor Affairs, *Forced Labor: the Prostitution of Children, Symposium Proceedings*, Washington, DC: US Department of Labor.

Murray, Diane H. (with Qin Baogi) (1994) *The Origins of the Truandihui: the Chinese Triads in Legend and History*, Stanford: Stanford University Press.

Mushkat, Miron (1982) *The Making of the Hong Kong Administrative Class*, Hong Kong: University of Hong Kong, Centre for Asia Studies.

Nakame International Economic Research, Nikon Keizai Shimbun Inc. (Nikkei), and Global Business Network (1998) *Scenarios for the Future of*

Japan, Emeryville, CA, Global Business Network.

Nathan, Andrew J. (1990) *China's Crisis: Dilemmas of Reform and Prospects for Democracy*, New York: Columbia University Press.

National Center for Adult Literacy (NCAL) (1995) "Adult literacy: the next generation", *NCAL Technical Report TR9501*, Philadelphia: NCAL.

Naughton, Barry (1995) *Growing Out of the Plan: Chinese Economic Reforms, 1978–1993*, New York: Cambridge University Press.

Navarro, Mireya (1997) "Russian submarine surfaces as player in drug world", *The New York Times*, March 5: 1–8.

Navarro, Vicente (1996) "La unidad monetaria, Maastricht y los Estados del Bienestar: notas comparativas de la UE con EEUU", paper presented at the Conference on New Social and Economic Policies for Europe, Fundacion Sistema, Madrid, December 18–19.

—— (1997) *Neoliberalismo y estado del bienestar*, Madrid: Alianza Editorial.

Nekrich, Aleksandr M. (1978) *The Punished Peoples: the Deportation and Tragic Fate of Soviet Minorities at the End of the Second World War*, New York: W.W. Norton.

Network Wizards (1996) Internet Survey, July, downloaded from: http://www.nw.com.

Newbury, Catherine (1988) *The Cohesion of Oppression: Clientship and Ethnicity in Rwanda, 1860–1960*, New York: Columbia University Press.

Newman, Anabel, Lewis, Warren and Beverstock, Caroline (1993) "Prison literacy: implications for program and assessment policy", *NCAL Technical Report TR93-1*, Philadelphia: NCAL.

Noble, Kenneth (1992) "As the nation's economy collapses, Zaïreans squirm under Mobutu's heel", *The New York Times*, August 30: 14.

Nonaka, Ikujiro and Takeuchi, Hirotaka (1994) *The Knowledge-creating Company: How Japanese Companies Created the Dynamics of Innovation*, New York: Oxford University Press.

Norman, E. Herbert (1940) *Japan's Emergence as a Modern State: Political and Economic Problems of the Meiji Period*, New York: Institute of Pacific Relations.

Nove, Alec (1969/1982) *An Economic History of the USSR*, Harmondsworth: Penguin.

—— (1977) *The Soviet Economic System*, London: Allen and Unwin.

Nzongola-Ntalaja, Georges (1993) *Nation-building and State-building in Africa*, SAPES Trust Occasional Paper Series no. 3, Harare: Sapes Books.

Odedra, Mayuri et al. (1993) "Sub-Saharan Africa: a technological desert", *Communications of the ACM*, 36(2) 25-9.

OECD (1995) *Literacy, Economy and Society: Results of the First International Adult Literacy Survey*, Paris: OECD.

Ohmae, Kenichi (1990) *The Borderless World: Power and Strategy in the Interlinked Economy*, New York: Harper.

Ong, Aihwa and Nonini, Donald (eds) (1997) *The Cultural Politics of Modern Chinese Transnationalism*, London: Routledge.

Orstrom Moller, J. (1995) *The Future European Model: Economic Interna-*

tionalization and Cultural Decentralization, Westport, CT: Praeger.

Ovchinsky, Vladimir (1993) *Mafia: Neob'yavlennyi vizit*, Moscow: INFRA-M.

Over, Mead (1990) "The economic impact of fatal adult illness from AIDS and other causes in Sub-Saharan Africa: a research proposal", Research Department of the World-Bank, Washington, unpublished.

Overhalt, William H. (1993) *The Rise of China*, New York: W.W. Norton.

Ozawa, Terutomo (1996) "Japan: the macro-IDP, meso-IDPs and the technology development path (TDP)", in John H. Dunning and Rajneesh Narula (eds), *Foreign Direct Investment and Governments: Catalysts for Economic Restructuring*, London: Routledge: pp. 142–73.

Palazuelos, Enrique (1990) *La economia sovietica mas alla de la perestroika*, Madrid: Ediciones de Ciencias Sociales.

Panos Institute (1992) *The Hidden Costs of AIDS: the Challenge to Development*, London: Panos Institute.

Pardo Segovia, Fernando (ed.) (1995) *Narcotrafico: situacion actual y perspectivas para la accion*, Lima: Centro Peruano de Relaciones Internacionales.

Parsons, Craig (1996) "Europe's identity crisis: European Union dilemmas in the 1990s", Berkeley: University of California, Center for Western European Studies, research paper.

Pasquini, Gabriel and De Miguel, Eduardo (1995) *Blanca y radiante: mafias, poder y narcotrafico en la Argentina*, Buenos Aires: Planeta.

Pease, Ken (1994) "Cross-national imprisonment rates: limitations of method and possible conclusions", *British Journal of Criminology*, 34, special issue.

Pedrazzini, Yves and Sanchez, Magaly (1996) *Malandros, bandes et enfants de la rue: la culture d'urgence dans la metropole latino-americaine*, Paris: Fondation Charles Leopold Mayer pour le Progres de l'Homme.

Perez Gomez, V. (1988) *Historia de la drogadiccion en Colombia*, Bogota: TM Editores/Uniandes.

Peterson, G. and Harrell, Adele V. (eds) (1993) *Drugs, Crime, and Social Isolation*, Washington, DC: The Urban Institute Press.

Pfeffer, Max (1994) "Low-wage employment and ghetto poverty: a comparison of African-American and Cambodian day-haul farm workers in Philadelphia", *Social Problems*, 41(1).

Philipson, Thomas and Posner, Richard A. (1995) "The microeconomics of the AIDS epidemic in Africa", *Population and Development Review*, 21(4): 835-48.

Pinkus, Benjamin (1988) *The Jews of the Soviet Union: the History of a National Minority*, Cambridge: Cambridge University Press.

Pipes, Richard (1954) *The Formation of the Soviet Union: Communism and Nationalism, 1917–23*, Cambridge, MA: Harvard University Press.

—— (1991) *The Russian Revolution*, New York: Alfred Knopf.

Pisani-Ferry, Jean (1995) "Variable geometry in Europe", paper presented at the Conference on Reshaping the Transatlantic Partnership: an Agenda for the Next Ten Years, Bruges: The College of Europe, March 20–2.

Plotnick, Robert D. (1990) "Determinants of teenage out-of-wedlock child-bearing", *Journal of Marriage and the Family*, 52: 735–46.

Po, Lan-chih (forthcoming) "Economic reform, housing privatization and changing life of women in China", unpublished PhD dissertation, Berkeley: University of California, Department of City and Regional Planning.

Podlesskikh, Georgyi and Tereshonok, Andrey (1994) *Vory V Zakone: Brosok k Vlasti*, Moscow: Khudozestvennaya Literatura.

Portes, Alejandro (ed.) (1995) "The economic sociology of immigration: essays on networks, ethnicity and entrepreneurship", New York: Russell Sage.

—— and Sensenbrenner, Julia (1993) "Embeddedness and immigration: notes on the social determinants of economic action", *American Journal of Sociology*, 98(6): 1320–50.

——, Castells, Manuel and Benton, Lauren (eds) (1989) *The Informal Economy: Studies on Advanced and Less Developed Countries*, Baltimore: The Johns Hopkins University Press.

Potter, Gary W. (1994) *Criminal Organizations: Vice, Racketeering and Politics in an American City*, Prospect Heights, Ill: Waveland Press.

Praaning, R. and Perry, C. (eds) (1989) *East–West Relations in the 1990s: Politics and Technology*, Dordrecht/Boston: M. Nijhoff.

Press, Robert M. (1993) "Some allege Mobutu is stirring up deadly tribal warfare in Zaïre", *Christian Science Monitor*, August 17: 1.

Pritchett, Lant (1995) *Divergence, Big Time*, Washington, DC: The World Bank, Policy Research Working Paper, no. 1522.

Prolongeau, Hubert (1992) *La vie quotidienne en Colombie au temps du cartel de Medellin*, Paris: Hachette.

Psacharopoulos, George et al. (1995) "Poverty and inequality in Latin America during the 1980s", *Review of Income and Wealth*, 41(3): 245–63.

Purcell, Randall P. (ed.) (1989) *The Newly Industrializing Countries in a World Economy*, Boulder, Colo.: Lynne Rienner.

Ravenhill, John (1993) "A second decade of adjustment: greater complexity, greater uncertainty", in Callaghy and Ravenhill (eds).

Reed, Deborah (1999) *California's Rising Income Inequality: Causes and Concerns*, San Francisco: Public Policy Institute of California.

Reischauer, Edwin O. (1988) *The Japanese Today: Change and Continuity*, Cambridge, MA: The Belknap Press of Harvard University Press.

Remnick, David (1993) *Lenin's Tomb: the Last Days of the Soviet Empire*, New York: Random House.

Renard, Ronald D. (1996) *The Burmese Connection: Illegal Drugs and the Making of the Golden Triangle*, Boulder, Colo.: Lynne Rienner.

Rezun, Miron (ed.) (1992) *Nationalism and the Breakup of an Empire: Russia and its Periphery*, Westport, CT: Praeger.

Riddell, Barry (1995) "The World Bank speaks to Africa yet again", *Canadian Journal of African Studies*, 29: 2.

Riddell, Roger (1993) "The future of the manufacturing sector in Sub-Saharan Africa", in Callaghy and Ravenhill (eds), pp. 215–47.

Riley, Thyra (1993) "Characteristics of and constraints facing black businesses in South Africa: survey results", paper prepared for the World Bank's presentation to the Seminar on Small and Medium Business Enterprises, Johannesburg, June 1–2.

Rizzini, Irene (ed.) (1994) *Children in Brazil Today: a Challenge for the Third Millennium*, Rio de Janeiro: Editora Universitaria Santa Ursula.

Roberts, Albert E. (1994) *Critical Issues in Crime and Justice*, Thousand Oaks, Ca: Sage.

Robinson, Thomas W. (ed.) (1991) *Democracy and Development in East Asia*, Washington, DC: The American Enterprise Institute Press.

Rodgers, Gerry, Gore, Charles and Figueiredo, Jose B.(eds) (1995) *Social Exclusion: Rhetoric, Reality, Responses*, Geneva: International Institute of Labour Studies.

Rodgers, Harrell (1996) *Poor Women, Poor Children*, Armonk, NY: M.E. Sharpe.

Rogerson, Christian (1993) "Industrial subcontracting in South Africa: a research review", paper prepared for the PWV Economic Development Forum, June.

Rohwer, Jim (1995) *Asia Rising*, New York: Simon and Schuster.

Room, G. (1992) *Observatory on National Policies to Combat Social Exclusion: Second Annual Report*, Brussels: Commission of the European Community.

Roth, Jurgen and Frey, Marc (1995) *Europa en las garras de la mafia*, Barcelona: Anaya and Mario Muchnik (orig. pub. in German in 1992).

Rowen, H.S. and Wolf Jr, Charles, (eds) (1990) *The Impoverished Superpower*, San Francisco: Institute for Contemporary Studies.

Ruggie, John G. (1993) "Territoriality and beyond: problematizing modernity in international relations", *International Organization*, 47(1): 139–74.

Sachs, Jeffrey (1998) "The IMF and the Asian flu", *The American Prospect*, March/April: 16–21.

Sachwald, Fredrique (1994) *European Integration and Competitiveness: Acquisitions and Alliances in Industry*, Aldershot: Edward Elgar.

Sakaiya, Taichi (1991) *The Knowledge–Value Revolution: or a History of the Future*, Tokyo: Kodansha International.

Salazar, Alonso and Jaramillo, Ana Maria (1992) *Medellin: las subculturas del narcotrafico*, Bogota: CINEP.

Salmin, A.M. (1992) *SNG: Sostoyanie i perspektivy razvitiya*, Moscow: Gorbachev Fund.

Sanchez Jankowski, Martin (1991) *Islands in the Street*, Berkeley: University of California Press.

Sandbrook, Richard (1985) *The Politics of Africa's Economic Stagnation*, Cambridge: Cambridge University Press.

Sandholtz, Wayne et al. (1992) *The Highest Stakes: Economic Foundations of National Security*, New York: BRIE/Oxford University Press.

Santino, Umberto and La Fiura, Giovanni (1990) *L'impresa mafiosa: dall'Italia agli Stati Uniti*, Milan: Franco Angeli.

Sapir, J. (1987) *Le système militaire sovietique*, Paris: La Decouverte.

Sarkar, Prabirjit and Singer, H.W. (1991) "Manufactured exports of developing countries and their terms of trade since 1965", *World Development*, 19(4): 333–40.

Sarmiento, Eduardo (1990) "Economia del narcotrafico", *Desarrollo y Sociedad*, September 26: 11–40.

Sarmiento, Luis Fernando (1991) *Cocaina and Co.: un mercado ilegal por dentro*, Bogota: Universidad Nacional de Colombia, Instituto de Estudios Politicos y Relaciones Internacionales.

Savona, Ernesto (ed.) (1993) *Mafia Issues*, Milan: International Scientific and Professional Advisory Council of the United Nations Crime Prevention and Criminal Justice Program.

Savvateyeva, Irina (1994) "Kontrrazvedka sobirayetsya proveryat' chinovnikov: dlya chego?", *Izvestiya*, April 28: 2.

Scherer, John L. and Jakobson, Michael (1993) "The collectivisation of agriculture and the Soviet prison camp system", *Europe–Asia Studies*, 45 (3): 533–46.

Schiffer, Jonathan (1983) *Anatomy of a Laissez-faire Government: the Hong Kong Growth Model Reconsidered*, Hong Kong: University of Hong Kong, Centre for Urban Studies.

Schiraldi, Vincent (1994) *The Undue Influence of California's Prison Guards' Union: California's Correctional-Industrial Complex*, San Francisco: Center on Juvenile and Criminal Justice, report, October.

Schlesinger, Jacob M. (1997) *Shadow Shoguns: the Rise and Fall of Japan's Postwar Political Machine*, New York: Simon and Schuster.

Scott, Ian (1987) "Policy making in a turbulent environment: the case of Hong Kong", Hong Kong: University of Hong Kong, Department of Political Science, research report.

—— and Burns, John P. (eds) (1984) *The Hong Kong Civil Service*, Hong Kong: Oxford University Press.

Scott, Peter D. and Marshall, Jonathan (1991) *Cocaine Politics: Drugs, Armies and the CIA in Central America*, Berkeley: University of California Press.

Sedlak, Andrea and Broadhurst, Diane (1996) *Executive Summary of the Third National Incidence Study of Child Abuse and Neglect*, Washington, DC: US Department of Health and Human Services.

Seki, Kiyohide (1987) "Population and family policy: measuring the level of living in the country of familism", Tokyo: Nihon University, Population Research Institute, Research Paper Series no. 25.

Seymour, Christopher (1996) *Yakuza Diary: Doing Time in the Japanese Underworld*, New York: Atlantic Monthly Press.

Shane, Scott (1994) *Dismantling Utopia: How Information Ended the Soviet Union*, Chicago: Ivan R. Dee.

Shargorodsky, Sergei (1995) "In troubled Russia, contract killings are a way of life", *San Francisco Chronicle*, November 17.

Shaw, Denis J. B. (1993) "Geographical and historical observations on the future of a federal Russia", *Post-Soviet Geography*, 34(8).

Shinotsuka, Eiko (1994) "Women workers in Japan: past, present and future", in Gelb and Lief-Palley (ed.): 95–119.

Shoji, Kokichi (1991) "Rising neo-nationalism in contemporary Japan – changing social consciousness of the Japanese people and its implications for world society", Tokyo: University of Tokyo, Department of Sociology, research paper.

—— (1994), "Sociology", in *An Introductory Bibliography for Japanese Studies*, vol. 9, part 1, Tokyo: The Japan Foundation: pp. 150–216.

—— (1995) "Small changes make big change: changing Japanese life-style and political change", Tokyo: University of Tokyo, Department of Sociology, research paper.

Sigur, Christopher J. (1994) Continuity and Change in Contemporary Korea, New York: Carnegie Council on Ethics and International Affairs.

Silver, Hilary (1993) "National conceptions of the new urban poverty: social structural change in Britain, France and the United States", *International Journal of Urban and Regional Research*, 17(3): September.

Simon, David (1995) "Debt, democracy and development: Sub-Saharan Africa in the 1990s", in Simon et al. (eds).

——, van Spengen, Wim, Dixon, Chris and Naarman, Anders (eds) (1995) *Structurally Adjusted Africa: Poverty, Debt and Basic Needs*, London: Pluto Press.

Simon, Gerhard (1991) *Nationalism and Policy toward the Nationalities in the Soviet Union: from Totalitarian Dictatorship toward Post-Stalinist Society*, Boulder, Colo.: Westview Press.

Simposio Internacional (1991) *El impacto del capital financiero del narcotrafico en America Latina*, La Paz: Centro para el estudio de las relaciones internacionales y el desarrollo.

Singh, Tejpal (1982) *The Soviet Federal State: Theory, Formation and Development*, Delhi: Sterling.

Sit, Victor (1982) "Dynamism in small industries: the case of Hong Kong", *Asian Survey*, 22: 399–409.

Skezely, Miguel (1995) "Poverty in Mexico during adjustment", *Review of Income and Wealth*, 41(3): 331–48.

Smaryl, O.I. (1984) "New technology and the Soviet predicament", *Survey*, 28(1): 109–11.

Smeeding, Timothy (1997) "Financial poverty in developed countries: the evidence from LIS", Luxembourg Income Study working paper, no. 155.

Smith, Gordon B. (1992) *Soviet Politics: Struggling with Change*, New York: St Martin's Press.

Smith, Patrick (1997) *Japan: a Reinterpretation*, New York: Pantheon.

Smolowe, Jill (1994) "Lock 'em up and throw away the key", *Time*, February 7: 55–9.

South African Government (1996a) "Restructuring the South African labour market", report of the Presidential Commission to Investigate Labour Market Policy.

—— (1996b) "Employment and occupational equity: policy proposals", Department of Labour Green Paper.

Souza Minayo, Maria Cecilia et al. (1999) *Fala, Galera: Juventude, Violencia e Cidadania na cidade do Rio de Janeiro*, Rio de Janeiro: Garamond/

UNESCO.

Specter, Michael (1996) "Cemetery bomb in Moscow kills 13 at ceremony", *The New York Times*, November 11: A1–A4.

Spence, Jonathan D. (1990) *The Search for Modern China*, New York: Norton.

Staebler, Martin (1996) "Tourism and children in prostitution", paper prepared for the World Congress against Commercial Sexual Exploitation of Children, Stockholm, August 27–31.

Steinberg, Dimitri (1991) *Soviet Defense Burden: Estimating Hidden Defense Costs*, Washington, DC: Intelligence Decision Systems, research report.

Sterling, Claire (1994) *Thieves' World: the Threat of the New Global Network of Organized Crime*, New York: Simon and Schuster.

Stiglitz, Joseph (1998) "Sound finance and sustainable development in Asia" (http://www.worldbank.org/html/extdr/extme/jsso031298.html).

Strong, Simon (1995) *Whitewash: Pablo Escobar and the Cocaine Wars*, London: Macmillan.

Sung, Yun-wing (1994) "Hong Kong and economic integration of the China circle", paper presented at the China Circle Conference organized by the Institute of Global Cooperation and Conflict, University of California, Hong Kong: December 8–11.

Suny, Ronald Grigor (1993) *The Revenge of the Past: Nationalism, Revolution, and the Collapse of the Soviet Union*, Stanford: Stanford University Press.

Survey (1984) "The Novosibirsk Report", *Survey* 28(1): 88–108 (English trans.).

Susser, Ida (1991) "The separation of mothers and children", in John Mollenkopf and Manuel Castells (eds), *Dual City: Restructuring New York*, New York: Russell Sage: pp. 207–24.

—— (1993) "Creating family forms: the exclusion of men and teenage boys from families in the New York City shelter system, 1987–1991", *Critique of Anthropology*, 13(3): 267–85.

—— (1995) "Fear and violence in dislocated communities", paper presented to the 94th Annual Meeting of the American Anthropological Association, Washington, DC.

—— (1996) "The construction of poverty and homelessness in US cities", *Annual Reviews of Anthropology*, 25: 411–35.

—— and Kreniske, John (1987) "The welfare trap: a public policy for deprivation" in Leith Mullings (ed.), *Cities of the United States*, New York: Columbia University Press, pp. 51–68.

Svedberg, Peter (1993) "Trade compression and economic decline in Sub-Saharan Africa", in Magnus Blomstrom and Mats Lundahl (eds), *Economic Crisis in Africa: Perspectives on Policy Responses*, Routledge: London and New York, pp. 21–40.

Szelenyi, Ivan (1982) "The intelligentsia in the class structure of state-socialist societies", in Michael Burawoy and Theda Skocpol (eds), *Marxist Inquiries*, special issue of the *American Journal of Sociology*, 88: 287–327.

Taguchi, Fukuji and Kato, Tetsuro (1985) "Marxist debates on the state in post-war Japan", *Hosei Ronsyu* (Journal of Law and Political Science),

105: 1-25.

Taibo, Carlos (1993a) "Las fuerzas armadas en la URSS", unpublished PhD dissertation, Madrid: Universidad Autonoma de Madrid.

—— (1993b) *La Union Sovietica (1917-1991)*, Madrid: Editorial Sintesis.

Tarasulo, Isaav T. (ed.) (1989) *Gorbachev and Glasnost: Viewpoints from the Soviet Press*, Wilmington, Delaware: Scholarly Resources Books.

Tevera, Dan (1995) "The medicine that might kill the patient: structural adjustment and urban poverty in Zimbabwe", in David Simon, Wim van Spengen, Chris Dixon and Anders Naarman (eds), *Structurally Adjusted Africa: Poverty, Debt and Basic Needs*, London: Pluto Press.

Thalheim, Karl (1986) *Stagnation or Change in the Communist Economies?* (with a note by Gregory Grossman), London: Center for Research in Communist Economies.

The Current Digest [of Post-Soviet press] (1994) "Crime, corruption pose political, economic threat", *Current Digest*, 45(4): 14-16.

The Economist (1993) "Let down again: a survey of Nigeria", special supplement, August 21.

—— (1995) "Coming of age: a survey of South Africa", special supplement, May 20.

—— (1996a) "Africa for the Africans: a survey of Sub-Saharan Africa", special supplement, September 7.

—— (1996b) "Belgium: crony state", October 26: 61–2.

—— (1996c) "Death shadows Africa's Great Lakes", October 19: 45–7.

—— (1997) "A survey of Japanese finance: a whopping explosion", special report, June 27: 1–18.

—— (1998) "Silicon Valley, PRC", June 27: 64–6.

—— (1999a) "Russian organised crime: crime without punishment", August 28: 17–19.

—— (1999b) "Europe's borders", October 16: 26–8.

—— (1999c) "A survey of Europe: a work in progress", October 23.

Thomas, John and Kruse-Vaucienne, Ursula (eds) (1977) *Soviet Science and Technology*, Washington, DC National Science Foundation.

Thompson, Grahame (1998) *Economic Dynamism in the Asian Pacific*, London: Routledge.

Thoumi, Francisco (1994) *Economia politica y narcotrafico*, Bogota: TM Editores.

Timmer, Doug A., Eitzen, D. Stanley, and Talley, Kathryn (1994) *Paths to Homelessness: Extreme Poverty and the Urban Housing Crisis*, Boulder, Colo.: Westview Press.

Tipton, Frank B. (1998) *The Rise of Asia: Economics, Society, and Politics in Contemporary Asia*, Honolulu: University of Hawaii Press.

Tokatlian, Juan G. and Bagley, Bruce (eds) (1990) *Economia politica del narcotrafico*, Bogota: CEREC/Uniandes.

Tonry, Michael (1994) "Racial disproportion in US prisons", *British Journal of Criminology*, 34, special issue.

—— (1995) *Malign Neglect: Race, Crime, and Punishment in America*, New York: Oxford University Press.

Totani, Osamu and Yatazawa, Noriko (eds) (1990) [*The Changing Family*: in Japanese], Tokyo: University of Tokyo Press.
Touraine, Alain (1995) "De la globalización al policentrismo", *El País*, July 24.
—— (1996a) "La deconstrucción europea", *El País*, April 4.
—— (1996b) "La globalizacion como ideología", *El País*, September 16.
—— (1996c) "Detras de la moneda: la economía", *El País*, December 22.
—— (1997) *Pourrons-nous vivre ensemble? Égaux et différents*, Paris: Fayard.
—— et al. (1996) *Le grand refus: reflexions sur la greve de decembre 1995*, Paris: Fayard.
Townsend, Peter (1993) *The International Analysis of Poverty*, London: Harvester/Wheatsheaf.
Tragardh, Lars (1996) "European integration and the question of national sovereignty: Germany and Sweden, 1945–1995", paper presented at the Center for Slavic Studies/Center for German and European Studies Symposium, University of California Berkeley, November 22.
Tranfaglia, Nicola (1992) *Mafia, politica e affari: 1943–91*, Roma: Editori Laterza.
Trotsky, Leon (1965) *La Revolution Russe* (trans. from Russian), Paris: Maspero.
Trueheart, Charles (1996) "String of crimes shocks Belgium: national pride damaged by pedophilia, murder, coverups", *Washington Post*, September 25.
Tsao, Yuan (1986) "Sources of growth accounting for the Singapore economy", in Lim Chong-Yah and Peter J. Lloyd (eds), *Singapore: Resources and Growth*, Singapore: Oxford University Press.
Tsuneyoshi, Ryoko (1994) "Small groups in Japanese elementary school classrooms: comparisons with the United States", *Comparative Education*, 30(2): 115–29.
Tsuru, Shigeto (1993) *Japan's Capitalism: Creative Defeat and Beyond*, Cambridge: Cambridge University Press.
Tsurumi, Kazuko (1970) *Social Change and the Individual: Japan Before and After Defeat in World War II*, Princeton, NJ: Princeton University Press.
Turbino, Fidel (1992) *Violencia y narcotrafico en Amazonia*, Lima: Centro Amazonico de antropologia y aplicacion practica.
Ueno, Chizuko (1987) "The position of Japanese women reconsidered", *Current Anthropology*, 28(4): S75-S82.
UNICEF (1996) *The State of the World's Children 1996*, Oxford: Oxford University Press.
United Nations, Department for Economic and Social Information and Policy Analysis (1996) *World Economic and Social Survey 1996: Trends and Policies in the World Economy*, New York: United Nations.
United Nations Development Programme (UNDP) (1996) *Human Development Report 1996*, New York: Oxford University Press.
—— (1997) *Human Development Report 1997*, New York: Oxford University Press.
—— (1998) *Human Development Report 1998*, New York: Oxford Univer-

sity Press.

—— (1999) *Human Development Report 1999*, New York: Oxford University Press.

United Nations Development Programme – Chile (1998) *El desarrollo humano en Chile*, Santiago de Chile: Naciones Unidas.

United Nations Economic and Social Council (UN-ESC) (1994) "Problems and dangers posed by organized transnational crime in the various regions of the world", Background Document for the World Ministerial Conference on Organized Transnational Crime, Naples, November, 21–23, Document E/CONF.88.2.

US Department of Defense (1989) *Critical Technologies Plan*, Washington, DC: Department of Defense.

US Department of Justice (1996) "Probation and parole population reaches almost 3.8 million", Washington, DC: US Department of Justice press release, June 30.

US Department of Labor (1994) *By the Sweat and Toil of Children: Vol. I. The Use of Child Labor in US Manufactured and Mined Imports*, Washington, DC: US Department of Labour.

—— (1995) *By the Sweat and Toil of Children: Vol. II. The Use of Child Labor in Agricultural Imports and Forced and Bonded Child Labor*, Washington, DC: US Department of Labour.

US News & World Report (1988) "Red Star Rising", pp. 48–53.

Van Kempen, Ronald and Marcuse, Peter (1996) *The New Spatial Order of Cities*, New York: Columbia University Press.

Van Regemorter, Jean-Louis (1990) *D'une perestroika à l'autre: l'évolution économique de la Russie de 1860 à nos jours*, Paris: SEDES, Les Cours de la Sorbonne.

Van Wolferen, Karel (1989) *The Enigma of Japanese Power. People and Politics in a Stateless Nation*, New York: Alfred Knopf.

Veen, Hans-Joachim (ed.) (1984) *From Brezhnev to Gorbachev: Domestic Affairs and Soviet Foreign Policy*, Leamington Spa: Berg.

Velis, Jean-Pierre (1990) *Through a Glass Darkly: Functional Illiteracy in Industrialized Countries*, Paris: UNESCO.

Veloza, Gustavo (1988) *La guerra entre los carteles del narcotrafico*, Bogota: G.S. Editores.

Venezky, Richard (1996) "Literacy assessment in the service of literacy policy", *NCAL Technical Report TR95-02*, Philadelphia: National Center for Adult Literacy.

Verdery, Katherine (1991) "Theorizing Socialism: a prologue to the "transition", *American Ethnologist*, August, pp. 419–39.

Volin, Lazar (1970) *A Century of Russian Agriculture: from Alexander II to Khrushchev*, Cambridge, MA: Harvard University Press.

Voshchanov, Pavel (1995) "Mafia godfathers become fathers of the nation", *Konsomolskaya Pravda* (read in the English version in *Business World of Russia Weekly*, 18/169, May: 13–14).

de Waal, Alex (1996) "Contemporary warfare in Africa: changing context, changing strategies", *IDS Bulletin*, 27(3): 6–16.

Wacquant, Loic (1993) "Urban outcasts: stigma and division in the black American ghetto and the French urban periphery", *International Journal of Urban and Regional Research*, 17(3): September.

—— (1996) "The rise of advanced marginality: notes on its nature and implications", *Acta Sociologica*, 12: 121–39.

Waever, Ole (1995) "Identity, integration, and security: solving the sovereignty puzzle in EU studies", *Journal of International Affairs*, 48(2): 1–43.

Wagner, Daniel (1992) "World literacy: research and policy in the EFA decade", *Annals of the American Academy of Political and Social Sciences*, 520, March 1992.

Waiselfisz, Julio Jacobo (1999) *Juventude, Volencia e Cidadania: Os Joves de Brasilia*, Sao Paulo: Cortez Editora/UNESCO.

Wakabayashi, Hideki (1994) *Japan's Revolution in Wireless Communications*, Tokyo: Nomura Research Institute.

Walder, Andrew G. (1986) *Communist Neo-traditionalism: Work and Authority in Chinese Industry*, Berkeley: University of California Press.

—— (1992) *Popular Protest in 1989: Democracy Movement*, Hong Kong: Chinese University Press.

—— (1995) "Local governments and industrial firms: an organizational analysis of China's transitional economy", *American Journal of Sociology*, 101(2): 263–301.

—— and Gong, Xiaoxia (eds) (1993) "China's great terror: new documentation on the Cultural Revolution", *Chinese Sociology and Anthropology*, 26(1), special issue.

Walker, Martin (1986) *The Waking Giant: Gorbachev's Russia*, New York: Pantheon.

Wallace, Bill (1996) "Warning on Russian crime rings", *San Francisco Chronicle*, March 18.

Wallace, Charles P. (1995) "The Pacific paradox: islands of despair", *Los Angeles Times,* March 16: A1–A30.

Wa Mutharika, Bingu (1995) *One Africa, One Destiny: towards Democracy, Good Governance and Development*, Harare: Sapes.

Watanabe, Osamu (1996) "Le neo-nationalisme japonais", *Perspectives Asiatiques,* 1: 19–39.

Watanuki, Joji (1990) "The development of information technology and its impact on Japanese society", Tokyo: Sophia University, Institute of International Relations, research paper.

Weiss, Herbert (1995) "Zaire: collapsed society, surviving states, future polity", in I. William Zartman (ed.), *Collapsed States: the Disintegration and Restoration of Legitimate Authority*, Boulder, Colo.: Lynne Rienner.

Weitzman, Martin L. (1970) "Soviet postwar economic growth and capital–labor substitution", *American Economic Review*, 60(4): 676–92.

Welch, Michael (1994) "Jail overcrowding: social sanitation and the warehousing of the urban underclass", in Roberts (ed.).

—— (1995) "Race and social class in the examination of punishment", in Lynch and Patterson (eds).

West, Cornel (1993) *Race Matters*, Boston: Beacon Press.

Wheatcroft, S.G., Davies, R.W. and Cooper, J.M. (eds) (1986) "Soviet industrialization reconsidered: some preliminary conclusions about economic development between 1926 and 1941", *Economic History Review*, 39, 2.

White, Gordon (ed.) (1988) *Developmental States in East Asia*, New York: St Martin's Press.

—— (ed.) (1991) *The Chinese State in the Era of Economic Reform*, Armonk, NY: M.E. Sharpe.

Wieviorka, Michel (1993) *La démocratie à l'épreuve: nationalisme, populisme, ethnicite*, Paris: La Decouverte.

Wilson, William Julius (1987) *The Truly Disadvantaged: the Inner City, the Underclass, and Public Policy*, Chicago: University of Chicago Press.

—— (1996) *When Work Disappears: the World of the New Urban Poor*, New York: Alfred Knopf.

Winckler, Edwin A. and Greenhalgh, Susan (eds.) (1988) *Contending Approaches to the Political Economy of Taiwan*, Armonk, NY: M.E. Sharpe.

Woherem, Evans (1994) *Information Technology in Africa: Challenges and Opportunities*, Nairobi: African Centre for Technology Studies Press.

Wolcott, P. (1993) "Soviet advanced technology: the case of high-performance computing", unpublished PhD dissertation, Tucson: University of Arizona.

—— and Goodman, S.E. (1993) "Under the stress of reform: high-performance computing in the Soviet Union", *Communications of the ACM*, 36(10): 26.

Wolff, Edward N. (1994) "Trends in household wealth in the United States: 1962–83 and 1983–89", *Review of Income and Wealth*, 40(2).

Wong, Christine et al. (1995) *Fiscal Management and Economic Reform in the People's Republic of China*, Hong Kong: Oxford University Press.

World Congress (1996) "Documents of the World Congress against the Commercial Sexual Exploitation of Children", Stockholm, August 27–31, downloaded from http://www.childhub.ch/webpub/csechome/21ae.htm.

Wright, Martin (ed.) (1989) *Soviet Union: the Challenge of Change*, Harlow, Essex: Longman.

Yabuki, Susumu (1995) *China's New Political Economy: the Giant Awakes*, Boulder, Colo.: Westview Press.

Yang, Mayfair Meilui (1994) *Gifts, Favors, and Banquets: the Art of Social Relationships in China*, Ithaca, NY: Cornell University Press.

Yansane, Aguibou Y. (ed.) (1996) *Development Strategies in Africa: Current Economic, Socio-political, and Institutional Trends and Issues*, Westport, CT: Greenwood Press.

Yazawa, Shujiro (1997) *Japanese Social Movements*, New York: Aldeen.

Yazawa, Sumiko (1995) "Political participation of Japanese women and local self-government – its trend and review", Tokyo: Tokyo Women's Christian University, research paper.

—— et al. (1992) *"Toshi josei to seiji sanka no new wave, kanagawa network undo no chosakara"* [New wave of political participation by urban women: research results of Kanagawa network movement], in *Yokohama Shiritsu daigaku keizai kenkyujo "keizai to boeki"*, no. 161 (as cited and summarized by Yazawa 1995).

Yeltsin, Boris (1990) *Memorias* (trans. from Russian), Madrid: Temas de Hoy.

—— (1994) "Ob ukrepleniyi Rossiyskogo gosudarstva", *Rossiyskaya gazeta*, February 25.

Yoshihara, Kunio (1988) *The Rise of Ersatz Capitalism in South East Asia*, Singapore: Oxford University Press.

Yoshino, K. (1992) *Cultural Nationalism*, London: Routledge.

Youngson, A.J. (1982) *Hong Kong: Economic Growth and Policy*, Hong Kong: Oxford University Press.

Yu, Fulai and Li, Si-Ming (1985) "The welfare cost of Hong Kong's public housing program", *Urban Studies*, 22: 133–40.

Zartman, I. William (ed.) (1995) *Collapsed States: the Disintegration and Restoration of Legitimate Authority*, Boulder, Colo.: Lynne Rienner.

Zimring, Franklin and Hawkins, Gordon (1994) "The growth of imprisonment in California", *British Journal of Criminology*, 34, special issue.

Zysman, John and Weber, Stephen (1997) "Economy and security in the new European political architecture", Berkeley: University of California, Berkeley Roundtable on the International Economy, research paper.

——, Doherty, Eileen and Schwartz, Andrew (1996) "Tales from the 'global economy': cross-national production networks and the reorganization of the European economy", Berkeley: University of California, Berkeley Roundtable on the International Economy, working paper.

Index

Page numbers in italics denote information in figures or tables.